The University of Chicago School Mathematics Project

ALGEBRA

VOLUME 2 • CHAPTERS 7–13

Authors

Susan A. Brown

R. James Breunlin

Mary Helen Wiltjer

Katherine M. Degner

Susan K. Eddins

Michael Todd Edwards

Neva A. Metcalf

Natalie Jakucyn

Zalman Usiskin

Director of Evaluation

Denisse R. Thompson

The McGraw·Hill Companies

Authors

3rd EDITION AUTHORS

Susan A. Brown, *Mathematics Department Chair*
York High School, Elmhurst, IL

R. James Breunlin, *Mathematics Department Chair*
Schaumburg High School, Schaumburg, IL

Mary Helen Wiltjer, *Mathematics Teacher*
Oak Park and River Forest High School, Oak Park, IL

Katherine M. Degner, *Mathematics Teacher*
Williamsburg Comm. High School, Williamsburg, IA

Susan K. Eddins, *Mathematics Teacher (retired)*
IL Mathematics & Science Academy, Aurora, IL

Michael Todd Edwards, *Assistant Professor of Mathematics Education*
Miami University, Ohio, Oxford, OH

Neva A. Metcalf, *Mathematics Teacher*
Evanston Township High School, Evanston, IL

Natalie Jakucyn, *Mathematics Teacher*
Glenbrook South High School, Glenview, IL

Zalman Usiskin, *Professor of Education*
The University of Chicago

AUTHORS OF EARLIER EDITIONS

John W. McConnell, *Instructional Supervisor of Mathematics*
Glenbrook South High School, Glenview, IL

Sharon Senk, *Professor of Mathematics*
Michigan State University, East Lansing, MI

Ted Widerski, *Mathematics Teacher*
Waterloo High School, Waterloo, WI

Cathy Hynes Feldman, *Mathematics Teacher*
The University of Chicago Laboratory Schools

James Flanders, UCSMP

Margaret Hackworth, *Mathematics Supervisor*
Pinellas County Schools, Largo, FL

Daniel Hirschhorn, UCSMP

Lydia Polonsky, UCSMP

Leroy Sachs, *Mathematics Teacher (retired)*
Clayton High School, Clayton, MO

Ernest Woodward, *Professor of Mathematics*
Austin Peay State University, Clarksville, TN

---

www.WrightGroup.com

 **Wright Group**

Copyright © 2008 by Wright Group/McGraw-Hill.

Printed in the United States of America.

Send all inquiries to:
Wright Group/McGraw-Hill
P.O. Box 812960
Chicago, IL 60681

ISBN 978-0-07-618591-7
MHID 0-07-618591-5

1 2 3 4 5 6 7 8 9 VHP 13 12 11 10 09 08 07

The **McGraw·Hill** Companies

UCSMP EVALUATION, EDITORIAL, AND PRODUCTION

Director of Evaluation
Denisse R. Thompson, *Professor of Mathematics Education*
University of South Florida, Tampa, FL

Evaluation Assistants
Gladys Mitchell, Zhuo Zheng

Editorial Staff
Catherine Ballway, Grant Owens, Asaf Hadari

Evaluation Consultant
Sharon L. Senk, *Professor of Mathematics*
Michigan State University, East Lansing, MI

Executive Managing Editor
Clare Froemel

Manuscript Production Coordinator
Benjamin R. Balskus

Since the first two editions of *Algebra* were published, millions of students and thousands of teachers have used the materials. Prior to the publication of this third edition, the materials were again revised, and the following teachers and schools participated in evaluations of the trial version during 2005–2006:

Shannon Johnson, *Junction City Middle School*
Junction City, KS

Julie Pellman, *Hyman Brand Hebrew Academy*
Overland Park, KS

Dan Kramer, *Highlands High School-Ft. Thomas*
Fort Thomas, KY

Craig Davelis, Megan Mehilos, Sue Nolte, Lynette TeVault, *York High School*
Elmhurst, IL

Jan Boudreau, *Rosemont Middle School*
La Crescenta, CA

Tammy Anderson, *Ashland High School*
Ashland, OR

Dennis Massoglia, *Washington Middle School*
Calumet, MI

Erica Cheung, *Stone Scholastic Academy*
Chicago, IL

The following schools participated in field studies in 1992–1993, 1987–1988, or 1986–1987 as part of the first edition or the second edition research.

Rancho San Joaquin Middle School
Lakeside Middle School
Irvine High School
Irvine, CA

D.W. Griffith Jr. High School
Los Angeles, CA

Mendocino High School
Mendocino, CA

Chaffey High School
Ontario, CA

Eagleview Middle School
Colorado Springs, CO

Lincoln Junior High School
Lesher Junior High School
Blevins Junior High School
Fort Collins, CO

Bacon Academy
Colchester, CT

Rogers Park Jr. High School
Danbury, CT

Clearwater High School
Clearwater, FL

Safety Harbor Middle School
Safety Harbor, FL

Aptakisic Junior High School
Buffalo Grove, IL

Austin Academy
Bogan High School
Disney Magnet School
Hyde Park Career Academy
Von Steuben Metropolitan Science Center
Washington High School
Chicago, IL

Morton East High School
Cicero, IL

O'Neill Middle School
Downers Grove, IL

Elk Grove High School
Elk Grove Village, IL

Glenbrook South High School
John H. Springman School
Glenview, IL

Mendota High School
Mendota, IL

Carl Sandburg Jr. High School
Winston Park Jr. High School
Palatine, IL

Grant Middle School
Springfield, IL

McClure Junior High School
Western Springs, IL

Hubble Middle School
Wheaton, IL

Central Junior High School
Lawrence, KS

Old Rochester High School
Mattapoisett, MA

Fruitport High School
Fruitport, MI

Sauk Rapids-Rice Schools
Sauk Rapids, MN

Parkway West Middle School
Chesterfield, MO

Taylor Middle School
Van Buren Middle School
Albuquerque, NM

Crest Hills Middle School
Shroder Paideia Middle School
Walnut Hills High School
Cincinnati, OH

Lake Oswego Sr. High School
Lake Oswego, OR

Springfield High School
Springfield, PA

R.C. Edwards Jr. High School
Central, SC

Easley Junior High School
Easley, SC

Liberty Middle School
Liberty, SC

Northeast High School
Clarksville, TN

Hanks High School
El Paso, TX

Robinson Middle School
Maple Dale Middle School
Fox Point, WI

Glen Hills Middle School
Glendale, WI

Contents

VOLUME 1

VOLUME 2

Chapter 9 — 524
Quadratic Equations and Functions

Chapter 10 — 580
Linear Systems

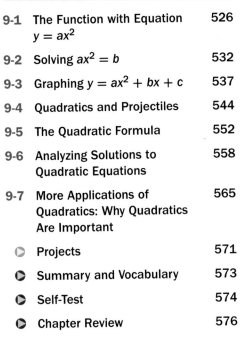

Using Algebra to Describe Patterns of Change

Contents

A small city of 100,000 people has been growing. School planners want to know how many classrooms the city might need during the next 50 years. They consider three possibilities.

1. The population stays the same.

2. The population increases by 3,000 people per year (increasing by a constant amount).

3. The population grows by 2% a year (increasing at a constant growth rate).

The graph on the next page shows what would happen under the three possibilities. *P* is the population *x* years from now.

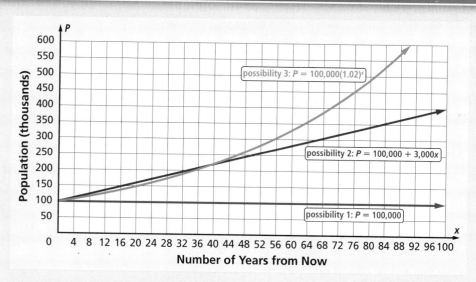

Possibility 3 is often considered the most reasonable. Under this assumption, $P = 100{,}000(1.02)^x$. Because the variable x is an exponent, this equation is said to represent *exponential growth*. This chapter discusses the important applications of exponential growth and compares them with the constant-increase and constant-decrease situations you studied in Chapter 6.

Lesson

7-1

Compound Interest

Vocabulary

power, nth power

base

exponent

principal

interest

annual yield

compound interest

▶ **BIG IDEA** Compound interest is the way most banks and other savings institutions pay savers who put their money into their accounts.

Powers and Repeated Multiplication

A number having the form x^n is called a **power.** When n is a positive integer, x^n describes repeated multiplication. For example, $10^3 = 10 \cdot 10 \cdot 10 = 1{,}000$ and $3^5 = 3 \cdot 3 \cdot 3 \cdot 3 \cdot 3 = 243$. These are examples of the following property.

Mental Math

Write as a fraction in lowest terms.

a. 0.02

b. 1.75

c. –3.57

> **Repeated Multiplication Property of Powers**
>
> When n is a positive integer, $x^n = \underbrace{x \cdot x \cdot \ldots \cdot x.}_{n \text{ factors}}$

The number x^n is called the **nth power** of x and is read "x to the nth power" or just "x to the n." In the expression x^n, x is the **base** and n is the **exponent.** Thus, 3^5 is read "3 to the 5th power," or "3 to the 5th," where 3 is the base and 5 is the exponent. In the expression $100{,}000(1.02)^x$ found on page 397, 1.02 is the base and x is the exponent. The number 100,000 is the coefficient of the power 1.02^x.

How Is Interest Calculated?

An important application of exponents and powers occurs with savings accounts. When you save money, you can choose where to put it. Of course, you can keep it at home, but banks, savings and loan associations, and credit unions will pay you to let them hold your money for you. The amount you give them at the start is called the **principal.** The amount they pay you is called **interest.**

Interest is always a percent of the principal. The percent that the money earns per year is called the **annual yield.**

Example 1

Suppose you deposit P dollars in a savings account upon which the bank pays an annual yield of 4%. If the account is left alone, how much money will be in it at the end of a year?

Solution

Total = principal + interest (4% of principal)

$$= P + 0.04P$$

$$= (1 + 0.04)P = 1.04P$$

You will have 1.04P, or 104% of the principal.

 QY1

▶ **QY1**

If you deposited $1,000 in a savings account with an annual yield of 4%, what would you have at the end of a year?

Compound Interest and How It Is Calculated

When the year is up, the account will have extra money in it because of the interest it earned. If that money is left in the account, then at the end of second year, the bank will pay interest on all the money that is now in the account (the original principal and the first year's interest). This leads to **compound interest,** which means that the interest earns interest.

Example 2

Suppose you deposit $100 in a savings account upon which the bank pays an annual yield of 4%. Assume the account is left alone in Parts a and b.

a. How much money will be in the account at the end of 4 years?

b. How much interest would you earn in the 4 years?

Solution

a. Refer to Example 1. Each year the amount in the bank is multiplied by $1 + 0.04 = 1.04$.

End of first year: $100(1.04) = 100(1.04)^1 = 104.00$

End of second year: $100(1.04)(1.04) = 100(1.04)^2 = 108.16$

End of third year:

$100(1.04)(1.04)(1.04) = 100(1.04)^3 = 112.4864 \approx 112.48$

End of fourth year:

$100(1.04)(1.04)(1.04)(1.04) = 100(1.04)^4 \approx 116.9858 \approx 116.98$

At the end of 4 years there will be $116.98 in the account.

b. Because you started with $100, you earned $116.98 - $100 = $16.98 in the 4 years.

Examine the pattern in the solution to Example 2. At the end of t years there will be $100(1.04)^t$ dollars in the account. By replacing 100 by P for principal, and 0.04 by r for the *annual yield*, we obtain a general formula for compound interest.

Compound Interest Formula

If a principal P earns an annual yield of r, then after t years there will be a total amount A, where $A = P(1 + r)^t$.

The compound interest formula is read "A equals P times the quantity 1 plus r, that quantity to the tth power."

GUIDED

Example 3

When Jewel was born, her parents put $2,000 into an account for college. What will be the total amount of money in the account after 18 years at an annual yield of 5.4%?

Solution Here $P = \$2,000$, $r = 5.4\%$, and $t = 18$. Substitute the values into the Compound Interest Formula. Use $5.4\% = 0.054$.

$$A = P(1 + r)^t$$
$$= \underline{\quad?\quad}(1 + \underline{\quad?\quad})^{\underline{\;?\;}}$$

To evaluate this expression, use a calculator key sequence such as the following.

$\underline{\quad?\quad}$ ⊠ $\underline{\quad?\quad}$ ⌃ $\underline{\quad?\quad}$ [ENTER]

Your display shows $\underline{\quad?\quad}$, which rounded down to the nearest cent is $\underline{\quad?\quad}$.

In 18 years, at an annual yield of 5.4%, $2,000 will increase to $\underline{\quad?\quad}$.

Tuition fees at public four-year colleges increased 35% between 2001 and 2006.

Source: The College Board

 QY2

Eighteen years may seem like a long time, but it is not an unusually long amount of time for money to be in college accounts or retirement accounts.

▶ **QY2**

Suppose you invest $6,240 in an account at 6.3% annual yield for 10 years. How much will be in the account at the end of the 10 years?

Why Do You Receive Interest on Savings?

Banks and other savings institutions pay you interest because they want money to lend to other people. The bank earns money by charging a higher rate of interest on the money they lend than the rate they pay customers who deposit money.

Thus, if the bank could loan the $1,000 you deposited at 4% (perhaps to someone buying a car) at 12% a year, the bank would receive 0.12($1,000), or $120 from that person. So the bank would earn $120 − $40 = $80 in that year on your money. Part of that $80 goes for salaries to the people who work at the bank, part for other bank costs, and part for profit to the owners of the bank.

Questions

COVERING THE IDEAS

1. How is the expression 4^{10} read?

2. Consider the expression $10x^9$. Name each of the following.
   a. base   b. power   c. exponent   d. coefficient

3. a. Calculate 7^3 without a calculator.
   b. Calculate 7^3 with a calculator. Show your key sequence.

In 4–6, rewrite the following expressions using exponents.

4. $\underbrace{\dfrac{5}{9} \cdot \dfrac{5}{9} \cdot \; \cdots \; \cdot \dfrac{5}{9}}_{t \text{ times}}$

5. $18 \cdot -3 \cdot -3 \cdot -3 \cdot -3$

6. $21 \cdot x \cdot x \cdot x \cdot x \cdot x \cdot x \cdot x \cdot x \cdot x \cdot x$

7. On page 397, three possibilities are offered for the growth of a population. What is the predicted population in 50 years using the indicated possibility?
   a. Possibility 1
   b. Possibility 2
   c. Possibility 3

8. **Matching** Match each term with its description.
   a. money you deposit   i. annual yield
   b. interest paid on interest   ii. compound interest
   c. yearly percentage paid   iii. principal

In 9 and 10, write an expression for the amount in the bank after 1 year if P dollars are in an account with the annual yield given.

9. 2%

10. 3.25%

11. a. Write the Compound Interest Formula.
    b. What does A represent?
    c. What does P stand for?
    d. What is r?
    e. What does t represent?

In 12–14, assume the interest is compounded annually.

12. Suppose you deposit $300 in a new savings account paying an annual yield of 2.5%. If no deposits or withdrawals are made, how much money will be in the account at the end of 5 years?

13. A bank advertises an annual yield of 4.81% on a 5-year CD (certificate of deposit). If the CD's original amount was $2,000, how much will it be worth after 5 years?

14. How much interest will be earned in 7 years on a principal of $1,000 at an annual yield of 5.125%?

APPLYING THE MATHEMATICS

In 15 and 16, assume the interest is compounded annually.

15. Susana invests $250 at an annual yield of 4%. Jake invests $250 at an annual yield of 8%. They leave the money in the bank for 2 years.
    a. How much interest does each person earn?
    b. Jake's interest rate is twice Susana's. Does Jake earn twice the interest that Susana does? Why or why not?

16. Which yields more money, (a) an amount invested for 6 years at an annual yield of 5%, or (b) the same amount invested for 3 years at an annual yield of 10%? Explain your answer.

In 17–19 on the next page, use the following: Danica invested $100 in an account that earns an annual yield of 10%. On the same day, Todd deposited $200 in an account earning 5% annually. Below are a graph and a spreadsheet that compare the amount in Danica's and Todd's accounts.

◇	A	B	C
1	Time since Investment (yr)	Danica's Account	Todd's Account
2	0	$100.00	$200.00
3	2	$121.00	$220.50
4	4	$146.41	$243.10
5	6	$177.15	$268.01
6	8	$214.37	$295.49
7	10	$259.37	$325.78
8	12	$313.84	$359.17
9	14		
10	16		
11	18		
12	20		

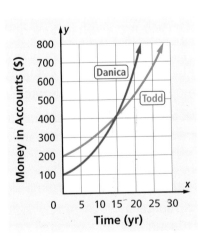

17. **a.** What formula will show the amount in Danica's account after t years?

    b. Complete the column indicating the amounts in Danica's account.

18. Repeat Question 17 for Todd's account.

19. In what year will Danica and Todd have the same amount in their accounts?

20. Use your calculator to make a table. If a principal of $1,000 is saved at an annual yield of 5% compounded annually and nothing is withdrawn from the account, in how many years will it double in value?

REVIEW

21. In World Cup Soccer, a team gets 3 points for a win and 1 point for a tie. Let W be the number of wins and T the number of ties. (**Lessons 6-9, 3-7**)

    a. If a team has more than 3 points, what inequality must W and T satisfy?

    b. Graph all possible pairs (W, T) for a team that has played 3 games and has more than 3 points.

22. Miho puts $6.00 into her piggy bank. Each week thereafter she puts in $2.50. (The piggy bank pays no interest.)

    a. Write an equation showing the total amount of dollars Y after X weeks.

    b. Graph the equation. (**Lesson 6-2**)

Ecuador's Ulises De La Cruz, left, and England's Joe Cole battle for the ball during a 2006 World Cup soccer match between England and Ecuador.

23. Find the probability of getting a number that is a factor of 12 in one toss of a fair die. (**Lesson 5-6**)

In 24 and 25, solve the sentence. (**Lessons 4-5, 4-4**)

24. $38c - 14 = 6(c - 3) + 4$ 25. $8(2 + \frac{1}{8}u) > 2u + 1 - u$

26. **Multiple Choice** Which formula describes the numbers in the table at the right? (**Lesson 1-2**)

    A $y = x + (x + 1)$ **B** $y = 2x$

    C $y = 2^x$ **D** $y = x^2$

x	0	2	4	6	8
y	1	4	16	64	256

27. Find t if $2^t = 32$. (**Previous Course**)

EXPLORATION

28. Find out the yield for a savings account in a bank or other savings institution near where you live. (Often these yields are in newspaper ads.)

QY ANSWERS

1. $1,040

2. $11,495.20

Lesson 7-2
Exponential Growth

Vocabulary

exponential growth

growth factor

exponential growth equation

▶ **BIG IDEA** Growth at a constant percentage rate can be described by an expression of the form bg^x, where $g > 1$ and the variable is in the exponent.

Powering and Population Growth

An important application of powers is in population growth situations. As an example, consider rabbit populations, which can grow quickly. In 1859, 24 rabbits were imported to Australia from Europe as a new source of food. Rabbits are not native to Australia, but conditions there were ideal for rabbits and so they flourished. Soon, there were so many rabbits that they damaged grazing land. By 1887, the government was offering a reward for a way to control the rabbit population. How many rabbits might there have been in 1887? Example 1 provides an estimate.

Mental Math

Solve each inequality.

a. $2x < 5$

b. $-4m + 3 > 14$

c. $9 + 3b \leq 3 - b$

Example 1

Twenty-six rabbits are introduced to another area. Assume that the rabbit population doubles every year. How many rabbits would there be after 28 years?

Solution Since the population doubles every year, in 28 years it will double 28 times. The number of rabbits will be

$$26 \cdot \underbrace{2 \cdot 2 \cdot 2 \cdot \ldots \cdot 2}_{28 \text{ factors}} .$$

To evaluate this expression on a calculator, rewrite it as $26 \cdot 2^{28}$. Use the $\boxed{y^x}$ or $\boxed{\wedge}$ key. There would be 6,979,321,856, or about 7 billion rabbits after 28 years.

What Is Exponential Growth?

The rabbit population in Example 1 is said to grow exponentially. In **exponential growth,** the original amount is repeatedly *multiplied* by a positive number called the **growth factor.**

A pet rabbit's diet should be made up of good quality pellets, fresh hay (alfalfa, timothy, or oat), water, and fresh vegetables.

Source: House Rabbit Society

> ### Growth Model for Powering
>
> If a quantity is multiplied by a positive number g (the growth factor) in each of x time periods, then, after the x periods, the quantity will be multiplied by g^x.

In Example 1, the population doubles (is multiplied by 2) every year, so $g = 2$. There are 28 time periods, so $x = 28$. The original number of rabbits, 26, is multiplied by g^x, or 2^{28}. So the population y of rabbits after x years is given by the formula $y = 26 \cdot 2^x$.

In general, if the amount at the beginning of the growth period is b, the growth factor is g, and y is the amount after x time periods, then $y = b \cdot g^x$. We call this the **exponential growth equation.**

The compound interest formula $A = P(1 + r)^t$ is another example of an exponential growth equation. Suppose $5,000 is invested at an annual yield of 4%. Using the variable names of the exponential growth equation, $b = 5,000$ and $g = 1.04$. So y, the value of the investment after x years, is given by $y = 5,000 \cdot 1.04^x$.

If the money is kept invested for 11 years, then $x = 11$, and the total amount will be $5,000 \cdot 1.04^{11}$, which is $7,697.27.

What Happens If the Exponent Is Zero?

In the exponential growth equation $y = b \cdot g^x$, x can be any real number. Consider the situation when $x = 0$. In 0 time periods no time has elapsed. The starting amount b has not grown at all and so it remains the same. It can remain the same only if it is multiplied by 1. This means that $g^0 = 1$, regardless of the value of the growth factor g. This property applies also when g is a negative number.

> ### Zero Exponent Property
>
> If x is any nonzero real number, then $x^0 = 1$.

In words, the zero power of any nonzero number equals 1. For example, $4^0 = 1$, $(-2)^0 = 1$, and $\left(\frac{5}{7}\right)^0 = 1$. The zero power of 0, which would be written 0^0, is undefined.

What Does a Graph of Exponential Growth Look Like?

An equation of the form $y = b \cdot g^x$, where g is a number greater than 1, can describe exponential growth. Graphs of such equations are not lines. They are *exponential growth curves.*

Example 2

Graph the equation $y = 1.5 \cdot 2^x$, when x is 0, 1, 2, 3, and 4.

Solution Substitute $x = 0, 1, 2, 3$, and 4 into the formula $y = 1.5 \cdot 2^x$. Below we show the computation and the results listed as (x, y) pairs.

Computation	(x, y)
$1.5 \cdot 2^0 = 1.5 \cdot 1 = 1.5$	$(0, 1.5)$
$1.5 \cdot 2^1 = 1.5 \cdot 2 = 3$	$(1, 3)$
$1.5 \cdot 2^2 = 1.5 \cdot 4 = 6$	$(2, 6)$
$1.5 \cdot 2^3 = 1.5 \cdot 8 = 12$	$(3, 12)$
$1.5 \cdot 2^4 = 1.5 \cdot 16 = 24$	$(4, 24)$

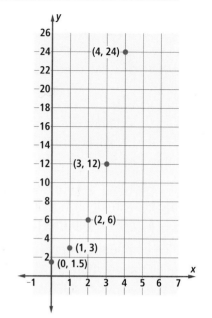

Notice that the y-intercept of the graph in Example 2 is 1.5. Also, the graph does not have a constant rate of change. When something grows exponentially, its rate of change is continually increasing.

Now/Next Method

Example 2 showed how to compute y-values. In an exponential growth equation, $y = b \cdot g^x$, you can compute the y-values by substituting for x. However, that method might not always be the fastest.

Numbers in an exponential growth pattern can be displayed on the homescreen of a graphing calculator using the Now/Next method.

Step 1 Type the starting value 48 (the Now) and press ENTER.

Step 2 Multiply by the growth factor 1.5. The calculator represents the Now by Ans (for "answer"). The calculator at the right is now programmed for Now/Next. By pressing ENTER, it automatically performs Now • 1.5 to get the Next term.

Try this on a calculator. Notice how quickly the table values can be displayed by repeatedly pressing ENTER.

 QY

Exponential Population Growth

Other than money calculated using compound interest, few things in the real world grow exactly exponentially. However, exponential growth curves can be used to approximate changes in population. For example, consider the population of California from 1930 to 2000 shown in the table on the next page.

▶ **QY**

A Now/Next table is shown below.

x	y	
0	4	$\searrow$ • 2.5
1	?	$\searrow$ • 2.5
2	?	$\searrow$ • 2.5
3	?	

a. What are the three numbers that fill in the missing cells if the growth factor is 2.5?

b. Write an equation of the form $y = b \cdot g^x$ for the ordered pairs (x, y).

California's population is graphed below. The curve is the graph of the exponential growth model $y = 5.68(1.29)^x$, where y is the population (in millions) x decades after 1930. The growth factor 1.29 was chosen because it is an "average" growth factor for California for the six decades shown. The points lie quite close to the curve, indicating that California's population since 1930 has grown about 29% per decade.

Year	Population
1930	5,677,251
1940	6,907,387
1950	10,586,223
1960	15,717,204
1970	19,971,069
1980	23,667,764
1990	29,760,021
2000	33,871,648

Source: U.S. Census Bureau

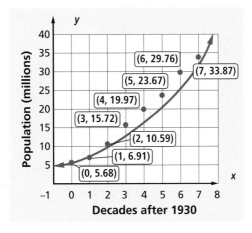

Questions

COVERING THE IDEAS

1. A round goby is a bottom-dwelling fish native to Eastern Europe. In 1995, it was found in the Great Lakes, where it is expected to be harmful to already existing habitats. The round goby is known to spawn several times during the summer, and biologists are tracking the growth of its population. Suppose 11 round gobies were in the Great Lakes in 1995 and that their population triples in size each year.

   a. Write an exponential growth equation to describe this situation.

   b. How many round gobies were in the Great Lakes after 2 years?

   c. How many round gobies were in the Great Lakes in 2000?

   d. How many round gobies will there be in the Great Lakes in 2025?

Round gobies have a well-developed sensory system that allows them to feed in complete darkness.

Source: University of Wisconsin Sea Grant

2. Copy the table at the right and complete it to make a Now/Next table for $y = 50 \cdot 1.2^x$.

3. Suppose that $3,000 is invested in an account with a 4.5% annual yield.

   a. What is the growth factor?

   b. What will be the value of the account after two years?

x	y
0	?
1	?
2	?
3	?

4. **True or False** An amount is multiplied by 10 in each of 12 time periods. After the 12 time periods, the original amount will be multiplied by 120.

In 5 and 6, evaluate the expression when $x = 17$, $y = 1.05$, and $z = 1.04$.

5. a. x^0 b. $x \cdot x^0$ c. $(x + x)^0$

6. a. y^0 b. $y^0 - z^0$ c. $(z - y)^0$

7. Explain why $(-5)^0$ and -5^0 are not equal.

8. Explain how $g^0 = 1$ applies to exponential growth.

9. Let $y = 0.5 \cdot 2^x$.
   a. Make a table for $x = 0, 1, 2, 3, 4$.
   b. Graph the values from Part a.

10. Write an equation of the form $y = b \cdot g^x$ to fit the numbers in the calculator display at the right.

```
                          18
Ans*4
                          72
                         288
                        1152
                        4608
                       18432
```

11. Consider the exponential growth model $y = 5.68(1.29)^x$ for California's population on page 407.
    a. How much does the model's value for 1990 deviate from the actual population?
    b. What does the model predict for the population of California in 2020?

APPLYING THE MATHEMATICS

12. Alexander Fleming discovered penicillin by observing mold growing on Petri dishes. Suppose you are biochemist studying a type of mold that has grown from 3,000 spores to 192,000 spores in one hour. You record the following information.

Time Intervals from Now	Time (min)	Number of Mold Spores
0	0	3,000
1	20	12,000
2	40	48,000
3	60	192,000

? · ?
? · ?
? · ?

Before tossing away some old Petri dishes in 1928, Alexander Fleming accidentally discovered a blue mold growing on the culture of a harmful bacteria.

Source: San Jose State University

a. What is the growth factor as the time interval increases by 1?

b. How many mold spores would there be after 2 hours? Explain how you found your answer.

c. If this growth rate continues, how many mold spores will there be after x hours have passed?

13. The equation $y = 34{,}277 \cdot 1.04^x$ can be used to model the population y of Colorado x years after 1860. This graph shows Colorado's actual population.

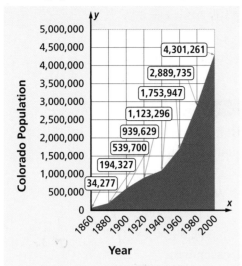

Source: Bureau of the Census

  a. What do 1.04 and 34,277 in the equation represent?

  b. What does the equation predict for the population of Colorado in 1960? By how much did the actual population deviate from the prediction?

  c. Use the model to predict the population of Colorado in 2030.

14. Gossip can be spread quickly in a school. Suppose one person begins spreading the gossip by telling 2 friends. Each friend then tells 2 of his or her different friends. Each person who hears the gossip continues to tell 2 more different friends.

three girls sharing a secret

  a. Complete the table below showing the number of new friends and total number of people who have heard the gossip if the pattern continues.

Stage of Gossip	0	1	2	3	4	5	6	7	8	9	10
New Friends Informed	1	2	4	?	?	?	?	?	?	?	?
Total Number of Friends Informed	1	3	7	?	?	?	?	?	?	?	?

  b. Make ordered pairs (x, y) from the first two rows of the table and plot the points on a graph.

  c. Make ordered pairs (x, y) from the first and third rows of the table and plot the points on a graph.

  d. How many stages of gossip will be needed before 800 people in all hear the gossip?

15. **a.** Graph $y = 2.5^x$ for $x = 0, 1, 2, 3, 4$, and 5.

b. Calculate the rate of change on the graph from $x = 0$ to $x = 1$.

c. Calculate the rate of change on the graph from $x = 4$ to $x = 5$.

d. What do the answers to Parts b and c tell you about this graph?

REVIEW

16. Ashley deposits $3,400 in a savings account with an annual yield of 5%. What will be the total amount of money in the account after 8 years? **(Lesson 7-1)**

17. **a.** Suppose a person's birthday is in July. What is the probability that it is on July 4th?

b. Suppose a person's birthday is in March. What is the probability that it is before the 10th? **(Lesson 5-6)**

18. At one time, the exchange rate for Swiss francs per U.S. dollar was 1.305, meaning that 1 dollar would buy 1.305 francs. With this exchange rate, how many U.S. dollars would 1 Swiss franc buy? **(Lesson 5-4)**

19. In the triangle at the right, side $\overline{AC}$ is 20% longer than side $\overline{AB}$ and side $\overline{BC}$ is 45% shorter than side $\overline{AC}$. If $AB = 9$, find the perimeter of the triangle. **(Lesson 4-1)**

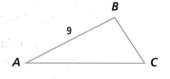

20. **Multiple Choice** Which expression does *not* equal $-(3x - 3y)$? **(Lessons 2-4, 2-1)**

A $3(y - x)$ **B** $3y + 3x$ **C** $-3x + 3y$ **D** $-3(x - y)$

EXPLORATION

21. This exploration will help to explain why 0^0 is undefined. You will examine values of x^0 and 0^x when x is close to 0.

a. Use your calculator to give values of x^0 for $x = 1, 0.1, 0.01, 0.001$, and so on. What does this suggest for the value of 0^0?

b. Use your calculator to give values of 0^x for $x = 1, 0.1, 0.01, 0.001$, and so on. What does this suggest for the value of 0^0?

c. What does your calculator display when you try to evaluate 0^0? Why do you think it gives that display?

QY ANSWERS

a. 10; 25; 62.5

b. $y = 4 \cdot 2.5^x$

Lesson 7-3

Exponential Decay

Vocabulary

exponential decay

half-life

▶ **BIG IDEA** Decay at a constant percentage rate can be described by an expression of the form bg^x, where $0 < g < 1$ and the variable is in the exponent.

The Growth Factor and the Type of Exponential Change

Three children were arguing. Tammy said, "If you multiply 5 by a positive number, the answer is always greater than 5." Nancy said, "No, you're wrong! I can multiply 5 by something and get an answer less than 5." Leon said, "I can multiply 5 by something and get 5 for an answer."

In the children's arguments, what matters is how the multiplier compares to 1. If Nancy chooses a multiplier between 0 and 1, multiplying by 5 gives a result that is less than 5. For example, $5 \cdot \frac{1}{10} = \frac{1}{2}$. Of course, Leon can do $5 \cdot 1$ and get 5 for an answer.

This relates to exponential equations of the form $y = b \cdot g^x$ because the growth factor g can be greater than, equal to, or less than 1. In the last lesson, you saw only situations in which the growth factor was greater than 1, so there was an increase over time in each case. While a growth factor always has to be positive, it can be less than 1. When this is true, there is a decrease over time. This happens in situations of **exponential decay**.

Examples of Exponential Decay

Psychologists use exponential decay models to describe learning and memory loss. In Example 1, the growth factor is less than 1 so the amount remembered decreases.

Mental Math

Find the number.

a. 7 less than 4 times the number is 13.

b. –10 times the number, plus 80, is 10.

c. 14 minus 3 times the number is 121.

Example 1

Assume that each day after cramming, a student forgets 20% of the vocabulary words learned the day before. A student crams for a French test on Friday by learning 100 vocabulary words Thursday night. But the test is delayed from Friday to Monday. If the student does not study over the weekend, how many words is he or she likely to remember on Monday?

(continued on next page)

Solution If 20% of the words are forgotten each day, 80% are remembered.

Day	Day Number	Number of Words Remembered
Thursday	0	100
Friday	1	$100(0.80) = 80$
Saturday	2	$100(0.80)(0.80) = 100(0.80)^2 = 64$
Sunday	3	$100(0.80)(0.80)(0.80) = 100(0.80)^3 = 51.2 \approx 51$
Monday	4	$100(0.80)(0.80)(0.80)(0.80) = 100(0.80)^4 = 40.96 \approx 41$

On Monday the student is likely to remember about 41 vocabulary words.

STOP QY1

As they get old, cars and other manufactured items often wear out. Therefore, their value decreases over time. This decrease, called *depreciation,* is often described by giving the percent of the value that is lost each year. If the item is worth r percent less each year, then it keeps $(1 - r)$ percent of its previous value. This is the growth factor. (The word "growth" is used even though the value is shrinking.)

> ▶ QY1
>
> If the student does not study between now (Thursday) and the test, how many words will be remembered x days from Thursday?

Example 2

In 1998, a new car cost $21,000. Suppose its value depreciates 15% each year.

a. Find an equation that gives the car's value y when it is x years old.

b. What was the predicted value of the car in 2005? How close is this to the actual price of a 1998 car, which was $7,050 in 2005?

c. Graph the car's value for the interval $0 \leq x \leq 8$.

About 35% of the cost of owning and operating a car comes from depreciation.

Source: Federal Highway Administration

Solutions

a. If the car loses 15% of its value each year, it keeps 85%, so the growth factor is $1 - 0.15 = 0.85$. In the exponential growth equation $y = b \cdot g^x$, b is 21,000, the new car's price, and g is 0.85. An equation that gives the value of the car is $y = 21,000 \cdot (0.85)^x$.

b. The year 2005 is 7 years after 1998, so $x = 7$.
$21,000(0.85)^7 \approx 6{,}732.12$. The predicted value was $6,732.12. The deviation between the actual price and the predicted price was $7,050 - $6,732.12 = $317.88, so the model gives a fairly accurate prediction.

c. The table below shows the value of the car each year. The initial value, $21,000, is the *y*-intercept of the graph. In the table, to move from one *y* value to the next, you can multiply by 0.85. The decrease is seen in the graph by the fact that the curve goes downward as you go to the right.

x	y (dollars)
0	21,000.00
1	17,850.00
2	15,172.50
3	12,896.63
4	10,962.13
5	9,317.81
6	7,920.14
7	6,732.12
8	5,722.30

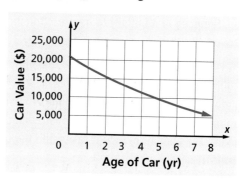

As with graphs of exponential growth, the points of an exponential decay relationship lie on a curve rather than a straight line. Another graph of the car value is shown below, with segments showing the rate of change between points. Notice that as you go from one year to the next, the amount of decrease is decreasing. For example, in going from new ($x = 0$) to 1 year old ($x = 1$), the value of the car dropped $3,150. But between $x = 7$ and $x = 8$, the value lost was only about $1,000.

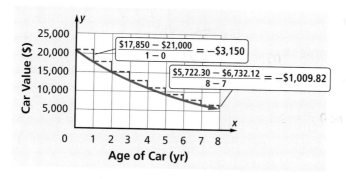

In each case, 15% of the value is lost. But as time passes, this is 15% of a smaller number.

 QY2

In Example 3 on the next page, the "population" is the amount of medication in a person's body.

> ▶ QY2
>
> A new boat costs $32,000. Its value depreciates by 8% each year. Give an equation for *y*, the value of the boat, when it is *x* years old.

GUIDED

Example 3

A common medicine for people with diabetes is insulin. Insulin breaks down in the bloodstream quickly, with the rate varying for different types of the medication. Suppose that initially there are 10 units of insulin in a person's bloodstream and that the amount decreases by 3% each minute.

a. Write an equation to describe y, the amount of insulin in the bloodstream, after x minutes have passed.

b. Make a calculator table for the equation from Part a. Use the table to find when 5 units of insulin remain in the bloodstream. (This is half of the initial amount. The amount of time it takes half the quantity to decay is called the **half-life.**)

c. How much insulin remains after 4 hours?

d. According to the equation, when will the amount of insulin in the body be zero?

Solutions

a. The amount of insulin starts at __?__ units. Because 3% of the insulin is lost each minute, the growth factor is __?__. The exponential equation is $y = $ __?__ $\cdot$ __?__ ^{x}.

b. The screen at the right shows the starting value of 10 units, with x increasing by 1 for each row. Scroll down the table to find where y is close to 5 units. This happens at x = __?__. So 5 units of insulin remain after about __?__ minutes.

c. First change 4 hours into __?__ minutes. When x = __?__ minutes, then $y = $ __?__ $\cdot$ __?__ $^{?} \approx 0.007$ unit of insulin remain. So after 4 hours, there is almost no insulin left.

d. Using this equation, the amount of insulin in the body will never be zero. No matter how great the value of x becomes, y will always be greater than zero.

The above example illustrates that a quantity decaying exponentially will theoretically never reach zero. Because this is true, there will never be an ordered pair with a y-coordinate of exactly 0. So the graph of an exponential equation $y = b \cdot g^x$ does not intersect the x-axis.

Graphs and Growth Factors

Exponential growth and exponential decay are both described by an equation of the same form, $y = b \cdot g^x$.

The value of g determines whether the equation describes growth or decay. A third situation happens when there is no change. The three possibilities are graphed below.

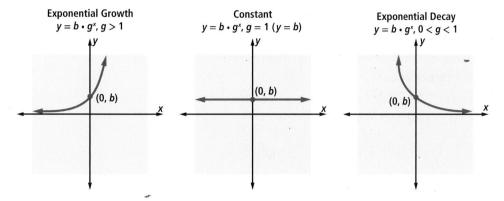

Exponential Growth
$y = b \cdot g^x, g > 1$
$(0, b)$

Constant
$y = b \cdot g^x, g = 1\ (y = b)$
$(0, b)$

Exponential Decay
$y = b \cdot g^x, 0 < g < 1$
$(0, b)$

The growth factor can be given in words like "double," "triple," or "half," which indicate a factor of 2, 3, or $\frac{1}{2}$, respectively. But it is also common to describe the growth factor by using percent. If the quantity is growing by a percent r, the value of growth factor g is greater than 1 and the exponential equation is $y = b(1 + r)^x$. If the quantity is shrinking, g is less than 1 and the equation is $y = b(1 - r)^x$. Recall that the graph of equation $y = k$ is a horizontal line, like that shown in the middle graph above. In this situation, in which the original quantity remains constant, there is neither growth nor decay. It can be described by an exponential equation where g is 1. For example, the horizontal line $y = 5$ is also the graph of $y = 5 \cdot 1^x$, since $1^x = 1$.

Questions

COVERING THE IDEAS

In 1–3, give the growth factor for a quantity with the given characteristic.

1. decreases exponentially by 17%

2. increases exponentially by 2.5%

3. does not change

4. Many teachers have policies about late work that lower a student's grade for each day that it is late. Suppose a teacher lowers the grade of a 50-point assignment by 20% for every day late.

    a. Let x = the number of days late an assignment is and y = the number of points the assignment would earn. Make a table of values using x = 0, 1, 2, 3, 4, and 5.

    b. Write an equation to describe the relationship.

5. Suppose a new car costs $32,000 in 2006. Find the value of the car in one year if the following is true.

   a. The car is worth 85% of its purchase price.

   b. The car depreciated 20% of its value.

   c. The value of the car depreciated d%.

6. A new piece of industrial machinery costs $2,470,000 and depreciates at a rate of 12% per year.

   a. Find the value of the machine after 15 years.

   b. Find the value of the machine after t years.

7. A person with diabetes requires a dose of 15 units of insulin. Assume that 3% of the insulin is lost from the bloodstream each minute. How much insulin remains in the bloodstream after 30 minutes? After x minutes?

8. a. Complete the table for the exponential decay situation at the right.

   b. Write an equation to describe the relationship.

x	y
0	160
1	?
2	?
3	?

· 0.75
· 0.75
· 0.75

In 9–11, classify the pattern in the table as exponential growth, exponential decay, or constant.

9.

x	y
0	35
1	?
2	?

· 1
· 1

10.

x	y
0	0.26
1	?
2	?

· 1.13
· 1.13

11.

x	y
0	458
1	?
2	?

· 0.32
· 0.32

12. **Fill in the Blank** Fill in each blank with "decay" or "growth."

   a. $\frac{2}{3}$ can be the growth factor in an exponential ___?___ situation.

   b. $\frac{3}{2}$ can be the growth factor in an exponential ___?___ situation.

APPLYING THE MATHEMATICS

13. Suppose a school has 2,500 students and the number of students is decreasing by 2% each year.

   a. If this rate continues, write an equation for the number of students after x years.

   b. If this rate continues, how many students will the school have 10 years from now?

14. Imagine that you begin with a cutout of an equilateral triangle. If you fold on the dotted lines as shown below, each vertex will touch the midpoint of the opposite side. Four regions will be formed.

Before folding   **Fold each vertex like this.**   **After 1 set of folds**

 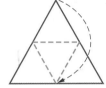

If you repeat this process, you will get a sequence of successively smaller equilateral triangles. Suppose the original triangle has an area of 100 square centimeters.

a. Complete the chart below.

Set of folds	0	1	2	3
Regions	1	4	?	?
Area of a Region (cm²)	100	?	?	?

b. Write an equation to describe the number of regions y after x sets of folds.

c. Write an equation to describe the area of each region y after x sets of folds.

15. Suppose one plate of tinted glass allows only 60% of light to pass through. The amount of light y that will pass through x panes of glass can then be described by the exponential decay equation $y = 0.6^x$.

a. Plot and label 5 points on a graph of this equation.

b. If enough panes of glass are put together, will the amount of light passing through the panes ever be zero according to this model?

16. The amount of a radioactive substance decreases over time. The *half-life* of a substance is the amount of time it takes half of the material to decay. Strontium-90 has a half-life of 29 years. This means that in each 29-year period, one half of the strontium-90 decays and one half remains. Suppose you have 2,000 grams of strontium-90.

a. How much strontium-90 will remain after 5 half-life periods?

b. How much strontium-90 will remain after 10 half-life periods?

c. How many years equal 10 half-life periods of strontium-90?

Colored light patterns reflect on the floor of the Old Louisiana State Capitol in Baton Rouge during the building's restoration in the early 1990s.

Exponential Decay **417**

17. Consider the equation $y = \left(\frac{1}{2}\right)^x$.

    a. Make a table of values giving y as both a fraction and a decimal when $x = 0, 1, 2, 3, 10,$ and 20.

    b. Find all solutions to the equation $\left(\frac{1}{2}\right)^x = 0$.

REVIEW

18. The rule of 72 is a simple finance method that can be used to estimate the number of periods that it will take an investment to double in value. The method is to divide 72 by the growth rate expressed as a percent, and the result will be the approximate number of periods. For example, if $50 is invested at 6% per year, then the rule of 72 says that after $\frac{72}{6} = 12$ years, a $50 investment will be worth $50 \cdot 2 = \$100$. Calculation shows that after 12 years, this investment is worth $100.61. **(Lessons 7-2, 7-1)**

    a. Use the rule of 72 to estimate the time it will take for $250 invested at 9% to double in value.

    b. Use the compound interest formula to give an exact value of a $250 investment after the number of periods found in Part a.

19. Refer to the table at the right that shows the average consumption of bottled water per person in the United States. **(Lesson 6-7, 6-4)**

    a. Draw a scatterplot with *year* on the *x*-axis and *gallons per person* on the *y*-axis.

    b. Find an equation of an eyeballed line to the data.

    c. Write the slope-intercept form of your equation for the line of fit from Part b.

    d. Use your equation to predict the consumption of bottled water in the United States in 2007.

Year	Bottled Water (gal/person)
2000	17.3
2001	18.8
2002	20.9
2003	22.4
2004	24.0
2005	25.7

Source: www.beveragemarketing.com

20. Solve $4.8q + 9.1 < 12.3q - 7.4$. **(Lessons 4-5, 3-8)**

EXPLORATION

21. Archaeologists use radioactivity to determine the age of ancient objects. Carbon-14 is a radioactive element that is often used to date fossils. Find the half-life of carbon-14 and describe how it is used to help date fossils.

QY ANSWERS

1. $100(0.80)^x$

2. $y = 32,000 \cdot (0.92)^x$

Modeling Exponential Growth and Decay

Vocabulary

exponential regression

▶ **BIG IDEA**   Situations of exponential growth and decay can be modeled by equations of the form $y = bg^x$.

As you saw with the population of California in Lesson 7-2, sometimes a scatterplot shows a data trend that can be approximated by an exponential equation. Similar to linear regression, your calculator can use a method called **exponential regression** to determine an equation of the form $y = b \cdot g^x$ to model a set of ordered pairs.

Modeling Exponential Decay

In the Activity below, exponential regression models how high a ball bounces.

Mental Math

Each product is an integer. Write the integer.

a. $\frac{1}{4} \cdot 360$

b. $\frac{2}{3} \cdot 45$

c. $\frac{4}{5} \cdot 135$

d. $\frac{5}{12} \cdot 228$

Activity

Each group of 5 or 6 students needs at least 3 different types of balls (kickball, softball, and so on), a ruler, markers or chalk, and large paper with at least 25 parallel lines that are 3 inches apart.

Step 1 Tape the paper to a wall or door so the horizontal lines can be used to measure height above the floor. To make measuring easier, number every fourth line (12 in., 24 in., 36 in., and so on).

Step 2 One student will drop each ball from the highest horizontal line and the other students will act as spotters to see how high the ball bounces. The 1st spotter will mark the height to which the ball rebounds after the 1st bounce. The 2nd spotter will mark the rebound height after the 2nd bounce, and so on, until the ball is too low to mark.

Step 3 Make a table similar to the one at the right and record the rebound heights after each bounce.

Bounce	Ball Height (in.)
0 (drop height)	?
1	?
2	?
3	?
?	?

Step 4 For each ball, enter the data in a list and create a scatterplot on your calculator.

Step 5a. Use the linear regression capability of your calculator to find the line of best fit for the data. Graph this line on the same screen as your scatterplot. Sketch a copy of the graph.

(continued on next page)

b. Find the deviation between the actual and predicted height of the ball after the 3rd bounce.

c. Use your linear regression model to predict the height of the ball after the 8th bounce.

Step 6a. Use the exponential regression capability of your calculator to find an exponential curve to fit the data. Graph this equation on the same screen as your scatterplot. Sketch a copy of the scatterplot and curve.

b. Find the deviation between the actual and predicted height of the ball after the 3rd bounce.

c. Use your exponential regression model to predict the height of the ball after the 8th bounce.

Step 7 Which seems to be the better model of the data the linear equation or the exponential equation? Explain how you made your decision.

Step 8 Repeat Step 6 to find exponential regression equations that fit the bounces of the other balls.

Step 9 Write a paragraph comparing the "bounciness" of the balls you tested.

 QY

Modeling Exponential Growth

Advances in technology change rapidly. Some people say that if you purchase a computer today it will be out of date by tomorrow. When computers were first introduced to the public, they ran much more slowly. As computers have advanced over the years, the speed has increased greatly. On the next page is an example of data that a person collected to show the advancement in computer technology. The processing speed of a computer is measured in megahertz (MHz).

GUIDED

Example

The table and graph on the next page show the average speed of a computer and the year it was made.

a. Write an equation to model the data.

b. Find the deviation between the actual speed for the year 2000 and the predicted speed.

c. Use the model to predict the processing speed of a computer made in 2020.

> **QY**
>
> A student dropped a ball from a height of 0.912 meter and used a motion detector to get the data below.
>
> | Bounce | Rebound Height (m) |
> |--------|--------------------|
> | 0 | 0.912 |
> | 1 | 0.759 |
> | 2 | 0.603 |
> | 3 | 0.496 |
> | 4 | 0.411 |
> | 5 | 0.328 |
> | 6 | 0.271 |
>
> a. Write an exponential equation to fit the data.
>
> b. After the 8th bounce, how high will the ball rebound?

Year	Years since 1976	Speed (MHz)
1976	0	2
1978	2	4
1980	4	5
1982	6	8
1984	8	13
1986	10	16
1988	12	20
1990	14	35
1992	16	48
1994	18	60
1996	20	85
1998	22	180
2000	24	420

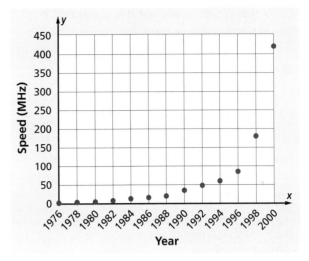

Source: *Microprocessor Quick Reference Guide*

Solutions

a. First enter the data into your calculator lists. Instead of letting years be the x-values, let $x =$ the years since 1976. So for 1976 itself, $x = 0$ and for 1978, $x = 2$. Next, use exponential regression on your calculator to find an exponential equation to fit the data. For $y = b \cdot g^x$, the calculator gives $b \approx 2.241$ and $g \approx 1.218$. (Your calculator may call this equation $y = ab^x$.)

The exponential equation that best fits the data is
$$y = \underline{\quad ? \quad}.$$

b. For 2000, $x = 24$ and the actual speed was 420 MHz. Substitute 24 into the equation to find the predicted value. The predicted speed is $y = \underline{\quad ? \quad}$ MHz. The deviation is $420 - \underline{\quad ? \quad} = \underline{\quad ? \quad}$. The actual processing speed in 2000 was $\underline{\quad ? \quad}$ more than the predicted speed.

c. The year 2020 is $2020 - 1976$, or 44 years after 1976, so substitute 44 for x in your exponential equation. $y = \underline{\quad ? \quad} \, (\underline{\quad ? \quad})^{\underline{\,?\,}}$, so the predicted processor speed for the year 2020 is $\underline{\quad ? \quad}$ MHz.

On April 25, 1961, the patent office awarded the first patent for an integrated circuit to Robert Noyce while Jack Kilby's application was still being analyzed. Today, both men are acknowledged as having independently conceived of the idea.

Source: PBS

Questions

COVERING THE IDEAS

1. Suppose a ball is dropped and it rebounds to a height of y feet after bouncing x times, where $y = 6(0.55)^x$. Use the equation to
   a. give the height from which the ball was dropped, and
   b. give the percent the ball rebounds in relation to its previous height.

In 2–4, use the graph to answer the questions. The percent written above each bar represents the percent of the previous height to which each type of ball will rebound.

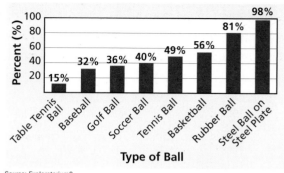

Source: Exploratorium®

2. Which ball's rebound height could be modeled by the equation $y = 10(0.49)^x$?

3. If a basketball is dropped from a height of 15 feet above the ground, how high will it rebound after the 1st bounce? After the 5th bounce?

4. Find and compare the rebound percentages in the Activity on page 419 to those in the graph. Are they similar or different?

5. A computer's memory is measured in terms of megabytes (MB). The table at the right shows how much memory an average computer had, based on the number of years it was made after 1977. Use exponential regression to predict the amount of memory for a computer made in 2020.

Years After 1977	Memory (MB)
0	0.0625
2	1.125
3	8
6	16
7	30
9	32
13	40
17	88
21	250
27	512

6. For each scatterplot, tell whether you would expect exponential regression to produce a good model for the data. Explain your reasoning.

a.

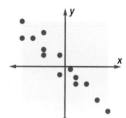

b.

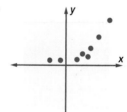

c.

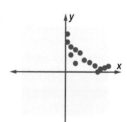

d.

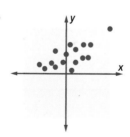

APPLYING THE MATHEMATICS

Matching In 7–9, the graphs relate the bounce height of a ball to the number of times that it has bounced. Match a graph to the equation.

a. $y = 5.1(0.90)^x$ b. $y = 8.7(0.90)^x$ c. $y = 8.7(0.42)^x$

7.

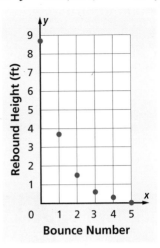

8.

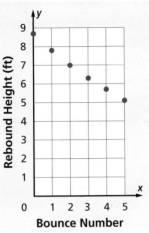

9.

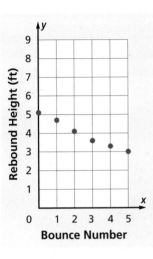

10. The table at the right shows the number of weeks a movie had played in theaters, how it ranked, and how much money it grossed each weekend. (Note that $x = 0$ is the weekend the movie opened.)

    a. Create a scatterplot with $y =$ gross sales after x weeks in theaters. Why is the exponential model a better model for these data than a linear model?

    b. Use exponential regression to find an equation to fit the data.

    c. What gross sales are predicted for the weekend of the 20th week?

Weeks in Theaters	Rank	Weekend Gross ($)
0	1	114,844,116
1	1	71,417,527
2	2	45,036,912
3	2	28,508,104
4	3	14,317,411
5	5	10,311,062
6	7	7,515,984
7	11	4,555,932
8	13	3,130,214
9	18	2,204,636
10	22	890,372
11	25	403,186

11. Lydia and Raul started with 2 pennies in a cup, shook them out onto the table, and added a penny for each coin that showed a head. They continued to repeat this process and their data are recorded in the table at the right.

    a. Create a scatterplot of their data.

    b. Use exponential regression to derive an equation relating the trial number to the number of pennies they will have on the table.

Trial Number	Number of Pennies
0	2
1	2
2	3
3	5
4	8
5	13
6	17
7	25
8	38
9	60

For **12** and **13**, create a real-world problem that could be modeled by the given equation.

12. $y = 72(1.08)^x$

13. $y = 14(0.65)^x$

14. The population of a city is 1,250,000. Write an expression for the population y years from now under each assumption. (**Lessons 7-3, 7-2, 6-1**)

a. The population grows 2.5% per year.

b. The population decreases 3% per year.

c. The population decreases by 1,500 people per year.

15. Graph $y = 125\left(\frac{2}{5}\right)^x$ for integer values of x from 0 to 5. (**Lesson 7-3**)

16. Rewrite $x^3 y^4$ using the Repeated Multiplication Property of Powers. (**Lesson 7-1**)

17. An art store buys a package of 40 bristle paintbrushes for $80.00 and a package of 30 sable paintbrushes for $150. If they plan to sell an art kit with 4 bristle paintbrushes and 3 sable paintbrushes, how much should they charge for the kit to break even on their costs? (**Lesson 5-3**)

18. *Skill Sequence* Divide and simplify each expression. (**Lesson 5-2**)

a. $\frac{4}{x} \div \frac{5}{x}$

b. $\frac{4}{x} \div \frac{5}{2x}$

c. $\frac{4}{x} \div \frac{5}{x^2}$

a young artist at work

19. Recall that if an item is discounted $x\%$, you pay $(100 - x)\%$ of the original price. Calculate in your head the amount you pay for a camera that originally cost $300 and is discounted each indicated amount. (**Lesson 4-1**)

a. 10%

b. 25%

c. $33\frac{1}{3}\%$

20. Evaluate $(3a)^3 (4b)^2$ when $a = -2$ and $b = 6$. (**Lesson 1-1**)

21. In the ball-drop activity on pages 419–420 and Questions 2–4 on page 422, you explored the rebound height of a ball as a percent of its previous height. Different types of balls have different percents. Does the height from which the ball is dropped affect the percent a ball will rebound? Explain your answer.

22. Do the activity described in Question 11 on page 423. How close is your exponential model to the one in that question?

QY ANSWERS

a. $y = 0.917(0.816)^x$

b. approximately 0.18 m

Lesson
7-5
The Language of Functions

Vocabulary

function
input
output
value of the function
squaring function
independent variable
dependent variable
domain of a function
range of a function
relation

▶ **BIG IDEA** A function is a relationship between two variables in which the value of the first variable is associated with, or determines, a unique value of the second variable.

In this course, you have seen many situations that involve two variables. In an investment situation, the length of time that money has been invested determines the value of the investment. In temperatures, the Fahrenheit temperature determines the Celsius temperature or vice versa. In a sequence of dot patterns, the term number determines the number of dots. When the value of a first variable determines the value of a second variable, we call the relationship between the variables a *function*.

Mental Math

To the nearest mile per gallon, estimate the mpg of a car that went

a. 300 miles on 11 gallons of gas.

b. 250 miles on 9 gallons of gas.

c. 400 miles on 14 gallons of gas.

A Squaring Function

Consider the squares of the integers from 1 to 10. There are two variables. The first is the integer. The second is its square. We can describe the relationship between these integers and their squares in many ways.

Table or List

Integer	Square
1	1
2	4
3	9
4	16
5	25
6	36
7	49
8	64
9	81
10	100

Graph

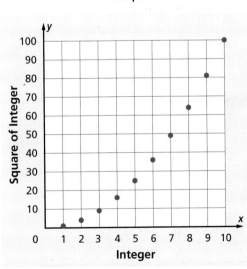

Equation $y = x^2$, where x is an integer from 1 to 10

Words The square of an integer from 1 to 10 is the result of multiplying the integer by itself.

In general, you can think of functions either as special kinds of correspondences or as special sets of ordered pairs. A **function** is a correspondence in which each value of the first variable (the **input**) corresponds to *exactly one* value of the second variable (the **output**), which is called a **value of the function.** We think of the first variable as determining the value of the second variable. The table, graph, equation, and words on page 425 describe a **squaring function.** The value of a number determines the value of its square. For example, when $x = 3$, the value of the squaring function is 9.

 QY1

The graph on page 425 shows the squaring function as a set of ordered pairs. A function is a set of ordered pairs in which each first coordinate appears with *exactly one* second coordinate. That is, once you know the value of the first variable (often called x), then there is only one value for the second variable (often called y). For this reason, the first variable is called the **independent variable** and the second variable is called the **dependent variable.**

▸ **QY1**

What is the value of the squaring function when $x = 7$?

The Domain and Range of a Function

Suppose in the squaring function that x can be any real number from −10 to 10. You cannot list all the ordered pairs of the function, but the function still can be described by the equation $y = x^2$, where x is a real number from −10 to 10. The function can still be described in words: The square of any real number from −10 to 10 is the result of multiplying the number by itself. And the function can still be described by a graph, as shown at the right.

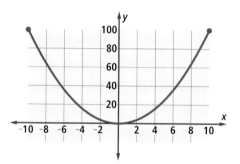

The difference between this squaring function and the one on page 425 is in the *domain of the function*. The **domain of a function** is the set of allowable inputs in the function, that is, the set of possible values of the first (independent) variable. In the squaring function on page 425, the domain is {1, 2, 3, 4, 5, 6, 7, 8, 9, 10}. In the squaring function on this page, the domain is the set of real numbers from −10 to 10.

If a function has a graph, you can read its domain from the graph. The domain is the set of x-coordinates of the points of the graph.

Corresponding to the domain of a function is its **range,** the set of possible values of the second (dependent) variable. The range is the set of possible values of the function. In the squaring function on page 425, the range is {1, 4, 9, 16, 25, 36, 49, 64, 81, 100}. In the squaring function on this page, the range is the set of real numbers from 0 to 100.

QY2

When a set of numbers is not specifically given for the domain of a function, you should assume that the domain is the set of all numbers possible in the situation.

Example 1

Consider the reciprocal function $y = \frac{1}{x}$, which pairs real numbers with their reciprocals.

a. Give the domain.
b. Find the value of the function when $x = 4$.

Solution

a. The domain is the set of all values that can replace x, the independent variable. Any number except 0 can be used. (Because $\frac{1}{0}$ is undefined, 0 has no reciprocal.) So the domain is all real numbers except 0.

b. Substitute 4 for x. The value of the function is $\frac{1}{4}$.

GUIDED

Example 2

What are the domain and range of the function described by the equation $y = 4x - 3$?

Solution The domain is the set of allowable values of x. Because no situation is given for x, you should assume that its domain is ___?___.

The range is the set of possible values of y. The graph of $y = 4x - 3$ is an oblique line. So any value of y is possible, and the range is ___?___.

In many places in this book, you have seen one function modeling another.

Example 3

In Lesson 7-3, the equation $y = 21{,}000(0.85)^x$ describes a function that models a car's value y when it is x years old if it was purchased for $21,000 and depreciates 15% a year. What is the range of this function?

Solution You can think of the car's value as decreasing constantly even though you have not yet studied values of powers when the exponent is not an integer. Refer to the graph in Lesson 7-3 on page 413. According to the model, the value of the car keeps decreasing but never reaches 0. So the range of the function is the set of real numbers y with $0 < y \leq 21{,}000$ which is written in set-builder notation as $\{y: 0 < y \leq 21{,}000\}$.

STOP QY3

▶ **QY2**

A third squaring function is graphed below. What is its domain? What is its range?

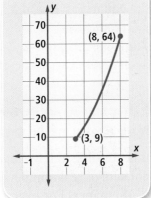

▶ **QY3**

Use a calculator to estimate the value of $21{,}000(0.85)^x$ to the nearest penny when $x = 25, 25.3$, and 26.

Relations That Are Not Functions

The word **relation** describes any set of ordered pairs. It is possible to have relations between variables that are not functions. This happens when the first variable x in a relation corresponds to more than one value of the second variable y. For example, the relation described by the equation $x = y^2$ does *not* describe a function. When $x = 4$, then $y = 2$ or $y = -2$. So the value $x = 4$ corresponds to two different values for y, 2 and -2. Because a value of x does not always determine exactly one value of y, the relation is not a function.

Functions Whose Domains or Ranges Are Not Sets of Numbers

It is possible to have functions whose domains and ranges are not sets of real numbers, or even that have little to do with mathematics. For example, every person on Earth has a unique blood type. So there is a function whose domain is the set of all living people on Earth and whose range is the set of all blood types. Each ordered pair of this function is of the form (a person, that person's blood type). This function has no equation and cannot be graphed, but it is still a function with a domain (the set of all people) and a range (the set of all blood types).

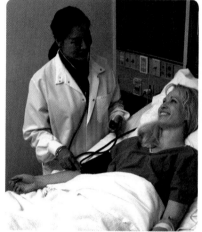

Everybody has a blood type. The most common blood-type classification system is the ABO system discovered by Karl Landsteiner in the early 1900s.

Source: University of Utah

Questions

COVERING THE IDEAS

1. Consider the function described by $y = x^2$ with domain the set of integers from 1 to 5.

   a. What is the value of this function when $x = 3$?

   b. The point (4, 16) is on the graph of this function. Which of these coordinates is the input and which is the output?

   c. Which variable is the independent variable and which is the dependent variable?

   d. What is the range of this function?

2. Consider a cubing function described by $y = x^3$ with domain the set of real numbers from -50 to 50. Find the value of this function when

   a. $x = 36$.   b. $x = -36$.   c. $x = 0$.

3. a. What is the value of the reciprocal function when $x = -1$?

   b. What is the value of the reciprocal function when $x = 3.5$?

4. Give the two definitions of *function* stated in this lesson.

5. Explain why 0 is not in the range of the reciprocal function.

In 6 and 7, the graph of a function is given.

a. From the graph, determine the domain of the function.

b. From the graph, determine the range of the function.

6.

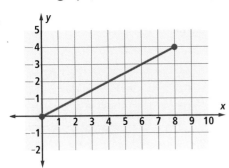

7.

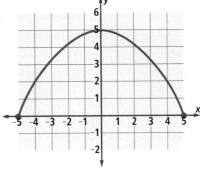

8. Determine if the following statement is *always, sometimes but not always,* or *never* true. The graph of a function may contain both points (6, 5) and (6, 7).

9. **Multiple Choice** Which table does *not* describe a function?

A

x	y
1	6
2	53
3	8

B

x	y
1	6
2	6
3	6

C

x	y
6	1
6	2
6	3

D

x	y
6	6
6	6
6	6

APPLYING THE MATHEMATICS

10. The graph at the right is of a function showing the distance walked by a hiker over time.

a. Find the value of the function when $x = 2$ P.M.

b. Find the value of the function when $x = 3{:}30$ P.M.

c. Find x for which the value of the function is 5.5 miles.

d. Use inequalities to describe the domain and range of this function.

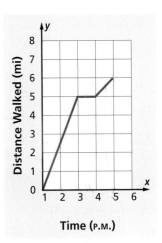

In 11 and 12, determine if the graph of ordered pairs (x, y) is that of a function. Justify your answer.

11.

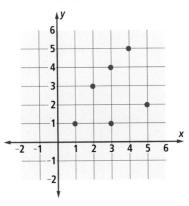

12.

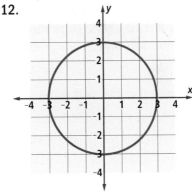

The Language of Functions   **429**

13. The function $y = 5 \cdot 0.8^x$ is graphed at the right.

    a. **True or False** Zero is in the range of this function.

    b. What is the value of this function when $x = 0$?

    c. What is the domain of the function that is graphed?

    d. What is the range of the function that is graphed?

    e. Suppose x can be any positive integer. What is the greatest possible value of y?

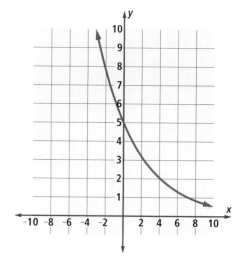

In **14** and **15**, a situation is described in which one quantity can be used to predict values of the second quantity. Tell which quantity you wish to be the input and which should be the output in order to have a function. Sketch a reasonable graph. Do not mark numbers on the axes. Think only about the basic shape of the graph.

14. the amount of time since a cup of hot coffee was poured and its temperature

15. the height of a skydiver who has jumped from an airplane

In **16–18**, use the graph of an absolute value function below. Find the range for the part of the function whose domain is given.

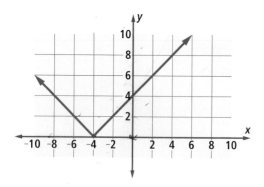

People have been using parachutes for hundreds of years, even during the 1100s in China.

Source: United States Parachute Association

16. domain $= \{x : x \geq 1\}$

17. domain $= \{x : -6 \leq x \leq -2\}$

18. domain $= \{x : x \leq 0\}$

In **19** and **20**, an equation for a function is given. Determine the domain and the range of the function. You may use a graphing calculator to help you.

19. $y = \frac{1}{75}x - 3$

20. $y = 100 \cdot \left(\frac{1}{2}\right)^x$, when $x \geq 0$

21. Since 1980, world records in the men's marathon have been set many times.

Date	Record-Setter	Country	Time	Location of Race
Dec. 6, 1981	Robert de Castella	Australia	2 hr, 8 min, 18 sec	Fukuoka, Japan
Oct. 21, 1984	Steve Jones	Britain	2 hr, 8 min, 5 sec	Chicago, USA
Apr. 20, 1985	Carlos Lopes	Portugal	2 hr, 7 min, 12 sec	Rotterdam, Netherlands
Apr. 17, 1988	Belayneh Dinsamo	Ethiopia	2 hr, 6 min, 50 sec	Rotterdam, Netherlands
Sept. 20, 1998	Ronaldo de Costa	Brazil	2 hr, 6 min, 5 sec	Berlin, Germany
Oct. 24, 1999	Khalid Khannouchi	Morocco	2 hr, 5 min, 42 sec	Chicago, USA
Apr. 14, 2002	Khalid Khannouchi	USA	2 hr, 5 min, 38 sec	London, England
Sept. 28, 2003	Paul Tergat	Kenya	2 hr, 4 min, 55 sec	Berlin, Germany

Source: www.marathonguide.com

a. Consider the function using the pairs (date, time). This function is an example of a *decreasing function*. Why do you think it is called a decreasing function?

b. Consider the eight ordered pairs (record-setter, time). By examining the definition of function, explain why these eight ordered pairs do *not* make up a function.

REVIEW

22. In China, most families are allowed to have only one child. This policy was implemented to reduce the population, with a goal of reaching 700 million citizens by 2050. Suppose the 2005 population of 1.3 billion decreases by 1% each year. **(Lesson 7-3)**

a. Write an expression for the population of China x years after 2005.

b. Will the goal of having 700 million citizens or less in the year 2050 be met?

23. Find the slope of the line given by the equation $\frac{7}{20}(x + 18) = \frac{8}{3}(y - 11)$. **(Lessons 6-2, 4-4, 3-8)**

24. Triangle 1 has an area of 12 cm^2 and is similar to Triangle 2, which has an area of 108 cm^2. What is the ratio of similitude of Triangle 1 to Triangle 2? **(Lesson 5-10)**

25. The maximum number p of people allowed on a certain elevator times the average weight w of an adult should not exceed 1,500 pounds. Write an inequality describing the rule and solve for p. **(Lesson 3-6)**

EXPLORATION

26. Find equations for two different functions with the same domain that contain both the ordered pairs (1, 1) and (2, 6).

QY ANSWERS

1. 49

2. domain: {$x: 3 \leq x \leq 8$}; range: {$y: 9 \leq y \leq 64$}

3. $361.15; $343.97; $306.98

Lesson 7-6

Function Notation

▶ **BIG IDEA** When a function f contains the ordered pair (x, y), then y is the value of the function at x, and we may write $y = f(x)$.

Refer to the graph on page 397. Recall that each equation represents a different prediction of the population of a town x years in the future. Each model describes a function. The functions are of three types.

Possibility 1 $P = 100{,}000$ describes a *constant function* where the population does not change.

Possibility 2 $P = 100{,}000 + 3{,}000x$ describes a *linear function* with 3,000 new people per year.

Possibility 3 $P = 100{,}000(1.02)^x$ describes an *exponential function* with a growth rate of 2% per year.

It is important to see these functions on the same axes because we want to compare them. But in talking about three functions, we might easily get confused. If we say the letter P, which P are we talking about? It would be nice to be able to name a function in a simple and useful manner.

Mental Math

Give the coordinates of a solution to the inequality.

a. $y \le -22x + 6$

b. $5m - 4n > 3$

c. $-b + 3 < a - 4.5$

$f(x)$ Notation

Conveniently, mathematics does have another way to name functions. With this method, Possibility 3 can be written $E(x) = 100{,}000(1.02)^x$.

We chose the letter E as a name for the function as a reminder of exponential growth. The symbol $E(x)$ shows that x is the input variable. It is read "E of x." What is the purpose of using this new symbol? It allows us to show the correspondence between specific pairs of values for the input (number of years x) and output (population predicted by the exponential growth model). For example, when $x = 3$, the output is $E(3) = 100{,}000(1.02)^3 = 106{,}120.8$. So $E(3) = 106{,}120.8 \approx 106{,}121$ people. When $x = 20$, the output is $E(20) = 100{,}000(1.02)^{20} \approx 148{,}595$ people.

The other population models can be written in function notation as well.

Possibility 2 could be written $L(x) = 100{,}000 + 3{,}000x$.
Possibility 1 could be written $C(x) = 100{,}000$.
Now each model has a different name.

It is important to know that $E(x)$ *does not* denote the multiplication of E and x. The parentheses indicate the input of a function.

Example 1

Given a function with equation $f(x) = 5x - 19$, find $f(2)$.

Solution $f(x) = 5x - 19$ is a general formula that tells how to find the output for any input. The symbol $f(2)$ stands for "the output of function f when the input is 2." So substitute 2 for x and evaluate the expression on the right side.

$f(2) = 5(2) - 19$
$\quad\quad = 10 - 19 = \text{-}9$

So $f(2) = \text{-}9$.

In Example 1, we say that –9 is the *value of the function* when $x = 2$.

GUIDED

Example 2

Use the three functions given earlier for population models to find $E(10)$, $L(10)$, and $C(10)$. Explain what the results mean in the context of the population situation.

Solution

$E(x) = 100{,}000(1.02)^x$
$E(10) = 100{,}000(1.02)^{\underline{\,\,?\,\,}}$

After 10 years, the population based on the exponential model is predicted to be about __?__ people.

$L(x) = 100{,}000 + 3{,}000x$
$L(10) = \underline{\quad?\quad} + \underline{\quad?\quad}(\underline{\,\,?\,\,}) = \underline{\quad?\quad}$

After 10 years, the population based on the linear model is predicted to be __?__ people.

$C(x) = 100{,}000$
$C(10) = 100{,}000$

After __?__ years, the population based on the __?__ model is predicted to be __?__ people.

In working with functions, questions arise in which you are given the value of one variable and are asked to find the value of the other variable. In Example 1, you were given the *input* value. You substituted to find the output value. In the next two examples, you are given the value of the *output*. This results in an equation to solve. When you have a formula for a function, symbolic methods may be used to solve the equation to find the input value.

Example 3

Possibility 2 used the linear function $L(x) = 100{,}000 + 3{,}000x$ to model the population of a town x years in the future. According to this model, in how many years will the population reach 150,000?

Solution In $L(x) = 100{,}000 + 3{,}000x$, replace $L(x)$ with 150,000. Then solve for x.

$$150{,}000 = 100{,}000 + 3{,}000x$$

$$50{,}000 = 3{,}000x$$

$$16.67 \approx x$$

The linear model predicts that in about 17 years the population will be 150,000. So $L(x) = 150{,}000$ when $x \approx 17$.

Because functions can also be described with tables and graphs, tables and graphs are useful in solving problems in which you are given the output and need to find the input.

Example 4

For $E(x) = 100{,}000(1.02)^x$, use the graph to find when the population reaches 150,000.

Solution Graph $y = 100{,}000(1.02)^x$. To help you see the point on this graph whose y-coordinate is 150,000, also graph the horizontal line $y = 150{,}000$. Trace on the graph to find where these two graphs intersect. **When x is between 20 and 21 years, $E(x)$ is approximately 150,000.**

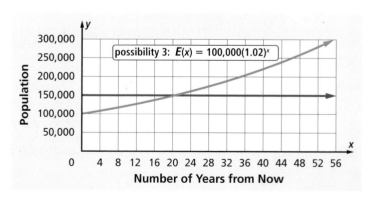

Check Substitute 20 and 21 for x in the equation $E(x) = 100{,}000(1.02)^x$.

Using $x = 20$, $E(x) = E(20) = 100{,}000(1.02)^{20} \approx 148{,}595$.

Using $x = 21$, $E(x) = E(21) = 100{,}000(1.02)^{21} \approx 151{,}567$.

$148{,}595 < 150{,}000 < 151{,}567$, so the answer is reasonable.

Unless the situation suggests a better letter, the most common letter used to name a function is f. That is, instead of writing $y = 3x + 5$, we might write $f(x) = 3x + 5$. Then f is the linear function with slope 3 and y-intercept 5. It is read "f of x equals 3 times x plus 5." This way of writing a function is called **f(x) notation** or **function notation**. The symbol $f(x)$ is attributed to the great Swiss mathematician Leonhard Euler (1707–1783).

Activity

The CAS allows you to work with functions.

1. **a.** Use the DEFINE command to define $f(x) = 3x^2 + 2x + 10$ in your CAS.
   b. Find $f(2)$.
   c. Find $f(3) + f(-6)$.
   d. Find $f(2006) - f(2005)$.
   e. Find $f(a)$.
   f. Find $f(y)$.
   g. Find $f(\text{math})$. (Do not type in multiplication symbols between the letters. CAS sees *math* as just one big variable called a string variable.)
   h. Find $f(\text{your name})$.
2. **a.** Define $g(x) = \dfrac{x^3 + 999}{8x - 1}$.
   b. Find $g(7)$, $g(\pi)$, $g(t)$, and $g(\text{mom})$.
3. Explain the relationships between function notation and substitution.
4. Without using a CAS, find $h(4)$ and $h(\text{algebra})$ if $h(x) = 5x + 2x^2 + 1$.

Questions

COVERING THE IDEAS

1. How is the symbol $f(x)$ read?

In 2 and 3, let $E(x) = 100{,}000(1.02)^x$, $L(x) = 100{,}000 + 3{,}000x$, and $C(x) = 100{,}000$.

2. **a.** Without a calculator, find the values of $E(1)$, $L(1)$, and $C(1)$.
   b. What do these values mean in the population projection situation?

3. **a.** With a calculator if necessary, find the values of $E(25)$, $L(25)$, and $C(25)$.
   b. What do these values mean in the population projection situation?

4. If $f(x) = 4 \cdot 0.12^x$, find each value.
   a. $f(1)$ **b.** $f(3)$ **c.** $f(5)$

5. Let p be a function with $p(n) = 100 \cdot 2^n$. Find the value of $p(n)$ when $n = 7$.

6. Determine if the statement is *always true, sometimes but not always true,* or *never true.* If $g(x) = 4x^2$ and $g(x) > 0$, then $x > 0$.

APPLYING THE MATHEMATICS

7. The table below shows the amount of money earned by a person who worked x hours.

Hours Worked x	Total Amount Earned $f(x)$
5	$45
10	$90
15	$135
20	$180
25	$225
30	$270

a. What is the value of $f(5)$?

b. What is the value of $f(15)$?

c. Find x if $f(x) = \$180$.

8. Let $h(n) = 0.5n$.

a. Calculate $h(0)$, $h(1)$, and $h(2)$.

b. Calculate $h(-1) + h(-2)$.

c. Why do you think the letter h was chosen for this function?

9. A computer purchased for $1,600 is estimated to depreciate at a rate of 25% per year. The computer's value after t years is given by $W(t) = 1,600(0.75)^t$.

a. Evaluate $W(4)$ and explain what the value means.

b. Graph the function W for values of t with $0 \le t \le 7$.

c. Use your graph to estimate the solutions to $W(t) < 1,000$ and explain what your answer means.

10. Suppose $L(x) = 12x - 18$.

a. Calculate $L(5)$.

b. Calculate $L(3)$.

c. Evaluate $\dfrac{L(5) - L(3)}{5 - 3}$.

d. What is the meaning of your calculation in Part c?

In 2005, approximately 89% of U.S. public middle and junior high schools had the use of computers in the classroom.

Source: Quality Education Data, Inc.

11. Oven temperature T varies with the length of time t the oven has been on. An oven, whose initial temperature was 80°, was set for 325°. The actual temperature was measured and then graphed over a 45-minute interval. Below is the graph of the function f where $T = f(t)$.

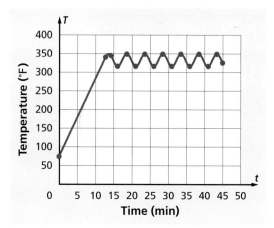

a. Estimate $f(25)$.

b. What is the meaning of $f(25)$?

c. Estimate the solution to the equation $f(t) = 200$.

d. What is the meaning of the solution in Part c?

REVIEW

In 12 and 13, could the table of values represent a function with x as the independent variable and y as the dependent variable? Why or why not? (Lesson 7-5)

12.

x	-3	-2	-1	0	1	2	3
y	0	1	5	1	6	0	2

13.

x	0	1	5	1	6	0	2
y	-3	-2	-1	0	1	2	3

14. Consider the relation described by the equation $x^2 + 3y^2 = 31$. (Lesson 7-5)

a. Is $(2, 3)$ a solution?

b. Is $(2, -3)$ a solution?

c. Is $x^2 + 3y^2 = 31$ the equation of a function? Explain.

15. Rewrite $8y - 4x + 1 = 25 + 6x$ in each form. (Lessons 6-8, 6-4)

a. standard form

b. slope-intercept form

16. **Skill Sequence** (Lessons 4-4, 2-2, 2-1)

   a. Simplify $3(5 - 2m)$.

   b. Simplify $3(5 - 2m) - 2(7m + 1)$.

   c. Solve $3(5 - 2m) - 2(7m + 1) = 43$.

EXPLORATION

17. Some functions involve more than one input variable. The chart below shows wind chill as a function of the wind speed and the temperature. For wind speed V and temperature T, let $W(V, T) = $ wind chill and let $F(V, T) = $ frostbite time.

	Temperature (°F)																	
Calm	40	35	30	25	20	15	10	5	0	−5	−10	−15	−20	−25	−30	−35	−40	−45
5	36	31	25	19	13	7	1	−5	−11	−16	−22	−28	−34	−40	−46	−52	−57	−63
10	34	27	21	15	9	3	−4	−10	−16	−22	−28	−35	−41	−47	−53	−59	−66	−72
15	32	25	19	13	6	0	−7	−13	−19	−26	−32	−39	−45	−51	−58	−64	−71	−77
20	30	24	17	11	4	−2	−9	−15	−22	−29	−35	−42	−48	−55	−61	−68	−74	−81
25	29	23	16	9	3	−4	−11	−17	−24	−31	−37	−44	−51	−58	−64	−71	−78	−84
30	28	22	15	8	1	−5	−12	−19	−26	−33	−39	−46	−53	−60	−67	−73	−80	−87
35	28	21	14	7	0	−7	−14	−21	−27	−34	−41	−48	−55	−62	−69	−76	−82	−89
40	27	20	13	6	−1	−8	−15	−22	−29	−36	−43	−50	−57	−64	−71	−78	−84	−91
45	26	19	12	5	−2	−9	−16	−23	−30	−37	−44	−51	−58	−65	−72	−79	−86	−93
50	26	19	12	4	−3	−10	−17	−24	−31	−38	−45	−52	−60	−67	−74	−81	−88	−95
55	25	18	11	4	−3	−11	−18	−25	−32	−39	−46	−54	−61	−68	−75	−82	−89	−97
60	25	17	10	3	−4	−11	−19	−26	−33	−40	−48	−55	−62	−69	−76	−84	−91	−98

Wind (mph)

Frostbite Times   30 minutes   10 minutes   5 minutes

Source: National Weather Service

   a. Pick three (V, T) pairs and find $W(V, T)$ and $F(V, T)$.

   b. Find two solutions for the equation $W(V, T) = -55$.

   c. Find two solutions for $W(V, T) = -39$ that have different values for $F(V, T)$.

18. Let $m(x) = $ the mother of person x and $f(x) = $ the father of person x. Using yourself for x, find $m(f(x))$ and $f(f(x))$. (*Hint:* Start with the inner-most parentheses.) What are simpler descriptions for each of these two functions?

Lesson 7-7

Comparing Linear Increase and Exponential Growth

▶ **BIG IDEA** In the long run, exponential growth always overtakes linear (constant) increase.

In the patterns that are constant increase/decrease situations, a number is repeatedly *added*. In exponential growth/decay situations, a number is repeatedly *multiplied*. In this lesson, we compare what happens as a result.

Mental Math

What is the date of the xth day of the year in a nonleap year when

a. $x = 100$?

b. $x = 200$?

c. $x = 300$?

GUIDED

Example

Suppose you have $10. For two weeks, your rich uncle agrees to do one of the following.
Option 1: Increase what you had the previous day by $50.
Option 2: Increase what you had the previous day by 50%.
Which option will give you more money?

Solution Make a table to compare the two options for the first week. Use the Now/Next method to fill in the table. The exponential growth factor is 1.50.

Start = $10
Next = Now + $50

Day	Option 1: Add $50.
0	$10
1	?
2	?

+ $50

Start = $10
Next = Now · 1.50

Day	Option 2: Multiply by 1.50.
0	$10
1	?
2	?

· 1.50

Continue the table until day 14. You should find that at first, you get more money from Option 1. But the table shows that starting on day __?__, Option 2 gives more money. In the long run, Option 2, increasing by 50% each day, is the better choice.

Above, the two options were described by telling how the amounts changed each day. In that situation, the Now/Next method works well. But to graph the situation on your calculator, you need equations for these functions.

Comparing Using a Graph

To find the equations for the functions in the Guided Example, you can make a table to compare the two options during the first week. The exponential growth factor is 1.50. Let $L(x)$ = the amount given to you under Option 1, and let $E(x)$ = the amount given to you under Option 2.

Day	Option 1: Add $50.	Option 2: Multiply by 1.50.
0	$L(0) = 10 = \$10.00$	$E(0) = 10 = \$10.00$
1	$L(1) = 10 + 50 \cdot 1 = \$60.00$	$E(1) = 10 \cdot 1.50^1 = \$15.00$
2	$L(2) = 10 + 50 \cdot 2 = \$110.00$	$E(2) = 10 \cdot 1.50^2 = \$22.50$
3	$L(3) = 10 + 50 \cdot 3 = \$160.00$	$E(3) = 10 \cdot 1.50^3 = \$33.75$
4	$L(4) = 10 + 50 \cdot 4 = \$210.00$	$E(4) = 10 \cdot 1.50^4 = \$50.63$
5	$L(5) = 10 + 50 \cdot 5 = \$260.00$	$E(5) = 10 \cdot 1.50^5 = \$75.94$
x	$L(x) = 10 + 50x$	$E(x) = 10 \cdot 1.50^x$

We see how the values compare by graphing the two functions E and L. The graphs of $L(x) = 10 + 50x$ and $E(x) = 10 \cdot 1.5^x$ are shown at the right.

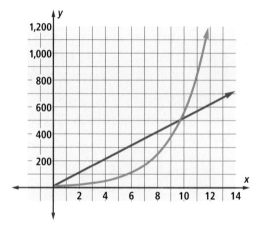

The line $L(x) = 10 + 50x$ has a constant rate of change. The graph of $y = 10 \cdot 1.5^x$ is a curve that gets steeper and steeper as you move to the right. Notice that at first the exponential curve is below the line. But toward the middle of the graph, it intersects the line and passes above it. On later days, the graph of the curve rises farther and farther above the line.

The longer your uncle gives you money, the better Option 2 is compared to Option 1.

Comparing Using Spreadsheets

Activity 1 shows how to use a spreadsheet to confirm the results of Guided Example 1.

Activity 1

Step 1 Create a spreadsheet similar to the one at the right. Be sure to have titles in row 1. In cells A2 through A16 enter the numbers 0 to 14.

◇	A	B	C
1	Day x	Option 1	Option 2
2	0	10	10
3	1	=B2+50	

Step 2 Type =B2+50 in cell B3. Press ENTER. What appears in cell B3?

Step 3 Type the formula for Option 2 into cell C3. (*Hint*: What is the Now/Next formula for Option 2?)

An advantage of spreadsheets is that you don't have to type a formula into each cell. When you type the formula =B2+50 into cell B3, the spreadsheet remembers this as: "Into this cell put 50 plus the number that is in cell B2 above." For example, if you copy cell B3 to cell D5, the formula copied will change to =D4+50 because one cell above D5 is D4. This way of copying in spreadsheets is called *replication.*

Step 4 Replicate the formula in cell B3 into cells B4 through B16.

Step 5 Replicate the formula in cell C3 into cells C4 through C16.

Step 6 Compare your spreadsheet to the table on page 440. Experiment by changing the starting amount of $10 to other values. Then go back to the original starting amount of $10 before doing the next step.

Step 7 Add two more columns to your spreadsheet.

◇	A	B	C	D	E
1	Day x	Option 1	Option 2	$L(x) = 10 + 50x$	$E(x) = 10 \bullet 1.5^x$
2	0	10	10		
3	1	=B2+50			

Step 8 Type =10+50*A2 in cell D2. This puts into D2 the value of the function L for the domain value in cell A2.

Step 9 Replicate the formula in cell D2 into cells D3 through D16.

Step 10 Compare the values in columns B and D. If they are the same, then you know that you have done the previous steps correctly.

Step 11 Type =10*1.5^A2 into cell E2. This puts into E2 the value of the function E for the domain value in cell A2.

Step 12 Replicate the formula in cell E2 into cells E3 through E16. What should happen? Have you done the previous steps correctly?

Activity 2

In 1993, Florida introduced 19 mountain lions into its northern region. With animals in the wild, there are two scenarios. If there are no limiting factors, the population of animals tends to grow exponentially. However, if limiting factors are established, the population growth tends to be linear. Limiting factors can be things such as climate, availability of food, predators, and hunting.

Suppose the scientists who introduced the mountain lions into northern Florida used one of the following options to model the population growth.

Option 1: There are limiting factors so that 2 more mountain lions appear each year.

Option 2: There are no limiting factors so that the population grows by 6% each year.

Step 1 First, create a spreadsheet similar to the one below.

A typical male mountain lion patrols 50 to 300 square miles, depending on how plentiful food is.

Source: *USAToday*

◇	A	B	C	D	E
1	Year	Option 1	Option 2	L(x)	E(x)
2	1993	19	19		
3	1994				

Step 2 Enter formulas into B3 and C3 to calculate the population using the Now/Next method.

Step 3 Copy and paste B3 into cells B4 and lower. Also copy and paste C3 into cells C4 and lower. Be sure to gather enough data and compare the populations in column B to those in column C.

Step 4 Enter formulas for $L(x)$ and $E(x)$ in columns D and E and copy these for as many rows as you used in Step 3.

Step 5 Graph each option's population equation on the same axes. Let the x-coordinates be the number of years since 1993. (Let $x = 0$ be 1993.) You can use the chart feature of the spreadsheet to create the graphs.

Step 6 Answer the following questions using the collected data and the graphs.

1. In 2010, which option would provide a larger population of mountain lions?

2. In which year (if ever), would Option 2 create a larger population of mountain lions?

A Summary of Constant Increase and Exponential Growth

In this lesson, you have seen that differences between linear and exponential models can be seen in the equations that describe them, the tables that list ordered pairs, and the graphs that picture them. You have seen that if the growth factor is greater than 1, exponential growth always overtakes constant increase. Here is a summary of their behavior.

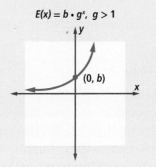

Constant Increase	Exponential Growth
• Begin with an amount b.	• Begin with an amount b.
• Add m (the slope) in each of the x time periods.	• Multiply by g (the growth factor) in each of the x time periods.
• After x time periods, the amount is given by the function $L(x) = mx + b$.	• After x time periods, the amount is given by the function $E(x) = b \cdot g^x$.

$L(x) = mx + b, \ m > 0$

$E(x) = b \cdot g^x, \ g > 1$

Questions

COVERING THE IDEAS

1. What is the difference between a constant increase situation and an exponential growth situation?

In 2–5, let $L(x) = 20 + 3x$ and $E(x) = 20(1.03)^x$.

2. Calculate $L(5)$ and $E(5)$.

3. Sketch a graph of both functions on the same axes.

4. Give an example of a value of x for which $E(x) > L(x)$.

5. What kind of situation could have led to these equations?

6. Two friends found $100 and split it equally between them. Alexis put her half in a piggy bank and added $7 to it each year. Lynn put her half in a bank with an annual yield of 7%.

 a. Make a spreadsheet to illustrate how much money each friend has at the end of each year for the next 25 years. Have one column represent Alexis and one column represent Lynn.

 b. Sketch a graph to represent the amount of money each friend has over the next 25 years.

7. Rochelle started to make the following spreadsheet. She replicated the formula in cell A2 into cells A3 and A4.

◇	A	B
1	28	6
2	=A1+13	=1.2*B1
3		
4		
5		

 a. Give the formulas that will occur in cells A3 and A4.

 b. What numbers result from the formulas in A3 and A4?

 c. How will the values in A3 and A4 change if Rochelle changes the start value in A1 to –5?

 d. Does column A illustrate constant increase or exponential growth? Explain.

8. Repeat Question 7 for column B.

9. The number of deer in the state of Massachusetts is a problem. In 1998, the deer population was estimated to be about 85,000. The Massachusetts Division of Fisheries and Wildlife had to decide whether to allow hunting (a limiting factor) or to ban hunting (no limiting factor). If hunting is allowed, they predict the deer population to increase at a constant rate of about 270 deer a year. If hunting is not allowed, the prediction is the deer population would grow exponentially by 15% each year.

 a. Write a Now/Next formula for the deer population if hunting is allowed.

 b. Write a Now/Next formula for the deer population if hunting is banned.

 c. Let $L(x)$ = the number of deer x years after 1998 if hunting is allowed. Find a formula for $L(x)$.

 d. Let $E(x)$ = the number of deer x years after 1998 if hunting is not allowed. Find a formula for $E(x)$.

 e. The state allowed hunting. The 2006 deer population was estimated between 85,000 and 95,000. Was the prediction correct?

In 1906, the U.S. deer population was a sparse 500,000. Today, experts estimate that 20 million deer roam the nation.

Source: Tufts University

APPLYING THE MATHEMATICS

10. Refer to the spreadsheet at the right.

    a. What Now/Next formula could be used to generate the numbers in column A?

    b. Let $f(x)$ be the value in column A at time x. What is a formula for $f(x)$?

◇	A
1	
2	15
3	165
4	1815
5	19965
6	219615
7	2415765
8	26573415
9	292307565
10	3215383215
11	35369215365

11. Suppose you are reading a 900-page novel at the rate of 25 pages per hour. You are currently at page 67.

    a. Is the number of pages you read in the book an example of constant increase or exponential growth? Explain.

    b. Write an equation to describe the pages finished x hours from now.

    c. How many hours will it take you to finish the book?

12. The graph at the right shows the number of territories in which bald eagles nest around the five Great Lakes.

    a. Would you describe the graphs as constant increase or exponential growth? Explain your answer.

    b. The graph of which lake can be represented by $y = 14.5 \cdot 1.053^x$, where x is the years since 1962? Explain your answer.

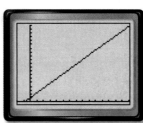

- Superior
- Michigan
- Huron
- Erie
- Ontario

MATCHING In 13–16, each graph is drawn on the window $-2 \le x \le 15$, $0 \le y \le 2{,}000$. Match the graph with its equation.

  a. $f(x) = 100 \cdot 1.25^x$ b. $g(x) = 100 + 125x$

  c. $h(x) = 100 + 60x$ d. $j(x) = 100 \cdot 1.1^x$

13.
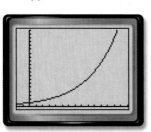

14.
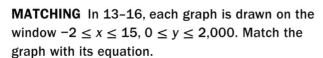

15.
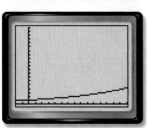

16.
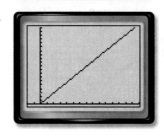

17. The principal of a high school is making long-range budget plans. The number of students dropped from 2,410 students to 2,270 in one year. Student enrollment is dropping, as shown in rows 2 and 3 of the spreadsheet. The situation may be modeled by a linear function or an exponential function.

    a. Make a spreadsheet similar to the one at the right. Show the future enrollments in the two possible situations.

◇	A	B	C
1		Constant Decrease	Exponential Decrease
2	0	2410	2410
3	1	2270	2270

    b. What are the predicted enrollments 5 years from the year shown in row 3? By how much do they differ?

    c. What are the predicted enrollments 15 years from year shown in row 3? By how much do they differ?

The safest way to transport children to and from school and school-related activities is in a school bus.

Source: National Association of State Directors of Pupil Transportation Services

REVIEW

18. Let $M(x) = 13x - 18$. Find the value of x for which $M(x) = -1.2$. (Lesson 7-6)

19. **True or False** If a is any real number, then a is in the range of the function with equation $y = 3x$. (Lesson 7-5)

20. Write an exponential expression for the number, which, written in base 10, is 7 followed by n zeroes (For example when $n = 3$, this number is 7,000.) (Lesson 7-2)

21. Write the equation $\dfrac{y - 3x + 2}{15} - \dfrac{1}{3} = \dfrac{7x + 2y}{5}$ in standard form.

    (Lessons 6-8, 3-8, 2-2)

22. Do the points $(-1, 3)$, $(5, 4)$, and $(0, -8)$ lie on a line? How can you tell? (Lesson 6-6)

23. If you ask a random person the date of his or her birth, what is the probability that it will be one of the first ten days of the month? (Lesson 5-6)

24. Calculate $5(-5)^5$. (Lesson 2-4)

EXPLORATION

25. The statement, "If the growth factor g is greater than 1, exponential growth always overtakes constant increase," was made at the start of this lesson. Write a similar statement that could describe the relationship between exponential decay and constant decrease.

Chapter 7 Projects

1 Reciprocal Functions

For a function f, the function g with $g(x) = \frac{1}{f(x)}$ is called the *reciprocal function* of f.

a. On the same pair of axes, graph the function with equation $y = x$, and its reciprocal, the function with equation $y = \frac{1}{x}$. Do the same for $y = 2$, $y = x^2$, and $y = 2^x$.

b. For each function in Part a, for what values of x is the reciprocal not defined?

c. What is the reciprocal of the reciprocal of the function f?

d. Give an example of a function h that is equal to its reciprocal function. Give an example of a function that is always greater than its reciprocal function and a function that is always less than its reciprocal function.

e. Describe any general patterns you noticed when graphing reciprocal functions.

2 A Famous Snowflake

The drawing below illustrates the construction of a famous shape called the Koch snowflake. In the first stage, you begin with a triangle. At every other stage, you draw a small triangle in the middle of each of the sides of the previous stage.

Stage 1	Stage 2	Stage 3	Stage 4

a. On a large piece of paper, draw the fifth stage of the Koch snowflake.

b. The first stage of the Koch snowflake has three sides. The next stage has 12 sides. The step after that has 48 sides. This number seems to grow exponentially. Explain why this is indeed the case, and find the growth factor and the initial value.

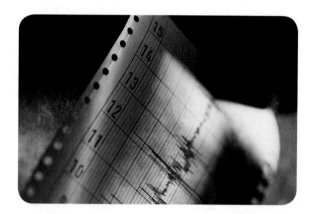

3 Richter Scale

The Richter scale is a scale used to measure the intensity of earthquakes. Look up the meaning of the Richter scale.

a. In 1992, an earthquake in Landers, California, measured 7.5 on the Richter scale. The largest earthquake ever recorded was the Great Chile earthquake of 1960, which measured 9.5 on the Richter scale. How much more powerful was the Chilean earthquake than the Landers earthquake?

b. Suppose a scientist plotted the magnitude of the most powerful annual earthquakes in a certain region over time and found that the measurements on the Richter scale increased linearly. How did the magnitude of the earthquakes increase?

c. Can an earthquake have a negative measure on the Richter scale? What does this mean?

4 Powers of Ten

In 1977, Charles and Ray Eames created a short documentary movie called *Powers of Ten*, which began with a picture of a picnic, and zoomed out by a factor of ten every ten seconds. (The movie is available on the Internet.) You can create a similar effect yourself. Download a free program that allows you to view satellite images of Earth at different levels of magnification.

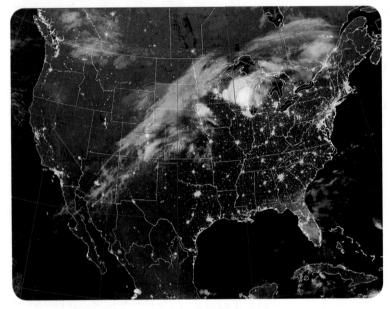

a. Find your school on the software, and zoom in as much as the software allows. Note the altitude from which you are viewing. Zoom out to an altitude ten times as high. Describe what you see. Do this as many times as the program allows.

b. Find out how many times you would have to zoom out before you could see the entire solar system, and how many times you would have to zoom out before you could see the entire galaxy.

c. Describe what you would see in the first three pictures if you zoomed in instead of out.

5 The Logistic Function and Growth

In this chapter you saw exponential growth used as a model for population growth. In nature, it is impossible for a population to continue to grow exponentially. (Otherwise it would overrun the entire Earth and still continue to grow!) When a population reaches a certain size, the resources available do not allow it to grow any larger. One way in which scientists model this kind of growth is called a *logistic function*. This is a function of the form $P(n) = a\dfrac{1 + b2^{-cn}}{1 + d2^{-cn}}$. This function gives the size of the population after n years.

a. Use a spreadsheet or a calculator to calculate the first 10 values of P, when $a = 200$, $b = 1$, $c = 0.5$, and $d = 20$. Plot the graph of the function and use exponential regression to find the exponential function that best fits the data. Do you think that in the first 10 years the population grows approximately exponentially?

b. For the values given in Part a, graph the first 100 values of the function. Does the population still appear to grow exponentially?

c. Explain why this function gives a better model of population growth than the exponential function.

- In Chapter 6, you saw many examples of constant-increase and constant-decrease patterns of change. They give rise to equations of the form $y = mx + b$. The change is called **linear** because the graph is a line. Now in Chapter 7, we turned our attention to patterns of change called **exponential growth** and **exponential decay**. They give rise to equations of the form $y = b \cdot g^x$.

- Graphs of exponential functions are curves. The change is called **exponential** because the independent variable is in the exponent. In exponential change, the number g is the growth factor. If $g > 1$, the situation is **exponential growth.** Among the common applications of exponential growth are compound interest and population growth. In the long run, exponential growth will always overtake a situation of linear increase. If $0 < g < 1$, the situation is **exponential decay.**

- These and other patterns can be described using the mathematical idea of a function. A **function** is a set of ordered pairs in which each first coordinate appears with exactly one second coordinate. Thus, functions exist whenever the value of one variable determines a unique value of another variable.

- A function may be described by a list of ordered pairs, a graph, an equation, or a written rule. If a function f contains the ordered pair (a, b), then we write $f(a) = b$. We say that b is the value of the function at a. If you know a formula for the function, you can obtain values and graphs of functions using calculators, spreadsheets, or paper and pencil.

- Constant-increase or constant-decrease situations are described by **linear functions.** Constant growth or decay situations are described by **exponential functions.** Repeatedly adding a quantity m to an initial value b gives rise to values of the linear function $f(x) = mx + b$. Repeatedly multiplying an initial value b by the growth factor g gives rise to values of the exponential function $f(x) = b \cdot g^x$. Spreadsheets are particularly useful for finding values of functions.

Vocabulary

7-1
power, nth power
base
exponent
principal
interest
annual yield
compound interest

7-2
exponential growth
growth factor
exponential growth
  equation

7-3
exponential decay
half-life

7-4
exponential regression

7-5
function
input, output
value of the function
squaring function
independent variable
dependent variable
domain of a function
range of a function
relation

7-6
$f(x)$ notation
function notation

Theorems and Properties

Repeated Multiplication Property of
  Powers (p. 398)
Compound Interest Formula (p. 400)

Growth Model for Powering (p. 405)
Zero Exponent Property (p. 405)

Take this test as you would take a test in class. You will need a calculator. Then use the Selected Answers section in the back of the book to check your work.

1. Evaluate $x^2 + x^0$ when $x = \frac{1}{5}$.

2. Write $8 \cdot 8 \cdot 8 \cdot 8 \cdot d \cdot d \cdot d \cdot d \cdot d \cdot d$ using exponents.

3. If $f(x) = 3x^0$, find $f(1{,}729)$.

4. If $g(y) = 3y - y^2$, find $g(-2)$.

In 5–7, Tyrone deposits $400 into a savings account that pays 4.4% interest per year.

5. Write and evaluate an expression for the amount of money Tyrone will have after 7 years, assuming he doesn't deposit or withdraw money from the account.

6. At the same time that Tyrone makes his deposit, his sister Oleta deposits $400 in a highly unusual savings account. The account pays exactly $22 interest each year. Who will have more money after 10 years?

7. Who will have more money after 25 years?

In 8–10, use the following information. A particular new 2006 car costs $34,975. Suppose its value depreciates 16% each year.

8. What is the growth factor of the value of the car?

9. Write a function $m(x)$ that approximates the car's value in x years. Specify the domain of your function.

10. Find $m(5)$, the approximate value of the car in 5 years.

For 11–13, $f(x) = 5 \cdot 0.74^x$. Calculate the value.

11. $f(1)$

12. $f(5)$

13. $f(7)$

In 14–16, use the absolute value function $f(x) = |x - 3|$ graphed below. Consider the domain as the set of all real numbers.

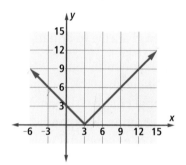

14. Determine $f(-12)$.

15. What is the range of the function f?

16. If the domain is restricted to $\{x: x \geq 5\}$, what is the range?

In 17–19, let $E(x) = 30(1.05)^x$ and $L(x) = 30 + 2x$.

17. Sketch a graph of these functions.

18. Which is greater, $L(9)$ or $E(9)$?

19. Give an example of a value of x when $L(x) < E(x)$.

In 20 and 21, write an equation describing the situation and graph the equation.

20. The population p of a country increases by 2.5% per year. In 1980, it had 76 million residents. Let k be the number of years since 1980.

21. The circulation c of a newspaper has decreased by 1% each month since January 2000, when it was 880,000. Let x be the number of months since January 2000.

In 22 and 23, graph the function on the given domain.

22. $h(k) = 1 - 3.5k, -10 \le k \le 8$

23. $c(x) = 10 \cdot 2^x, 0 \le x \le 5$

24. **Matching** Decide which of the situations the function with the given equation describes.

   i. constant increase

   ii. constant decrease

   iii. exponential growth

   iv. exponential decay

   a. $f(x) = -4x + 18$

   b. $g(x) = 0.4(5)^x$

   c. $h(x) = 5(0.4)^x$

   d. $m(x) = \frac{2}{3}x - 7$

25. It is estimated that a house purchased in 1990 for $100,000 has increased in value about 4% a year since that time. Suppose you want to use a spreadsheet to display the estimated value of the house from 1990 to 2010.

◇	A	B
1	Year	Value of House
2	1990	$100,000
3		
4		
5		

   a. What formula could you enter in cell A3 to get the appropriate value using cell A2?

   b. Explain the process by which you would obtain appropriate amounts in cells B4 to B22.

Chapter

7

Chapter Review

SKILLS
PROPERTIES
USES
REPRESENTATIONS

SKILLS Procedures used to get answers

OBJECTIVE A Evaluate functions.
(Lesson 7-6)

In 1–4, suppose $f(x) = 10 - 3x$. Evaluate the function.

1. $f(2)$
2. $f(-4)$
3. $f(1) + f(0)$
4. $f(3 + 6)$

5. If $g(x) = \left(\frac{11}{6}\right)^x$, give the value of $g(2)$.

6. If $h(x) = 2x^3$, calculate $h(4)$.

7. If $f(t) = -8t$ and $g(t) = 6t$, give the value of $f(-1) + g(-2)$.

8. If $E(m) = 6^m$ and $L(m) = m + 5$, find a value for m for which $E(m) < L(m)$.

OBJECTIVE B Calculate function values in spreadsheets. (Lesson 7-7)

In 9 and 10, use the spreadsheet below.

◇	A	B	C
1	x	1000(1.05)^x	1000+50x
2	0	1000	1000
3	1		
4	2		
5	3		

9. Rani wants to put values of the function with equation $y = 1{,}000(1.05)^x$ in column B of the spreadsheet.

   a. What formula can she enter in cell B3?

   b. What number will appear in cell B3?

   c. What should she do to get values of y in column B when $x = 2, 3, 4, 5, \ldots, 10$?

10. Olivia wants to put values of the function with equation $f(x) = 1{,}000 + 50x$ in column C of the spreadsheet.

    a. What formula can she enter in cell C3?

    b. What number will appear in cell C3?

    c. What should she do to get values of $f(x)$ in column C when $x = 2, 3, 4, 5, \ldots, 10$?

PROPERTIES The principles behind the mathematics

OBJECTIVE C Use the language of functions. (Lessons 7-5, 7-6)

11. Suppose $y = f(x)$.

    a. What letter names the independent variable?

    b. What letter names the function?

12. A linear function L is graphed below.

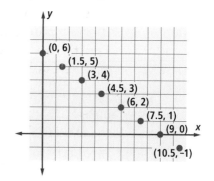

    a. What is $L(3)$?

    b. What is the domain of L?

    c. What is the range of L?

    d. Find a formula for $L(x)$ in terms of x.

13. Suppose a function f consists of only the ordered pairs (2, 200), (4, 400), (5, 500), and (10, 1,000).

   a. What is the domain of f?

   b. What is the range of f?

   c. Give a formula for $f(x)$ in terms of x.

USES Applications of mathematics in real-world situations

OBJECTIVE D Calculate compound interest. (Lesson 7-1)

14. An advertisement indicated that a 3-year certificate of deposit would yield 4.53% per year. If \$2,000 is invested in this certificate, what will it be worth at the end of 3 years?

15. When Brie was born, she received a gift of \$500 from her grandparents. Her parents put it into an account at an annual yield of 5.2%. Brie is now 12 years old. How much is this gift worth now?

16. In 2004, the endowment of Harvard University (the value of the university's assets) was reported to be about \$22.14 billion. Suppose the trustees of the university feel they can grow this endowment by 6% a year. What would be the value of the endowment in 2010?

17. Which investment yields more money: (a) x dollars for 4 years at an annual yield of 8% or (b) the same amount of money at an annual yield of 4% for 8 years? Explain your reasoning.

OBJECTIVE E Solve problems involving exponential growth and decay. (Lessons 7-2, 7-3, 7-4)

18. In 1990, there were 4.4 million cell phone subscribers in the United States; by 2006, there were 219.4 million subscribers. The table below shows the number of cell phone subscribers for each year from 1990 to 2006.

Year	Cell Phone Subscribers (in thousands)
1990	4,369
1991	3,380
1992	8,893
1993	13,067
1994	19,283
1995	28,154
1996	38,195
1997	48,706
1998	60,831
1999	76,285
2000	97,036
2001	118,398
2002	134,561
2003	148,066
2004	169,467
2005	194,479
2006	219,420

a. Create a scatterplot with y = cell phone subscribers and x = the year since 1990. Why is the exponential model a better model for these data than a linear model?

b. Use exponential regression to find an equation to fit the data.

c. Use your equation from Part b to predict the number of cell phone subscribers for the year 2013.

19. Twelve fish were introduced into a large lake. In 3 years, the population had multiplied by a factor of 20.

    a. In 15 years, at this growth rate, by how much would the population be multiplied?

    b. **Multiple Choice** If P is the number of fish t years after introduction, which formula relates P and t?

    A $P = 12(20)^t_t$ **B** $P = 12(20)^{3t}$

    C $P = 12(20)^{\frac{t}{3}}$

20. Suppose a car depreciates 20% in value each year, and its purchase price was $22,000.

    a. What is the growth factor in the situation?

    b. What is the car's value 1 year after purchase?

    c. What is its value n years after purchase?

OBJECTIVE F Determine whether a situation is constant increase, constant decrease, exponential growth, exponential decay, or a nonconstant change. (Lesson 7-4)

In 21–24, does the equation describe a situation of constant increase, constant decrease, exponential growth, or exponential decay?

21. $y = \frac{1}{5}x - 10$ 22. $m = -3n + 4$

23. $p = \frac{2}{3}(3)^r$ 24. $y = 3\left(\frac{2}{3}\right)^x$

25. A store is going out of business. It advertises that it is reducing prices 1% on day 1, then 2% more on day two, then 3% more on day 3, and so on for 100 days. Is this a situation of constant decrease, exponential decay, or neither of these?

26. Is the sequence: $\frac{1}{12}, \frac{1}{6}, \frac{1}{4}, \frac{1}{3}, \ldots$ one of constant increase, constant decrease, exponential growth, exponential decay, or a different kind of increase or decrease?

OBJECTIVE G Compare linear increase with exponential growth. (Lesson 7-7)

27. Country A has 10 million people and its population is growing by 2% each year. Country B has 20 million people and its population is growing by 1 million people per year.

    a. Give an equation for the population $A(n)$ of country A, n years from now.

    b. Give an equation for the population $B(n)$ of country B, n years from now.

    c. In 30 years, if these trends continue, which country would have the greater population? Explain why.

    d. In 100 years, if these trends continue, which country would have the greater population? Explain why.

28. Explain why exponential growth always overtakes linear increase if the time frame is long enough.

REPRESENTATIONS Pictures, graphs, or objects that illustrate concepts

OBJECTIVE H Graph exponential relationships. (Lessons 7-2, 7-3)

In 29–32, graph the equation and describe a situation that it might represent.

29. $A = 1,000(1.02)^x$

30. $C = 0.07 + 0.03t$

31. $y = 50 - 3x$

32. $V = 10,000(0.90)^t$

33. Graph the function of Question 20 for integer values of the domain from 1 to 10.

OBJECTIVE I Graph functions.
(Lessons 7-5, 7-6)

In 34–37, graph the function on the domain
$-5 \le x \le 5$.

34. $f(x) = 30 - 2x$

35. $g(x) = x^2$

36. $h(x) = 3 \cdot 2^x$

37. $m(x) = x^3 - x$

38. **Multiple Choice** Which is the graph of the function A when $A(x) = \left(\frac{1}{3}\right)^x$?

A

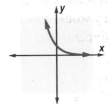

B

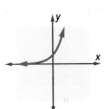

C

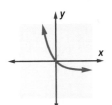

D

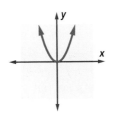

39. Refer to the graph of a linear function L below.

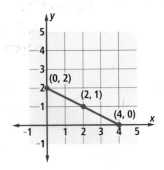

a. What is the value of $L(2)$?

b. What is the value of $L(0)$?

c. What is the domain of L?

d. What is the range of L?

40. On the grid below, each tick mark is one unit.

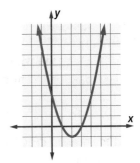

a. What is $f(0)$?

b. What is $f(3)$?

c. What is the domain of f?

d. What is the range of f?

Chapter

8 Powers and Roots

Contents

Visible light, infrared and ultraviolet radiation, x-rays, microwaves, and radio waves are all parts of the electromagnetic spectrum. Waves differ only in their wavelengths. Radio waves can be as long as 1,000 meters or longer; x-rays can be as short as one billionth of a meter or less.

To describe these numbers, we use powers of 10. On the scale shown below, each tick mark is 10 *times* the length of the tick mark to its left. You have seen these powers of 10 used in scientific notation.

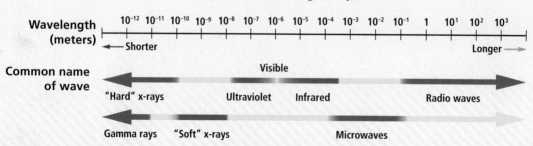

The Electromagnetic Spectrum

Wavelength (meters): 10^{-12} 10^{-11} 10^{-10} 10^{-9} 10^{-8} 10^{-7} 10^{-6} 10^{-5} 10^{-4} 10^{-3} 10^{-2} 10^{-1} 1 10^{1} 10^{2} 10^{3}

← Shorter   Longer →

Common name of wave

Visible

"Hard" x-rays   Ultraviolet   Infrared   Radio waves

Gamma rays   "Soft" x-rays   Microwaves

Here is a graph of $y = 10^x$ on the window $-5 \leq x \leq 5$, $-10 \leq y \leq 20$. You can see that as x increases by 1, y is multiplied by 10. The coordinates of some points on this graph are easily found by hand. When $x = 0$, $y = 10^0 = 1$. When $x = 1$, $y = 10^1 = 10$. When $x = 2$, $y = 10^2 = 100$. When $x = 3$, $y = 10^3 = 1,000$, too large to be on the graph. But the graph contains values of the function when x is negative. What is the meaning of 10^{-1}, 10^{-2}, 10^{-3}, and so on?

Also, the graph computes values for y when x is not an integer. Although we do not discuss all the powers of x in this chapter, the meanings of $\frac{1}{2}$ and $\frac{1}{3}$ are discussed and found to be related to square roots and cube roots. Additionally, there is the question of how all these powers and roots are related. For example, how is x^7 related to x^{-7}? Are the 7th powers of different numbers related in any way? The answers to these questions provide additional understanding of some of the applications of powers that you saw in the preceding chapter. They also shed light on some important formulas for lengths, area, and volume found in geometry.

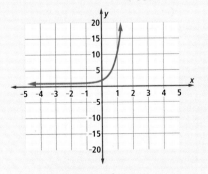

Lesson 8-1

The Multiplication Counting Principle

Vocabulary

scientific notation

▶ **BIG IDEA** Expressions involving powers result from certain counting problems and are used in scientific notation.

The Jaipur Friendship and Knitting Society decided that it would call itself by the 3-letter acronym JFK. (An *acronym*, like USA or NCAA, is a "word" made up of the first letter of each word in a phrase.) They were disappointed to learn that JFK was already a popular acronym. It is the initials of President John Fitzgerald Kennedy and identifies one of the airports in New York City as well as some highways throughout the country. So the society decided to use JFKS.

Members of the society realized that there is only a certain number of 3-letter acronyms. So they wondered, how many 3-letter acronyms are there in the English language?

To answer this question, we apply a very useful problem-solving strategy. We consider a simpler problem we may be able to solve and then apply its solution to the problem we want to solve.

Mental Math

Simplify $\dfrac{n \cdot 3n \cdot 6n \cdot 9n}{n \cdot 2n \cdot 4n \cdot 6n}$

Example 1

How many 2-letter acronyms are there?

Solution Count the acronyms in an organized manner, alphabetically. AA, AB, AC, ..., AZ gives 26. BA, BB, BC, ... BZ gives another 26. There will be 26 groups of 26, so the total number is $26 \cdot 26 = 26^2 = 676$.

Knitting was first introduced to Europe in the 5th century CE.

Source: Fine Living TV Network

Notice that we gave the answer to Example 1 in three forms: as a *product* $26 \cdot 26$, as a *power* 26^2, in our customary *base-10 decimal* system as 676. Each of these forms is useful, so you need to be able to move back and forth from one way of writing a number to another.

Example 1 applies multiplication in a manner that is so important that it has a special name, the *Multiplication Counting Principle*.

Multiplication Counting Principle

If one choice can be made in *m* ways and then a second choice can be made in *n* ways, then there are *mn* ways of making the first choice followed by the second choice.

The Multiplication Counting Principle was applied in Example 1. There were 26 choices for the first letter. After that choice was made, there were 26 choices for the second letter. So $m = 26$ and $n = 26$, and the number of 2-letter acronyms is $26 \cdot 26$, or 676.

Example 2

How many 3-letter acronyms are there?

Solution 1 Apply the Multiplication Counting Principle to the result of Example 1, which found that there are 676 different 2-letter acronyms. For each one, there are 26 possible third letters. So the total number is $676 \cdot 26 = 17{,}576$.

Solution 2 Keep the result from Example 1 in factored form. There are $26 \cdot 26$ different 2-letter acronyms. Now, with 26 possible third letters, the total number is $26 \cdot 26 \cdot 26 = 26^3$. This is also equal to 17,576.

The idea behind the solutions to Example 2 is very powerful and can be continued. To get the number of 4-letter acronyms, you can work from the number of 3-letter acronyms. Each 3-letter acronym is the beginning of 26 4-letter acronyms, so the number of 4-letter acronyms is $26^3 \cdot 26$, or 26^4, and so on. This thinking is much like the Now/Next thinking you used in the spreadsheets of Lesson 7-8.

 QY1

Choosing From n Objects Repeatedly

A sequence of two objects is said to have "length" 2; a sequence of three objects has length 3, and so on. In the previous examples you counted ways to make acronyms of length 2 and 3. Order matters with acronyms. President John Fitzgerald Kennedy had initials JFK, but not KFJ. Order also matters with acronyms such as NASA (National Aeronautics and Space Administration) and SCUBA (self-contained underwater breathing apparatus).

The process used to find the number of different acronyms of length 2 or 3 can be generalized, leading to the following result.

Arrangements Theorem

If there are n ways to select each object in a sequence of length L, then n^L different sequences are possible.

 QY2

> **QY1**
>
> The Russian alphabet has 33 letters. How many 4-letter Russian acronyms are possible?

> **QY2**
>
> A test has 20 multiple-choice questions with 5 choices each. How many different sets of answers are possible?

In Example 3, not all of the objects have the same number of choices possible.

Example 3

Suppose a standardized test has 20 questions with 4 choices and 10 questions with 5 choices. What is the probability that a person could guess on every one of the 30 questions and answer them all correctly?

Solution Think of the test as having 2 parts. Count the number of ways each part can be created.

Part 1 This part has 20 questions with 4 choices. We want to know how many sequences m of length 20 there are with these 4 letters.

$$m = \underline{\quad ? \quad}$$

Part 2 This part has 10 questions with 5 choices. Let n be the number of sequences of length 10 with 5 letters.

$$n = \underline{\quad ? \quad}$$

Now apply the Multiplication Counting Principle and multiply the results from Part 1 and Part 2 to determine how many different sets of answers are possible.

$$mn = \underline{\quad ? \quad}$$

In base 10 this number is 10,737,418,240,000,000,000. If a person is guessing, then we assume that each one of these sets of answers is equally likely, and only one of them has all the correct answers. So the probability of having a perfect test is $\frac{1}{mn} = \underline{\quad ? \quad}$.

The national average mathematics score on The National Assessment of Educational Progress (NAEP) at grade 8 was 16 points higher in 2005 than in 1990.

Source: National Assessment of Educational Progress

Writing Large Numbers in Scientific Notation

Depending on your calculator and the mode it is in, if you enter mn to calculate the answer to Example 3, the result will be displayed either as the long base-10 number or in *scientific notation.* You should try this on your calculator. Presumably you have used scientific notation in other mathematics or science classes. Recall that in **scientific notation,** a number is represented as $x \cdot 10^n$, where n is an integer and $1 \leq x < 10$. In scientific notation, $10,737,418,240,000,000,000 \approx 1.0737 \cdot 10^{19}$.

A major advantage of scientific notation is that it quickly tells you the size of a number. The exponent is one less than the number of digits in the whole number. A whole number $x \cdot 10^n$ has $n + 1$ digits. Notice that the exponent is 19 in the scientific notation form of the number above, and the base-10 form has 20 digits.

Questions

COVERING THE IDEAS

1. **a.** Write all the 2-letter acronyms that can be made from the five vowels A, E, I, O, and U.

   b. **Fill in the Blanks** In Part a, you have found the number of sequences of length __?__ of __?__ objects.

2. The Greek alphabet is about 2,750 years old and is used by about 12 million people in Greece and other countries around the world. It contains 24 letters.

   a. How many 2-letter acronyms are there using Greek letters?

   b. How many 4-letter acronyms are there using Greek letters?

3. Write the number 5^6 in base-10 and in scientific notation.

4. **a.** Write an example of a 6-letter acronym made from the five letters A, B, C, D, and E.

   b. How many of these 6-letter acronyms are possible?

5. Suppose part of a spreadsheet has 6 columns and 15 rows.

   a. How many cells are in the spreadsheet?

   b. Explain how your answer applies the Multiplication Counting Principle by indicating how choices are involved in finding the number of cells.

6. **a.** Draw three horizontal lines and four vertical lines. In how many points do these lines intersect?

   b. If you drew 30 horizontal lines and 40 vertical lines, in how many points would they intersect?

   c. If you drew h horizontal lines and v vertical lines, in how many points would they intersect?

7. **a.** A quiz consists of 10 true-or-false questions. How many different sets of answers are possible? Write your answer in exponential form, in base-10, and in scientific notation.

   b. If you guess on all 10 questions, what is the probability of getting all the questions correct?

   c. Answer Parts a and b if there are Q true or false questions on the test.

8. A test has 5 true-or-false questions and 15 multiple-choice questions with 4 choices each.

   a. How many different sets of answers are possible? Write your answer in exponential form, in base-10, and in scientific notation.

   b. If you guessed on every question, what is the probability you would get all 20 questions correct?

9. Use the information on the electromagnetic spectrum on page 456. Write the number in base-10 notation.

   a. the longest wavelength marked on the spectrum

   b. the shortest wavelength marked on the spectrum

APPLYING THE MATHEMATICS

10. Radio station call letters in the United States must start with either W or K.

    a. How many choices are there for the first letter?

    b. How many choices are there for the second letter?

    c. How many different 4-letter station names are possible?

11. The Cayuga Indians played a game called *Dish* using 6 peach pits. The pits were blackened on one side and plain on the other. When pits were tossed, they landed on the blackened and plain sides with about the same frequency. When the six pits were tossed, a player scored if either all blackened or all plain sides landed up. What is the probability that a player would score points on one toss of the pits?

12. How many 6-digit whole numbers are there? Answer the question in two ways.

    a. by subtracting the least 6-digit number from the greatest 6-digit number and working from that

    b. by thinking of the problem as a series of choices: 9 choices for the left digit (because it cannot be zero) and 10 choices for every other

13. Assume that everyone in the United States has a first name, a middle name, and a last name. Therefore, everyone has a 3-letter acronym of his or her initials. If your initials are typical, about how many of the 300 million people in the United States have your initials?

14. How many different sets of answers are possible for each of the following tests?

    a. a group of P true-or-false questions

    b. a group of Q questions that can be answered "sometimes," "always," or "never"

    c. a test made up of two parts: P true or false questions and Q *always, sometimes but not always,* or *never* questions

In June 2005, there were 2,019 commercial U.S. radio stations.

Source: Federal Communications Commission

REVIEW

15. Do the ordered pairs (x, y) that satisfy $y < -4x + 8$ describe a function? Why or why not? (**Lesson 7-5**)

16. Consider these points (0, –2), (6, 4), and (–10, –12).
    (**Lessons 6-6, 3-4**)
    a. Write an equation for the line containing these three points.
    b. If the point $(x, 20)$ lies on this line, find the value of x.

17. Refer to the similar triangles at the right. If the ratio of similitude of the smaller triangle to the larger triangle is $\frac{1}{3}$, find the area of the larger triangle. (**Lesson 5-10**)

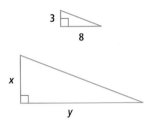

18. A biologist captured, tagged, and released 40 fish caught in a lake. Three weeks later, the biologist caught 28 fish. Of these, 8 had tags. Based on these findings, estimate the total number of fish in the lake. (**Lesson 5-9**)

19. Solve $\frac{1}{5}x - \frac{3}{10} = \frac{9}{10}$. (**Lesson 3-8**)

In 20 and 21, write the number in scientific notation. (Previous Course)

20. seven thousandths

21. 2.8 billion

EXPLORATION

22. Many of the cabinet-level departments in the United States government are identified by acronyms. Tell what department each of these acronyms stands for. As a hint, we have put the departments (not the acronyms) in alphabetical order.

    a. USDA   b. DOC   c. DOD   d. ED
    e. DOE   f. HHS   g. DHS   h. HUD
    i. DOJ   j. DOL   k. DOS   l. DOI
    m. DOT   n. VA

23. The Greek alphabet has 24 letters and the Russian alphabet has 33 letters.
    a. Are there more 4-letter Greek acronyms or 3-letter Russian acronyms?
    b. What is the least value of n for which there are *fewer* n-letter Greek acronyms compared to $(n - 1)$-letter Russian acronyms?

The Pentagon has three times the floor space of the Empire State Building in New York.

Source: Pentagon Tours

Lesson

8-2

Products and Powers of Powers

▶ **BIG IDEA** Because of the relationship between repeated multiplication and powers, products and powers of powers can be themselves written as powers.

Multiplying Powers with the Same Base

When n is a positive integer, $x^n = \underbrace{x \cdot x \cdot \ldots \cdot x}_{n\ factors}$. From this, a number of important properties can be developed. They all involve multiplication in some way because of the relationship between exponents and multiplication. Addition is different. In general, there is no way to simplify the sum of two powers. For example, $3^2 + 3^4 = 9 + 81 = 90$, and 90 is not an integer power of 3. But notice what happens when we multiply powers with the same base.

$$3^2 \cdot 3^4 = \underbrace{(3 \cdot 3)}_{2\ factors} \cdot \underbrace{(3 \cdot 3 \cdot 3 \cdot 3)}_{4\ factors} = \underbrace{(3 \cdot 3 \cdot 3 \cdot 3 \cdot 3 \cdot 3)}_{6\ factors} = 3^6$$

$$1.06^0 \cdot 1.06^3 = 1 \cdot \underbrace{(1.06 \cdot 1.06 \cdot 1.06)}_{3\ factors} = 1.06^3$$

$$(-6)^5 \cdot (-6)^5 = \underbrace{(-6 \cdot -6 \cdot -6 \cdot -6 \cdot -6)}_{5\ factors} \cdot \underbrace{(-6 \cdot -6 \cdot -6 \cdot -6 \cdot -6)}_{5\ factors} = (-6)^{10}$$

These three expressions involved multiplying powers of the same base, where the base was a specific number (3, 1.06, or –6). The same process is used to multiply powers of a variable.

Mental Math

Use the circle graph. Give each value in the indicated form.

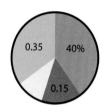

a. blue sector, decimal

b. green sector, fraction

c. red sector, percent

d. yellow sector, decimal

e. yellow sector, fraction

Activity

Step 1 Evaluate each expression.

   a. $z^7 \cdot z^4$ **b.** $y^6 \cdot y^8$ **c.** $y^2 \cdot y^4 \cdot y^3$ **d.** $x^3 \cdot x$

   e. $x^4 \cdot x^2 \cdot x$ **f.** $t \cdot t \cdot t$ **g.** $t^3 \cdot t^4 \cdot t \cdot t$ **h.** $z^0 \cdot z^5 \cdot z^2 \cdot z^2$

Step 2 Check your answers using a CAS.

   a. When multiplying powers with the same base, how is the exponent of the answer related to the exponents of the original factors?

   b. Some of the variables do not have visible exponents, like $x^3 \cdot x$. Does the relationship you described in Part a apply in this case?

   c. Refer to Part h. What does z^0 equal? How does this fit in with the answer to Part 2a?

The general pattern established in the activity leads us to the *Product of Powers Property.*

Product of Powers Property

For all m and n, and all nonzero b, $b^m \cdot b^n = b^{m+n}$.

The Product of Powers Property can be illustrated with a multiplication fact triangle. Notice that the powers are multiplied, but the exponents are added.

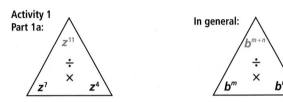

Here is a situation leading to multiplying powers with the same base.

Example 1

Suppose you fold an 8.5-inch by 11-inch piece of paper alternating the direction of the folds (fold down, fold to the left, fold down, fold to the left, and so on).

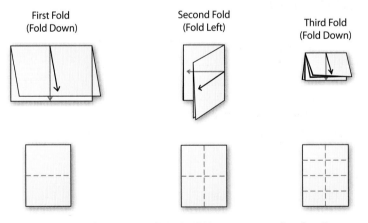

First Fold
(Fold Down)

Second Fold
(Fold Left)

Third Fold
(Fold Down)

Imagine that you keep folding indefinitely. Write an expression for the number of regions created by first folding the paper n times, and then folding it *three times more.*

Solution You begin with 1 piece of paper, which is 1 region. Each time you fold the paper, you double the number of regions. After n folds, you have 2^n regions. Folding an additional 3 times doubles the number of regions 3 more times. The number of folds is $2^n \cdot 2 \cdot 2 \cdot 2$ or $2^n \cdot 2^3$. Applying the Product of Powers Property, $2^n \cdot 2^3 = 2^{n+3}$.

Multiplying Powers with Different Bases

The Product of Powers Property tells how to simplify the product of two powers with the same base. A product with different bases, such as $a^3 \cdot b^4$, usually *cannot* be simplified.

Example 2

Simplify $r^9 \cdot s^5 \cdot r^7 \cdot s^2$.

Solution Use the properties of multiplication to group factors with the same base.

$$r^9 \cdot s^5 \cdot r^7 \cdot s^2 = r^9 \cdot r^7 \cdot s^5 \cdot s^2 \qquad \text{Commutative Property of Multiplication}$$

$$= r^{9+7} \cdot s^{5+2} \qquad \text{Product of Powers Property}$$

$$= r^{16} \cdot s^7 \qquad \text{Simplify.}$$

$r^{16} \cdot s^7$ cannot be simplified further because the bases are different.

Check Perform the multiplication with a CAS.

A CAS indicates that $r^9 \cdot s^5 \cdot r^7 \cdot s^2 = r^{16} \cdot s^7$. It checks.

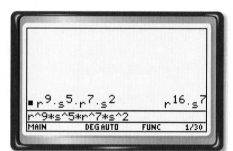

What Happens If We Take a Power of a Power?

When powers of powers are calculated, interesting patterns also emerge.

Example 3

Write $(5^2)^4$ as a single power.

Solution Think of 5^2 as a number that is raised to the 4th power.

$$(5^2)^4 = 5^2 \cdot 5^2 \cdot 5^2 \cdot 5^2 \qquad \text{Repeated Multiplication Model for Powering.}$$

$$= 5^{2+2+2+2} \qquad \text{Product of Powers Property}$$

$$= 5^8 \qquad \text{Simplify.}$$

The general pattern is called the *Power of a Power Property*.

Power of a Power Property

For all m and n, and all nonzero b, $(b^m)^n = b^{mn}$.

Some expressions involve both powers of powers and multiplication.

Example 4

Simplify $3m(m^4)^2$.

Solution 1 First rewrite $(m^4)^2$ as repeated multiplication.

$$3m(m^4)^2 = 3m^1 \cdot m^4 \cdot m^4 = 3m^9$$

Solution 2 First use the Power of a Power Property with $(m^4)^2$.

$$3m(m^4)^2 = 3m^1 \cdot m^8 = 3m^9$$

Questions

COVERING THE IDEAS

In 1 and 2, write the product as a single power.

1. $18^5 \cdot 18^4$

2. $(-7)^3 \cdot (-7)^2$

3. Write $w^4 \cdot w^3$ as a single power and check your answer by substituting 2 for w.

In 4–6, suppose you fold an 8.5-inch by 11-inch piece of paper as in Example 1. Calculate the number of regions created by folding the paper in the way described.

4. two times, then three more times

5. three times, then two more times, then two more times

6. m times, then n more times

7. Find the expression that completes the fact triangle at the right.

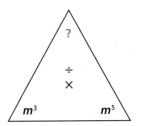

In 8–10, rewrite the expression as a single power.

8. $(2^3)^4$

9. $(m^5)^2$

10. $(y^2)^6$

In 11–16, simplify the power.

11. $3a^4 \cdot 5a^2$

12. $2(k^{10})^7$

13. $d(d^{13})$

14. $m^2 \cdot m^9 \cdot a^0 \cdot m^7 \cdot a^9$

15. $a^3(b^3a^5)$

16. $4k^2(k^3)^5$

APPLYING THE MATHEMATICS

17. A quiz has two parts. The first part has 5 multiple-choice questions. The second part has 3 multiple-choice questions. Each multiple-choice question has 4 choices. How many different sequences of answers are possible on the 8 questions?

In 18–20, solve the equation. Show all work.

18. $2^4 \cdot 2^n = 2^{12}$

19. $(5^6)^x = 5^6$

20. $(a^7 \cdot a^n)^2 = a^{24}$

21. Suppose a population P of bacteria triples each day.

    a. Write an expression for the number of bacteria after 4 days.

    b. How many days after the 4th day will the bacteria population be $P \cdot 3^{20}$?

22. Does the Product of Powers Property work for fractions? Write each expression as a power and a simple fraction.

    a. $\frac{3}{5} \cdot \frac{3}{5} \cdot \frac{3}{5}$ **b.** $\frac{3}{5} \cdot \frac{3}{5} \cdot \frac{3}{5} \cdot \frac{3}{5}$ **c.** $\frac{3}{5} \cdot \frac{3}{5} \cdot \frac{3}{5} \cdot \frac{3}{5} \cdot \frac{3}{5} \cdot \frac{3}{5} \cdot \frac{3}{5}$

REVIEW

23. Abigail is going to buy a new car. She has to choose the body style (sedan, SUV, or convertible), transmission (automatic or standard), and color (white, black, red, blue, or green). (**Lesson 8-1**)

    a. How many different ways can Abigail make her choices?

    b. If another color choice of silver is given to her, how many more choices does she have?

24. If $f(x) = 3x + 2$ and $g(x) = 3x^2 - 2$, find each value. (**Lesson 7-6**)

    a. $f(3)$ **b.** $g(-2)$ **c.** $f(5) - g(5)$ **d.** $g(-4) + f(-4)$

In 2004, there were 4,236,736 passenger cars produced in the United States.

Source: Automotive News Data Center

25. A band sold 1,252 tickets for a concert that were priced at $35. The band decided to lower the ticket price to their next concert to $30 in hopes of attracting a larger audience. After lowering the price, 1,510 tickets were sold. (**Lessons 6-6, 3-4**)

    a. Write a linear equation that relates the price of the ticket x and the number of tickets sold y.

    b. Use your answer to Part a to predict the number of tickets that will be sold if the price is lowered to $20.

26. Consider the line $y = 4x - 5$. Find (**Lessons 6-4, 6-2**)

    a. its slope.   **b.** its y-intercept.   **c.** its x-intercept.

27. Write 0.00324 in scientific notation. (**Previous Course**)

28. Write these numbers as decimals. (**Previous Course**)

    a. $9.8 \cdot 10^0$ **b.** $9.8 \cdot 10^{-1}$

    c. $9.8 \cdot 10^{-2}$ **d.** $9.8 \cdot 10^{-3}$

EXPLORATION

29. There are prefixes in the metric system for some of the powers of 10. For example, the prefix for 10^3 is kilo-, as in kilogram, kilometer, and kilobyte. Give the metric prefix for each power.

    a. 10^6 **b.** 10^9 **c.** 10^{12} **d.** 10^{15} **e.** 10^{18}

Lesson 8-3

Quotients of Powers

▶ **BIG IDEA** Because of the relationship between multiplication and division, quotients of powers can be themselves written as powers.

As you know, $\frac{24}{3} = 8$ because $8 \cdot 3 = 24$. Similarly, $\frac{24}{3} = \frac{8 \cdot \cancel{3}^1}{1\cancel{3}} = 8$. Both of these methods can be helpful in understanding quotients of powers.

For example, suppose $\frac{x^{10}}{x^2} = x^?$. By rewriting this statement to read $x^? \cdot x^2 = x^{10}$, we can apply the Product of Powers Property, $x^{?+2} = x^{10}$. You can see that the unknown exponent is 8 because $8 + 2 = 10$. So $\frac{x^{10}}{x^2} = x^8$. Another way of finding the unknown exponent in $\frac{x^{10}}{x^2} = x^?$ is to write both the numerator and denominator in expanded form and simplify the fraction.

$$\frac{x^{10}}{x^2} = \frac{1\cancel{x} \cdot 1\cancel{x} \cdot x \cdot x \cdot x \cdot x \cdot x \cdot x \cdot x \cdot x}{1\cancel{x} \cdot \cancel{x}_1}$$

$$= x \cdot x \cdot x \cdot x \cdot x \cdot x \cdot x \cdot x$$

$$= x^8$$

Activity

1. Simplify each expression.

   a. $\dfrac{a^7}{a^4}$

   b. $\dfrac{m^{14}}{m^5}$

   c. $\dfrac{y^{12}}{y}$

   d. $\dfrac{n^{13}}{n^{13}}$

2. When dividing powers of the same base, how is the exponent of the answer related to the exponents of the original division?

The general pattern established in the Activity is the *Quotient of Powers Property*.

Quotient of Powers Property

For all m and n, and all nonzero b, $\dfrac{b^m}{b^n} = b^{m-n}$.

 STOP QY

Mental Math

True or false?

a. $x^{100} + x^{101} = x^{201}$

b. $x^{100} \cdot x^{101} = x^{201}$

c. $x^{100} + x^{101} = 2x^{101}$

d. $x^{100} + x^{100} = 2x^{100}$

▶ **QY**

Simplify $\dfrac{z^{50}}{z^{10}}$.

Fact triangles are another way of representing the Quotient of Powers Property.

A specific case:

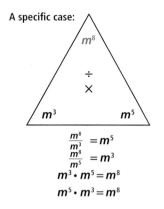

In general:

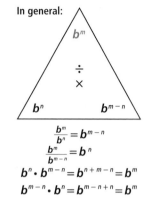

$$\frac{m^8}{m^3} = m^5$$
$$\frac{m^8}{m^5} = m^3$$
$$m^3 \cdot m^5 = m^8$$
$$m^5 \cdot m^3 = m^8$$

$$\frac{b^m}{b^n} = b^{m-n}$$
$$\frac{b^m}{b^{m-n}} = b^n$$
$$b^n \cdot b^{m-n} = b^{n+m-n} = b^m$$
$$b^{m-n} \cdot b^n = b^{m-n+n} = b^m$$

The Zero Power

In Question 1d of the Activity, you should have seen that $\frac{n^{13}}{n^{13}} = 1$. More generally, consider the fraction $\frac{b^m}{b^m}$. By the Quotient of Powers Property, $\frac{b^m}{b^m} = b^{m-m} = b^0$. But you also know that any nonzero number divided by itself is 1. So $1 = \frac{b^m}{b^m} = b^0$. This is another way of showing why $b^0 = 1$.

An Application of the Quotient of Powers Property

The Quotient of Powers Property is useful in dividing numbers written in scientific notation.

Example 1

The Gross Domestic Product (GDP) of a country is the total value of all the goods and services produced in the country. When the GDP is divided by the population of the country, the result is the GDP per person, often called the *GDP per capita*. In 2006, Denmark had a population of about 5.5 million and a GDP of $243.4 billion. What is Denmark's GDP per capita?

Solution Since GDP per capita is a rate unit, the answer is found by division.

$$\frac{\$243,400,000,000}{5.5 \text{ million people}} = \frac{2.434 \times 10^{11}}{5.5 \times 10^6}$$ Write in scientific notation.

$$= \frac{2.434}{5.5} \cdot \frac{10^{11}}{10^6}$$ Multiplying Fractions Property

$$\approx 0.44 \cdot 10^5$$ Quotient of Powers Property

$$\approx \$44,000/\text{person}$$ Write in base 10.

Approximately 5.5 million people live in Denmark, making it one of the most densely populated nations in Northern Europe.

Source: Danish Tourist Board

Check Change the numbers to decimal notation and simplify the fraction.

$$\frac{243{,}400{,}000{,}000}{5{,}500{,}000} = \frac{2{,}434{,}000}{55} \approx 44{,}000$$

Dividing Powers with Different Bases

To use the Quotient of Powers Property, the bases must be the same. For example, $\frac{a^5}{b^2}$ cannot be simplified further. To divide two algebraic expressions that involve different bases, group powers of the same base together and use the Quotient of Powers Property to simplify each fraction.

Example 2

Simplify $\frac{30a^3n^6}{5a^2n}$.

Solution 1

$$\frac{30a^3n^6}{5a^2n} = \frac{30}{5} \cdot \frac{a^3}{a^2} \cdot \frac{n^6}{n} \qquad \text{Multiplying Fractions Property}$$

$$= \frac{30}{5} \cdot a^{3-2} \cdot n^{6-1} \qquad \text{Quotient of Powers Property}$$

$$= 6 \cdot a^1 \cdot n^5 = 6an^5 \qquad \text{Arithmetic}$$

Solution 2

$$\frac{30a^3n^6}{5a^2n} = \frac{30 \cdot a \cdot a \cdot a \cdot n \cdot n \cdot n \cdot n \cdot n \cdot n}{5 \cdot a \cdot a \cdot n} \qquad \begin{array}{l}\text{Repeated Multiplication}\\\text{Property of Powers}\end{array}$$

$$= \frac{6 \cdot a \cdot n \cdot n \cdot n \cdot n \cdot n}{1} \qquad \text{Equal Fractions Property}$$

$$= 6an^5 \qquad \text{Arithmetic}$$

Check Use a CAS to check your answer, as shown below.

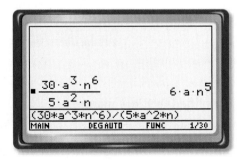

Questions

COVERING THE IDEAS

In 1–3, write the quotient as a single power.

1. $\dfrac{2^7}{2^4}$

2. $\dfrac{8^5}{8^m}$

3. $\dfrac{3^m}{3^n}$

In 4–9, use the Quotient of Powers Property to simplify the fraction.

4. $\dfrac{x^{12}}{x^2}$ **5.** $\dfrac{a^{20}}{a^{20}}$ **6.** $\dfrac{6.5 \times 10^{21}}{3.1 \times 10^{19}}$

7. $\dfrac{12a^2b^{12}}{2ab^7}$ **8.** $\dfrac{2a^5b^9}{8a^3b}$ **9.** $\dfrac{24a^{10}b^5}{6a^4b^5}$

10. In 2006, the African country of Burundi had a population of about 8.1 million and a GDP of about \$5.7 billion. What is Burundi's GDP per capita?

11. Why can't $\dfrac{a^3}{b^4}$ be simplified?

12. If $\dfrac{b^n}{b^m} = 1$, how must m and n be related?

APPLYING THE MATHEMATICS

In 13–15, write the quotient as a single power.

13. $\dfrac{4^3}{2^6}$ **14.** $\dfrac{16 \cdot 2^m}{2^6}$ **15.** $\dfrac{4^3}{8 \cdot 2^6}$

In 16–19, rewrite the expression so that it has no fraction.

16. $\dfrac{(7m)^5}{(7m)^3}$ **17.** $\dfrac{(7 + 3m)^7}{(7 + 3m)^6}$ **18.** $\dfrac{x^{5a-10}}{x^{3-3a}}$ **19.** $\dfrac{2a^6 + 6a^6}{2a^5}$

20. In Norway in 2002, $4.7 \cdot 10^7$ kilograms of ground coffee were consumed, and the total population was approximately 4,525,000. To brew a typical cup of coffee, you need 10.6 grams of ground coffee. Determine the coffee consumption (in terms of cups per person) in Norway in 2002.

21. In 2005, the world's population was approximately $6.446 \cdot 10^9$ people. In the same year, global oil output was approximately $8.0 \cdot 10^7$ million barrels per day. A barrel is equivalent to 35 gallons of oil.

  a. How many barrels of oil was this per person per day?

  b. At this rate, how many gallons of oil were consumed per person during 2005?

22. Write an algebraic fraction that can be simplified to $12a^2b$ using the Quotient of Powers Property.

The number of cups of coffee consumed per capita per year in the Nordic countries of Norway, Sweden, Denmark, and Finland is among the highest in the world.

Source: nationmaster.com

REVIEW

In 23–26, simplify the expression. (Lesson 8-2)

23. $3x \cdot x^2$

24. $n \cdot n^2 \cdot n^3$

25. $2h^3 \cdot 6h^4 + 3h \cdot 4h^6$

26. $a^x \cdot a^y \cdot a^z$

27. Suppose each question on a 5-question, multiple-choice quiz has four choices. (**Lesson 8-1**)

    a. Give the probability of guessing all the correct answers as the reciprocal of a power.

    b. Give the probability of guessing all wrong answers.

28. Distances after various times when traveling at 65 miles per hour are shown on the spreadsheet below. (**Lesson 6-1**)

◇	A	B
1	Time (hours)	Distance (miles)
2	1.0	?
3	1.5	97.5
4	2	130
5	2.5	162.5
6	3	?
7	3.5	?

    a. Complete the spreadsheet.

    b. Name two ways to get the value in cell B7.

29. Calculate the total cost in your head. (**Lesson 2-2**)

    a. 8 cans of tuna fish at $2.99 per can

    b. 5 tickets to a movie at $10.50 per ticket

EXPLORATION

30. The average 14 year old has a volume of about 3 cubic feet.

    a. Consider all the students in your school. Would their total volume be more or less than the volume of one classroom? Assume the classroom is 10 feet high, 30 feet long, and 30 feet wide.

    b. Assume the population of the world to be 6.4 billion people and the average volume of a person to be 4 cubic feet. Is the volume of all the people more or less than 1 cubic mile? How much more or less? (There are $5,280^3$ cubic feet in a cubic mile.)

QY ANSWER

z^{40}

Lesson

8-4

Negative Exponents

▶ **BIG IDEA** The numbers x^{-n} and x^n are reciprocals.

What Is the Value of a Power with a Negative Exponent?

You have used base 10 with a negative exponent to represent small numbers in scientific notation. For example, $10^{-1} = 0.1 = \frac{1}{10^1}$, $10^{-2} = 0.01 = \frac{1}{10^2}$, $10^{-3} = 0.001 = \frac{1}{10^3}$, and so on.

Now we consider other powers with negative exponents. That is, we want to know the meaning of b^n when n is negative. Consider this pattern of the powers of 2.

$$2^4 = 16$$
$$2^3 = 8$$
$$2^2 = 4$$
$$2^1 = 2$$
$$2^0 = 1$$

Each exponent is one less than the one above it. The value of each power is half that of the number above. Continuing the pattern suggests that the following are true.

$$2^{-1} = \frac{1}{2}$$
$$2^{-2} = \frac{1}{4} = \frac{1}{2^2}$$
$$2^{-3} = \frac{1}{8} = \frac{1}{2^3}$$
$$2^{-4} = \frac{1}{16} = \frac{1}{2^4}$$

A general description of the pattern is simple: $2^{-n} = \frac{1}{2^n}$. That is, 2^{-n} is the reciprocal of 2^n. We call the general property the *Negative Exponent Property*.

Negative Exponent Property

For any nonzero b and all n, $b^{-n} = \frac{1}{b^n}$, the reciprocal of b^n.

Mental Math

Give the area of

a. a square with side $\frac{s}{2}$.

b. a circle with radius $3r$.

c. a rectangle with $\frac{3}{4}x$ and $\frac{8}{3}y$ dimensions.

Notice that even though the exponent in 2^{-4} on the previous page is negative, the number 2^{-4} is still positive. All negative integer powers of positive numbers are positive.

 QY

▶ QY

Write 5^{-4} as a simple fraction without a negative exponent.

Example 1

Rewrite $a^7 \cdot b^{-4}$ without negative exponents.

Solution

$$a^7 \cdot b^{-4} = a^7 \cdot \frac{1}{b^4} \qquad \text{Substitute } \frac{1}{b^4} \text{ for } b^{-4}.$$
$$= \frac{a^7}{b^4}$$

Because the Product of Powers Property applies to all exponents, it applies to negative exponents. Suppose you multiply b^n by b^{-n}.

$$b^n \cdot b^{-n} = b^{n + -n} \qquad \text{Product of Powers Property}$$
$$= b^0 \qquad \text{Property of Opposites}$$
$$= 1 \qquad \text{Zero Exponent Property}$$

To multiply b^n by b^{-n}, you can also use the Negative Exponent Property.

$$b^n \cdot b^{-n} = b^n \cdot \frac{1}{b^n} \qquad \text{Negative Exponent Property}$$
$$= 1 \qquad \text{Definition of reciprocal}$$

In this way, the Product of Powers Property verifies that b^{-n} must be the reciprocal of b^n. In particular, $b^{-1} = \frac{1}{b}$. That is, the −1 power (read "negative one" or "negative first" power) of a number is its reciprocal.

Suppose the base b is a fraction, $b = \frac{x}{y}$. Then the reciprocal of b is $\frac{y}{x}$. Consequently, this gives us a different form of the Negative Exponent Property that is more convenient when the base is a fraction. The simplest way to find the reciprocal of a fraction $\frac{a}{b}$ is to invert it, producing $\frac{b}{a}$.

Negative Exponent Property for Fractions

For any nonzero x and y and all n, $\left(\frac{x}{y}\right)^{-n} = \left(\frac{y}{x}\right)^n$.

Example 2

Write each expression without negative exponents.

a. $\left(\dfrac{5}{4}\right)^{-2}$

b. $\left(\dfrac{1}{m^2}\right)^{-3}$

Solution

a. Use the Negative Exponent Property for Fractions.

$$\left(\dfrac{5}{4}\right)^{-2} = \left(\dfrac{\underline{?}}{}\right)$$

$$= \underline{\ ?\ }$$

b. Take the reciprocal to the opposite power.

$$\left(\dfrac{1}{m^2}\right)^{-3} = \left(\dfrac{\underline{?}}{1}\right)^{3}$$

$$= (\underline{\ ?\ })^{3}$$

$$= \underline{\ ?\ }$$

Recall the compound interest formula $A = P(1 + r)^t$. In this formula, negative exponents stand for unit periods going back in time.

Example 3

Ten years ago, Den put money into a college savings account at an annual yield of 6%. If the money is now worth $9,491.49, what was the amount initially invested?

Solution

Here $P = 9{,}491.49$, $r = 0.06$, and $t = -10$ (for 10 years ago).

So, $A = 9{,}491.49(1.06)^{-10} \approx 5{,}300$.

So, Den originally started with approximately $5,300.

Check Use the Compound Interest Formula. If Den invested $5,300, he would have $5{,}300(1.06)^{10}$, which equals $9,491.49. It checks.

Quotient of Powers and Negative Exponents

The last lesson involved fractions in which two powers of the same base are divided. When the denominator contains the greater power, negative exponents can be used to simplify the expression. For example, $\dfrac{x^5}{x^9} = x^{5-9} = x^{-4}$.

This can be verified using repeated multiplication.

$$\frac{x^5}{x^9} = \frac{\overset{1}{\cancel{x}} \cdot \overset{1}{\cancel{x}} \cdot \overset{1}{\cancel{x}} \cdot \overset{1}{\cancel{x}} \cdot \overset{1}{\cancel{x}}}{\underset{1}{\cancel{x}} \cdot \underset{1}{\cancel{x}} \cdot \underset{1}{\cancel{x}} \cdot \underset{1}{\cancel{x}} \cdot \underset{1}{\cancel{x}} \cdot x \cdot x \cdot x \cdot x} = \frac{1}{x^4}$$

In this way, you can see again that $b^{-n} = \frac{1}{b^n}$.

GUIDED

Example 4

Simplify $\frac{5a^4b^7c^2}{15a^{11}b^5c^3}$. Write the answer without negative exponents.

Solution

$$\frac{5a^4b^7c^2}{15a^{11}b^5c^3} = \frac{5}{15} \cdot \frac{a^4}{a^{11}} \cdot \frac{b^7}{b^5} \cdot \frac{c^2}{c^3}$$
Group factors with the same base together.

$$= \frac{1}{3} \cdot a^{\underline{}} \cdot b^{\underline{}} \cdot c^{\underline{}}$$
Quotient of Powers Property

$$= \frac{1}{3} \cdot \frac{1}{a^{\underline{}}} \cdot \frac{b^{\underline{}}}{1} \cdot \frac{1}{c^{\underline{}}}$$
Negative Exponent Property

$$= \underline{}$$
Multiply the fractions.

Applying the Power of a Power Property with Negative Exponents

Consider $(x^3)^{-2}$, a power of a power. Wanda wondered if the Power of a Power Property would apply with negative exponents. She entered the expression into a CAS and the screen below appeared.

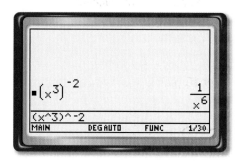

This is the answer that would result from applying the Power of a Power Property.

$$\left(x^3\right)^{-2} = x^{3 \cdot -2} = x^{-6}$$

Then you can rewrite the power using the Negative Exponent Property.

$$x^{-6} = \frac{1}{x^6}$$

All the properties of powers you have learned can be used with negative exponents. They can translate an expression with a negative exponent into one with only positive exponents.

Example 5

Simplify $(y^{-4})^2$. Write without negative exponents.

Solution

$$(y^{-4})^2 = y^{-8} \qquad \text{Power of a Power Property}$$

$$= \frac{1}{y^8} \qquad \text{Negative Exponent Property}$$

Questions

COVERING THE IDEAS

1. **Fill in the Blanks** Complete the last four equations in the pattern below. Then write the next equation in the pattern.

$$3^4 = 81$$
$$3^3 = 27$$
$$3^2 = 9$$
$$3^1 = 3$$
$$3^0 = 1$$
$$3^{-1} = \underline{\;?\;}$$
$$3^{-2} = \underline{\;?\;}$$
$$3^{-3} = \underline{\;?\;}$$
$$3^{-4} = \underline{\;?\;}$$

In 2–5, write as a simple fraction.

2. 7^{-2} 　　 3. 5^{-3} 　　 4. $\left(\frac{2}{3}\right)^{-1}$ 　　 5. $(y^6)^{-4}$

In 6–9, write as a negative power of an integer.

6. $\frac{1}{36}$ 　　 7. $\frac{1}{81}$ 　　 8. 0.1 　　 9. 0.0001

10. Eight years ago, Abuna put money into a college savings account at an annual yield of 5%. If there is now $7,250 in the account, what amount was initially invested? Round your answer to the nearest penny.

11. Rewrite each expression without negative exponents.

   a. w^{-1} 　　 b. $w^{-1}x^{-2}$ 　　 c. $w^{-1}y^3$ 　　 d. $5w^{-1}x^{-2}y^3$

In 12–14, write each expression without negative exponents.

12. $9^2 \cdot 9^{-2}$ 　　 13. $n^a \cdot n^{-a}$ 　　 14. $(m^{-5})^3$

15. Simplify $\frac{32a^8bc^3}{8a^6b^4c}$. Write without negative exponents.

16. **a.** Graph $y = 2^x$ when the domain is $\{-4, -3, -2, -1, 0, 1, 2, 3, 4\}$.

 b. Describe what happens to the graph as x decreases.

17. Graph $y = 10^x$ as on page 457. Describe what happens as x goes from 0 to -12.

APPLYING THE MATHEMATICS

18. If the reciprocal of $a^{-12}b^5$ is $a^n b^m$, find m and n.

19. Use properties of algebra to justify the answer shown on the CAS screen below.

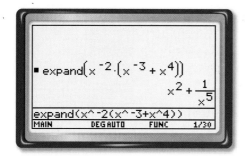

In 20 and 21, solve and check each equation.

20. $7^a \cdot 7^3 = 7^{-6}$ 　　　　　　 21. $5^m \cdot \frac{1}{25} = 5^{-3}$

22. Suppose you draw a square with area 25 square units and connect the midpoints of each side to create a smaller square inside the original. A sequence of successively smaller squares may be created by repeating the process with the most recently created square. The shaded regions show squares in the sequence.

Step 0 　　　　 Step 1 　　　　 Step 2 　　　　 Step 3

 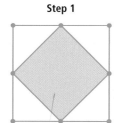 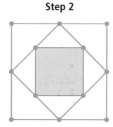 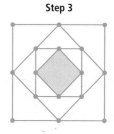

Area = 25 units² 　　 Area = _?_ 　　 Area = _?_ 　　 Area = _?_

Write the area of the shaded square for each step as 25 times a power of 2.

 a. Step 1 　　 **b.** Step 2 　　 **c.** Step 10 　　 **d.** Step n

REVIEW

In 23–25 first simplify. Then evaluate when $a = 2$ and $b = 5$.
(Lessons 8-3, 8-2)

23. $\dfrac{a^2 \cdot a^5 \cdot a^3}{a^4}$

24. $(b^2 a^{-2})^3$

25. $(2b^3)^a$

26. Some people use randomly generated passwords to protect their computer accounts. Suppose a Web site uses random passwords that are six characters long. They allow only lower-case letters and the digits 0 through 9 to be used. (Lessons 8-1, 5-6)

Nearly 49 million laptop computers were sold worldwide in 2004, almost double the number sold in 2000.

Source: *USA Today*

a. What is the total number of possible passwords?

b. Jacinta forgot her password. What is the probability that she will guess her password correctly on the first try?

c. Myron says there would be more possibilities available if the site switched to passwords four characters long but allowed the use of upper-case letters as well. Is Myron correct? Why or why not?

27. Tyra is learning addition and multiplication. For practice, Tyra's teacher gives her a whole number less than 13. Tyra then multiplies the number by 8, adds 25, and states her answer. (Lessons 7-6, 7-5)

a. Describe the situation with function notation, letting x be the number Tyra is given and $m(x)$ the number Tyra states.

b. What is the domain of the function you wrote?

c. What are the greatest and least values the function can have?

EXPLORATION

28. Objects in the universe can be quite small. Do research to find objects of the following sizes.

a. 10^{-3} meter

b. 10^{-6} meter

c. 10^{-9} meter

d. 10^{-12} meter

QY ANSWER

$\dfrac{1}{625}$

Lesson 8-5

Powers of Products and Quotients

> ▶ **BIG IDEA** Because of the relationship among multiplication, division, and powers, powers distribute over products and quotients.

The Power of a Product

The expression $(3x)^4$ is an example of a power of a product. It can be rewritten using repeated multiplication.

$$(3x)^4 = (3x) \cdot (3x) \cdot (3x) \cdot (3x) \quad \text{Repeated Multiplication Model for Powering}$$
$$= 3 \cdot 3 \cdot 3 \cdot 3 \cdot x \cdot x \cdot x \cdot x \quad \text{Associative and Commutative Properties}$$
$$= 3^4 \cdot x^4 \quad \text{Repeated Multiplication Model for Powering}$$
$$= 81x^4 \quad \text{Arithmetic}$$

You can check this answer using a CAS.

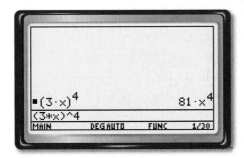

In general, any positive integer power of a product can be rewritten using repeated multiplication.

$$(ab)^n = \underbrace{(ab) \cdot (ab) \cdot \ldots \cdot (ab)}_{n \text{ factors}}$$
$$= \underbrace{a \cdot a \cdot \ldots \cdot a}_{n \text{ factors}} \cdot \underbrace{b \cdot b \cdot \ldots \cdot b}_{n \text{ factors}}$$
$$= a^n \cdot b^n$$

When a and b are nonzero, this result holds for all values of n.

Power of a Product Property

For all nonzero a and b, and for all n, $(ab)^n = a^n b^n$.

This property can be applied to simplify the expression $(3x)^4$ from page 481. The power is applied to each factor of $3x$, so $(3x)^4 = 3^4x^4$, resulting in $81x^4$.

Example 1

Simplify $(-4x)^3$.

Solution Use the Power of a Product Property.

$(-4x)^3 = (-4)^3 \cdot x^3 = -64x^3$

Check Substitute a test value for x and follow order of operations.

Let $x = 1.5$. Does $(-4x)^3 = -64x^3$?

$$(-4 \cdot 1.5)^3 = -64(1.5)^3$$
$$(-6)^3 = -64 \cdot (3.375)$$
$$-6 \cdot -6 \cdot -6 = -216$$
$$-216 = -216 \qquad \text{It checks.}$$

Remember that in the order of operations, powers take precedence over opposites. In $-64x^3$, the power is done before the multiplication. In $(-4x)^3$, the multiplication is inside parentheses so it is done before the power.

 QY1

▶ QY1

Simplify $(3xy)^4$.

GUIDED

Example 2

Simplify $(-5x^2y^3z)^3$.

Solution

$(-5x^2y^3z)^3$

$= (-5)\underset{?}{\overset{?}{}}(x^2)\underset{?}{\overset{?}{}}(y^3)\underset{?}{\overset{?}{}}z\underset{?}{\overset{?}{}}$ Apply the Power of a Product Property.

$= (-5)\underset{?}{\overset{?}{}}x\underset{?}{\overset{?}{}}y\underset{?}{\overset{?}{}}z\underset{?}{\overset{?}{}}$ Apply the Power of a Power Property.

$= \underline{?}$ Evaluate the numerical power.

The Power of a Quotient

The expression $\left(\frac{a}{b}\right)^n$ is the power of a quotient. By using the properties of the previous lessons, you can write this without parentheses.

$$\left(\frac{a}{b}\right)^n = \left(a \cdot \frac{1}{b}\right)^n = (a \cdot b^{-1})^n = a^n \cdot (b^{-1})^n = a^n \cdot b^{-n} = \frac{a^n}{b^n}$$

Power of a Quotient Property

For all nonzero a and b, and for all n, $\left(\frac{a}{b}\right)^n = \frac{a^n}{b^n}$.

The Power of a Quotient Property enables you to find powers of fractions more quickly.

Example 3

Write $\left(\frac{3}{4}\right)^5$ as a simple fraction.

Solution 1 Use the Power of a Quotient Property.

$$\left(\frac{3}{4}\right)^5 = \frac{3^5}{4^5} = \frac{243}{1,024}$$

Solution 2 Use repeated multiplication.

$$\left(\frac{3}{4}\right)^5 = \frac{3}{4} \cdot \frac{3}{4} \cdot \frac{3}{4} \cdot \frac{3}{4} \cdot \frac{3}{4} = \frac{3^5}{4^5} = \frac{243}{1,024}$$

Check Change the fractions to decimals.

$$\left(\frac{3}{4}\right)^5 = 0.75^5 = 0.2373046875$$

$$\frac{243}{1,024} = 0.2373046875$$

They are equal.

 QY2

Powers are found in many formulas for area and volume.

> ▶ **QY2**
>
> Rewrite $11 \cdot \left(\frac{2}{m}\right)^6$ as a simple fraction.

Activity

You will need two pieces of 8.5-in. by 11-in. paper, tape, scissors, and a ruler.

Step 1

Begin with one sheet of paper, positioned so that it is taller than it is wide. Fold it into fourths lengthwise and tape the long edges together to form the sides of a tall box with a square base.

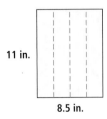

11 in.

8.5 in.

8.5 in.
perimeter of base

(*continued on next page*)

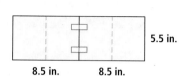

5.5 in.

8.5 in.   8.5 in.

17 in.
perimeter of base

Step 2 Cut the other piece of paper in half to create two 8.5-in. by 5.5-in. pieces. Fold each half, as shown by the dotted lines. Tape these pieces together to form a 17-in. by 5.5-in. piece of paper. Tape the short edges together to form the sides of a short box with a square base.

Step 3 **Multiple Choice** Which of the following do you think is true?

  A The tall, skinny box has more volume.

  B The short, wide box has more volume.

  C Both boxes have the same volume.

  In several sentences, justify your conjecture with a logical argument.

Step 4 Test your conjecture using the formula $V = s^2h$ for the volume V of a box with height h and a square base whose sides have length s.

  a. Calculate the length of the sides of the base of the tall prism.
  $s = \underline{\ ?\ }$

  b. Calculate the volume of the tall prism. $V = \underline{\ \ ?\ \ }$

  c. Repeat Parts a and b for the short prism. $s = \underline{\ ?\ }$, $V = \underline{\ \ ?\ \ }$

Step 5 According to your calculations, which is the correct answer to Step 3? $\underline{\ ?\ }$

  Do you think you would get the same result if you started with a sheet of paper of a different size? Why or why not?

Using Powers of Quotients to Explain the Activity Results

Suppose you begin with a sheet of paper with height h and width p. The shorter box has half the height of the taller box, but the perimeter of its base is twice as long. Each side of the base of the tall box has length $\frac{p}{4}$. Each side of the base of the short box has length $\frac{2p}{4}$. So for the short prism, $2p =$ perimeter and $\frac{h}{2} =$ height.

Tall Box   **Short Box**

h

$\dfrac{h}{2}$

$\dfrac{p}{4}$ $\dfrac{2p}{4}$

The volume of a box with a square base is given by the formula $V = s^2h$, where the height is h and the side of the base is s. So, the volume of the tall box $= \left(\frac{p}{4}\right)^2 \cdot h$, and the volume of the short box $= \left(\frac{2p}{4}\right)^2 \cdot \frac{h}{2}$.

To compare these volumes, we use properties of powers to simplify the expressions.

Example 4

The tall box has volume $\left(\frac{p}{4}\right)^2 \cdot h$ and the short box has volume $\left(\frac{2p}{4}\right)^2 \cdot \frac{h}{2}$.

a. Show that the volume of the tall box is always less than or equal to the volume of the short box.

b. The volume of the short box is how many times the volume of the tall one?

Solution

a. First apply the Power of a Quotient Property to simplify each volume.

Tall Box	Short Box
$V = \left(\frac{p}{4}\right)^2 \cdot h$	$V = \left(\frac{2p}{4}\right)^2 \cdot \frac{h}{2}$
$= \frac{p^2}{4^2} \cdot h$	$= \left(\frac{(2p)^2}{4^2}\right) \cdot \frac{h}{2}$
$= \frac{p^2}{16} \cdot h$	$= \left(\frac{4p^2}{16}\right) \cdot \frac{h}{2}$
$= \frac{p^2h}{16}$	$= \left(\frac{p^2}{4}\right) \cdot \frac{h}{2} = \frac{p^2h}{8}$

$$\text{Volume of the tall box} = \frac{p^2h}{16}$$
$$= \frac{1}{2} \cdot \frac{p^2h}{8}$$
$$= \frac{1}{2} \cdot \text{volume of short box}$$

Because the volume of the tall box is half the volume of the short one, the volume of the tall box is less than the volume of the short box.

b. The volume of the short box is 2 times the volume of the tall box.

Questions

COVERING THE IDEAS

1. a. Rewrite $(6x)^3$ without parentheses.
   b. Check your answer by letting $x = 2$.

In 2–5, rewrite the expression without parentheses.

2. $(5t^2)^3$ 3. $8(-7xy)^3$ 4. $2(x^2y)^4$ 5. $(-t)^{93}$

6. Aisha made a common error when she wrote $(3x)^4 = 12x^4$. Show her this is incorrect by substituting 2 in for x. Then, write a note to Aisha explaining what she did wrong.

In 7–9, write as a simple fraction.

7. $\left(\frac{2}{3}\right)^4$

8. $5\left(\frac{n^5}{10}\right)^3$

9. $\left(\frac{19}{2y}\right)^3$

10. What is the area of a square with perimeter p?

APPLYING THE MATHEMATICS

11. The area A of an isosceles right triangle with leg L can be found using the formula $A = \frac{1}{2}L^2$. If L is multiplied by 6, what happens to the area of the triangle?

12. Suppose you tape a 3-in. by 5-in. notecard to a pencil widthwise (as shown in Figure 1). Assume that the radius of the round pencil is $\frac{3}{16}$ in.

   a. If you rotate the pencil, what shape is traced by point A? Find the area of the shape.

   b. If you rotate the pencil, the entire notecard in Figure 1 traces a cylinder. Cylinders with height h and a base of radius r have volume $V = \pi r^2 h$. Calculate the volume of this region.

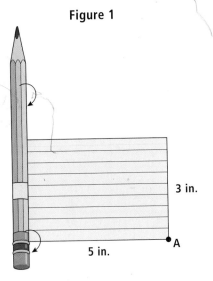

Figure 1

3 in.

5 in.

A

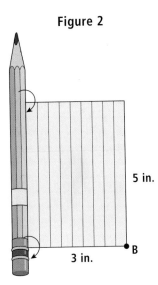

Figure 2

5 in.

3 in.

B

   c. Suppose you tape a 3 in.-by-5 in. notecard to a pencil heightwise, as shown in Figure 2. If you rotate the pencil, what shape is traced by point B? Find the area of the shape.

   d. If you rotate the pencil, what shape is traced by the entire notecard? Calculate the volume of this region.

   e. **True or False** Changing the taping of the notecard does not change the volume of the shape that is traced by the notecard when the pencil is rotated.

In 13–15, rewrite without parentheses and simplify.

13. $(xy)^2\left(\dfrac{x}{y}\right)^3$　　　**14.** $(abc)^0 \cdot \dfrac{(ab)^2}{abc}$　　　**15.** $(2w)^4(3w^3)^2$

In 16–18, fill in the blank with an exponent or an expression that makes the statement true for all values of the variables.

16. $(3x^2y)^{\underline{\ ?\ }} = 27x^6y^3$　　**17.** $(2xy^2)^{\underline{\ ?\ }} = 1$　　　**18.** $(\underline{\ ?\ })^3 = 64x^6y^9$

19. If $x = 5$, what is the value of $\dfrac{(3x)^9}{(3x)^7}$?

REVIEW

In 20 and 21, simplify the expression so that your answer does not contain parentheses or negative exponents. Then evaluate when $r = 1.5$ and $s = 1$. (Lessons 8-4, 8-3)

20. $r^4s^9r^{-3}s^7$　　　　　　　　**21.** $\dfrac{17s^{-2}}{5^5} \cdot r^{-2}$

22. On each day (Monday through Friday) this week, Antoine will do one of three activities after school: play tennis, walk his dog, or read. How many different orders of activities are possible? (Lesson 8-1)

23. Solve $9(p - 2) < 47p - 2(5 - p)$ for p. (Lesson 4-5)

The World Junior Tennis competition, the international team competition for players aged 14 and under, was started by the International Tennis Federation in 1991.

Source: International Tennis Federation

EXPLORATION

24. A list of some powers of 3 is shown below. Look carefully at the last digit of each number.

$$3^0 = 1 \qquad 3^4 = 81$$
$$3^1 = 3 \qquad 3^5 = 243$$
$$3^2 = 9 \qquad 3^6 = 729$$
$$3^3 = 27$$

a. Predict the last digit of 3^{10}. Check your answer with a calculator.

b. Predict the last digit of 3^{20}. Check your answer with a calculator.

c. Describe how you can find the last digit of any positive integer power of 3.

d. Does a similar pattern happen for powers of 4? Why or why not?

QY ANSWERS

1. $81x^4y^4$

2. $\dfrac{704}{m^6}$

Lesson

8-6

Square Roots and Cube Roots

▶ **BIG IDEA** If a first number is the square (or the cube) of a second number, then the second number is a square root (or cube root) of the first.

Areas of Squares and Powers as Squares

The second power x^2 of a number x is called the **square** of x, or x **squared**, because it is the area of a square with side length x. This is not a coincidence. The ancient Greek mathematicians pictured numbers as lengths, and they pictured the square of a number as the area of a square.

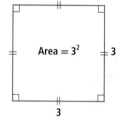

It is easy to calculate the area of a square on a grid if the square's sides are horizontal and vertical, but what if the square's sides are slanted?

Activity 1

Follow these steps to determine the area of the square *EFGH*, at the right.

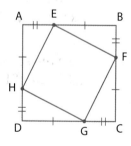

Step 1 Square *ABCD* is 3 units on a side. What is its area?

Step 2 Triangle *AEH* is a right triangle with legs of length 1 unit and 2 units. What is the area of △*AEH*?

Step 3 Subtract the areas of the four corner triangles from the area of *ABCD* to get the area of *EFGH*.

Sides of Squares and Square Roots

You should have found that the area of *EFGH* is 5 square units. If the area of the square *EFGH* is 5 square units, what is the length of one of its sides? The Greek mathematicians could do the previous calculations easily. But now they were stumped. Can *GH* be $2\frac{1}{2}$?

No, because $\left(2\frac{1}{2}\right)^2 = 2.5^2 = 6.25$, which is greater than 5. In fact, the Greeks were able to show that it is impossible to find any simple fraction whose square is exactly 5. So they simply called the length the *square root* of 5. We still do that today. The length of a side of a square whose area is *x* is called a square root of *x*. The length of *GH* is a square root of 5. Similarly, a square root of 9 is 3, because a square with area 9 has side 3.

> **Definition of Square Root**
>
> If $A = s^2$, then s is a **square root** of A.

If two numbers have the same absolute value, such as 3 and –3, then they have the same square, 9. Although –3 cannot be the length of a side of a square, every positive number but 0 has two square roots, one positive and one negative. We denote the square roots of *A* by the symbols $\sqrt{A}$ (the positive root) and $-\sqrt{A}$ (the negative root). So the square roots of 9 are $\sqrt{9} = 3$ and $-\sqrt{9} = -3$. The two square roots of 5 are $\sqrt{5}$ and $-\sqrt{5}$. In the figure on the previous page, $GH = \sqrt{5}$.

The Radical Sign $\sqrt{}$

The **radical sign** $\sqrt{}$ indicates that a square root is being found. The horizontal bar attached to it, called a *vinculum*, acts like parentheses. The order of operations applies, so work is done inside the radical sign before the square root is taken. For example, $\sqrt{16 - 9} = \sqrt{7}$. On the other hand, $\sqrt{16} - \sqrt{9} = 4 - 3 = 1$.

In dealing with square roots, it helps to know the squares of small positive integers: 1, 4, 9, 16, 25, 36, 49, 64, 81, 100, 121, 144, ...

> **Example 1**
>
> What are the square roots of each number?
>
> a. 64
>
> b. 17.3
>
> *(continued on next page)*

Solutions

a. Because $8^2 = 64$ and $(-8)^2 = 64$, the square roots of 64 are 8 and -8. We can write $\sqrt{64} = 8$ and $-\sqrt{64} = -8$.

b. Because there is no decimal that multiplied by itself equals 17.3, just write $\sqrt{17.3}$ and $-\sqrt{17.3}$. A calculator shows $\sqrt{17.3} \approx 4.1593$ and so $-\sqrt{17.3} \approx -4.1593$.

Square Roots That Are Not Whole Numbers

The Greek mathematician Pythagoras and his followers, the Pythagoreans, were able to prove that numbers like $\sqrt{5}$ are not equal to simple fractions or ratios. Today we know that there is no finite or repeating decimal that equals $\sqrt{5}$. While $\sqrt{5}$ is approximately 2.23606797..., the decimal does not end nor repeat. You should check that the squares of truncated forms of 2.23606797..., are very close to 5. For example, $2.236 \cdot 2.236 = 4.999696$. But only $\sqrt{5}$ and $-\sqrt{5}$ square to be exactly 5, so $\sqrt{5} \cdot \sqrt{5} = 5 = -\sqrt{5} \cdot -\sqrt{5}$.

> **Square of the Square Root Property**
>
> For any nonnegative number x, $\sqrt{x} \cdot \sqrt{x} = \sqrt{x^2} = x$.

You can use this property to simplify or evaluate expressions that are exact, rather than use your calculator to deal with approximations.

 QY1

▶ **QY1**

Explain why
$4\sqrt{10} \cdot 3\sqrt{10} = 120$.

A Positive Square Root of x Is a Power of x

Suppose $m = \frac{1}{2}$ and $n = \frac{1}{2}$ in the Product of Powers Property $x^m \cdot x^n = x^{m+n}$. Then, $x^{\frac{1}{2}} \cdot x^{\frac{1}{2}} = x^{\frac{1}{2} + \frac{1}{2}} = x^1 = x$.

This means that $x^{\frac{1}{2}}$ is a number which, when multiplied by itself, equals x. Thus $x^{\frac{1}{2}}$ is a square root of x, and we identify $x^{\frac{1}{2}}$ as the positive square root of x. So, for any positive number x, $x^{\frac{1}{2}} = \sqrt{x}$.

For example, $100^{\frac{1}{2}} = \sqrt{100} = 10$ and $64.289^{\frac{1}{2}} = \sqrt{64.289} \approx 8.02$.

Activity 2

Use a calculator to verify that $x^{\frac{1}{2}} = \sqrt{x}$.

Step 1a. Enter 16^(1/2). What number results?

b. You have calculated the square root of what number?

Step 2a. Enter 8^0.5. What number results?

    b. You have calculated the square root of what number?

Step 3   Enter (−4)^(1/2). What results, and why?

Activity 3

Use the idea of Activity 1 to determine the length of a side of square *IJKL* shown below. Show your work.

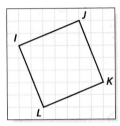

Activity 4

Three squares are drawn on a coordinate grid at the right.

1. Use the idea of Activities 1 and 3 to determine the area of square III. Explain your work.

2. What is the area of square I?

3. What is the area of square II?

4. How are the areas of the three squares related to each other?

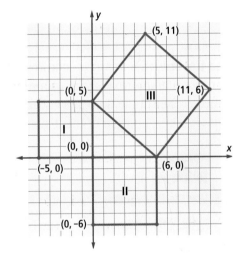

The Pythagorean Theorem

The result of Activity 4 is one example of the *Pythagorean Theorem*. We state this theorem in terms of area first, and then in terms of powers.

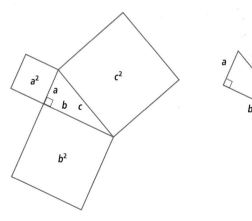

Pythagorean Theorem

(In terms of area) In any right triangle, the sum of the areas of the squares on its legs equals the area of the square on its hypotenuse.

(In terms of length) In any right triangle with legs of lengths a and b and a hypotenuse of length c, $a^2 + b^2 = c^2$.

For example, in $\triangle GDH$ from Activity 1, $HD^2 + DG^2 = GH^2$.

$$1^2 + 2^2 = GH^2$$
$$1 + 4 = GH^2$$
$$5 = GH^2$$

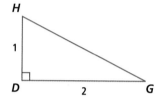

By the definition of square root, $GH = \sqrt{5}$.

The Pythagorean Theorem is perhaps the most famous theorem in all of mathematics. It seems to have been discovered independently in many cultures, for it was known to the Babylonians, Indians, Chinese, and Greeks well over 2,500 years ago. In the United States and Europe, this theorem is known as the Pythagorean Theorem because Pythagoras or one of his students proved it in the 6th century BCE. In China, it is called the Gougu Theorem. In Japan, it is called "The Theorem of the Three Squares."

Example 2

Use the Pythagorean Theorem to find the length of the missing side.

Solution Use the Pythagorean Theorem to write an equation involving the lengths of the three sides of the right triangle.

$$m^2 + 12^2 = 14^2$$
$$m^2 + 144 = 196$$
$$m^2 + 144 - 144 = 196 - 144$$
$$m^2 = 52$$
$$m = \sqrt{52}$$
$$m \approx 7.21$$

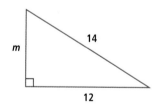

Check Substitute the solution into the original triangle and apply the Pythagorean Theorem.

Does $\left(\sqrt{52}\right)^2 + 12^2 = 14^2$?
$52 + 144 = 196$ Yes, it checks.

Cubes and Cube Roots

The third power x^3 of a number x is called the **cube** of x, or x **cubed,** because it is the volume of a cube with edge x. So, for example, the volume of a cube with edge of length 6 inches is $6 \cdot 6 \cdot 6$, or 216 cubic inches. We write $6^3 = 216$, and we say "6 cubed equals 216." Like the square, this is not a coincidence. The ancient Greek mathematicians pictured the cube of a number s as the volume of a cube whose edge is s.

Also, in a manner like that of a square, if the volume of a cube is V, then an edge of the cube is called a **cube root** of V.

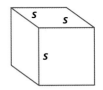

> ### Definition of Cube Root
> If $V = s^3$, then s is a cube root of V.

Since $6^3 = 216$, 6 is a cube root of 216. Unlike square roots, cube roots do not come in pairs. For example, –6 is not a cube root of 216, since $(-6)^3 = -216$. In the real numbers, all numbers have exactly one cube root.

 QY2

> ▶ **QY2**
>
> **Fill in the Blanks**
> Since $4^3 = 64$, ___?___ is
> the cube root of ___?___.

The cube root of V is written using a radical sign as $\sqrt[3]{V}$. For example, $\sqrt[3]{216} = 6$ and $\sqrt[3]{-216} = -6$. Many calculators have a $\sqrt[3]{}$ command, though it may be hidden in a menu. You should try to locate this command on your calculator. However, you will learn an alternate method for calculating cube roots in the next lesson.

> ### Cube of the Cube Root Property
> For any nonnegative number x, $\sqrt[3]{x} \cdot \sqrt[3]{x} \cdot \sqrt[3]{x} = \sqrt[3]{x^3} = x$.

For example, $1.2^3 = 1.2 \cdot 1.2 \cdot 1.2 = 1.728$. This means:

- 1.728 is the cube of 1.2.
- 1.2 is the cube root of 1.728.
- $1.2 = \sqrt[3]{1.728}$

When the value of a square root or cube root is not an integer, your teacher may expect two versions: (1) the exact answer written with a radical sign and (2) a decimal approximation rounded to a certain number of decimal places.

Questions

COVERING THE IDEAS

1. **a.** A side of a square is 16 units. What is its area?
   b. The area of a square is 16 square units. What is the length of a side?

2. Rewrite the following sentences, substituting numbers for x and y to produce a true statement. *A square has a side of length x and an area y.* Then y is the square of x, and x is the square root of y.

In 3–6, write or approximate the number to two decimal places.

3. $\sqrt{36}$
4. $\sqrt{121}$
5. $50^{\frac{1}{2}}$
6. $10^{0.5}$

In 7–10, evaluate the expression to the nearest thousandth.

7. $\sqrt{1,000}$
8. $\sqrt{100 + 100}$
9. $\sqrt{5} \cdot \sqrt{5}$
10. $2 \cdot \left(\frac{3}{4}\right)^{\frac{1}{2}} \left(\frac{3}{4}\right)^{\frac{1}{2}}$

11. **a.** Approximate $\sqrt{11}$ to the nearest hundred-thousandth.
    b. Multiply your answer to Part a by itself.
    c. What property is validated by Parts a and b?

In 12–14, find the length of the missing side of the right triangle. If the answer is not an integer, give both its exact value and an approximation to the nearest hundredth.

12.
13.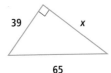
14.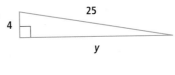

15. Write the cubes of the integers from 1 to 10.

16. 2 is a cube root of 8 because ____?____ .

17. **a.** Write the exact cube root of 1,700.
    b. Estimate the cube root of 1,700 to the nearest thousandth.
    c. Check your answer to Part b by multiplying your estimate by itself three times.

In 18 and 19, evaluate the expression.

18. $\sqrt[3]{2.197}$
19. $\sqrt[3]{45} \cdot \sqrt[3]{45} \cdot \sqrt[3]{45}$

APPLYING THE MATHEMATICS

20. Suppose p is a positive number.

    a. What is the sum of the square roots of p?

    b. What is the product of the square roots of p?

21. In Chapter 7, the equation $P = 100{,}000(1.02)^x$ gave the population x years from now of a town of 100,000 today with a growth rate of 2% per year. Calculate P when $x = \frac{1}{2}$, and tell what the answer means.

22. A small park is shown below. If you want to go from one corner to the other corner, how many fewer feet will you walk if you go diagonally through the park rather than walk around it? Round your answer to the nearest foot.

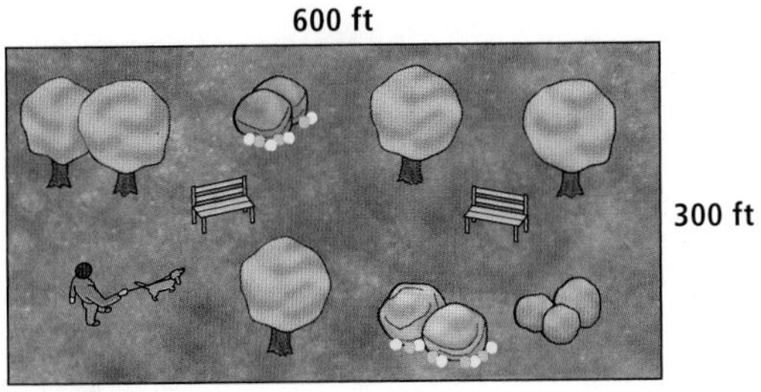

600 ft

300 ft

23. In the movie *The Wizard of Oz,* the scarecrow recites the following after receiving his diploma, "The sum of the square roots of any two sides of an isosceles triangle is equal to the square root of the remaining side." The scarecrow was attempting to recite the Pythagorean Theorem.

    a. Write several sentences explaining how this statement differs from the Pythagorean Theorem.

    b. Is the scarecrow's statement accurate? If not, produce a counterexample.

24. A dog is on a leash that is 10 meters long and attached to a pole 2.5 meters above the the dog's collar. To the nearest tenth of a meter, how far from the pole can the dog roam?

REVIEW

25. As you know, $4 \cdot 9 = 36$. So the square of 2 times the square of 3 equals the square of 6. Determine the general pattern. (**Lesson 8-5**)

26. Simplify $a^6 \cdot \left(\frac{3}{a}\right)^3$. (**Lesson 8-5**)

In 27 and 28, solve. (**Lessons 8-4, 8-2**)

27. $3^4 \cdot 3^x = 3^{12}$

28. $\frac{1}{512} = 2^a$

29. Other than the sun, the star nearest to us, Proxima Centauri, is about $4 \cdot 10^{13}$ km away. Earth's moon is about $3.8 \cdot 10^5$ km from us. If it took astronauts about 3 days to get to the moon in 1969, at that speed how long would it take them to get to Proxima Centauri? (**Lesson 8-3**)

30. ***Skill Sequence*** Solve each equation for y. Assume $a \neq 0$. (**Lesson 4-7**)

   a. $3x + 4y = 2$

   b. $6x + 8y = 4$

   c. $9x + 12y = 6$

   d. $3ax + 4ay = 2a$

You would have to circumnavigate Earth $9\frac{1}{2}$ times to equal the distance from Earth to the moon.

EXPLORATION

31. Make a table to evaluate $n^{\frac{1}{3}}$ on your calculator when n is 1, 2, 3, ..., up to 7. What do you think $n^{\frac{1}{3}}$ is equivalent to? Give a reason for your answer.

Lesson
8-7

Multiplying and Dividing Square Roots

Vocabulary

radicand

> ▶ **BIG IDEA** Like powers, square roots distribute over products and quotients.

Activity 1

Step 1 Compute these square roots to the nearest thousandth either individually or using the list capability of a calculator.

$\sqrt{1} = 1.000$ $\sqrt{2} \approx 1.414$ $\sqrt{3} \approx 1.732$ $\sqrt{4} = \underline{\ ?\ }$

$\sqrt{5} \approx \underline{\ ?\ }$ $\sqrt{6} \approx 2.449$ $\sqrt{7} \approx \underline{\ ?\ }$ $\sqrt{8} \approx \underline{\ ?\ }$

$\sqrt{9} = \underline{\ ?\ }$ $\sqrt{10} \approx \underline{\ ?\ }$ $\sqrt{11} \approx \underline{\ ?\ }$ $\sqrt{12} \approx \underline{\ ?\ }$

$\sqrt{13} \approx \underline{\ ?\ }$ $\sqrt{14} \approx \underline{\ ?\ }$ $\sqrt{15} \approx \underline{\ ?\ }$ $\sqrt{16} = \underline{\ ?\ }$

$\sqrt{17} \approx \underline{\ ?\ }$ $\sqrt{18} \approx \underline{\ ?\ }$ $\sqrt{19} \approx \underline{\ ?\ }$ $\sqrt{20} \approx \underline{\ ?\ }$

Step 2 Consider the product $\sqrt{2} \cdot \sqrt{3}$. Find the product of the decimal approximations, rounded to 3 decimal places.

Decimal approximations: $\underline{\ ?\ } \cdot \underline{\ ?\ } \approx 2.449$

Is the decimal product found in the table above? $\underline{\quad ?\quad}$
If so, write the equation that relates the product of the square roots.
Square roots: $\underline{\ ?\ } \cdot \underline{\ ?\ } = \underline{\ ?\ }$

Step 3 Repeat Step 2 but use a product of two different square roots from the list $\sqrt{2}, \sqrt{3}, \sqrt{4}, \sqrt{5}$.

Square roots: $\underline{\ ?\ } \cdot \underline{\ ?\ }$

Decimal approximations: $\underline{\ ?\ } \cdot \underline{\ ?\ } \approx \underline{\ ?\ }$

Is the decimal product found in the table above? $\underline{\quad ?\quad}$
If so, write the equation that relates the product of the square roots.
Square roots: $\underline{\ ?\ } \cdot \underline{\ ?\ } = \underline{\ ?\ }$

Step 4 Multiply another pair of square roots in the table. $\underline{\ ?\ } \cdot \underline{\ ?\ }$
Predict what their product will be. $\underline{\ ?\ }$ Is your prediction correct?
$\underline{\quad ?\quad}$

Mental Math

Given $f(x) = 611x^2 + 492x - 1,000$. Calculate the following.

a. $f(0)$

b. $f(1)$

In Activity 1, you should have discovered that when the product of two numbers a and b is a third number c, it is also the case that the product of the square root of a and the square root of b is the square root of c. That is, if $ab = c$, then $\sqrt{a} \cdot \sqrt{b} = \sqrt{c} = \sqrt{ab}$. For example, because $5 \cdot 6 = 30$, $\sqrt{5} \cdot \sqrt{6} = \sqrt{30}$. You can check this by using decimal approximations to the square roots.

Product of Square Roots Property

For all nonnegative real numbers a and b, $\sqrt{a} \cdot \sqrt{b} = \sqrt{ab}$.

The Product of Square Roots Property may look unusual when the square roots are written in radical form. But when the square roots are written using the exponent $\frac{1}{2}$, the property takes on a familiar look.

$$a^{\frac{1}{2}} \cdot b^{\frac{1}{2}} = (ab)^{\frac{1}{2}}$$

It is just the Power of a Product Property, with $n = \frac{1}{2}$! This is further evidence of the appropriateness of thinking of the positive square root of a number as its $\frac{1}{2}$ power.

Activity 2

Step 1 Pick a square root from $\sqrt{6}$, $\sqrt{12}$, and $\sqrt{18}$.
Pick a square root from $\sqrt{2}$, $\sqrt{3}$, and $\sqrt{6}$.
Find the quotient of the decimal approximations.

Square roots __?__ ÷ __?__

Decimal approximations __?__ ÷ __?__ ≈ __?__

Is the quotient found in the table in Activity 1? __?__

If so, write the quotient as a square root. __?__

If not, is the quotient close to a number in the table? __?__

What square root is it closest to? __?__

Step 2 Repeat the process in Step 1 using a different square root from each group.

Step 3 Repeat the process again using a third pair of square roots.

In Activity 2, you should have discovered that when the quotient of two numbers c and a is a third number b, it is also the case that the quotient of the square root of c and the square root of a is the square root of b. That is, if $\frac{c}{a} = b$, then $\frac{\sqrt{c}}{\sqrt{a}} = \sqrt{\frac{c}{a}} = \sqrt{b}$. For example, since $\frac{24}{8} = 3$, $\frac{\sqrt{24}}{\sqrt{8}} = \sqrt{\frac{24}{8}} = \sqrt{3}$.

Quotient of Square Roots Property

For all positive real numbers a and c, $\dfrac{\sqrt{c}}{\sqrt{a}} = \sqrt{\dfrac{c}{a}}$.

Fact triangles can be used to visualize the Product of Square Roots Property and the Quotient of Square Roots Property. For all positive numbers a, b, and c:

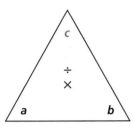
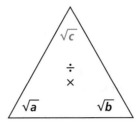

$$a \cdot b = c$$
$$b \cdot a = c$$
$$\frac{c}{a} = b$$
$$\frac{c}{b} = a$$

$$\sqrt{a} \cdot \sqrt{b} = \sqrt{c}$$
$$\sqrt{b} \cdot \sqrt{a} = \sqrt{c}$$
$$\frac{\sqrt{c}}{\sqrt{a}} = \sqrt{b}$$
$$\frac{\sqrt{c}}{\sqrt{b}} = \sqrt{a}$$

STOP QY1

"Simplifying" Radicals

A radical expression is said to be simplified if the quantity under the radical sign, called the **radicand,** has no perfect square factors other than 1.

Just as you can multiply square roots by using the Product of Square Roots Property, $\sqrt{4} \cdot \sqrt{10} = \sqrt{4 \cdot 10} = \sqrt{40}$, you can rewrite a square root as a product by factoring the radicand.

$$\sqrt{40} = \sqrt{4 \cdot 10}$$
$$= \sqrt{4} \cdot \sqrt{10}$$
$$= 2 \cdot \sqrt{10}$$

Many people consider $2\sqrt{10}$ to be simpler than $\sqrt{40}$ because it has a smaller radicand. This process is called *simplifying a radical.* The key to the process is to find a perfect square factor of the radicand.

> ▶ **QY1**
>
> Use either the Product or Quotient of Square Roots Property to evaluate each expression.
>
> a. $\sqrt{8} \cdot \sqrt{2}$
>
> b. $\dfrac{\sqrt{45}}{\sqrt{5}}$
>
> c. $\dfrac{\sqrt{80}}{\sqrt{40}}$

Example 1

Simplify $\sqrt{27}$.

Solution   Perfect squares larger than 1 are 4, 9, 16, 25, 36, 49,.... .
Of these, 9 is a factor of 27.

(continued on next page)

$$\sqrt{27} = \sqrt{9 \cdot 3} \qquad \text{Factor 27.}$$
$$= \sqrt{9} \cdot \sqrt{3} \qquad \text{Product of Square Roots Property}$$
$$= 3\sqrt{3} \qquad \sqrt{9} = 3$$

Check Using a calculator we see $\sqrt{27} \approx 5.196152423$ and $3\sqrt{3} \approx 5.196152423$.

Is $3\sqrt{3}$ really simpler than $\sqrt{27}$? It depends. For estimating purposes, $\sqrt{27}$ is simpler since we can easily see it is slightly larger than $\sqrt{25}$ or 5. But for seeing patterns, $3\sqrt{3}$ may be simpler. In the next example, the answer $7\sqrt{2}$ is related to the given information in a useful way that is not served by leaving it in the unsimplified form $\sqrt{98}$.

GUIDED

Example 2

Each leg of the right triangle below is 7 cm long.

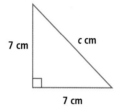

7 cm

c cm

7 cm

a. Find the exact length of the hypotenuse.
b. Put the exact length in simplified radical form.

Solutions

a. Use the Pythagorean Theorem.
$$c^2 = \underline{\;?\;}^2 + \underline{\;?\;}^2 \qquad \text{Substitute the lengths of the legs.}$$
$$c^2 = 98 \qquad\qquad \text{Add.}$$
$$c = \underline{\;?\;} \qquad\qquad \text{Use a radical sign to write the exact answer.}$$

b. Now use the Product of Square Roots Property to simplify the result. Note that the perfect square 49 is a factor of 98.
$$c = \sqrt{\underline{\;?\;} \cdot 2}$$
$$c = \sqrt{\underline{\;?\;}} \cdot \sqrt{\underline{\;?\;}}$$
$$c = \underline{\;?\;}\sqrt{2}$$
The exact length of the hypotenuse is $\sqrt{98}$ or $\underline{\;?\;}$ cm.

The Product of Square Roots Property also applies to expressions containing variables.

GUIDED

Example 3

Assume x and y are positive. Simplify $\sqrt{48x^2y^2}$.

Solution

$$\sqrt{48x^2y^2} = \sqrt{\underline{}} \cdot \sqrt{3} \cdot \sqrt{x^2} \cdot \sqrt{y^2}$$
$$= \underline{} \cdot \sqrt{3} \cdot x \cdot y$$
$$= \underline{} xy\sqrt{3}$$

Check Substitute values for x and y. We choose $x = 4$ and $y = 3$.

$$\sqrt{48x^2y^2} = \sqrt{48 \cdot 16 \cdot 9} \qquad 4xy\sqrt{3} = 4 \cdot 4 \cdot 3\sqrt{3}$$
$$= \sqrt{\underline{}} \qquad\qquad = \underline{}\,\sqrt{3}$$
$$\approx 83.14 \qquad\qquad\qquad \approx 83.14$$

It checks.

STOP QY2

Although square roots were first used in connection with geometry, they also have important applications in physical situations. One such application is with the pendulum clock.

In a pendulum clock, a clock hand moves each time the pendulum swings back and forth. The first idea for a pendulum clock came from the great Italian scientist Galileo Galilei in 1581. (At the time of Galileo, there was no accurate way to tell time; watches and clocks did not exist. People used sand timers but they were not very accurate.) Galileo died in 1642, before he could carry out his design. The brilliant Dutch scientist Christiaan Huygens applied Galileo's concept of tracking time with a pendulum swing in 1656.

A very important part of constructing the clock was calculating the time it takes a pendulum to complete one swing back and forth. This is called the *period* of the pendulum. The formula $p = 2\pi\sqrt{\dfrac{L}{32}}$ gives the time p in seconds for one period in terms of the length L (in feet) of the pendulum.

> ▶ **QY2**
>
> **a.** Assume x and y are positive.
> Simplify $\sqrt{25x^2y}$.
>
> **b.** Assume x is positive.
> Simplify $\dfrac{\sqrt{24x^2}}{\sqrt{6x^2}}$.

Example 4

A pendulum clock makes one "tick" for each complete swing of the pendulum. If a pendulum is 2 feet long, how many ticks would the clock make in one minute?

Solution First calculate p when $L = 2$.

(*continued on next page*)

Dutch mathematician, Christiaan Huygens (1629–1695), patented the first pendulum clock, which greatly increased the accuracy of time measurement.

Source: University of St. Andrews

$$p = 2\pi\sqrt{\tfrac{2}{32}} = 2\pi\sqrt{\tfrac{1}{16}} = 2\pi\tfrac{\sqrt{1}}{\sqrt{16}} = 2\pi \cdot \tfrac{1}{4} = \tfrac{\pi}{2}$$

It takes $\frac{\pi}{2}$ seconds for the pendulum to go back and forth.

$$\frac{1 \text{ tick}}{\frac{\pi}{2} \text{ s}} \cdot \frac{60 \text{ s}}{1 \text{ min}} = \frac{60}{\frac{\pi}{2}} \frac{\text{tick}}{\text{min}} \approx 38.2 \text{ ticks/min}$$

So the clock makes about 38.2 ticks per minute.

Questions

COVERING THE IDEAS

In 1–4, use the Product or Quotient of Square Roots Property to evaluate the expression.

1. $\sqrt{8} \cdot \sqrt{2}$

2. $\sqrt{36 \cdot 81 \cdot 100}$

3. $\dfrac{\sqrt{40}}{\sqrt{10}}$

4. $\dfrac{\sqrt{6^3}}{\sqrt{6}}$

5. If $\sqrt{3} \cdot \sqrt{6} = \sqrt{x} = y\sqrt{z}$, what is x, what is y, and what is z?

6. If $\dfrac{\sqrt{63}}{\sqrt{7}} = \sqrt{x} = y$, what is x and what is y?

7. **Multiple Choice** Which is *not* equal to $\sqrt{50}$?

   A $\sqrt{5} \cdot \sqrt{10}$

   B $\sqrt{25} + \sqrt{25}$

   C $\sqrt{2} \cdot \sqrt{25}$

   D $5\sqrt{2}$

8. a. Use the formula $p = 2\pi\sqrt{\dfrac{L}{32}}$ to calculate the time p for one period of a pendulum of length $L = 8$ feet.

   b. If the clock makes one tick for each pendulum swing back and forth, how many ticks are there in one minute?

In 9–12, simplify the square root.

9. $\sqrt{18}$

10. $\sqrt{24}$

11. $\sqrt{50}$

12. $8\sqrt{90}$

13. Assume m and n are positive. Simplify each expression.

    a. $\sqrt{150m^2n}$

    b. $\dfrac{\sqrt{112m^7}}{\sqrt{7m^3}}$

14. The length of each leg of a right triangle is 8 cm. What is the exact length of the hypotenuse?

15. Let $m = \frac{1}{2}$ in the Power of a Quotient Property $\left(\dfrac{x}{y}\right)^m = \dfrac{x^m}{y^m}$. What property of this lesson is the result?

APPLYING THE MATHEMATICS

In 16–19, write the exact value of the unknown in simplified form. Then approximate the unknown to the nearest hundredth.

16.

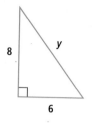

17.

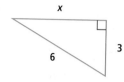

18.

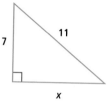

19.

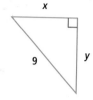

20. Find the area of a triangle with base $\sqrt{18}$ and height $6\sqrt{2}$.

21. The radical $\sqrt{50}$ is equivalent to $5\sqrt{2}$. Explain why it is easier to tell that $\sqrt{50}$ is slightly larger than 7 than it is to tell $5\sqrt{2}$ is slightly larger than 7.

In 22–25, explore adding square roots. You can add square roots using the Distributive Property if their radicands are alike. So, $3\sqrt{11} + 5\sqrt{11} = 8\sqrt{11}$, but $2\sqrt{11} + 4\sqrt{3}$ cannot be simplified. In each expression below, simplify terms if possible, then add or subtract.

22. $2\sqrt{25} + \sqrt{49}$

23. $\sqrt{12} - 10\sqrt{3}$

24. $\sqrt{45} - \sqrt{20}$

25. $4\sqrt{50} + 3\sqrt{18}$

REVIEW

In 26 and 27, consider the rectangular field pictured here. (Lesson 8-6, Previous Course)

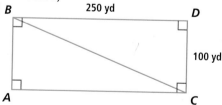

26. How much shorter would it be to walk diagonally across the field as opposed to walking along the sides to get from B to C?

27. Suppose A is the origin of the coordinate system with the y-axis on $\overleftrightarrow{AB}$ and the x-axis on $\overleftrightarrow{AC}$. Give the coordinates of point D.

In 28–30, write the expression as a power of a single number. (Lessons 8-4, 8-3, 8-2)

28. $\dfrac{k^{15}}{k^9}$

29. $x^4 \cdot x$

30. $(w^2)^{-3}$

31. Which is greater, $(6^4)^2$, or $6^4 \cdot 6^2$? (Lesson 8-2)

32. In 1995, Ellis invested $5,000 for 10 years at an annual yield of 8%. In 2005, Mercedes invested $7,000 for 5 years at 6%. By the end of 2010, who would have more money? Justify your answer. (Lesson 7-1)

33. After x seconds, an elevator is on floor y, where $y = 46 - 1.5x$. Give the slope and y-intercept of $y = 46 - 1.5x$, and describe what they mean in this situation. (Lesson 6-4)

34. A box with dimensions 30 cm by 60 cm by 90 cm will hold how many times as much as one with dimensions 10 cm by 20 cm by 30 cm? (Lesson 5-10)

Elisha Graves Otis invented the first safety brake for elevators in 1852, kick-starting the elevator industry.

Source: Elevator World, Inc.

EXPLORATION

35. Is there a Product of Cube Roots Property like the Product of Square Roots Property? Explore this idea and reach a conclusion. Describe your exploration and defend your conclusion.

36. Use the formula $p = 2\pi\sqrt{\dfrac{L}{32}}$ to determine the length of a pendulum that will make 1 tick each second. Answer to the nearest hundredth of an inch.

QY ANSWERS

1a. 4

1b. 3

1c. $\sqrt{2}$

2a. $5x\sqrt{y}$

2b. 2

Lesson
8-8

Distance in a Plane

> ▶ **BIG IDEA** Using the Pythagorean Theorem, the distance between any points in a plane can be found if you know their coordinates.

Competitions involving small robots (sometimes called Robot Wars™ or BotBashes™) began in the late 1990s as engineering school projects but quickly spread to competitions open to the public. Even television programs have featured the battling 'bots. The competitions take place in an enclosed arena that is laid out in a grid pattern like the one below.

Mental Math

What is 20% of each quantity?

a. $40x$

b. $5y$

c. $40x + 5y$

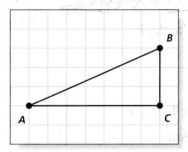

To get from point A to point B in the arena, robots can be maneuvered manually by their "driver," but because the shortest distance between A and B is the straight line segment, robot designers like to program direction and distance commands into their robots. The distance traveled is an application of the Pythagorean Theorem because side $\overline{AB}$ is the hypotenuse of a right triangle.

Distances along Vertical and Horizontal Lines

To find the distance between any two points in the coordinate plane, we begin by examining the situation where points are on the same vertical or horizontal line.

You can find the distance between two points on vertical or horizontal lines by thinking of them as being on a number line. The distance can be obtained by counting spaces or by subtracting appropriate coordinates. Consider the rectangle $DEFG$ graphed on the next page.

Japan's humanoid robot VisiON NEXTA kicks a ball during a penalty kick competition at the RoboCup 2005 in Osaka, Japan.

Horizontal Distance The distance DE can be found by counting spaces on the number line or it can be calculated by subtracting the x-coordinates and then taking the absolute value.

$$DE = |-2 - 3| = 5$$

Vertical Distance Similarly, the distance EF can be found by counting spaces or it can be calculated by subtracting the y-coordinates and taking the absolute value.

$$EF = |3 - (-1)| = 4$$

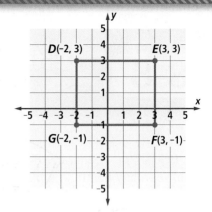

 QY1

The Distance between Any Two Points in a Plane

The Pythagorean Theorem enables you to find the distance between any two points in the plane.

> ▶ **QY1**
>
> Find the length of the segment whose endpoints are (50, 21) and (50, 46).

Example 1

Find AB in $\triangle ABC$ at the right.

Solution $\overline{AB}$ is the hypotenuse of $\triangle ABC$ whose legs, $\overline{AC}$ and $\overline{BC}$, are horizontal and vertical, respectively. The length of the legs can be calculated by subtracting appropriate coordinates.

$AC = |8 - 1| = 7$ $\qquad\qquad$ $BC = |5 - 2| = 3$

Now apply the Pythagorean Theorem.

$(AB)^2 = (AC)^2 + (BC)^2$

$(AB)^2 = 7^2 + 3^2$

$(AB)^2 = 58$

$\quad AB = \sqrt{58} \approx 7.62$

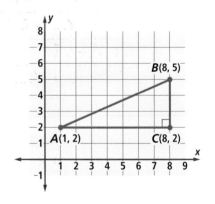

This method can be generalized to find the distance between any two points on a coordinate grid.

Let point $A = (x_1, y_1)$ and $B = (x_2, y_2)$, as shown at the right. Then a right triangle can be formed with a third vertex at $C = (x_2, y_1)$. Using these coordinates, $AC = |x_2 - x_1|$ and $BC = |y_2 - y_1|$. Now use the Pythagorean Theorem.

$AB^2 = AC^2 + BC^2 = |x_2 - x_1|^2 + |y_2 - y_1|^2$

Since a number and its absolute value have the same square, $|x_2 - x_1|^2 = (x_2 - x_1)^2$ and $|y_2 - y_1|^2 = (y_2 - y_1)^2$.

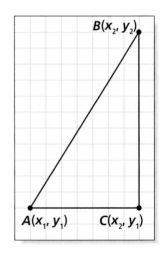

Thus $AB^2 = (x_2 - x_1)^2 + (y_2 - y_1)^2$.

Take the positive square root of each side. The result is a formula for the distance between two points in the coordinate plane.

> **Formula for the Distance between Two Points in a Coordinate Plane**
>
> The distance AB between the points $A = (x_1, y_1)$ and $B = (x_2, y_2)$ in a coordinate plane is $AB = \sqrt{(x_2 - x_1)^2 + (y_2 - y_1)^2}$.

GUIDED

Example 2

Find the distance between the points (23, 16) and (31, −11) to the nearest thousandth.

Solution Using the formula for the distance between two points in a plane, let $A = (x_1, y_1) = (\underline{\ ?\ }, \underline{\ ?\ })$ and $B = (x_2, y_2) = (\underline{\ ?\ }, \underline{\ ?\ })$.

$AB = \sqrt{(\underline{\ ?\ } - \underline{\ ?\ })^2 + (\underline{\ ?\ } - \underline{\ ?\ })^2}$

$= \sqrt{(\underline{\ ?\ })^2 + (\underline{\ ?\ })^2}$

$= \sqrt{\underline{\ ?\ } + \underline{\ ?\ }} = \sqrt{\underline{\ ?\ }} \approx \underline{\ ?\ }$

Example 3

Use the map at the right. It shows streets and the locations of three buildings in a city. The streets are 1 block apart.

a. Give the coordinates of all three buildings.

b. Find the distance from the train station to the zoo.

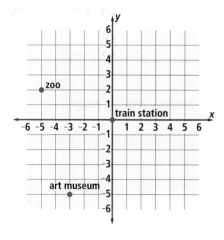

Solutions

a. The coordinates are as follows.

train station (0, 0)

zoo (-5, 2)

art museum (-3, -5)

b. We need to find the distance from (0, 0) to (−5, 2).

distance $= \sqrt{(0 - -5)^2 + (0 - 2)^2}$

$= \sqrt{(5)^2 + (-2)^2}$

$= \sqrt{25 + 4}$

$= \sqrt{29} \approx 5.39$ blocks

QY2

▶ **QY2**

In Example 3, find the distance from the zoo to the art museum.

Questions

COVERING THE IDEAS

1. Refer to $\triangle EFP$ at the right.

   a. Determine FE.

   b. Determine FP.

   c. Use the Pythagorean Theorem to calculate EP.

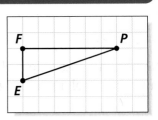

In 2–5, find PT.

2. $P = (3, 4)$ and $T = (3, 9)$

3. $P = (-3, 4)$ and $T = (4, 4)$

4. $P = (-\frac{2}{3}, \frac{1}{2})$ and $T = (\frac{5}{3}, \frac{1}{2})$

5. $P = (33, -4)$ and $T = (33, 18)$

In 6 and 7, find the length of $\overline{AB}$.

6.

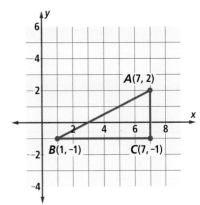

7.

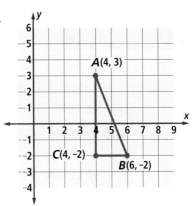

In 8–13, find the distance between the two points.

8. $E = (4, 9)$; $D = (8, 6)$

9. $F = (15, 2)$; $G = (20, -10)$

10. $H = (5, -1)$; $I = (11, 2.2)$

11. $J = (-6, -7)$; $K = (-2, 0)$

12. $L = (-1, 2)$; $M = (-3, 4)$

13. $N = (-0.43, -0.91)$; $P = (-0.36, -0.63)$

APPLYING THE MATHEMATICS

In 14 and 15, use the map at the right, which shows the locations of a house, school, and mall. Suppose each square of the grid is a half mile on a side.

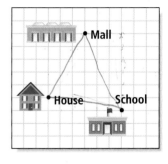

14. **a.** What is the distance from the house to the school?

    b. Which is closer to the house, the mall or the school?

15. How far is it from school to the mall?

16. Pirate Slopebeard has the treasure map below. How far is the treasure from the start if you travel along a straight path "as the crow flies?"

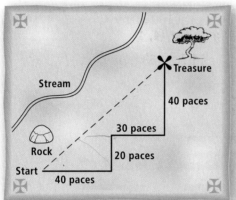

17. Write an expression for the distance between the points $(0, 0)$ and (b, d).

18. The vertices of a triangle are $(3, 4)$, $(6, 9)$, and $(9, 4)$. Is the triangle equilateral? How do you know?

19. Write the distance formula using a power instead of a radical sign.

20. Does it matter which ordered pair is first when using the distance formula? Choose two ordered pairs. Do the calculation both ways to verify your answer.

REVIEW

21. Evaluate $3^{\frac{1}{2}} \cdot 4^{\frac{1}{2}} \cdot 12^{\frac{1}{2}}$ in your head. **(Lesson 8-7)**

22. Consider the function f with $f(x) = 1.5^x$. Find the following values to the nearest hundredth. **(Lessons 8-6, 7-6)**

    a. $f(0)$ **b.** $f\left(\frac{1}{2}\right)$ **c.** $f(1)$

    d. $f(2)$ **e.** $f(-1)$ **f.** $f(-2)$

23. If $d = \sqrt{6}$, find the value of $\frac{d^5}{(3d)^2} \cdot 10d$. **(Lessons 8-6, 8-5)**

24. Suppose Pythagoras Park is a rectangle 250 meters wide and 420 meters long. There are sidewalks around the edges of the park and a diagonal sidewalk connecting the southeast corner to the northwest corner. Esmeralda and Dory are standing at the southeast corner and want to get to the ice cream stand at the northwest corner. (**Lessons 8-6, 5-3**)

   a. How many meters would Esmeralda and Dory have to walk if they traveled along the diagonal sidewalk? Round your answer to the nearest meter.

   b. How many meters would Esmeralda and Dory have to walk if they traveled along the edge sidewalks?

   c. Esmeralda walks along the diagonal sidewalk at 60 meters per minute while Dory jogs along the edge sidewalks at 100 meters per minute. Who arrives at the ice cream stand first?

25. Suppose the graph of f is a line with slope $\frac{8}{5}$ and $f(7) = 1.2$. Write a formula for $f(x)$. (**Lessons 7-6, 6-2**)

26. Suppose $f(x) = 29x - 2$ and $g(x) = 2(34.5x + 17.75)$. For what value of x does $f(x) = g(x)$? (**Lessons 7-6, 4-4**)

EXPLORATION

27. You may have seen videos showing giant robotic arms maneuvering through space to perform a task. Did you ever wonder how the robot is controlled? One component is calculating how far to move the arm. To do this, designers extend the ideas in this lesson from 2 dimensions (x, y) to 3 dimensions (x, y, z) and calculate the distance between two *ordered triples* that describe locations in space. The distance between two points (x_1, y_1, z_1) and (x_2, y_2, z_2) in space is $\sqrt{(x_2 - x_1)^2 + (y_2 - y_1)^2 + (z_2 - z_1)^2}$. Calculate the distance between $(3, 5, 2)$ and $(-4, 3, -2)$. Draw a picture of the two points and the distance on the graph below.

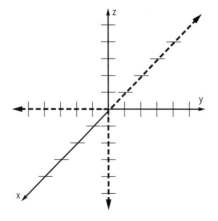

According to the U.N.'s 2004 World Robotics Survey, most industrial robots are used on assembly lines, chiefly in the auto industry.

Remembering Properties of Powers and Roots

▶ **BIG IDEA** If you forget any of the properties of powers, you can recall them by testing special cases, following patterns, and knowing alternate ways of rewriting the same expression.

Here are six properties of powers that were presented in this chapter. They apply to all exponents m and n and nonzero bases a and b.

Properties of Powers

Product of Powers
$b^m \cdot b^n = b^{m+n}$

Negative Exponent
$b^{-n} = \frac{1}{b^n}$

Power of a Power
$(b^m)^n = b^{mn}$

Quotient of Powers
$\frac{b^m}{b^n} = b^{m-n}$

Power of a Product
$(ab)^n = a^n b^n$

Power of a Quotient
$\left(\frac{a}{b}\right)^n = \frac{a^n}{b^n}$

In addition, two properties of square roots were studied. They apply to all nonnegative numbers a and b.

Properties of Square Roots

Product of Square Roots
$\sqrt{a} \cdot \sqrt{b} = \sqrt{ab}$

Quotient of Square Roots
$\frac{\sqrt{a}}{\sqrt{b}} = \sqrt{\frac{a}{b}}, b \neq 0$

With so many properties, some students confuse them. This lesson shows you how to use general problem-solving strategies to remember the properties and to test a special case to verify your reasoning.

Testing a Special Case

Because of calculators, a strategy called *testing a special case* is often possible. You can use this strategy to verify your reasoning.

Mental Math

Evaluate.

a. $|-19 + -42|$

b. $|55.5 - 32| + |-9|$

c. $|-10 + 5| - |-30 + 15|$

Example 1

Emily was not sure how to simplify $x^5 \cdot x^6$. She felt the answer could be x^{30}, $2x^{11}$, or x^{11}. Which is correct?

Solution 1 Use a special case. Let $x = 3$. Now calculate $x^5 \cdot x^6$ (with a calculator) and see if it equals the calculator result for x^{30} or $2x^{11}$ or x^{11}.

$x^5 \cdot x^6 = 3^5 \cdot 3^6 = 177{,}147$

$x^{30} = 3^{30} = 205{,}891{,}132{,}094{,}649 \approx 2.0589 \cdot 10^{14}$

$2x^{11} = 2 \cdot 3^{11} = 354{,}294$

$x^{11} = 3^{11} = 177{,}147$

So, the answer is x^{11}.

Solution 2 Use repeated multiplication to rewrite x^5 and x^6.

$x^5 \cdot x^6 = (x \cdot x \cdot x \cdot x \cdot x) \cdot (x \cdot x \cdot x \cdot x \cdot x \cdot x)$

Notice there are 11 factors of x in the product. So, $x^5 \cdot x^6 = x^{11}$.

Showing That a Pattern Is Not Always True

When testing a special case, you should be careful in choosing numbers. The numbers 0, 1, and 2 are not good for checking answers to problems involving powers, because a pattern may work for a few of these numbers but not for all numbers. Recall that a *counterexample* is a special case for which the answer is false. To show a pattern is not true, it is sufficient to find one counterexample.

Example 2

Sir Lancelot's assistant, Squire Root, noticed $2^3 + 2^3 = 2^4$ since $8 + 8 = 16$. He guessed that in general, there is a property $x^3 + x^3 = x^4$.

He tested a second case by letting $x = 0$ and found $0^3 + 0^3 = 0^4$. He concluded that the property is always true. Is he correct?

Solution Try a different value for x. Let $x = 5$.

Does $5^3 + 5^3 = 5^4$? Does $125 + 125 = 625$? No. $x = 5$ is a counterexample that shows that Squire's property is not always true.

If you have trouble remembering a property or are not certain that you have simplified an expression correctly, try using repeated multiplication or testing a special case.

In Example 3, using the properties of powers, a calculation that is complicated even with a calculator, is reduced to two calculations.

Example 3

The mean radius of Earth is about $3.96 \cdot 10^3$ miles. The mean radius of Jupiter is about $4.34 \cdot 10^4$ miles. Using the formula $V = \frac{4}{3}\pi r^3$ for the volume V of a sphere with radius r, how many times could Earth fit inside Jupiter?

Solution To answer the question, you need to divide the volume of Jupiter by the volume of Earth. So substitute for r in the formula for the volume of a sphere.

$$\frac{\text{volume of Jupiter}}{\text{volume of Earth}} \approx \frac{\frac{4}{3}\pi(4.34 \cdot 10^4)^3}{\frac{4}{3}\pi(3.96 \cdot 10^3)^3}$$

$$= \frac{(4.34 \cdot 10^4)^3}{(3.96 \cdot 10^3)^3} \qquad \text{Multiplication of Fractions}$$

$$= \left(\frac{4.34 \cdot 10^4}{3.96 \cdot 10^3}\right)^3 \qquad \text{Power of a Quotient Property}$$

$$= \left(\frac{43.4}{3.96}\right)^3 \qquad \text{Quotient of Powers Property}$$

$$\approx 1{,}316 \qquad \text{Arithmetic}$$

In Example 3, notice that by using the properties, we reduced a complicated calculation to two operations: division of 43.4 by 3.96 and then cubing of the quotient.

Earth could fit inside Jupiter about 1,300 times. (Jupiter is *very* big compared to Earth!)

It is important to realize that the properties of numbers and operations are consistent. If you apply them correctly, you can find many paths to a correct solution. The result you get using some properties will not disagree with the results another person gets by correctly using other properties.

GUIDED

Example 4

If $\left(\frac{9q^{-5}}{6q^{-3}}\right)^{-7} = aq^n$, what are the values of a and n?

Solution 1 This question requires that the expression on the left side be simplified into the form aq^n.

(continued on next page)

$$\left(\frac{9q^{-5}}{6q^{-3}}\right)^{-7} = \frac{9^{\frac{?}{}}\, q^{\frac{?}{}}}{6^{\frac{?}{}}\, q^{\frac{?}{}}}$$ Apply the Power of a Power Property to eliminate the parentheses.

$$= \frac{9^{\frac{?}{}}}{6^{\frac{?}{}}}\, q^{\frac{?}{}}$$ Apply the Quotient of Powers Property.

$$= \frac{6^{\frac{?}{}}}{9^{\frac{?}{}}}\, q^{\frac{?}{}}$$ Apply the Negative Exponent Property $\left(b^{-n} = \frac{1}{b^n}\right)$.

$$= \left(\frac{6}{9}\right)^{\frac{?}{}}\, q^{\frac{?}{}}$$ Use the Power of a Quotient Property.

$$= \left(\frac{2}{3}\right)^{\frac{?}{}}\, q^{\frac{?}{}}$$ Rewrite the fraction in lowest terms.

Thus, $a = \left(\frac{2}{3}\right)^{\frac{?}{}}$ and $n = \underline{\ ?\ }$.

Solution 2 Work with a partner and follow these steps.

1. Apply the Quotient of Powers Property inside the parentheses.

2. Write the fraction in lowest terms.

3. Apply the Power of a Power Property.

You should obtain the same answer as in Solution 1.

Questions

COVERING THE IDEAS

1. **Multiple Choice** For all nonzero values of n, $\dfrac{n^{40}}{n^{10}} =$

   A n^4.   B n^{30}.   C 1^{30}.   D 1^4.

2. **Multiple Choice** For all nonzero values of s, $\dfrac{s^4}{(2s)^2} =$

   A $4s^2$.   B $\dfrac{s^2}{2}$.   C $\dfrac{s^2}{4}$.   D 1.

3. **Multiple Choice** For all nonzero values of v, $\dfrac{v^8 \cdot v^{12}}{(v^8)^{12}} =$

   A 1.   B $-v^{76}$.   C v^{-76}.   D v^{76}.

4. **Multiple Choice** For all values of m and n, $(3m)^2 \cdot (2n)^3 =$

   A $6m^2n^3$.   B $48m^2n^3$.   C $72m^2n^3$.   D $3{,}125m^2n^3$.

5. What is a counterexample?

6. **True or False** If two special cases of a pattern are true, then the pattern is true.

7. **True or False** If one special case of a pattern is false, then the pattern is false.

8. Consider the equation $x^4 = 8x$.

   a. Is the equation true for the special case $x = 2$?

   b. Is the equation true for the special case $x = 0$?

   c. Is the equation true for the special case $x = 3$?

   d. Is the equation true for all values of x?

In 9–11, test special cases to decide whether the pattern is always true. Show all work.

9. $(r^3)^{-4} = r^{3-4}$

10. $(2n)^3 = 2n^3$

11. $5y^3 \cdot 4y^4 = 20y^7$

In 12–15, name the property or properties being used.

12. $\left(\frac{2}{q}\right)^{10} = \frac{2^{10}}{q^{10}}$

13. $(x + 4)(x + 4)^4 = (x + 4)^5$

14. $(2x^2y)^3 = 2^3x^6y^3$

15. $\left(\frac{2}{41}\right)^{-3} = \left(\frac{1}{\frac{2}{41}}\right)^3$

In 16–18, write the expression without negative exponents.

16. $\left(\frac{3}{5}\right)^{-1}$

17. $\left(\frac{3x^2}{y^3}\right)^{-2}$

18. $\left(\frac{2m^{-2}}{12m}\right)^{-40}$

In 19 and 20, refer to Example 3 and use the fact that the mean radius of Mars is about $2.11 \cdot 10^3$ miles.

19. About how many times could Mars fit into Earth?

20. About how many times could Mars fit into Jupiter?

APPLYING THE MATHEMATICS

21. Describe two different ways to simplify $\left(\frac{x^6}{x^3}\right)^{-2}$.

22. Consider the pattern $\frac{2}{x} - \frac{1}{y} = \frac{2y - x}{xy}$.

   a. Is the pattern true when $x = 3$ and $y = 5$?

   b. Test the special case when $x = y$.

   c. Test another case. Let $x = 6$ and $y = 2$.

   d. Do you think the pattern is *always, sometimes but not always,* or *never true* for all nonzero x and y?

In 23 and 24, use the fact that the prime factorization of 24 is $2^3 \cdot 3$ and the prime factorization of 360 is $2^3 \cdot 3^2 \cdot 5$.

23. Give the prime factorization of 360^{25}.

24. Give the prime factorization of $\left(\frac{360}{24}\right)^8$.

REVIEW

25. Find the distance between the points (–3, –9) and (12, 56). Round to the nearest tenth, if necessary. **(Lesson 8-8)**

26. Let $y = \sqrt{3}$ and $z = \sqrt{5}$. Evaluate $\frac{y}{z} \cdot (2yz)^3$. **(Lesson 8-7)**

27. An isosceles right triangle is a right triangle in which both legs have the same length. Lenora says that an isosceles right triangle with legs of length s always has a hypotenuse of length $s \cdot \sqrt{2}$. Is Lenora correct? Why or why not? **(Lesson 8-6)**

28. Three days a week, Rollo rollerblades to work. He rollerblades eight and a half blocks. On each block, there are fourteen houses. Each house has three trees in its front yard. How many trees does Rollo rollerblade by on his way to work each week? **(Lesson 8-1)**

29. A line has an x-intercept of 12 and a y-intercept of 15. Write an equation of this line. **(Lesson 6-6)**

30. On a regular die, which is more likely: rolling an even number six times in a row, or rolling a number less than 3 four times in a row? **(Lesson 5-7)**

EXPLORATION

31. Six of the eight properties mentioned at the beginning of this lesson involve either multiplication or division. Show that *none* of these six properties is true if every multiplication is replaced by addition and every division is replaced by subtraction.

The first known roller skates were created in the 1760s and possessed a single line of wheels.

Source: National Museum of Roller Skating

Chapter 8 Projects

1 Estimating Square Roots

To estimate a square root without a calculator, you can use an algorithm called the *Babylonian method*. Suppose you want to estimate $\sqrt{r}$.

Step 1 Guess a number a_1 that is reasonably close to $\sqrt{r}$.

Step 2 Replace a_1 with $a_2 = \frac{1}{2}\left(a_1 + \frac{r}{a_1}\right)$.

Step 3 Replace a_2 by $a_3 = \frac{1}{2}\left(a_2 + \frac{r}{a_2}\right)$.

Doing this process again and again will make each a_n closer and closer to the square root. For example, suppose you wanted to estimate $\sqrt{5}$. A good starting guess for a_1, is 2. In Step 2, replace a_1 with $a_2 = \frac{1}{2}\left(2 + \frac{5}{2}\right) = 2.25$.

In Step 3, replace 2.25 with $a_3 = \frac{1}{2}\left(2.25 + \frac{5}{2.25}\right)$ $= 2.23611111\ldots$. Step 3 should already give you a very good approximation of $\sqrt{5}$.

a. Use the Babylonian method to estimate $\sqrt{10}$, $\sqrt{21}$, and $\sqrt{30.235}$. Then find these numbers using your calculator. In each step of the Babylonian method, find the absolute value of the difference between the number a_n and the square root. What do you conclude?

b. Calculate $\sqrt{5}$ again, but this time, in Step 1, choose the inappropriate guess $a_1 = 1,000,000$. Does the method still work?

c. Use the method to calculate $\sqrt{9}$, using the guess $a_1 = 3$. What do you notice?

2 Fraction Exponents

In this chapter you saw both $\frac{1}{2}$ and $-\frac{1}{2}$ used as exponents. In this project you will discover the meaning of exponents that are other fractions.

a. Recall the rule $b^m \cdot b^n = b^{m+n}$. According to this rule, what should the number $b^{\frac{1}{3}} \cdot b^{\frac{1}{3}} \cdot b^{\frac{1}{3}}$ equal? Check this with a calculator.

b. Remember the rule $b^{m \cdot n} = (b^m)^n$. Because $\frac{2}{3} = \frac{1}{3} \cdot 2$, what should $b^{\frac{2}{3}}$ be? Check your answer with a calculator.

c. What should the number $b^{\frac{m}{n}}$ be?

3 Interview with Pythagoras

Who was Pythagoras? Use a library or the Internet to find out about his life, philosophy, mathematics, and the people who followed him. Write an interview with him, as if it were to be printed in a local newspaper. Include responses you think Pythagoras might have given. You may want to perform your interview (with a partner) for your class.

4 Moving in the Coordinate Plane

In a computer game, a spaceship is in the middle of the screen, which has coordinate $(0, 0)$. The player can give it one of four instructions—up, down, left, or right—that cause the ship to move one unit in the appropriate direction. For example, the right command will cause the spaceship to move to $(1, 0)$.

a. Suppose the player gave the spaceship 5 commands in a row (for example: up, down, right, right, up). How many different possibilities for this are there?

b. Draw all the possible points in the plane that the spaceship can be in at the end of the five commands. How many different points are there?

c. Complete Parts a and b for two commands, three commands, and four commands. What patterns do you notice? Check these patterns for six commands.

d. What is the minimal number of commands necessary for the ship to reach the point (m, n)?

5 Mathematics and Crossword Puzzles

When stumped on a definition in a crossword puzzle for which they are missing a few letters, many people resort to guessing.

a. Suppose you know three letters out of a five letter word. How many possible guesses are there? How many possible guesses are there if you know that the first missing letter is a vowel?

b. Find a dictionary on the Internet that is intended for use with crossword puzzles. These dictionaries often sort words by length, as well as alphabetically. For n from 2 to 10, what is the number of possible words of length n that can be spelled with the letters of the English alphabet? For each length, how many of these possibilities are actually words? What is the relative frequency of real words, for each word length?

6 Counting Braille Letters

Braille is a system of writing that can be read by people by touch. Each letter consists of six dots, some of which are raised and some are not. For example, the letter J is written ⠚ (the black dots represent raised dots), and the letter M is written ⠍.

a. Look up a table with a list of all Braille symbols and letters.

b. Why do you think Braille has six dots? Would four dots have been enough? Would five?

c. Modern versions of Braille have eight dots. How many different possible letters and symbols can be written with eight dots?

Chapter 8 Summary and Vocabulary

▶ In Chapter 7, you saw many applications of the operation of powering to situations of exponential growth and decay. Another important application of powering is to the counting of objects: If there are n ways to select each object in a sequence of length L, then n^L different sequences are possible. **Powers** are also convenient for writing very large and very small numbers and are essential in **scientific notation.**

▶ The operation of taking a number to a power has many properties that connect it with multiplication and division. If two powers of the same number are multiplied or divided, the result is another power of that number: $x^m \cdot x^n = x^{m+n}$ and $\frac{x^m}{x^n} = x^{m-n}$. From these results, we can verify again that when $x \neq 0$, $x^0 = 1$. We can also deduce that $x^{-n} = \frac{1}{x^n}$.

▶ The terms **square root** and **cube root** come from the historical origins of these ideas in geometry. If a square has side s, its area is s^2, "s squared." If its area is A, the length of its side is $\sqrt{A}$, or $A^{\frac{1}{2}}$. If a cube has edge e, then its volume is e^3 or, "e cubed." If a cube has volume V, then each of its edges has length $\sqrt[3]{V}$.

▶ The **nth power** of a product xy is the product of the nth powers: $(xy)^n = x^n \cdot y^n$. Closely related to squares are square roots, and so we have $\sqrt{xy} = \sqrt{x} \cdot \sqrt{y}$. Similarly, the nth power of a quotient is the quotient of the nth powers: $\left(\frac{x}{y}\right)^n = \frac{x^n}{y^n}$ and so $\sqrt{\frac{x}{y}} = \frac{\sqrt{x}}{\sqrt{y}}$. These properties help to simplify and rewrite expressions involving radicals.

▶ Two important applications of squares and square roots are the **Pythagorean Theorem** and the **distance formula** between two points in a coordinate plane, which is derived from that theorem.

Vocabulary

8-1
scientific notation

8-6
square
squared
square root
radical sign ($\sqrt{}$)
cube
cubed
cube root

8-7
radicand

Theorems and Properties

Multiplication Counting Principle (p. 458)
Arrangements Theorem (p. 459)
Product of Powers Property (p. 465)
Power of a Power Property (p. 466)
Quotient of Powers Property (p. 469)
Negative Exponent Property (p. 474)

Negative Exponent Property for Fractions (p. 475)
Power of a Product Property (p. 481)
Power of a Quotient Property (p. 482)
Square of the Square Root Property (p. 490)

Pythagorean Theorem (p. 492)
Cube of the Cube Root Property (p. 493)
Product of Square Roots Property (p. 498)
Quotient of Square Roots Property (p. 499)

Chapter

8   Self-Test

Take this test as you would take a test in class. You will need a calculator. Then use the Selected Answers section in the back of the book to check your work.

1. **Multiple Choice** $x^4 \cdot x^7 =$

   A x^{11} **B** x^{28} **C** $2x^{11}$ **D** $2x^{28}$

2. Rewrite 5^{-3} as a simple fraction.

3. Order from least to greatest: $(-4)(-3)$, $(-3)^4$, $(-4)^{-3}$

In 4–6, simplify the expression.

4. $\sqrt{600}$ 5. $\sqrt{25x}$ 6. $2^{\frac{1}{2}} \cdot 50^{\frac{1}{2}}$

In 7–12, simplify the expression.

7. $y^4 \cdot y^2$ 8. $(10m^2)^3$ 9. $\dfrac{a^{15}}{a^3}$

10. $\left(\dfrac{m}{6}\right)^3$ 11. $g^4 \cdot g \cdot g^0$ 12. $\dfrac{6n^2}{4n^3 \cdot 2n}$

13. Rewrite $4y^{-3}w^2$ without a negative exponent and justify your answer.

14. Rewrite $\dfrac{2}{x^2} \cdot \dfrac{5}{x^5}$ as a single fraction without negative exponents. Justify your steps.

15. The prime factorization of 288 is $2^5 \cdot 3^2$. Use this information to find the prime factorization of $10(288)^2$.

16. Rewrite $\left(\dfrac{3}{y^2}\right)^{-3}$ without parentheses or negative exponents.

17. Evaluate $\sqrt[3]{30}$ to the nearest thousandth.

18. If $f(x) = 1{,}000(1.06)^x$, estimate $f(-3)$ to the nearest integer.

19. State the general property that justifies each step.

   a. $\left(\dfrac{x^{-9}}{x^{-5}}\right)^3 = \dfrac{(x^{-9})^3}{(x^{-5})^3}$ **b.** $= \dfrac{x^{-27}}{x^{-15}}$

   c. $= x^{-12}$ **d.** $= \dfrac{1}{x^{12}}$

20. Find a value of m for which $m^2 \neq m^{-2}$.

21. What is the distance between the points $(9, 5)$ and $(1, -10)$?

22. Common notebook paper outside the United States is called A4, with dimensions 210 mm by 297 mm. A piece of A4 paper is placed on a grid as shown below. If the paper is cut along a diagonal, how long is the cut line?

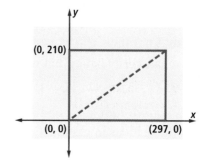

23. The volume of a cube is 30 cubic inches. What is the length of an edge of the cube?

24. A square has a diagonal with length 12 meters. What is the area of the square?

25. In some states, a license plate consists of 2 letters followed by 4 digits. How many different license plates are possible that fit this description? (Note: There are ten digits: 0, 1, 2, . . ., 9.)

Chapter 8 Chapter Review

SKILLS Procedures used to get answers.

OBJECTIVE A Simplify products, quotients, and powers of powers. (Lessons 8-2, 8-3, 8-4, 8-5)

In 1–7, simplify the expression.

1. $2m^2 \cdot 3m^3 \cdot 4m^4$

2. $\dfrac{6y^8}{12y^4}$

3. $\dfrac{7xy^2}{3x^2y^{-2}}$

4. $b^{-2}(4b^5)$

5. $\left(\dfrac{v^4}{v^8}\right)^6$

6. $\dfrac{7.28 \cdot 10^{115}}{8.3 \cdot 10^{72}}$

7. $a^{10}(3a^3) + 5a^{13}(a^7 - 2)$

In 8 and 9, rewrite the expression a. without fractions and b. without negative exponents.

8. $\dfrac{a^{-1}b^4}{b^{-2}c^3}$

9. $\dfrac{60x^2}{45x^{-2}}$

10. Rewrite $-ab^{-1}$ without a negative exponent.

11. Rewrite $(7x^{-7})(6y^{-3})$ without a negative exponent.

OBJECTIVE B Evaluate negative integer powers of real numbers. (Lessons 8-4, 8-5)

In 12–15, rewrite the expression as a decimal or fraction without an exponent.

12. 4^{-3}

13. 6^{-2}

14. $\left(\dfrac{1}{10}\right)^{-2}$

15. $\left(\dfrac{2}{3}\right)^{-5}$

16. If $f(x) = 2x^{-4}$, what is $f(-3)$?

17. The value of a house today is estimated at \$150,000 and has been growing at 3% a year. Its value x years from now will be $150{,}000(1.03)^x$. What was its value 5 years ago? Round your answer to the nearest thousand dollars.

18. Write $603.8 \cdot 10^{-4}$ in decimal form.

19. If $0.0051 = 5.1 \cdot 10^n$, what is n?

In 20 and 21, tell whether each expression names a positive number, a negative number, or zero.

20. a. $5^3 + 3^{-5}$

   b. $3^5 - 3^{-5}$

21. a. $\left(-\dfrac{1}{2}\right)^{-3}$

   b. $-\left(\dfrac{1}{2}\right)^{-3}$

OBJECTIVE C Rewrite powers of products and quotients. (Lessons 8-5, 8-9)

In 22–29, rewrite the expression without parentheses.

22. $(xy)^5$

23. $(60m^2n^3)^2$

24. $30\left(\dfrac{1}{3}u^4v\right)^3$

25. $\left(\dfrac{3}{4}\right)^{11} \cdot \left(\dfrac{6}{8}\right)^{-4}$

26. $\dfrac{1}{2}\left(\dfrac{1}{v}\right)^3 - (2v)^{-3}$

27. $\left(\dfrac{-8s}{t^2}\right)^{-4}$

28. $(m^3n^{-2})(m^2n^{-3})^3$

29. $\left(\dfrac{2y^2z^{-3}}{6y^{-3}z^4}\right)^{-2}$

OBJECTIVE D Simplify square roots. (Lessons 8-6, 8-7)

In 30–36, simplify the expression. Assume the variables stand for positive numbers.

30. $\sqrt{6} \cdot \sqrt{24}$

31. $(4^3 + 4^3)^{\frac{1}{2}}$

32. $\sqrt{3^2 + 4^2}$

33. $5\sqrt{7} \cdot 2\sqrt{3}$

34. $\sqrt{17m} \cdot \sqrt{17m}$

35. $\sqrt{\dfrac{4x^2}{y^2}}$

36. $\sqrt{36a^{36}b^4}$

OBJECTIVE E Evaluate cube roots. (Lesson 8-6)

In 37–40, give the exact cube root of the number, or the cube root rounded to the nearest thousandth.

37. -8

38. 1

39. 200

40. $1{,}330$

In 41 and 42, estimate the number to the nearest thousandth and check your answer by an appropriate multiplication.

41. $\sqrt[3]{0.05}$

42. $\sqrt[3]{10}$

PROPERTIES The principles behind the mathematics

| **OBJECTIVE F** Test a special case to determine whether a pattern is true. (Lesson 8-9)

43. Tell whether the pattern $x^4 = x^3$ is true for the given value of x.

   a. $x = 1$ b. $x = 0$ c. $x = -1$

   d. Based on your answers to Parts a–c, do you have evidence that the pattern is true, or are you sure it is not always true? Explain your reasoning.

44. Consider the pattern $(xy)^{-2} = \frac{1}{x^2 y^2}$, where x and y are not zero.

   a. Is the pattern true when $x = 5$ and $y = 3$?

   b. Is the pattern true when $x = -4$ and $y = 0.5$?

   c. Do you have evidence that the pattern is true for all nonzero real number values of x and y? Explain your reasoning.

In 45 and 46, find a counterexample to the pattern.

45. $-4a = a^{-4}$

46. $(x + y)^2 = x^2 + y^2$

| **OBJECTIVE G** Identify properties of powers that justify a simplification, from the following list: Zero Exponent Property (Chapter 7); Negative Exponent Property; Power of a Product Property; Power of a Quotient Property; Product of Powers Property; Quotient of Powers Property; Power of a Power Property. (Lessons 8-2, 8-3, 8-4, 8-5)

In 47–52, identify the property or properties that justify the simplification. Assume all variables represent positive numbers.

47. $\left(\frac{1}{2}\right)^3 = \frac{1}{8}$

48. $a^{10} = a^8 \cdot a^2$

49. $(b^4)^0 = 1$

50. $2^{-n} = \frac{1}{2^n}$

51. $4^{-2} \cdot 4^3 = 4$

52. $\frac{w^2 a^2}{w^2 h^{-1}} = aah$

53. Show and justify two different ways to simplify $\left(\frac{12}{13}\right)^{-4}$.

54. Show and justify two different ways to simplify $\frac{m^{-1}}{n^{-1}}$.

USES Applications of mathematics in real-world situations

| **OBJECTIVE H** Use powers to count the number of sequences possible for repeated choices. (Lesson 8-1)

55. A test contains 5 questions where the choices are *always*, *sometimes but not always*, or *never*.

   a. How many different answer sheets are possible?

   b. If you guess, what is the probability that you will answer all 5 questions correctly?

   c. If you guess, what is the probability that you will answer all 5 questions incorrectly?

56. Excluding the five vowels A, E, I, O, and U in the English language, how many 4-letter acronyms are possible?

57. A restaurant serves two different types of pizza (thin crust and deep dish), three sizes, and nine toppings. How many different pizzas with one topping are possible?

58. Imagine that a fair coin is tossed 12 times. The result of each toss is recorded as H or T.

  a. How many different sequences of H and T are possible?

  b. What is the probability that all the tosses are heads?

  c. What is the probability of getting the sequence HTHHTTTHTTTH?

REPRESENTATIONS Pictures, graphs, or objects that illustrate concepts

OBJECTIVE I Represent squares, cubes, square roots, and cube roots geometrically. (Lesson 8-8)

59. The area of the tilted square below is 8 square units. What is the length of a side of the tilted square?

60. A square has area 1,000 square units.

  a. Give the exact length of a side.

  b. Estimate the length of a side to the nearest hundredth.

61. If a square has side xy, what is its area?

62. If a cube has an edge of length 2.3 cm, what is its volume?

63. A cube has a volume of 1 cubic meter. What is the length of an edge?

64. A cube has a volume of 2 cubic meters. What is the length of an edge?

OBJECTIVE J Calculate distances on the *x-y* coordinate plane. (Lesson 8-8)

In 65 and 66, use the graph below.

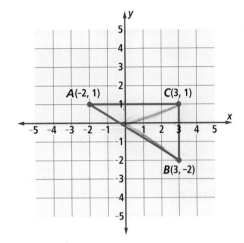

65. Find each length.

  a. AC **b.** BC **c.** AB

66. If O is the point $(0, 0)$, find OB and OC.

In 67–70, find the distance between the points.

67. $(2, 11)$ and $(11, 2)$ **68.** $(6, 5)$ and $(3, -5)$

69. (a, b) and $(-1, 4)$ **70.** (x, y) and (h, k)

71. Stanton, Nebraska is about 8 miles east and 3 miles south of the center of Norfolk, Nebraska.

  a. On a straight line distance, is it true that Stanton is less than 9 miles from the center of Norfolk?

  b. Draw a picture to justify your answer to Part a.

Quadratic Equations and Functions

When an object is dropped from a high place, such as the roof of a building or an airplane, it does not fall at a constant speed. The longer it is in the air, the faster it falls. Furthermore, the distance d that a heavier-than-air object falls in a time t does not depend on its weight. In the early 1600s, the Italian scientist Galileo described the relationship between d and t mathematically. In our customary units of today, if d is measured in feet and t is in seconds, then $d = 16t^2$.

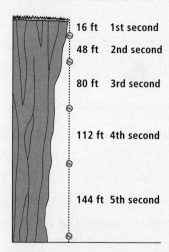

16 ft   1st second

48 ft   2nd second

80 ft   3rd second

112 ft 4th second

144 ft 5th second

A table of values and a graph of this equation are shown on the next page.

t (sec)	d (ft)
0	0
1	16
2	64
3	144
4	256
5	400

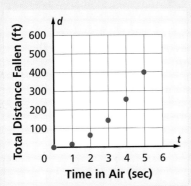

The expression $16t^2$ is a *quadratic expression*, the equation $d = 16t^2$ is an example of a *quadratic equation*, and the function whose independent variable is t and dependent variable is d is a *quadratic function*. The word "quadratic" comes from the Latin word *quadratum* for square. Think of the area x^2 of a square with side x.

From the time of the Ancient Greek mathematicians until about 1600, the only known physical applications of quadratic expressions were to the area of squares and other geometric figures. But, in the next hundred years, discoveries by Galileo, Kepler, Newton, Leibniz, and others found uses for quadratic expressions involving objects that were in motion. These discoveries explain everything from the path of a basketball shot to the orbits of planets around our sun. They enable us to talk to each other via cell phones and collect information about stars in distant space. They are important both for mathematics and for science. In this chapter you will learn about a wide variety of quadratic equations and functions, and their applications.

Lesson

9-1

The Function with Equation $y = ax^2$

Vocabulary

parabola

reflection-symmetric

axis of symmetry

vertex

▶ **BIG IDEA** The graph of any quadratic function with equation $y = ax^2$, with $a \neq 0$, is a parabola with vertex at the origin.

Graphing $y = x^2$

The simplest quadratic function has equation $y = x^2$. A table of values for $y = x^2$ is given below. Notice the symmetry in the second row of the table. Each x value and its opposite have the same square. For example, 3^2 and $(-3)^2$ are both equal to 9. The bottom row of the table shows that the output of the function is positive for a pair of opposite positive and negative input values.

Mental Math

If (a, b) is in the 2nd quadrant, in which quadrant is:

a. $(-a, -b)$?

b. $(-a, b)$?

c. $(a, -b)$?

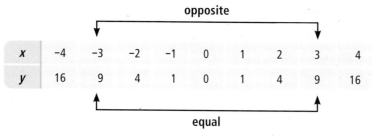

opposite

x	-4	-3	-2	-1	0	1	2	3	4
y	16	9	4	1	0	1	4	9	16

equal

This symmetry can be seen in the graph of the equation $y = x^2$ at the right, which is a **parabola.** Every positive number is the y-coordinate of two points on the graph with opposite x-coordinates. For example, 25 is the y-coordinate of the points $(5, 25)$ and $(-5, 25)$. For this reason, the parabola is its own reflection image over the y-axis. For this reason we say the parabola is **reflection-symmetric** to the y-axis. The y-axis is called the **axis of symmetry** of the parabola.

The intersection point of a parabola with its axis of symmetry is called the **vertex** of the parabola. The vertex of the graph of $y = x^2$ is $(0, 0)$.

The function $y = x^2$ is of the form $y = ax^2$, with $a = 1$. You should be able to sketch the graph of any equation of this form.

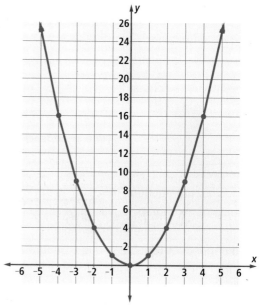

Graphing $y = ax^2$

All equations of the form $y = ax^2$ have similar graphs.

Activity

Step 1 Use the window $-20 \leq x \leq 20$, and $-20 \leq y \leq 20$ to graph all three equations on your calculator. Sketch the graphs on a single grid on a separate sheet of paper.

    a. $f(x) = 3x^2$ **b.** $g(x) = -x^2$ **c.** $h(x) = -3x^2$

Step 2 Evaluate $f(2)$, $g(2)$, and $h(2)$.

Step 3 Is $(-2, -12)$ a point on the graph of $h(x)$? Explain how you know.

Step 4 Use a graphing calculator to make a sketch of the following functions. Use the same window you used for Step 1.

    a. $j(x) = 0.2x^2$ **b.** $k(x) = -0.5x^2$

Step 5 Evaluate $j(3)$ and $k(3)$.

Step 6 Is $(-3, 2.9)$ a point on the graph of $j(x)$? Explain how you know.

Step 7 If a parabola is opening up, what must be true about the value of a in $y = ax^2$? If a parabola is opening down, what must be true about a in $y = ax^2$?

Properties of the Graph of $y = ax^2$

The graph of $y = ax^2$, where $a \neq 0$, has the following properties:

1. It is a parabola symmetric to the y-axis.

2. Its vertex is $(0, 0)$.

3. If $a > 0$, the parabola opens up. If $a < 0$, the parabola opens down.

Finding Points on the Graph of $y = ax^2$

If you know the y-coordinate of a point on the graph of a parabola and the equation, you can find the x-coordinate or coordinates. We illustrate this with a different parabola.

GUIDED

Example 1

Consider the following situation: You know the area of a circle and want to find its radius.

(continued on next page)

Solution Sketch a graph of the familiar formula $A = \pi r^2$, where A is the area of a circle with radius r.

Step 1 Make a scale on each axis. In doing this, ask yourself: What are the possible values of r? What are the possible values of A?

Step 2 Make a table of values for A when $r = 1, 2, 3$, and 4. Estimate each to the nearest hundredth. The first value has been done for you.

Step 3 Graph the points (r, A) from the table.

Step 4 Put an open circle at $(0, 0)$ because 0 is not in the domain of r. Connect $(0, 0)$ and the other points with a curve like a parabola.

Step 5 Use your graph to estimate the radius of a circle whose area is 12 square units.

r	A
1	3.14
2	?
3	?
4	?

Example 2

The graph of $f(x) = 1.5x^2$ is shown at the right. Estimate x if $f(x) = 10$.

Solution Draw the horizontal line $y = 10$. The graph intersects this line at two points. The x-coordinates of these points are approximately 2.5 and -2.5.

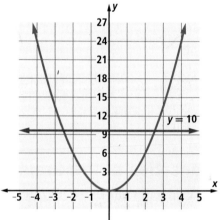

In the next lesson, you will see how to obtain the exact values of x with $f(x) = 10$.

Questions

COVERING THE IDEAS

In 1 and 2, an equation of a function is given.

    a. Make a table of x and y for integer values of x from −4 to 4.

    b. Graph the equation.

    c. Tell whether the graph opens up or down.

1. $g(x) = \frac{1}{2}x^2$

2. $f(x) = -\frac{1}{2}x^2$

3. Refer to the parabola at the right.

    a. Does the parabola open up or down?

    b. The parabola is the graph of a function. Which does the function have, a maximum value or a minimum value?

    c. Give the coordinates of the vertex.

    d. Give an equation of the axis of symmetry of the parabola.

4. How are the graphs of $y = 7x^2$ and $y = -7x^2$ related to each other?

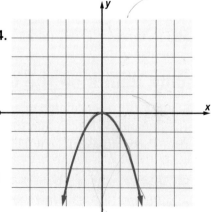

5. Match each table with the graph it most accurately represents.

a.

x	y
-2	4
0	0
2	4

b.

x	y
-2	-4
0	0
2	-4

c.

x	y
-2	-10
0	0
2	-10

i.
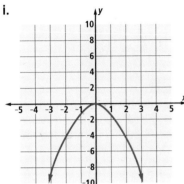

ii.
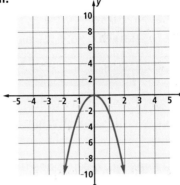

iii.
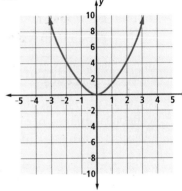

6. Match each graph at the right with one of the equations below.

a. $y = x^2$

b. $y = -0.25x^2$

c. $y = -3x^2$

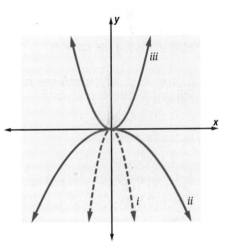

7. **Fill in the Blanks** Consider the graph of the function $f(x) = ax^2$.

a. If a is positive, the graph is a parabola that opens ___?___.

b. If a is negative, the graph is a parabola that opens ___?___.

8. Use the graph of $A = \pi r^2$ to estimate the radius of a circle whose area is 20 square units.

9. Consider the graph of the function defined by $y = 5x^2$.

a. Without plotting any points, sketch what you think the graph of this function looks like.

b. Make a table of values satisfying this function. Use $x = -2, -1.5, -1, -0.5, 0, 0.5, 1, 1.5,$ and 2.

c. Draw a graph of this function from your table.

d. From the graph, estimate the values of x for which $y = 14$.

10. Consider the formula $A = s^2$ for the area A of a square with a side of length s.

   a. Graph all possible values of s and A on a coordinate plane.

   b. Explain how the graph in Part a is like and unlike the graph of $y = x^2$ at the start of this lesson.

11. The parabola at the right has equation $y = -5x^2$.

   a. Find y if $x = 0$.

   b. Find x if $y = -5$.

   c. Find x if $y = -20$.

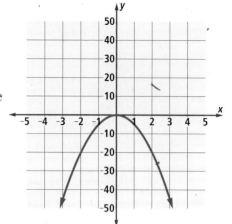

APPLYING THE MATHEMATICS

12. Refer to the parabola at the right. Points P and Q are reflection images of each other over the y-axis. What are the coordinates of Q?

In 13 and 14, fill in the blanks with *negative, zero,* or *positive*.

13. **Fill in the Blanks** Consider the expression $-1x^2$.

   a. If x is negative, $-1x^2$ is ___?___.

   b. If x is zero, $-1x^2$ is ___?___.

   c. If x is positive, $-1x^2$ is ___?___.

   d. What do Parts a–c tell you about the graph of $y = -1x^2$?

14. **Fill in the Blanks** Consider the expression $4x^2$.

   a. If x is negative, $4x^2$ is ___?___.

   b. If x is zero, $4x^2$ is ___?___.

   c. If x is positive, $4x^2$ is ___?___.

   d. What do Parts a–c tell you about the graph of $y = 4x^2$?

15. What is the only real number whose square is not a positive number?

In 16 and 17, a graph of a function f with $f(x) = ax^2$ is shown. Find the value of a.

16.

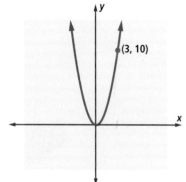

17.

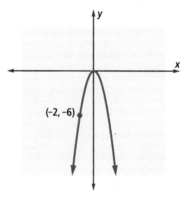

18. **Fill in the Blank** If $a = 0$, the graph of the function $y = ax^2$ is ___?___.

19. Consider the equation $d = 16t^2$, which gives the distance d in feet that an object dropped at time $t = 0$ will have fallen after t seconds.

    a. If an object falls 400 feet in t seconds, find t.

    b. Estimate how long it will take an object to fall 200 feet.

REVIEW

20. *Skill Sequence* Simplify each expression. (**Lesson 8-7**)

    a. $\sqrt{3} \cdot \sqrt{27}$ b. $\sqrt{3x} \cdot \sqrt{27x}$ c. $\sqrt{3x} + \sqrt{27x}$

21. Suppose a box has sides of length 6 inches, 8 inches, and 12 inches. Find the length of the longest thin pole, like the one shown at the right, which can fit inside the box. (*Hint:* First find the diagonal of the base.) (**Lesson 8-6**)

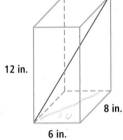

12 in.

8 in.

6 in.

22. Suppose that t years ago, Kendra deposited P dollars into a savings account with an annual yield of 3%. If she has not deposited or withdrawn any additional money and the account now contains $500, write an equation involving t and P. (**Lesson 7-1**)

23. Derek is a tennis instructor at his local gym. He gives lessons to 3 people twice a week. If he charges $25 per person for a lesson, and he works for 15 straight weeks, how much money will Derek earn? (**Lesson 5-4**)

The United States Tennis Association is the largest tennis organization in the world with more than 665,000 individual members and 7,000 organizational members.

Source: USTA

EXPLORATION

24. Draw a set of axes on graph paper. Aim a lit flashlight at the origin up the *y*-axis. What is the shape of the lit region? Keep the lit end of the flashlight over the origin but tilt the flashlight to raise its bottom. How does the shape of the lit region change?

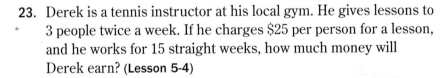

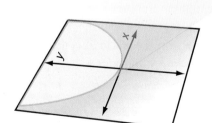

Lesson
9-2

Solving $ax^2 = b$

> ▶ **BIG IDEA** When $\frac{b}{a}$ is not zero, the equation $ax^2 = b$ has two solutions, $x = \sqrt{\frac{b}{a}}$ and $x = -\sqrt{\frac{b}{a}}$.

Graphs and tables can be very helpful in seeing the behavior of equations of the form $ax^2 = b$.

Example 1

Solve $2x^2 = 32$.

Solution 1 Create and graph two functions from the equation. One is the parabola $y = 2x^2$. The other is the horizontal line $y = 32$. Notice that the graphs intersect at two points. This is because two different values of x make the equation true. Trace on the graph of the parabola to find the intersection points, $(-4, 32)$ and $(4, 32)$. Use the x-coordinates.

The solutions are $x = -4$ and $x = 4$.

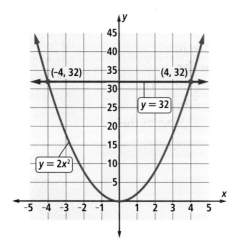

Solution 2 Create a table of values for the equation. Notice that there are two places where the expression $2x^2$ is equal to 32, when $x = -4$ and when $x = 4$. The solutions are $x = -4$ and $x = 4$.

Check

Does $2(4)^2 = 32$?   Does $2(-4)^2 = 32$?

$\quad 2(16) = 32$ $\qquad\qquad 2(16) = 32$

$\qquad 32 = 32$ $\qquad\qquad\quad 32 = 32$ Both -4 and 4 check.

Mental Math

Evaluate.

a. 5^0

b. $4^3 - 3^3$

c. $10^2 - 5^3 + 2^4$

x	$2x^2$
−5	50
−4	32
−3	18
−2	8
−1	2
0	0
1	2
2	8
3	18
4	32
5	50

In Example 1, the graph and table helped to show that an equation like $2x^2 = 32$ has two solutions.

You can solve equations of the form $x^2 = b$ symbolically by recalling the meaning of *square root*. If $x^2 = b$, then $x = \sqrt{b}$ or $x = -\sqrt{b}$. Notice that it takes only one step to solve an equation of the form $x^2 = b$. With just one additional step, you can solve an equation of the form $ax^2 = b$.

Example 2

A quarter is dropped 60 feet from the roof of a school building. To determine how long the quarter will be in the air, use Galileo's equation $d = 16t^2$. In the equation, t is the time, in seconds, that it takes a heavier-than-air object to fall d feet.

Solution Here $d = 60$, so we need to solve $60 = 16t^2$.

$\dfrac{60}{16} = t^2$ — Divide both sides by 16.

$t = \pm\sqrt{\dfrac{60}{16}}$ — Take the square roots of both sides.

$t \approx \pm 1.936$ — Approximate the square root.

$t \approx 1.936$ — Only the positive solution makes sense in this situation.

The quarter will be in the air for approximately 1.9 seconds.

 QY

> ▶ **QY**
>
> Find how long it will take an object to hit the ground if it falls from the top of Chicago's John Hancock Center, which is 1,127 feet tall.

You can combine your knowledge of solving linear equations with what was done in Example 2 to solve some equations that look quite complicated. In the next example, you should think of $2n + 11$ as a single number. Psychologists call this idea *chunking*. Chunking is what you do when you read an entire word without thinking of the individual letters.

Example 3

Solve $3(2n - 11)^2 = 75$.

Solution Think of $2n - 11$ as a single number, say x. Then this equation is $3x^2 = 75$. Some people like to write the x in place of $2n - 11$, but you do not have to do that.

$3(2n - 11)^2 = 75$

Divide both sides by 3.

$(2n - 11)^2 = 25$

(continued on next page)

Take the square roots of both sides of the equation.

$(2n - 11) = \pm\sqrt{25}$

$2n - 11 = \pm 5$

Thus either $2n - 11 = 5$ or $2n - 11 = -5$.

Now there are two linear equations to be solved. It is good to separate the two processes.

$2n - 11 = 5$	or	$2n - 11 = -5$
$2n = 16$		$2n = 6$
$n = 8$		$n = 3$

So there are two solutions, $n = 8$ or $n = 3$.

Check Substitute 8 for n in the original equation.

Does $3(2 \cdot 8 - 11)^2 = 75$? Yes, because $3(5)^2 = 75$.

Substitute 3 for n in the original equation.

Does $3(2 \cdot 3 - 11)^2 = 75$? Yes, because $3 \cdot (-5)^2 = 75$.

Questions

COVERING THE IDEAS

1. Solve $-4x^2 = -100$ using the graph at the right.

2. Solve $5x^2 + 7 = 7.8$ using the table below.

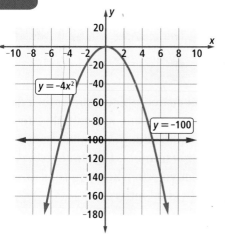

x	−0.6	−0.4	−0.2	0	0.2	0.4	0.6
$5x^2 + 7$	8.8	7.8	7.2	7	7.2	7.8	8.8

In 3–8, solve the equation.

3. $x^2 = 40$

4. $3{,}705 = y^2 + 436$

5. $12v^2 - 24 = 36$

6. $5w^2 = 400$

7. $3(a + 5)^2 = 12$

8. $(7v - 2)^2 = 81$

9. **a.** You drop a stone into a deep well and carefully time how long it takes until you hear the stone plop into the water. If it takes 2.4 seconds, about how far from the top is the water in the well?

   b. If the water was 64 feet from the top of the well, how long would it take until the stone hit the water?

10. A 30-foot ladder is placed against a wall so that its bottom is 9 feet away from the wall. How high up the wall is the top of the ladder?

APPLYING THE MATHEMATICS

11. If the area of a circle is 100 square units, then what is the radius of the circle, to the nearest hundredth of a unit?

In 12 and 13, solve the quadratic equation.

12. $\frac{1}{2}(2z + 3)^2 = 18$

13. $3v^2 + 10 = 7v^2 - 15$

14. Consider the figures drawn at the right. Suppose that the circle has the same area as the square. If the diameter of the circle is 4 feet, what is the length of the side of the square, to the nearest inch? (*Hint:* You will need to use the formulas for the area of a square and the area of a circle.)

15. You wish to make a bull's-eye target so that the area of the inner circle equals the area of the outer ring between the two circles. If the radius of the outer circle is 12 inches, what should the radius of the inner circle be?

12 in.

REVIEW

16. **True or False** 0 is in the range of $y = ax^2$ for all values of a. (**Lesson 9-1**)

In 17–19, simplify the expression. (Lessons 8-5, 8-3, 8-2)

17. $n \cdot m^3 \cdot n^5 \cdot m^2$ 18. $\frac{12x^8}{8x^2}$ 19. $\left(\frac{3}{5a}\right)^2$

20. A company that manufactures combination locks wants each lock to have a unique 3-number combination. There are 36 numbers on each lock. (**Lesson 8-1**)

    a. How many locks can the company produce without having to use the same combination twice?

    b. Suppose a worker at the company forgets the combination of one of the locks, but he knows that it does not begin with 1. How many different combinations might he have to try to open the lock?

21. Let $f(x) = 2x^2$. (**Lessons 7-6, 7-5**)
    a. What is the domain of f?   b. What is the range of f?

22. a. Determine a real situation that can be answered by solving $\frac{18}{24} = \frac{x}{32}$.
    b. Answer your question from Part a. (**Lesson 5-9**)

23. Tickets for a school play cost $6 for adults and $4 for children. The organizers of the play have determined that they must sell at least $975 worth of tickets in order to cover their expenses. **(Lesson 6-9)**

a. Write an inequality that represents this situation.

b. Graph the inequality.

c. Suppose 86 adult tickets are sold. If exactly $1,000 were raised from ticket sales, how many children tickets must have been sold?

24. Jessica is driving between Cleveland and Chicago, a distance of about 350 miles. From Cleveland to Chicago, she averages 65 miles per hour. On the return trip, she averages x miles per hour. If the round trip takes Jessica 12 hours, find her average speed x on the way back. **(Lessons 5-3, 3-4)**

Since 1929, more than two million students have been honored for excellence in theater arts with invitations to join the International Thespian Society.

Source: Educational Theatre Association

25. Multiple Choice The graph below pictures solutions to which inequality? **(Lessons 3-7, 3-6)**

A $h - 3 \leq -8$ B $h + 7 > 2$ C $h - 5 \geq -10$ D $h + 5 < 0$

EXPLORATION

26. On a piece of graph paper, carefully draw a circle with center at (0, 0) and radius 10 units. This circle will contain the point (10, 0) and three other points on the axes.

a. What are the coordinates of those other three points?

b. The circle will contain 8 other points whose coordinates are both integers. Identify those 8 points.

c. Find the coordinates of three other points in the 1st quadrant that are on the circle. (*Hint:* You may need to describe the coordinates with square roots.)

QY ANSWER

about 8.39 sec

Lesson
9-3

Graphing
$y = ax^2 + bx + c$

▶ **BIG IDEA**   The graphs of any quadratic function with equation $y = ax^2 + bx + c$, $a \neq 0$, is a parabola whose vertex can be found from the values of a, b, and c.

If $a \neq 0$, the graph of $y = ax^2$ is a parabola with vertex $(0, 0)$. This lesson is about the graph of a more general function, $y = ax^2 + bx + c$. We begin with an important everyday use.

How Far Does a Car Travel after Brakes Are Applied?

When a driver decides to stop a car, it takes time to react and press the brake. Then it takes time for the car to slow down. The total distance traveled in this time is called the *stopping distance* of the car. The faster the car is traveling, the greater the distance it takes to stop the car. A formula that relates the speed x (in miles per hour) of a car and its stopping distance d (in feet) is $d = 0.05x^2 + x$.

This function is used by those who study automobile performance and safety. It is also important for determining the distance that should be maintained between a car and the car in front of it.

To find the distance needed to stop a car traveling 40 miles per hour, you can substitute 40 for x in the above equation.

$$d = 0.05(40)^2 + 40$$
$$= 0.05(1{,}600) + 40$$
$$= 80 + 40$$
$$= 120$$

Thus, a car traveling 40 mph takes about 120 feet to come to a complete stop after the driver decides to apply the brakes.

A table of values and a graph for the stopping distance formula is shown on the next page. The situation makes no sense for negative values of x or d, so the graph has points in the first quadrant only. The graph is part of a parabola.

Mental Math

Simplify.

a. $\sqrt{18}$

b. $\sqrt{200}$

c. $\dfrac{\sqrt{18}}{\sqrt{200}}$

Traffic lights were used before the advent of the motorcar. In 1868, a lantern with red and green signals was used at a London intersection to control the flow of horse buggies and pedestrians.

Source: www.ideafinder.com

Speed x (mph)	Distance $d = 0.05x^2 + x$ (ft)
10	15
20	40
30	75
40	120
50	175
60	240
70	315

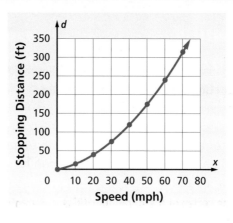

Properties of the Graph of $y = ax^2 + bx + c$

The equation $d = 0.05x^2 + x$ is of the form $y = ax^2 + bx + c$, with d taking the place of y, $a = 0.05$, $b = 1$, and $c = 0$. The graph of every equation of this form (provided $a \neq 0$) is a parabola. Moreover, every parabola with a vertical line of symmetry has an equation of this form. The values of a, b, and c determine where the parabola is positioned in the plane and whether it opens up or down. If $a > 0$ the parabola opens up, as in the situation above. If $a < 0$, the parabola opens down, as in Example 1.

Example 1

a. Graph $f(x) = -2x^2 - 3x + 8$. Use a window big enough to show the vertex of the parabola, the two x-intercepts, and the y-intercept.

b. Estimate its vertex, x-intercepts, and y-intercept.

Solutions

a. Here is a graph of $y = -2x^2 - 3x + 8$ on the window $-5 \leq x \leq 5$; $-10 \leq y \leq 10$.

b. From the window we have shown, we can only estimate the location of the vertex. The vertex is near (-0.8, 9.1). You do not have to estimate the y-intercept. It is $f(0)$, the value of y when $x = 0$, and is easily calculated. The graph has y-intercept 8. On the other hand, you can only estimate its x-intercepts. They are the values of x when the graph intersects the x-axis. The x-intercepts are near -2.9 and 1.4.

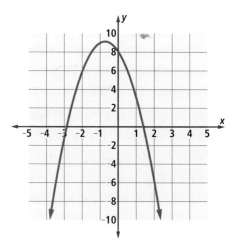

Using Tables to Determine the Vertex of a Parabola

We could only estimate the vertex in Example 1 from the graph. Even if you use the trace function on a calculator or computer, you might not happen to find the vertex exactly. But in some cases, the symmetry of a parabola can be used to determine its vertex.

Example 2

Find the exact location of the vertex of the parabola that is the graph of $f(x) = -2x^2 - 3x + 8$ from Example 1.

Solution Because we know that the vertex is near the point $(-0.8, 9.1)$, we find y for values of x between -1 and 0. Look in the table at the right for a pair of points which have the same y-coordinates. Notice that there are three pairs of points whose y-coordinates are the same. These pairs occur on either side of -0.75. This indicates that the vertex is the point for which $x = -0.75$. Because $f(-0.75) = 9.125$, the vertex is $(-0.75, 9.125)$.

x	y
−1.0	9
−0.9	9.08
−0.8	9.12
−0.7	9.12
−0.6	9.08
−0.5	9
−0.4	8.88
−0.3	8.72
−0.2	8.52
−0.1	8.28
0	8

From a graph, it is often not as easy to locate the x-intercepts of a parabola as it is the vertex. The next two activities explore how the intercepts of the parabolas change as the values of b and c change in the equation $y = ax^2 + bx + c$.

Activity 1

Step 1 Graph $y = 2x^2$ and $y = 2x^2 - 10$ on the same axes.
  a. What is the y-intercept of $y = 2x^2$?
  b. What is the y-intercept of $y = 2x^2 - 10$?
  c. Describe how the two graphs are related to each other.

Step 2 Graph $y = -0.75x^2$ and $y = -0.75x^2 + 1$ on the same axes.
  a. What is the y-intercept of $y = -0.75x^2$?
  b. What is the y-intercept of $y = -0.75x^2 + 1$?
  c. Describe how the two graphs are related to each other.

Step 3 Graph $y = 2x^2 + c$ for three different values of c, with at least one of these values negative.
  a. Give the equations that you graphed.
  b. What is the effect of c on the graphs?

Activity 2

Step 1 To determine the effect of b on the graph of a quadratic function, consider the function $y = x^2 + bx - 4$.

a. Graph this function for the three different values of b given in the table below. Fill in the table.

Equation $y = ax^2 + bx + c$	b	Vertex of Parabola	y-intercept of Parabola	x-intercepts (if any)
$y = x^2 + 2x - 4$	?	?	?	?
$y = x^2 + 4x - 4$	?	?	?	?
$y = x^2 - 3x - 4$	?	?	?	?

b. What features of the graph of $y = x^2 + bx - 4$ does the value of b affect?

c. What feature of the graph of $y = x^2 + bx - 4$ is not affected by the value of b?

Step 2 Find a window that shows a graph of $y = \frac{1}{2}x^2 - 6x + 4$, including its vertex, its y-intercept and its x-intercept(s).

a. Describe your window.

b. Use the trace feature of the calculator to estimate or determine the vertex, the y-intercept, and the x-intercepts.

c. Tell how the x-coordinate of the vertex is related to the x-intercepts.

Questions

COVERING THE IDEAS

In 1–4, use the formula for automobile stopping distances given in this lesson, $d = 0.05x^2 + x$.

1. Define stopping distance.

2. Find the stopping distance for a car traveling 45 miles per hour.

3. Find the stopping distance for a car traveling 55 miles per hour.

4. **True or False** The stopping distance for a car traveling 50 mph is exactly double the stopping distance of a car traveling 25 mph.

5. The equation $d = 0.05x^2 + x$ is of the form $f(x) = ax^2 + bx + c$. What are the values of a, b, and c?

6. Explain how you can tell by looking at an equation of the form $y = ax^2 + bx + c$ whether its graph will open up or down.

In 7–9, an equation for a function is given.

    a. Make a table of x and y values when x equals –3, –2, –1, 0, 1, 2, and 3.

    b. Graph the equation.

    c. Identify the y-intercept, x-intercept(s), and vertex.

    d. Describe the range of the function.

7. $y = x^2 - 6$ 8. $y = x^2 - 2x + 5$ 9. $y = 3x^2 + 4$

10. The parabola at the right contains (–3, 0) and (–1, 0) and its vertex has integer coordinates.

    a. Find the coordinates of its vertex.

    b. Write an equation of its axis of symmetry.

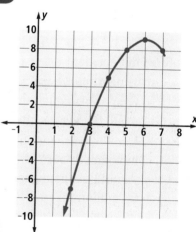

11. Consider this table of values for a parabola.

x	-8	-7	-6	-5	-4	-3	-2	-1	0
y	-28	0	20	32	36	32	?	?	?

    a. What are the coordinates of the vertex of the parabola?

    b. Use symmetry to find the coordinates of the points whose y values are missing in the table.

APPLYING THE MATHEMATICS

12. The parabola at the right contains points with integer coordinates as shown by the dots.

    a. Copy this graph on graph paper. Then use symmetry to graph more of the parabola.

    b. Give the coordinates of the vertex.

    c. Give an equation for the axis of symmetry.

    d. At what points does the parabola intersect the x-axis?

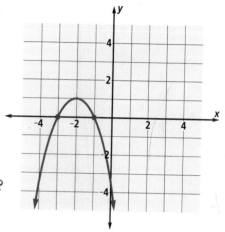

13. **Multiple Choice** Which of the two graphs is the graph of $y = x^2 - 6x + 8$? Justify your answer.

A

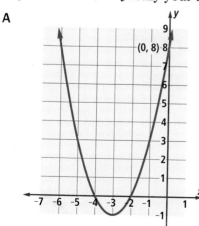

B

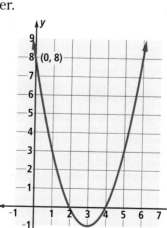

Graphing $y = ax^2 + bx + c$ **541**

Matching In 14–17, match the graph with its equation.

a. $y = 2x^2$

b. $y = 2x^2 + 1$

c. $y = 2x^2 - 1$

d. $y = -2x^2 - 1$

14.

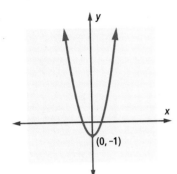

15.

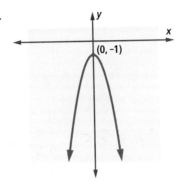

16.

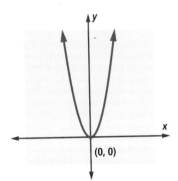

17.

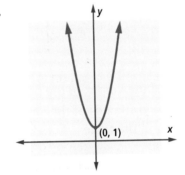

18. An insurance company reports that the equation
$y = 0.4x^2 - 36x + 1{,}000$ relates the age of a driver x (in years)
to the accident rate y (number of accidents per 50 million miles
driven) when $16 \le x \le 74$.

a. Graph this equation on your calculator. Give the window you
used, the vertex, and the intercepts of the graph.

b. Use the trace function of the graph to determine the age
in which drivers have the fewest accidents per mile driven.
About how many accidents do drivers of this age have per
50 million miles driven?

c. According to this model, an 18-year-old driver is how many
times as likely to have an accident as a 45-year-old driver?

REVIEW

19. Consider Galileo's equation $d = 16t^2$. **(Lesson 9-2)**

a. Find t when $d = 350$.

b. Write a question involving distance and time that can be
answered using Part a.

20. Below are Charlotta's answers to questions about $y = \frac{x^2}{4}$. After she wrote this, she realized that she copied the equation incorrectly. It should be $y = -\frac{x^2}{4}$. What does Charlotta need to change to correct her work? (**Lesson 9-1**)

x	−4	−2	0	2	4
y	4	1	0	1	4

vertex = (0, 0)

axis of symmetry: $x = 0$

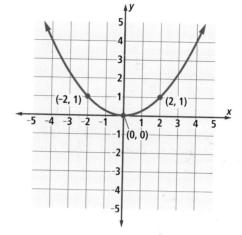

21. **Skill Sequence** If $a = -6$, $b = 8$, and $c = 12$, find the value of each expression. (**Lessons 8-6, 1-1**)

   a. $-4ac$

   b. $b^2 - 4ac$

   c. $\sqrt{b^2 - 4ac}$

22. A giant tortoise is walking at an average rate of $0.17 \frac{\text{mile}}{\text{hour}}$. Assume the tortoise continues walking at this rate.

   a. How long will it take the tortoise to travel 50 feet?

   b. How long will it take the tortoise to travel f feet?

   (**Lessons 5-4, 5-3**)

EXPLORATION

23. Begin with $y = -x^2$. With your calculator, experiment to find an equation for the parabola whose graph is used in Question 12.

In the past, giant species of *Geochelone* (tortoise) were once found on all continents except Australasia, but today the giant forms are restricted to *G. elephantopus* in the Galapagos and *G. gigantea* on the island of Aldabara.

Source: Rochester Institute of Technology

Lesson
9-4

Quadratics and Projectiles

Vocabulary

force of gravity

initial upward velocity

initial height

> ▶ **BIG IDEA** Assuming constant gravity, both the path of a projectile and the height of a projectile over time can be described by an equation of the form $y = ax^2 + bx + c, a \neq 0$.

A *projectile* is an object that is thrown, dropped, or launched, and then proceeds with no additional force on its own. A ball thrown up into the air is considered a projectile.

Mental Math

Estimate to the nearest 10.

a. 24% of 82

b. 5% of 206

c. 61% of 92

Equations for the Paths of Projectiles

When there is a constant force of gravity, the path of a projectile is a parabola. The parabola shows the height of the projectile as a function of the *horizontal distance* from the launch.

Activity

Step 1 A classroom board should be partitioned into rectangles by drawing evenly spaced lines, as shown. Work in a group and assign two students the tasks of tossing and catching a ball. Position the tosser at the left end of the board and the catcher at the right end of the board. During the experiment, the tosser will toss the ball to the catcher so that it does not go higher than the top of the board. For each vertical division line on the board, assign a student to act as a spotter. The diagram at the right would require 7 spotters. When the ball is tossed, these spotters will observe the ball's height when it crosses their vertical line.

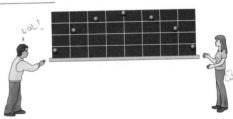

Step 2 Toss the ball while the spotters note its height as it passes each of the vertical lines. (It may take a few tosses to get everything right.) Following the toss, each spotter should mark the approximate point on the board at which the ball passed his or her vertical line. Using the board as a coordinate system, measure the horizontal and vertical distances to each point. Record the results.

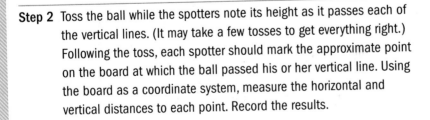

x = horizontal distance ball has traveled	?	?	?	?	?	?	?	?	?
y = height of the ball	?	?	?	?	?	?	?	?	?

Step 3 Enter the data into lists L1 and L2 on your calculator. Perform *quadratic regression* on the data. Quadratic regression fits a parabola "of best fit" to three or more points in the plane. Here is how to apply quadratic regression on one calculator.

The calculator returns coefficients *a*, *b*, and *c* of the quadratic equation that most closely fit the data entered into lists L1 and L2.

Step 4 Next, set up a reasonable plot window to fit your data. Enter the equation obtained in Step 3 into your Y= menu. Plot the scatterplot and function on the same grid. How close is the scatterplot to the parabola of best fit?

Equations for the Heights of Projectiles over Time

The graph of Galileo's formula $d = -16t^2$ is also a parabola. That parabola describes the height of the projectile as a function of the *length of time* since the projectile was launched.

When a projectile is launched, several factors determine its height above the ground at various times:

1. The **force of gravity** pulls the projectile back to Earth. By Galileo's formula, gravity pulls the projectile towards Earth $16t^2$ feet in *t* seconds.

2. The **initial upward velocity** with which the projectile is thrown or shot contributes to its height at time *t*. We use *v* to stand for the initial velocity. In *t* seconds, the projectile would go *vt* feet if there were no gravity.

3. The **initial height** of the projectile. We call this height *s* (for starting height).

Adding all these forces together yields a formula for the height of a projectile over time. Notice that the force of gravity is downward, so it has a negative effect on the height, while the launch velocity is considered to be upward and positive.

> ### General Formula for the Height of a Projectile over Time
>
> Let h be the height (in feet) of a projectile launched with an initial upward velocity v feet per second and an initial height of s feet. Then, after t seconds, $h = -16t^2 + vt + s$.

Since 16 feet $\approx$ 4.9 meters, if the units are in meters in the formula above, then $h = -4.9t^2 + vt + s$.

It is very easy to confuse the graph showing the height of a projectile as a function of time with a graph that represents the object's path, because they both are parabolas. However, even when a ball is tossed straight up and allowed to fall, its graph of height as a function of time is a parabola.

Ball's Path

Ball's Height Graphed as a Function of Time

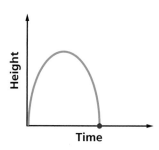

Example 1

A ball is launched from an initial height of 6 feet with an initial upward velocity of 32 feet per second.

a. Write an equation describing the height h in feet of the ball after t seconds.

b. How high will the ball be 2 seconds after it is thrown?

c. What is the maximum height of the ball?

Solutions

a. Since units are provided in feet, use the general formula $h = -16t^2 + vt + s$. Substitute 6 for s and 32 for v.

$h = -16t^2 + 32t + 6$

b. Substitute 2 for t in $h = -16t^2 + 32t + 6$.

$$h = -16(2)^2 + 32(2) + 6$$
$$= -16(4) + 64 + 6$$
$$= -64 + 64 + 6$$
$$= 6$$

In 2 seconds, the ball will be 6 feet high.

c. Use a graphing calculator. Plot $y = -16x^2 + 32x + 6$. A graph of this function using the window $0 \le x \le 3$, and $0 \le y \le 25$ is shown at the right. The maximum height is the greatest value of h shown on the graph, the y-coordinate of the vertex. Trace along the graph, and read the y-coordinate as you go. When we did this using the window $0 \le x \le 3$, and $0 \le y \le 25$, our trace showed that $(0.989, 21.998)$ and $(1.021, 21.993)$ are on the graph. So try $t = 1$. This gives $h = 22$.

The maximum height reached is 22 feet.

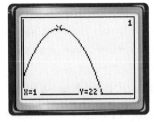

Check You can verify the maximum height by using the MAXIMUM or VERTEX command on your calculator. The screen at the right shows the vertex as $(1, 22)$.

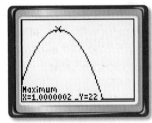

GUIDED

Example 2

An object is dropped from an initial height of 90 meters.

a. Write a formula describing the height of the object (in meters) after t seconds.

b. After how many seconds does the object hit the ground?

c. What is the maximum height of the object?

Solutions

a. Because units are provided in meters, use the general formula

$$h = -4.9t^2 + v \cdot t + s.$$

Substitute 90 for s and 0 for v.

$$h = -4.9t^2 + \underline{\quad ? \quad} \cdot t + \underline{\quad ? \quad}$$
$$= -4.9t^2 + \underline{\quad ? \quad}$$

b. The value(s) of t corresponding to $h = 0$ must be found when the object hits the ground.

$$0 = -4.9t^2 + \underline{\quad ? \quad}.$$
$$4.9t^2 = \underline{\quad ? \quad}$$
$$t^2 \approx \underline{\quad ? \quad}$$

Because t is positive (it measures time after launch), ignore the negative square root.

$$t \approx \underline{\quad ? \quad}$$

(continued on next page)

Quadratics and Projectiles **547**

You should find that the object hits the ground in about 4.3 seconds.

c. A graph of $y = -4.9x^2 + 90$ is shown at the right. The graph shows that the object is farthest from the ground when it is launched. That is when $t = 0$. Then $h = -4.9t^2 + 90 = -4.9(0)^2 + 90 = 90$. The maximum height is 90 meters. We knew this because the object was dropped from this height, and the equation and graph confirm it.

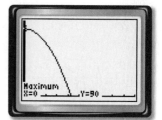

If a projectile is thrown upward and comes back down to Earth, then it will reach some heights twice.

GUIDED

Example 3

Suppose a ball is thrown upward with an initial velocity of 22 meters per second from an initial height of 2 meters.

a. Write a formula for the height in meters of the ball after t seconds.

b. Estimate when the ball is 20 meters high.

Solutions

a. Because units are provided in meters, use $h = -4.9t^2 + vt + s$. Substitute 2 for s and 22 for v.

$h = $ __?__

b. The values of t corresponding to $h = 20$ must be found. Graph the equation you found in Part a on the window $0 \le x \le 6$, $10 \le y \le 30$. Draw a horizontal line $y = 20$ to indicate $h = 20$ feet. Use the INTERSECT command on your calculator to find both intersections. Our calculator shows that when $x \approx$ __?__ and $x \approx$ __?__, $y \approx 20$.

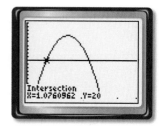
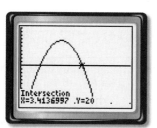

The ball is 20 meters off the ground at about __?__ seconds and __?__ seconds after being thrown.

A method for finding exact answers without finding the intersections of two graphs is discussed in Lesson 9-5.

Questions

COVERING THE IDEAS

1. In your own words, define the term projectile. Give several real-life examples of projectiles.

2. Use quadratic regression on your calculator to find an equation for the parabola passing through the points $(0, 6)$, $(5, 30)$, and $(10, 6)$.

3. A ball is thrown from an initial height of 5 feet with an initial upward velocity of 30 feet per second.
   a. Write a function describing the height of the ball after t seconds.
   b. How high will the ball be 2 seconds after it is thrown?
   c. What is the maximum height of the ball?

4. Suppose a ball is batted with an initial upward velocity of 26 meters per second from an initial height of 1 meter.
   a. Write a function describing the height in meters of the ball after t seconds.
   b. Estimate when the ball is 5 meters high.

5. An object is dropped from an initial height of 40 feet.
   a. What is the object's initial velocity? What is its maximum height?
   b. Write a formula for the height h in feet of the object after t seconds.
   c. After how many seconds does the object hit the ground?

6. An object is dropped from an initial height of 150 meters.
   a. Write a formula for the height h in meters of the object after t seconds.
   b. After how many seconds does the object hit the ground?
   c. What is the maximum height of the object?

Los Angeles's Vladimir Guerrero hits a solo home run in the fourth inning of a baseball game in Oakland, California.

Source: Associated Press

APPLYING THE MATHEMATICS

7. Use quadratic regression on your calculator to answer this question. A football kicker attempts to kick a 40-yard field goal. The kicker kicks the football from a height of 0 feet above the ground. The football is 26 feet above the ground at its peak (the vertex) at a distance of 22 yards from the kicker. The height of the crossbar (the bottom bar of the goal post) is 10 feet off the ground. Assuming the ball is kicked straight, will the kick clear the crossbar of the goal post? (*Hint:* Use the information given to determine a third point on the parabola and use quadratic regression.)

8. Refer to the graph at the right.
It shows the height *h* in feet of
a soccer ball *t* seconds after it is
drop-kicked into the air.

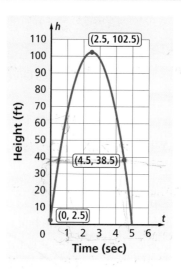

There were approximately
321,555 high school girl
soccer players in the
2005–2006 school year.

Source: National Federation of High School
Associations

a. What is the approximate height
of the soccer ball at 1 second?
At 4 seconds?

b. What is the greatest height the
ball reaches?

c. At what times is the ball 38.5
feet high?

d. Approximately how long is the
ball in the air?

e. For how many seconds is the ball more than 38.5 feet above
the ground?

f. What does the *h*-intercept represent in this situation?

g. What does the *t*-intercept represent in this situation?

9. A small rocket is shot from the edge of a cliff. Suppose that
after *x* seconds, the rocket is *y* meters above the cliff, where
$y = 25x - 5x^2$.

a. Graph this equation using the window $0 \le x \le 8$, $-5 \le y \le 40$.

b. What is the greatest height the rocket reaches?

c. How far above the edge of the cliff is the rocket after
4 seconds?

d. Between which times is the rocket more than 20 feet above
the cliff's edge?

e. What is the height of the rocket after 6 seconds?

f. At approximately what time does the rocket fall below the
height of the cliff's edge?

10. A ball is thrown from an initial height of 7 feet. After 5 seconds
in the air, the ball reaches a maximum height of 18 feet above
the ground.

a. What third point on the graph can be deduced from this
information?

b. Use quadratic regression to find a formula for the height in
feet of the ball after *t* seconds.

c. Use the formula to find the initial velocity of the ball.

d. Use the graph to approximate how long the ball is in the air.

REVIEW

In **11** and **12**, an equation is given.
   a. Make a table of values for integer values of *x* from −3 to 3.
   b. Graph the equation. **(Lessons 9-3, 9-2)**

11. $y = \frac{1}{4}x^2$ **12.** $y = 8x - 3x^2$

In **13** and **14**, use the graph of the parabola at the right.
(Lessons 9-3, 9-1)

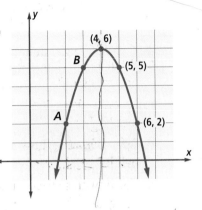

13. Use the symmetry of the parabola to find the coordinates of points *A* and *B*.

14. Write an equation for the axis of symmetry.

15. Multiple Choice Which of the following is *not* equal to uv^2?
(Lessons 8-5, 8-2)

   A $u \cdot v \cdot v$ **B** $(u)v^2$ **C** $u(v)^2$ **D** $(uv)^2$

16. The table below estimates the number of calories people of various weights burn per minute while participating in various activities. **(Lessons 6-8, 6-5, 3-4)**

The state of California has produced the most high school All-American boy's basketball players (72) through the 2005–2006 season.

Source: mcdepk.com

Activity	Weight (lb)			
	105–115	127–137	160–170	180–200
Full-court Basketball	9.8	11.2	13.2	14.5
Jogging (5 mph)	8.6	9.2	11.5	12.7
Running (8 mph)	10.4	11.9	14.2	17.3
Volleyball	7.8	8.9	10.5	11.6
Bicycling (10 mph)	5.5	6.3	7.8	14.5

Source: www.coolnurse.com

   a. Suppose Vince, who weighs 168 pounds, works out by jogging and then playing basketball. Let *x* = the number of minutes he jogs, and let *y* = the number of minutes he plays basketball. If he burns a total of 445 calories, write an equation in standard form that describes *x* and *y*.
   b. Find the *x*- and *y*-intercepts of the line from Part a.
   c. If Vince plays basketball for 25 minutes, use your equation to calculate how long he must jog to burn 445 calories.

EXPLORATION

17. Infinitely many parabolas have *x*-intercepts at 0 and 6. Find equations for three such parabolas.

Lesson

9-5 The Quadratic Formula

Vocabulary

quadratic equation

standard form of a quadratic
equation

▶ **BIG IDEA** If an equation can be put into the form $ax^2 + bx + c$,
it can be solved using the Quadratic Formula.

One of the most exciting events in amateur sports is 10-meter
platform diving. Once a diver leaves a platform, the diver becomes
a projectile. Consequently, during a dive, a diver's height above
the water at any given time can be determined using a quadratic
equation. This is important because for a diver to practice spins and
somersaults, he or she must know how much time will pass before
entering the water.

Suppose a diver jumps upward at an initial velocity of 4.3 meters per
second. Then the diver's height $h(t)$ in meters t seconds into the dive;
can be estimated using the equation $h(t) = -4.9t^2 + 4.3t + 10$ and
graphed below. When the diver hits the water, $h(t)$ is zero. So solving
the equation $0 = -4.9t^2 + 4.3t + 10$ gives the number of seconds from
departing the platform to entering the water.

The equation $0 = -4.9t^2 + 4.3t + 10$ is an example of a *quadratic
equation*. A **quadratic equation** is an equation that can be written in
the form $ax^2 + bx + c = 0$ with $a \neq 0$. In this case, t is being used in
place of x, $a = -4.9$, $b = 4.3$, and $c = 10$.

The Quadratic Formula

You can find the solutions to *any* quadratic equation by using
the *Quadratic Formula*. This formula gives the value(s) of x
in terms of a (the coefficient of x^2), b (the coefficient of x),
and c (the constant term). The formula states that there are
at most two solutions to a quadratic equation.

If $ax^2 + bx + c = 0$ and $a \neq 0$, then $x = \dfrac{-b + \sqrt{b^2 - 4ac}}{2a}$ or
$x = \dfrac{-b - \sqrt{b^2 - 4ac}}{2a}$.

The calculations of the two solutions differ in only one way.
$\sqrt{b^2 - 4ac}$ is added to $-b$ in the numerator of the first
calculation, while $\sqrt{b^2 - 4ac}$ is subtracted from $-b$ in the
second calculation.

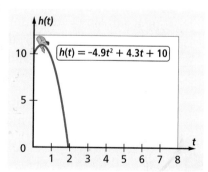

$h(t) = -4.9t^2 + 4.3t + 10$

The work in calculating the two solutions is almost the same. So, the two expressions can be written as one expression using the symbol $\pm$, which means "plus or minus." This symbol means you do two calculations: one using the $+$ sign to add and one using the $-$ sign to subtract.

The Quadratic Formula

If $ax^2 + bx + c = 0$ and $a \neq 0$, then $x = \dfrac{-b \pm \sqrt{b^2 - 4ac}}{2a}$.

The quadratic equation $ax^2 + bx + c = 0$ and the Quadratic Formula $x = \dfrac{-b \pm \sqrt{b^2 - 4ac}}{2a}$ are equivalent equations. The quadratic equation was solved for x to generate the quadratic formula. In Chapter 13, you can see how this formula was found.

The quadratic formula is one of the most often used and most famous formulas in all mathematics. *You should memorize it today!*

Applying the Quadratic Formula

Example 1

Solve $x^2 + 8x + 7 = 0$.

Solution Recall that $x^2 = 1x^2$. So think of the given equation as $1x^2 + 8x + 7 = 0$ and apply the Quadratic Formula with $a = 1$, $b = 8$, and $c = 7$.

$$x = \frac{-b \pm \sqrt{b^2 - 4ac}}{2a}$$

$$= \frac{-8 \pm \sqrt{8^2 - 4 \cdot 1 \cdot 7}}{2 \cdot 1}$$

Follow the order of operations. Work under the radical sign (with its unwritten parentheses) first.

$$= \frac{-8 \pm \sqrt{64 - 28}}{2}$$

$$= \frac{-8 \pm \sqrt{36}}{2}$$

So, $x = \dfrac{-8 + 6}{2}$ or $x = \dfrac{-8 - 6}{2}$

$x = \dfrac{-2}{2} = -1$ or $x = \dfrac{-14}{2} = -7$

Check Do -1 and -7 make the equation $x^2 + 8x + 7 = 0$ true? Substitute -1 for x.

Does $(-1)^2 + 8(-1) + 7 = 0$?

$1 + -8 + 7 = 0$ Yes, it checks.

(continued on next page)

> ▶ **READING MATH**
>
> On some calculators there is a key that is labeled $\pm$ or $+/-$. That key takes the opposite of a number. It does not perform the two operations $+$ and $-$ required in the Quadratic Formula.

Substitute −7 for x.

Does $(-7)^2 + 8(-7) + 7 = 0$?

$49 + -56 + 7 = 0$ Yes, it checks.

STOP QY

▸ QY

Solve
$3y^2 - 10.5y + 9 = 0$.

Sometimes you must decide whether or not a solution to a quadratic equation is reasonable, given the context of the problem. In Guided Example 2, we return to the diving situation described at the beginning of this lesson.

The x-axis represents a height of 0. The graph crosses the x-axis a little to the left of 2, which is close to 1.93. The INTERSECT feature on a graph is also helpful for finding a solution.

GUIDED

Example 2

In 10-meter platform diving, the function $h(t) = -4.9t^2 + 4.3t + 10$ gives the approximate height $h(t)$ above the water in meters a diver is at t seconds after launching into the dive. How many seconds elapse from the time the diver leaves the 10-meter platform until the diver hits the water?

Solution The diver will hit the water when the diver's height above the water is zero, so solve the equation $0 = -4.9t^2 + 4.3t + 10$.

Apply the Quadratic Formula with $a = -4.9$, $b = 4.3$, and $c = 10$.

$$t = -4.3 \pm \frac{\sqrt{(\underline{\ ?\ })^2 \underline{\ ?\ } 4(\underline{\ ?\ })(\underline{\ ?\ })}}{2(\underline{\ ?\ })}$$

$$= \frac{-4.3 \pm \sqrt{\ ?\ }}{-9.8}$$

So, $t = \frac{-4.3 + \sqrt{\ ?\ }}{-9.8}$ or $t = \frac{-4.3 - \sqrt{\ ?\ }}{-9.8}$.

These are exact solutions to the quadratic equation. However, since the given information is not exact, it is more reasonable to want an approximation.

$$t \approx \frac{-4.3 + \ ?\ }{-9.8} \quad \text{or} \quad t \approx \frac{-4.3 - \ ?\ }{-9.8}$$

$$t \approx -1.1 \quad \text{or} \quad t \approx 1.9$$

The diver cannot reach the water in negative time, so the solution −1.1 seconds does not make sense in this situation. We therefore eliminate this as an answer. The diver will hit the water about 1.9 seconds after leaving the diving platform.

Check Substituting 1.9 in for t in the equation $0 = -4.9t^2 + 4.3t + 10$ is one method you can use to check a solution. Other methods are looking at a table or a graph.

Juliana Veloso of Brazil competes in the women's 10-meter platform semifinals at the 2006 USA Grand Prix Diving Championships in Fort Lauderdale, Florida.

In Example 3, the equation has to be put in $ax^2 + bx + c = 0$ form before the Quadratic Formula can be applied. This form is called the **standard form of a quadratic equation.** When the number under the radical sign in the Quadratic Formula is not a perfect square, approximations are often used in the last step of the process.

Example 3

Solve $x^2 - 3x = 37$.

Solution Put $x^2 - 3x = 37$ into standard form.

$x^2 - 3x - 37 = 37 - 37$ Subtract 37 from both sides.

$x^2 - 3x - 37 = 0$

Apply the Quadratic Formula, with $a = 1$, $b = -3$, and $c = -37$.

$$x = \frac{-(-3) \pm \sqrt{(-3)^2 - 4(1)(-37)}}{2(1)}$$

$$x = \frac{3 \pm \sqrt{9 + 148}}{2}$$

$$x = \frac{3 \pm \sqrt{157}}{2}$$

So $x = \frac{3 + \sqrt{157}}{2}$ or $x = \frac{3 - \sqrt{157}}{2}$.

These are exact solutions. You can approximate the solutions using a calculator.

Because $\sqrt{157} \approx 12.5$, $x \approx \frac{3 + 12.5}{2}$ or $x \approx \frac{3 - 12.5}{2}$. So $x \approx 7.75$ or $x \approx -4.75$.

Check Do the two values found work in the equation $x^2 - 3x = 37$?

Substitute 7.75 for x.

$(7.75)^2 - 3(7.75) = 36.8$. This is close to 37.

Substitute −4.75 for x.

$(-4.75)^2 - 3(-4.75) = 36.8$. This is close to 37.

In both cases the checks are not exact, but the solutions are approximations, so the check is close enough.

Questions

COVERING THE IDEAS

1. State the Quadratic Formula.

2. Is it true that the Quadratic Formula can be used to solve *any* quadratic equation?

3. Find the two values of $\frac{-3 \pm 9}{2}$.

In 4–7, use the Quadratic Formula to solve the equation. Give the exact solutions and check both solutions.

4. $x^2 + 15x + 54 = 0$

5. $t^2 + 4t + 4 = 0$

6. $3m^2 + 2m = 4$

7. $3y^2 = 13y + 100$

In 8 and 9, use the Quadratic Formula to solve the equations. Round the solutions to the nearest hundredth and check both solutions.

8. $20n^2 - 6n - 2 = 0$

9. $3p^2 + 14 = -19p$

10. If a diver dives from a 20-foot platform with an initial upward velocity of 14 feet per second, then the diver's approximate height can be represented by the function $h(t) = -16t^2 + 14t + 20$, where $h(t)$ is the height and t is the time in seconds. (This formula is different from the one in this lesson because meters have been converted to feet.)

   a. Find $h(1)$. Write a sentence explaining what it means.

   b. Estimate to the nearest tenth of a second how much time the diver will be in the air before hitting the water.

APPLYING THE MATHEMATICS

11. The solutions to $ax^2 + bx + c = 0$ are the x-intercepts of the graph of $y = ax^2 + bx + c$.

   a. Use the Quadratic Formula to find the solutions to $3x^2 - 6x - 45 = 0$.

   b. Check your answers to Part a by graphing an appropriate function.

12. The graphs of $y = -0.5x^2 + 6$ and $y = 4$ intersect at two points.

   a. Find the x-coordinate of each of the intersecting points.

   b. Find both coordinates of the two points of intersection.

   c. Check your answers to Part b by graphing these equations.

13. In 1971, the astronaut Alan Shepard (who had been the first U.S. man in space 9 years earlier) snuck a collapsible golf club and a golf ball onto *Apollo 14*. Just before taking off from the moon to return to Earth, he hit two golf balls. In doing so, he vividly showed the difference between gravity on the moon and on Earth. On the moon the approximate height $h(t)$ of the ball (in feet) after t seconds is given by the function $h(t) = -0.8t^2 + 12t$.

   a. At what two times would the golf ball reach a height of 20 feet? (Round your answer to the nearest hundredth.)

   b. How long would it take for the ball to come back to the surface of the moon?

14. The area of a rectangle is 240 cm^2. The length is 14 cm more than the width. What are the length and width of the rectangle?

REVIEW

15. If the x-intercepts of a parabola are 8 and –4, what is the x-coordinate of its vertex? (**Lesson 9-3**)

16. **Multiple Choice** Which equation is graphed at the right? (**Lessons 9-3, 9-2**)

    A $y = 2x^2$

    B $y = -2x^2$

    C $y = 2x^2 + 2$

    D $y = -2x^2 - 2$

17. Find the radius of a circle if the center of the circle is at (–2, 6) and the point (1, 2) is on the circle. (**Lesson 8-8**)

18. Kristen is buying a new car. She can choose from 4 models, 2 transmission types, 9 exterior colors, and 6 interior colors. How many combinations of models, transmissions, exteriors, and interiors are possible? (**Lesson 8-1**)

19. **Skill Sequence** If $f(x) = \frac{5x - 6}{x}$, find each value. (**Lesson 7-6**)

    a. $f(2)$ b. $f(3)$ c. $f(x + 1)$

EXPLORATION

20. a. Solve the equation $ax^2 + bx + c = 0$ for x using a CAS. In what form does the CAS put the two solutions?

    b. Add the two solutions using the CAS. What is the sum?

    c. Multiply the two solutions using the CAS. What is the product?

    d. Use the results from Parts b and c to check the *exact* answers to Example 3 of this lesson.

Lesson 9-6

Analyzing Solutions to Quadratic Equations

Vocabulary

discriminant

▶ **BIG IDEA** The value of the discriminant $b^2 - 4ac$ of a quadratic equation $ax^2 + bx + c = 0$ can tell you whether the equation has 0, 1, or 2 real solutions.

In Acapulco, Mexico, cliff divers dive from a place called La Quebrada ("the break in the rocks") 27 meters above the water. As you have learned, a diver's path is part of a parabola that can be described using a quadratic equation. An equation that relates the distance x (in meters) away from the cliff and the distance y (in meters) above the water is $y = -x^2 + 2x + 27$. The graph at the right shows that when a diver pushes off the cliff, the diver arches upward and then descends.

Will the diver's height reach 27.75 meters? 28 meters? 30 meters? You can use the equation, the graph, or the table to determine whether or not a diver reaches a particular height.

Mental Math

Solve the equation.

a. $a + 14 = 29$

b. $b^2 + 14 = 39$

c. $(c - 6)^2 + 14 = 39$

Distance Above Water (m) vs *Distance Away from Cliff (m)*

Using a Graph or Table to Determine Solutions to a Quadratic Equation

GUIDED

Example 1

Consider the situation of a La Quebrada diver. Graph and generate a table of the parabola with equation $y = -x^2 + 2x + 27$ to determine whether the diver will ever reach

a. 27.75 meters.   b. 28 meters.   c. 30 meters.

Adele Laurent of Denver, Colorado, dives from the La Quebrada cliff during the International Cliff Diving Championships in 1996, the first year that women were allowed to participate in the championships.

Source: Associated Press

Solutions

a. A graph of $y = -x^2 + 2x + 27$ is shown on the right using the window $0 \le x \le 4$ and $25 \le y \le 30$. Also graphed is the line $y = 27.75$. This line crosses the parabola twice.

   The diver reaches 27.75 meters twice, once on the way up and once on the way down.

   A table of $y = -x^2 + 2x + 27$ is shown below. From the table it is evident that there are two distances x when $y = 27.75$ meters: once 0.5 meter from the cliff and again 1.5 meters away.

b. Suppose you draw the line $y = 28$ on the graph. How many times does the line appear to intersect the graph? __?__

   Now look at the table. It appears the diver reaches the height of 28 meters __?__ time(s). The diver reaches the height of 28 meters __?__ meter(s) from the cliff.

c. Suppose you draw the line $y = 30$ on the graph. How many times does the line appear to intersect the graph? __?__

   Now look at the table below. It appears the diver reaches the height of 30 meters __?__ time(s).

Using the Quadratic Formula to Find the Number of Real Solutions

We can answer the same questions about the height of the diver using the Quadratic Formula.

Example 2

Will the diver ever reach a height of

a. 27.75 meters?   b. 28 meters?   c. 30 meters?

Solutions

a. Let $y = 27.75$ in the equation $y = -x^2 + 2x + 27$.

$$27.75 = -x^2 + 2x + 27$$

Add −27.75 to both sides to put the equation in standard form.

$$0 = -x^2 + 2x - 0.75$$

(continued on next page)

Let $a = -1$, $b = 2$, and $c = -0.75$ in the Quadratic Formula. Then

$$x = \frac{-2 \pm \sqrt{2^2 - 4(-1)(-0.75)}}{2(-1)}$$

$$x = \frac{-2 + \sqrt{1}}{-2} \quad \text{or} \quad x = \frac{-2 - \sqrt{1}}{-2}$$

$$x = 0.5 \quad \text{or} \quad x = 1.5$$

The diver reaches a height of 27.75 meters twice, first at 0.5 meter from the cliff and second at 1.5 meters from the cliff.

b. Let $y = 28$ in the equation $y = -x^2 + 2x + 27$.

$$28 = -x^2 + 2x + 27$$

Add −28 to both sides to place the equation in standard form.

$$0 = -x^2 + 2x - 1$$

Let $a = -1$, $b = 2$, and $c = -1$ in the Quadratic Formula.

$$x = \frac{-2 \pm \sqrt{2^2 - 4(-1)(-1)}}{2(-1)} = \frac{-2 \pm 0}{-2} = 1$$

So the diver reaches 28 meters just once, 1 meter up from the cliff. This agrees with the graph that shows the vertex to be (1, 28).

c. Let $y = 30$ in the equation $y = -x^2 + 2x + 27$.

$$30 = -x^2 + 2x + 27$$

Add −30 to both sides to place the equation in standard form

$$0 = -x^2 + 2x - 3$$

Let $a = -1$, $b = 2$, and $c = -3$ in the Quadratic Formula. Then

$$x = \frac{-2 \pm \sqrt{2^2 - 4(-1)(-3)}}{2(-1)} = \frac{-2 \pm \sqrt{-8}}{-2}$$

Because no real number multiplied by itself equals −8, there is no square root of −8 in the real number system. In fact, no negative number has a square root in the real number system. So $30 = -x^2 + 2x + 27$ does not have a real number solution. This means that the diver never reaches a height of 30 meters. This is consistent with the graph that shows there is no point on the parabola with a height of 30 meters.

The Discriminant of a Quadratic Equation

Look closely at the number under the square root in each of the solutions in Example 2. Notice that the number of solutions to a quadratic equation is related to this number, which is the number $b^2 - 4ac$ in the Quadratic Formula. In the solution to Part a, $b^2 - 4ac = 1$, which is positive. Adding $\sqrt{1}$ and subtracting $\sqrt{1}$ results in two solutions. In the solution to Part b, $b^2 - 4ac = 0$, and adding $\sqrt{0}$ and subtracting $\sqrt{0}$, yields the same result, 1. That quadratic equation has just one solution. There is no solution to the equation in Part c because $b^2 - 4ac = -8$, and −8 does not have a square root in the set of real numbers.

Because the value of $b^2 - 4ac$ *discriminates* among the various possible number of real number solutions to a specific quadratic equation, it is called the **discriminant** of the equation $ax^2 + bx + c = 0$. Stated below are the specific properties of the discriminant.

Discriminant Property

If $ax^2 + bx + c = 0$ and a, b, and c are real numbers ($a \neq 0$), then:

When $b^2 - 4ac > 0$, the equation has exactly two real solutions.

When $b^2 - 4ac = 0$, the equation has exactly one real solution.

When $b^2 - 4ac < 0$, the equation has no real solutions.

An important use of the discriminant relates solutions of a quadratic equation to the x-intercepts of the related function. Specifically, the solutions to $ax^2 + bx + c = 0$ are the x-intercepts of $y = ax^2 + bx + c$. So the discriminant tells you how many times the function $f(x) = ax^2 + bx + c$ crosses the x-axis.

Quadratic Function	Value of $b^2 - 4ac$	Number of x-intercepts	Graph (All screens are shown in the standard viewing window.)
$y = x^2 + x - 6$	$1^2 - 4(1)(-6) = 25$ positive	two	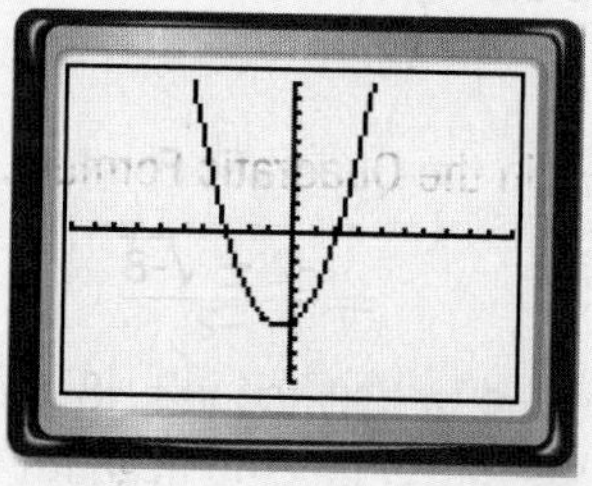
$y = x^2 - 6x + 9$	$(-6)^2 - 4(1)(9) = 0$ zero	one	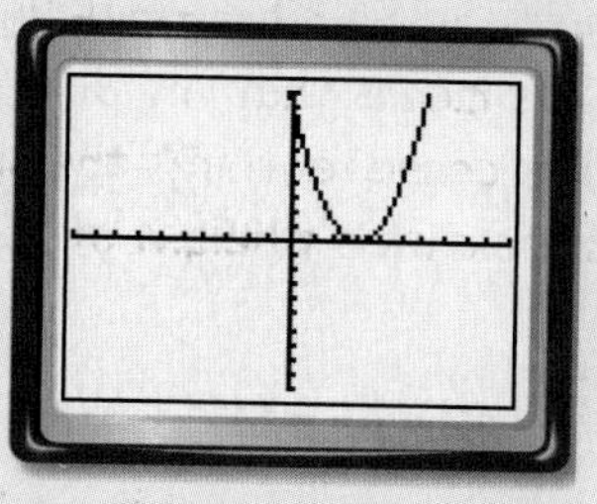
$y = x^2 + 2x + 7$	$2^2 - 4(1)(7) = -24$ negative	zero	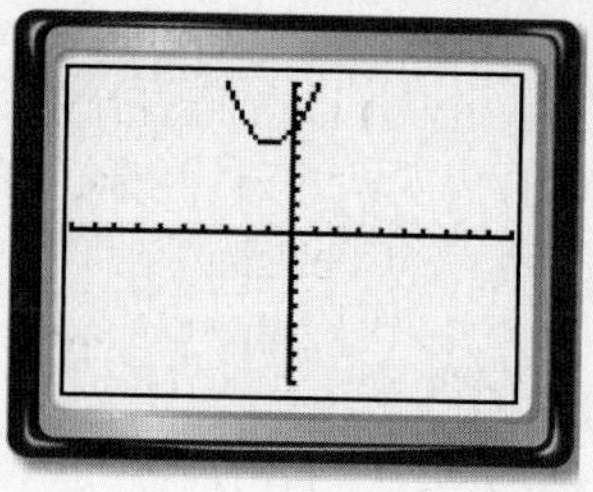

STOP QY

▸ **QY**

Determine the number of real solutions to $6x^2 + 3x = -7$.

GUIDED

Example 3

How many times does the graph of $y = 2x^2 + 16x + 32$ intersect the x-axis?

Solution Find the value of the discriminant $b^2 - 4ac$. Here $a = \underline{\quad?\quad}$, $b = \underline{\quad?\quad}$, and $c = \underline{\quad?\quad}$.

So $b^2 - 4ac = \underline{\quad?\quad}$.

$$= \underline{\quad?\quad} = 0$$

Because the discriminant is $\underline{\quad?\quad}$, the graph of $y = 2x^2 + 16x + 32$ intersects the x-axis $\underline{\quad?\quad}$ time(s).

Check You should check your answer by graphing the equation with a calculator.

Questions

COVERING THE IDEAS

In 1 and 2, refer to the La Quebrada cliff diver equation $y = -x^2 + 2x + 27$ from Example 1.

1. **a.** What equation can be solved to determine how far away (horizontally) from the cliff the diver will be when the diver is 27 meters above the water?

    b. Will the diver reach a height of 27 meters above the water? If so, how many times?

2. How far from the cliff will the diver be at 10 meters above the water?

3. How many real solutions does a quadratic equation have when the discriminant is

    a. negative?   **b.** zero?   **c.** positive?

4. The discriminant of the equation $ax^2 + bx + c = 0$ is $-1{,}200$. What does this indicate about the graph of $y = ax^2 + bx + c$?

5. The equation $y = \frac{1}{2}x^2 - x - \frac{3}{2}$ is graphed at the right. Use the graph to determine the number of real solutions to each equation.

    a. $\frac{1}{2}x^2 - x - \frac{3}{2} = -2$ **b.** $\frac{1}{2}x^2 - x - \frac{3}{2} = -3$

    c. $\frac{1}{2}x^2 - x - \frac{3}{2} = 1$ **d.** $\frac{1}{2}x^2 - x - \frac{3}{2} = 5{,}000$

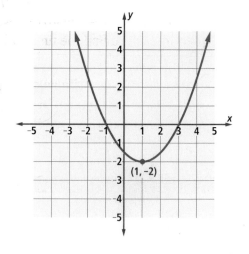

In 6–9, a quadratic equation is given.

  a. Calculate the value of the discriminant.

  b. Give the number of real solutions.

  c. Find all the real solutions.

6. $2x^2 + x + 3 = 0$

7. $-4n^2 + 56n - 196 = 0$

8. $22q^2 = q + 3$

9. $x = \dfrac{x^2}{6} + \dfrac{1}{4}$ $a = 120$ or 30?

In 10 and 11, an equation of the form $y = ax^2 + bx + c$ is graphed. Tell whether the value of $b^2 - 4ac$ is *positive, negative,* or *zero.*

10.

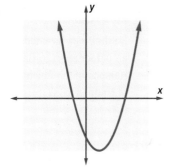

11.

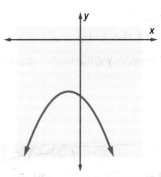

In 12 and 13, a quadratic function f is described.

  a. Calculate the value of the discriminant of the quadratic equation $f(x) = 0$.

  b. Give the number of x-intercepts of the graph of f.

12. $f(x) = 5x^2 + 20x + 20$

13. $f(x) = 2x^2 + x - 3$

APPLYING THE MATHEMATICS

14. For what value of h does $x^2 + 6x + h = 0$ have exactly one solution?

15. If the discriminant for the equation $2x^2 + 4x + c = 0$ is 8, what is the value of c?

16. In Lesson 9-5, a diver's height $h(t)$ above the water after t seconds was given by $h(t) = -4.9t^2 + 4.3t + 10$. Use the discriminant to find the time t when the diver reached the maximum height.

17. Can any parabolas with an equation of the form $y = ax^2 + bx + c$ *not* have a y-intercept? Why or why not?

18. By letting $x = m + 3$, solve $4(m + 3)^2 - 13(m + 3) - 35 = 0$ for m.

REVIEW

19. Solve $45x^2 - 100 = 0$. (**Lesson 9-5**)

In 20 and 21, use the following information. A softball pitcher tosses a ball to a catcher 50 feet away. The height h (in feet) of the ball when it is x feet from the pitcher is given by the equation $h = -0.016x^2 + 0.8x + 2$. (Lesson 9-4)

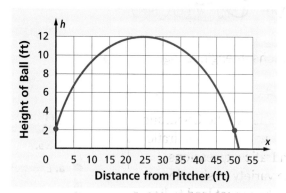

Softball was invented as an indoor sport by George Hamock of the Chicago Board of Trade in 1887.

Source: The History Channel

20. How high is the ball at its peak?

21. a. If the batter is 2 feet in front of the catcher, how far is the batter from the pitcher?

   b. How high is the ball when it reaches the batter?

In 22 and 23, state whether the parabola described by the equation opens up or down. (Lesson 9-3)

22. $y = -\frac{1}{3}x^2 - 6x + 1$ **23.** $y = 0.5x - 2x^2$

24. Skill Sequence In Parts a–d, simplify each statement. (Lesson 2-2)

   a. $\dfrac{-4 + x}{2a} + \dfrac{-4 - x}{2a}$

   b. $\dfrac{-b + y}{2a} + \dfrac{-b - y}{2a}$

   c. $\dfrac{-b + \sqrt{z}}{2a} + \dfrac{-b - \sqrt{z}}{2a}$

   d. $\dfrac{-b + \sqrt{b^2 - 4ac}}{2a} + \dfrac{-b - \sqrt{b^2 - 4ac}}{2a}$

   e. What does Part d tell you about the solutions to a quadratic equation?

EXPLORATION

25. Create a parabola in the following way. Take a plain sheet of notebook paper and draw a dark dot in the middle of the paper. Draw a line anywhere on the paper that is parallel to the bottom of the paper. Make sure the line stretches to both edges of the paper. Now fold the paper so that the dot falls on the line. Unfold the paper, and then fold the paper so that the dot falls on another place on the line. Repeat this 20 times so that the dot has fallen in different places on the line each time. The folds should outline a parabola that can be seen by unfolding the paper. Take another sheet and see what happens if the dot is farther from the line or closer to the line than the dot you used the first time.

QY ANSWER

0

Lesson 9-7

More Applications of Quadratics: Why Quadratics Are Important

▶ **BIG IDEA** Quadratics have applications in engineering, geometry, and counting problems.

You may wonder why you are asked to memorize the Quadratic Formula or even why you need to know how to solve quadratic equations. There is a simple reason. Quadratic expressions, equations, and functions appear in a wide variety of situations. Furthermore, these situations are unlike those that lead to linear expressions. Many problems involving linear expressions can be solved by some people without algebra, using just intuition from arithmetic. Few people can solve problems that lead to quadratic expressions without using algebra.

You have seen applications of quadratic expressions in areas of squares and of circles, and to describe paths of projectiles. There are too many other applications to describe them all here. In this lesson, we give just a few.

Mental Math

Solve.

a. $E = mc^2$ for m.

b. $A = \pi r^2$ for π.

Parabolas as Important Curves

In your future mathematics courses, you will study perhaps the most important property of a parabola: its reflective property. Because of its reflective property, a parabola is the shape of a cross-section of automobile headlights, satellite dishes, and radio telescopes.

Parabolas also appear on suspension bridges. When a chain is suspended between two fixed points, the curve it describes is a *catenary*. A catenary looks much like a parabola but is slightly deeper. But in a suspension bridge where the roadway is hung by support cables from the main cables, the shape of the main cable is a parabola.

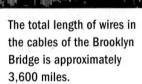

The total length of wires in the cables of the Brooklyn Bridge is approximately 3,600 miles.

Source: Endex Engineering, Inc.

Example 1

Suppose a team of engineers and construction workers are repairing a suspension bridge to strengthen it for use with increased traffic flow. The engineer uses scale models, such as the graph on the next page, to make decisions about repairs.

(continued on next page)

Let the roadway be along the *x*-axis. Place the *y*-axis at one end of the roadway. Then the ends of the bridge are at $(0, 0)$ and $(600, 0)$. The graph at the right shows that the parabola passes through points $(0, 200)$, $(300, 0)$, and $(600, 200)$. By using quadratic regression, an equation for the parabola through these points can be found. In standard form, the equation is given by $y = \frac{1}{450}x^2 - \frac{4}{3}x + 200$, where *y* is the length of each vertical cable at the distance *x* from the end of the bridge. Suppose a support cable 82.5 feet long is delivered to the construction site. How far from the left end of the bridge should the cable be placed?

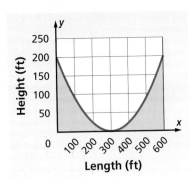

Solution 1 Substitute 82.5 for *y* in the equation of the parabola. Then solve the equation for *x*.

$$82.5 = \frac{1}{450}x^2 - \frac{4}{3}x + 200$$

$37{,}125 = x^2 - 600x + 90{,}000$ Multiply both sides by 450.

$0 = x^2 - 600x + 52{,}875$ Subtract 37,125 from both sides.

Now the equation $x^2 - 600x + 52{,}875 = 0$ can be solved using the Quadratic Formula, with $a = 1$, $b = -600$, and $c = 52{,}875$.

$$x = \frac{-b \pm \sqrt{b^2 - 4ac}}{2a}$$

$$= \frac{-(-600) \pm \sqrt{(-600)^2 - 4(1)(52{,}875)}}{2(1)}$$

$$= \frac{600 \pm \sqrt{360{,}000 - 211{,}500}}{2}$$

$$= \frac{600 \pm \sqrt{148{,}500}}{2}$$

$$\approx \frac{600 \pm 385.4}{2}$$

$$x \approx 107.3 \text{ ft or } x \approx 492.7 \text{ ft}$$

The cable can be placed either 107.3 ft or 492.7 ft from the left end of the bridge.

Solution 2 Enter the equation of the parabola and the desired *y* value into a calculator, as shown at the right.

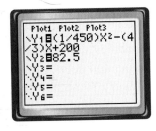

Graph each equation over the domain $0 \le x \le 600$. The solutions to the problem are intersection points of the two functions.

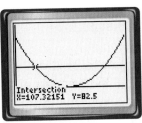

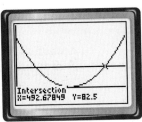

The x-coordinates of the intersections indicate that the cable is 82.5 feet long when $x \approx 107.3$ ft and $x \approx 492.7$ ft.

This makes sense because these distances are equally far from the center of the bridge at 300 ft.

A Geometry Problem Involving Counting

Many counting problems lead to quadratic equations. For example, the number d of diagonals of an n-sided convex polygon is given by the formula $d = \dfrac{n(n - 3)}{2}$.

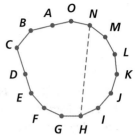

$\overline{NH}$ is one diagonal of this convex 15-sided polygon.

Example 2

a. How many diagonals does a convex polygon of 15 sides have?

b. Can a convex polygon have exactly 300 diagonals? If so, how many sides must that polygon have?

Solutions

a. When $n = 15$, $d = \dfrac{n(n - 3)}{2} = \dfrac{15(15 - 3)}{2} = \dfrac{15 \cdot 12}{2} = 90$.
A 15-sided polygon has 90 diagonals.

b. Substitute 300 for d in the formula.

$$300 = \frac{n(n - 3)}{2}$$

$600 = n(n - 3)$ Multiply both sides by 2.

$600 = n^2 - 3n$ Distributive Property

To solve, write the equation in standard form.

$0 = n^2 - 3n - 600$ Subtract 600 from both sides.

This equation is in standard form with $a = 1$, $b = -3$, and $c = -600$. Use the Quadratic Formula.

$$n = \frac{-b \pm \sqrt{b^2 - 4ac}}{2a}$$

$$= \frac{-(-3) \pm \sqrt{(-3)^2 - 4 \cdot 1 \cdot (-600)}}{2 \cdot 1}$$

$$= \frac{3 \pm \sqrt{9 + 2{,}400}}{2}$$

$$= \frac{3 \pm \sqrt{2{,}409}}{2}$$

Because the discriminant 2,409 is not a perfect square, the values of n that we get are not integers. But n has to be an integer because it is the number of sides of a polygon. So the discriminant signals that there is no polygon with exactly 300 diagonals.

Questions

COVERING THE IDEAS

1. A cable of length 100 feet is brought to the construction site in the situation of Example 1. How far from the left end of the bridge can that cable be placed?

2. Draw a convex decagon (10-sided polygon) and one of its diagonals. How many other diagonals does this polygon have?

3. Can a convex polygon have exactly 21 diagonals? If so, how many sides does that polygon have?

4. Can a convex polygon have exactly 2,015 diagonals? If so, how many sides does that polygon have?

5. The sum of the integers from 1 to n is $\frac{n(n + 1)}{2}$. If this sum is 7,260, what is n?

6. The sum $5 + 6 + 7 + 8 + 9 + 10 = 45$ is an instance of the more general pattern that the sum of the integers from n to $2n$ is $1.5(n^2 + n)$.

   a. What is the sum of the integers from 100 to 200?

   b. If the sum of the integers from n to $2n$ is 759, what is n?

7. In the figure below, $\overline{PA}$ is *tangent* to the circle at point A. (It intersects the circle only at that point.) Another segment from P intersects the circle at points B and C. When you study geometry, you will learn that $PA^2 = PB \cdot PC$. Suppose $PA = 12$, $BC = 7$, and $PB = x$.

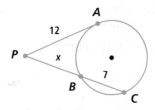

   a. Write an algebraic expression for PC.

   b. Substitute into $PA^2 = PB \cdot PC$ and solve the resulting quadratic equation to find PB.

APPLYING THE MATHEMATICS

8. In any circle O with diameter $\overline{PR}$, $SQ^2 = PQ \cdot RQ$, as shown at the right.

   a. If $PR = 10$ and $PQ = x$, write an algebraic expression for QR.

   b. Substitute the values from Part a into the formula $SQ^2 = PQ \cdot RQ$ to find SQ when $PR = 10$ and $PQ = 3$.

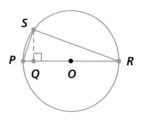

9. Suppose an architect is designing a building with arched windows in the shape of a parabola. The area under the arch will be divided into windowpanes as shown in the diagram below. The architect needs to know the lengths of the four horizontal bars at heights 2, 4, 6, and 8 units. If the parabola has equation $y = -0.5x^2 + 8x - 22$, find the length, to the nearest tenth of a unit, of the bar at the 6-unit height.

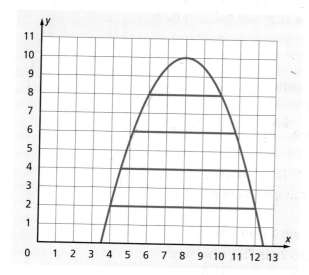

10. Secure telephone networks (ones in which each person is connected to every other person by a direct line) require $\frac{n(n-3)}{2} = \frac{1}{2}n^2 - \frac{1}{2}n$ cable lines for n employees. A company is interested in setting up a secure phone networking group. Each employee in the group is provided with a secure connection to all other employees in the group. Suppose enough money is allotted to provide cable for 500 such connections. How many employees can be enrolled in the group?

Radio and telecommunications equipment installers and repairers held about 222,000 jobs in 2004.

Source: U.S. Department of Labor

REVIEW

11. Suppose a quadratic equation has only one real solution. What can you conclude about its discriminant? **(Lesson 9-6)**

In 12–15, determine whether the equation has 0, 1, or 2 real number solutions. (You do not need to find the solutions.) **(Lesson 9-6)**

12. $-a^2 + 3a - 5 = 0$

13. $b^2 + 4b + 4 = 0$

14. $2c(c - 5) = 11$

15. $3(d - 6) = 5(d^2 + 11)$

16. Find an equation for a parabola with vertex $(0, 0)$ that opens down. **(Lesson 9-1)**

17. **Skill Sequence** Solve the equation. **(Lessons 9-1, 8-6)**

a. $\sqrt{a} = 6$

b. $\sqrt{b + 8} = 6$

c. $\sqrt{4c - 5} = 6$

In **18** and **19**, use the figure at the right, which represents the front view of a building plan for a cottage. The cottage is to be **24 feet wide**. The edges $\overline{AC}$ and $\overline{BC}$ of the roof are to be equal in length and to meet at a right angle. **(Lessons 8-8, 8-7)**

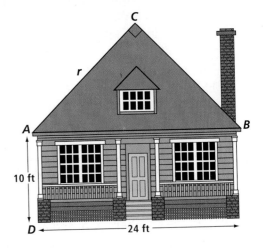

18. a. Find the length r of each edge as a simplified radical.

   b. Round the length of an edge to the nearest tenth of a foot.

19. Find BD.

20. True or False If the growth factor of an exponential growth situation is 2, then an equation that represents this situation is $y = 2 \cdot b^x$. **(Lesson 7-2)**

21. Consider the three points $(2, 1)$, $(-4, 31)$, and $(7, -24)$. **(Lessons 6-8, 6-3)**

   a. Show that these points lie on the same line.

   b. Write an equation for the line in standard form.

22. A school begins the year with 250 reams of paper. (A ream contains 500 sheets.) The teachers are using an average of 18 reams per week, and the school receives a shipment of 10 additional reams each week. **(Lesson 2-2)**

   a. How many reams will the school have after w weeks?

   b. Suppose the school year lasts 36 weeks. Assuming these rates continue, will the school run out of paper before the year ends?

EXPLORATION

23. Some telescopes use parabolic mirrors. Look on the Internet or in reference books to find out why it is useful to have mirrors shaped like parabolas and summarize your findings.

Chapter 9 Projects

1 Programming the Quadratic Formula

Use a computer or a graphing calculator to write a program that solves the equation $ax^2 + bx + c = 0$. The input of your program should be the numbers a, b, and c. Your program should state the number of real solutions and give them (if they exist). Your program should also work if $a = 0$.

2 Verifying Projectile Motion

For this project, you will need a device that can record video (such as a camcorder or a digital camera) and a television or computer on which to play the video you recorded. Have a friend throw a ball (or any other object), and use your recording device to film the path the ball takes. It is very important to keep the camera still the whole time, so be sure to stand far enough away from your friend. Tape a piece of tracing paper to a television. Play the video in slow motion and trace the path the ball takes. Does this path indeed seem to be a parabola? If possible, choose appropriate axes and find an equation for a parabola of best fit.

3 The Focus of a Parabola

Recall that a circle is the set of points at a fixed distance from a point called the center of the circle. Parabolas also have a definition involving distance from a special point called the *focus* of the parabola.

a. Look up this definition of a parabola, and write a paragraph that explains it.

b. Find out how the focus of a parabola is related to light reflecting from a mirror that is shaped like a parabola.

c. Parabolas are used in many manufactured items, such as satellite dishes and flashlights. Find three such uses that are related to the property you found in Part b, and explain why parabolas were used in these cases.

4 Checking Whether Points Lie on a Parabola

a. Use a calculator or a spreadsheet to find the values of x^2, for $x = 1, 2, 3, \ldots, 100$. Then calculate the differences between the values for consecutive numbers, and plot them. For example, $2^2 - 1^2 = 3$, so you would plot the point $(2, 3)$, $3^2 - 2^2 = 5$, so your plot should include the point $(3, 5)$. There would be 99 points in all. What is an equation of a function that includes all 99 ordered pairs?

b. Choose three numbers: a, b, and c, and repeat Part a using $ax^2 + bx + c$ instead of x^2.

c. Repeat Part a using x^3 instead of x^2, and then using 2^x instead of x^2. Are the points on these plots still on a single line?

d. Parts a, b, and c suggest a method for checking if a collection of points are all on a parabola. Describe this method.

5 Formulas for Sums of Consecutive Integers

In this chapter, you saw the formula $S = \dfrac{n(n + 1)}{2}$ for the sum of the integers from 1 to n.

a. Graph this formula for values of n, from 1 to 10.

b. Find and graph a formula for the sum of the even integers from 2 to $2n$.

c. Find and graph a formula for the sum of the multiples of 3 from 3 to $3n$.

d. Generalize Parts a, b, and c to find a formula for the sum of the multiples of k, from k to kn.

6 Catenaries, Parabolas, and a Famous Landmark

The Gateway Arch in St. Louis, Missouri is one of the most famous landmarks in the United States. At first view, the shape of the Arch appears to be a parabola.

a. In Lesson 9-7, a shape called a catenary was mentioned. This shape looks very much like a parabola. Find out if the shape of the Gateway Arch is a parabola or a catenary, and why one is a better choice than the other.

b. Use the Internet to find a picture of a catenary. Print a large copy of this image on a piece of paper. Next, create a graph of a parabola that looks similar to the catenary, and print it. Make sure both printouts have the same size. Using these printouts as guidelines, use clay (or any other sculpting medium) to create a parabolic and a catenary model of the Gateway Arch. Which seems to be more stable?

Chapter 9 Summary and Vocabulary

A **quadratic function** is a function f whose equation can be written in the form $f(x) = ax^2 + bx + c$ with $a \neq 0$. The simplest quadratic function is $f(x) = ax^2$. The **vertex** of the graph of $y = ax^2$ is at $(0, 0)$. The graph of $y = ax^2 + bx + c$ is a parabola symmetric to the vertical line through its vertex. If $a > 0$, the parabola opens up. If $a < 0$, the parabola opens down. To determine where this parabola crosses the horizontal line $y = k$, you can solve $ax^2 + bx + c = k$.

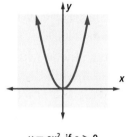

$y = ax^2$, if $a > 0$

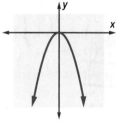

$y = ax^2$, if $a < 0$

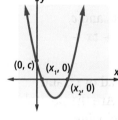

$y = ax^2 + bx + c$, if $a > 0$

Quadratic expressions, equations, and functions appear in a variety of situations. The word "squaring" comes from applications of quadratic expressions in such formulas as $A = s^2$ and $A = \pi r^2$. The **path of a projectile** can be described by a quadratic equation. The function whose input is the time t (in seconds) since launch and whose output is the height h (in feet) of the projectile has the formula $h = -16t^2 + vt + s$, where s is the height at launch and v is the upward launch velocity (in feet per second).

These situations, certain counting problems, and many geometric situations give rise to problems that can be solved by quadratic equations. The values of x that satisfy the equation $ax^2 + bx + c = 0$, where $a \neq 0$, can be found using the **Quadratic Formula**, $x = \dfrac{-b \pm \sqrt{b^2 - 4ac}}{2a}$.

The **discriminant** of the quadratic equation $ax^2 + bx + c = 0$ is $b^2 - 4ac$. If the discriminant is positive, there are two real solutions to the equation; if it is zero, there is one solution; and if it is negative, there are no real solutions.

Vocabulary

9-1
parabola
reflection-symmetric
axis of symmetry
vertex

9-4
force of gravity
initial upward velocity
initial height

9-5
quadratic equation
standard form of a
   quadratic equation

9-6
discriminant

Theorems and Properties

General Formula for the Height of a
   Projectile over Time (p. 546)

The Quadratic Formula (p. 553)
Discriminant Property (p. 561)

Chapter
9 Self-Test

Take this test as you would take a test in class. You will need a calculator. Then use the Selected Answers section in the back of the book to check your work.

In 1–6, find all real solutions. Round your answers to the nearest hundredth. If there are no real solutions, write that.

1. $2x^2 = 162$

2. $n^2 - 8n - 10 = 0$

3. $5y^2 - 1 = 11y$

4. $24 = \frac{1}{6}z^2$

5. $v^2 = 16v - 64$

6. $3p^2 - 9p + 7 = 0$

7. If the discriminant of a quadratic equation is 6, how many solutions does the equation have?

8. **Multiple Choice** Which of these graphs is of the equation $y = 1.75x^2$?

A
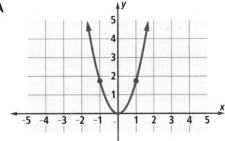

B
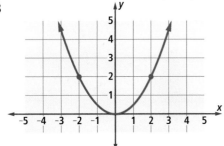

C
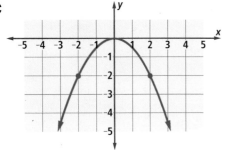

In 9 and 10, an equation is given.
   a. Make a table of values of x and y for integer values of x from $x = -3$ to $x = 3$.
   b. Graph the equation.

9. $y = 2x^2$

10. $y = -x^2 + 4x - 3$

In 11–13, consider the following. When a roller coaster goes down a hill, then $h = 0.049v^2$, where v is the velocity of the coaster (in meters per second) when it is h meters below the top of the hill.

11. Use the equation to determine at what distance below the top of the hill the roller coaster will reach a velocity of 20 meters per second.

12. Suppose the designer of the roller coaster builds the hill to be 44 meters high. At what velocity will the roller coaster be traveling when it reaches the bottom of the hill?

13. Currently the fastest wooden roller coaster is Son of Beast located at Kings Island in Cincinnati, Ohio. The maximum speed of the roller coaster is 35 meters per second. What is the height of the top of the hill?

14. The product of two consecutive integers, n and $n + 1$, is 1,722. If the integers are both negative, what are the numbers?

15. A circle and a rectangle have equal areas. One side of the rectangle is 6 inches longer than the other side, and the perimeter of the rectangle is 24. Calculate the radius of the circle, to the nearest hundredth.

In 16–18, use the parabola with vertex *V* below.

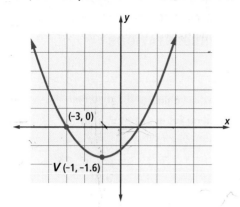

16. Find the minimum *y* value of the parabola.

17. Find the *x*-intercepts.

18. Find an equation for the axis of symmetry of the parabola.

In 19 and 20, a tennis ball is thrown from the top of a building. The graph below shows $h = -16t^2 + 40t + 50$, giving the height *h* of the ball in feet after *t* seconds.

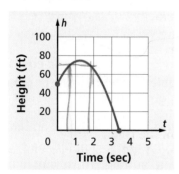

19. To the nearest hundredth of a second, how long does it take the ball to reach the ground?

20. At what times is the ball 70 feet above the ground? Give your answer to the nearest hundredth of a second.

21. **True or False** The parabola $y = \frac{1}{2}x^2 - 7x - 35$ opens down.

22. Suppose that the quadratic equation $ax^2 - 5x + 3 = 0$ has a discriminant of 1. Find the value of *a*.

In 23 and 24, use the discriminant to give the number of real solutions to the equation.

23. $-3x^2 + 12x - 7 = 0$

24. $x^2 - 4x = -4$

$$x^2 - 4x + 4 = 0$$

$$\frac{4 \pm \sqrt{4^2 - 4(1)(4)}}{2} =$$

Chapter 9 Chapter Review

SKILLS Procedures used to get answers

OBJECTIVE A Solve quadratic equations of the form $ax^2 = b$. (Lesson 9-2)

In 1–8, solve without using the Quadratic Formula.

1. $4x^2 = 676$

2. $9 = \frac{1}{4}h^2$

3. $k^2 + 15 = 100$

4. $t^2 - 11 = 11$

5. $2(m + 3)^2 = 72$

6. $69 = 5 + 2y^2$

7. $\frac{63}{16} = 7(4 - v)^2$

8. $(6w - 1)^2 = \frac{25}{4}$

OBJECTIVE B Solve quadratic equations using the Quadratic Formula. (Lessons 9-5, 9-6)

In 9–18, solve the equation using the Quadratic Formula. Round your answers to the nearest hundredth.

9. $m^2 + 7m + 12 = 0$

10. $14x = x^2 + 49$

11. $y^2 - 6y = 3$ $y^2 - 6y - 3 = 0$

12. $r^2 - \frac{11}{7} = \frac{4}{5}r$

13. $0 = p^2 + 10(p + 2.5)$ $p^2 (p + 2.5) + 10$

14. $\frac{3}{4}x^2 - \frac{2}{3}x = 2$

15. $5n^2 + 9n = 2$ $5n^2 + 9n - 2 = 0$

16. $2a^2 - 8a = -8$

17. $b^2 + 5.4b - 19.75 = 0$

18. $30 + 5(2z^2 - 10z) = 0$

PROPERTIES The principles behind the mathematics

OBJECTIVE C Identify and use the properties of solutions to quadratic equations. (Lesson 9-6)

19. Give the values of x that satisfy the equation $ax^2 + bx + c = 0$.

20. **True or False** If a quadratic equation has two solutions, then it has two x-intercepts.

In 21 and 22, calculate the discriminant.

21. $x^2 + 4x - 8 = 0$

22. $7y^2 - y = 1$

23. If the discriminant of the quadratic equation $x^2 + bx + 2 = 0$ is 8, find the possible value(s) of b.

In 24–27, find the number of real solutions to the equation by using the discriminant.

24. $g^2 - 3g - 8 = 0$

25. $3v = 2v^2 + 4$

26. $m^2 = 6m - 9$

27. $w(w - 2) = -8$

USES Applications of mathematics in real-world situations

OBJECTIVE D Use quadratic equations to solve problems about paths of projectiles. (Lessons 9-2, 9-4)

28. Regina is a track and field athlete competing in the shot put, an event that requires "putting" (throwing in a pushing motion) a heavy metal ball (the "shot") as far as possible. The height of the ball h when it is x feet from Regina can be described by the quadratic equation $h = -0.021x^2 + 0.6x + 6$.

   a. At what distances from Regina will the shot put be at a height of 8 feet? Round your answers to the nearest hundredth.

   b. Will Regina's shot put travel 38 feet, the distance needed to win the event? Justify your answer.

In 29 and 30, when an object is dropped near the surface of a planet or moon, the distance d (in feet) it falls in t seconds is given by the formula $d = \frac{1}{2}gt^2$, where g is the acceleration due to gravity. Near Earth $g \approx 32$ ft/sec^2, and near Earth's moon $g \approx 5.3$ ft/sec^2.

29. A skydiver jumps from a plane at an altitude of 10,000 feet. She begins her descent in "free fall," that is, without opening the parachute.

   a. How far will she fall in 15 seconds?

   b. The diver plans to open the parachute after she has fallen 6,000 feet. How many seconds after jumping will this take place?

30. An astronaut on the moon drops a hammer from a height of 6 feet.

   a. How long will it take the hammer to hit the ground?

   b. Suppose the astronaut is back on Earth and drops a hammer from a height of 6 feet. How long will it take the hammer to hit the ground?

31. Refer to the graph below of $h = -4.9t^2 + 20t$, which shows the height (in meters) of a ball t seconds after it is thrown from ground level at an initial upward velocity of 20 meters per second.

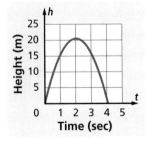

   a. Give the height of the ball after 1 second.

   b. Find when the ball will reach a height of 15 meters.

   c. Use the Quadratic Formula to calculate how long the ball will be in the air.

OBJECTIVE E Solve geometric problems involving quadratic equations. (Lessons 9-2, 9-7)

32. Suppose a rectangle has length $2x$ inches and width $x + 3$ inches. Find the length and width given that the area of the rectangle is 5.625 square inches.

33. Consider the rectangular region below. Luisa has 120 meters of fencing to build a fence around her yard.

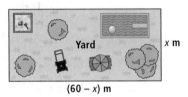

   a. Use the diagram to write an equation for the area A enclosed by the fencing.

   b. What value of x will result in the greatest possible area enclosed by the fencing?

34. Refer to the triangle below. If the area of the triangle is 18 square inches and the base of the triangle is 4 inches shorter than its height, find the length of the base of the triangle. Round your answer to the nearest hundredth of an inch.

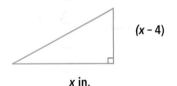

OBJECTIVE F Solve other real-world problems involving quadratic functions. (Lesson 9-7)

35. The relationship between elevation above sea level in kilometers, e, and the boiling point of water in degrees Celsius, t, can be approximated by the equation $e = t^2 - 200.58t + 10{,}058$. Water boils at lower temperatures at higher elevations. Find the boiling point of water at the top of Mt. Ararat in Turkey, which is 5,166 meters high.

36. Consider the formula $d = \frac{n(n-3)}{2}$, where d is the number of diagonals of an n-sided convex polygon.

    a. How many diagonals does a dodecagon (12-sided polygon) have?

    b. Is it possible for a polygon to have 27 diagonals? If so, how many sides does that polygon have?

37. A financial analyst working for an investment company projects the net profit P (in millions of dollars) of the company to be modeled by the equation $P = 4.23t^2 - 5.32t + 3.86$, where t is the number of years since 2005.

    a. Use the analyst's model to predict whether the net profit will reach 100 million dollars in 2011.

    b. Calculate, to the nearest tenth, when the company's net profit is projected to reach 75 million dollars.

REPRESENTATIONS Pictures, graphs, or objects that illustrate concepts

OBJECTIVE G Graph equations of the form $y = ax^2$ and interpret these graphs. (Lesson 9-1)

In 38 and 39, an equation is given.

    a. Make a table of values.

    b. Graph the equation.

38. $y = 7x^2$ **39.** $y = \frac{3}{5}x^2$

40. Consider the quadratic equation $y = -1.5x^2$.

    a. Graph the equation.

    b. Determine the coordinates of the vertex.

    c. Tell whether the vertex is a maximum or a minimum.

41. Multiple Choice Which equation is graphed below?

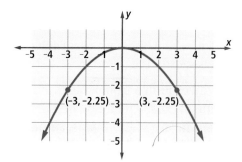

    A $y = -4x^2$ **B** $y = -\frac{1}{4}x^2$

    C $y = \frac{1}{4}x^2$ **D** $y = 4x^2$

42. True or False The axis of symmetry for the parabola with equation $y = 2x^2$ is the line $x = 0$.

OBJECTIVE H Graph equations of the form $y = ax^2 + bx + c$ and interpret these graphs. (Lesson 9-3)

43. Use the parabola with vertex V below.

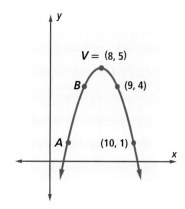

    a. What is the maximum value of the function?

    b. What is an equation for its axis of symmetry?

    c. Find the coordinates of points A and B, the reflection images of the named points over the parabola's axis of symmetry.

In 44 and 45, answer *true* or *false*.

44. Every parabola has a minimum value.

45. The parabola $y = -4x^2 + 2x - 13$ opens down.

46. What equation must you solve to find the x-intercepts of the parabola $y = ax^2 + bx + c$?

47. The parabola $y = \frac{1}{8}x^2 - 6x + 22$ has x-intercepts 4 and 44. Find the coordinates of its vertex without graphing.

48. A table of values for a parabola is given below.

x	0	2	4	6	8	10	12
y	?	?	−6	−8	−6	0	10

a. Complete the table.

b. Write an equation for the parabola's axis of symmetry.

c. What are the coordinates of its vertex?

49. Consider the quadratic equation $y = -x^2 - 4x + 3$.

a. Make a table of x and y values for integer values of $-5 \le x \le 1$.

b. Graph the equation.

c. Determine whether the vertex is a minimum or a maximum.

50. Which of these is the graph of $y = x^2 - 4x + 5$?

A

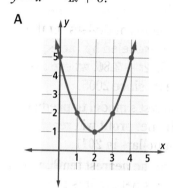

B

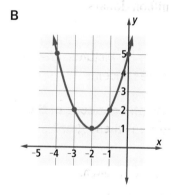

Chapter

10 Linear Systems

The table and graph below display the men's and women's winning times in the Olympic 100-meter freestyle swimming race for each Summer Olympic year from 1912 to 2004.

Year	Men's Time (sec)	Women's Time (sec)	Year	Men's Time (sec)	Women's Time (sec)
1912	63.4	82.2	1968	52.2	60.0
1920	60.4	73.6	1972	51.22	58.59
1924	59.0	72.4	1976	49.99	55.65
1928	58.6	71.0	1980	50.40	54.79
1932	58.2	66.8	1984	49.80	55.92
1936	57.6	65.9	1988	48.63	54.93
1948	57.3	66.3	1992	49.02	54.64
1952	57.4	66.8	1996	48.74	54.50
1956	55.4	62.0	2000	48.30	53.83
1960	55.2	61.2	2004	48.17	53.84
1964	53.4	59.5			

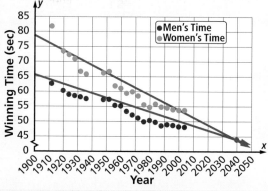

Source: *The World Almanac and Book of Facts*

The graph shows two trends. First, both men's and women's Olympic winning times have been decreasing rather steadily since 1912. Second, the women's winning time has been decreasing faster than the men's winning times. Regression lines have been fitted to the data. These lines have the following equations: $y = -0.1627x + 372.99$ (men) and $y = -0.269x + 589.83$ (women), where x is the year and y is the winning time in seconds. The lines intersect near (2040, 41).

This means that if the winning times were to continue to decrease at the rates they have been decreasing, the women's winning time will be about equal to the men's in the Olympic year 2040. The winning times will then each be about 41 seconds.

Finding points of intersection of lines or other curves by working with their equations is called *solving a system*. In this chapter you will learn various ways of solving systems.

Lesson

10-1

An Introduction to Systems

Vocabulary

system

solution to a system

empty set, null set

▶ **BIG IDEA** Solving a system of equations means finding all the solutions that are common to the equations.

A **system** is a set of equations or inequalities joined by the word *and,* that together describe a single situation. The two equations at the beginning of this chapter describing the winning Olympic times of men and women in the 100-meter freestyle events are an example of a system of equations.

Systems are often signaled by using a single left-hand brace { in place of the word *and.* So we can write this system as $\begin{cases} y = -0.1627x + 372.99 \\ y = -0.269x + 589.83 \end{cases}$.

When you write a system in this way, it is helpful to align the equal signs under one another.

Mental Math

a. How many quarters make $10.50?

b. How many dimes make $10.50?

c. How many nickels make $10.50?

What Is a Solution to a System?

A **solution to a system** of equations with two variables is an ordered pair (x, y) that satisfies both equations in the system.

Example 1

Consider the system $\begin{cases} y = 3x - 7 \\ 2y - 2x = 10 \end{cases}$.

a. Verify that the ordered pair (6, 11) is a solution to the system.

b. Show that (1, −4) is *not* a solution to the system.

Solutions

a. In each equation, replace x with 6 and y with 11.

First equation: $y = 3x - 7$

Does $11 = 3 \cdot 6 - 7$?

$11 = 18 - 7$ Yes.

Second equation: $2y - 2x = 10$

Does $2 \cdot 11 - 2 \cdot 6 = 10$?

$22 - 12 = 10$ Yes.

(6, 11) is a solution because it satisfies both equations.

Swimmer Larsen Jensen of the United States celebrates his silver medal after finishing second in the 1500-meter freestyle during the 2004 Summer Olympic Games in Athens, Greece.

b. Substitute 1 for x and −4 for y in both equations. The pair (1, −4) is a solution to the first equation because $-4 = 3 \cdot 1 - 7$. However, $2 \cdot -4 - 2 \cdot 1 = -10 \neq 10$. So (1, −4) is not a solution to the system.

STOP QY

> ▶ QY
>
> Is the ordered pair (2, −1) a solution to the system in Example 1?

Solving Systems by Graphing

You can find the solutions to a system of equations with two variables by graphing each equation and finding the coordinates of the point(s) of intersection of the graphs.

Example 2

A second-grade class has 23 students. There are 5 more boys than girls. Solve a system of equations to determine how many boys and how many girls are in the class.

Solution Translate the conditions into a system of two equations. Let x be the number of boys and y be the number of girls. Because there are 23 students, $x + y = 23$. Because there are 5 more boys than girls, $y + 5 = x$. The situation is described by the system $\begin{cases} x + y = 23 \\ y + 5 = x \end{cases}$.

Graph the equations and identify the point of intersection.

There are 14 boys and 9 girls in the class. The solution is (14, 9), as graphed on the next page.

Check To check that (14, 9) is a solution, $x = 14$ and $y = 9$ must be checked in both equations.

Is (14, 9) a solution to $x + y = 23$? Does $14 + 9 = 23$? Yes.

Is (14, 9) a solution to $y + 5 = x$? Does $9 + 5 = 14$? Yes.

Old lady at 12:00!

A total of 49.6 million children attended public and private schools in the United States in 2003.

Source: U.S. Census Bureau

The two conditions about the numbers of boys and girls can be seen by looking at tables of solutions for each equation.

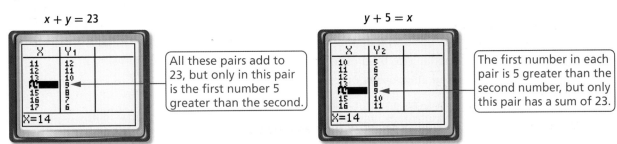

$x + y = 23$

X	Y₁
11	12
12	11
13	10
14	9
15	8
16	7
17	6
X=14	

All these pairs add to 23, but only in this pair is the first number 5 greater than the second.

$y + 5 = x$

X	Y₂
10	5
11	6
12	7
13	8
14	9
15	10
16	11
X=14	

The first number in each pair is 5 greater than the second number, but only this pair has a sum of 23.

An Introduction to Systems **583**

In general, there are four ways to indicate the solution to a system. They are shown below using the solution to the system in Example 2.

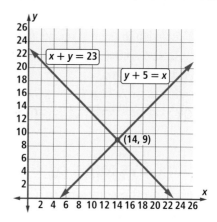

As an ordered pair	(14, 9)
As an ordered pair identifying the variables	$(x, y) = (14, 9)$
By naming the variables individually	$x = 14$ and $y = 9$
As a set of ordered pairs	{(14, 9)}

Systems with No Solutions

When the sentences in a system have no solutions in common, we say that there is no solution to the system. We cannot write the solution as an ordered pair or by listing the elements. The solution set is the set with no elements { }, written with the special symbol Ø. This set is called the **empty set** or **null set.**

GUIDED

Example 3

Find all solutions to the system $\begin{cases} y = -x + 4 \\ y = -x - 2 \end{cases}$.

Solution Graph both equations using a graphing calculator.

1. How many times do the lines appear to intersect? ___?___

2. What is the slope of each line? ___?___

3. If two lines in a plane do not intersect, they are called ___?___ lines.

Now look at the table of values on the graphing calculator.

4. Is there an ordered pair common to both lines? ___?___

This is an example of a system of equations for which there is no solution. The solution set is Ø.

Cost and Revenue Equations

In manufacturing, a *cost equation* describes the cost y of making x products. *Fixed costs* are things like rent and employee salaries, which must be paid regardless of the number of products made. *Variable costs* include materials and shipping, which depend upon how many products are made. The total of fixed and variable costs is the amount of money the business pays out each month.

A *revenue equation* describes the amount y that a business earns by selling x products. The *break-even point* is the point at which the revenue and total costs are the same. This point tells the manufacturer how many items must be sold in order to make a profit.

Example 4

A manufacturer of T-shirts has monthly fixed costs of $8,000, and the cost to produce each shirt is $3.40. Therefore, the cost y to produce x shirts is given by $y = 8{,}000 + 3.40x$. The business sells shirts to stores for $9 each. So the revenue equation is $y = 9x$. Find the break-even point for the shirt manufacturer.

Solution The break-even point can be found by solving the system $\begin{cases} y = 8{,}000 + 3.40x \\ y = 9x \end{cases}$.

Make a table to help you find reasonable x and y values to use in setting the window. The table below shows that the intersection point will be seen in the window $1{,}400 \le x \le 1{,}500$, $12{,}600 \le y \le 13{,}500$.

Children are shown silk-screening T-shirts. Silk-screening is a process in which color is forced into material like fabric or paper through a silk screen.

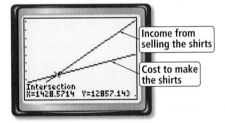

The INTERSECT command on a calculator shows that the point (1,429, 12,858) is an approximate solution. At the break-even point, 1,429 shirts are manufactured and sold. It costs about the same amount to make the shirts as the manufacturer earns from selling them. If more than 1,429 shirts are produced and sold, the business will earn a profit.

Check When $x = \$1{,}429$ in the cost equation, $y = \$8{,}000 + 3.40 \cdot \$1{,}429 = \$12{,}858.60$. When $x = 1{,}429$ in the revenue equation, $y = 9 \cdot \$1{,}429 = \$12{,}861$. These values are close enough to make 1,429 the first coordinate of the break-even point.

In Example 4, the solution is an approximation. When solutions do not have integer coordinates, it is likely that reading a graph will give you only an estimate. But graphs can be created quickly. In the next few lessons, you will learn algebraic techniques to find exact solutions to systems.

Questions

1. **True or False** When a system has two variables, each solution to the system is an ordered pair.

2. What does the brace { represent in a system?

3. a. Verify that $(8, -2)$ is a solution to the system $\begin{cases} -x = 4y \\ 2x + 3y = 10 \end{cases}$.
   b. Write this solution in two other ways.

4. Show that $(11, 8)$ is *not* a solution to $\begin{cases} y = x - 3 \\ x + 5y = 50 \end{cases}$.

5. Refer to the graph at the right.

   a. What system is represented?

   b. What is the solution to the system?

   c. Verify your answer to Part b.

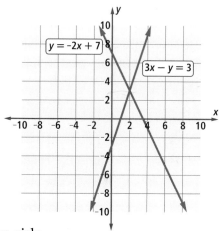

In 6 and 7, a system is given.
   a. **Solve the system by graphing.**
   b. **Check your solution.**

6. $\begin{cases} y = -\frac{1}{2}x + 3 \\ y = 2x - 7 \end{cases}$
7. $\begin{cases} y = x \\ 4x - 2y = 12 \end{cases}$

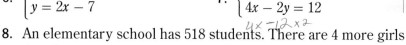

8. An elementary school has 518 students. There are 4 more girls than boys.

   a. If g is the number of girls and b is the number of boys, translate the given information into two equations.

   b. Letting $x = g$ and $y = b$, graph the equations on a calculator.

   c. Using the graph from Part b, use the **INTERSECT** command to find the number of boys and girls in the school.

9. A small business makes wooden toy trains. The business has fixed expenses of $3,800 each month. In addition to this, the production of each train costs $4.25. The business sells the trains to stores for $12.50 each.

   a. Write cost and revenue equations as a system.

   b. Use a calculator table to find a good window to display the graph. What window did you use?

   c. Find the break-even point.

   d. Last month the business made and sold 518 trains. Did the business earn a profit?

10. Find all solutions to the system $\begin{cases} y = 3x - 5 \\ y = 3x - 1 \end{cases}$.

Archaeologists have discovered jointed wooden dolls, carved horses, chariots, and even a crocodile with moveable jaws that date back to the year 1100 BCE.

Source: *TDmonthly*

11. Consider the system $\begin{cases} y_1 = 2x + 5 \\ y_2 = 3x \end{cases}$.

The screen at the right shows solutions to $y_1 = 2x + 5$. Make a column for y_2 and use it to find the ordered pair that also satisfies $y_2 = 3x$, and therefore is a solution to the system.

APPLYING THE MATHEMATICS

12. The sum of two numbers is –19 and their difference is –5. Write a system of equations and solve it using a graph.

13. Below are a table and graph of the winning times in seconds for the Olympic men's and women's 100-meter backstroke events.

Year	Men's Time	Women's Time	Year	Men's Time	Women's Time
1924	73.2	83.2	1972	56.58	65.78
1928	68.2	82.0	1976	55.49	61.83
1932	68.6	79.4	1980	56.33	60.86
1936	65.9	78.9	1984	55.79	62.55
1948	66.4	74.4	1988	55.05	60.89
1952	65.4	74.3	1992	53.98	60.68
1956	62.2	72.9	1996	54.10	61.19
1960	61.9	69.3	2000	53.72	61.21
1964	NA	67.7	2004	54.06	60.37
1968	58.7	66.2			

Source: International Olympic Committee

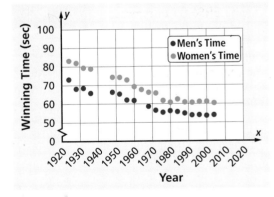

In Lesson 4-4, you were asked to estimate when the women's time might equal the men's time. Now repeat this question by finding equations for lines of best fit for the men's and women's times. Graph the two equations. According to these lines, will the women's winning time ever equal the men's winning time in the 100-meter backstroke? If yes, estimate the year when this will happen. If no, explain why not.

14. Buffy is hosting a meeting and plans to serve 4 dozen muffins. She wants to have twice as many blueberry muffins as plain muffins. The table at the right shows some of the possible ways to order 4 dozen muffins.

    a. Using x for the number of plain muffins and y for the number of blueberry muffins, write a system of equations to describe this situation.

    b. Graph your equations from Part a to find how many of each kind Buffy should order.

Number of Plain Muffins	Number of Blueberry Muffins
0	48
10	38
20	28
30	18
40	8
48	0

REVIEW

15. **Skill Sequence** Solve each equation. (Lessons 9-5, 4-4, 3-4)

    a. $5x + 6 = 3$

    b. $5x + 6 = 2x + 3$

    c. $5x + 6 = 2x^2 + 3$

    d. $5x + 6 = 2x(x + 1)$

In 16–18, simplify the expression. (Lessons 8-4, 8-3, 8-2)

16. $m^2 \cdot n^3 \cdot m \cdot n^4$

17. $(-5x^7y^9)^4$

18. $\dfrac{18r^2s^3}{6rs^4}$

19. Graph $\{(x, y): 4x - 8y < 2\}$. (Lesson 6-9)

20. Find the values of the variables so that the given point lies on the graph of $10x - 4y = 20$. (Lessons 6-8, 4-7)

    a. $(5, p)$

    b. $(q, -2)$

    c. $(r, 0)$

21. Two workers can dig a 20-foot well in 2 days. How long will it take 6 workers to dig a 90-foot well, assuming that each of these 6 workers dig at the same rate as each of the 2 workers? (Lessons 5-4, 5-3)

Two men stand above a well that serves as an extractor of gold.

EXPLORATION

22. Some experts believe that even though the women's swim times are decreasing faster than the men's, it is the ratio of the times that is the key to predictions.

    a. Compute the ratio of the men's time to the women's time for the 100-meter freestyle for each Olympic year in Question 13.

    b. Graph your results.

    c. What do you think the ratio will be in the year 2020? Does this agree with the prediction in Question 13?

QY ANSWER

no

Lesson 10-2

Solving Systems Using Substitution

▶ **BIG IDEA** Substituting an expression that equals a single variable is an effective first step for solving some systems.

When equations for lines in a system are in $y = mx + b$ form, a method of solving called *substitution* can be very efficient. Example 1 illustrates this method.

Example 1

Solve the system $\begin{cases} y = 7x + 25 \\ y = -5x - 11 \end{cases}$ using substitution.

Solution Because $7x + 25$ and $-5x - 11$ both equal y, they must equal each other. Substitute one of them for y in the other equation.

$7x + 25 = -5x - 11$	Substitution
$12x + 25 = -11$	Add $5x$ to both sides.
$12x = -36$	Subtract 25 from both sides.
$x = -3$	Divide both sides by 12.

Now you know $x = -3$. However, you must still solve for y. You can substitute -3 for x into either of the original equations. We choose the first equation.

$y = 7x + 25$

$y = 7(-3) + 25$

$y = -21 + 25$

$y = 4$

The solution is $x = -3$ and $y = 4$, or just $(-3, 4)$.

STOP QY

Check A graph shows that the lines with equations $y = 7x + 25$ and $y = -5x - 11$ intersect at $(-3, 4)$.

Suppose two quantities are increasing or decreasing at different constant rates. Then each quantity can be described by an equation of the form $y = mx + b$. To find out when the quantities are equal, you can solve a system using substitution. Example 2 illustrates this idea.

Mental Math

Find the greatest common factor.

a. 15; 200

b. 1,500; 20,000

c. 14; 26; 53

d. 1,400; 2,600; 5,300

▶ **QY**

Check that $(-3, 4)$ is a solution to $y = -5x - 11$.

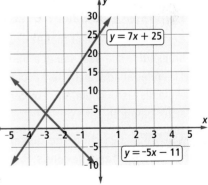

Example 2

The Rapid Taxi Company charges $2.15 for a taxi ride plus 20¢ for each $\frac{1}{10}$ mile traveled. A competitor, Carl's Cabs, charges $1.50 for a taxi ride plus 25¢ for each $\frac{1}{10}$ mile traveled. For what distance do the rides cost the same?

Solution Let $d =$ the distance of a cab ride in tenths of a mile.

Let $C =$ the cost of a cab ride of distance d.
Rapid Taxi: $C = 2.15 + 0.20d$
Carl's Cabs: $C = 1.50 + 0.25d$

The rides cost the same when the values of C and d for Rapid Taxi equal the values for Carl's Cabs, so we need to solve the system formed by these two equations. Substitute $2.15 + 0.20d$ for C in the second equation.

$2.15 + 0.20d = 1.50 + 0.25d$

Now solve.

$\quad\quad 0.65 = 0.05d \quad$ Add −1.50 and −0.20d to both sides.
$\quad\quad\quad\quad d = 13 \quad$ Divide both sides by 0.05.

The two companies charge the same amount for a ride that is 13 tenths of a mile long, or 1.3 miles long.

Check Check to see if the cost will be the same for a ride of 13 tenths of a mile.
The cost for Rapid Taxi is $2.15 + 0.20 \cdot 13 = 2.15 + 2.60 = 4.75$.
The cost for Carl's Cabs is $1.50 + 0.25 \cdot 13 = 1.50 + 3.25 = 4.75$.
The cost is $4.75 from each company, so the answer checks.

The average taxi fare in New York in 2006 was $9.65.

Source: MSNBC

In Example 2, Carl's Cabs is cheaper at first, but as the number of miles increases, the prices become closer. Eventually the price for Carl's Cabs catches up with Rapid Taxi's price, and then Carl's is more expensive than Rapid. The next example also involves "catching up."

GUIDED

Example 3

Bart was so confident that he could run faster than his little sister that he bragged, "I can beat you in a 50-meter race. I'm so sure that I'll give you a 10-meter head start!" Bart could run at a speed of 4 meters per second, while his sister could run 3 meters per second. Could Bart catch up to his sister before the end of the race?

Solution Let d be the distance that Bart and his sister have traveled after t seconds. Recall that distance = rate · time.

For Bart, $d = 4t$.

Because Bart gives his sister a 10-meter head start, $d = 10 + 3t$. To know the time t when Bart will catch up to his sister, solve the system.

$$\begin{cases} d = \underline{?} \\ d = \underline{?} \end{cases}$$

Substitute $4t$ for d in the second equation.

$$\underline{?} = \underline{?} + \underline{?}$$

Solve this equation as you would any other.

$$t = \underline{?}$$

This means that after 10 seconds, Bart and his sister are at the same point. However, is the race finished at 10 seconds? Substitute 10 for t to find the distance. In 10 seconds Bart has run 40 meters. Because the race is 50 meters long, the race is not over when Bart catches up to his sister. Therefore, Bart wins.

Questions

COVERING THE IDEAS

In 1–5, a system is given.
  a. Use substitution to find the solution.
  b. Check your answer.

1. $\begin{cases} y = 3x - 4 \\ y = 5x - 10 \end{cases}$

2. $\begin{cases} b = 48 + a \\ b = 60 - a \end{cases}$

3. $\begin{cases} y = -\frac{1}{9}x + 6 \\ y = \frac{5}{3}x + 38 \end{cases}$

4. $\begin{cases} x = \frac{2}{3}y - 8 \\ x = -12.5y + 150 \end{cases}$

5. $\begin{cases} m = 8n + 33 \\ m = 3n - 78 \end{cases}$

6. Suppose that in Freeport, a taxi ride costs $2.50 plus 15¢ for each $\frac{1}{10}$ mile traveled. In Geneva, a taxi ride costs $1.70 plus 20¢ for each $\frac{1}{10}$ mile traveled. Write a system of equations and solve it to find the distance for which the costs are the same.

7. Recall from Example 3 that Bart ran 4 meters per second and his sister ran 3 meters per second. Bart's sister said to him, "You'll beat me if I have only a 10-meter head start. I'll race you if you give me a 15-meter head start." Solve a system of equations to find out if she would then beat him in a 50-meter race.

8. A tomato canning company has fixed monthly costs of $4,200. There are additional costs of $2.35 to produce each case of canned tomatoes. The company sells tomatoes to grocery stores for $5.85 per case.

a. Write a system of equations to describe this situation.

b. How many cases must the company sell to break even?

c. Check your solution.

Approximately 124,900 acres of tomatoes were harvested in the United States in 2002.

Source: U.S. Department of Agriculture

APPLYING THE MATHEMATICS

9. A car leaves a gas station traveling at 60 mph. The driver has accidentally left his credit card at the gas station. Six minutes later, his friend leaves the station with the credit card, traveling at 65 mph to catch up to him.

a. Write two equations to indicate the distance d that each car is from the gas station t hours after the first car leaves.

b. Solve the system to determine when the second car will catch up to the first car.

c. How far will they have traveled from the gas station when they meet?

10. Cameron has $450 and saves $12 a week. Sean has only $290, but is saving $20 a week.

a. After how many weeks will they each have the same amount of money?

b. How much money will each person have then?

11. In 2000, the metropolitan area of Dallas had about 5,200,000 people and was growing at about 120,000 people a year. In 2000, the metropolitan area of Boston had about 4,400,000 people and was growing at about 25,000 people a year.

a. If these trends had been this way for quite some time, in what year did Dallas and Boston have the same population?

b. What was this population?

12. In July 2005, Philadelphia approved taxi fares with an initial charge of $2.30 and an additional charge of $0.30 for each $\frac{1}{7}$ mile. If $P(x)$ is the cost for taking a taxi x miles, then $P(x) = 2.30 + 0.30 \cdot 7x$. In October 2005, Atlanta established new taxi fares with an initial charge of $2.50 and an additional charge of $0.25 for each $\frac{1}{8}$ mile. If $A(x)$ is the cost of taking a taxi x miles in Atlanta, then $A(x) = 2.50 + 0.25 \cdot 8x$. Solve a system to approximate at what distance the fares for Philadelphia and Atlanta are the same.

13. One plumbing company charges $55 for the first half hour of work and $25 for each additional half hour. Another company charges $35 for the first half hour and then $30 for each additional half hour. For how many hours of work will the cost of each company be the same?

In **14** and **15**, a system that involves a quadratic equation is given. Each system has two solutions.
    a. Solve the system by substitution.
    b. Check your answers.

14. $\begin{cases} y = \frac{1}{9}x^2 \\ y = 4x \end{cases}$
                15. $\begin{cases} y = 2x^2 + 5x - 3 \\ y = x^2 - 2x + 5 \end{cases}$

REVIEW

16. Consider the system $\begin{cases} y = 20x + 8 \\ 24x - y = -6 \end{cases}$. Verify that $\left(\frac{1}{2}, 18\right)$ is a solution to the system, but that $(1, 20)$ is not. (**Lesson 10-1**)

In **17** and **18**, solve the system of equations by graphing. (**Lesson 10-1**)

17. the system in Question 3

18. the system in Question 4

19. **a.** Simplify $y(y - 9) + 4y + 1$.
    b. Solve $y(y - 9) = 4y + 1$. (**Lesson 9-5**)

20. **Skill Sequence** Solve each equation. (**Lessons 9-1, 8-6**)
    a. $n^2 = 16$ **b.** $\sqrt{n} = 16$ **c.** $\sqrt{n^2} = 16$

21. What is the cost of x basketballs at $18 each and y footballs at $25 each? (**Lessons 5-3, 1-2**)

EXPLORATION

22. Find the taxi rates where you live or in a nearby community. Graph the rates to show how they compare to those in Question 12.

Lesson

10-3

More Uses of Substitution

> ▶ **BIG IDEA** Substitution is a reasonable method to solve systems whenever you can easily solve for one variable in an equation.

In the previous lesson, you saw how to use substitution as a technique to solve systems of equations when the same variable was alone on one side of each equation. Substitution may also be used in other situations. Here is a typical situation that lends itself to substitution.

Mental Math

Estimate between two consecutive integers.

a. $\sqrt{26}$

b. $\sqrt{171}$

c. $-\sqrt{171}$

Example 1

A grandfather likes to play guessing games with his grandchildren. One day he tells them, "I have only dimes and quarters in my pocket. They are worth $3.85. I have 14 fewer quarters than dimes. How many of each coin do I have?" Use a system of equations to answer his question.

Solution Translate each condition into an equation. Let D equal the number of dimes and Q equal the number of quarters. Dimes are worth $0.10 each, so D dimes are worth $0.10D$. Quarters are worth $0.25 each, so Q quarters are worth $0.25Q$. The total value of all the coins is $3.85. So $0.10D + 0.25Q = 3.85$.

There are 14 fewer quarters than dimes. That leads to a second equation $Q = D - 14$. Together the two equations form a system.

$$\begin{cases} 0.10D + 0.25Q = 3.85 \\ Q = D - 14 \end{cases}$$

Because $Q = D - 14$, substitute $D - 14$ for Q in the first equation.

$0.10D + 0.25(D - 14) = 3.85$ Substitution

$0.10D + 0.25D - 0.25(14) = 3.85$ Distributive Property

$0.10D + 0.25D - 3.5 = 3.85$ Arithmetic

$0.35D - 3.5 = 3.85$ Collect like terms.

$0.35D = 7.35$ Add 3.5 to both sides.

$D = 21$ Divide both sides by 0.35.

a grandfather posing with his three grandchildren

To find Q, substitute 21 for D in either equation. We use the second equation because it is solved for Q. When $D = 21$, $Q = D - 14 = 21 - 14 = 7$. So $(D, Q) = (21, 7)$. The grandfather has 21 dimes and 7 quarters.

Check The 21 dimes are worth $2.10 and the 7 quarters are worth $1.75.
$2.10 + $1.75 = $3.85

In Chapter 6, you used the slope and *y*-intercept to find an equation of a line that passes through two given points. A different method for finding an equation through two points makes use of a system of equations.

Example 2

Find an equation of the line that passes through the points $(3, 26)$ and $(-2, 1)$.

Solution In slope-intercept form, the equation of the line is $y = mx + b$. If the values of m and b were known, each point on the line would make the equation true.

Substitute the coordinates of each given point for x and y to get two equations.

Using $(3, 26)$, $26 = m \cdot 3 + b$.

Using $(-2, 1)$, $1 = m \cdot -2 + b$.

This gives the system $\begin{cases} 26 = 3m + b \\ 1 = -2m + b \end{cases}$.

Either equation can be solved for b. From the second equation, $b = 2m + 1$. Now substitute $2m + 1$ for b in the first equation.

$26 = 3m + (2m + 1)$

$26 = 5m + 1$

$25 = 5m$

$5 = m$

This is the slope of the line. To find b, substitute 5 for m in either of the original equations. We use the second equation.

$1 = -2m + b$

$1 = -2 \cdot 5 + b$

$1 = -10 + b$

$11 = b$

This is the *y*-intercept. Thus, an equation of the line through $(3, 26)$ and $(-2, 1)$ is $y = 5x + 11$.

(continued on next page)

Check Does each ordered pair satisfy the equation of the line?

Does $26 = 5 \cdot 3 + 11$? Yes, $26 = 15 + 11$.

Does $(3, 26)$ satisfy $y = 5x + 11$? Yes, $(3, 26)$ is on the line.

Does $1 = 5 \cdot -2 + 11$? Yes, $1 = -10 + 11$.

Does $(-2, 1)$ satisfy $y = 5x + 11$? Yes, $(-2, 1)$ is on the line.

Some situations have been around for generations. Example 3 is taken from an 1881 algebra text; the prices are out of date, but the situation is not.

GUIDED

Example 3

A farmer purchased 100 acres of land for $2,450. He paid $20 per acre for part of it and $30 per acre for the rest. How many acres were there in each part?

Solution You want to find two amounts, so use two variables.

Let $x =$ the number of acres at $20/acre,

and $y =$ the number of acres at $30/acre.

The farmer purchased a total of 100 acres, so $x + y = 100$.

The total cost is $2,450. So $20x + 30y = 2,450$.

Solve the system of these two equations.

$$\begin{cases} x + y = 100 \\ 20x + 30y = 2,450 \end{cases}$$

Although neither equation is solved for a variable, the first equation is equivalent to $y = \underline{\quad?\quad}$

$20x + 30(\underline{\quad?\quad}) = 2,450$ Substitute $\underline{\quad?\quad}$ for y in the second equation.

$20x + \underline{\quad?\quad} - \underline{\quad?\quad} = 2,450$ Distributive Property

$3,000 - \underline{\quad?\quad} = 2,450$ Collect like terms.

$\underline{\quad?\quad} = -550$ Add $-3,000$ to both sides.

$x = 55$ Divide both sides by -10.

To find y, substitute 55 for x in either of the original equations. We use the first equation because it is simpler.

$$x + y = 100$$
$$55 + y = 100$$
$$y = 45$$

The farmer bought 55 acres at $20/acre, and 45 acres at $30/acre.

Check Substitute 55 for x and 45 for y into the second equation.

Does $20x + 30y = 2,450$?

Yes, $20(55) + 30(45) = 1,100 + 1,350 = 2,450$.

A CAS can be used to solve systems of equations even when neither equation has an isolated variable.

Example 4

Use a CAS to solve $\begin{cases} y = \frac{2}{3}x + \frac{10}{3} \\ 5x + 2y = 32 \end{cases}$.

Solution Since the first equation is already solved for y, simply substitute that expression for y into the second equation and solve the second equation for x. To do that quickly on a CAS, you can use the SOLVE command.

Step 1 Find the SOLVE command on your calculator and place it on the entry line. On some calculators you may find it in the **Algebra** menu.

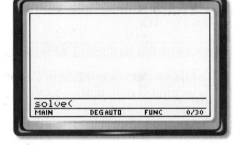

Step 2 Enter the second equation with $\left(\frac{2}{3}x + \frac{10}{3}\right)$ in place of y as you would if you were solving the equation by hand. That is, enter

$$5x + 2\left(\frac{2}{3}x + \frac{10}{3}\right) = 32.$$

Step 3 The SOLVE command on many CAS requires you to specify the variable for which to solve. In this case it is x. You may need to enter a comma followed by x before you close the parentheses and hit $\boxed{\text{ENTER}}$. You should get $x = 4$.

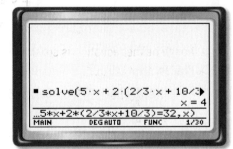

Step 4 Now substitute this x value into the first equation to get $y = 6$.

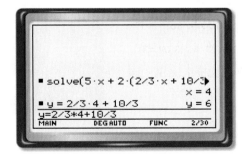

So, the solution to the system is $(4, 6)$.

(continued on next page)

Check Determining if a point is a solution to a system is easy to do on a CAS. Enter the two original equations and the specific values for each variable. The symbol " | " on one CAS means "with" or "such that" and indicates these values. The response "true" indicates that (4, 6) checks.

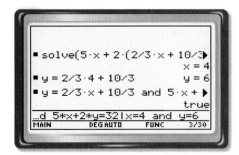

 STOP QY

▶ **QY**

Below is the solution to a system found by using a CAS.

solve(4•x+3•(2–5•x) =17,x)

            x=-1

y=2–5•-1

            y=7

a. Find the system of equations.

b. Check the solution by hand.

Questions

COVERING THE IDEAS

1. The owners of a carnival have found that twice as many children as adults come to the carnival. Solve a system to estimate the number of children and the number of adults at the carnival when 3,570 people attend.

2. A jar of coins has only nickels and quarters, which are worth a total of $9.40. There are 4 more quarters than nickels. How many nickels and quarters are in the jar?

3. The Drama Club and Service Club held a charity car wash. There were four times as many Service Club members as Drama Club members working, so the Service Club earned four times as much money. The car wash raised $280 in all. How much did each club earn for their charity?

In 4–7, a system is given.
   a. Solve each system of equations by substitution.
   b. Check your answer.

4. $\begin{cases} y = 2x \\ 3x + 2y = 21 \end{cases}$

5. $\begin{cases} n + 5w = 6 \\ n = -8w \end{cases}$

6. $\begin{cases} a - b = 2 \\ a + 5b = 20 \end{cases}$

7. $\begin{cases} y = x - 1 \\ 4x - y = 19 \end{cases}$

8. Here is another problem from the 1881 algebra textbook. A farmer bought 100 acres of land, part at $37 per acre and part at $45 per acre, at a total cost of $4,220. How much land was there in each part?

Americans gave a total of $260.28 billion in contributions to charities in 2005.

Source: Giving USA Foundation

APPLYING THE MATHEMATICS

In 9 and 10,

    a. solve each system by substitution.

    b. check your answer by graphing the system.

9. $\begin{cases} x + y = 8 \\ \quad y = -3x \end{cases}$

10. $\begin{cases} \quad x = 2y - 10 \\ 5x + 3 = 15 \end{cases}$

11. Solve the system $\begin{cases} b = -1.36a + 4.4 \\ 1.2a + 4.58b = -181 \end{cases}$ using a CAS.

12. Angles P and Q are complementary. If $m\angle P = 10x$ and $m\angle Q = 15x$, find x, $m\angle P$, and $m\angle Q$.

13. A business made $120,000 more this year than it did last year. This was an increase of 16% over last year's earnings. If T and L are the earnings (in dollars) for this year and last year, respectively, then $\begin{cases} T = L + 120{,}000 \\ T = 1.16L \end{cases}$. Find the profits for this year and last year.

14. Mrs. Rodriguez leaves money to her two favorite charities in her will. Charity A is to get 2.5 times as much money as Charity B. The total amount of money donated in the will is $28,000.

    a. Write a system of equations describing this situation.

    b. Solve to find the amount of money each charity will get.

15. Anica received her results for mathematics and verbal achievement tests. Her mathematics score is 40 points higher than her verbal score. Her total score for the two parts is 1,230.

    a. Let v = Anica's verbal score, and m = her mathematics score. Write a system of equations for this situation.

    b. Find Anica's two scores.

REVIEW

In 16 and 17 solve the system and check. (Lessons 10-2, 10-1)

16. $\begin{cases} y = x - 5 \\ y = -4x + 10 \end{cases}$

17. $\begin{cases} y = 6x + 6 \\ y = 6x - 2 \end{cases}$

18. One hot-air balloon takes off from Albuquerque, New Mexico, and rises at a rate of 110 feet per minute. At the same time, another balloon takes off from Santa Fe, New Mexico, and rises at a rate of 80 feet per minute. The altitude of Albuquerque is 4,958 feet and the altitude of Santa Fe is 6,950 feet. (Lesson 10-2)

    a. When are the two balloons at the same altitude?

    b. What is their altitude at that time?

19. If $a^3b^{-4}c$ is equal to the reciprocal of $\dfrac{a^{-5}b^2c^3}{a^{-2}b^xc^4}$, find x. (Lessons 8-4, 8-3)

Hot-air balloons hold from 19,000 to 211,000 cubic feet of air and are from 50 to 90 feet tall.

Source: hotairballoons.com

In 20 and 21, graph the solution set
   a. on a number line.
   b. in the coordinate plane. (Lessons 6-9, 3-6)

20. $x < 6$

21. $-4y + 2 < 6$

22. In 2002, India ended its Police Pigeon Service. This is a system in which trained pigeons transport messages. The service was used when traditional communication broke down during natural disasters. Suppose a trained pigeon flies 41.3 mph in still air. (Lesson 5-3)

   a. How far can it fly in m minutes in still air?
   b. How fast can it fly *with* the wind if the wind speed is s mph?
   c. How fast can it fly *against* the wind if the wind speed is s mph?
   d. If the pigeon is flying down a highway that has a speed limit of 65 mph and there is a 21.9 mph tailwind, would you give it a speeding ticket?

EXPLORATION

23. Here is a nursery rhyme whose earliest traceable publication date is around 1730 in *Folklore,* now in the library of the British Museum. (St. Ives is a village in England.)

   As I was going to St. Ives,
   I met a man with seven wives.
   Each wife had seven sacks,
   Each sack had seven cats,
   Each cat had seven kits:
   Kits, cats, sacks, and wives,
   How many were going to St. Ives?

   a. Let $W =$ the number of wives, $S =$ the number of sacks, $C =$ the number of cats, and $K =$ the number of kits. Write three equations that relate two of these variables to each other.
   b. Find the value of $K + C + S + W$.
   c. What is an answer to the riddle?

QY ANSWERS

a. $\begin{cases} y = 2 - 5x \\ 4x + 3y = 17 \end{cases}$

b. $4 \cdot {-1} + 3 \cdot 7 =$
$-4 + 21 = 17$ and
$2 - 5 \cdot {-1} = 2 + 5 = 7$.
So $(-1, 7)$ checks.

Lesson

10-4

Solving Systems by Addition

Vocabulary

addition method for solving
  a system

▶ **BIG IDEA**   The sum of the left sides of two equations equals the sum of the right sides of those equations.

The numbers $\frac{1}{4}$ and 25% are equal even though they may not look equal; so are $\frac{17}{20}$ and 85%. If you add them, the sums are equal.

$$\frac{1}{4} = 25\% \qquad\qquad \frac{17}{20} = 85\%$$

So $\frac{1}{4} + \frac{17}{20} = 25\% + 85\%$.

Adding on each side, $\frac{22}{20} = 110\%$.

This is one example of the following generalization of the Addition Property of Equality.

Mental Math

Find the perimeter of

a. a square with sides of length 6.2x.

b. a regular octagon with sides of length 21ab.

c. a regular pentagon with sides of length $4.5m + 1.5n$.

Generalized Addition Property of Equality

For all numbers or expressions a, b, c, and d: If $a = b$ and $c = d$, then $a + c = b + d$.

The Generalized Addition Property of Equality can be used to solve some systems. Consider this situation: The sum of two numbers is 5,300. Their difference is 1,200. What are the numbers?

If x and y are the two numbers, with x the greater number, we can write the following system.

$$\begin{cases} x + y = 5{,}300 \\ x - y = 1{,}200 \end{cases}$$

Notice what happens when the left sides are added (combining like terms) and the right sides are added.

$$\begin{array}{r} x + y = 5{,}300 \\ + \; x - y = 1{,}200 \\ \hline 2x + 0 = 6{,}500 \end{array}$$

Because y and $-y$ sum to 0, the sum of the equations is an equation with only one variable. Solve $2x = 6{,}500$ as usual.

$$x = 3{,}250$$

To find y, substitute 3,250 for x in one of the original equations. We choose $x + y = 5{,}300$.

$$x + y = 5{,}300$$
$$3{,}250 + y = 5{,}300$$
$$y = 2{,}050$$

The ordered pair (3,250, 2,050) checks in both equations:
$3{,}250 + 2{,}050 = 5{,}300$ and $3{,}250 - 2{,}050 = 1{,}200$.

So the solution to the system $\begin{cases} x + y = 5{,}300 \\ x - y = 1{,}200 \end{cases}$ is (3,250, 2,050).

Using the Generalized Addition Property of Equality to eliminate one variable from a system is sometimes called the **addition method for solving a system.** The addition method is an efficient way to solve systems when the coefficients of the same variable are opposites.

Example 1

A pilot flew a small plane 180 miles from North Platte, Nebraska, to Scottsbluff, Nebraska, in 1 hour against the wind. The pilot returned to North Platte in 48 minutes $\left(\frac{48}{60} = \frac{4}{5} \text{ hour} \right)$ with the wind at the plane's back. How fast was the plane flying (without wind)? What was the speed of the wind?

Solution Let A be the average speed of the airplane without wind and W be the speed of the wind, both in miles per hour. The total speed against the wind is then $A - W$, and the speed with the wind is $A + W$. There are two conditions given on these total speeds.

There are more than 8,100 airports in the United States used only by small planes. They have runways shorter than 3,000 feet.

Source: Aircraft Owners and Pilots Association

From North Platte to Scottsbluff the average speed of the plane was $\frac{180 \text{ miles}}{1 \text{ hour}} = 180 \frac{\text{miles}}{\text{hour}}$.
This was against the wind, so $A - W = 180$.

From Scottsbluff to North Platte the average speed of the plane was $\frac{180 \text{ miles}}{\frac{4}{5} \text{ hour}} = 225 \frac{\text{miles}}{\text{hour}}$.
This was with the wind, so $A + W = 225$.

We have the system $\begin{cases} A - W = 180 \\ A + W = 225 \end{cases}$.

Now solve the system. Since the coefficients of W are opposites (1 and -1), add the equations.

$$\begin{array}{rl} A - W = 180 & \\ \underline{A + W = 225} & \\ 2A = 405 & \text{Add.} \\ A = 202.5 & \text{Divide by 2.} \end{array}$$

Substitute 202.5 for A in either of the original equations. We choose the second equation.

$$202.5 + W = 225$$
$$W = 22.5$$

The average speed of the airplane was about 202.5 mph and the speed of the wind was 22.5 mph.

Check Refer to the original question. Against the wind, the plane flew at $202.5 - 22.5$ or 180 mph, so it flew 180 miles in 1 hour. With the wind, the plane flew at $202.5 + 22.5$ or 225 mph. At that rate, in 48 minutes the pilot flew $\frac{48}{60}$ hr $\cdot$ 225 $\frac{mi}{hr} = 180$ miles, which checks with the given conditions.

Sometimes the coefficients of the same variable are equal. In this case, use the Multiplication Property of Equality to multiply both sides of one of the equations by –1. This changes all the numbers in that equation to their opposites. Then you can use the addition method to find solutions to the system.

Example 2

Solve $\begin{cases} 5x + 17y = 1 \\ 5x + 8y = -26 \end{cases}$.

Solution We rewrite the equations and number them to make it easy to refer to them later.

$\begin{cases} 5x + 17y = 1 \\ 5x + 8y = -26 \end{cases}$ Equation #1

    Equation #2

Notice that the coefficients of x in the two equations are equal.

Multiply the second equation by –1. Call the resulting Equation #3.

$-5x - 8y = 26$ Equation #3

Now use the addition method with the first and third equations.

$$
\begin{array}{ll}
5x + 17y = 1 & \text{Equation \#1} \\
+ \ -5x - 8y = 26 & \text{Equation \#3} \\
\hline
9y = 27 & \text{Equation \#1 + Equation \#3} \\
y = 3 &
\end{array}
$$

To find x, substitute 3 for y in one of the original equations.

$5x + 17(3) = 1$ We use Equation #1.
$5x + 51 = 1$
$5x = -50$
$x = -10$

So $(x, y) = (-10, 3)$.

(continued on next page)

Check Substitute in both equations.

Equation #1 Does $5 \cdot -10 + 17 \cdot 3 = 1$? Yes.

Equation #2 Does $5 \cdot -10 + 8 \cdot 3 = -26$? Yes.

GUIDED

Example 3

A resort hotel offers two weekend specials.

Plan A: 3 nights with 6 meals for $564

Plan B: 3 nights with 2 meals for $488

At these rates, what is the cost of one night's lodging and what is the average cost per meal? (Assume there is no discount for 6 meals.)

Solution Let N = price of one night's lodging.

Let M = average price of one meal.

Write an equation to describe each weekend special.

From Plan A: $3N + 6M = 564$ Equation #1

From Plan B: ___?___   Equation #2

Notice the coefficients of N are the same, so multiply Equation #2 by -1.

___?___   Equation #3

___?___   Add Equations #1 and #3.

Does your last equation have only one variable? If so, solve this equation. If not, ask someone for help.

$M = $ ___?___

Substitute this value of M in either equation, and solve for N.

$(N, M) = ($ ___?___ , ___?___ $)$

What is the price of one night's lodging? ___?___

What is the average cost of a meal? ___?___

The average hotel room rate in the United States in 2006 was $96.42 per night.

Source: Smith Travel Research

Questions

COVERING THE IDEAS

1. **a.** When is adding equations an appropriate method for solving systems?

   b. What is the goal in adding equations to solve systems?

2. Which property allows you to add to both sides of two equations to get a new equation?

In 3 and 4, a system is given.

    a. Solve the system.

    b. Check your solution.

3. $\begin{cases} 3x + 9y = 75 \\ -3x - y = 15 \end{cases}$

4. $\begin{cases} a + b = -22 \\ a - b = 4 \end{cases}$

5. The sum of two numbers is 1,776 and their difference is 1,492. What are the numbers?

6. Find two numbers whose sum is 20 and whose difference is 20.

7. When is it useful to multiply an equation by –1 as a first step in solving a system?

8. Airlines schedule about 5.5 hours of flying time for an A320 Airbus to fly from Dulles International Airport near Washington, D.C., to Los Angeles International Airport. Airlines schedule about 4.5 hours of flying time for the reverse direction. The distance between these airports is about 2,300 miles. They allow about 0.4 hour for takeoff and landing.

    a. From this information, estimate (to the nearest 5 mph) the average wind speed the airlines assume in making their schedule.

    b. What average airplane speed (to the nearest 5 mph) do the airlines assume in making their schedule?

In 9 and 10, solve the system.

9. $\begin{cases} 14x - 5y = 9 \\ 17x - 5y = 27 \end{cases}$

10. $\begin{cases} 17m + 7n = 8 \\ 17m + 5n = 13 \end{cases}$

11. $(N, M) = (150, 19)$ is the solution to the system of equations $\begin{cases} 3N + 6M = 564 \\ 3N + 2M = 488 \end{cases}$ in Example 3. Check this solution.

12. A hotel offers the following specials. Plan A includes a two-night stay and one meal for $199. Plan B includes a 2-night stay and 4 meals for $247. What price is this per night and per meal?

APPLYING THE MATHEMATICS

In 13 and 14, solve the system.

13. $\begin{cases} 2x - 6y = 34 \\ x = 2 - 6y \end{cases}$

14. $\begin{cases} \frac{1}{4}z + \frac{3}{4}w = \frac{1}{2} \\ \frac{7}{4}w + \frac{1}{4}z = \frac{3}{8} \end{cases}$

15. As you know, $\frac{3}{5} = 60\%$ and $\frac{3}{8} = 37.5\%$.

    a. Is it true that $\frac{3}{5} - \frac{3}{8} = 60\% - 37.5\%$? Justify your answer.

    b. Is it true that $\frac{3}{5} \cdot \frac{3}{8} = 60\% \cdot 37.5\%$? Justify your answer.

16. In 2006, the tallest person playing professional basketball in the Women's National Basketball Association (WNBA) was Margo Dydek. The shortest person was Debbie Black. When they stood next to each other, Margo was 23 in. taller. If one stood on the other's head, they would have stood 12 ft 5 in. tall. How tall is each player?

GÉANT

REVIEW

In 17 and 18, solve by using any method. (Lessons 10-3, 10-2, 10-1)

17. $\begin{cases} y = 2x - 3 \\ y = -8x + 6 \end{cases}$

18. $\begin{cases} A = -5n \\ B = 6n \\ 4A + B = 39 \end{cases}$

19. a. Solve $x^2 + 3x - 28 = 0$.

    b. Find the x-intercepts of the graph of $y = x^2 + 3x - 28$.
    (Lesson 9-5)

20. The formula $d = 0.04s^2 + 1.5s$ gives the approximate distance d in feet needed to stop a particular car traveling on dry pavement at a speed of s miles per hour. How much farther will this car travel before stopping if it is traveling at 65 mph instead of 50 mph? (Lesson 9-3)

21. Let $f(x) = \sqrt{2x - 9}$. (Lessons 8-6, 7-6, 7-5)

    a. What is the domain of f?

    b. What is the range of f?

22. Simplify $x^{-1} + x - \frac{1}{x}$. (Lessons 8-4, 8-3)

23. Find the slope of line ℓ pictured below. (Lesson 6-2)

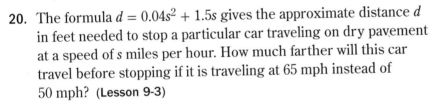

Margo Dydek

Debbie Black

24. In 2005, the total revenues of a cell phone company increased 5.5% from the previous year to $36.84 billion. What were the company's revenues in 2004? (**Lesson 4-1**)

25. Solve $38(212 - x) = 0$ in your head. (**Lesson 3-4**)

EXPLORATION

26. Subtracting equations is part of a process that can be used to find simple fractions for repeating decimals. For example, to find a fraction for $0.\overline{72} = 0.7272727272...$, first let $d = 0.\overline{72}$. Then multiply both sides of the equation by an appropriate power of 10. Here we multiply by 10^2 because $0.\overline{72}$ has a two-digit block that repeats.

$$100d = 72.\overline{72} \qquad \text{Equation \#1}$$
$$d = 0.\overline{72} \qquad \text{Equation \#2}$$

Subtract the second equation from the first.

$$99d = 72 \qquad \text{Equation \#1} - \text{Equation \#2}$$

Solve for d and simplify the fraction.

$$d = \frac{72}{99} \text{ or } d = \frac{8}{11}$$

A calculator shows that $\frac{8}{11} = 0.7272727272....$

a. Use the above process to find a simple fraction equal to $0.\overline{15}$.

b. Modify the process to find a simple fraction equal to $0.9\overline{02}$.

c. Find a simple fraction equal to $0.\overline{123456}$.

Lesson

10-5

Solving Systems by Multiplication

Vocabulary

equivalent systems

multiplication method for
  solving a system

▶ **BIG IDEA** An effective first step in solving some systems is to multiply both sides of one of the equations by a carefully chosen number.

Recall that there are three common forms for equations of lines.

Form		Example
Standard	$Ax + By = C$	$3x + 8y = 20$
Slope-Intercept	$y = mx + b$	$y = -2x + 1$
Point-Slope	$y - k = m(x - h)$	$y - 50 = \frac{3}{4}(x - 20)$

Mental Math

Classify the angle with the given measure as acute, right, or obtuse.

a. $134°$

b. $84°$

c. $0.23°$

The substitution method described in Lessons 10-2 and 10-3 is convenient for solving systems in which one or both equations are in slope-intercept form. The addition method studied in Lesson 10-4 is convenient for solving systems in which both equations are in standard form and the coefficients of one variable are either equal or opposites. However, not all systems fall into one of these two categories.

Consider the following system.

$$\begin{cases} 3x - 4y = 7 \\ 6x - 5y = 20 \end{cases}$$

Adding or subtracting the two equations will not result in an equation with just one variable, because the x and the y terms are neither equal nor opposites. Substitution could be used, but it introduces fractions.

An easier method uses the Multiplication Property of Equality to create an *equivalent system* of equations. **Equivalent systems** are systems with exactly the same solutions. Notice that if you multiply both sides of the first equation by -2, the x terms of the resulting system have opposite coefficients.

Example 1

Solve the system $\begin{cases} 3x - 4y = 7 \\ 6x - 5y = 20 \end{cases}$.

Solution 1 Multiply both sides of the first equation by −2 and apply the Distributive Property.

$$\begin{cases} 3x - 4y = 7 \\ 6x - 5y = 20 \end{cases} \xrightarrow{\text{multiply by -2}} \begin{cases} -2(3x - 4y) = -2(7) \\ 6x - 5y = 20 \end{cases}$$

$$\begin{cases} -6x + 8y = -14 \\ 6x - 5y = 20 \end{cases}$$

$$3y = 6 \qquad \text{Add the equations.}$$

$$y = 2 \qquad \text{Solve for } y.$$

To find x, substitute 2 for y in one of the original equations.

$$3x - 4y = 7$$
$$3x - 4 \cdot 2 = 7$$
$$3x - 8 = 7$$
$$3x = 15$$
$$x = 5$$

So the solution is $(x, y) = (5, 2)$.

Solution 2 Multiply both sides of the second equation by $-\frac{1}{2}$. This also makes the coefficients of x opposites.

$$\begin{cases} 3x - 4y = 7 \\ 6x - 5y = 20 \end{cases} \xrightarrow{\text{multiply by } -\frac{1}{2}} \begin{cases} 3x - 4y = 7 \\ -\frac{1}{2}(6x - 5y) = -\frac{1}{2}(20) \end{cases}$$

$$\begin{cases} 3x - 4y = 7 \\ -3x + \frac{5}{2}y = -10 \end{cases}$$

$$-\frac{3}{2}y = -3 \qquad \text{Add.}$$

$$y = 2$$

Proceed as in Solution 1 to find x. Again $(x, y) = (5, 2)$.

Example 1 shows that the solution is the same no matter which equation is multiplied by a number. The goal is to obtain opposite coefficients for one of the variables in the two equations. Then the resulting equations can be added to eliminate that variable. This technique is sometimes called the **multiplication method for solving a system**.

 QY

▶ **QY**

$$\begin{cases} 7x + 3y = 22.5 \\ 2x - 12y = 45 \end{cases}$$

$$\downarrow$$

$$\begin{cases} 28x + 12y = 90 \\ 2x - 12y = 45 \end{cases}$$

a. Explain what operation occurred to go from the first system to the second system.

b. Finish solving the system.

Sometimes it is necessary to multiply *each* equation by a different number before adding.

Example 2

Solve the system $\begin{cases} -3m + 2n = 6 \\ 4m + 5n = -31 \end{cases}$.

Solution The idea is to multiply by a number so that one variable in the resulting system has a pair of opposite coefficients. To make the coefficients of m opposites, multiply the first equation by 4 and the second equation by 3.

$$\begin{cases} -3m + 2n = 6 \\ 4m + 5n = -31 \end{cases} \xrightarrow[\text{multiply by 3}]{\text{multiply by 4}} \begin{cases} -12m + 8n = 24 \\ 12m + 15n = -93 \end{cases}$$

Now add. $23n = -69$

$n = -3$

To find m, substitute -3 for n in either original equation. We use the first equation.

$$-3m + 2 \cdot (-3) = 6$$
$$-3m - 6 = 6$$
$$-3m = 12$$
$$m = -4$$

So $(m, n) = (-4, -3)$.

Check You should check your solution by substituting for m and n in each original equation.

Many situations naturally lead to linear equations in standard form. This results in a linear system that can be solved using the multiplication method.

Example 3

A marching band currently has 48 musicians and 18 people in the flag corps. The drum majors wish to form hexagons and squares like those diagrammed at the right. Are there enough members to create the formations with no people left over? If so, how many hexagons and how many squares can be made? If not, give a recommendation for the fewest people the drum majors would need to recruit and how many hexagons and how many squares could be made.

Hexagon
Flag bearer in center

Square
Two musicians in the center

Solution Consider the entire formation to include
h hexagons and s squares. There are two conditions in the
system: one for musicians and one for the flag corps.

There are 6 $\frac{\text{musicians}}{\text{hexagon}}$ and 2 $\frac{\text{musicians}}{\text{square}}$.

So $6h + 2s = 48$ musicians.

There are 1 $\frac{\text{flag bearer}}{\text{hexagon}}$ and 4 $\frac{\text{flag bearers}}{\text{square}}$.

So $h + 4s = 18$ flag bearers.

To find h, multiply the first equation by −2, and add the result to
the second equation.

Marching bands perform in
competitions, at sporting
events, and in parades.

$$
\begin{array}{r}
-12h + -4s = -96 \\
h + 4s = 18 \\
\hline
-11h = -78 \\
h = 7.\overline{09}
\end{array}
$$

Because h is not a positive integer in this solution, these
formations will not work with 48 musicians and 18 flag bearers.

−78 is not divisible by −11, but −77 is. By recruiting one additional member
to the flag corps we get a number divisible by −11. This would create the
following system.

$$
\begin{array}{r}
-12h + -4s = -96 \\
h + 4s = 19 \\
\hline
-11h = -77 \\
h = 7
\end{array}
$$

Now $h = 7$. Substituting for h in the second equation of this new system,
you find that $s = 3$.

All 48 musicians and 19 flag bearers could be arranged into
7 hexagons and 3 squares, so the drum major needs to recruit 1
more flag bearer.

Check Making 7 hexagons would use 42 musicians and 7 flag bearers.
Making 3 squares would use 6 musicians and 12 flag bearers. This setup
uses exactly 48 musicians and 19 flag bearers.

When the equations in a system are not given in either standard
or slope-intercept form, it is wise to rewrite the equations in one
of these forms before proceeding. For example, to solve the system
below, you could use one of three methods.

$$
\begin{cases}
n - 3 = \frac{3}{2}m \\
4m + 5n = -31
\end{cases}
$$

Method 1 Multiply the first equation by 2 to eliminate fractions.

$$\begin{cases} 2n - 6 = 3m \\ 4m + 5n = -31 \end{cases}$$

Add $-3m$ and 6 to both sides of the first equation. The result is the system of Example 2, which is in standard form.

Method 2 Add 3 to both sides of the first equation.

$$\begin{cases} n = \frac{3}{2}m + 3 \\ 4m + 5n = -31 \end{cases}$$

To finish solving this system you could use substitution by substituting n into the second equation.

Method 3 Use substitution on a CAS to solve the system.

Step 1 Use the SOLVE command to solve one of the equations for one of the variables. We choose the first equation and solve for n.

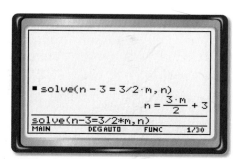

Step 2 Substitute this value for n into the second equation and solve for m. Most CAS will allow you to copy and paste so that you do not have to type expressions multiple times. The display shows $m = -4$.

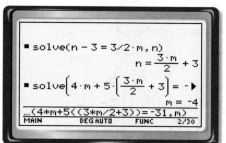

Step 3 Then substitute -4 for m into the first equation to get $n = -3$.

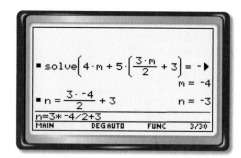

Questions

COVERING THE IDEAS

1. Consider the system $\begin{cases} 5x + 3d = 9 \\ 2x + d = 26 \end{cases}$.

   a. **Fill in the Blanks** If the ___?___ equation is multiplied by ___?___, then adding the equations will eliminate ___?___.

   b. Solve the system.

2. A problem on a test was to solve the system $\begin{cases} -8n + m = -19 \\ 4n - 3m = -8 \end{cases}$.

   Three students used three different methods to solve the system. Their first steps are shown.

Annisha's Method	Maxandra's Method	Victor's Method
$\begin{cases} -8n + m = -19 \\ 8n - 6m = -16 \end{cases}$	$\begin{cases} m = -19 + 8n \\ 4n - 3m = -8 \end{cases}$	$\begin{cases} -24n + 3m = -57 \\ 4n - 3m = -8 \end{cases}$

   a. Which student(s) used substitution to solve the system?

   b. Which variable will Annisha's method eliminate? Explain what she did to make an equivalent system.

   c. Which variable will Victor's method eliminate? Explain what he did to make an equivalent system.

   d. Pick one of the methods and finish solving the system.

3. Consider the system $\begin{cases} 7r - 3s = 9 \\ 2r + 5s = 26 \end{cases}$.

   a. By what two numbers can you multiply the equations so that, if you add the results, you will eliminate r?

   b. By what two numbers can you multiply the equations so that, if you add the results, you will eliminate s?

   c. Use one of these methods to solve the system.

4. Consider the system $\begin{cases} 10t + u = 85 \\ 2t + 3u = 31 \end{cases}$.

   a. Write an equivalent system that would eliminate t first.

   b. Write an equivalent system that would eliminate u first.

   c. Use one of the methods to solve the system.

5. A marching band has 60 musicians and 30 flag bearers. They wish to form pentagons and squares like those diagrammed at the right.

   a. If the formation has 3 pentagons and 4 squares, how many musicians and flag bearers will be involved?

   b. Is it possible to change the numbers of pentagons and squares so that every person will have a spot? If so, how many of each formation will be needed?

6. Solve the system $\begin{cases} n + 7 = \frac{1}{3}m \\ 7m - 3n = 57 \end{cases}$.

In 7–10, solve the system.

7. $\begin{cases} 24x + 15y = 20 \\ 4x + 3y = 5 \end{cases}$

8. $\begin{cases} 7a - 8b = 1 \\ 6a - 7b = 1 \end{cases}$

9. $\begin{cases} 9y + x = -8 \\ 2 = y - x \end{cases}$

10. $\begin{cases} 113.2 = 4x - 2y \\ 331.4 = 6x + 5y \end{cases}$

APPLYING THE MATHEMATICS

11. Solve the system by first rewriting each equation in standard form. $\begin{cases} 0.2x + 0.3(x + 4) = 0.16y \\ 0.04y - 0.07 = 0.08x \end{cases}$

12. Milo feels that the probability that he will be elected to the student council is $\frac{1}{10}$ of the probability that he will not be elected. What does Milo think is the probability that he will be elected? (Remember that the sum of the probabilities that he will be elected and not be elected is 1.)

Three students are participating in student council elections.

13. A test has m multiple-choice (MC) questions and e extended-response (ER) questions. If the MC questions are worth 2 points each and the ER questions are worth 7 points each, the test will be worth a total of 95 points. If the MC questions are worth 3 points each and the ER questions are worth 8 points each, the test will be worth a total of 130 points. How many MC questions and how many ER questions are on the test?

14. A security guard counted 82 vehicles in a parking lot. The only vehicles in the lot were cars and motorcycles. To double-check his count, the security guard counted 300 wheels. How many motorcycles and how many cars are in the parking lot?

15. Delise and Triston's class went on a field trip to a local farm. The farm raised cows and chickens. Delise counted 27 heads and Triston counted 76 legs. How many cows and how many chickens are on the farm?

   a. Answer this question by solving a system.

   b. Write a few sentences explaining how to answer the question without using algebra.

REVIEW

In 16 and 17, solve the system using any method. (Lessons 10-4, 10-3, 10-2, 10-1)

16. $\begin{cases} 6x + 2y = 26 \\ 4x + 2y = 8 \end{cases}$

17. $\begin{cases} y = \frac{2}{3}x - 4 \\ y = \frac{1}{4}x + 1 \end{cases}$

18. The two diagrams below illustrate a system of equations.
(**Lessons 10-4, 10-2**)

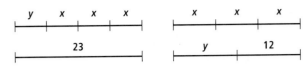

a. Write an equation for the diagram at the left.

b. Write an equation for the diagram at the right.

c. Solve the system for x and y.

d. Check your work.

19. Ashlyn has $600 and saves $30 each week. Janet has $1,500 and spends $30 each week. (**Lesson 10-2**)

a. How many weeks from now will they each have the same amount of money?

b. What will this amount be?

20. A 16-foot ladder leans against a house. If the base of the ladder is 6 feet from the base of the house, at what height does the top of the ladder touch the house? (**Lessons 9-1, 8-6**)

In **21** and **22**, consider a garage with a roof pitch of $\frac{3}{12}$ at the right. The garage is to be 20 feet wide. (**Lessons 6-3, 5-9**)

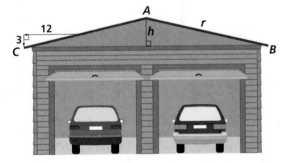

21. What is the slope of $\overline{AB}$?

22. a. What is the height h of the roof?

b. Find the length r of one rafter.

23. **True or False** (**Lesson 5-6**)

a. Probabilities are numbers from 0 to 1.

b. A probability of 1 means that an event must occur.

c. A relative frequency of −1 cannot occur.

EXPLORATION

24. Create formations of a college band consisting of 110 musicians and a flag corps of 36 with no members left over.

Lesson

10-6

Systems and Parallel Lines

Vocabulary

coincident lines

▶ **BIG IDEA** Systems having 0, 1, or infinitely many solutions correspond to lines having 0 or 1 point of intersection, or being coincident.

The idea behind parallel lines is that they "go in the same direction." So we call two lines parallel if and only if they are in the same plane and either are the same line or do not intersect. All vertical lines are parallel to each other. So are all horizontal lines. But not all oblique lines are parallel. For oblique lines to be parallel, they must have the same slope.

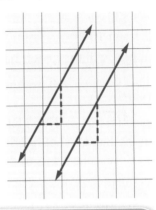

Mental Math

Evaluate.

a. $\dfrac{7 \cdot 6 \cdot 5}{3!}$

b. $\dfrac{9!}{9 \cdot 8 \cdot 7 \cdot 6}$

Slopes and Parallel Lines Property

If two lines have the same slope, then they are parallel.

Nonintersecting Parallel Lines

You have learned that when two lines intersect in exactly one point, the coordinates of the point of intersection can be found by solving a system. But what happens when the lines are parallel? Consider this linear system.

$$\begin{cases} 5x - 2y = 11 \\ 15x - 6y = -25 \end{cases}$$

You can solve the system by multiplying the first equation by –3, and adding the result to the second equation.

$$\begin{array}{r} -15x + 6y = -33 \\ + \ 15x - 6y = -25 \\ \hline \end{array}$$

Notice that when you add you get $0 = -58$.

This is impossible! When an equation with no solution (such as $0 = -58$) results from correct applications of the addition and multiplication methods on a system of linear equations, the original conditions must also be impossible. There are no pairs of numbers that work in *both* equations.

Thus, the system has no solutions. The lines do not intersect. The graph of the system is two parallel nonintersecting lines, as shown at the right. As another check, rewrite the equations for the lines in slope-intercept form.

line ℓ: $5x - 2y = 11$
$-2y = -5x + 11$
$y = 2.5x - 5.5$

line m: $15x - 6y = -25$
$-6y = -15x - 25$
$y = 2.5x + 4.1\overline{6}$

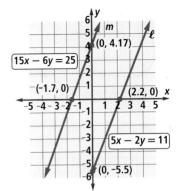

Both lines ℓ and m have the same slope of 2.5, but different y-intercepts. Thus, they are parallel.

 QY1

Coincident Lines

Some systems have infinitely many solutions. They can be solved using any of the techniques you have studied in this chapter.

> **QY1**
>
> Show that the system
> $$\begin{cases} -4x + 2y = -16 \\ 6x - 3y = 18 \end{cases}$$
> has no solution.

Example 1

Solve the system $\begin{cases} 4x + 2y = 6 \\ y = -2x + 3 \end{cases}$.

Solution 1 Rewrite the first equation in slope-intercept form.

$4x + 2y = 6$
$2y = -4x + 6$ Add $-4x$ to each side.
$y = -2x + 3$ Divide each side by 2.

Notice that this equation is identical to the second equation in the system. So, any ordered pair that is a solution to one equation is also a solution to the other equation. The graphs of the two equations are the same line.

Solution 2 Use substitution. Substitute $-2x + 3$ for y in the first equation.

$4x + 2(-2x + 3) = 6$
$4x - 4x + 6 = 6$
$6 = 6$

The sentence $6 = 6$ is *always* true. So, any ordered pair that is a solution to one equation is also a solution to the other equation in the system. The graphs of the two equations are the same line.

The solution set consists of all ordered pairs on the line with equation $y = -2x + 3$, as shown at the right.

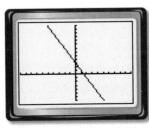

$-10 \le x \le 10, -7 \le y \le 13$

(continued on next page)

Check As a partial check, find an ordered pair that satisfies one of the equations of the original system. We use $y = -2x + 3$ to find the ordered pair $(0, 3)$. Check that this ordered pair also satisfies the other equation. Does $4 \cdot 0 + 2 \cdot 3 = 6$? Yes, $6 = 6$.

STOP QY2

Whenever a sentence that is always true (such as $0 = 0$ or $6 = 6$) occurs from correct work with a system of linear equations, the system has infinitely many solutions. We say that the lines *coincide* and that the graph of the system is two **coincident lines.**

You have now studied all the ways that two lines in the plane can be related, and all the types of solutions a system of two linear equations might have. The table below summarizes these relationships.

> **QY2**
>
> Find a second ordered pair that satisfies one of the equations in Example 1 and show that it satisfies the other equation.

Description of System	Graph	Number of Solutions to System	Slopes of Lines
Two intersecting lines		1 (the point of intersection)	Different
Two parallel and nonintersecting lines		0	Equal
One line (parallel and coincident lines)		Infinitely many	Equal

GUIDED

Example 2

Find all solutions to $\begin{cases} 12x - 10y = 2 \\ -18x + 15y = -3 \end{cases}$.

Solution

Step 1 Multiply both sides of the first equation by 3. ___?___

Step 2 Multiply both sides of the second equation by 2. ___?___

Step 3 Add the equations from Steps 1 and 2. ___?___

The solution set consists of all ordered pairs on the line with equation $12x - 10y = 2$.

Questions

COVERING THE IDEAS

1. What is true about the slopes of parallel lines?

2. Which two lines among Parts a–d are parallel?
   a. $y = 8x + 500$
   b. $y = 2x + 500$
   c. $y = 8x + 600$
   d. $x = 2y + 500$

3. a. Graph the line with equation $y = \frac{1}{3}x + 5$.
   b. Draw the line parallel to it through the origin.
   c. What is an equation of the line you drew in Part b?

4. Give an example of a system with two nonintersecting lines.

5. Give an example of a system with two coincident lines.

In 6 and 7, a system is given.
   a. Determine whether the system includes *nonintersecting* or *coincident* lines.
   b. Check your answer to Part a by graphing.

6. $\begin{cases} 12a = 6b - 3 \\ 4a - 2b = -3 \end{cases}$

7. $\begin{cases} y - x = 5 \\ 3y - 3x = 15 \end{cases}$

8. **Matching** Match the description of the graph with the number of solutions to the system.
   a. lines intersect in one point
   b. lines do not intersect
   c. lines coincide

   i. no solution
   ii. infinitely many solutions
   iii. one solution

APPLYING THE MATHEMATICS

9. a. How many pairs of numbers M and N satisfy both conditions i and ii below?
      i. The sum of the numbers is –2.
      ii. The average of the numbers is 1.
   b. Explain your answer to Part a.

10. Could the situation described here have happened? Justify your answer by using a system of equations. A pizza parlor sold 36 pizzas and 21 gallons of soda for $456. The next day, at the same prices, they sold 48 pizzas and 28 gallons of soda for $608.

In 11–14, describe the graph of the system as two intersecting lines, two parallel nonintersecting lines, or coincident lines.

11. $\begin{cases} a = b \\ b - a = 0 \end{cases}$

12. $\begin{cases} y = 5 - 3x \\ 6x + 2y - 10 = 0 \end{cases}$

13. $\begin{cases} 10x + 20y = 30 \\ y + 2x = 3 \end{cases}$

14. $\begin{cases} \frac{4}{5}c - \frac{3}{5}d = 3.6 \\ 8c = 6d + 72 \end{cases}$

15. Melissa is the costume manager for a theater company and is supposed to receive a 15% professional discount from a fabric store. Last week, she bought 40 yards of a red material and 35 yards of a black fabric and paid $435.63. Two friends of hers went to the same store the following week. One bought 20 yards of red material and 10 yards of black fabric for $185, and the other bought 15 yards of red material and 40 yards of black fabric for $447.50. Did Melissa receive a discount? If so, was it the correct percentage?

A dancer is performing in a stage production.

REVIEW

16. A band has 59 musicians (M) with an additional 24 flag bearers (F). They plan to form pentagons and squares with one person in the middle, as shown below.

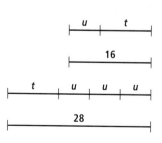

Let p be the number of pentagons formed and s be the number of squares formed. Can all musicians and flag bearers be accommodated into these formations? Why or why not?
(Lesson 10-5)

17. Each diagram at the right represents an equation involving lengths t and u.
(Lesson 10-4)

a. Write a pair of equations describing these relationships.

b. Use either your equations or the diagrams to find the lengths of t and u. Explain your reasoning.

c. Check your work.

18. Find the x-intercepts of the graph of $y = x^2 + 9x - 5$ using each method. (**Lessons 9-5, 9-3**)

    a. Let $y = 0$ and use the Quadratic Formula.

    b. Use a graphing calculator and zoom in on the intercepts.

19. a. Simplify $\sqrt{d^8 + 3d^8}$.

    b. Check your answer from Part a by testing the special case where $d = 2$. (**Lesson 8-9**)

20. In December of 1986, Dick Rutan and Jeana Yeager flew the *Voyager* airplane nonstop around Earth without refueling, the first flight of its kind. The average rate for the 24,987-mile trip was 116 mph. How many days long was this flight?
    (**Lesson 5-3**)

A chase plane follows the *Voyager* as it flies over Southern California.

21. a. Identify an equation of the vertical line through the point $(-6, 18)$.

    b. Identify an equation of the horizontal line through the point $(-6, 18)$. (**Lesson 4-2**)

EXPLORATION

22. Consider the general system $\begin{cases} ax + by = e \\ cx + dy = f \end{cases}$ of two linear equations in two variables, x and y.

    a. Find y by multiplying the first equation by c and the second equation by $-a$ and then adding.

    b. Find x by multiplying the first equation by d and the second equation by $-b$ and then adding.

    c. Your answers to Parts a and b should be fractions. Write them with the denominator $ad - bc$ if they are not already in that form.

    d. Use a CAS to solve this system and compare the CAS solution with what you found by hand.

10-7

Matrices and Matrix Multiplication

matrix (matrices)

elements

dimensions

matrix form

2 × 2 identity matrix

▶ **BIG IDEA** Rectangular arrays called matrices can sometimes be multiplied and represent systems of linear equations.

Mental Math

What is the probability that

a. a randomly-chosen one-digit number is odd?

b. a randomly-selected day in the year 2015 is in June?

c. a fair, 6-sided die shows a 3 or 5?

When you use a method like multiplication or addition to solve systems of linear equations, you do the same steps over and over. Once a linear system to be solved for x and y is in the form

$$\begin{cases} ax + by = e \\ cx + dy = f \end{cases}$$, the processes for solving it are the same. The different

solutions are caused by the numbers a, b, c, and d that are the coefficients and the numbers e and f that are the constants.

A mathematical tool called a *matrix* allows you to separate those numbers from the overall structure of the problem. A **matrix** (the

plural is **matrices**) is a rectangular array, such as $\begin{bmatrix} 3 & -4 \\ 15 & 0 \end{bmatrix}$.

The brackets [ ] identify the numbers that are in the matrix. The objects in the array are the **elements** of the matrix. The elements of

the matrix $\begin{bmatrix} 3 & -4 \\ 15 & 0 \end{bmatrix}$ are 3, –4, 15, and 0. They are identified by the

row and the column of the matrix they are in. The rows are counted from the top; the columns from the left. So –4 is the element in the 1st row and 2nd column.

The number of rows and the number of columns of a matrix are its

dimensions. Because it has 2 rows and 2 columns, the matrix $\begin{bmatrix} 3 & -4 \\ 15 & 0 \end{bmatrix}$

is a 2 × 2 (read "2 by 2") matrix, while the matrix $\begin{bmatrix} x \\ y \end{bmatrix}$ is a 2 × 1

matrix because it has 2 rows and 1 column.

The linear system $\begin{cases} 2x + 6y = 2 \\ x + 4y = -5 \end{cases}$ is described by three matrices:

the 2 × 2 *coefficient matrix* $\begin{bmatrix} 2 & 6 \\ 1 & 4 \end{bmatrix}$, the 2 × 1 *variable matrix* $\begin{bmatrix} x \\ y \end{bmatrix}$,

and the 2 × 1 *constant matrix* $\begin{bmatrix} 2 \\ -5 \end{bmatrix}$.

In *matrix form,* the system on the previous page is

$\begin{bmatrix} 2 & 6 \\ 1 & 4 \end{bmatrix} \cdot \begin{bmatrix} x \\ y \end{bmatrix} = \begin{bmatrix} 2 \\ -5 \end{bmatrix}$. In general, the **matrix form** of the system

$\begin{cases} ax + by = e \\ cx + dy = f \end{cases}$ is $\begin{bmatrix} a & b \\ c & d \end{bmatrix} \cdot \begin{bmatrix} x \\ y \end{bmatrix} = \begin{bmatrix} e \\ f \end{bmatrix}$.

Example 1

Write $\begin{cases} 4x = 5y + 10 \\ 2x - 3y = 20 \end{cases}$ in matrix form.

Solution The first step is to rewrite the system with each equation in

standard form: $\begin{cases} 4x - 5y = 10 \\ 2x - 3y = 20 \end{cases}$. Then form three matrices to describe the

coefficients, variables, and constants in the standard-form system.

$$\begin{bmatrix} 4 & -5 \\ 2 & -3 \end{bmatrix} \cdot \begin{bmatrix} x \\ y \end{bmatrix} = \begin{bmatrix} 10 \\ 20 \end{bmatrix}$$

coefficient matrix • variable matrix = constant matrix

Matrix Multiplication

Above, we have put a dot between the coefficient and variable matrices. This is because these matrices are multiplied. Matrices can be added, subtracted, and multiplied; but in this lesson you will learn only about matrix multiplication.

The matrix form of the system in Example 1 shows that the matrix

$\begin{bmatrix} 4 & -5 \\ 2 & -3 \end{bmatrix}$ is multiplied by $\begin{bmatrix} x \\ y \end{bmatrix}$. What does it mean to multiply these

matrices? To multiply these matrices, we combine each row of the

2×2 matrix $\begin{bmatrix} 4 & -5 \\ 2 & -3 \end{bmatrix}$ with the 2×1 matrix $\begin{bmatrix} x \\ y \end{bmatrix}$ to form a product

2×1 matrix. Each element in the product matrix is the product of the first entries plus the product of the second entries. Multiplying

the top row of $\begin{bmatrix} 4 & -5 \\ 2 & -3 \end{bmatrix}$ by $\begin{bmatrix} x \\ y \end{bmatrix}$ gives $4x + -5y$. Multiplying the

bottom row of $\begin{bmatrix} 4 & -5 \\ 2 & -3 \end{bmatrix}$ by $\begin{bmatrix} x \\ y \end{bmatrix}$ gives $2x + -3y$.

So $\begin{bmatrix} 4 & -5 \\ 2 & -3 \end{bmatrix} \cdot \begin{bmatrix} x \\ y \end{bmatrix} = \begin{bmatrix} 4x - 5y \\ 2x - 3y \end{bmatrix}$. This is why we say that the system

$\begin{cases} 4x - 5y = 10 \\ 2x - 3y = 20 \end{cases}$ is equivalent to the matrix equation

$\begin{bmatrix} 4 & -5 \\ 2 & -3 \end{bmatrix} \cdot \begin{bmatrix} x \\ y \end{bmatrix} = \begin{bmatrix} 10 \\ 20 \end{bmatrix}$. In the same way, two matrices can be

multiplied when both matrices contain numbers.

Example 2

Perform the multiplication $\begin{bmatrix} 10 & 3 \\ -2 & 5 \end{bmatrix} \cdot \begin{bmatrix} 4 \\ 11 \end{bmatrix}$.

Solution The result will be a 2×1 matrix. So write down places for the elements of this matrix.

$$\begin{bmatrix} 10 & 3 \\ -2 & 5 \end{bmatrix} \cdot \begin{bmatrix} 4 \\ 11 \end{bmatrix} = \begin{bmatrix} \underline{\ ?\ } \\ \underline{\ ?\ } \end{bmatrix}$$

Multiply the top row by the column to obtain the top element:

$10 \cdot 4 + 3 \cdot 11 = 73$. Multiply the bottom row by the column to obtain the bottom element: $-2 \cdot 4 + 5 \cdot 11 = 47$.

$$\begin{bmatrix} 10 & 3 \\ -2 & 5 \end{bmatrix} \cdot \begin{bmatrix} 4 \\ 11 \end{bmatrix} = \begin{bmatrix} 10 \cdot 4 + 3 \cdot 11 \\ -2 \cdot 4 + 5 \cdot 11 \end{bmatrix} = \begin{bmatrix} 73 \\ 47 \end{bmatrix}$$

Multiplying 2 × 2 Matrices

Not all matrices can be multiplied. For a product AB of two matrices A and B to exist, each row of A must have the same number of elements as each column of B. This is so that row-by-column multiplication can be performed. The element in row i and column j of the product is the result of multiplying row i of A and the column j of B.

Example 3

Find the product $\begin{bmatrix} 1 & 2 \\ 5 & 3 \end{bmatrix} \cdot \begin{bmatrix} -4 & 6 \\ 30 & 5 \end{bmatrix}$.

Solution The product will be a 2×2 matrix. First write down the spaces for the elements of the product. The product will have the same number of rows as the first matrix and the same number of columns as the second matrix.

$$\begin{bmatrix} 1 & 2 \\ 5 & 3 \end{bmatrix} \cdot \begin{bmatrix} -4 & 6 \\ 30 & 5 \end{bmatrix} = \begin{bmatrix} \underline{\ ?\ } & \underline{\ ?\ } \\ \underline{\ ?\ } & \underline{\ ?\ } \end{bmatrix}$$

Pick an element of the product matrix.

For the element in the 1st row, 1st column of the product, multiply the 1st row of the left matrix by the 1st column of the right matrix.

$1 \cdot -4 + 2 \cdot 30 = 56$

$$\begin{bmatrix} 1 & 2 \\ 5 & 3 \end{bmatrix} \cdot \begin{bmatrix} -4 & 6 \\ 30 & 5 \end{bmatrix} = \begin{bmatrix} 56 & ? \\ ? & ? \end{bmatrix}$$

For the element in the 1st row, 2nd column of the product, multiply the 1st row of the left matrix by the 2nd column of the right matrix.

$1 \cdot 6 + 2 \cdot 5 = 16$

$$\begin{bmatrix} 1 & 2 \\ 5 & 3 \end{bmatrix} \cdot \begin{bmatrix} -4 & 6 \\ 30 & 5 \end{bmatrix} = \begin{bmatrix} 56 & 16 \\ ? & ? \end{bmatrix}$$

The other two elements are found in a similar manner.

$5 \cdot -4 + 3 \cdot 30 = 70$ and $5 \cdot 6 + 3 \cdot 5 = 45$

$$\begin{bmatrix} 1 & 2 \\ 5 & 3 \end{bmatrix} \cdot \begin{bmatrix} -4 & 6 \\ 30 & 5 \end{bmatrix} = \begin{bmatrix} 56 & 16 \\ 70 & 45 \end{bmatrix}$$

In matrix multiplication, the left and right matrices play different roles. So you should not expect that reversing the order of the matrices will give the same product. For the matrices of Example 3, $\begin{bmatrix} -4 & 6 \\ 30 & 5 \end{bmatrix} \cdot \begin{bmatrix} 1 & 2 \\ 5 & 3 \end{bmatrix} = \begin{bmatrix} 26 & 10 \\ 55 & 75 \end{bmatrix}$. Matrix multiplication is not commutative.

Questions

COVERING THE IDEAS

1. Consider the matrix $\begin{bmatrix} a & b & c \\ d & e & f \end{bmatrix}$.

   a. What are the dimensions of this matrix?

   b. Name the elements in the first row.

   c. Which element is in the 2nd row, 3rd column?

2. The matrix equation $\begin{bmatrix} -4 & 6 \\ 3 & -7 \end{bmatrix} \cdot \begin{bmatrix} d \\ g \end{bmatrix} = \begin{bmatrix} 18 \\ 54 \end{bmatrix}$ describes a system

   of equations. Write the system.

In 3 and 4, a system is given.

    a. Write the coefficient matrix.

    b. Write the constant matrix.

3. $\begin{cases} 5a - 2b = -4 \\ 3a + 4b = 34 \end{cases}$

4. $\begin{cases} 5x + 3(y + 1) = 85 \\ 2x = 7y \end{cases}$

5. What is the result when the row [−4 6] is combined with the column $\begin{bmatrix} 0.25 \\ -0.50 \end{bmatrix}$ in a matrix multiplication?

In 6–8, multiply the two matrices.

6. $\begin{bmatrix} 3 & 5 \\ -2 & 4 \end{bmatrix} \cdot \begin{bmatrix} 6 \\ 1 \end{bmatrix}$

7. $\begin{bmatrix} 5 & -8 \\ 4 & 11 \end{bmatrix} \cdot \begin{bmatrix} 0.5 & 0 \\ -2 & 4 \end{bmatrix}$

8. $\begin{bmatrix} 0 & -1 \\ 1 & 2 \end{bmatrix} \cdot \begin{bmatrix} 3 & 4 \\ 5 & -6 \end{bmatrix}$

9. Give an example different from the one provided in this lesson to show that multiplication of 2×2 matrices is not commutative.

APPLYING THE MATHEMATICS

10. The matrix $\begin{bmatrix} 1 & 0 \\ 0 & 1 \end{bmatrix}$ is called the **2 × 2 identity matrix** for multiplication. To see why, calculate the products in Parts a and b.

    a. $\begin{bmatrix} 1 & 0 \\ 0 & 1 \end{bmatrix} \cdot \begin{bmatrix} a & b \\ c & d \end{bmatrix}$

    b. $\begin{bmatrix} a & b \\ c & d \end{bmatrix} \cdot \begin{bmatrix} 1 & 0 \\ 0 & 1 \end{bmatrix}$

    c. **True or False** Matrix multiplication of a 2×2 matrix with the 2×2 identity matrix is commutative.

11. Solve $\begin{bmatrix} -9 & 2 \\ 0 & 15 \end{bmatrix} \cdot \begin{bmatrix} x \\ 5 \end{bmatrix} = \begin{bmatrix} 100 \\ 75 \end{bmatrix}$ for x.

12. Solve $\begin{bmatrix} a & b \\ c & d \end{bmatrix} \cdot \begin{bmatrix} x \\ y \end{bmatrix} = \begin{bmatrix} 3x - 4y \\ 2x + y \end{bmatrix}$ for a, b, c, and d.

13. Create three different 2×2 matrices M, N, and P.
    a. Calculate MN.
    b. Calculate $(MN)P$.
    c. Calculate NP.
    d. Calculate $M(NP)$.
    e. Do your answers to Parts b and d tell you that matrix multiplication is definitely not associative, or do they tell you that matrix multiplication might be associative?

14. When a matrix M is multiplied by itself, the product $M \cdot M$ is called M^2 for short. $M^2 \cdot M = M^3$, $M^3 \cdot M = M^4$, and so on. Let $M = \begin{bmatrix} 0 & -1 \\ 1 & 0 \end{bmatrix}$. Show that M^4 is the identity matrix of Question 10.

REVIEW

15. Without drawing any graphs, explain how you can tell whether the graphs of $17x + 20y = 84$ and $16x + 20y = 85$ are two intersecting lines, one line, or two nonintersecting parallel lines. (**Lesson 10-6**)

In 16 and 17, solve by using any method. (**Lessons 10-6, 10-5, 10-4, 10-2, 10-1**)

16. $\begin{cases} 3x + 2y = 40 \\ 9x + 6y = 120 \end{cases}$

17. $\begin{cases} y = 10 - 4x \\ y = 4x - 10 \end{cases}$

18. A hardware store placed two orders with a manufacturer. The first order was for 18 hammers and 14 wrenches, and totaled $582. The second order was for 12 hammers and 10 wrenches, and totaled $396. What is the cost of one hammer and of one wrench? (**Lesson 10-5**)

19. Consider the equations $2x + y = 4$, $x = 5$, and $y = 3$. The graph of these equations forms a triangle. (**Lessons 10-1, 8-8, 8-6**)
    a. Find the vertices of the triangle.
    b. Find the length of each side of the triangle.
    c. Find the area of the triangle.

20. **Skill Sequence** Find an equivalent expression without a fraction. (**Lessons 8-4, 8-3**)
    a. $\dfrac{x^5}{x}$ b. $\dfrac{x^5}{x^3}$ c. $\dfrac{x^5}{y^3}$

21. An Aztec calendar is being placed on a rectangular mat that is 1.25 times as high and 2.25 times as wide as the calendar. What percent of the mat is taken up by the calendar? (**Lesson 5-7**)

2.25d

1.25d

EXPLORATION

22. Rows and columns with 3 elements are multiplied as follows.

$$[a \quad b \quad c] \cdot \begin{bmatrix} d \\ e \\ f \end{bmatrix} = [ad + be + cf]$$

3×3 matrices can be multiplied using the same row-by-column idea as is used with 2×2 matrices. The product MN of two 3×3 matrices M and N is a 3×3 matrix. The element in row i and column j of MN is the result of multiplying row i of M and the column j of N.

a. Use this idea to find MN when $M = \begin{bmatrix} 2 & 1 & 0 \\ -1 & 5 & 2 \\ 0 & 3 & 10 \end{bmatrix}$ and

$N = \begin{bmatrix} 0 & 3 & -3 \\ 4 & 6 & 1 \\ -0.5 & 0 & 12 \end{bmatrix}$.

b. Show that $\begin{bmatrix} 1 & 0 & 0 \\ 0 & 1 & 0 \\ 0 & 0 & 1 \end{bmatrix}$ is the identity matrix for 3×3 matrix

multiplication. (*Hint:* Calculate products as in Question 10.)

Lesson
10-8

Using Matrices to Solve Systems

Vocabulary

inverse (of a matrix)

▶ **BIG IDEA** By finding the inverse of a matrix, you can solve systems of linear equations.

The matrix method for solving systems follows a pattern like the one used to solve the equation $\frac{2}{7}x = 28$.

To solve this equation, you would multiply both sides of the equation by the number that makes the coefficient of x equal to 1. This is the multiplicative inverse of $\frac{2}{7}$, or $\frac{7}{2}$.

$$\frac{7}{2} \cdot \frac{2}{7}x = \frac{7}{2} \cdot 28$$
$$1 \cdot x = 98$$

When the coefficient is 1, the equation simplifies to become a statement of the solution, $x = 98$.

Mental Math

If $g(t) = -4t^2$, calculate

a. $g(10)$.

b. $g(5)$.

c. $\frac{g(10)}{g(5)}$.

d. $g(2)$.

The 2 × 2 Identity Matrix

Refer to the solution to the above equation. Working backwards, the key to the solution $x = 98$ is to have obtained $1 \cdot x = 98$ in the previous step. For a system of two linear equations, if (e, f) is the solution, then the solution can be written $\begin{cases} x = e \\ y = f \end{cases}$. What is the previous step?

Working backwards, this is the same as $\begin{cases} 1x + 0y = e \\ 0x + 1y = f \end{cases}$. The coefficient matrix of this system is $\begin{bmatrix} 1 & 0 \\ 0 & 1 \end{bmatrix}$. Recall from Question 10 in Lesson 10-7 that the matrix $\begin{bmatrix} 1 & 0 \\ 0 & 1 \end{bmatrix}$ is called the 2 × 2 identity matrix because when it multiplies a 2 × 2 or 2 × 1 matrix, it does not change that matrix.

$$\begin{bmatrix} 1 & 0 \\ 0 & 1 \end{bmatrix} \cdot \begin{bmatrix} h \\ k \end{bmatrix} = \begin{bmatrix} h \\ k \end{bmatrix}$$

Thus, you can solve a system with matrices if you can convert it into an equivalent system in which the coefficient matrix is the identity matrix. This is done by multiplying both sides of the original matrix equation by a new matrix, called the **inverse** of the coefficient matrix. You can use technology to help you find the inverse matrix.

Example

Use matrices to solve the system $\begin{cases} 2x - 5y = 4 \\ -4x + 11y = -6 \end{cases}$.

Solution First, write the system in matrix form.

$$\begin{bmatrix} 2 & -5 \\ -4 & 11 \end{bmatrix} \cdot \begin{bmatrix} x \\ y \end{bmatrix} = \begin{bmatrix} 4 \\ -6 \end{bmatrix}$$

Use technology to find the inverse of the coefficient matrix as shown on one particular calculator below.

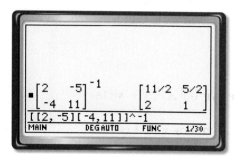

So the inverse of $\begin{bmatrix} 2 & -5 \\ -4 & 11 \end{bmatrix}$ is $\begin{bmatrix} 5.5 & 2.5 \\ 2 & 1 \end{bmatrix}$. Multiply each side of the matrix

equation by $\begin{bmatrix} 5.5 & 2.5 \\ 2 & 1 \end{bmatrix}$ on the left.

$$\begin{bmatrix} 5.5 & 2.5 \\ 2 & 1 \end{bmatrix} \cdot \begin{bmatrix} 2 & -5 \\ -4 & 11 \end{bmatrix} \cdot \begin{bmatrix} x \\ y \end{bmatrix} = \begin{bmatrix} 5.5 & 2.5 \\ 2 & 1 \end{bmatrix} \cdot \begin{bmatrix} 4 \\ -6 \end{bmatrix}$$

This produces the identity matrix. Multiply these matrices.

$$\begin{bmatrix} 1 & 0 \\ 0 & 1 \end{bmatrix} \cdot \begin{bmatrix} x \\ y \end{bmatrix} = \begin{bmatrix} 5.5 \cdot 4 + 2.5 \cdot -6 \\ 2 \cdot 4 + 1 \cdot -6 \end{bmatrix}$$

$$\begin{bmatrix} x \\ y \end{bmatrix} = \begin{bmatrix} 7 \\ 2 \end{bmatrix}.$$

The solution is $(x, y) = (7, 2)$.

Check Substitute $x = 7$ and $y = 2$ into each of the original equations.

Does $2 \cdot 7 - 5 \cdot 2 = 4$? Yes, $14 - 10 = 4$.

Does $-4 \cdot 7 + 11 \cdot 2 = -6$? Yes, $-28 + 22 = -6$.

Inverse 2 × 2 Matrices

In the previous example, we asserted that the inverse of $\begin{bmatrix} 2 & -5 \\ -4 & 11 \end{bmatrix}$

is $\begin{bmatrix} 5.5 & 2.5 \\ 2 & 1 \end{bmatrix}$. While a calculator or computer may automatically

give you the inverse, you still need to be able to check that what you are given is correct. This is done by doing the row-by-column multiplication,

$$\begin{bmatrix} 2 & -5 \\ -4 & 11 \end{bmatrix} \cdot \begin{bmatrix} 5.5 & 2.5 \\ 2 & 1 \end{bmatrix} = \begin{bmatrix} 2 \cdot 5.5 + -5 \cdot 2 & 2 \cdot 2.5 + -5 \cdot 1 \\ -4 \cdot 5.5 + 11 \cdot 2 & -4 \cdot 2.5 + 11 \cdot 1 \end{bmatrix} = \begin{bmatrix} 1 & 0 \\ 0 & 1 \end{bmatrix}.$$

When two matrices are inverses, you can multiply them in either order and you will still get the identity matrix.

 QY

The inverse of the matrix A is denoted by the symbol A^{-1}. We write

$\begin{bmatrix} 2 & -5 \\ -4 & 11 \end{bmatrix}^{-1} = \begin{bmatrix} 5.5 & 2.5 \\ 2 & 1 \end{bmatrix}$. With powers of real numbers, $x \cdot x^{-1} = 1$,

the multiplicative identity for real numbers. With matrices,

$A \cdot A^{-1} = \begin{bmatrix} 1 & 0 \\ 0 & 1 \end{bmatrix}$, the multiplicative identity for 2 × 2 matrices.

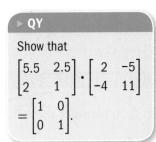

▶ **QY**

Show that
$$\begin{bmatrix} 5.5 & 2.5 \\ 2 & 1 \end{bmatrix} \cdot \begin{bmatrix} 2 & -5 \\ -4 & 11 \end{bmatrix}$$
$$= \begin{bmatrix} 1 & 0 \\ 0 & 1 \end{bmatrix}.$$

Summary of the Matrix Method

The matrix method of solving a system of linear equations is useful because it can be applied to systems with more than two variables in exactly the same way as it is applied to systems with two variables. You will work with these larger systems in later courses. The process is always the same.

$A \cdot \begin{bmatrix} x \\ y \end{bmatrix} = B$ — Write the system as the product of three matrices: coefficients · variables = constants.

$A^{-1} \cdot A \cdot \begin{bmatrix} x \\ y \end{bmatrix} = A^{-1} \cdot B$ — Multiply (on the left) each side by the inverse of the coefficient matrix.

$\begin{bmatrix} 1 & 0 \\ 0 & 1 \end{bmatrix} \cdot \begin{bmatrix} x \\ y \end{bmatrix} = A^{-1} \cdot B$ — Because A and A^{-1} are inverses, their product is the identity matrix.

$\begin{bmatrix} x \\ y \end{bmatrix} = A^{-1} \cdot B$

The left side gives the variables. The right side gives the solutions. *Caution:* Just as 0 has no multiplicative inverse, not all 2 × 2 matrices have multiplicative inverses. When a coefficient matrix does not have an inverse, then there is not a unique solution to the system. There may be infinitely many solutions, or there may be no solution.

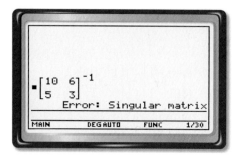

Questions

COVERING THE IDEAS

In 1–3, consider the system $\begin{cases} 1x + 0y = 7 \\ 0x + 1y = -3 \end{cases}$.

1. Solve this system.

2. Write the coefficient matrix for the system.

3. Write the matrix form for the system.

4. Write the 2 × 2 identity matrix for multiplication.

5. Show that the inverse of $\begin{bmatrix} 1 & -2 \\ 5 & 4 \end{bmatrix}$ is $\begin{bmatrix} \frac{2}{7} & \frac{1}{7} \\ -\frac{5}{14} & \frac{1}{14} \end{bmatrix}$.

6. **Multiple Choice** Which of these matrices is the inverse of $\begin{bmatrix} 3 & 4 \\ 5 & 7 \end{bmatrix}$?

   A $\begin{bmatrix} -3 & -4 \\ -5 & -7 \end{bmatrix}$ B $\begin{bmatrix} -2 & -4 \\ -5 & -6 \end{bmatrix}$ C $\begin{bmatrix} 7 & -4 \\ -5 & 3 \end{bmatrix}$ D $\begin{bmatrix} \frac{1}{3} & 0 \\ 0 & \frac{1}{17} \end{bmatrix}$

In 7–9, use the given system.
   a. Write the system in matrix form.
   b. Use technology to find the inverse of the coefficient matrix.
   c. Solve the system.

7. $\begin{cases} 3x + 5y = 27 \\ 2x + 3y = 17 \end{cases}$ 8. $\begin{cases} 2x + 3y = 18 \\ 3x + 4y = 21 \end{cases}$ 9. $\begin{cases} 2m - 6t = -6 \\ 7.5m - 15t = -37.5 \end{cases}$

APPLYING THE MATHEMATICS

10. a. Show that $\begin{bmatrix} 1 & 0 \\ 0 & -1 \end{bmatrix}$ equals its multiplicative inverse.

    b. What real numbers equal their multiplicative inverses?

In **11** and **12**, a system is given.

    a. Using inverse matrices, write the product of two matrices that will find the solution.

    b. Give the solution.

    c. Check the solution.

11. $\begin{cases} 2.3x + y = -5.5 \\ 3.1x + 2.4y = -1.1 \end{cases}$

12. $\begin{cases} 0.5m + 1.5t = 10 \\ t + 14 = 0.5m \end{cases}$

13. Consider the three systems below.

    i. $\begin{cases} x - 8y = -35 \\ 5x + 8y = 65 \end{cases}$
    ii. $\begin{cases} y = x - 3 \\ 2x + 3y = 16 \end{cases}$
    iii. $\begin{cases} 4x - 5y = 8 \\ 12x - 15y = 3 \end{cases}$

    a. Choose the system which describes two parallel lines, and write its coefficient matrix.

    b. What is your calculator's response when you try to find the inverse of the coefficient matrix of the system you chose in Part a?

14. Show that the matrix $\begin{bmatrix} 3 & 5 \\ 9 & 15 \end{bmatrix}$ has no multiplicative inverse by

writing the matrix equation $\begin{bmatrix} 3 & 5 \\ 9 & 15 \end{bmatrix} \cdot \begin{bmatrix} a & b \\ c & d \end{bmatrix} = \begin{bmatrix} 1 & 0 \\ 0 & 1 \end{bmatrix}$ as two

systems of equations and showing that those systems have no solution.

REVIEW

In **15** and **16**, multiply the given matrices. (**Lesson 10-7**)

15. $\begin{bmatrix} 5 & 6 \\ 2 & -3 \end{bmatrix} \cdot \begin{bmatrix} -4 & 1 \\ 0 & 2 \end{bmatrix}$

16. $\begin{bmatrix} 1 & 2 \\ 4 & 3 \end{bmatrix} \cdot \begin{bmatrix} 8 \\ -2 \end{bmatrix}$

17. Solve $\begin{bmatrix} -4 & 1 \\ 3 & 6 \end{bmatrix} \cdot \begin{bmatrix} 5 \\ a \end{bmatrix} = \begin{bmatrix} -12 \\ 63 \end{bmatrix}$ for a. (**Lesson 10-7**)

In **18** and **19**, determine whether the lines are parallel and nonintersecting, coincident, or intersecting in only one point. (**Lesson 10-6**)

18. $\begin{cases} y = 4x - 6 \\ 28x - 7y = -10 \end{cases}$

19. $\begin{cases} 8x + 6y = 10 \\ 4x - 3y = -5 \end{cases}$

20. A jar of change contains 64 coins consisting only of quarters and dimes. The total value of the coins in the jar is $13.60. Let q = the number of quarters, and d = the number of dimes. (**Lesson 10-4**)

    a. Write two equations that describe the information given above.

    b. How many of each type of coin is in the jar?

MONEY!

Each dime has 118 reeds and each quarter has 119 reeds along its outer edge.

Source: U.S. Mint

21. **Skill Sequence** Solve each equation. (**Lessons 9-5, 9-2, 8-6**)

    a. $x^2 = 144$

    b. $x^2 + 44 = 144$

    c. $4x^2 + 44 = 144$

    d. $4x^2 + 44x + 265 = 144$

22. Simplify the expression $\sqrt{x} \cdot \sqrt{x} \cdot \sqrt{x^3}$. (**Lessons 8-7, 8-6**)

23. Suppose a bank offers a 4.60% annual yield on a 4-year CD. What would be the amount paid at the end of the 4 years to an investor who invests $1,800 in this CD? (**Lesson 7-1**)

24. Ms. Brodeur wants to lease about 2,000 square meters of floor space for a business. She noticed an advertisement in the newspaper regarding a set of 3 vacant stores. Their widths are given in the floor plan at the right. How deep must these stores be to meet Ms. Brodeur's required area? (**Lesson 2-1**)

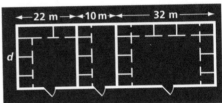

EXPLORATION

25. A formula for the inverse of a 2×2 matrix $\begin{bmatrix} a & b \\ c & d \end{bmatrix}$ can be found by following these steps.

    Step 1 Write $\begin{bmatrix} a & b \\ c & d \end{bmatrix} \cdot \begin{bmatrix} x & u \\ y & v \end{bmatrix} = \begin{bmatrix} 1 & 0 \\ 0 & 1 \end{bmatrix}$ as two systems of

    equations. Keep a, b, c, and d as the coefficients. One system will have the variables x and y and the other will have u and v.

    Step 2 Solve for x, y, u, and v in terms of a, b, c, and d. Find a formula in this way and check it with at least two different matrices. You may want to use a CAS to find the formula.

Lesson

10-9 | Systems of Inequalities

> ▶ **BIG IDEA** The graph of the solutions to a system of linear inequalities is a region bounded by lines.

In Lesson 6-9, you graphed linear inequalities like $y < 11$ and $y \geq 4x + 3$ on a coordinate plane. These inequalities describe half-planes. In this lesson, you will see how to graph regions described by a system of two or more inequalities. Solving a system of inequalities involves finding the common solutions of two or more inequalities.

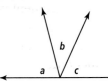
Example 1

Graph all solutions to the system $\begin{cases} x \geq 0 \\ y \geq 0 \end{cases}$.

Solution First graph the solution to $x \geq 0$. It is shown at the left below. Then graph the solution $y \geq 0$, shown at the right below.

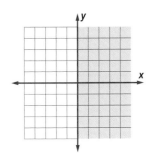
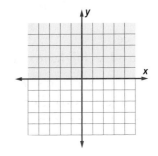

The solution to the system is the set of points common to both of the sets above. At the right we show the solutions to the two inequalities superimposed. At the far right is the solution to the system. The solution is the intersection of the two solution sets above shown in green. It consists of the first quadrant and the nonnegative parts of the x- and y-axes.

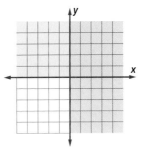
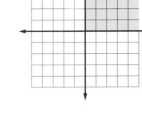

Recall that in general, the graph of $Ax + By < C$ is a half-plane, and that it lies on one side of the boundary line $Ax + By = C$.

Example 2

Graph all solutions to the system $\begin{cases} y \le 3 \\ x > -2 \\ y > x - 1 \end{cases}$.

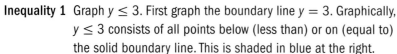

Solution The graph of the system is the set of points in common to all three half-planes. So graph all three inequalities.

Inequality 1 Graph $y \le 3$. First graph the boundary line $y = 3$. Graphically, $y \le 3$ consists of all points below (less than) or on (equal to) the solid boundary line. This is shaded in blue at the right.

Inequality 2 Graph $x > -2$. Graph the boundary line $x = -2$. This line is dashed since we want only values greater than -2. $x > -2$ tells us to shade to the right of the line in red where values are greater than -2.

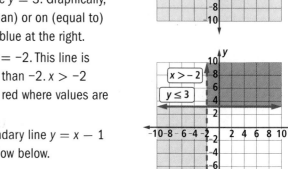

Inequality 3 Graph $y > x - 1$. Graph the dashed boundary line $y = x - 1$ and shade above the line as shown in yellow below.

The solution is the region shown below and includes one of the sides of the triangle. The graph at the far right shows what your final graph should look like.

Check A partial check is to choose a point in the intersection region. We choose $(1, 2)$. Substitute the point into all the inequalities.

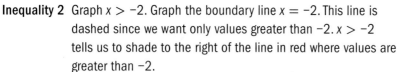

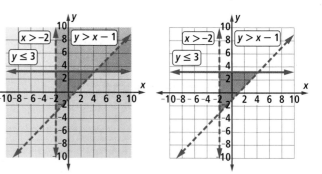

Is $2 \le 3$? Yes.

Is $1 > -2$? Yes.

Is $2 > 1 - 1$? Yes.

When an intersection point cannot be found easily from a graph, you need to solve a system of equations to find it.

GUIDED

Example 3

Graph all solutions to the system $\begin{cases} y < 2x + 3 \\ y > 2x - 2 \end{cases}$.

Solution

1. The boundary lines $y = 2x + 3$ and $y = 2x - 2$ have the same slope. So they are ____?____ lines.

2. Graph the lines.

3. The solutions to $y < 2x + 3$ comprise the half-plane $\underline{\quad?\quad}$ the boundary line. The solutions to $y > 2x - 2$ make up the (above/below) half-plane $\underline{\quad?\quad}$ the line. (above/below)

You saw in Lesson 10-6 that a system whose graph is made up of nonintersecting and parallel lines has no solutions. Is this necessarily true for a system of inequalities whose boundary lines are nonintersecting and parallel? Explain. $\underline{\quad?\quad}$

4. Graph the intersection of the two half-planes in Step 3.

Questions

COVERING THE IDEAS

1. The graph of all solutions to $\begin{cases} x > 0 \\ y < 0 \end{cases}$ consists of all points in which quadrant?

2. Graph the solutions to the system $\begin{cases} x < 0 \\ y > 0 \end{cases}$.

3. Consider the system $\begin{cases} y \le 4x + 1 \\ y > 2x + 1 \end{cases}$.

    a. How is the graph of all solutions to the system related to the graphs of $y \le 4x + 1$ and $y > 2x + 1$?

    b. **Fill in the Blank** The graph of $y > 2x + 1$ is a $\underline{\quad?\quad}$.

    c. Why does the graph of $y \le 4x + 1$ include its boundary line?

    d. Is $(2, 5)$ a solution to this system? How can you tell?

In 4 and 5, graph the solution to the system.

4. $\begin{cases} x > 0 \\ y > 0 \\ 3x + y < 10 \end{cases}$

5. $\begin{cases} x \ge -3 \\ y \le 4 \\ y \ge 2x + 1 \end{cases}$

6. Consider the system $\begin{cases} x > 0 \\ y > 0 \\ x + y < 30 \\ x + y > 20 \end{cases}$.

    a. The graph of all solutions to this system is the interior of a quadrilateral with what vertices?

    b. Name two points that are solutions to the system.

    c. Is $(9, 10)$ a solution to the system? Why or why not?

7. The solution to a system of equations that involves different parallel lines is Ø (empty set). You saw in Example 3 this is not necessarily true of a system of inequalities that involves parallel lines. Is it possible to have a system of inequalities whose solution is Ø? Why or why not?

APPLYING THE MATHEMATICS

In 8 and 9, describe the shaded region with a system of inequalities.

8.
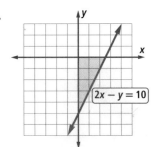

9.
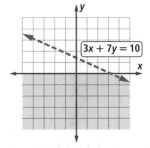

10. Write the system of inequalities whose solution is the interior of the rectangle with vertices (–3, 10), (5, 10), (5, –1), and (–3, –1).

11. It takes Tippie about 10 minutes to type a letter of moderate length and about 8 minutes to type a normal double-spaced page.
    a. Write a system of inequalities that describes the total number of letters L and pages P Tippie can type in an hour or less. Assume the number of letters typed is greater than or equal to zero, as is the number of pages.
    b. Accurately graph the set of points that satisfies the system.

12. An actress is paid $300 per day to understudy a part and $750 per day to perform the role before an audience. During one run, an actress earned between $4,000 and $7,000.
    a. At most, how many times might she have performed the role?
    b. What is the maximum number of times she might have been an understudy?
    c. Graph all possible ways she might have earned her salary.

13. A hockey team is scheduled to play 14 games during a season. Its coach estimates that it needs at least 20 points to make the playoffs. A win is worth 2 points and a tie is worth 1 point.
    a. Make a graph of all the combinations of wins w and ties t that will get the team into the playoffs.
    b. How many ways are there for the team to make the playoffs?

Actors' Equity Association, founded in 1913, is the labor union that represents more than 45,000 actors and stage managers in the United States.

Source: Actors' Equity Association

REVIEW

In 14 and 15, a system of equations is given.

a. Write the system in matrix form.

b. Use technology to find the inverse of the coefficient matrix.

c. Solve the system. (Lesson 10-8)

14. $\begin{cases} y = 3x - 8 \\ 4x + 4y = 12 \end{cases}$

15. $\begin{cases} 6x + 4y = 14 \\ -2x - 3y = -18 \end{cases}$

16. Let ℓ be the line with equation $y = -4x + 9$. Write an equation of a line that (Lesson 10-6)

a. coincides with ℓ.

b. does not intersect ℓ.

17. Solve the system $\begin{cases} 2.5x + y = 6 \\ 9x + 4y = 17.5 \end{cases}$ using any method.

(Lessons 10-5, 10-4, 10-2, 10-1)

In 18–20, use the formula $h = -16t^2 + 94t + 2$ for the height h in feet of a model rocket t seconds after being fired straight up from a stand 2 feet off the ground. (Lessons 9-5, 9-4, 9-3)

18. a. Graph the equation.

b. Use the graph to find the maximum height of the rocket.

19. a. Find the height of the rocket after 6 seconds.

b. Interpret your answer to Part a.

20. Use the Quadratic Formula to calculate at what time(s) the rocket is at a height of 100 feet.

EXPLORATION

21. Find a system of linear inequalities whose solution on a coordinate plane is a region like the one shown at the right.

Lesson

10-10

Nonlinear Systems

Vocabulary

nonlinear system

Mental Math

Refer to the rectangle.

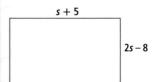

a. What is the area of the rectangle?

b. What is the perimeter of the rectangle?

▶ **BIG IDEA**   The ideas used to solve systems of linear equations can be applied to solve some systems of nonlinear equations.

Previously in this chapter you have worked with systems of linear equations. In these systems, every graph involved is a line. In this lesson, we consider systems that involve curves. A **nonlinear system** is a system of equations or inequalities in which at least one of the equations or inequalities is nonlinear.

GUIDED

Example 1

Solve the system $\begin{cases} y = x^2 + 3 \\ y = x + 9 \end{cases}$.

Solution   Look at the graphs at the right. The solutions occur at the points of intersection. These graphs intersect at $(-2, \underline{\quad?\quad})$ and $(3, \underline{\quad?\quad})$; therefore, the system has two solutions.

The solutions are $(\underline{\quad?\quad})$ and $(\underline{\quad?\quad})$.

 QY

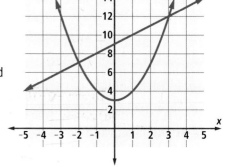

Solving algebraically using substitution is also an option. You may need to use the Quadratic Formula.

▶ **QY**

Check your answer to Guided Example 1 by substituting the coordinates of each point into both equations to verify that they are solutions to the system.

Example 2

Solve the system $\begin{cases} y = -2x + 8 \\ y = -x^2 + 4x - 1 \end{cases}$.

Solution   Because both expressions in x are equal to y, they are equal to each other at the point of intersection.

$-2x + 8 = -x^2 + 4x - 1$	Substitution
$8 = -x^2 + 6x - 1$	Add 2x to both sides.
$0 = -x^2 + 6x - 9$	Subtract 8 from both sides.
$x = \dfrac{-6 \pm \sqrt{6^2 - 4(-1)(-9)}}{2(-1)}$	Quadratic Formula
$x = \dfrac{-6 \pm \sqrt{36 - 36}}{-2} = \dfrac{-6 \pm 0}{-2}$ or 3	

Now find the y-coordinate of the point of intersection.

$y = -2x + 8$

$y = -2(3) + 8 = -6 + 8 = 2$

The solution is (3, 2).

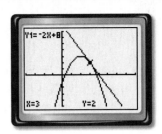

Check The graph reinforces that there is only one solution and that it is at (3, 2), as shown on the screen at the right.

Some nonlinear systems have no solutions.

Example 3

Solve the system $\begin{cases} y = x^2 + 6x + 11 \\ y = -x^2 + 6x - 9 \end{cases}$.

Solution 1 Use substitution.

$x^2 + 6x + 11 = -x^2 + 6x - 9$

$2x^2 + 6x + 11 = 6x - 9$ Add x^2.

$2x^2 + 11 = -9$ Subtract $6x$.

$2x^2 = -20$ Subtract 11.

$x^2 = -10$ Divide by 2.

$x = \pm\sqrt{-10}$ Take the square root.

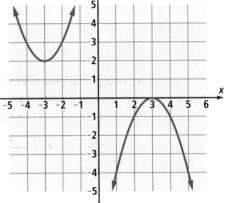

The solutions $\sqrt{-10}$ and $-\sqrt{-10}$ are not real numbers, so there is no solution for this system in the set of real numbers.

Solution 2 Graph the equations.

The parabolas never intersect, so there is no solution to this system.

When you don't know how to solve a system of equations algebraically, you can use a graphing approach to make very good approximations.

Example 4

Jonas is working on a science fair project. He wants to study the result of combining equal populations (in weight) of two types of bacteria. The first bacteria (in grams) grow according to the function $f(x) = 15(0.8)^x$ where $x =$ the time from now (in hours). The other bacteria growth (in grams) is modeled by $g(x) = 4(1.5)^x$, where $x =$ the time from now (in hours). If Jonas wants to combine them when the two populations are equal, how long will he have to wait? How many grams of each type of bacteria will there be at that time?

(continued on next page)

Solution This situation can be represented by the following system.

$$\begin{cases} f(x) = 15(0.8)^x \\ g(x) = 4(1.5)^x \end{cases}$$

Graph the two functions on your calculator. Be sure to include any intersections in the viewing window. Use the INTERSECT command to find an accurate approximation for the solution.

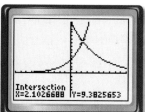

Intersection
X=2.1026688 Y=9.3825653

Jonas should combine the bacteria in approximately 2.10 hours (or 2 hours and 6 minutes). There will be about 9.4 grams of bacteria in each population at that time.

Questions

COVERING THE IDEAS

In 1 and 2, solve the system using substitution.

1. $\begin{cases} y = 2x^2 + 12x + 17 \\ y = -x^2 - 6x - 10 \end{cases}$

2. $\begin{cases} y = x^2 + 4x + 3 \\ y = 3x + 1 \end{cases}$

3. Solve the system $\begin{cases} y = 3x^2 \\ y = -4x^2 \end{cases}$ by picturing the graph in your head.

In 4–6, solve the system.

4. $\begin{cases} y = x^2 - 6x + 1 \\ y = -x^2 + 4x + 1 \end{cases}$

5. $\begin{cases} p = 9q + 25 \\ p = 2q^2 + 7q + 1 \end{cases}$

6. $\begin{cases} y = x^2 + 3 \\ y = -x + 1 \end{cases}$

In 7 and 8, solve the system by graphing. Round solutions to the nearest hundredth.

7. $\begin{cases} y = 5x^2 + 5 \\ y = 0.5x^2 \end{cases}$

8. $\begin{cases} y = 2.718^x \\ y = 3.14(0.25)^x \end{cases}$

APPLYING THE MATHEMATICS

In 9 and 10, solve the system by graphing.

9. $\begin{cases} y = |x - 3| \\ y = -2x^2 + 12x - 18 \end{cases}$

10. $\begin{cases} y = x^2 \\ y = 2^x \end{cases}$

11. Solve the system of Example 3 by addition.

12. A quarterback passes a football to a receiver downfield. The path of the ball is described by the equation $h = -0.025x^2 + x + 6$, where $x =$ the horizontal distance (in yards) of the ball from the quarterback and h is the height of the ball (in feet) above the ground. The receiver catches the ball 40 yards downfield. A bird flies over the quarterback in the same direction as the ball. Its flight is described by the equation $y = \frac{7}{60}x + 10$, where $x =$ the distance from the quarterback (in yards) and y is the bird's height (in feet).

a. When the quarterback first threw the ball, how high was it off the ground?

b. How high was the bird when it was right over the quarterback?

c. How many times did the path of the bird and the football cross?

d. Give these points of intersection.

e. Notice that the time when the bird or the football is moving is not given. Explain why this means the bird and ball might not have hit each other.

Philadelphia Eagles quarterback Donovan McNabb throws a pass against the Tampa Bay Buccaneers in the first quarter of the NFC championship game at Veterans Stadium in Philadelphia, January 19, 2003.

Source: Associated Press

13. During a spring training game in 2001, baseball pitching great Randy Johnson threw a fastball. A bird flew in the ball's path and was accidentally struck by the ball. This is the only time in Major League Baseball that a bird has been struck by a pitch. A possible equation for the height of Randy Johnson's pitch is $h = -5.56t^2 - 1.39t + 4.25$, where t is the time in seconds since he threw the ball and h is the ball's height in feet above the ground. A possible equation for the bird's height is $h = -24.42t^2 + 3.94t + 5.14$, where t is the time in seconds since Randy's pitch and h is the bird's height above the ground in feet.

a. For the ball and the bird to collide, what must be true of the system $\begin{cases} h = -5.56t^2 - 1.39t + 4.25 \\ h = -24.42t^2 + 3.94t + 5.14 \end{cases}$?

b. Find how long after the pitch was thrown that it struck the bird.

c. What was the height of the bird when it got struck by the ball?

d. Does the graph of the parabola $h = -5.56t^2 - 1.39t + 4.25$ represent the flight of the ball? Explain.

14. Company One's stock values during the month of January can be represented by $V = 40(0.9)^x$, where x is time in days since the beginning of the month. Company Two's stock values can be represented by $V = |2x - 9|$ for the same time period.

a. Approximate when Companies One and Two had the same stock value and give that value.

b. Describe how well each company's stock values changed over the month (from $x = 0$ to $x = 31$).

c. When would have been the best time to buy Company Two's stock? Explain your answer.

REVIEW

15. Solve $\begin{bmatrix} 1 & -2 \\ 3 & 1.5 \end{bmatrix} \cdot \begin{bmatrix} -3 \\ 2 \\ n \end{bmatrix} = \begin{bmatrix} -11.5 \\ 3 \end{bmatrix}$ for n. **(Lesson 10-8)**

16. Solve $\begin{cases} x - 1.5y = 11 \\ 5x + 9y = 11 \end{cases}$ by any method. **(Lessons 10-5, 10-4, 10-3)**

17. Suppose Rodney bought a car 32 years ago for $8,000. It lost 6% of its value each year for the first 15 years. Then its value stayed the same for 3 years. When it was 18 years old, the car became a collector's item and its value increased 21% each year. Find the value of the car now. **(Lessons 7-3, 7-2)**

18. Graph the solutions to the inequality $-4.5y - 18x + 3 < 12$ on a coordinate grid. **(Lesson 6-9)**

EXPLORATION

19. An equation for a circle with radius 2 centered at the origin is $x^2 + y^2 = 4$. Use your calculator to find a pair of values of m and b so that the number of solutions to the system $\begin{cases} x^2 + y^2 = 4 \\ y = mx + b \end{cases}$ is

a. 2. b. 1. c. 0.

Chapter 10 Projects

1 Cars and Computers

For the years 1985, 1990, 1995, 2000, and 2005, find the number of cars in the United States and the number of personal computers.

a. Find lines of best fit for these two sets of data.

b. Find the year in which these two lines meet.

c. Do you think your calculation in Part b is a good prediction of when the number of computers in the United States will be the same as the number of cars? Explain your answer.

2 When Do Systems Have Integer Solutions?

Suppose you have a system of the form
$$\begin{cases} ax + by = e \\ cx + dy = f, \end{cases}$$
where $a, b, c, d, e,$ and f are all integers.

a. Create three systems of this form that have a single solution whose coordinates are integers. In each case calculate $ad - bc$.

b. Create three systems of this form that have a single solution whose coordinates are not two integers. In each case calculate $ad - bc$.

c. When do you think that a system as described above has a solution with integer coordinates?

3 Systems with More Variables

In mathematics and in many of its applications, sometimes you need to solve systems with more than just two variables. Just as a system with two variables had two equations, a system with n variables has n equations. The methods for solving these systems are basically the same as the methods you studied in this chapter.

a. Explain how you could solve the system
$$\begin{cases} x + y + z = 3 \\ x + 2y = 5 \\ 3x - 2y = -1 \end{cases}$$
. (*Hint:* You might want to solve a certain system with two variables in the process.)

b. Using methods similar to the methods in this chapter, what could you do to the system
$$\begin{cases} 3x - 2y - 2z = 0 \\ x + y + z = 0 \\ 7x + 10y + z = 9 \end{cases}$$
to make it look more like the system in Part a, in which only one equation had the variable z in it? Do this, then solve the system.

c. Write a short explanation on how to solve systems with three variables for someone who knows how to solve systems with only two variables.

4 Adding and Subtracting Equations

Write two linear equations and do the following.

a. Graph the two linear equations and find their intersection.

b. Graph the equation found by adding the two selected equations.

c. Graph the equation found by subtracting them.

d. Multiply each equation by a number, and add them again.

e. Do the graphs have any common features? If so, describe them.

f. Verify your calculations starting with a different pair of equations.

5 Finding the Counterfeit

A math-savvy pirate finds 12 gold coins, and he fears that several might be counterfeit. (Counterfeit coins are lighter.) He measures all 12 coins on a scale and finds that together they weigh 1.3 kilograms. He removes one coin, and finds that together they weigh 1.15 kilograms. He removes yet another coin, and finds that together they weigh 1 kilogram. At this point, his scale broke. Find out how many counterfeit coins (if any) the pirate found. Explain how systems of equations can be used to find the solution.

Chapter 10 Summary and Vocabulary

○ A **system** is a set of sentences that together describe a single situation. Situations that lead to linear equations can lead to a **linear system.** All that is needed is that more than one condition must be satisfied. This chapter discusses ways of solving systems in which the sentences are equations or inequalities in two variables.

○ The **solution set to a system** is the set of all solutions common to all of the sentences in the system. A solution to a system of two linear equations is an ordered pair (x, y) that satisfies each equation. Systems of two linear equations may have zero, one, or infinitely many solutions. Other systems may have other numbers of solutions.

○ One way to solve a system is by graphing. There are as many solutions as intersection points. Graphing is also a way to describe solutions of systems that have infinitely many solutions, for example, systems of **coincident lines** and **systems of linear inequalities,** with overlapping half-planes.

○ However, graphing does not always yield exact solutions. In this chapter, four strategies are presented for finding exact solutions to systems of linear equations. 1. Substitution is a good method to use if at least one equation is given in $y = mx + b$ form. 2. Addition is appropriate if the same term has opposite signs in the two equations in the system. 3. Multiplication is a good method when both equations are in $Ax + By = C$ form. Each of these methods changes the system into an equivalent system whose solutions are the same as those of the original system. 4. With **matrices,** the system $\begin{cases} ax + by = e \\ cx + dy = f \end{cases}$ becomes $\begin{bmatrix} a & b \\ c & d \end{bmatrix} \cdot \begin{bmatrix} x \\ y \end{bmatrix} = \begin{bmatrix} e \\ f \end{bmatrix}$. This matrix equation is of the form $AX = B$, where A is the coefficient matrix $\begin{bmatrix} a & b \\ c & d \end{bmatrix}$, X is the variable matrix $\begin{bmatrix} x \\ y \end{bmatrix}$, and B is the constant matrix $\begin{bmatrix} e \\ f \end{bmatrix}$. Multiplying both sides of $AX = B$ by the **multiplicative inverse** A^{-1} of the matrix A results in $X = A^{-1}B$.

Theorems and Properties

Generalized Addition Property of Equality (p. 601)
Slopes and Parallel Lines Property (p. 616)

Vocabulary

10-1
system
solution to a system
empty set, null set

10-4
addition method for solving a system

10-5
equivalent systems
multiplication method for solving a system

10-6
coincident lines

10-7
matrix (matrices)
elements
dimensions
matrix form
2 × 2 identity matrix

10-8
inverse (of a matrix)

10-10
nonlinear system

Chapter

10   Self-Test

Take this test as you would take a test in class. You will need a calculator. Then use the Selected Answers section in the back of the book to check your work.

In 1–4, solve the system by the indicated method.

1. $\begin{cases} y = x - 7 \\ y = 1.5x + 2 \end{cases}$ substitution

2. $\begin{cases} -4d + 9f = 3 \\ 4d - 5f = 9 \end{cases}$ addition

3. $\begin{cases} 7h + 3g = 4 \\ 2h - g = 2 \end{cases}$ multiplication

4. $\begin{cases} 3a - b = 6 \\ \frac{3}{5}b = 37 - 4a \end{cases}$ graphing

5. Solve $\begin{cases} y = x^2 + 3x - 5 \\ y = 6x - 7 \end{cases}$ by using any method.

6. Determine whether the system $\begin{cases} 3s = 2t - 5 \\ \frac{2}{3}t - \frac{1}{3}s = -5 \end{cases}$ has 0, 1, or infinitely many solutions.

In 7 and 8, multiply.

7. $\begin{bmatrix} 2 & 7 \\ 1 & 0 \end{bmatrix} \cdot \begin{bmatrix} 3 \\ 4 \end{bmatrix}$

8. $\begin{bmatrix} 3 & 5 \\ 4 & 6 \end{bmatrix} \cdot \begin{bmatrix} 2 & 8 \\ 1 & 7 \end{bmatrix}$

$\begin{matrix} 6+5 & 24+ & 35 \\ 8+6 & 28+42 \end{matrix}$

9. Solve the system $\begin{cases} 3p + 5q = 5 \\ p - q = 7 \end{cases}$ using matrices. Use a calculator to find the inverse of the matrix.

10. An electronics store receives two large orders. The first order is for 6 high-definition televisions and 3 DVD players, and totals $6,795. The second order is for 4 high-definition televisions and 4 DVD players, and totals $4,860. What is the cost of one high-definition television and what is the cost of one DVD player?

11. Give values for m, n, c, and d so that the system $\begin{cases} y = mx + c \\ y = nx + d \end{cases}$ has infinitely many solutions.

12. Rosie is buying posies and roses. She wants to spend no more than $40. Roses are $5 each, and posies are $2 each. Accurately graph all combinations of flowers that she can buy.

13. Solve the system $\begin{cases} y = 3x + 50 \\ y = -2x + 70 \end{cases}$ by graphing.

14. A passenger airplane took 2 hours to fly from St. Louis, Missouri, to Orlando, Florida, in the direction of the jet stream. On the return trip against the jet stream, the airplane took 2 hours and 30 minutes. If the distance between the two cities is about 1,000 miles, find the airplane's speed in still air and the speed of the jet stream.

15. Akando bought 80 feet of chicken wire to make a coop on his farm. He needs the coop to be at least 10 feet wide and 15 feet long.

    a. Draw a graph to show all possible dimensions (to the nearest foot) of the coop.

    b. At most, how wide can the coop be?

16. Graph all solutions to the system $\begin{cases} y \le x + 3 \\ y \ge -2x + 4 \end{cases}$

17. Kele paid for his lunch with 15 coins. He used only quarters and dimes. If his lunch cost $2.40, how many of each coin did he use?

18. Write a system of inequalities to describe the shaded region below.

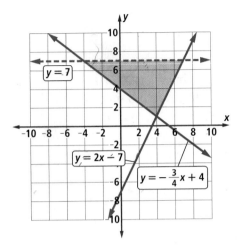

Chapter 10 Chapter Review

SKILLS
PROPERTIES
USES
REPRESENTATIONS

SKILLS Procedures used to get answers

OBJECTIVE A Solve systems using substitution. (Lessons 10-2, 10-3)

In 1 and 2, solve the system by using substitution.

1. $\begin{cases} m = n \\ 3m - 4 = n \end{cases}$

2. $\begin{cases} 2p = q + 5 \\ 2q = 4(p + 2) \end{cases}$

In 3 and 4, two lines have the given equations. Find the point of intersection, if any.

3. Line ℓ: $y = 2x + 5$;

   Line m: $y = -3x + 4$

4. Line p: $y = \frac{2}{3}x + \frac{1}{9}$;

   Line q: $y = \frac{1}{5}x - 4$

OBJECTIVE B Solve systems by addition and multiplication. (Lessons 10-4, 10-5)

In 5 and 6, solve the system by addition.

5. $\begin{cases} 3b + 4 = a \\ -3b - 5 = 2a \end{cases}$

6. $\begin{cases} 0.4x + 0.75y = 2.7 \\ 0.4x - 2y = 2.5 \end{cases}$

In 7–10, solve the system by multiplication.

7. $\begin{cases} 3f + g = 41 \\ f - 2g = 20 \end{cases}$

8. $\begin{cases} 3t - u = 5 \\ 6t + 3u = 7 \end{cases}$

9. $\begin{cases} 5w + 2v = 6 \\ 7 + 5v = w \end{cases}$ $5w + 2v = 6$ $25w + 10v = 6$ $5v - w = -7$ $10v - w = -7$

10. $\begin{cases} 3x - 5 = y \\ 2x - 7y = 9 \end{cases}$

OBJECTIVE C Multiply 2 × 2 matrices by 2 × 2 or 2 × 1 matrices. (Lesson 10-7)

In 11–14, multiply.

11. $\begin{bmatrix} 2 & -4 \\ 3 & 5 \end{bmatrix} \cdot \begin{bmatrix} 7 \\ 4 \end{bmatrix}$

12. $\begin{bmatrix} 6 & -0.5 \\ 0.5 & 2 \end{bmatrix} \cdot \begin{bmatrix} 6 \\ 12 \end{bmatrix}$

13. $\begin{bmatrix} -6 & 8 \\ -9 & 7 \end{bmatrix} \cdot \begin{bmatrix} 1 & 3 \\ 4 & 2 \end{bmatrix}$

14. $\begin{bmatrix} 2 & 11 \\ 0 & 7 \end{bmatrix} \cdot \begin{bmatrix} 0 & -4 \\ 5 & 9 \end{bmatrix}$

OBJECTIVE D Solve systems using matrices. (Lesson 10-8)

In 15–18, a system is given.

a. Write the system in matrix form.

b. Use technology to find the inverse.

c. Solve the system.

15. $\begin{cases} 3x + 2y = 7 \\ 5x + 7y = 9 \end{cases}$

16. $\begin{cases} 6m + 4d = 7 \\ 4m + 3d = 13 \end{cases}$

17. $\begin{cases} 5p - 7q = 20 \\ 4p - 8q = 14 \end{cases}$

18. $\begin{cases} w + 3z = 5 \\ 4z - 5w = 9 \end{cases}$

OBJECTIVE E Solve nonlinear systems. (Lesson 10-10)

In 19 and 20, solve by substitution.

19. $\begin{cases} y = -2x^2 \\ y + x^2 = -1 \end{cases}$

20. $\begin{cases} 2x^3 - 2y = x^2 - 5 \\ y = x^3 - 2x \end{cases}$

PROPERTIES Principles behind the mathematics

OBJECTIVE F Determine whether a system has 0, 1, or infinitely many solutions. (Lesson 10-6)

In 21–24, determine whether the given system has 0, 1, or infinitely many solutions.

21. $\begin{cases} 2y + 3x = 5 \quad (4-3x)+3x=5 \\ 2y = 4 - 3x \end{cases}$

22. $\begin{cases} y + 3x = 7 \\ y = 3x + 7 \end{cases}$

23. $\begin{cases} 3p = 7q + 2 \\ 6p = 10q + 5 \end{cases}$

24. $\begin{cases} 4p + 5q = 7 \\ 2p = 3\frac{1}{2} - \frac{5}{2}q \end{cases}$

25. When will the system $\begin{cases} y = mx + a \\ y = mx + b \end{cases}$ have no solution? Explain your answer.

26. Can the given set of points be the intersection of two lines?

    a. exactly one point

    b. exactly two points

    c. infinitely many points

    d. no points

27. **Fill in the Blank** Two lines are parallel only if they have the same ___?___.

28. **True or False** Two lines can intersect in more than one point if they have different y-intercepts.

USES Applications of mathematics in real-world situations

OBJECTIVE G Use systems of linear equations to solve real-world problems. (Lessons 10-2, 10-3, 10-4, 10-5, 10-6)

29. Austin drove four times as far as Antonio. Together, they drove 350 miles. How far did they each drive?

30. Car A costs $2,800 down and $100 per month. Car B costs $3,100 down and $50 per month. After how many months is the amount paid for the cars equal?

31. Good Job offers $30,000 per year, plus a $1,000 raise each year. Nice Job offers $32,000 per year, plus a $500 raise each year. When will you make more money per year with Good Job?

32. Tickets to see an orchestra cost $30 for adults and $15 for students. One night, the total number of tickets sold was 633. If they sold $15,945 worth of tickets, how many adults and how many students attended?

33. A chemist wishes to mix a 15% acid solution with 30% acid solution to make a 25% acid solution. If the chemist wants to make 8 pints of the solution, how many pints of each solution should the chemist use?

34. From 1990 to 2000, the population of Seattle, Washington, grew at a rate of about 4,700 people per year, to a population of about 565,000. Baltimore, Maryland, decreased at a rate of about 8,400 people per year, to a population of about 650,000. If these rates continue, in about how many years will Seattle and Baltimore have the same population?

OBJECTIVE H Use systems of linear inequalities to solve real-world problems. (Lesson 10-9)

35. A chef has 10 ducks and wants to make Peking duck and duck salad. It takes 1 duck to make Peking duck, and 2 ducks to make duck salad. Make a graph to show all the combinations of duck dishes that the chef can make.

36. Suppose 40 students want to play 2 games. If each game must have at least 10 students and at most 25 students, make a graph of the number of ways the students could divide up to play the games.

37. Jackie is running around a rectangular track with a perimeter of at most 500 feet. The track is at least 80 feet wide and 100 feet long.

   a. Draw a graph to show all possible dimensions (to the nearest foot) of the track.

   b. What is the maximum length of the track?

   c. What is the maximum width of the track?

38. Nihad won $300 in a soccer all-stars contest. She wants to buy soccer balls for $25 and pairs of soccer shoes for $30. She wants to buy at least two balls and at least two pairs of shoes.

   a. Graph all the combinations she could buy.

   b. What is the maximum number of pairs of shoes she can buy?

   c. What is the maximum number of balls she can buy?

REPRESENTATIONS Pictures, graphs, or objects that illustrate concepts

OBJECTIVE I Find solutions to systems of equations by graphing. (Lessons 10-1, 10-6, 10-10)

In 39–43, solve the system by graphing. Round your answers to the nearest tenth.

39. $\begin{cases} 5x + 4y = 7 \\ 3x + 2y = 6 \end{cases}$

40. $\begin{cases} 16x - 16y = 16 \\ \frac{1}{2}x + \frac{1}{2}y = -2 \end{cases}$

41. $\begin{cases} 0.5x - 0.4y = 0.8 \\ x - 1.6 = 0.8y \end{cases}$

42. $\begin{cases} y = 2^x \\ y = 1.32x + 2.67 \end{cases}$

43. $\begin{cases} 2y - 3x = 7 \\ x^2 + y = 15 \end{cases}$

OBJECTIVE J Graphically represent solutions to systems of linear inequalities. (Lesson 10-9)

In 44–47, graph all solutions to the system.

44. $\begin{cases} y \le 3x \\ y \ge 2x + 1 \end{cases}$

45. $\begin{cases} x + 4 > 7 + 2y \\ x - 4 < y + 2 \end{cases}$

46. $\begin{cases} y > -2 \\ x + y < 0 \\ x - y \ge 1 \end{cases}$

47. $\begin{cases} x \ge 0 \\ y \ge 0 \\ x + y < 9 \end{cases}$

In 48 and 49, accurately graph the set of points that satisfies the situation.

48. An elephant can eat 70 pounds of food in a meal. If the elephant eats P sacks of peanuts averaging 7 pounds each and L bunches of leaves weighing 5 pounds each, how many sacks and bunches can the elephant eat?

49. Conan wants to watch t television shows and m movies. Each show lasts 30 minutes, and each movie lasts 90 minutes. If he has 5 hours of viewing time available, how many full shows and movies can he watch?

OBJECTIVE K Write a system of inequalities given a graph. (Lesson 10-9)

In 50–52, write a system of inequalities to describe the shaded region.

50.

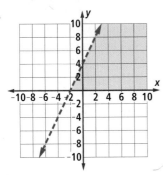

51.

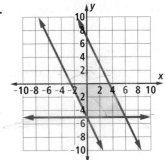

52.

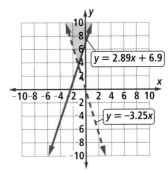

Chapter

11 Polynomials

Expressions such as those below are _polynomials._

$1 \cdot 10^3 + 4 \cdot 10^2 + 9 \cdot 10^1 + 2$

s^3

$2\ell w + 2wh + 2\ell h$

$1,000x^4 + 500x^3 + 100x^2 + 200x$

Polynomials form the basic structure of our base 10 arithmetic. The expanded form of a number like 1,492, or $1 \cdot 10^3 + 4 \cdot 10^2 + 9 \cdot 10^1 + 2 \cdot 10^0$, is a polynomial in x with the base 10 substituted for x.

Polynomials are also found in geometry. For example, the monomial s^3 represents the volume of a cube with edge s, as shown below. The trinomial $2\ell w + 2wh + 2\ell h$ represents the surface area of a box of dimensions ℓ by w by h, as shown below.

 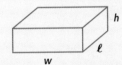

Algebra is filled with polynomials. The linear expression $ax + b$ is a polynomial, as is the quadratic expression $ax^2 + bx + c$. In Chapter 7, you calculated compound interest for a single deposit. When several deposits are made, the total amount of money accumulated can be expressed as a polynomial. For example, the polynomial

$$1{,}000x^4 + 800x^3 + 600x^2 + 250x$$

represents the amount of money you would have if you had invested $1,000 four years ago, added $800 to it three years ago, added $600 to it two years ago, and added $250 to it one year ago, all earning at the same rate $x - 1$.

In this chapter you will study these and other situations that give rise to polynomials and how to add, subtract, multiply, and factor them.

Lesson

11-1

Investments and Polynomials

Vocabulary

polynomial in *x*

standard form for a
  polynomial

▶ **BIG IDEA** When amounts are invested periodically and earn interest from the time of investment, the total value can be represented by a polynomial.

Among the most important money matters adults commonly deal with are salary or wages, savings, payments on loans for cars or trips or other items, and home mortgages or rent.

Each of these items involves paying or receiving money each month, every few months, or every year. But what is the total amount paid or received? The answer is not easy to calculate because interest starts at different times. Here is an example of this kind of situation.

Mental Math

**Find the distance
between**

a. (x, y) and $(0, 0)$.

b. $(a, 5)$ and $(a, -11)$.

c. $(m, m - n)$ and (m, m).

Example 1

Each birthday from age 12 on, Jessica has received $500 from her grandparents. She saves the money in an account that pays an annual yield of 6%. How much money will she have by the time she is 18?

Solution Write down how much Jessica has on each birthday. On her 12th birthday she has $500. She then receives interest on that $500. She receives an additional $500 on her 13th birthday. So on her 13th birthday she has $500(1.06) + 500 = \$1,030.00$.

Each year interest is paid on all the money previously saved and each year another $500 gift is added. The totals for her 12th through 15th birthdays are given below.

Birthday	Expression	Total
12th	500	= $500
13th	500(1.06) + 500	= $1,030.00
14th	$500(1.06)^2 + 500(1.06) + 500$	= $1,591.80
15th	$500(1.06)^3 + 500(1.06)^2 + 500(1.06) + 500$	= $2,187.31

from 12th birthday from 13th birthday from 14th birthday from 15th birthday

You can see the pattern. By her 18th birthday, Jessica will have three more gifts of $500 and earn interest on this money for three more years. The total will be $500(1.06)^6 + 500(1.06)^5 + 500(1.06)^4 + 500(1.06)^3 + 500(1.06)^2 + 500(1.06) + 500 = \$4{,}196.91$.

This total of $4,196.91 that she has by her 18th birthday is $696.91 more than the total $3,500 she received as gifts because of the interest earned.

Letting $x = 1.06$, the amount of money Jessica has (in dollars) after her 18th birthday is given by the polynomial
$$500x^6 + 500x^5 + 500x^4 + 500x^3 + 500x^2 + 500x + 500.$$

This expression is called a *polynomial in x*. A **polynomial in x** is a sum of multiples of powers of x. In this situation the polynomial is useful because if the interest rate is different, you only have to substitute a different value for x. We call x in this situation a *scale factor*. For example, had Jessica invested her money at an annual yield of 4%, the scale factor would be 104% = 1.04. At the end of 6 years, Jessica's investment (in dollars) would be $500(1.04)^6 + 500(1.04)^5 + 500(1.04)^4 + 500(1.04)^3 + 500(1.04)^2 + 500(1.04) + 500$.

You should verify with a calculator that this sum equals $3,949.14.

GUIDED

Example 2

Suppose Rajib's parents gave him $100 on his 12th birthday, $120 on his 13th, $140 on his 14th, and $160 on his 15th. If he invests all the money in an account with a yearly scale factor x, how much money will he have on his 15th birthday?

Solution By his 15th birthday, the __?__ from Rajib's 12th birthday will earn 3 years' worth of interest. It will have grown to __?__ $\cdot\, x^{?}$.

The __?__ from his 13th birthday will have grown to __?__ .

The __?__ from his 14th birthday will have grown to __?__ .

On his 15th birthday he receives __?__ .

Through his 15th birthday, the total dollar amount Rajib will have from his birthday gifts is $100x^3 + 120x^2 + 140x + 160$.

Rajib's aunt gave him $50 on each of these 4 birthdays. If he puts this money into the same account, the amount available from the aunt's gifts would be $50x^3 + 50x^2 + 50x + 50$.

The total amount he would have from all these gifts is found by adding these two polynomials.

$(100x^3 + 120x^2 + 140x + 160) + (50x^3 + 50x^2 + 50x + 50)$

Recall that this sum can be simplified. First, use the Associative and Commutative Properties of Addition to rearrange the polynomials so that like terms are together.

$= (100x^3 + 50x^3) + (120x^2 + 50x^2) + (140x + 50x) + (160 + 50)$

Then use the Distributive Property to add like terms.

$= (100 + 50)x^3 + (120 + 50)x^2 + (140 + 50)x + (160 + 50)$
$= 150x^3 + 170x^2 + 190x + 210$

Notice what the answer means in relation to Rajib's birthday presents. The first year he got $150 ($100 from his parents, $50 from his aunt). The $150 has 3 years to earn interest. The $170 from his next birthday earns interest for 2 years. And so on. Also notice that in these examples we have written the polynomials in the form of decreasing powers of x. This is called **standard form for a polynomial.** Polynomials are often written in standard form.

When comparing investments, it is often useful to make a table or construct a spreadsheet.

Example 3

Kelsey and Chip plan to save money for a round-the-world trip when they retire 10 years from now. Kelsey plans to save $2,000 per year for the first 5 years, and then will stop making deposits. Chip plans to wait 5 years to begin saving, but then hopes to save $2,500 per year for 5 years. They will each deposit their savings at the beginning of the year into a special account earning 6% interest compounded annually. How much will each have after 10 years?

Solution Make a spreadsheet showing the amount of money each person will have at the end of each year. At the end of the first year Kelsey will have $1.06(2,000) = 2,120$. At the end of the second year, she will have 106% of the sum of the previous balance and the new deposit of $2,000. In all, she will have $1.06(2,120 + 2,000) = \$4,367.20$. This pattern continues. But after 5 years, she deposits no more money. So her money only accumulates interest. Kelsey's end-of-year balance in the spreadsheet on the next page was computed by entering the formula $=1.06*B2$ into cell C2 and the formula $=1.06*(C2+B3)$ into cell C3. The formula in cell C3 was then replicated down column C to C11. A similar set of formulas generated Chip's end-of-year balance.

Miami was the top cruise ship departure port of the United States in 2004 with 641 departures.

Source: Bureau of Transportation Statistics

◇	A	B	C	D	E
1	Year	Kelsey's Deposits ($)	Kelsey's End-of-Year Balance ($)	Chip's Deposits ($)	Chip's End-of-Year Balance ($)
2	1	2,000	2,120.00	0	0
3	2	2,000	4,367.20	0	0
4	3	2,000	6,749.23	0	0
5	4	2,000	9,274.19	0	0
6	5	2,000	11,950.64	0	0
7	6	0	12,667.68	2,500	2,650.00
8	7	0	13,427.74	2,500	5,459.00
9	8	0	14,233.40	2,500	8,436.54
10	9	0	15,087.40	2,500	11,592.73
11	10	0	15,992.65	2,500	14,938.30

Ten years from now Kelsey will have about $16,000 and Chip will have about $15,000.

In Example 3, notice that even though Kelsey deposits $10,000 and Chip deposits $12,500 at the same rate of interest, compounding interest over a longer period of time gives Kelsey about $1,055 more than Chip. Here is what has happened. After 10 years:

Kelsey has $2,000x^{10} + 2,000x^9 + 2,000x^8 + 2,000x^7 + 2,000x^6$.

Chip has $2,500x^5 + 2,500x^4 + 2,500x^3 + 2,500x^2 + 2,500x$.

When $x = 1.06$, Kelsey has more than Chip.

Questions

COVERING THE IDEAS

1. Refer to Example 1. Suppose Jessica is able to get an annual yield of 5% on her investment.
   a. How much money will she have in her account by her 18th birthday?
   b. How much less is this than what she would have earned with a 6% annual yield?

2. Mary's grandfather will receive a $3,000 bonus from his employer on each of his birthdays from age 61 to age 65 if he indicates he will retire at 65.
   a. If he saves the money in an account paying an annual yield of 6.5%, how much will he have by the time he retires at age 65?
   b. How much will he have accumulated by the time he retires at age 65 if his investment grows by a scale factor of x each year?

3. Refer to Example 2. Suppose Rajib also gets $75, $85, $95, and $105 from cousin Lilly on his four birthdays. He puts this money into his account also.

   a. By his 15th birthday, how much money will Rajib have from just his cousin?

   b. What is the total Rajib will have saved by his 15th birthday from all of his birthday presents?

In 4–6, refer to Example 3.

4. Explain why Chip had less money saved than Kelsey at the end of the 10-year period even though he put more money into his account than Kelsey.

5. Chip said to Kelsey, "I might have less money now, but I am catching up to you, and even if we put no more money into our accounts, the amount in my account will be greater after a few more years." Kelsey said, "You have less now and you will always have less." Who is right?

6. Suppose Kelsey and Chip were able to earn 3% on their investments. Recalculate the balances in the spreadsheet and describe the end result.

7. Refer to page 654. Write the number 84,267 as a polynomial in base 10.

APPLYING THE MATHEMATICS

In 8–11, Clara, Mona, and Odella are friends who have the same birthday. They received the following cash presents on their birthdays. Each put all her money into a bank account that paid a 6% annual yield.

	Clara	Mona	Odella
In 2003	$200	$250	$100
In 2004	$300	$250	$500
In 2005	$250	$250	nothing

8. How much money did Clara have on her birthday in 2003?

9. How much did Mona have on her birthday in 2004?

10. How much did Odella have on her birthday in 2005?

11. In 2006, Clara received $300 on her birthday. If all the money from 2003 to 2006 had been and remains in an account with scale factor x, how much would she have had by her birthday in each of the following years?

   a. 2005

   b. 2006

   c. 2007

   d. 2008

Out of a class of 24 students, the probability of any 3 that share a birthday is about 16.6%.

12. Suppose in 1999 Tanya received $100 on her birthday. From 2000 to 2003 she received $150 on her birthday. She put the money in a shoe box. The money is still there.

    a. How much money did Tanya have after her 2003 birthday?

    b. How much more would she have had if she had invested her money at an annual yield of 4% each year?

13. **Multiple Choice** Which is the sum of $x^4 + x^3 + x^2$?

    A x^9 B $3x^9$

    C x^{24} D None of these

In 14–17, simplify the expression.

14. $(2y^2 + 13y - 14) + (4y^2 - 3y - 24)$

15. $6(11n + 8n^2 - 2) + (6n^2 - n - 9)$

16. $(7w^2 - 2w + 16) - 4(7w^2 + 15)$

17. $(x^3 + 2x^2 + 8) - (2x - 5x^3 + 6)$

18. Solve the equation $(3x^2 + 2x + 4) + (3x^2 + 11x + 2) = 0$.

19. Solve the equation $(3x^2 + 2x + 4) - (3x^2 + 11x + 2) = 0$.

In 20 and 21, find the missing polynomial.

20. $(91x^2 + 4x - 15) + (\ \underline{\ ?\ }\ ) = 110x^2 + 62$

21. $(3y^2 - 2y - 1) - (\ \underline{\ ?\ }\ ) = -4y^2 - 6y + 21$

22. A *cord* of wood is an amount of wood equal to about 128 cubic feet. A wood harvester has planted trees in a forest each spring for four years, as shown in the table at the right.

    Suppose each tree contains 0.01 cord of wood when planted, and the cordage grows with a scale factor x each year. How many cords of wood are in the forest after planting the fourth spring?

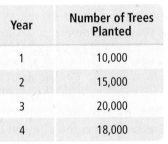

Year	Number of Trees Planted
1	10,000
2	15,000
3	20,000
4	18,000

Forests cover 747 million acres in the United States.

Source: U.S. Department of Agriculture

REVIEW

23. If 8 pencils and 5 erasers cost $4.69 and 3 pencils and 4 erasers cost $2.80, find the cost of 2 pencils. **(Lesson 10-2)**

24. Write an equation for the line which passes through the points (4, –8) and (–10, 6). **(Lesson 6-6)**

25. Consider the equation $\dfrac{30(4h-2)}{6(2h-1)} = 10$. (**Lesson 5-5**)

   a. For what value of h is $\dfrac{30(4h-2)}{6(2h-1)}$ undefined?

   b. Solve for h.

26. In one of his studies, discussed in the book *The Effects of Cross- and Self-Fertilization in the Vegetable Kingdom,* Charles Darwin compared the heights of two groups of plants. One group was cross-pollinated, meaning they were fertilized by pollen from other plants. The other group was self-fertilized. For the cross-fertilized plants, the mean height was 20.2, and for the self-fertilized plants the mean height was 17.6. Darwin's data are shown below. (*Note:* The values were rounded before plotting in Question 27.) (**Lessons 1-7, 1-6**)

Cross-Fertilized (in.)	23.5	12.0	21.0	22.0	19.1	21.5	22.1	20.4	18.3	21.6	23.3	21.0	22.1	23.0	12.0
Self-Fertilized (in.)	17.4	20.4	20.0	20.0	18.4	18.6	18.6	15.3	16.5	18.0	16.3	18.0	12.8	15.5	18.0

   a. Find the range of the data for each type of plant.

   b. Find the mean for each type of plant.

   c. Find the mean absolute deviation for each type of plant.

27. Use the two dot plots below. (**Lesson 1-7**)

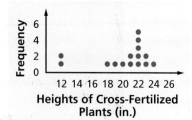
Heights of Cross-Fertilized Plants (in.)

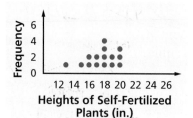
Heights of Self-Fertilized Plants (in.)

   a. Classify each dot plot as skewed right, skewed left, symmetric, or uniform.

   b. Based on Darwin's data, what advice would you give to a farmer who wants to grow tall plants?

EXPLORATION

28. Refer to Kelsey and Chip in Example 3 and Questions 4–6.

   a. For what interest rates does Kelsey end up with more money after 10 years than Chip?

   b. For what interest rates does Chip end up with more money than Kelsey?

Lesson 11-2
Classifying Polynomials

Vocabulary

monomial

polynomial

binomial

trinomial

degree of a monomial

degree of a polynomial

linear polynomial

quadratic polynomial

▶ **BIG IDEA** Polynomials are classified by their number of terms and by their degree.

Classifying Polynomials by Numbers of Terms

Recall that a *term* can be a single number, variable, or product of numbers and variables. In an expression, addition (or subtraction, which is "adding the opposite") separates terms.

Polynomials are identified by their number of terms. A **monomial** is a single term in which the exponent for every variable is a positive integer. A **polynomial** is an expression that is either a monomial or sum of monomials. Polynomials with two or three terms are used so often they have special names. A **binomial** is a polynomial that has two terms. A **trinomial** is a polynomial that has three terms. Here are some examples.

Monomials	Not Monomials	
$6x$	$6x + y$	(a binomial)
$-16t^2$	$-16t^{-2}$	(negative exponent on a variable)
x^2y^4	$\dfrac{x^2}{y^4}$	(variables divided)
Binomials	**Not Binomials**	
$x + 26\sqrt{2}$	$26x\sqrt{2}$	(monomial)
$\dfrac{x}{3} - y^3$	$-\dfrac{xy^3}{3}$	(monomial)
$0.44 - 2^{-10}pq^4$	$0.44 - 2^{-10}p + q^4$	(trinomial)
Trinomials	**Not Trinomials**	
$18x^2 + 5x + 9$	$(15x^2)(5x)(9)$	(monomial)
$a^2 + 2ab - b^{20}$	$a^{-2} + 2ab - b^{-20}$	(negative exponent on variables)
$pq + qr + rp$	$\dfrac{1}{pq + qr + rp}$	(variables divided)

There are no special names for polynomials with more than three terms.

Mental Math

Refer to the graph of a function.

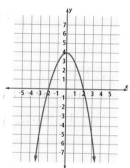

a. State the domain of the function.

b. State the range of the function.

c. State the x-intercepts.

d. State the y-intercept.

Classifying Polynomials by Degree

Every nonconstant term of a polynomial has one or more exponents. For example, $3x^2$ has 2 as its exponent. $10t$ has an unwritten exponent of 1, since $t^1 = t$. $15a^2b^3c^4$ has 2, 3, and 4 as its exponents.

The **degree of a monomial** is the sum of the exponents of the variables in the expression.

$3x^2$ has degree 2.

$10t$ has degree 1.

$15a^2b^3c^4$ has degree $2 + 3 + 4$, or 9.

The degree of a single number, such as 15, is considered to be 0 because $15 = 15x^0$. However, the number 0 is said not to have any degree, because $0 = 0 \cdot x^n$, where n could be any number. The **degree of a polynomial** is the highest degree of any of its monomial terms after the polynomial has been simplified. For example, $6x - 17x^4 + 8 + x^2$ has degree 4. $p + q^2 + pq^2 + p^2q^3$ has degree 5 (because $2 + 3 = 5$).

 QY1

> **QY1**
>
> Classify each polynomial by the number of its terms and its degree.
>
> a. $x^6 + x^7 + x^5$
> b. $8y^3z^2 - 40yz^6$
> c. $\frac{4}{3}\pi r^3$

When a polynomial has only one variable, writing it in standard form makes it easy to determine its degree. When the polynomial in x above is written in standard form, the degree is the exponent of the leftmost term.

$-17x^4 + x^2 + 6x + 8$ has degree 4.

Function notation can be used to represent a polynomial in a variable. For example, let $p(x) = -17x^4 + x^2 + 6x + 8$. Then values of the polynomial are easily described. For example,
$p(2) = -17 \cdot 2^4 + 2^2 + 6 \cdot 2 + 8 = -248$.

 QY2

> **QY2**
>
> If $p(x) = -x + 3 + 4x^4$, what is $p(-2)$?

The polynomial $p + q^2 + pq^2 + p^2q^3$ is a polynomial in p and q. There is no standard form for writing polynomials that have more than one variable, like this one. However, sometimes one variable is picked and the polynomial is written in decreasing powers of that variable. For example, written in decreasing powers of q, this polynomial is $p^2q^3 + pq^2 + q^2 + p$, or, to emphasize the powers of q, $p^2q^3 + (p + 1)q^2 + p$.

A polynomial of degree 1, such as $13t - 6$, is called a **linear polynomial.** A polynomial of degree 2, such as $2x^2 + 3x + 1$ or ℓw, is called a **quadratic polynomial.** Linear and quadratic polynomials whose coefficients are positive integers can be represented by tiles.

The tiles below represent the polynomial $2x^2 + 3x + 1$ because this polynomial is the area of the figure.

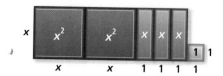

Using the Degree of a Polynomial to Check Operations with Polynomials

The simplest polynomials in one variable are the monomials x, x^2, x^3, x^4, and so on. You know how to add, subtract, multiply, and divide these monomials. For example, $x^2 \cdot x^3 = x^5$, so in this case a polynomial of degree 2 multiplied by a polynomial of degree 3 gives a polynomial of degree 5. In general, the degree of an answer to a polynomial computation is as easy to determine with complicated polynomials as it is with the simplest ones. Consider these examples of polynomial addition and subtraction.

GUIDED

Example

Collect like terms and determine the degree of the resulting polynomial.

1. $(17w + 14) - (6 - 5w) =$ ___?___

   degree 1   degree 1   degree 1

2. $(6ab - 22) + (2a + 8b) = 6ab + 2a + 8b - 22$

   degree 2   degree 1   degree ___?___

3. $(4x + x^3 - 7) - (x^2 + 4x + 5) =$ ___?___

   degree 3   degree 2   degree ___?___

4. $(x^7 + 4x - 5) + (3 - 2x - x^7) =$ ___?___

   degree 7   degree 7   degree ___?___

Notice that the degree of the sum or difference of two polynomials is never greater than the highest degree of the polynomial addends. Can you see why this is so?

Questions

COVERING THE IDEAS

1. Explain why $3x^2 + 4$ is a polynomial but $\frac{3}{x^2} + 4$ is not.

2. **Fill in the Blank** A binomial is a polynomial with ___?___ term(s).

In 3–6, an expression is given.

   a. Tell whether the expression is a monomial.

   b. If it is a monomial, state its degree.

3. $17x^{11}$ 4. $2w^{-4}$

5. $\frac{1}{2}bh$ 6. $2a^4b^5$

7. Is xyz a trinomial? Explain your reasoning.

8. Classify each polynomial by its degree and number of terms.

   a. $x^2 + 10$ b. $x^2 + 10x + 21$

   c. $x^2 + 10xy + y^2$ d. $x^3 + 10x^2 + 21x$

9. Write the polynomial $12 - 4x - 3x^5 + 8x^2$ in standard form.

10. a. Write the polynomial $a^3 - 3ab^2 - b^3 - 3a^2b$ in standard form as a polynomial in a.

   b. Write the polynomial $a^3 - 3ab^2 - b^3 - 3a^2b$ in standard form as a polynomial in b.

In 11 and 12, what polynomial is represented by the tiles?

11.

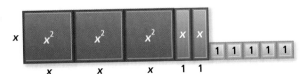

12.

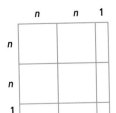

13. Fill in the blank with *always, sometimes but not always,* or *never.* Explain your answer. The degree of the sum of two polynomials is ___?___ greater than the degree of either polynomial addend.

APPLYING THE MATHEMATICS

In 14–18, an expression is given.

   a. Show that the expression can be simplified into a monomial.

   b. Give the degree of the monomial.

14. $10x - 14x$ 15. $10x(-14x)$

16. $(5n^3)(6n)^2$ 17. $xy + yx$

18. $12x^4 - (3x^4 + 2x^4 + x^4)$

19. Let $p(x) = 50x^3 + 50x^2 + 50x + 50$ and $q(x) = 100x^3 + 120x^2 + 140x + 160$. Give the degree of each polynomial.

   a. $p(x)$ b. $q(x)$ c. $p(x) + q(x)$ d. $p(x) - q(x)$

20. Repeat Question 19 if $p(x) = x^{200} - x^{100} + 1$ and $q(x) = x^{100} - x^{200} + 1$.

In 21–24, give the degree of these polynomials used to find length, area, and volume of geometric figures.

21. perimeter of a triangle $= a + b + c$

22. volume of a circular cone $= \frac{1}{3}\pi r^2 h$

23. area of a trapezoid $= \frac{1}{2}hb_1 + \frac{1}{2}hb_2$

24. surface area of a cylinder $= 2\pi r^2 + 2\pi rh$

25. a. Write a monomial with one variable whose degree is 70.

   b. Write a monomial with two variables whose degree is 70.

26. Complete the fact triangle below and write the related polynomial addition and subtraction facts.

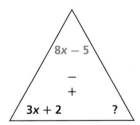

27. a. Give an example of two trinomials in x of degree 5 whose sum is of degree 5.

   b. Give an example of two trinomials in x of degree 5 whose sum is not of degree 5.

28. a. Write 318 and 4,670 as polynomials with 10 substituted for the variable.

   b. Add your polynomials from Part a. Is your sum equal to the sum of 318 and 4,670?

REVIEW

29. a. If you received $1,000 as a present on the day you were born, and the money was put into an account at an annual scale factor of x, how much would be in your account on your 18th birthday?

   b. Evaluate the amount in Part a if $x = 1.05$. (**Lesson 11-1**)

30. Consider the system $\begin{cases} a - 2b = 50 \\ b = -4c \end{cases}$. To solve this system, one student substituted $-4c$ for b in the first equation. The student then wrote $a - 8c = 50$. (Lessons 10–3, 10–2)

   a. Is the student's work correct?

   b. If it is correct, finish solving the system. If not, describe the error the student made.

31. A parking lot with length 70 meters and width 40 meters is to have a pedestrian sidewalk surrounding it, increasing its total area to 3,256 square meters. What will be the width of the sidewalk? (Lesson 9-7)

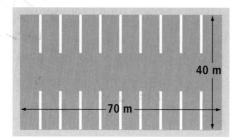

In 32–34, use the Distributive Property to expand the expression. (Lesson 2-1)

32. $4x(x - 9)$ 33. $n(n + 52)$ 34. $(3m + 19.2)80$

EXPLORATION

35. Suppose three polynomials of the same degree n are added.

   a. What is the highest possible degree of their sum? Explain your answer.

   b. What is the lowest possible degree of their sum?

Lesson 11-3

Multiplying a Polynomial by a Monomial

> ▶ **BIG IDEA** To multiply a polynomial by a monomial, multiply each term of the polynomial by the monomial and add the products.

In earlier chapters, you saw several kinds of problems involving multiplication by a monomial. To multiply a monomial by a monomial, you can use properties of powers.

$$(9a^4b^5)(8a^3b) = 9 \cdot 8 \cdot a^{4\,+\,3}b^{5\,+\,1}$$
$$= 72a^7b^6$$

To multiply a monomial by a binomial, you can use the Distributive Property $a(b + c) = ab + ac$.

$$2x(5x + 3) = 2x \cdot 5x + 2x \cdot 3$$
$$= 10x^2 + 6x$$

Some products of monomials and binomials can be pictured using the Area Model for Multiplication. For example, the product $2x(5x + 3)$ is the area of a rectangle with dimensions $2x$ and $5x + 3$. Such a rectangle is shown below at the left.

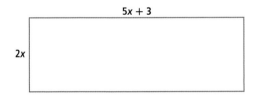 

This rectangle can be split into tiles as shown above at the right. The total area of the rectangle is $10x^2 + 6x$, which agrees with the result obtained using the Distributive Property.

Mental Math

Find the multiplicative inverse of each number.

a. $-5x$

b. $\dfrac{4q}{-9}$

c. 0

d. $a + b$

Example 1

Find two equivalent expressions for the total area of the rectangle pictured at the right.

(continued on next page)

Solution The total area is the same as the sum of the areas of the individual tiles, or $3x^2 + 6x$. Also, the total area is length times width, or $3x(x + 2)$.

So this drawing shows $3x(x + 2) = 3x^2 + 6x$.

The area representation of a polynomial shows how to multiply a monomial by any other polynomial. The picture shows a view of some storefronts at a shopping mall.

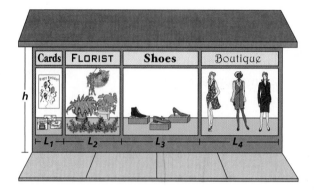

The displays in the windows are used to attract shoppers, so store owners and mall managers are interested in the areas of storefronts. Note that the height h of each storefront is a monomial, and the sum of the lengths of the storefronts $(L_1 + L_2 + L_3 + L_4)$ is a polynomial.

The total area of the four windows can be computed in two ways. One way is to consider all the windows together. They form one big rectangle with length $(L_1 + L_2 + L_3 + L_4)$ and height h. Thus, the total area equals $h \cdot (L_1 + L_2 + L_3 + L_4)$.

A second way is to compute the area of each storefront and add the results. Thus, the total area also equals $hL_1 + hL_2 + hL_3 + hL_4$.

These areas are equal, so
$$h \cdot (L_1 + L_2 + L_3 + L_4) = hL_1 + hL_2 + hL_3 + hL_4.$$

In general, to multiply a monomial by a polynomial, extend the Distributive Property: multiply the monomial by each term in the polynomial and add the results.

Example 2

Expand $6r(x^2 - \sqrt{3}x + 7rx)$.

Solution Multiply each term in the trinomial by the monomial $6r$.

$$6r(x^2 - \sqrt{3}x + 7rx) = 6r \cdot x^2 - 6r \cdot \sqrt{3}x + 6r \cdot 7rx$$
$$= 6rx^2 - 6\sqrt{3}rx + 42r^2x$$

Check 1 Test a special case by substituting for both r and x. We let $r = 5$ and $x = 3$.

Does

$6 \cdot 5(3^2 - \sqrt{3} \cdot 3 + 7 \cdot 5 \cdot 3) = 6 \cdot 5 \cdot 3^2 - 6\sqrt{3} \cdot 5 \cdot 3 + 42 \cdot 5^2 \cdot 3$?

Remember to follow order of operations on each side.

Does $30(114 - 3\sqrt{3}) = 270 - 90\sqrt{3} + 3{,}150$?

A calculator shows that each side has the value $3{,}264.115\ldots$.

Check 2 Use a CAS. Enter

`EXPAND(6*r*(x^2-[√ ](3)*x+7*r*x)).`

You should get an expression equivalent to the answer.

As always, you must be careful with the signs in polynomials.

Activity

A student was given the original expressions below and asked to expand them. The student's answers are shown below.

Original Expressions	Student's Expanded Expressions
1. $2x(3x^2y^3z^7)$	1. $6x^3 + 2xy^3 + 2xz^7$
2. $-3a^2(4a^2b + 7ab - 5a^3b^2)$	2. $-12a^4b - 21a^3b + 15a^5b^2$
3. $7m^3n(4mn^4)$	3. $28m^4n^5$
4. $7xy(2x^3y - 5xy^5 + x^2y)$	4. $14x^4y^2 - 5xy^5 + x^2y$
5. $\frac{1}{4}a^5b(8ab^2 + 2a^2 - 20a^3b)$	5. $2a^6b^3 + \frac{1}{2}a^7b - 5a^8b^2$

Step 1 Identify the expressions you believe the student expanded correctly.

Step 2 Expand the original expressions. Did you accurately find the expanded expressions with mistakes?

Step 3 For each expression the student did not expand correctly, write a sentence explaining what the student did incorrectly.

Explaining a Rule from Arithmetic

Recall the rule for multiplying a decimal by a power of 10: To multiply by 10^n, move the decimal point n places to the right. Multiplication of a monomial by a polynomial can show why this rule works. For example, suppose 81,026 is multiplied by 1,000. Write 81,026 as a polynomial in base 10, and 1,000 as the monomial 10^3.

$$1{,}000 \cdot 81{,}026 = 10^3 \cdot (8 \cdot 10^4 + 1 \cdot 10^3 + 2 \cdot 10 + 6)$$

Now use the Distributive Property.

$$= 10^3 \cdot 8 \cdot 10^4 + 10^3 \cdot 1 \cdot 10^3 + 10^3 \cdot 2 \cdot 10 + 10^3 \cdot 6$$

The products can be simplified using the Product of Powers Property and the Commutative and Associative Properties of Multiplication.

$$= 8 \cdot 10^7 + 1 \cdot 10^6 + 2 \cdot 10^4 + 6 \cdot 10^3$$

Now simplify the polynomial.

$$= 81{,}026{,}000$$

This same procedure can be repeated to explain the product of any decimal and any integer power of 10.

Questions

COVERING THE IDEAS

In 1 and 2, find the product.

1. $(5x)(11x)$

2. $(200xy^3)(3x^2y)$

In 3 and 4,

    a. find the product, and

    b. draw a rectangle to represent the product.

3. $3h(h + 5)$

4. $4n(n + 3)$

In 5 and 6, a large rectangle is shown.

    a. Express its area as the sum of areas of smaller rectangles.

    b. Express its area as length times width.

    c. Write an equality from Parts a and b.

5.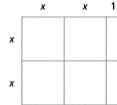

6.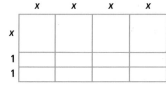

7. **Fill in the Blank** Using the Distributive Property,
   $a(b - c + d) = \underline{\quad ? \quad}$.

In 8–11, expand the expression.

8. $3x^2(x^2 + 2x - 8)$

9. $5x(-5x^2 - x + 6.2)$

10. $p(2 + p^2 + p^3 + 5p^4)$

11. $-0.5ab(4b - 2a + 10)$

12. Use multiplication of a monomial by a polynomial to explain why the product of 7,531 and 100,000 is 753,100,000.

APPLYING THE MATHEMATICS

13. Suppose the building below had to increase its height by 2 feet.

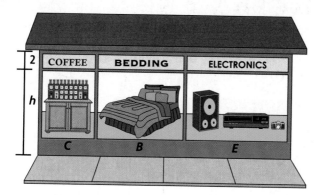

   a. Express the entire building's new storefront area as the sum of the three individual stores' storefront areas.
   b. Express the entire building's new storefront area as new height times length.
   c. Express the new storefront area as the sum of its old area and the additional area.

14. The arrangement of rectangles at the right is used by children in many countries for playing hopscotch. What is the total area?

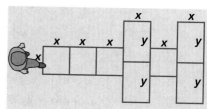

In 15–17, write the expression as a polynomial in standard form.

15. $(6x)(3x) - (5x)(2x) - (4x)(x)$

16. $2(x^2 + 3x) + 3x^2$

17. $m^3(m^2 - 3m + 2) - m^2(m^3 - 5m^2 - 6)$

In 18 and 19, simplify the expression.

18. $a(2b - c) + b(2c - a) + c(2a - b)$

19. $(x^2 + 2xy + y^2) - (x^2 - 2xy + y^2)$

20. At the right is a circle in a square.
   a. What is the area of the square?
   b. What is the area of the circle?
   c. What is the area of the shaded region?
   d. If a person had 3 copies of the shaded region, how much area would be shaded?
   e. If a person had c copies of the shaded region, how much area would be shaded?

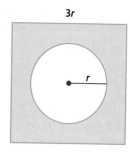

3r

21. **Fill in the Blank** Find the missing polynomial in the given equation.

$$3n^2 \cdot (\underline{\ ?\ }) = 60n^4 + 27n^3 - 30n^2$$

22. a. What is the rule for dividing a decimal by 1,000?

    b. Make up an example like the one on pages 671–672 to explain why the rule works.

REVIEW

In 23 and 24, an expression is given.

    a. Tell whether the expression is a polynomial.

    b. If it is a polynomial, give its degree. If it is not a polynomial, explain why not. (Lesson 11-2)

23. $4a^4 + 2a^{-2}$ 24. $n^3m^5 + n^2m^4 + nm^3$

25. Write a trinomial with degree 4. (Lesson 11-2)

26. After five years of birthdays, T.J. has received and saved $50x^4 + 70x^3 + 45x^2 + 100x + 80$ dollars. He put the money in a savings account at a yearly scale factor x. (Lessons 11-1, 7-1)

    a. How much did T.J. get on his last birthday?

    b. How much did T.J. get on the first of these birthdays?

    c. If $x = 1$, how much has T.J. saved?

    d. What does a value of 1 for x mean?

27. For what value(s) of c does the quadratic equation $3x^2 - 4x + c = 0$ have no solutions? (Lesson 9-6)

In 28 and 29, simplify the expression. (Lessons 8-4, 5-2)

28. $\dfrac{18xy^3}{6xy}$ 29. $\dfrac{4m}{9} \div \dfrac{6m^3}{15m}$

In 30 and 31, write an equation for the line with the given characteristics.

30. contains the points $(8, -2)$ and $(3, 13)$ (Lesson 6-6)

31. slope $\frac{1}{2}$, x-intercept 1 (Lesson 6-4)

EXPLORATION

32. a. Suppose a monomial of degree 3 is multiplied by a monomial of degree 4. What must be true about the degree of the product? Support your answer with an example.

    b. Suppose a monomial of degree m is multiplied by a monomial of degree n. What must be true about the degree of the product? Support your answer with an example.

Lesson 11-4

Common Monomial Factoring

Vocabulary

factoring

trivial factors

greatest common factor

factorization

prime polynomials

complete factorization

▶ **BIG IDEA** Common monomial factoring is the process of writing a polynomial as a product of two polynomials, one of which is a monomial that factors each term of the polynomial.

When two or more numbers are multiplied, the result is a single number. *Factoring* is the reverse process. In **factoring,** we begin with a single number and express it as the product of two or more numbers. For example, the product of 7 and 4 is 28. So, factoring 28, we get $28 = 7 \cdot 4$. In Lesson 11-3, you multiplied monomials by polynomials to obtain polynomials. In this lesson you will learn how to reverse the process.

If factors are not integers, then every number has infinitely many factors. For example, 8 is not only $4 \cdot 2$ and $8 \cdot 1$, but also $24 \cdot \frac{1}{3}$ and $2.5 \cdot 3.2$. For this reason, in this book all factoring is *over the set of integers.*

Mental Math

Consider the parabola
$y = 3(x - 6)^2 + 4$.

a. What is its vertex?

b. Does the parabola open up or down?

c. True or False The parabola is congruent to $y = -3x^2$.

d. What is an equation for its line of symmetry?

Factoring Monomials

Every expression has itself and the number 1 as a factor. These are called the **trivial factors.** If a monomial is the product of two or more variables or numbers, then it will have factors other than itself and 1.

Example 1

What are the factors of $49x^3$?

Solution The factors of 49 are 1, 7, and 49. The monomial factors of x^3 are 1, x, x^2, and x^3. The factors of $49x^3$ are the 12 products of a factor of 49 with a factor of x:

$1, 7, 49, x, 7x, 49x, x^2, 7x^2, 49x^2, x^3, 7x^3, 49x^3$

 QY

The **greatest common factor** (GCF) of two or more monomials is the product of the greatest common factor of the coefficients and the greatest common factors of the variables.

▶ **QY**

Which of the factors of $49x^3$ are trivial factors?

Example 2

Find the greatest common factor of $6xy^2$ and $18y$.

Solution The GCF of 6 and 18 is 6. The GCF of xy^2 and y is y. Because the factor x does not appear in all terms, it does not appear in the GCF.

So the GCF of $6xy^2$ and $18y$ is $6 \cdot y$, which is $6y$.

Notice that the GCF of the monomials includes the GCF of the coefficients of the monomials. It also includes any common variables raised to the *least* exponent of that variable found in the terms.

As with integers, the result of factoring a polynomial is called a **factorization.** Here is a factorization of $6x^2 + 12x$.

$$6x^2 + 12x = 2x(3x + 6)$$

Again, as with integers, a factorization with two factors means that a rectangle can be formed with the factors as its dimensions. Here is a picture of the factorization.

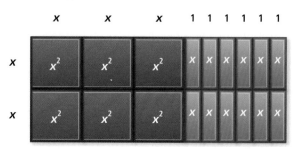

Activity

Step 1 Build or draw two other rectangles with an area of $6x^2 + 12x$.

Step 2 Write the factorization that is shown by each rectangle.

Step 3 Do any of the rectangles have the greatest common factor of $6x^2$ and $12x$ as a side length? If so, which rectangle?

The Activity points out that there is more than one way to factor $6x^2 + 12x$. When factoring a polynomial, the goal is that the GCF of all the terms is one factor. In $6x^2 + 12x$, $6x$ is the greatest common factor, so $6x^2 + 12x = 6x(x + 2)$.

Monomials such as $6x$, and polynomials such as $x + 2$ that cannot be factored into polynomials of a lower degree, are called **prime polynomials.** To factor a polynomial completely means to factor it into prime polynomials. When there are no common numerical factors in the terms of any of the prime polynomials, the result is called a **complete factorization.** The complete factorization of $6x + 12$ is $6(x + 2)$.

There are many techniques for factoring polynomials, and you will study several in this and the next chapter. No matter which technique you use, you will obtain the same answer. As with integers, the prime factorization of a polynomial is unique except for order.

> **Unique Factorization Theorem for Polynomials**
>
> Every polynomial can be represented as a product of prime polynomials in exactly one way, disregarding order and integer multiples.

GUIDED

Example 3

Factor $20a^3b + 8a - 12a^5b^2$ completely.

Solution The greatest common factor of 20, 8, and −12 is __?__. The greatest common factor of a^3, a, and a^5 is __?__. Because the variable b does not appear in all terms, b does not appear in the greatest common factor.

The greatest common factor of $20a^3b$, $8a$, and $-12a^5b^2$ is __?__.

Divide each term by the GCF to find the terms in parentheses. With practice you'll be able to do these steps in your head.

$$\frac{20a^3b}{4a} = \underline{\ ?\ } \quad \frac{8a}{4a} = \underline{\ ?\ } \quad \frac{-12a^5b^2}{4a} = \underline{\ ?\ }$$

So $20a^3b + 8a - 12a^5b^2 = 4a(\underline{\ ?\ } + \underline{\ ?\ } - \underline{\ ?\ })$.

Factoring provides a way of simplifying some fractions.

Example 4

Simplify $\dfrac{22m + 4m^2}{m}$. $(m \neq 0)$

Solution 1 Factor the numerator, simplify the fraction, and multiply.

$$\frac{22m + 4m^2}{m} = \frac{2m(11 + 2m)}{m} = 2(11 + 2m) = 22 + 4m$$

Solution 2 Separate the given expression into the sum of two fractions and then simplify each fraction.

$$\frac{22m + 4m^2}{m} = \frac{22m}{m} + \frac{4m^2}{m} = 22 + 4m$$

Check The solutions give the same answer, so they check.

Questions

COVERING THE IDEAS

1. List all the factors of $33x^4$.

In 2 and 3, find the GCF.

2. $25y^5$ and $40y^2$

3. $17a^2b^2$ and $24ba^2$

4. Represent the factorization $12x^2 + 8x = 4x(3x + 2)$ with rectangles.

5. **a.** Factor $15c^2 + 5c$ by finding the greatest common factor of the terms.

   b. Illustrate the factorization by drawing a rectangle whose sides are the factors.

6. Showing tiles, draw two different rectangles each with area equal to $16x^2 + 4x$.

7. Explain why $x^2 + xy$ is not a prime polynomial.

8. In Parts a–c, complete the products.

   a. $36x^3 + 18x^2 = 6(\underline{\ ?\ } + \underline{\ ?\ })$

   b. $36x^3 + 18x^2 = 18(\underline{\ ?\ } + \underline{\ ?\ })$

   c. $36x^3 + 18x^2 = 18x^2(\underline{\ ?\ } + \underline{\ ?\ })$

   d. Which of the products in Parts a–c is a complete factorization of $36x^3 + 10x^2$? Explain your answer.

9. Simplify $\dfrac{24n^6 + 20n^4}{4n^2}$.

10. Find the greatest common factor of $28x^5y^2$, $-14x^4y^3$, and $49x^3y^4$.

In 11–14, factor the polynomial completely.

11. $33a - 33b + 33ab$

12. $x^{2,100} - x^{2,049}$

13. $12v^9 + 16v^{10}$

14. $46cd^3 - 69cd^2 + 18c^2d^2$

APPLYING THE MATHEMATICS

15. The area of a rectangle is $14r^2h$. One dimension is $2r$. What is the other dimension?

16. The top vertex in the fact triangle at the right has the expression $27abc - 45a^2b^2c^2$. What expression belongs in the position of the question mark?

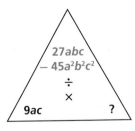

17. **a.** Graph $y = 2x^2 - 8x$.

    b. Graph $y = 2x(x - 4)$.

    c. What do you notice about the graphs of the equations? Explain why this occurs.

In **18** and **19**, a circular cylinder with height h and radius r is pictured at the right. Factor the expression giving its surface area.

18. $\pi r^2 + 2\pi rh$, the surface area with an open top

19. $2\pi r^2 + 2\pi rh$, the surface area with a closed top

In **20** and **21**, simplify the expression.

20. $\dfrac{9x^2 y + 54xy - 9xy^2}{9xy}$

21. $\dfrac{-100n^{100} - 80n^{80} + 60n^{60}}{2n^2}$

REVIEW

In **22** and **23**, simplify the expression. **(Lesson 11-3)**

22. $-4x^3(3 - 5x^2 + 7x^4)$ **23.** $k(k + 2k^2 + n) - 2n(k - 2n) - k^2$

24. Which investment plan is worth more at the end of 10 years if the annual yield is 6%? Justify your answer. **(Lesson 11-1)**

    Plan A: Deposit $50 each year on January 2, beginning in 2008.

    Plan B: Deposit $100 every other year on January 2, beginning in 2008.

25. **Multiple Choice** Which system of inequalities describes the shaded region in the graph at the right? **(Lesson 10-9)**

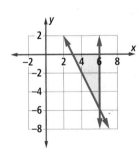

  A $\begin{cases} y - x < 6 \\ x \le 0 \\ y \le 6 \end{cases}$ **B** $\begin{cases} y + 2x \ge 6 \\ x \le 6 \\ y \le 0 \end{cases}$ **C** $\begin{cases} y + 2x \le 6 \\ x \le 0 \\ y \le 0 \end{cases}$ **D** $\begin{cases} y \le 6 + 4x \\ x \ge 3 \\ y \ge 1 \end{cases}$

26. Simplify $\sqrt{50x^3 y^4}$. **(Lesson 8-6)**

27. There are 4 boys, 7 girls, 6 men, and 5 women on a community youth board. How many different leadership teams consisting of one adult and one child could be formed from these people? **(Lesson 8-1)**

EXPLORATION

28. The number 6 has four factors: 1, 2, 3, and 6. The number 30 has eight factors: 1, 2, 3, 5, 6, 10, 15, and 30.

    a. Find five numbers that each have an odd number of factors.

    b. Give an algebraic expression that describes all numbers with an odd number of factors. Explain why you think these numbers have an odd number of factors.

QY ANSWER

1 and $49x^3$

Multiplying Polynomials

▶ **BIG IDEA**   To multiply a polynomial by a polynomial, multiply each term of one polynomial by each term of the other polynomial and add the products.

Picturing the Multiplication of Polynomials with Area

The Area Model for Multiplication shows how to multiply two polynomials with many terms. For example, to multiply $a + b + c + d$ by $x + y + z$, draw a rectangle with length $a + b + c + d$ and width $x + y + z$.

Mental Math

Evaluate.

a. $27^{\frac{1}{3}}$

b. $27^{\frac{2}{3}}$

c. $27^{\frac{2}{3}}$

	a	b	c	d
x	ax	bx	cx	dx
y	ay	by	cy	dy
z	az	bz	cz	dz

The area of the largest rectangle equals the sum of the areas of the twelve smaller rectangles.

   total area $= ax + ay + az + bx + by + bz + cx + cy + cz + dx + dy + dz$

But the area of the biggest rectangle also equals the product of its length and width.

   total area $= (a + b + c + d) \cdot (x + y + z)$

The Distributive Property can be used to justify why the two expressions must be equal. Distribute $(x + y + z)$ over $(a + b + c + d)$ to get $(a + b + c + d) \cdot (x + y + z) = a(x + y + z) + b(x + y + z) + c(x + y + z) + d(x + y + z) = ax + ay + az + bx + by + bz + cx + cy + cz + dx + dy + dz$.

Because of the multiple use of the Distributive Property, we call this general property the *Extended Distributive Property.*

Extended Distributive Property

To multiply two sums, multiply each term in the first sum by each term in the second sum and then add the products.

If one polynomial has *m* terms and the second has *n* terms, there will be *mn* terms in their product. This is due to the Multiplication Counting Principle. If some of these are like terms, you can simplify the product by combining like terms.

GUIDED

Example 1

Cassandra used the EXPAND feature on a CAS to multiply the polynomials $x^2 - 4x + 8$ and $5x - 3$. Her result is shown at the right.

The CAS does not display steps that most people would show in order to find the answer. Using the Extended Distributive Property, show the steps that the CAS does not display to expand $(x^2 - 4x + 8)(5x - 3)$.

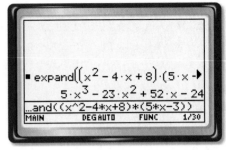

Solution $(x^2 - 4x + 8)(5x - 3)$

$= x^2 \cdot \underline{\ ?\ } + x^2 \cdot \underline{\ ?\ } + (-4x) \cdot \underline{\ ?\ } + (-4x) \cdot \underline{\ ?\ } +$ $8 \cdot \underline{\ ?\ } + 8 \cdot \underline{\ ?\ }$

$= \underline{\ ?\ } + \underline{\ ?\ } + \underline{\ ?\ } + \underline{\ ?\ } + \underline{\ ?\ } + \underline{\ ?\ }$

Now combine like terms.

$= \underline{\ ?\ } - \underline{\ ?\ } + \underline{\ ?\ } - \underline{\ ?\ }$

Example 2

Expand $(4x + 3)(x - 6)$.

Solution Think of $x - 6$ as $x + -6$. Multiply each term in the first polynomial by each in the second. There will be four terms in the product.

$(4x + 3)(x - 6) = 4x \cdot x + 4x \cdot (-6) + 3 \cdot x + 3 \cdot (-6)$
$= 4x^2 + (-24)x + 3x + (-18)$

Now simplify by adding or subtracting like terms.

$= 4x^2 - 21x - 18$

Check 1 Let $x = 10$. (Ten is a nice value to use in checks because powers of 10 are so easily calculated.) Then $(4x + 3)(x - 6) =$ $(4 \cdot 10 + 3)(10 - 6) = 43 \cdot 4 = 172$.
When $x = 10$, $4x^2 - 21x - 18 = 4 \cdot 10^2 - 21 \cdot 10 - 18 =$ $400 - 210 - 18 = 172$; so it checks.

(continued on next page)

Check 2 It is possible that when $x = 10$, the expression $(4x + 3)(x - 6)$ just happened to have the same value as $4x^2 - 21x - 18$. A better check is to set each expression equal to y and graph the resulting equation.

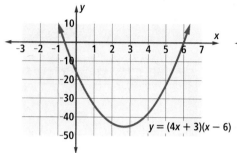

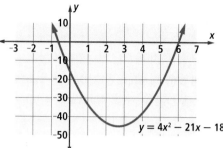

The two graphs are identical, so it checks.

 QY

Because multiplication is associative and commutative, to multiply three polynomials you can start by multiplying any two of them, and then multiply their product by the third polynomial.

> ▶ **QY**
>
> Austin used a CAS to multiply $a^2 + 5n - 14$ by $4n + 1$. The screen shows $4a^2n + a^2 + 20n^2 - 51n - 14$.
>
> **a.** How many terms did the CAS combine to get the product shown?
>
> **b.** Which like terms produced a^2?
>
> **c.** Which like terms produced $20n^2$?
>
> **d.** Which like terms produced $-51n$?

Example 3

Expand $n(n - 1)(n - 2)$.

Solution 1 Multiply n by $n - 1$ first.

$$n(n - 1)(n - 2) = n(n - 1) \cdot (n - 2)$$
$$= (n^2 - n)(n - 2)$$
$$= n^2 \cdot n + n^2(-2) - n \cdot n - n(-2)$$
$$= n^3 - 2n^2 - n^2 + 2n$$
$$= n^3 - 3n^2 + 2n$$

Solution 2 Multiply $n - 1$ by $n - 2$ first.

$$n(n - 1)(n - 2) = n \cdot (n - 1)(n - 2)$$
$$= n \cdot (n \cdot n + n \cdot (-2) - 1 \cdot n - 1 \cdot (-2))$$
$$= n \cdot (n^2 - 2n - n + 2)$$
$$= n \cdot (n^2 - 3n + 2)$$
$$= n^3 - 3n^2 + 2n$$

Questions

COVERING THE IDEAS

1. **a.** What multiplication is shown at the right?

   b. Do the multiplication.

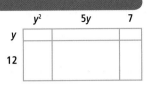

2. Simone used a CAS to multiply $2n - 5$ by $n^2 + 3n + 6$. The screen at the right shows her result. Explain which multiplications were done and combined to get each term in the product.

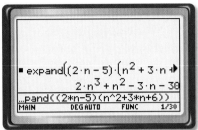

3. **a.** Multiply $2x - 5$ by $6x + 4$.

   b. Check your answer by letting $x = 10$.

   c. Check your answer by graphing $y = (2x - 5)(6x + 4)$ and graphing your answer.

In 4–7, expand and simplify the expression.

4. $(3x^2 + 7x + 4)(x + 6)$

5. $(n + 1)(2n^2 + 3n - 1)$

6. $(m^2 - 10m - 3)(2m^2 - 5m - 4)$ 7. $4(x^2 + 2x + 2)(x^2 - 2x + 2)$

8. Find the area of the rectangle at the right, and simplify the result.

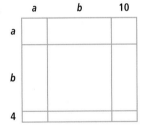

9. Expand $(5c - 4d + 1)(c - 7d)$.

10. **a.** Expand $(n - 3)(n + 4)(2n + 5)$ by first multiplying $n - 3$ by $n + 4$, then multiplying that product by $2n + 5$.

    b. Do the same expansion starting with a different multiplication.

APPLYING THE MATHEMATICS

11. **a.** Expand $(3x + 5)(4x + 2)$.

    b. Expand $(3x - 5)(4x - 2)$.

    c. Make a generalization from the pattern of answers in Parts a and b.

12. **a.** Expand $(4p - 1)(2p + 3)$.

    b. Expand $(4p + 1)(2p - 3)$.

    c. Make a generalization from the pattern of answers in Parts a and b.

13. Expand $\left(\frac{1}{5}x - 2.7\right)^2$ by writing the power as $\left(\frac{1}{5}x - 2.7\right)\left(\frac{1}{5}x - 2.7\right)$.

14. How much larger is the volume of a cube with edges of length $n + 1$ than the volume of a cube with edges of length n?

15. Solve the equation $(2n - 7)(n + 14) = 57$ by multiplying the binomials and then using the Quadratic Formula.

REVIEW

16. The sector at the right is one-third of a circle with radius r. Write a formula for the perimeter p of this sector in factored form. **(Lesson 11-4)**

17. If $p(x) = 2x^2 + 5$ and $q(x) = 3x^2 + 6$, simplify $2 \cdot p(x) - 3 \cdot q(x)$. **(Lesson 11-3)**

18. Twice the larger of two numbers is six more than four times the smaller. If the sum of eight times the smaller and three times the larger is 93, what are the two numbers? **(Lessons 10-5, 10-4, 10-2)**

19. Given $f(x) = 4^{-x} + 2$, find each value. **(Lessons 8-4, 7-6)**
    a. $f(2)$ b. $f(-1)$ c. $f(0) + f(-3)$

20. Find two algebraic fractions whose product is $\frac{14m}{39p}$. **(Lesson 5-1)**

EXPLORATION

21. Multiply each of the polynomials in Parts a–d by $x + 1$.
    a. $x - 1$ b. $x^2 - x + 1$
    c. $x^3 - x^2 + x - 1$ d. $x^4 - x^3 + x^2 - x + 1$
    e. Look for a pattern and use it to multiply
       $(x + 1)(x^8 - x^7 + x^6 - x^5 + x^4 - x^3 + x^2 - x + 1)$.
    f. Predict what you think the product of $(x + 1)$ and
       $(x^{100} - x^{99} + x^{98} - x^{97} + ... + x^2 - x + 1)$ is when simplified.
       Can you explain why your answer is correct?

22. A multidigit number in base 10 is shorthand for a polynomial in x. When $x = 10$, $436 = 4x^2 + 3x + 6$, and $2{,}187 = 2x^3 + 1x^2 + 8x + 7$.

    When you multiply 2,187 by 436, you are essentially multiplying two polynomials.

    $$(4x^2 + 3x + 6)(2x^3 + 1x^2 + 8x + 7)$$

    Multiply these polynomials and show how their product equals the product of 436 and 2,187 when $x = 10$.

Lesson 11-6

Special Binomial Products

Vocabulary

perfect square trinomials

difference of squares

▶ **BIG IDEA** The square of a binomial $a + b$ is the expression $(a + b)^2$ and can be found by multiplying $a + b$ by $a + b$ as you would multiply any polynomials.

Can you compute $46 \cdot 54$ in your head? How about 103^2? Studying products of special binomials can help you find the answers quickly without a calculator. Two such products are used so frequently that they are given their own names: Perfect Squares and the Difference of Two Squares.

Mental Math

A circle has diameter 10 centimeters. Estimate

a. its circumference.

b. its area.

Perfect Squares: The Square of a Sum

Just as numbers and variables can be squared, so can algebraic expressions. Given any two numbers a and b, you can expand $(a + b)^2$ or $(a - b)^2$. These are read "a plus b, quantity squared" and "a minus b, quantity squared."

How can you expand $(a + b)^2$? One way is to write the power as repeated multiplication.

$$(a + b)^2 = (a + b)(a + b)$$

Next, use the Distributive Property.

$$= a(a + b) + b(a + b)$$

Then apply the Distributive Property again to the first and second products.

$$= (a^2 + ab) + (ba + b^2)$$

And finally combine like terms (because $ab = ba$).

$$= a^2 + 2ab + b^2$$

The square of a sum of two terms is the sum of the squares of the terms plus twice their product.

Geometrically, $(a + b)^2$ can be thought of as the area of a square with sides of length $a + b$. As the figure shows, its area is $a^2 + 2ab + b^2$.

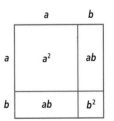

🛑 QY

▶ **QY**

Expand $(x + 8)^2$.

Example 1

Calculate 103^2.

Solution 1 Write 103 as the sum of two numbers whose squares you can calculate in your head. $103 = 100 + 3$, so $103^2 = (100 + 3)^2$. Then use the special binomial product rule for the square of a sum.

$$(100 + 3)^2 = 100^2 + 2 \cdot 3 \cdot 100 + 3^2 = 10{,}000 + 600 + 9$$
$$= 10{,}609$$

Solution 2 Write the square as a multiplication and expand.

$$103^2 = (100 + 3)(100 + 3)$$
$$= 100 \cdot 100 + 100 \cdot 3 + 3 \cdot 100 + 3 \cdot 3$$
$$= 10{,}000 + 300 + 300 + 9 = 10{,}609$$

With practice, either of the solutions to Example 1 can be done in your head.

GUIDED

Example 2

The area of a square with side $7c + 5$ is $(7c + 5)^2$. **Expand this binomial.**

Solution 1 Use the rule for the square of a binomial.

$$(7c + 5)^2 = (7c)^2 + \underline{\ ?\ } + \underline{\ ?\ }$$
$$= \underline{\ ?\ } c^2 + \underline{\ ?\ } c + \underline{\ ?\ }$$

Solution 2 Rewrite the square as a multiplication and expand using the Distributive Property.

$$(7c + 5)^2 = (7c + 5)(7c + 5)$$
$$= \underline{\ ?\ } (7c + 5) + \underline{\ ?\ } (7c + 5)$$
$$= \underline{\ ?\ } \cdot 7c + \underline{\ ?\ } \cdot 5 + \underline{\ ?\ } \cdot 7c + \underline{\ ?\ } \cdot 5$$
$$= \underline{\ ?\ } c^2 + \underline{\ ?\ } c + \underline{\ ?\ }$$

Solution 3 Draw a square with side $7c + 5$. Subdivide it into smaller rectangles and find the sum of their areas.

Check Test a special case. Let $c = 3$. Then $7c + 5 = \underline{\ ?\ }$ and $(7c + 5)^2 = \underline{\ ?\ }$.

Also $\underline{\ ?\ } c^2 + \underline{\ ?\ } c + \underline{\ ?\ } = \underline{\ ?\ } \cdot 9 + \underline{\ ?\ } \cdot 3 + \underline{\ ?\ } = \underline{\ ?\ }$. It checks.

Perfect Squares: The Square of a Difference

To square the difference $(a - b)$, think of $a - b$ as $a + -b$. Then apply the rule for the perfect square of a sum.

$$(a - b)^2 = (a + -b)^2$$
$$= a^2 + 2a(-b) + (-b)^2$$
$$= a^2 - 2ab + b^2$$

The square of a difference of two terms is the sum of the squares of the terms minus twice their product.

Squaring a binomial always results in a trinomial. Trinomials of the form $a^2 + 2ab + b^2$ or $a^2 - 2ab + b^2$ are called **perfect square trinomials** because each is the result of squaring a binomial.

> **Perfect Squares of Binomials**
>
> For all real numbers a and b, $(a + b)^2 = a^2 + 2ab + b^2$ and $(a - b)^2 = a^2 - 2ab + b^2$.

Activity 1

Complete the table.

$(a + b)^2$	$a^2 + 2ab + b^2$	$(a - b)^2$	$a^2 - 2ab + b^2$
$(x + 1)^2$	?	$(x - 1)^2$	?
$(x + 2)^2$	?	$(x - 2)^2$	?
$(x + 3)^2$	?	$(x - 3)^2$	?
$(x + 4)^2$	?	$(x - 4)^2$	?
$(x + 15)^2$	?	$(x - 15)^2$	?
$(x + n)^2$	?	$(x - n)^2$	?

The Difference of Two Squares

Another special binomial product is the sum of two numbers times their difference. Let x and y be any two numbers. What is $(x + y)(x - y)$?

$(x + y)(x - y) = x(x - y) + y(x - y)$ Distributive Property

$= x^2 - xy + yx - y^2$ $-xy$ and yx are opposites.

$= x^2 - y^2$

The product of the sum and difference of two numbers is the **difference of squares** of the two numbers.

Difference of Two Squares

For all real numbers x and y, $(x + y)(x - y) = x^2 - y^2$.

Activity 2

Complete the table at the right.

The difference of two squares can be used to multiply two numbers that are equidistant from a number whose square you know.

$(a + b)(a - b)$	$a^2 - b^2$
$(x + 1)(x - 1)$	?
$(x + 2)(x - 2)$	?
$(x + 3)(x - 3)$	?
$(x + 4)(x - 4)$	?
$(x + 15)(x - 15)$	?
$(x + n)(x - n)$	?

Example 3

Compute $46 \cdot 54$ in your head.

Solution 46 and 54 are the same distance from 50. So think of $46 \cdot 54$ as $(50 - 4)(50 + 4)$. This is the product of the sum and difference of the same numbers, so the product is the difference of the squares of the numbers.

$$(x - y)(x + y) = x^2 - y^2$$
$$(50 - 4)(50 + 4) = 50^2 - 4^2 = 2{,}500 - 16 = 2{,}484$$

Example 4

Expand $(8x^5 + 3)(8x^5 - 3)$.

Solution This is the sum of and difference of the same numbers, so the product is the difference of squares of the numbers.

$$(8x^5 + 3)(8x^5 - 3) = (8x^5)^2 - 3^2 = 64x^{10} - 9$$

Check Let $x = 2$.

$$(8x^5 + 3)(8x^5 - 3) = (8 \cdot 2^5 + 3)(8 \cdot 2^5 - 3)$$
$$= (8 \cdot 32 + 3)(8 \cdot 32 - 3)$$
$$= 259 \cdot 253 = 65{,}527$$

$64x^{10} - 9 = 64 \cdot 2^{10} - 9 = 64 \cdot 1{,}024 - 9 = 65{,}527$, so it checks.

Questions

COVERING THE IDEAS

In 1–3, expand and simplify the expression.

1. $(g + h)^2$
2. $(g - h)^2$
3. $(g + h)(g - h)$

4. What is a *perfect square trinomial*?

5. Give an example of a perfect square trinomial.

In 6 and 7, a square is described.

    a. Draw a picture to describe the situation.

    b. Write the area of the square as the square of a binomial.

    c. Write the area as a perfect square trinomial.

6. A square with sides of length $2n + 1$.

7. A square with sides of length $5p + 11$.

8. Verify that $(a - b)^2 = a^2 - 2ab + b^2$ by substituting numbers for a and b.

In 9–16, expand and simplify the expression.

9. $(x - 5)^2$ 10. $(3 + n)(3 - n)$ 11. $(n^2 + 4)(n^2 - 4)$

12. $(13s + 11)^2$ 13. $(9 - 2x)^2$ 14. $\left(10 + \frac{1}{2}t\right)^2$

15. $(3x + yz)(3x - yz)$ 16. $(2a + 5b)(-5b + 2a)$

17. Compute in your head. Then write down how you did each computation.

    a. 30^2 **b.** $29 \cdot 31$ **c.** $28 \cdot 32$ **d.** $27 \cdot 33$

In 18–20, compute in your head. Then write down how you did each computation.

18. $16 \cdot 24$ 19. 201^2 20. $75 \cdot 65$

APPLYING THE MATHEMATICS

In 21–25, tell whether the expression is a perfect square trinomial, difference of squares, or neither of these.

21. $u^2 - 2uj + j^2$ 22. $9 - v^2$

23. $2sd + s^2 + d^2$ 24. $xy - 16$

25. $-i^2 + p^2$

26. Solve $\frac{x - 4}{7} = \frac{6}{x + 4}$.

27. The numbers being multiplied in each part of Question 17 add to 60. Use the pattern found there to explain why, of all the pairs of numbers that add to 100, the largest product occurs when both numbers are 50.

In 28 and 29, expand and simplify the expression.

28. $\left(\sqrt{11} + \sqrt{13}\right)\left(\sqrt{11} - \sqrt{13}\right)$

29. $(3x + y)^2 + (3x - y)^2$

REVIEW

30. a. Expand $(x - 12)(x + 10)$.

   b. Solve $(x - 12)(x + 10) = 85$. **(Lessons 11-6, 9-5)**

31. After 7 years of putting money into a retirement account at a scale factor x, Lenny has saved $800x^6 + 1{,}000x^5 + 1{,}500x^4 + 1{,}200x^3 + 1{,}400x^2 + 1{,}800x + 2{,}000$ dollars. **(Lesson 11-1)**

   a. How much did Lenny put in during the most recent year?

   b. How much did Lenny put in during the first year?

   c. Give an example of a reasonable value for x, and evaluate the polynomial for that value of x.

32. Richard wants to construct a rectangular prism with height and width of x inches and length of 5 inches. He wants his prism to have the same volume as surface area. Construct a system with equations for the volume and surface area. Then solve for x. **(Lesson 10-10)**

In 33–35, describe a situation that might yield the given polynomial. (Lesson 8-2)

33. e^3 **34.** $6x^2$ **35.** $\pi r^2 - \pi s^2$

36. In 1965, Gordon Moore stated that computing speed in computers doubles every 24 months (Moore's Law). Computing speed is measured by transistors per circuit. **(Lesson 7-2)**

   a. In 1971, engineers could fit 4,004 transistors per circuit. Use Moore's Law to write an expression for the number of transistors per circuit that were possible in 1979.

   b. Many experts believe that Moore's Law will hold until 2020. Estimate the number of transistors per circuit possible in 2020, given that processors developed in 2000 had about 100 million transistors per circuit.

EXPLORATION

37. A CAS will be helpful in this question. After collecting terms, the expansion of $(a + b)^2$ has 3 unlike terms. Expand $(a + b + c)^2$. You should find that the expansion of $(a + b + c)^2$ has 6 unlike terms. How many unlike terms does the expansion of $(a + b + c + d)^2$ have? Try to generalize the result.

QY ANSWER

$x^2 + 16x + 64$

Lesson

11-7

Permutations

Vocabulary

permutation

$n!$, n factorial

circular permutation

▶ **BIG IDEA** From a set of n symbols, the number of permutations of length r without replacement is given by the product of the polynomials $\underbrace{n(n - 1)(n - 2)...}_{r \text{ factors}}$.

In Lesson 8-1, you saw the following problem: How many 3-letter acronyms (like JFK, IBM, BMI, or TNT) are there in English? The answer is 26^3 because the first letter can be any one of the 26 letters of the alphabet, and so can the second letter, and so can the third letter. Think of the spaces to be filled and use the Multiplication Counting Principle: $\underline{26} \cdot \underline{26} \cdot \underline{26} = 17{,}576$.

Now suppose that the letters in the acronym have to be different. Then TNT and other acronyms with duplicate letters are not allowed. The first letter can still be any one of the 26 letters of the alphabet, but the second letter can only be one of the 25 letters remaining, and the third letter can only be one of the 24 letters remaining. So the total number of 3-letter acronyms in English with different letters is $\underline{26} \cdot \underline{25} \cdot \underline{24} = 15{,}600$.

The first situation is called an *arrangement with replacement* because a letter can be used more than once. The second situation, where a letter cannot be used more than once, is called a **permutation.** So, a permutation is an arrangement without replacement. The above situation shows that, with 26 letters, there are 17,576 arrangements with replacement of length 3, and 15,600 permutations of length 3.

Suppose there were only three letters, A, B, and C. Notice the difference between the two types of arrangements.

Mental Math

Suppose n is an integer. Determine if the following statements are *always, sometimes but not always,* or *never true.*

a. If $x > 0$, $x^n > 0$.

b. If $x < 0$, $x^n > 0$.

c. If $x < 0$, $2x^n < 0$.

Length 2 with replacement	AA, AB, AC, BA, BB, BC, CA, CB, CC
Length 2 without replacement	AB, AC, BA, BC, CA, CB
Length 3 with replacement	AAA, AAB, AAC, ABA, ABB, ABC, ACA, ACB, ACC, 9 starting with B, and 9 more starting with C, a total of 3^3 or 27 arrangements
Length 3 without replacement	ABC, ACB, BAC, BCA, CAB, CBA
Length 4 with replacement	AAAA, AAAB, AAAC, ..., AABA, AABB, AABC, ... and so on, a total of 3^4 or 81 arrangements
Length 4 without replacement	None! (Do you see why?)

Example 1

Dori saw a license plate with the numbers 15973. She noticed that all the digits were different odd digits. She wondered if this was unusual.

a. How many 5-digit numbers are there with only odd digits?

b. How many 5-digit numbers are there with only odd digits, all of them different?

Solution

a. This is a situation of arrangements with replacement. Each digit could be any of 5 numbers. Think of spaces to be filled.

$$\underline{5} \cdot \underline{5} \cdot \underline{5} \cdot \underline{5} \cdot \underline{5} = 3{,}125$$

b. This is a situation of permutations. The first digit can be any one of the 5 odd numbers. But then the second digit must be different, so it can only be one of the 4 odd numbers that remain. The third digit can only be one of the 3 odd numbers that remain after the first two have been chosen. The 4th digit can only be one of the 2 that remain. The fifth digit can only be the remaining digit. Filling spaces, you can picture this as

$$\underline{5} \cdot \underline{4} \cdot \underline{3} \cdot \underline{2} \cdot \underline{1} = 120.$$

There is quite a difference between the two kinds of arrangements! So it is not so unusual that Dori saw a license plate with all odd digits, but rather unusual that all the digits would be different.

GUIDED

Example 2

Three of the 11 members of a jazz band will each perform a solo at a concert. In how many orders can three people be picked from the band to perform a solo?

Solution This is an arrangment __?__ replacement situation.
                              (with/without)

Any of __?__ people could perform the first solo.

After that soloist, any of __?__ people could perform the second solo.

Then any of __?__ people could perform the third solo.

So there are __?__ • __?__ • __?__ or __?__ possible orders.

Jazz music developed in the last part of the 19th century in New Orleans.

Source: *Columbia Encyclopedia*

A Connection with Polynomials

Suppose you begin with n letters. *Without* replacement, there are $\underline{n} \cdot \underline{(n-1)}$ acronyms of length 2. Using the Distributive Property, you can see that $n(n-1) = n^2 - n$, which is a polynomial of degree 2. There are $\underline{n} \cdot \underline{(n-1)} \cdot \underline{(n-2)}$ acronyms of length 3.

Using the Extended Distributive Property, this product equals $n^3 - 3n^2 + 2n$, a polynomial of degree 3. Example 1b asked for permutations of length 5. Since $n = 5$ in Example 1b, the multiplication was $\underline{5} \cdot \underline{(5-1)} \cdot \underline{(5-2)} \cdot \underline{(5-3)} \cdot \underline{(5-4)}$. In general, there are $\underline{n} \cdot \underline{(n-1)} \cdot \underline{(n-2)} \cdot \underline{(n-3)} \cdot \underline{(n-4)}$ such permutations.

This product equals $n^5 - 10n^4 + 35n^3 - 50n^2 + 24n$, a 5th degree polynomial. In general, the number of permutations of length n can be calculated by evaluating a polynomial of degree n.

Permutations Using All the Items

With five different items, there cannot be permutations of length 6 because there are only 5 different items. However, the situation of permutations using all the items is quite common, as Example 3 shows.

Example 3

You have 13 books to put on a shelf. In how many ways can they be arranged?

Solution This is a permutation problem. Any one of the 13 books can be farthest left. Once it has been chosen, there are 12 choices for the book to its right. Then there are 11 choices for the book to the right of the first two; and so on. **The total number of permutations of the books is** $\underline{13} \cdot \underline{12} \cdot \underline{11} \cdot \underline{10} \cdot \underline{9} \cdot \underline{8} \cdot \underline{7} \cdot \underline{6} \cdot \underline{5} \cdot \underline{4} \cdot \underline{3} \cdot \underline{2} \cdot \underline{1}$, or 6,227,020,800.

The answers to Examples 1b and 3 each are the product of the integers from 1 to n. This product is denoted as $n!$ and called **n factorial.** Using factorial notation, the answer to Example 1b is 5! and the answer to Example 3 is 13!

$$n! = n(n-1)(n-2) \cdot ... \cdot 3 \cdot 2 \cdot 1$$

Specifically, $1! = 1$.

$2! = 2 \cdot 1 = 2$
$3! = 3 \cdot 2 \cdot 1 = 6$
$4! = 4 \cdot 3 \cdot 2 \cdot 1 = 24$
$5! = 5 \cdot 4 \cdot 3 \cdot 2 \cdot 1 = 120$
$6! = 6 \cdot 5 \cdot 4 \cdot 3 \cdot 2 \cdot 1 = 720$, and so on.

Notice how $n!$ gets large quite quickly as n grows.

 QY

> ▶ QY
>
> a. A baseball manager is setting the batting order for the 9 starting players. How many different batting orders are possible?
>
> b. What is 8!?

Factorial notation is very convenient for describing numbers of permutations. You saw at the beginning of this lesson the product of three numbers 26 · 25 · 24. This product can be written as the quotient of two factorials.

$$26 \cdot 25 \cdot 24 = 26 \cdot 25 \cdot 24 \cdot \frac{23 \cdot 22 \cdot 21 \cdot \ldots \cdot 3 \cdot 2 \cdot 1}{23 \cdot 22 \cdot 21 \cdot \ldots \cdot 3 \cdot 2 \cdot 1}$$

$$= \frac{26 \cdot 25 \cdot 24 \cdot 23 \cdot 22 \cdot 21 \cdot \ldots \cdot 3 \cdot 2 \cdot 1}{23 \cdot 22 \cdot 21 \cdot \ldots \cdot 3 \cdot 2 \cdot 1}$$

$$= \frac{26!}{23!}$$

So, with a factorial key on a calculator, you can calculate any number of permutations just by dividing two factorials.

Questions

COVERING THE IDEAS

1. **a.** Identify two of the permutations of length 4 from the six letters A, B, C, D, E, and F.

   b. How many permutations are there of length 4 from the six letters A, B, C, D, E, and F?

2. You have 8 of your favorite pictures that you would like to hang on a wall, but there is room for only 3 of the pictures. How many different permutations of 3 pictures are possible from your 8 favorites, assuming you arrange the pictures in a straight line so that their order matters?

3. How many different permutations of length 2 are there from n objects when $n \geq 2$?

4. How many different permutations of length 7 are there from n objects when $n \geq 7$?

5. **a.** Identify two of the permutations of length 5 from the five letters V, W, X, Y, and Z.

   b. How many permutations of length 5 are there from these five letters?

6. A volleyball coach is deciding the serving order for the six starting players. How many different starting orders are possible?

7. In how many different orders can n objects be arranged on a shelf?

8. Give the values of 7!, 8!, 9!, and 10!.

In 9–12, write as a single number in base 10 or as a simple fraction in lowest terms.

9. $\frac{8!}{6!}$ 10. $\frac{100!}{99!}$ 11. $\frac{15!}{17!}$ 12. $\frac{2!}{6!}$

The forearm pass, or "dig" is a type of shot used when receiving a serve or playing a hard, low hit ball.

APPLYING THE MATHEMATICS

13. Consider the following pattern.

$$2! = 2 \cdot 1! \qquad\qquad 3! = 3 \cdot 2! \qquad\qquad 4! = 4 \cdot 3!$$

   Are all three instances above true? If so, describe the general pattern using one variable. If not, correct any instances that are false.

14. Three hundred people enter a raffle. The first prize is a computer and the second prize is a cell phone.

   a. How many different ordered pairs of people are eligible to win these prizes?

   b. Suppose you and your best friend are among the 300. If the winning tickets are chosen at random, what is the probability that you will win the computer and your best friend will win the cell phone?

15. a. How many license plate numbers with 4 digits have all different odd digits, with the first digit being 3?

   b. Write down all these license plate numbers.

16. How many license plate numbers with 6 digits have all different odd digits?

17. A **circular permutation** is an ordering of objects around a circle. Some permutations that are different along a line are considered the same around a circle. For example, the two arrangements of A, B, C, and D pictured here are considered to be the same.

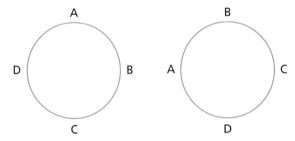

   Write all the circular permutations of 4 objects around a circle.

A raffle is used in many organizations looking to raise funds.

REVIEW

18. Expand and simplify $(-a + 6b)(-a - 6b)$. **(Lesson 11-6)**

19. How much smaller is the area of a circle with radius $(r - 4)$ than that of a circle with radius r (assume $r > 4$)? **(Lesson 11-5)**

In 20 and 21, simplify the expression. **(Lessons 11-4, 8-3)**

20. $\dfrac{25n^2 - 21n}{n}$

21. $\dfrac{8x^3 + 16x^2 + 24x^6}{4x^2}$

22. A rectangle with dimensions $4w$ and $2w + 1$ is contained in a rectangle with dimensions $10w$ and $6w + 2$, as shown in the diagram at the right. **(Lesson 11-3)**

    a. Write an expression for the area of the larger rectangle.

    b. Write an expression for the area of the smaller rectangle.

    c. Write a polynomial in standard form for the area of the shaded region.

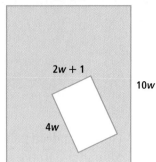

23. Consider the polynomial $3x^3 - 4x^2 + x + 6$. Give an example of a polynomial of degree 3 that when added to this will give a polynomial of degree 1. **(Lesson 11-2)**

24. The spreadsheet below shows an investment of $1,200 increasing in two different ways. **(Lesson 7-7)**

◇	A	B	C
		Years From Now	Exponential Growth	Constant Increase
1	Years From Now	Exponential Growth	Constant Increase
2	0	1200	1200
3	1	1260	1275
4	2	1323	1350
5	3		
6	4		
7	5		
8	6		
9	7		

    a. What formula should be entered in cell B5? C5?

    b. Describe the difference in investments after 7 years.

    c. Which investment will be worth more in 10 years? Justify your answer.

EXPLORATION

25. Here are polynomial expressions for the number of permutations of n symbols with various lengths:

    Length 2: $n(n - 1) = n^2 - n$

    Length 3: $n(n - 1)(n - 2) = n^3 - 3n^2 + 2n$

    Length 4: $n(n - 1)(n - 2)(n - 3) = n^4 - 6n^3 + 11n^2 - 6n$

    Length 5: $n(n - 1)(n - 2)(n - 3)(n - 4) = n^5 - 10n^4 + 35n^3 - 50n^2 + 24n$

    a. Use a CAS to find a polynomial expression for the number of permutations of n symbols with length 6.

    b. Identify some patterns in these polynomials that enable you to predict some features of the polynomial for the number of permutations of n symbols with length 7.

QY ANSWERS

1. 362,880

2. 40,320

Lesson 11-8

The Chi-Square Statistic

Vocabulary

expected number

deviation

chi-square statistic

> ▶ **BIG IDEA** The chi-square statistic is found by adding squares of binomials and provides evidence for whether data found in certain tables represent events that are occurring randomly.

The *chi-square* statistic is different from any statistic you have yet seen. This statistic compares actual frequencies with the frequencies that would be expected by calculating probabilities, as shown below.

The following table shows the average daily numbers of live births in California between 1995 and 1997. Are birthdays randomly distributed among the days of the week?

Mental Math

Solve.

a. $|n| = 14$

b. $|n| = -14$

c. $|-n| = 14$

d. $-|n| = 14$

Day of the Week	Mon.	Tues.	Wed.	Thurs.	Fri.	Sat.	Sun.
Actual Numbers of Births	1,473	1,629	1,602	1,588	1,593	1,272	1,159

Source: *Journal of the American Medical Association*

The **expected number** of births is the mean number of births for a given day that is predicted by a probability. If the births occurred randomly, then the expected number for each day would be the same. There were 10,316 births each week on average. So the expected number of births for each day is $\frac{10,316}{7}$ which, rounded to the nearest integer, is 1,474.

Day of the Week	Mon.	Tues.	Wed.	Thurs.	Fri.	Sat.	Sun.
Expected Numbers of Births	1,474	1,474	1,474	1,474	1,474	1,474	1,474

As you know, even if events occur randomly, it is not common for all events to occur with the same frequency. When you toss a coin ten times, you would not usually get 5 heads even if the coin were fair. Similarly, if there were 1,460 births on 4 days and 1,425 on the other three days, that would not seem to be much of a difference from the expected numbers. So the question is: Do the actual numbers deviate enough from the expected numbers that we should think that the births happen more often on certain days of the week?

If we let an expected number be e and an actual observed number be a, then $|e - a|$. The absolute value of the difference between these numbers is called the **deviation** of a from e. For example, the deviation on Saturday is $|1,474 - 1,272|$, or 202.

In 1900, the English statistician Karl Pearson introduced the **chi-square statistic** as a way of determining whether the difference in two frequency distributions is greater than that expected by chance. ("Chi" is pronounced *ky* as in *sky*.) The algorithm for calculating this statistic uses the squares of deviations, which is why we study it in this lesson.

Calculating the Chi-Square Statistic

Step 1 Count the number of events. Call this number n. In the above situation, there are 7 events, one each for Mon., Tues., Wed., Thurs., Fri., Sat., and Sun.

Step 2 Let a_1, a_2, a_3, a_4, a_5, a_6, and a_7 be the actual frequencies.

In this example, $a_1 = 1{,}473$, $a_2 = 1{,}629$, $a_3 = 1{,}602$, $a_4 = 1{,}588$, $a_5 = 1{,}593$, $a_6 = 1{,}272$, and $a_7 = 1{,}159$.

Step 3 Let e_1, e_2, e_3, e_4, e_5, e_6, and e_7 be the expected frequencies.

In this example, $e_1 = e_2 = e_3 = e_4 = e_5 = e_6 = e_7 = 1{,}474$.

Step 4 Calculate $\dfrac{(a_1 - e_1)^2}{e_1}$, $\dfrac{(a_2 - e_2)^2}{e_2}$, ..., $\dfrac{(a_n - e_n)^2}{e_n}$. Each number is the square of the deviation, divided by the expected frequency.

$$\frac{(a_1 - e_1)^2}{e_1} = \frac{1}{1{,}474}, \quad \frac{(a_2 - e_2)^2}{e_2} = \frac{24{,}025}{1{,}474}, \quad \frac{(a_3 - e_3)^2}{e_3} = \frac{16{,}384}{1{,}474}, \quad \frac{(a_4 - e_4)^2}{e_4} =$$

$$\frac{12{,}996}{1{,}474}, \quad \frac{(a_5 - e_5)^2}{e_5} = \frac{14{,}161}{1{,}474}, \quad \frac{(a_6 - e_6)^2}{e_6} = \frac{40{,}804}{1{,}474}, \quad \frac{(a_7 - e_7)^2}{e_7} = \frac{99{,}225}{1{,}474}$$

Step 5 Add the n numbers found in Step 4. This sum is the chi-square statistic.

$$\frac{1}{1{,}474} + \frac{24{,}025}{1{,}474} + \frac{16{,}384}{1{,}474} + \frac{12{,}996}{1{,}474} + \frac{14{,}161}{1{,}474} + \frac{40{,}804}{1{,}474} + \frac{99{,}225}{1{,}474} =$$

$$\frac{207{,}596}{1{,}474} \approx 140.8$$

The chi-square statistic measures how different a set of actual observed numbers is from a set of expected numbers. The larger the chi-square statistic is, the greater the difference. But is 140.8 unusually large? You can find that out by looking in chi-square tables. These tables give the values for certain values of n and certain probabilities. On the next page is such a table. In this table, n is the number of events. The other columns of the table correspond to probabilities of 0.10 (an event expected to happen $\frac{1}{10}$ of the time), 0.05 (or $\frac{1}{20}$ of the time), 0.01 (or $\frac{1}{100}$ of the time), and 0.001 (or $\frac{1}{1{,}000}$ of the time). You are not expected to know how the values in the table were calculated. The mathematics needed to calculate them is normally studied in college.

Critical Chi-Square Values				
$n-1$	0.10	0.05	0.01	0.001
1	2.71	3.84	6.63	10.8
2	4.61	5.99	9.21	13.8
3	6.25	7.81	11.34	16.3
4	7.78	9.49	13.28	18.5
5	9.24	11.07	15.09	20.5
6	10.6	12.6	16.8	22.5
7	12.0	14.1	18.5	24.3
8	13.4	15.5	20.1	26.1
9	14.7	16.9	21.7	27.9
10	16.0	18.3	23.2	29.6
15	22.3	25.0	30.6	37.7
20	28.4	31.4	37.6	45.3
25	34.4	37.7	44.3	52.6
30	40.3	43.8	50.9	59.7
50	63.2	67.5	76.2	86.7

How to Read a Chi-Square Table

Examine the number 14.1, which appears in column 0.05, row 7. This means that, with 8 events, a chi-square value greater than 14.1 occurs with probability 0.05 or less.

On page 698, we obtained a chi-square value of 140.8 with $n = 7$ events. So we look in row $n - 1$, which is row 6. A value as large as 140.8 would occur with probability less than 0.001, that is, less than 1 in 1,000 times. So we have evidence that the births in California are not evenly distributed among the days of the week. The data should be examined to determine why Saturdays and Sundays have fewer births.

Suppose the frequencies of the births had led to a chi-square value of 10.9. Then, looking across row 6, we would see that this value is between the listed values 10.6 and 12.6. So 10.9 has a probability between 0.10 and 0.05. That means that a chi-square value as high as 10.9 would occur between $\frac{1}{10}$ and $\frac{1}{20}$ of the time just by chance. Statisticians normally do not consider this probability to be low enough to think there is reason to question the expected values.

When a chi-square value is found that occurs with probability less than 0.05, statisticians question whether the assumptions that led to the expected values are correct. With this criterion, the above distribution of births is highly unusual. So we would question whether the births are occurring randomly.

 QY

▶ QY

a. Why do you think there are fewer births on Saturday than on Monday through Friday?

b. Why do you think there are even fewer births on Sunday?

Example

Suppose 90 students were asked to name the United States President in 1950 from the names listed below. Suppose: 24 picked Dwight Eisenhower, 31 picked John Kennedy, and 35 picked Harry Truman (the correct answer). Is there evidence to believe the people were just guessing?

Solution Calculate the chi-square statistic following the steps given above.

Step 1 Find the number of events. $n = 3$.

Step 2 Identify the actual observed values. $a_1 = 24$; $a_2 = 31$; $a_3 = 35$.

Step 3 Calculate the expected values. If people were just guessing, we would expect each of the three names to be picked by the same number of people. Since there were 90 people in all, each name would be picked by 30. So, $e_1 = 30$; $e_2 = 30$; $e_3 = 30$.

Harry S. Truman was the 33rd President of the United States.

Step 4 Calculate $\frac{(a_1 - e_1)^2}{e_1}$, $\frac{(a_2 - e_2)^2}{e_2}$, and $\frac{(a_3 - e_3)^2}{e_3}$.

$$\frac{(a_1 - e_1)^2}{e_1} = \frac{(24 - 30)^2}{30} = \frac{36}{30}; \quad \frac{(a_2 - e_2)^2}{e_2} = \frac{(31 - 30)^2}{30} = \frac{1}{30};$$

$$\frac{(a_3 - e_3)^2}{e_3} = \frac{(35 - 30)^2}{30} = \frac{25}{30}$$

Step 5 The sum of the numbers in Step 4 is $\frac{36 + 1 + 25}{30} = \frac{62}{30} \approx 2.07$.

Now examine the table. When $n = 3$, $n - 1 = 2$. So, look at the second row. The number 2.07 is less than the value 4.61 that would occur with probability 0.10. The numbers 24, 31, and 35 are like those that could randomly appear more than 10% of the time. It is quite possible that the people were guessing.

The chi-square statistic can be used whenever there are actual frequencies and you have some way of calculating expected frequencies. However, the chi-square value is not a good measure of the deviation from the expected frequencies when there is an expected frequency that is less than 5.

Questions

COVERING THE IDEAS

1. What does the chi-square statistic measure?

2. When was the chi-square statistic developed, and by whom?

3. For what expected frequencies should the chi-square statistic not be used?

In 4 and 5, average number of traffic deaths per day of the week in the United States are given for a particular year.

a. Calculate the chi-square statistic assuming that traffic deaths occur randomly on days of the week.

b. Is there evidence to believe that the deaths are not occurring randomly on the days of the week?

	Mon.	Tues.	Wed.	Thurs.	Fri.	Sat.	Sun.
4. **Year 1985**	100	105	105	110	145	170	140
5. **Year 1995**	100	100	100	105	140	150	130

6. Suppose in the Example of this lesson that 40 students had picked Harry Truman, 30 had picked Dwight Eisenhower, and 20 had picked John Kennedy. Would there still be evidence that students were guessing randomly?

APPLYING THE MATHEMATICS

7. You build a spinner as shown at the right and spin it 50 times with the following outcomes. Use the chi-square statistic to determine whether or not the spinner seems to be fair.

Outcome	1	2	3	4	5
Frequency	13	13	9	8	7

8. A coin is tossed 1,000 times and lands heads up 537 times. Compare the numbers of heads and tails with what would be expected if the coin were fair. Use the chi-square statistic to test whether the coin is fair.

9. *The World Almanac and Book of Facts 2006* lists 64 notable tornadoes in the United States since 1925. The table at the right shows their frequencies by season of the year. Use the chi-square statistic to determine whether these figures support a view that more tornadoes occur at certain times of the year than at other times of the year.

Season	Number of Tornadoes
Autumn	8
Winter	15
Spring	38
Summer	3

10. Here are the total points scored in each quarter from the 16 National Football League games played December 17–19, 2005.

Quarter	1	2	3	4	Total
Points	122	196	133	150	601

Source: National Football League

Use the chi-square statistic to answer this question. Do football teams tend to score more points in one quarter than in any other?

REVIEW

11. **a.** How many different permutations can be made using the letters of HORSE?

    b. How many different permutations can be made using the letters of MONKEY? **(Lesson 11-7)**

12. **a.** Which holds more, a cube with edges of length 6, or a rectangular box with dimensions 5 by 6 by 7?
    (Lessons 11-6, 11-5)

    b. Which holds more, a cube with edges of length x, or a box with dimensions $x - 1$ by x by $x + 1$?; Justify your answer.

In 13–15, expand and simplify the expression. (Lessons 11-6, 11-5)

13. **a.** $(2x + y)^2$ **b.** $(2x - y)^2$ **c.** $(2x - y)(2x + y)$

14. $(8 - a)(a - 8)$ 15. $(3k^2 - 6km + 3m^2)^2$

16. Draw a picture of the following multiplication using rectangles.
    $4x(x + 6) = 4x^2 + 24x$ **(Lesson 11-3)**

17. On the fifth day after planting, a Moso bamboo tree was 38.5 cm. On the 14th day, the tree was 70.9 cm. **(Lessons 6-1, 5-4)**

    a. What was the average rate of change in height per day between the 5th and 14th days?

    b. Express the rate in Part a in cm/week.

EXPLORATION

18. A new high school for mathematics and science was opened in Cityville. Four hundred girls and 600 boys applied for 150 slots. A committee considered the applications and accepted 65 girls and 85 boys. Some people complained that there was discrimination.

    a. One complaint was that too few girls were accepted. This person's opinion was that there should have been equal numbers of boys and girls accepted and that the numbers accepted deviated too much from equality. Use the chi-square statistic to test whether this deviation could have occurred easily by chance.

    b. A second complaint was that too many girls were accepted. This person's position was that the numbers of boys and girls accepted should have been proportional to the number of applicants who were boys and girls. Use the chi-square statistic to test whether this deviation could have occurred easily by chance.

    c. If you were on the school board, would you agree with either complaint? Explain your answer.

Moso bamboo was introduced into the United States in about 1890.

Source: BAMBOO The Magazine of The American Bamboo Society

QY ANSWERS

a. Answers vary. Sample answer: With the ability to schedule deliveries, many physicians opt to schedule them during the week.

b. Answers vary. Sample answer: Many physicians choose Sunday as their day off and do not schedule deliveries for that day.

Chapter 11 Projects

1 Dividing Polynomials

If you wanted to check if 23 is a factor of 10,373, you could divide 10,373 by 23, and check if there is a remainder in the division. One way to do this would be to use long division. There is an algorithm for long division with polynomials, which is similar to an algorithm for long division with numbers. Here are two examples: one in which $x^3 - 4x^2 + 7x - 4$ is divided by $(x - 1)$, and the other in which $x^2 - 9$ is divided by $(x + 2)$.

$$
\begin{array}{r}
x^2 - 3x + 4 \\
x - 1 \overline{)x^3 - 4x^2 + 7x - 4} \\
\underline{-(x^3 - x^2)} \\
0x^3 - 3x^2 + 7x - 4 \\
\underline{-(-3x^2 + 3x)} \\
0x^2 + 4x - 4 \\
\underline{-(4x - 4)} \\
0
\end{array}
$$

$$
\begin{array}{r}
x - 2 \\
x + 2 \overline{)x^2 - 9} \\
\underline{-(x^2 + 2x)} \\
0x^2 - 2x - 9 \\
\underline{-(-2x - 4)} \\
-5
\end{array}
$$

In the first example, the result is $x^2 - 3x + 4$ with no remainder. In the second example the result is $(x - 2)$ with remainder –5.

a. Is $(x - 1)$ a factor of $x^3 - 4x^2 + 7x - 4$? Is $(x - 2)$ a factor of $x^2 - 9$?

b. Divide $x^3 + 3x^2 + 9x + 27$ by $(x + 3)$.

c. Write a description of the long division algorithm and explain it to a friend.

2 The Right Order

When performing complex actions, the order in which you do them is often important. For example, when dressing yourself in the winter, you might choose to put on pants, then a shirt, then a sweater, then socks, then shoes, and finally a jacket. The order in which you perform these actions is important.

a. How many different permutations of these actions are there?

b. Give four permutations of this order that would result in you not being dressed properly. Describe what happens in each case.

c. Give four permutations of this order that would result in you being dressed properly.

d. Give another sequence of events in which order matters. Answer Parts a, b, and c for this sequence.

3 Representing Positive Integers Using Powers

a. Every positive integer can be written as a sum of different powers of 2, where each power is added at most once. For example, $50 = 2^5 + 2^4 + 2^1$. You may be surprised to learn that for each number there is only one way to write it as a sum of powers of 2. Find the powers of 2 representation for the integers from 1 to 16. Explain why there is only one such representation and how this relates to writing numbers in base 10.

(continued on next page)

b. Every positive integer can be represented as a sum of powers of 3, where each power is added at most twice. For example, $50 = 3^3 + 3^2 + 3^2 + 3^1 + 3^0 + 3^0$. Find the powers of 3 representation for all the integers from 1 to 16. Explain why there is only one such representation for each number.

4 Differences of Higher Powers

In this chapter you saw why $x^2 - y^2 = (x - y)(x + y)$. This is only one instance of a general pattern.

a. Use the Extended Distributive Property to show that $x^3 - y^3 = (x - y)(x^2 + xy + y^2)$ and that $x^4 - y^4 = (x - y)(x^3 + x^2y + yx^2 + y^3)$.

b. Find similar factors for $x^5 - y^5$ and then generalize them to find similar factors for $x^n - y^n$.

c. Suppose $y = 1$. What does your answer from Part b say that $\dfrac{x^n - 1}{x - 1}$ is equal to?

d. Use the formula from Part c to calculate $1 + 2 + 2^2 + 2^3 + \ldots + 2^{10}$. (You can use the fact that $2^{10} = 1{,}024$.)

5 Switches and Sorting

One special type of permutation, in which the positions of two elements are changed, is called a *switch*. For example, a switch could change the acronym BADC into the acronym ABDC. Another switch could change ABDC to ABCD. Suppose you are given an acronym and you want to put it into alphabetical order. (This sort of problem comes up very often in computer programming.)

a. Find and describe an algorithm to put an acronym into alphabetical order using a sequence of switches.

b. Use your algorithm to sort the acronym UNESCO. How many switches were required to do this?

6 Testing Astrology

From a book (like *Who's Who*) or online source, find at least 100 famous people in a field and note their birthdays. Identify the astrological sign of each person. Then tabulate the number of people with each sign. Do these data lead you to believe that certain birth signs are more likely to produce famous people? Use a chi-square statistic assuming a random distribution of the birthdays among the 12 astrological signs is expected. Although $n - 1 = 11$ here, refer to row 10 from the chi-square table on page 699.

Chapter 11 — Summary and Vocabulary

○ A **monomial** is a product of terms. The **degree of a monomial** is the sum of the exponents of its variables. A **polynomial** is an expression that is either a monomial or a sum of monomials. The **degree of a polynomial** is taken to be the largest degree of its monomial terms. **Linear polynomials** are polynomials of degree 1. **Quadratic polynomials** are polynomials of degree 2.

○ Polynomials emerge from a variety of situations. Our customary way of writing whole numbers in base 10 can be considered as a polynomial with 10 substituted for the variable. If different amounts of money are invested each year at a **scale factor** x, the total amount after several years is a **polynomial in** x. The number of permutations of n objects can be represented by a polynomial in n.

○ Addition and subtraction of polynomials are based on adding like terms, one of the forms of the Distributive Property that you studied earlier in this book. Multiplication of polynomials is also justified by the Distributive Property. To multiply one polynomial by a second, multiply each term in the first polynomial by each term in the second polynomial, then add the products. For example:

monomial by a polynomial: $a(x + y + z) = ax + ay + az$

two polynomials: $(a + b + c)(x + y + z) =$
$$ax + ay + az + bx + by + bz + cx + cy + cz$$

two binomials: $(a + b)(c + d) = ac + ad + bc + bd$

perfect square: $(a + b)^2 = (a + b)(a + b) = a^2 + 2ab + b^2$

difference of two squares: $(a + b)(a - b) = a^2 - b^2$

○ If each of the terms of a polynomial has a common factor, then so does their sum. It can be factored out using the Distributive Property.

○ The square of the difference of actual and expected values in an experiment, $(a - e)^2$, appears in the calculation of the **chi-square statistic**. This statistic can help you decide whether the assumptions that led to the expected values are correct.

Vocabulary

11-1
polynomial in x
standard form for a
  polynomial

11-2
monomial
polynomial
binomial
trinomial
degree of a monomial
degree of a polynomial
linear polynomial
quadratic polynomial

11-4
factoring
trivial factors
greatest common factor
factorization
prime polynomials
complete factorization

11-6
perfect square trinomials
difference of squares

11-7
permutation
$n!$, n factorial
circular permutation

11-8
expected number
deviation
chi-square statistic

Theorems and Properties

Unique Factorization Theorem for
  Polynomials (p. 677)

Extended Distributive Property (p. 680)
Perfect Squares of Binomials (p. 687)

Difference of Two Squares (p. 688)

Chapter 11 Self-Test

Take this test as you would take a test in class. You will need a calculator. Then use the Selected Answers section in the back of the book to check your work.

In 1–6, expand and simplify the expression.

1. $3x(10 - 4x + x^3)$

2. $(2b - 5)^2$

3. $(8z + 3)(8z - 3)$

4. $6a(2a^2 + 9a - 1)$

5. $(5a^2 - a)(5a^2 - a)$

6. $(2 - 6c)(4 + 3c)$

In 7 and 8, consider the polynomial $8x^3 - 5 + 2x + 11x^3 - 9x^2$.

7. What is the degree of this polynomial?

8. Is the polynomial a *monomial*, *binomial*, *trinomial*, or *none of these*?

9. Factor completely: $12x^3y^2 - 24x^2y^3 + 30x^2y^4$.

In 10 and 11, write as a single polynomial.

10. $(20n^2 - 8n - 12) + (16n^3 - 7n^2 + 5)$

11. $9p^4 + p^2 - 5 - p(3p^3 + p - 2)$

12. **True or False** The expression $3v^2 + 3v - 1$ is a trinomial of degree 3.

13. Simplify the fraction $\frac{28w^3 - 18w}{2w}$, assuming that $w \neq 0$.

14. Write the area of the shaded portion of the rectangular region as a polynomial in standard form.

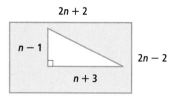

15. A swim team has 7 swimmers available to race a 4-person relay. How many different orders of swimmers are possible?

16. Twenty-five art students entered a competition in which 1st, 2nd, and 3rd place prizes were to be awarded. How many permutations of students could receive these prizes?

In 17 and 18, consider the following. On Ashley's 16th birthday, she received $200. She received $150 on her 17th birthday, and $300 on each of her 18th and 19th birthdays.

17. If she invested all of this money each year in a savings account with a yearly scale factor x, how much money would she have on her 21st birthday?

18. Evaluate your answer to Question 17 if the savings account had an interest rate of 3%.

19. a. What is the area of the largest rectangle below?

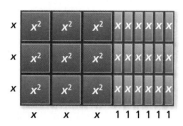

b. What factorization of the rectangle's area is shown?

c. Is this a complete factorization? Explain your answer.

20. Represent the product $(x + 2y)(5 + z)$ using areas of rectangles.

21. Jerry believes a die is weighted to favor certain numbers. The table below shows the outcome of 198 random tosses of the die.

Number	Outcomes
1	24
2	44
3	31
4	30
5	43
6	26

Use the chi-square statistic to provide evidence as to whether Jerry's view is correct. Justify your answer.

22. Represent the product $(x + 4)^2$ using areas of rectangles. Write your answer in standard form.

Chapter

11

Chapter Review

SKILLS
PROPERTIES
USES
REPRESENTATIONS

SKILLS Procedures used to get answers

OBJECTIVE A Add and subtract polynomials. (Lessons 11-1, 11-2)

In 1–4, simplify the expression and write the answer in standard form.

1. $(-k^3 + 2k^2 - 17k + 8) + (5k^3 - 2k^2 - 8)$

2. $\frac{4}{3}h^3 + 4 - \frac{2}{3}h^3 + \frac{1}{7}h^2 - 5$

3. $(5.4s^4 + 9.8s^2 - 8) - (-3.7s^3 - 4 + 5.2s)$

4. $(12w^3 - 3w^2 + -8w - 9) - (80w + 8)$

OBJECTIVE B Multiply polynomials. (Lessons 11-3, 11-5, 11-6)

5. **Fill in the Blank** $(-6x + 9) \cdot \left(\frac{5}{3}x + 6\right) = -10x^2 - \underline{?}\ x + 54$

In 6–16, write as a single polynomial in standard form.

6. $m(7m^2 - 13m + 12)$

7. $9p(p^3 + p^2 - 6p + 5)$

8. $-3x^2\left(12x^2 + \frac{2}{3}x\right)$

9. $-\frac{1}{7}q^8(-q^3 + 14q^2 - 112q + 5)$

10. $2(g + 3g^2 + 19g^3 - g^6) + g(-3g^5 + 2g + 6g^3)$

11. $(b - 3)(b + 3)$

12. $(8x - 2)(2x - 1)$

13. $2(1 + 6w)(1 - 6w)$

14. $3(a^2 + a - 1)(a + 1)$

15. $(n - 2)(n - 3)(n - 4)$

16. $(c^2 + 10c - 4)(2c^2 - 8c + 1)$

17. The length of one leg of a right triangle is $(3x - 1)$, and the length of the other leg is $(17x + 2)$. Express the area of the triangle as a polynomial in standard form.

OBJECTIVE C Find common monomial factors of polynomials. (Lesson 11-4)

In 18–21, factor the polynomial completely.

18. $9k^3 + 6k^2$ 19. $u^2v - uv^2$

20. $-84y^3 - 18y^2 + 93y$

21. $45a^9b^5 + 60a^6b^4 - 15a^5b^3 + 420a^3b^2$

22. **Multiple Choice** Which is a complete factorization of $24y^7 + 18y^5 - 90y^3$?

A $y^3(24y^4 + 18y^2 - 90)$

B $3y^3(8y^7 + 6y^5 - 30y^3)$

C $6y^7(4 + 3y^{-2} + 15y^{-4})$

D $6y^3(4y^4 + 3y^2 - 15)$

OBJECTIVE D Expand squares of binomials. (Lesson 11-6)

In 23–26, expand and simplify the expression.

23. $(p + 6)^2$ 24. $(-u - 5)^2$

25. $(11 - 45z)^2$ 26. $(-w + 2)^2$

27. **Multiple Choice** The square of which binomial below is $64c^4 + -80c^3 + 25c^2$?

A $8c - 5$ B $8c^2 - 5c$

C $8c^2 + 5c$ D $8c^3 + 5c$

PROPERTIES The principles behind the mathematics

OBJECTIVE E Classify polynomials by their degrees or number of terms. (Lesson 11-2)

28. Give an example of a monomial of degree 5.

29. Give an example of a trinomial of degree 5.

In 30–33, consider the polynomials below.

    a. $n^2 - 5$ **b.** $2m^2 + 4m - 7$

    c. $12a^4 - 16a^2 + 3$ **d.** $8w^2y + 9wy$

30. Which are binomials?

31. Which are trinomials?

32. Which have degree 2?

33. Which have degree 4?

USES Applications of mathematics in real-world situations

OBJECTIVE F Translate investment situations into polynomials. **(Lesson 11-1)**

34. Flora decides to open a retirement account with an annual interest rate y. In the first year, Flora invests $5,000. The second year, she invests $3,000, and then in the third year she invests $2,000. She keeps the money in the account at the same scale factor for five years after her last deposit.

    a. Write a polynomial that describes how much money she has in this account at the end of that time.

    b. If $y = 1.07$, how much money does Flora have in her retirement account after the five years?

35. Jeffrey is saving money during his high school years to go on a trip to Egypt after he graduates. The trip costs $3,000. At the end of his freshman year, he deposits $1,200 in a savings account with an annual scale factor of x. At the end of his sophomore year, he deposits $700 in the same account. At the end of his junior year, he deposits $500. It is now the end of his senior year.

    a. Write an expression that shows how much money Jeffrey has in his account.

    b. If the savings account pays 4% annual interest, how much more money does he need to afford the trip?

OBJECTIVE G Determine numbers of permutations. **(Lesson 11-7)**

In 36–38, Beth has 7 different blouses in her closet.

36. How many different ways can she select a blouse for each of the 7 days of the week?

37 How many different ways can she select a blouse for each of the 5 school days of the week?

38. Suppose Beth wants to wear her favorite blouse on Monday. How many different ways can she select a blouse for each of the remaining 4 school days of the week?

In 39–41, Kyle has recently opened a bank account and is asked to set the 4-digit PIN (Personal Identification Number) for his ATM card, in which each digit can be any number from 0 to 9.

39. How many different ways can Kyle select a PIN?

40. If the digits of the PIN must all be different, how many ways can Kyle select the PIN?

41. If the first digit of the PIN is *not* allowed to be zero, how many different ways can Kyle a select PIN, assuming the digits cannot be repeated?

42. Six guests arrive for a dinner party and are to be seated around a large circular table. How many different ways can the host of the party seat the guests around the table?

43. During a track meet, 9 runners are racing in the 100-yard dash, but only the top 3 runners receive an award. How many different ways are there for the top 3 runners to place?

OBJECTIVE H Use a chi-square statistic to determine whether or not statistics support a conclusion. (Lesson 11-8)

44. Sixty people were surveyed in a taste test of two types of chocolate. 26 people preferred chocolate A and 34 people preferred chocolate B.

    a. If the chocolates were equally tasty, what would be the expected numbers of preference for each chocolate?

    b. Calculate the chi-square statistic for this situation using the actual numbers and the expected numbers from Part a.

    c. Use the chi-square table on page 699. Does the evidence support the fact that chocolate B is preferred to chocolate A? Explain why or why not.

45. A company was open only Monday through Friday. Because it was not open Saturday or Sunday, it expected that it would get about the same amount of mail each day Tuesday through Friday, but three times this amount on Monday. However, some people thought there was too much mail coming on Monday. When the numbers of pieces of mail for each day for a few weeks were totaled, here were the numbers on each day.

Day	Mon.	Tues.	Wed.	Thurs.	Fri.
Pieces of Mail	122	30	41	35	27

    a. How many pieces of mail did the company expect each day?

    b. Calculate the chi-square statistic for this situation using the actual numbers and the expected numbers from Part a.

    c. Use the chi-square table on page 699. Does the evidence support the company's expectations on how much mail to expect? Justify your answer.

46. A large factory believes that its floor manager is becoming careless towards the end of his shift each day. Below is a table that shows the hour of his shift and the number of accidents that occurred during that hour.

Hour	1	2	3	4	5	6	7	8
Accidents	5	4	4	7	9	8	11	10

    a. If the factory were to have an equal number of accidents each hour, find the expected number.

    b. Calculate the chi-square statistic for this situation using the actual numbers and the expected number from Part a.

    c. Use the chi-square table on page 699. Does the evidence support the factory's belief about the floor manager? Justify your answer.

REPRESENTATIONS Pictures, graphs, or objects that illustrate concepts

OBJECTIVE I Represent polynomials by areas. (Lessons 11-3, 11-5, 11-6)

47. a. Write the area of the largest rectangle below as the sum of 4 terms.

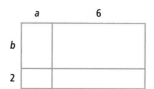

    b. Write the area of the largest rectangle as the product of 2 binomials.

    c. Are the answers to Parts a and b equal?

48. Represent $(n + m)(p + q)$ using areas of rectangles.

49. a. What polynomial multiplication is represented by the area of the largest rectangle below?

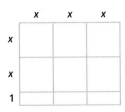

b. What is the product in standard form?

50. Show the product $(3x + 1)^2$ using areas of rectangles. Write your answer in standard form.

51. Show a factorization of $3x^2 + 9x$ by rearranging these tiles into a different rectangle.

52. Show $4x^2 + 4x + 1 = (2x + 1)^2$ by rearranging these tiles into a square with sides $2x + 1$.

Chapter

12

More Work with Quadratics

Contents

In writing it is important to know and use synonyms for the same idea. A picture may be beautiful or pretty, or it may be dazzling or brilliant, or it may be dull or drab or gray. Synonyms help convey ideas more clearly and one word may fit a situation just a little better than another.

Equivalent expressions in mathematics are like synonyms in writing. Equivalent expressions are often classified by their form.

Here are four ways to write the same number:

2,048	base 10
$2 \cdot 10^3 + 4 \cdot 10^1 + 8 \cdot 1$	expanded form
2^{11}	exponential form
$2.048 \cdot 10^3$	scientific notation

There are occasions when each of these forms is most appropriate or most helpful to understanding a situation. Base 10 is our normal compact way of writing numbers. Expanded form shows the meaning of base 10. Exponential form arises in many counting situations and situations of growth. Scientific notation is useful when comparing numbers that differ greatly in size.

Equivalent equations are also like synonyms. Consider the line that contains the two points (2, 9) and (8, 11). Three equivalent equations for this line are in forms that you saw in Chapter 6.

$y = \frac{1}{3}x + \frac{25}{3}$ slope-intercept form

$x - 3y = -25$ standard form

$y - 9 = \frac{1}{3}(x - 2)$ point-slope form

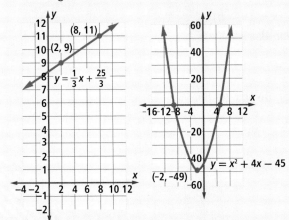

In this chapter, we return to quadratic equations and parabolas. Here are three equivalent equations for the parabola that is graphed at the left.

$y = x^2 + 4x - 45$ standard form

$y + 49 = (x + 2)^2$ vertex form

$y = (x - 5)(x + 9)$ factored form

In Chapter 9, you saw that standard form enables you to use the Quadratic Formula to find the x-intercepts of the graph. Standard form also is very useful for solving equations. The vertex form, which opens the chapter, lets you quickly find the vertex of the parabola. This is useful for graphing and for obtaining the minimum (or maximum) value of y. The factored form, which you will study later in this chapter, shows the x-intercepts of the graph.

713

Lesson

12-1

Graphing
$y - k = a(x - h)^2$

Vocabulary

vertex form of an equation for a parabola

▶ **BIG IDEA** The graph of the equation $y - k = a(x - h)^2$ is a parabola whose vertex can be easily found.

In Chapter 9, you graphed many parabolas with equations in the *standard form* $y = ax^2 + bx + c$. When an equation is in this form, the vertex of the parabola is not obvious. In Activity 1, you are asked to examine some parabolas with equations in the form $y - k = a(x - h)^2$. When an equation is in this form, its graph is a parabola whose vertex can be found rather easily.

Mental Math

Suppose $b(x) = 2|x| - 4$. Evaluate

a. $b(5)$.

b. $b(-5)$.

c. $b(5) - b(-5)$.

d. $\frac{b(5)}{b(-5)}$.

Activity 1

In 1–6, set a graphing calculator for the window $-15 \le x \le 15$, $-10 \le y \le 10$.

a. Graph the equation on your calculator. (You will have to solve the equation for y if it is not already solved for y.) Copy the graph by hand onto your paper.

b. Label the vertex with its coordinates.

c. Draw the axis of symmetry as a dotted line. Label the axis of symmetry with its equation.

1. $y - 4 = (x - 3)^2$ **2.** $y + 3 = (x - 5)^2$

3. $y - 1 = (x + 4)^2$ **4.** $y + 8 = -(x + 6)^2$

5. $y - 12 = -(x - 4)^2$ **6.** $y = (x - 0.35)^2$

7. Look back at your graphs for Questions 1–6 and the equations that produced them. Explain how to look at an equation like $y - k = (x - h)^2$ to help determine the vertex of its graph.

In 8 and 9, each graph is of an equation of the form $y - k = (x - h)^2$. The vertex and axis of symmetry of the parabola are given. Use what you learned in Questions 1–7.

a. Write an equation for the graph.

b. Check your equation by graphing it on your calculator. Do you get the graph you expected?

8.

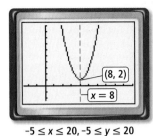

$-5 \leq x \leq 20, -5 \leq y \leq 20$

9.

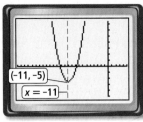

$-25 \leq x \leq 5, -10 \leq y \leq 14$

Example 1

Consider the graph of $y - 7 = 6(x - 15)^2$.

a. Explain why the graph is a parabola.

b. Find the vertex of this parabola without graphing.

Solution

a. If the equation can be written in the form $y = ax^2 + bx + c$, its graph is a parabola. Work with the given equation to get it into that form.

$y - 7 = 6(x - 15)^2$

$y - 7 = 6(x^2 - 30x + 225)$ Square of a Binomial

$y - 7 = 6x^2 - 180x + 1{,}350$ Distributive Property

$y = 6x^2 - 180x + 1{,}357$ Add 7 to both sides.

This equation is of the form $y = ax^2 + bx + c$, with $a = 6$, $b = -180$, and $c = 1{,}357$, so its graph is a parabola.

b. To find its vertex, examine the original equation $y - 7 = 6(x - 15)^2$. Add 7 to both sides.

$$y = 6(x - 15)^2 + 7$$

Since $(x - 15)^2$ is the square of a real number, $(x - 15)^2$ cannot be negative. The least value $(x - 15)^2$ can have is 0, and that occurs when $x = 15$. Thus the least value that $6(x - 15)^2$ can have is 0, and the least value that $6(x - 15)^2 + 7$ can have is 7. All of these least values occur when $x = 15$. As a consequence, the vertex of the parabola is at the point on the parabola with x-coordinate 15. When $x = 15$, substitution shows that $y = 7$. So the vertex is $(15, 7)$. Since 7 is the least value of y, the parabola must open up.

Check You should graph the equation $y - 7 = 6(x - 15)^2$ with a graphing calculator, making sure that the window contains the point $(15, 7)$. (You will likely have to solve the equation for y before graphing.)

The argument in Example 1 can be repeated in general. It demonstrates the theorem on the next page.

Graphing $y - k = a(x - h)^2$ **715**

Parabola Vertex Theorem

The graph of all ordered pairs (x, y) satisfying an equation of the form $y - k = a(x - h)^2$ is a parabola with vertex (h, k).

> **QY**
>
> Give the vertex of the parabola with equation $y - 8 = 3(x + 15)^2$.

STOP QY

The form $y - k = a(x - h)^2$ is called the **vertex form of an equation for a parabola** because you can easily find the vertex from the equation.

Example 2

Multiple Choice Which of the four curves at the right is the graph of $y + 3 = (x - 4)^2$?

Solution Rewrite $y + 3 = (x - 4)^2$ so it corresponds to the general equation $y - k = a(x - h)^2$.

$$y - {-3} = (x - 4)^2$$

The vertex is given by (h, k). So the vertex of the graph is $(4, -3)$. The parabola with this vertex is choice D.

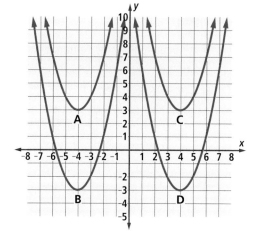

Activity 2

Use a dynamic graphing system to do the following.

Step 1 Create three sliders that include positive and negative numbers.

Name one slider a. (Or create a parameter a that is based on the slider.)

Name one slider h. (Or create a parameter h that is based on the slider.)

Name one slider k. (Or create a parameter k that is based on the slider.)

Step 2 Move the sliders so $a = 1, h = 0,$ and $k = 0$.

Step 3 Create the equation $y - k = a(x - h)^2$, using the parameters for a, h, and k. Plot the equation. The graph should show $y - 0 = 1(x - 0)^2$ or $y = x^2$.

a. Make a table of values for $-3 \leq x \leq 3$.

b. Find the differences between the y-coordinates as the x-coordinates increase by 1. Does this pattern look familiar?

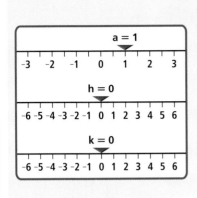

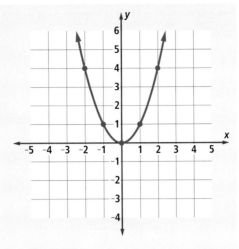

$$y - k = a(x - h)^2$$
$$y - 0 = 1(x - 0)^2$$

Step 4 Slowly move the *a* slider from 1 to 0.

    a. What happens to the graph for $0 < a < 1$?

    b. Move the *a* slider to 0.5. Make a table of values for $-3 < x < 3$. How do the *y*-coordinates compare to those in the table in Step 3?

    c. Find the differences between the *y*-coordinates as the *x*-coordinates increase by 1. How do the differences compare to those in Step 3?

Step 5 Now move the *a* slider to the right of 1.

    a. What happens to the graph when $a > 1$?

    b. Move the *a* slider to 2. Make a table of values for $-3 < x < 3$. How do the *y*-coordinates compare to those in the table in Step 3?

    c. Find the differences between the *y*-coordinates as the *x*-coordinates increase by 1. How do the differences compare to those in Step 3?

Step 6 Is the effect *a* has on the differences in the *y*-coordinates of $y = ax^2 + bx + c$ the same as or different from the effect *a* has on the differences in the *y*-coordinates of $y - k = a(x - h)^2$? Explain.

Step 7 Write a prediction of what you think happens to the graph when *a* is between -1 and 0.

Write a prediction of what you think happens to the graph when *a* is less than -1.

Step 8 Move the *a* slider to test your predictions. Were you correct? Explain how your predictions in Step 7 are similar to and different from what occurred in Steps 4 and 5.

Step 9 Sketch what you think the graph of each function will look like.

    $y - 5 = 2(x - 1)^2$ $y + 3 = 0.25(x - 2)^2$ $y = -3(x + 4)^2$

(continued on next page)

Step 10 Check your predictions from Step 9 by moving sliders *a*, *h*, and *k* to match the values in the function.

Step 11 Write a possible equation in vertex form for the graph of the parabola at the right.

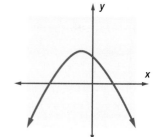

Example 3

Write an equation in vertex form for the graph of the parabola at the right.

Solution 1 First locate the vertex and substitute it into the vertex form of an equation for a parabola, $y - k = a(x - h)^2$.

The vertex is at (4, –1), so $y - -1 = a(x - 4)^2$.

Next find the value of *a*. Compare the pattern in the change of the *y*-coordinates as the *x*-coordinates change by 1 in the graph to that of $y = x^2$.

Pattern change in *y*-coordinates for $y = x^2$: 1, 3, 5, ...

Pattern change in *y*-coordinates for graph: 2, 6, 10, ...

The pattern change for the graph is double the pattern change of $y = x^2$, so $a = 2$.

The equation for the parabola is $y + 1 = 2(x - 4)^2$.

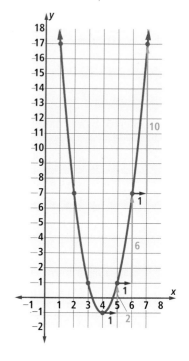

Solution 2 As in Solution 1, first locate the vertex and substitute it into the vertex form of an equation for a parabola, $y - k = a(x - h)^2$.

The vertex is at (4, –1), so $y - -1 = a(x - 4)^2$.

Next find the value of *a*. Pick a point on the graph that is not the vertex and substitute it into the equation. Then solve for *a*. We pick point (6, 7).

$$7 + 1 = a(6 - 4)^2$$
$$8 = a(2)^2$$
$$8 = 4a$$
$$2 = a$$

Substitute *a* and the vertex into the equation.

The equation for the parabola is $y + 1 = 2(x - 4)^2$.

Check Pick a point on the graph and substitute it into the equation. We'll use the point (3, 1).

$$1 + 1 = 2(3 - 4)^2$$
$$2 = 2(-1)^2$$
$$2 = 2 \cdot 1$$
$$2 = 2 \text{ So it checks.}$$

Problems involving area can lead to parabolas. Consider the following problem.

GUIDED

Example 4

There are many possible rectangles with a perimeter of 24 units. Suppose the length of one side of such a rectangle is L.

a. Find the area A of the rectangle in terms of L.

b. Graph the equation from Part a.

c. Use the graph to determine the maximum area of a rectangle with perimeter of 24 units.

Solutions

a. You know that the perimeter P of a rectangle is given by the formula $P = 2L + 2W$. So in this case, $24 = 2L + 2W$.

Now solve this equation for W.

___?___ $= 2W$

Divide both sides by 2.

___?___ $= W$

Since the area $A = LW$, substituting ___?___ for W gives the following formula for A.

$A = L$___?___

b. Letting $x = L$ and $y = A$, a graph of $y = x(12 - x)$ is shown here. The graph is a parabola because $y = 12x - x^2$ is of the form $y = ax^2 + bx + c$. The only part of the parabola that makes sense in this problem is for values of x between 0 and 12, so we use that window.

c. Each value of y in $y = x(12 - x)$ is the area of a particular rectangle. If $x = L = 2$, then $W = 12 - 2 = 10$ units. The area is $y = 2 \cdot 10 = 20$ units^2. That is, the point $(2, 20)$ on the parabola means that when one side of the rectangle is 2 units, the area of the rectangle is 20 units^2.

If $x = L = 3$, then $W =$ ___?___. The area $y =$ ___?___ $=$ ___?___.

If $x = L = 10$, then $W =$ ___?___. The area $y =$ ___?___ $=$ ___?___.

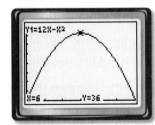

The maximum value of y is at the vertex of the parabola. From the graph the vertex is $(6, 36)$. So the maximum area of the rectangle is ___?___, occurring when $L =$ ___?___ and $W =$ ___?___, that is, when the rectangle is a square.

The equation graphed in Example 4 is not in vertex form. That makes it difficult to know the vertex. In Lesson 12-2, you will see how to convert an equation into vertex form.

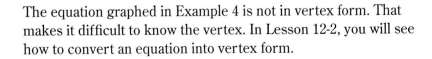

Graphing $y - k = a(x - h)^2$ **719**

Questions

COVERING THE IDEAS

1. The graph at the right shows a parabola.

    a. What are the coordinates of its vertex?

    b. Give an equation for its axis of symmetry.

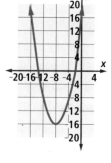

2. Give the minimum value of each expression.

    a. x^2 b. $(x + 6)^2$ c. $3(x + 6)^2$ d. $3(x + 6)^2 - 8$

3. Explain why 7 is the maximum value of the expression $-4(x - 5)^2 + 7$.

In 4–7, an equation of a parabola is given.

    a. Find the coordinates of its vertex.

    b. Write an equation for its axis of symmetry.

    c. Tell whether the parabola opens up or down.

4. $y + 8 = -5(x - 9)^2$

5. $y - 21 = 0.2(x - 15)^2$

6. $y - 43 = 8x^2$

7. $y + \frac{1}{2} = -(x + 6)^2$

8. The equation $y = x(18 - x)$ gives the area of a rectangle with perimeter of 36 where x is the length of one of its sides. This equation is graphed at the right.

    a. Give the areas of the three rectangles for which $x = 4$, 5, and 11.

    b. Point P on the graph represents a rectangle. Give the rectangle's side lengths and area.

    c. What is the maximum area of a rectangle with perimeter 36?

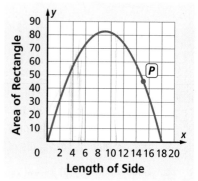

9. Explain the similarities and differences in the graphs of the functions.

    a. $y + 8 = (x - 4)^2$

    b. $y + 8 = 1.25(x - 4)^2$

    c. $y + 8 = 0.75(x - 4)^2$

APPLYING THE MATHEMATICS

10. A rectangle has perimeter 60.

    a. Find a formula for its area A in terms of the length L of one side.

    b. Graph the formula you found in Part a.

    c. What is the maximum area of this rectangle?

11. A parabola has vertex $(-12, 9)$ and contains the point $(-10, 5)$. Give an equation for the parabola.

In **12** and **13**, an equation of the form $y = ax^2$ and its graph are given. A translation image of the parabola is graphed with a dashed curve. Write an equation for the image.

12.

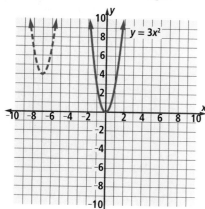

13.

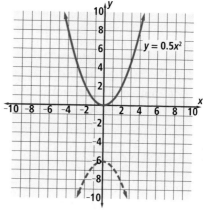

14. Write an equation for the graph of the parabola at the right.

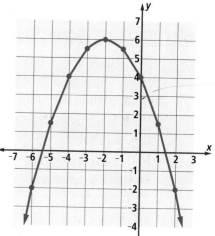

In **15** and **16**, find equations for two different parabolas that fit the description.

15. The vertex is $(5, -18)$ and the parabola opens down.

16. The axis of symmetry is $x = 2$ and the parabola opens up.

In **17** and **18**, a graph of a parabola and a point on it are given. Find the coordinates of a second point on the parabola that has the same y-coordinate as the given point.

17.

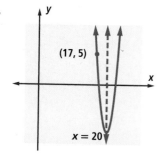

18.

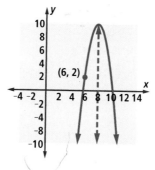

REVIEW

19. Draw rectangles picturing $3a(a + 8) = 3a^2 + 24a$. (**Lesson 11-3**)

20. The sum of the legs of a right triangle is 34 cm. If the hypotenuse is 26 cm, calculate the length of each of the legs. (**Lessons 10-2, 8-6**)

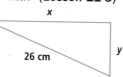

21. Find all values of m that satisfy
    $(m^2)^2 - 15m^2 + 36 = 0$. **(Lesson 9-5)**

22. Suppose a basketball team wins 9 of its first 11 games during a season. At this rate, how many games would you expect the team to win in a 28-game season? **(Lesson 5-9)**

23. A climber is ascending Mount Kilimanjaro, the highest mountain in Africa. At 9 A.M. the climber is at an elevation of 15,416 feet and at 10:15 A.M. the climber is at an elevation of 16,004 feet. At this rate, when would the climber reach the 19,336-foot summit? **(Lesson 5-5)**

24. Simplify $5\pi \div \frac{4\pi}{3}$. **(Lesson 5-2)**

25. Solve the equation or inequality. **(Lessons 4-5, 4-4)**
    a. $2x = 3x$ b. $2x > 3x$

Mount Kilimanjaro is not only the highest peak on the African continent; it is also the tallest freestanding mountain in the world at 19,336 feet.

Source: Mount Kilimanjaro National Park

EXPLORATION

26. Tiger Woods drives golf balls 300 yards before they hit the ground. Suppose one of his drives is 80 feet high at its peak, and that the path of the ball is a parabola.
    a. With a suitable placement of coordinates, find an equation for this parabola.
    b. How far from the tee (where the drive begins) is the ball 50 feet up in the air?

QY ANSWER

$(-15, 8)$

Lesson

12-2

Completing the Square

Vocabulary

complete the square

▶ **BIG IDEA** Completing the square is a process that converts an equation for a parabola from standard form into vertex form.

You have now seen two forms of equations whose graphs are parabolas.

Standard form $y = ax^2 + bx + c$

Vertex form $y - k = a(x - h)^2$

From the vertex form you can read the vertex of the parabola and also the maximum or minimum possible value of y. For example, from this form, you could tell the highest point that a baseball or a rocket reaches if you have an equation for its path.

But equations for paths are usually found in standard form $y = ax^2 + bx + c$. So the goal of this lesson is for you to learn how to convert an equation in standard form to one in vertex form.

Mental Math

A rocket's height h in feet t seconds after it is launched is shown below.

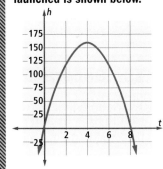

a. How long is the rocket in the air?

b. Estimate the greatest height it reaches.

c. When does it reach this greatest height?

The Problem, Visually Stated

Consider the equation $y = x^2 + 6x + 14$. Visually, you can picture this quadratic expression as 1 square, 6 lengths, and 14 units as shown at the right.

We want to convert it into vertex form. The idea is to move half of the lengths to try to create a bigger square as shown at the right.

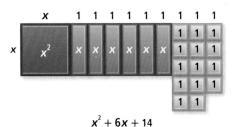

$x^2 + 6x + 14$

It will take 9 of the units to fill in the bottom right corner to complete the square. The new bigger square, pictured below, has an area $x^2 + 3x + 3x + 9$. But its length and width are each $x + 3$. So it has area $(x + 3)^2$.

And because 5 units are left over, we have shown that $x^2 + 6x + 14 = (x + 3)^2 + 5$.

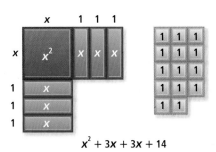

$x^2 + 3x + 3x + 14$

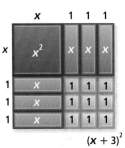
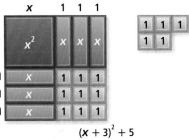

$(x + 3)^2 + 5$

Now, if $y = x^2 + 6x + 14$, then $y = (x + 3)^2 + 5$, which means that $y - 5 = (x + 3)^2$.

Activity

In 1–4, an equation for a parabola is given.

a. Using algebra tiles, build the given quadratic expression with a square, lengths, and units.

b. Rearrange the square, lengths, and units to convert the equation to vertex form.

1. $y = x^2 + 4x + 18$ **2.** $y = x^2 + 10x + 30$

3. $y = x^2 + 10x + 25$ **4.** $y = x^2 + 14x + 52$

The General Process

In the expression $x^2 + 6x + 14$ on the previous page, we separated $6x$ into $3x + 3x$ and added 9 units to get the square. In general, the goal is to add a number to $x^2 + bx$ so that the right side of the equation contains a perfect square. We know, from the square of a binomial, that $(x + h)^2 = x^2 + 2hx + h^2$. Our goal is to find a number h^2 so that $x^2 + bx + h^2$ is a perfect square.

Comparing $x^2 + 2hx + h^2$ with $x^2 + bx$, we see that $b = 2h$. So $h = \frac{1}{2}b$. This means that $h^2 = \left(\frac{1}{2}b\right)^2$. And so $\left(x + \frac{1}{2}b\right)^2 = x^2 + bx + \left(\frac{1}{2}b\right)^2$.

Thus, to **complete the square** on $x^2 + bx$, add $\left(\frac{1}{2}b\right)^2$.

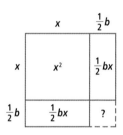

For example, in $x^2 + 6x$, $b = 6$ and $h = 3$. Then $h^2 = 9$.

Converting from Standard Form to Vertex Form

By completing the square, you can convert an equation in standard form to one in vertex form.

Example 1

a. Convert the equation $y = x^2 + 9x$ for a parabola into vertex form.

b. Find the vertex of this parabola.

Solutions

a. Think of $x^2 + 9x$ as $x^2 + bx$. Then $b = 9$. So $\left(\frac{1}{2}b\right)^2 = (4.5)^2$. Thus, using the above argument, if you add 4.5^2 to $x^2 + 9x$, you will have the square of a binomial. But in an equation, you cannot add something to one side without adding it to the other.

$$y = x^2 + 9x$$
$$y + 4.5^2 = x^2 + 9x + 4.5^2 \quad \text{Add } (4.5)^2 \text{ to both sides.}$$
$$y + 4.5^2 = (x + 4.5)^2 \quad \quad \text{Square of a binomial}$$

b. From Part a, we see that the vertex is $(-4.5, -4.5^2)$, that is, $(-4.5, -20.25)$.

Check Graph the two parabolas with equations $y = x^2 + 9x$ and $y + 4.5^2 = (x + 4.5)^2$ on the same grid. The graphs are identical to the one shown at the right, and the vertex is $(-4.5, -20.25)$.

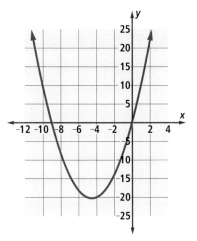

Completing the Square on $y = x^2 - bx$

Recall from Lesson 11-6 that $(x - h)^2 = x^2 - 2hx + h^2$.

Consequently, to complete the square on $x^2 - 2hx$ you add h^2. That is, to complete the square on $x^2 - bx$ you add the same amount as you do to complete the square on $x^2 + bx$.

Example 2

Without graphing, find the minimum value for y when $y = x^2 - 6x - 13$.

Solution You can find the minimum value of y if you know the vertex of the parabola that is the graph of $y = x^2 - 6x - 13$. First add 13 to both sides to isolate $x^2 - 6x$ on the right side.

$$y = x^2 - 6x - 13$$
$$y + 13 = x^2 - 6x$$

Now complete the square on $x^2 - 6x$. Here $b = -6$, so add $\left(\frac{-6}{2}\right)^2$, or 9, to both sides.

$$y + 13 + 9 = x^2 - 6x + 9$$
$$y + 22 = (x - 3)^2$$

So the vertex is $(3, -22)$.

Consequently, the minimum value of y is -22.

Check 1 Try values of x near the vertex and see what values of y result.

When $x = 4$, $y = 4^2 - 6 \cdot 4 - 13 = -21$.

When $x = 2$, $y = 2^2 - 6 \cdot 2 - 13 = -21$ also.

The symmetry confirms that -22 is a minimum value for y when $x = 3$, because it is less than -21.

Check 2 Graph the equation $y = x^2 - 6x - 13$. We leave that to you.

Questions

COVERING THE IDEAS

In 1 and 2, square the binomial.

1. $x + 7$
2. $n - 6.5$

3. **Fill in the Blanks** To complete the square for $x^2 + 20x$, add __?__. The result is the square of the binomial __?__.

4. **a.** Give the sum of the areas of the three rectangles below.
   b. What is the area of the undrawn rectangle needed to complete the large square?
   c. What algebraic expression will the completed large square below picture?

In 5–9, a quadratic expression is given.
   a. What number must be added to the expression to complete the square?
   b. After adding that number, the expression is the square of what binomial?

5. $x^2 + 2x$

6. $t^2 + 30t$

7. $r^2 - 7r$

8. $v^2 + bv$

9. $w^2 - bw$

10. **a.** Convert the equation $y = x^2 + 14x$ into vertex form.
    b. Find the vertex of this parabola.

11. **a.** Convert the equation $y = x^2 - 3x + 1$ into vertex form.
    b. Find the minimum value of y.

APPLYING THE MATHEMATICS

12. In this lesson, all the parabolas are graphs of equations of the form $y = x^2 + bx + c$. To deal with an equation of the form $y = -x^2 + bx + c$, first multiply both sides of the equation by -1, then complete the square, and finally multiply by -1 again so that y will be on the left side. Try this method to find the vertex of the parabola with equation $y = -x^2 + 5x + 2$.

13. In Lesson 9-4, the equation $\overset{y}{h} = -16\overset{x^2}{t^2} + 32\overset{x}{t} + 6$ described the height h of a ball t seconds after being thrown from a height of 6 feet with an initial upward velocity of 32 feet per second. Put this equation into vertex form using the following steps.

Step 1 Substitute y for h and x for t.

Step 2 Divide both sides of the equation by –16 so that the coefficient of x^2 is 1.

Step 3 Complete the square on the right side of the equation and add the appropriate amount to the left side.

Step 4 Multiply both sides of the equation by –16 so that the coefficient of y on the left side of the equation is 1.

a. What is the vertex of the parabola?

b. Is this a minimum or a maximum?

Kevin Garnett shoots a free throw for the Minnesota Timberwolves of the National Basketball Association.

Source: Associated Press

14. The equation $h = -0.12x^2 + 2x + 6$ describes the path of a basketball free throw, where h is the height of the ball in feet when the ball is x feet forward of the free-throw line.

a. Use the steps in Question 13 to put this equation into vertex form.

b. What is the greatest height the ball reaches?

15. If $y = x^2 - x + 1$, can y ever be negative? Explain your answer.

16. The process of completing the square can be used to solve quadratic equations. Consider the equation $y^2 - 10y + 24 = 0$.

a. Add –24 to both sides.

b. Complete the square on $y^2 - 10y$ and add the constant term to both sides.

c. You now have an equation of the form $(y - 5)^2 = k$. What is k?

d. Solve the equation in Part c by taking the square roots of both sides.

17. Use the process described in Question 16 to solve $x^2 + 24x + 7 = 0$.

REVIEW

18. Consider the parabola with quadratic equation $y + 8 = 3(x + 2)^2$. **(Lesson 12-1)**

a. Find the vertex of the parabola.

b. Graph the parabola.

19. Two parents of blood type AB will produce children of three different blood types: A, B, and AB. One inheritance hypothesis argues that when parents of blood type AB produce children, 25% will have blood type A, 25% will have blood type B, and 50% will have blood type AB. Consider the table below that gives the blood types of 248 children born of 100 couples with both parents of blood type AB. Use a chi-square test to determine whether the data support the hypothesis. Justify your reasoning. **(Lesson 11-8)**

Blood Type	Number of Children
A	58
B	51
AB	139

20. **a.** How many solutions does the system $\begin{cases} y = |x| \\ y = 2 \end{cases}$ have?

   b. Find the solutions. **(Lesson 10-1)**

In 21 and 22, solve. (Lessons 9-2, 5-2)

21. $\dfrac{4}{x} = \dfrac{8}{15}$

22. $\dfrac{m}{7} = \dfrac{20}{m}$

23. A watch company increases the price of its watches by 8%. If their watch now sells for $130.50, what did it sell for before the increase? **(Lesson 4-1)**

24. Solve $6(3x^2 - 3x) - 9(2x^2 + 1) = 12$. **(Lessons 3-4, 2-1)**

EXPLORATION

25. Explain how the drawing below can be used to show $(x - b)^2 = x^2 - 2bx + b^2$.

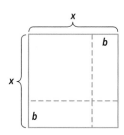

Lesson 12-3

The Factored Form of a Quadratic Function

Vocabulary

factored form (of a quadratic function)

▶ **BIG IDEA** The graph of the equation $y = a(x - r_1)(x - r_2)$ is a parabola that intersects the x-axis at $(r_1, 0)$ and $(r_2, 0)$.

You have seen two forms of equations for a quadratic function: standard form and vertex form. In this lesson, you will see some advantages of a third form called *factored form.* Below are graphs of three equations: $y + 4 = (x - 3)^2$, $y = (x - 1)(x - 5)$, and $y = x^2 - 6x + 5$.

Mental Math

Using one fair, 6-sided die, what is the probability of rolling

a. a 3?

b. an even number?

c. a number less than 3?

$y + 4 = (x - 3)^2$

Vertex form

$y = (x - 1)(x - 5)$

Factored form

$y = x^2 - 6x + 5$

Standard form

They are in fact the same parabola described in three different ways. You can check this by converting the first two equations into standard form.

$$y + 4 = (x - 3)^2$$
$$y + 4 = (x - 3)(x - 3)$$
$$y + 4 = x^2 - 6x + 9$$
$$y = x^2 - 6x + 5$$

$$y = (x - 1)(x - 5)$$
$$y = x^2 - 1x - 5x + 5$$
$$y = x^2 - 6x + 5$$

Different key aspects of the graph are revealed by each form. From the vertex form, you can easily determine the vertex, (3, –4). From the factored form, you can easily determine the x-intercepts, 1 and 5. In standard form, the y-intercept is clearly 5.

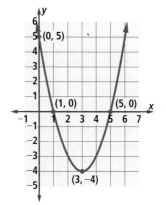

Activity 1

Use a dynamic graphing system.

Step 1 Create two sliders with values between −6 and 6. Label one r_1 and the other r_2.

Step 2 Slide bars so $r_1 = 1$ and $r_2 = 4$.

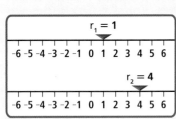

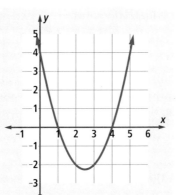

$$f(x) = (x - r_1)(x - r_2)$$
$$f(x) = (x - 1)(x - 4)$$

Step 3 Graph the function $f(x) = (x - r_1)(x - r_2)$.

Step 4 Give the points of intersection of the graph of f and the x-axis.

Step 5 Move the sliders to complete the table below.

r_1	r_2	$f(x) = (x - r_1)(x - r_2)$	Points of intersection of graph and x-axis
5	2	$f(x) = (x - 5)(x - 2)$	(?, 0) and (?, 0)
−4	−3	?	?
0	−1	?	?
3	3	?	?
?	?	$f(x) = (x + 2)(x - 4)$	?
?	?	$f(x) = (x + 5)(x + 5)$	?

Step 6 Explain how the factored form of a quadratic in the third column reveals the x-intercepts of the graph of that quadratic.

Step 7 Give the x-intercepts of the following functions using their graphs.

a. $f(x) = (x - 3)(x + 1)$ **b.** $g(x) = x(x + 6)$ **c.** $h(x) = (x - 2)(x - 2)$

How the Factored Form Displays the x-Intercepts

The equation $y = ax^2 + bx + c$ is in **factored form** when it is written as $y = a(x - r_1)(x - r_2)$.

For the function with equation $y = (x - 1)(x - 4)$ graphed in Activity 1, $a = 1$, $r_1 = 1$, and $r_2 = 4$.

The x-intercepts of the function are the values of x for which $y = 0$. So they are the values of x that satisfy the equation $0 = (x - 1)(x - 4)$.

Recall the Zero Product Property from Lesson 2-8: When the product of two numbers is zero, at least one of the numbers must be 0. In symbols, if $ab = 0$, then $a = 0$ or $b = 0$. Consequently, $y = 0$ when either $x - 1 = 0$ or $x - 4 = 0$. So $y = 0$ when either $x = 1$ or $x = 4$.

In general, the x-intercepts of a parabola can be determined from factored form in the same way that the vertex can be determined from vertex form.

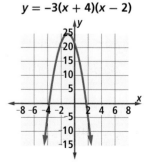

Factor Theorem for Quadratic Functions

The x-intercepts of the graph of $y = a(x - r_1)(x - r_2)$ are r_1 and r_2.

Example 1

Consider the equation $y = (x + 4)(x - 2)$.

a. Find the x-intercepts of its graph.

b. Graph the equation.

Solutions

a. The x-intercepts occur when $y = 0$. So solve $(x + 4)(x - 2) = 0$. By the Zero Product Property, either $x + 4 = 0$ or $x - 2 = 0$, so either $x = -4$ or $x = 2$. So the x-intercepts are -4 and 2.

b. Recall that the x-coordinate of the vertex is the mean of the x-intercepts -4 and 2. So the vertex has x-coordinate -1. When $x = -1$, $y = (-1 + 4)(-1 - 2) = -9$. So the vertex is $(-1, -9)$. With this information, you can sketch a graph.

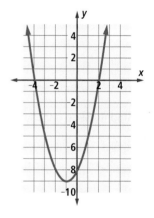

In the equation $y = (x + 4)(x - 2)$, the value of a, the coefficient of x^2, is 1. If the factors $x + 4$ and $x - 2$ remain the same but the value of a is changed, notice the similarities and changes in the graphs.

$y = (x + 4)(x - 2)$	$y = 2(x + 4)(x - 2)$	$y = -(x + 4)(x - 2)$	$y = -3(x + 4)(x - 2)$

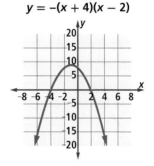

x-intercepts: −4 and 2
vertex: (−1, −9)

x-intercepts: −4 and 2
vertex: (−1, −18)

x-intercepts: −4 and 2
vertex: (−1, 9)

x-intercepts: −4 and 2
vertex: (−1, 27)

To see them better, all four equations can be placed on the same set of axes.

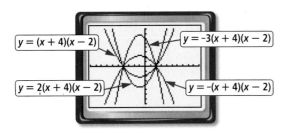

All four graphs have the same pair of x-intercepts, –4 and 2, so each goes through the points (–4, 0) and (2, 0).

Activity 2

Use a dynamic graphing system. You can use the previous Activity's set-up for this Activity.

Step 1 Create two sliders with values between –6 and 6. Label one r_1 and the other r_2.

Step 2 Create a third slider with values between –6 and 6 and label it a.

Step 3 Slide bars so $r_1 = 1$, $r_2 = 4$, and $a = 1$.

Step 4 Plot the function $f(x) = a \cdot (x - r_1)(x - r_2)$.

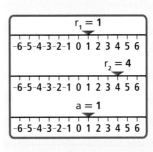

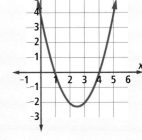

$$f(x) = a \cdot (x - r_1)(x - r_2)$$
$$f(x) = 1 \cdot (x - 1)(x - 4)$$

Step 5 Slide a. Do the x-intercepts change?

Step 6 Make $r_1 = -3$ and $r_2 = -3$. Slide a. Do the x-intercepts change?

Step 7 Move r_1 and r_2 to other values and then slide a. Explain your observations about the relationship between the value of a and the x-intercepts.

Step 8 Slide a into the positive values. What is true about the shape of the parabola when a is positive?

Step 9 Slide a into the negative values. What is true about the shape of the parabola when a is negative?

Step 10 Slide a to zero. Describe what happens to the graph.

Step 11 Complete the table. Verify your results by graphing.

a	r_1	r_2	$f(x) = a(x - r_1)(x - r_2)$	Does the parabola open up or down?
2	2	–3	$f(x) = 2(x - 2)(x + 3)$	?
–1	–4.1	5	?	?
5	–6	–6	?	up
–3	–5	0	?	?

When a quadratic expression is in factored form and equal to 0, you can solve equations and find x-intercepts quite easily. You can also determine vertices and maximum and minimum values of the expression.

Example 2

a. Find the x-intercepts of the graph of $y = (3x - 5)(2x + 1)$.

b. Find the vertex of the parabola.

Solutions

a. Solve $0 = (3x - 5)(2x + 1)$. Use the Zero Product Property.

Either $3x - 5 = 0$ or $2x + 1 = 0$.

$$3x = 5 \quad \text{or} \quad 2x = -1$$
$$x = \frac{5}{3} \quad \text{or} \quad x = -\frac{1}{2}$$

Thus the x-intercepts are $\frac{5}{3}$ and $-\frac{1}{2}$.

b. The x-coordinate of the vertex is the mean of the x-intercepts.

$$\frac{\frac{5}{3} + \frac{-1}{2}}{2} = \frac{\frac{10}{6} - \frac{3}{6}}{2} = \frac{\frac{7}{6}}{2} = \frac{7}{12}$$

When $x = \frac{7}{12}$, $y = \left(3 \cdot \frac{7}{12} - 5\right)\left(2 \cdot \frac{7}{12} + 1\right) = \left(\frac{21}{12} - \frac{60}{12}\right)\left(\frac{7}{6} + \frac{6}{6}\right)$

$$= -\frac{39}{12} \cdot \frac{13}{6} = -\frac{169}{24}.$$

So the vertex of the parabola is $\left(\frac{7}{12}, -\frac{169}{24}\right) = \left(\frac{7}{12}, -7\frac{1}{24}\right)$.

Questions

COVERING THE IDEAS

1. Give the x-intercepts of the graph of $y = 3(x - 8)(x + 4)$.

2. If the product of two numbers is zero, what must be true of at least one of those numbers?

In 3–5, solve the equation.

3. $0 = -5(x - 32)(x + 89.326)$

4. $777(n + 198)(2n - 10) = 0$

5. $p(p + 19) = 0$

6. Consider the equations $y = 3(x - 20)(x + 80)$ and $y = -2(x - 20)(x + 80)$.

   a. What two points do the graphs of these equations have in common?

   b. What is the x-coordinate of the vertex of both graphs?

   c. What is the y-coordinate of the vertex for each graph?

In 7–10, an equation for a function is given.
   a. Find the x-intercepts of the graph of the function.
   b. Find the vertex of the graph of the function.
   c. Sketch a graph of the function.
   d. Check your work by writing the equation in standard form and graphing that equation.

7. $y = (x + 15)(x + 7)$ 8. $y = -3(x + 8)(2x - 9)$

9. $f(x) = -x(4x + 11)$ 10. $g(x) = (x - 3)^2$

11. A quadratic function is graphed at the right.
   a. Give an equation for the axis of symmetry of the parabola.
   b. Give 3 possible equations in factored form for the graph.

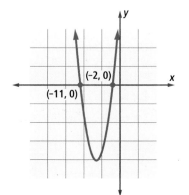

APPLYING THE MATHEMATICS

12. Down in a canyon there is a cannon that shoots cantaloupes straight up. Candice is standing on a cliff above the cannon. The cliff is at ground level or a height of 0 feet, so that the cantaloupes are fired from a negative starting height. The cantaloupe is shot up into the air higher than the cliff (on which Candice is standing) and then comes back down past the cliff back into the canyon. The cantaloupe passes by Candice 1 second after it is fired on the way up and 2 seconds after it was fired on the way down.
   a. What part of the situation represents the x-intercepts (or where the cantaloupe has a height of 0 feet)?
   b. In projectile problems where the units are in feet and seconds, $a = -16$. Write an equation for the situation in factored form.
   c. Give the axis of symmetry for this graph.
   d. Give the coordinates of the vertex of the graph.
   e. What does the vertex represent in the scenario about the cantaloupe?

13. The vertex of a parabola is $(-2, -18)$ and one of the x-intercepts is 1.
   a. Give the other x-intercept.
   b. Write an equation for the parabola in factored, vertex, and standard forms.

14. A formula that describes how many diagonals d that can be drawn in a polygon with n sides is $d = \frac{1}{2}n(n - 3)$.

Number of sides	3	4	5	6	...
Number of diagonals	0	2	5	9	...

a. What are the n-intercepts of the formula's graph?

b. Why does the point $(2, -1)$ not make sense in this situation?

c. The graph of the formula is part of a parabola. Find its vertex.

REVIEW

15. Consider the equation $y = -x^2 + 10x - 20$. (**Lessons 12-2, 12-1**)
    a. Rewrite the equation in vertex form.
    b. Give the vertex of the parabola.
    c. Graph the parabola.

In 16 and 17, multiply the expression. (**Lessons 11-6, 11-5**)

16. $(4a - 1)(3a + 6)$ 17. $(5n + 8)(5n - 8)$

18. If the cost of 15 pads of paper is $12.30, how many pads can be purchased with $3.75? (**Lesson 5-5**)

19. Give the coordinates of the point of intersection of the two lines. (**Lesson 4-2**)
    a. $x = 2, y = -4$ b. $x = a, y = 0$ c. $x = r, y = s$

20. A class of 34 students contains 2.5% of all the students in the school. How many students are in the school? (**Lesson 4-1**)

EXPLORATION

21. Consider the equation $y_1 = (x - 5)(x - 2)(x + 1)$.
    a. Graph this equation using a graphing calculator.
    b. Identify the x-intercepts of the graph.
    c. Use the results of Parts a and b to graph $y_2 = -(x - 5)(x - 2)(x + 1)$ without a graphing calculator.
    d. Use the results of Parts a and b to graph $y_3 = 3(x - 5)(x - 2)(x + 1)$ without a graphing calculator.
    e. Write a few sentences generalizing Parts a through d.

The Factored Form of a Quadratic Function   **735**

Lesson

12-4 Factoring $x^2 + bx + c$

Vocabulary

square term

linear term

constant term

prime polynomial over the integers

▶ **BIG IDEA** Some quadratic trinomials of the form $x^2 + bx + c$ can be factored into two linear factors.

In Lesson 12-3 you saw the advantage of the factored form $y = a(x - r_1)(x - r_2)$ in finding the x-intercepts r_1 and r_2 of the graph of a quadratic function. In this lesson you will see how to convert quadratic expressions from the form $x^2 + bx + c$ into factored form.

Notice the pattern that results from the multiplication of the binomials of the forms $(x + p)$ and $(x + q)$. After combining like terms, the product is a trinomial.

Mental Math

Use the discriminant to determine the number of real solutions to

a. $-5y^2 + 6y + 7 = 0$.

b. $3h^2 + 10 - h = 0$.

c. $-9x^2 - 12x - 4 = 0$.

		square term	linear term	constant term
$(x + 4)(x + 3) = x^2 + 3x + 4x + 12 =$		x^2	$+ \quad 7x$	$+ \quad 12$
$(x - 6)(x + 8) = x^2 + 8x - 6x - 48 =$		x^2	$+ \quad 2x$	$- \quad 48$
$(x + p)(x + q) = x^2 + qx + px + pq =$		x^2	$+ (p + q)x +$	pq

Examine the trinomials above. Their constant term pq is the product of the constant terms of the binomials. The coefficient $p + q$ of the linear term is the sum of the constant terms of the binomials. This pattern suggests a way to factor trinomials in which the coefficient of the square term is 1.

Example 1

Factor $x^2 + 11x + 18$.

Solution To factor, you need to identify two binomials, $(x + p)$ and $(x + q)$, whose product equals $x^2 + 11x + 18$. You must find p and q, two numbers whose product is 18 and whose sum is 11. Because the product is positive and the sum is positive, both p and q are positive. List the positive pairs of numbers whose product is 18. Then calculate their sums.

Product is 18	Sum of Factors
1, 18	19
2, 9	11
3, 6	9

The sum of the numbers 2 and 9 is 11. So $p = 2$ and $q = 9$.

Thus, $x^2 + 11x + 18 = (x + 2)(x + 9)$.

Check Factoring can always be checked by multiplication.

$(x + 2)(x + 9) = x^2 + 9x + 2x + 18 = x^2 + 11x + 18$; it checks.

GUIDED

Example 2

Factor $x^2 - x - 30$.

Solution Think of this trinomial as $x^2 + {-1}x + {-30}$. You need two numbers whose product is -30 and whose sum is -1. Since the product is negative, one of the factors is negative. List the possibilities.

Product is -30	Sum of Factors
-1, 30	29
-2, ?	?
-3, ?	?
-5, ?	?
-6, ?	?
-10, ?	?
?, ?	?
?, ?	?

The only pair of factors of -30 whose sum is -1 is __?__ and __?__.
So $x^2 - x - 30 = (x - \underline{?})(x + \underline{?})$.

Check 1 Multiply $(x - \underline{?})(x + \underline{?}) = x^2 + \underline{?}x - \underline{?}x - 30 = x^2 - x - 30$. It checks.

Check 2 Graph $y = x^2 - x - 30$ and $y = (x - \underline{?})(x + \underline{?})$. The graphs should be identical. Below we show the output from a graphing calculator, with the window $-10 \le x \le 10$, $-35 \le y \le 35$.

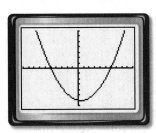

$y = x^2 - x - 30$

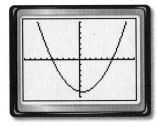

$y = (x - 6)(x + 5)$

The graphs appear to be identical.

As you know, some trinomials are perfect squares. You can use the method from Examples 1 and 2 to solve perfect square trinomials.

Example 3

Factor $t^2 - 8t + 16$.

Solution Find factors of 16 whose sum is −8. Because the product is positive and the sum is negative, both numbers are negative. You need only to consider negative factors of 16.

Product is 16	Sum of Factors
−1, −16	−17
−2, −8	−10
−4, −4	−8

So $t^2 - 8t + 16 = (t - 4)(t - 4) = (t - 4)^2$.

Check Use a CAS to factor $t^2 - 8t + 16$.

Not all trinomials of the form $x^2 + bx + c$ can be factored into polynomials with integer coefficients. For example, to factor $t^2 - 12t + 16$ as two binomials $(t + p)(t + q)$, where p and q are integers, the product of p and q would have to be 16 and their sum would have to be −12. The table in Example 3 shows that there are no such pairs of numbers. We say that $t^2 - 12t + 16$ is *prime over the integers*. A **prime polynomial over the integers** is one that cannot be factored into factors of lower degree with integer coefficients.

GUIDED

Example 4

Factor $m^2 + 5m - 24$.

Solution

1. Think of factors of __?__ whose sum is __?__.
2. Because the product is negative, how many of the factors are negative?
3. $m^2 + 5m - 24 = ($__?__$)($__?__$)$

Check Check your solution by graphing $y = x^2 - 5x - 24$ and $y = ($__?__$)($__?__$)$.

Activity

Use a CAS and the FACTOR command to complete this Activity. Work with a partner, a team, or your entire class.

The entries in the table on the next page are quadratic expressions of the form $x^2 + bx + c$. We want to factor them into polynomials with integer coefficients.

b	c = 1	c = 2	c = 3	c = 4	c = 5	c = 6	c = 7	c = 8	c = 9	c = 10
1	$x^2 + x + 1$	$x^2 + x + 2$	$x^2 + x + 3$	$x^2 + x + 4$	$x^2 + x + 5$	$x^2 + x + 6$	$x^2 + x + 7$	$x^2 + x + 8$	$x^2 + x + 9$	$x^2 + x + 10$
2	$x^2 + 2x + 1$	$x^2 + 2x + 2$	$x^2 + 2x + 3$	$x^2 + 2x + 4$	$x^2 + 2x + 5$	$x^2 + 2x + 6$	$x^2 + 2x + 7$	$x^2 + 2x + 8$	$x^2 + 2x + 9$	$x^2 + 2x + 10$
3	$x^2 + 3x + 1$	$x^2 + 3x + 2$	$x^2 + 3x + 3$	$x^2 + 3x + 4$	$x^2 + 3x + 5$	$x^2 + 3x + 6$	$x^2 + 3x + 7$	$x^2 + 3x + 8$	$x^2 + 3x + 9$	$x^2 + 3x + 10$
4	$x^2 + 4x + 1$	$x^2 + 4x + 2$	$x^2 + 4x + 3$	$x^2 + 4x + 4$	$x^2 + 4x + 5$	$x^2 + 4x + 6$	$x^2 + 4x + 7$	$x^2 + 4x + 8$	$x^2 + 4x + 9$	$x^2 + 4x + 10$
5	$x^2 + 5x + 1$	$x^2 + 5x + 2$	$x^2 + 5x + 3$	$x^2 + 5x + 4$	$x^2 + 5x + 5$	$x^2 + 5x + 6$	$x^2 + 5x + 7$	$x^2 + 5x + 8$	$x^2 + 5x + 9$	$x^2 + 5x + 10$
6	$x^2 + 6x + 1$	$x^2 + 6x + 2$	$x^2 + 6x + 3$	$x^2 + 6x + 4$	$x^2 + 6x + 5$	$x^2 + 6x + 6$	$x^2 + 6x + 7$	$x^2 + 6x + 8$	$x^2 + 6x + 9$	$x^2 + 6x + 10$
7	$x^2 + 7x + 1$	$x^2 + 7x + 2$	$x^2 + 7x + 3$	$x^2 + 7x + 4$	$x^2 + 7x + 5$	$x^2 + 7x + 6$	$x^2 + 7x + 7$	$x^2 + 7x + 8$	$x^2 + 7x + 9$	$x^2 + 7x + 10$
8	$x^2 + 8x + 1$	$x^2 + 8x + 2$	$x^2 + 8x + 3$	$x^2 + 8x + 4$	$x^2 + 8x + 5$	$x^2 + 8x + 6$	$x^2 + 8x + 7$	$x^2 + 8x + 8$	$x^2 + 8x + 9$	$x^2 + 8x + 10$
9	$x^2 + 9x + 1$	$x^2 + 9x + 2$	$x^2 + 9x + 3$	$x^2 + 9x + 4$	$x^2 + 9x + 5$	$x^2 + 9x + 6$	$x^2 + 9x + 7$	$x^2 + 9x + 8$	$x^2 + 9x + 9$	$x^2 + 9x + 10$
10	$x^2 + 10x + 1$	$x^2 + 10x + 2$	$x^2 + 10x + 3$	$x^2 + 10x + 4$	$x^2 + 10x + 5$	$x^2 + 10x + 6$	$x^2 + 10x + 7$	$x^2 + 10x + 8$	$x^2 + 10x + 9$	$x^2 + 10x + 10$

Step 1 Make a table like the one above with the same row and column headings, but keep the other cells blank.

Step 2 Factor each of the 100 entries in the table. Put the factored form in your table. If the quadratic cannot be factored over the integers, write "P," for prime, in the box. The expressions $x^2 + x + 1$ and $x^2 + 2x + 1$ have been done for you below.

b	c = 1
1	P
2	$(x + 1)(x + 1)$

Step 3 In your table, circle the factored expressions.

Step 4 For which values of c is there only one factorization of $x^2 + bx + c$ in that column? What type of numbers are these c values?

Step 5 When $c = 6$, there are two factorizations of $x^2 + bx + 6$. The factorizations occur when $b = 5$ and $b = 7$.
$$x^2 + 5x + 6 = (x + 2)(x + 3)$$
How are the 2 and 3 related to the 6?
How are the 2 and 3 related to the 5?
$$x^2 + 7x + 6 = (x + 1)(x + 6)$$
How are the 1 and 6 related to the 6?
How are the 1 and 6 related to the 7?

Step 6 If $x^2 + bx + c$ factors into $(x + p)(x + q)$ then $p + q = \underline{\ ?\ }$ and $pq = \underline{\ ?\ }$.

Step 7 For how many integer values of b is the expression $x^2 + bx + 20$ factorable? Explain. Give the values of b that allow $x^2 + bx + 20$ to be factored.

For how many integer values of b is the expression $x^2 + bx + 37$ factorable? Explain. Give the values of b that allow $x^2 + bx + 37$ to be factored.

Questions

1. **a.** In order to factor $x^2 + 10x + 24$, list the possible integer factors of the last term and their sums.

   b. Factor $x^2 + 10x + 24$.   **c.** Check your work.

2. Suppose $(x + p)(x + q) = x^2 + bx + c$.

   a. What must pq equal?   **b.** What must $p + q$ equal?

3. Sandra, Steve, and Simona each attempted to factor $n^2 + 2n - 48$. Which student's factorization is correct? Explain what mistake the other two students made.

Sandra's	Steve's	Simona's
$(n + 6)(n - 8)$	$(n - 6)(n - 8)$	$(n - 6)(n + 8)$

In 4–9, write the trinomial as the product of two binomials.

4. $x^2 + 22x + 40$ 5. $q^2 + 20q + 19$ 6. $z^2 - z - 56$

7. $v^2 - 102v + 101$ 8. $r^2 + 10r + 16$ 9. $m^2 + 17m - 38$

10. Explain why the trinomial $x^2 + 6x + 4$ cannot be factored over the integers.

11. **a.** Factor $x^2 - 8x + 15$.

    b. What are the x-intercepts of the graph of $y = x^2 - 8x + 15$?

12. The diagram at the right uses tiles to the factorization of
    $x^2 + 4x + 3 = (x + 1)(x + 3)$.

    Make a drawing to show the factorization of $x^2 + 7x + 10$.

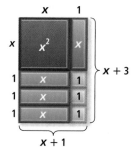

13. **a.** Find an equation of the form $y = (x + p)(x + q)$ whose graph is identical to the graph of $y = x^2 - 18x + 32$.

    b. Check your work by graphing both equations on the same set of axes.

14. **a.** Find the vertex of the parabola with equation $y = x^2 + 2x - 35$ by factoring to find the x-intercepts.

    b. Check Part a by completing the square to put the equation in vertex form.

15. Factor $-40 + 13x - x^2$.

16. If $m^2 + 13mn + 22n^2 = (m + pn)(m + qn)$, what are p and q?

REVIEW

17. Solve and check $(n - 10)\left(\frac{1}{2}n + 6\right) = 0$. **(Lesson 12-3)**

In **18** and **19**, find the value of c that makes each trinomial a perfect square. **(Lesson 12-2)**

18. $x^2 - 14x + c$
19. $x^2 + 9x + c$

In **20** and **21**, expand the expression. **(Lesson 11-6)**

20. $(4 - x)(4 + x)$
21. $(5a - 3)(5a + 3)$

22. Explain how $37^2 - 35^2$ can be calculated in your head. **(Lesson 11-6)**

In **23** and **24**, simplify the expression. **(Lessons 11-5, 11-4)**

23. $\frac{9z^3 + 10z}{z}$
24. $(n^2 + m^2) - (n - m)^2$

25. Factor $28b^4 + 8b^2 + 40$ completely. **(Lesson 11-4)**

26. A certain type of glass allows 85% of the light hitting it to pass through 1 centimeter of glass. The fraction y of light passing through x centimeters of glass is then $y = (0.85)^x$. **(Lesson 7-3)**

    a. Draw a graph of this equation for $0 \le x \le 10$.

    b. Use the graph to estimate the thickness of this glass you would need to allow only a quarter of the light hitting it to pass through.

In **27** and **28**, give the slope and y-intercept for each line. **(Lessons 6-8, 6-4)**

27. $y = \frac{1}{4}x$
28. $12x - 3y = 30$

Light is shining through tinted glass.

EXPLORATION

29. Using a CAS, make a table like that in the Activity but with integer values of c from -1 to -10. (Row 1 of the table is $x^2 + x - 1, x^2 + x - 2$, and so on.)

    a. Repeat Steps 1–3 from the Activity.

    b. How many of these 100 quadratic expressions can be factored over the integers?

    c. Describe a pattern in the table that could enable you to extend the table to more factors without doing any calculations.

Lesson
12-5
Factoring $ax^2 + bx + c$

▶ **BIG IDEA** Some quadratic trinomials of the form $ax^2 + bx + c$ can be factored into two linear factors.

You have seen that some trinomials of the form $x^2 + bx + c$ can be factored into a product of two binomials.

$$x^2 + 0x - 100 = (x + 10)(x - 10)$$
$$x^2 + 12x + 36 = (x + 6)(x + 6)$$
$$x^2 - 9x + 14 = (x - 7)(x - 2)$$
$$x^2 + 7x - 8 = (x - 1)(x + 8)$$

In this lesson, we consider quadratic trinomials in which the coefficient of the square term is not 1. Again, we seek to factor the trinomial into binomials with integer coefficients.

In factoring such a trinomial, first check for a common factor of the three terms.

Mental Math

Find the greatest common factor of

a. $16t$ and 32.

b. $9a$, $6b$, and $10ab$.

c. x^2 and $4x^3$.

Example 1

Factor $50x^5 + 200x^4 + 200x^3$.

Solution $50x^3$ is a common factor of the three terms.

$$50x^5 + 200x^4 + 200x^3 = 50x^3(x^2 + 4x + 4)$$

To factor $x^2 + 4x + 4$, we need a binomial whose constant terms have a product of 4 and a sum of 4.

$$x^2 + 4x + 4 = (x + 2)(x + 2)$$

So, $50x^5 + 200x^4 + 200x^3 = 50x^3(x + 2)(x + 2)$.

The original polynomial is said to be factored completely.

Check

$$50x^3(x + 2)(x + 2) = (50x^4 + 100x^3)(x + 2)$$
$$= 50x^5 + 100x^4 + 100x^4 + 200x^3$$
$$= 50x^5 + 200x^4 + 200x^3$$

The factorization checks.

When the coefficient of the square term is not 1 and there is no common factor of the three terms, a different process is applied. Suppose $ax^2 + bx + c = (dx + e)(fx + g)$.

The product of d and f, from the first terms of the binomials, is a. The product of e and g, the constant terms of the binomials, is c. The task is to find d, e, f, and g so that the rest of the multiplication and addition gives b.

Example 2

Factor $5x^2 + 32x + 12$.

Solution

Step 1 Rewrite the expression as a product of two binomials.
$$5x^2 + 32x + 12 = (dx + e)(fx + g)$$
You need to find integers d, e, f, and g.

Step 2 The coefficient of $5x^2$ is 5, so $df = 5$. Assume either d or f is 5, and the other is 1. Now write the following.
$$5x^2 + 32x + 12 = (5x + e)(x + g)$$
The product of e and g is 12, so $eg = 12$. Because the middle term $32x$ is positive, e and g must be positive. Thus, e and g might equal 1 and 12, or 2 and 6, or 3 and 4, in either order. Try all six possibilities.

Can e and g be 1 and 12?
$$(5x + 1)(x + 12) = 5x^2 + 61x + 12$$
$$(5x + 12)(x + 1) = 5x^2 + 17x + 12$$
No, we want $b = 32$, not 61 or 17.

Can e and g be 3 and 4?
$$(5x + 3)(x + 4) = 5x^2 + 23x + 12$$
$$(5x + 4)(x + 3) = 5x^2 + 19x + 12$$
No. Again the middle term is not what we want.

Can e and g be 2 and 6?
$$(5x + 2)(x + 6) = 5x^2 + 32x + 12$$
Yes; here $b = 32$. This is what we want.
$$5x^2 + 32x + 12 = (5x + 2)(x + 6)$$

Check 1 The multiplication $(5x + 2)(x + 6) = 5x^2 + 32x + 12$ is a check.

Check 2 Graph $y = 5x^2 + 32x + 12$ and $y = (5x + 2)(x + 6)$ on the same set of axes. The graphs should be identical. It checks.

(continued on next page)

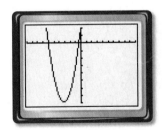

$y = 5x^2 + 32x + 12$
and
$y = (5x + 2)(x + 6)$

Check 3 Another check is to substitute a value for x, say 4.

Does $5x^2 + 32x + 12 = (5x + 2)(x + 6)$?

$5 \cdot 4^2 + 32 \cdot 4 + 12 = (5 \cdot 4 + 2)(4 + 6)$

$\qquad 80 + 128 + 12 = 22 \cdot 10$

Yes. Each side equals 220.

In Example 2, there are not many possible factors because the coefficient of x^2 is 5 and all numbers are positive. Example 3 has more possibilities, but the idea is still the same. Try factors until you find the correct ones.

GUIDED

Example 3

Factor $15y^2 - 16y - 7$.

Solution First write down the form. $(ay + b)(cy + d)$. So $ac =$ __?__. Thus either a and c are 3 and 5 or they are __?__ and __?__. The product $bd = -7$. So b and d are either __?__ and __?__, or __?__ and __?__.

List all the possible factors with $a = 3$ and $c = 5$, and multiply.

$(3y + 7)(5y - 1) =$ __?__

$(3y - 7)(5y + 1) =$ __?__

$(3y - 1)(5y + 7) =$ __?__

$(3y + 1)(5y - 7) =$ __?__

List all the possible factors with $a = 1$ and $c = 15$.

$(\underline{\,?\,}y + 7)(\underline{\,?\,}y - 1) =$ __?__

$(\underline{\,?\,}y - 7)(\underline{\,?\,}y + 1) =$ __?__

$(\underline{\,?\,}y - 1)(\underline{\,?\,}y + 7) =$ __?__

$(\underline{\,?\,}y + 1)(\underline{\,?\,}y - 7) =$ __?__

At most, you need to do these eight multiplications. If one of them gives $15y^2 - 16y - 7$, then that is the correct factoring.

So $15y^2 - 16y - 7 =$ __?__.

In Example 3, notice that each choice of factors gives a product that differs only in the coefficient of y (the middle term). If the original problem were to factor $15y^2 - 40y - 7$, this process shows that no factors with integer coefficients will work. The quadratic $15y^2 - 40y - 7$ is a prime polynomial over the set of integers.

Once a quadratic trinomial $f(x)$ has been factored, then solving $f(x) = 0$ is easy using the Zero Product Property.

Example 4

Solve $15y^2 - 16y - 7 = 0$.

Solution Use the factorization of $15y^2 - 16y - 7$ in Example 3.

$$15^2 - 16y - 7 = 0$$

$$(\underline{\quad ? \quad})(\underline{\quad ? \quad}) = 0$$

$$\underline{\quad ? \quad} = 0 \qquad \text{or} \qquad \underline{\quad ? \quad} = 0$$

$$y = \underline{\quad ? \quad} \qquad \text{or} \qquad y = \underline{\quad ? \quad}$$

Questions

COVERING THE IDEAS

1. Perform the multiplications in Parts a–d.
   a. $(2x + 3)(4x + 5)$
   b. $(2x + 5)(4x + 3)$
   c. $(2x + 1)(4x + 15)$
   d. $(2x + 15)(4x + 1)$
   e. Explain how these multiplications are related to factoring $8x^2 + 26x + 15$.

2. Suppose $ax^2 + bx + c = (dx + e)(fx + g)$ for all values of x.
   a. The product of d and f is $\underline{\ ?\ }$.
   b. The product of $\underline{\ ?\ }$ and $\underline{\ ?\ }$ is c.

3. Factor the trinomials completely.
   a. $2x^2 + 14x + 2$
   b. $5n^2 + 35n - 50$

In 4–9, factor the trinomial, if possible.

4. $5A^2 + 7A + 2$

5. $-3x^2 + 11x - 6$

6. $y^2 - 10y + 16$

7. $14w^2 - 9w - 1$

8. $-4x^2 - 11x + 3$

9. $17k^2 - 36k + 19$

10. Check the solutions to Example 1 by substitution.

11. Solve $20x^2 + 11x - 3 = 0$ by factoring.

APPLYING THE MATHEMATICS

12. Jules solved the equation $2x^2 - 5x + 3 = 7$ in the following way.

    Step 1 He factored $2x^2 - 5x + 3$ into $(2x - 3)(x - 1)$.

    Step 2 He substituted the factored expression back into the equation $(2x - 3)(x - 1) = 7$.

    Step 3 He considered all the possibilities: $2x - 3 = 7$ and $x - 1 = 1$, in this case $x = 5$ or $x = 2$; or $2x - 3 = 1$ and $x - 1 = 7$, in this case $x = 2$ or $x = 8$.

    Step 4 He checked his work and found that none of these values of x check in the original equation.

    What did Jules do wrong?

13. Find the vertex of the parabola with equation $y = 8x^2 - 6x + 1$ by first factoring to obtain the x-intercepts.

14. Consider the equation $6t^2 + 7t - 24 = 0$.

    a. Solve the equation by using the Quadratic Formula.

    b. Solve the equation by factoring.

    c. Which method do you prefer to solve this problem? Why?

15. **a.** Solve the equation $3n^2 = 2 - 5n$ using the Quadratic Formula.

    b. Check your solution to Part a by solving the same equation using factoring.

16. **a.** Factor $14x^3 - 21x^2 - 98x$ into the product of a monomial and a trinomial.

    b. Give the complete factorization of $14x^3 - 21x^2 - 98x$.

In 17 and 18, find the complete factorization.

17. $9p^2 + 30p^3 + 25p^4$

18. $-2x^2 + 23xy - 30y^2$

REVIEW

19. Rewrite $x^8 - 16$ as the product of

    a. two binomials.

    b. three binomials. **(Lessons 12-4, 11-6)**

20. Find two consecutive positive even integers whose product is 360. **(Lessons 12-4, 12-2)**

21. Find the x-intercepts of $y = x^2 - 8x + 3$ by completing the square. **(Lessons 12-3, 12-2)**

22. **a.** Here are three instances of a pattern. Describe the general pattern using two variables, x and y. (**Lessons 11-6, 1-2**)

$$(48 + 32)(24 - 16) = 2(24^2 - 16^2)$$
$$(10 + 20)(5 - 10) = 2(5^2 - 10^2)$$
$$(4 + 1)(2 - 0.5) = 2(2^2 - 0.5^2)$$

b. Does your general pattern hold for all real values of x and y? Justify your answer.

23. **Multiple Choice** Which equation is graphed below?
(**Lesson 9-1**)

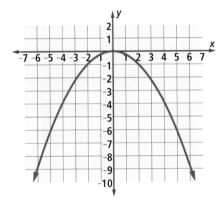

A $y = -\frac{1}{4}x^2$ **B** $y = 4x^2$

C $y = -4x^2$ **D** $y = \frac{1}{4}x^2$

24. When a fair, six-sided die is tossed, the probability of getting a 1 is $\frac{1}{6}$. If the die is tossed twice, the probability of getting a 1 both times is $\frac{1}{6} \cdot \frac{1}{6} = \left(\frac{1}{6}\right)^2$. (**Lessons 8-2, 8-1**)

a. Write an expression to represent the probability of rolling a die m times and getting a 1 each time.

b. Write your answer to Part a as a power of 6.

EXPLORATION

25. The polynomial $6x^3 + 47x^2 + 97x + 60$ can be factored over the integers into $(3x + a)(2x + b)(x + c)$. Find a, b, and c. (*Hint:* What is $a \cdot b \cdot c$?)

Lesson 12-6

Which Quadratic Expressions Are Factorable?

▶ **BIG IDEA** A quadratic expression with integer coefficients is factorable over the integers if and only if its discriminant is a perfect square.

This lesson connects two topics you have seen in this chapter: factoring and solutions to quadratic equations. These topics seem quite different. Their relationship to each other is an example of how what you learn in one part of mathematics is often useful in another part.

You have seen four ways to find the real-number values of x that satisfy $ax^2 + bx + c = 0$.

1. You can graph $y = ax^2 + bx + c$ and look for its x-intercepts.

2. You can use the Quadratic Formula.

3. You can factor $ax^2 + bx + c$ and use the Zero Product Property.

4. You can set $f(x) = ax^2 + bx + c$ to 0 and look for values of x such that $f(x) = 0$.

The first two ways can always be done. But you know that it is not always possible to factor $ax^2 + bx + c$ over the integers, so it useful to know when it is possible.

Mental Math

Match each function graphed below with its type.

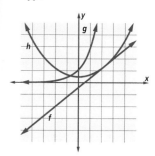

a. exponential growth

b. linear

c. quadratic

A Quadratic Equation with Rational Solutions

Consider the equation $9x^2 + 14x - 8 = 0$. Use the Quadratic Formula.

Step 1 $x = \dfrac{-14 \pm \sqrt{14^2 - 4 \cdot 9 \cdot (-8)}}{2 \cdot 9}$

Step 2 $= \dfrac{-14 \pm \sqrt{484}}{18}$

Step 3 $= \dfrac{-14 \pm 22}{18}$

Step 4 So $x = \dfrac{-14 + 22}{18} = \dfrac{4}{9}$ or $x = \dfrac{-14 - 22}{18} = -2$

Notice that the solutions $\frac{4}{9}$ and -2 have no visible radical sign. This is because the number 484 under the square root sign is a perfect square (Step 2). So, after calculating the square root (Step 3), one integer is divided by another, and the solutions are rational numbers.

In general, for quadratic equations with integer coefficients, if the *discriminant* $b^2 - 4ac$ in the quadratic equation $ax^2 + bx + c = 0$ is a perfect square, then the solutions are rational. The square root of an integer that is not a perfect square is irrational. So the square root will remain in the solutions, and the solutions will be irrational. These results can be summarized in one sentence: *When a, b, and c are integers, the solutions to $ax^2 + bx + c = 0$ are rational numbers if and only if $b^2 - 4ac$ is a perfect square.*

Relating the Solving of $ax^2 + bx + c = 0$ to the Factoring of $ax^2 + bx + c$

Now we connect this with factoring. Consider the same equation as before: $9x^2 + 14x - 8 = 0$.

Factor the left side.

$$(9x - 4)(x + 2) = 0$$

Use the Zero Product Property.

$$9x - 4 = 0 \quad \text{or} \quad x + 2 = 0$$
$$x = \frac{4}{9} \quad \text{or} \quad x = -2$$

You can see from the equation above that when a quadratic equation in standard form is factorable, the solutions are rational numbers. Combining this observation with the facts on the previous page leads us to the following conclusion, which we call the *Discriminant Theorem*. A formal proof of this theorem is given in Chapter 13.

Discriminant Theorem

When *a*, *b*, and *c* are integers, with $a \neq 0$, either all three of the following conditions hold, or none of these hold.

1. $b^2 - 4ac$ is a perfect square.

2. $ax^2 + bx + c$ is factorable over the set of polynomials with integer coefficients.

3. The solutions to $ax^2 + bx + c = 0$ are rational numbers.

Example 1

Is $8x - 5x^2 + 21$ factorable into polynomials with integer coefficients?

Solution First rewrite this expression in the standard form of a polynomial.

$$-5x^2 + 8x + 21$$

Thus $a = -5$, $b = 8$, and $c = 21$.

(continued on next page)

Then $b^2 - 4ac = (8)^2 - 4 \cdot (-5) \cdot 21 = 64 + 420 = 484$.

Since $484 = 22^2$, 484 is a perfect square. So the expression is factorable.

 QY

▶ **QY**

Verify Example 1 by finding the factorization of

$8x - 5x^2 + 21$.

GUIDED

Example 2

Is the polynomial $2x^2 - 10 + 5x$ factorable?

Solution

Step 1 Write the polynomial in standard form. ___?___

Step 2 Identify a, b, and c. $a = $ __?__, $b = $ __?__, and $c = $ __?__

Step 3 Calculate $b^2 - 4ac$. __?__

Step 4 Is $b^2 - 4ac$ a perfect square? __?__

Step 5 What is your conclusion?

The phrase "with integer coefficients" is necessary in Example 1 because every quadratic expression is then factorable if noninteger coefficients are allowed.

Example 3

What can be learned by applying the Discriminant Theorem to the quadratic equation $x^2 - 29 = 0$?

Solution In this case, $a = 1$, $b = 0$, and $c = -29$, so $b^2 - 4ac = 0^2 - 4 \cdot 1 \cdot (-29) = 116$. Since 116 is not a perfect square, the solutions to $x^2 - 29 = 0$ are irrational and the polynomial $x^2 - 29$ cannot be factored into linear factors with integer coefficients.

Yet the polynomial $x^2 - 29$ in Example 3 can be factored as the difference of two squares.

$$x^2 - 29 = x^2 - \left(\sqrt{29}\right)^2 = \left(x - \sqrt{29}\right)\left(x + \sqrt{29}\right)$$

The factors do not have integer coefficients, so we say that $x^2 - 29$ is prime over the set of polynomials with integer coefficients, but not over the set of all polynomials. It is just like factoring 7 into $3 \cdot \frac{7}{3}$. The integer 7 is prime over the integers but can be factored into rational numbers.

Applying the Discriminant Theorem

Knowing whether an expression is factorable can help determine what methods are available to solve an equation.

Example 4

Solve $m^2 - 9m + 24 = 0$ by any method.

Solution Because the coefficient of m^2 is 1, it is reasonable to try to factor the left side. But first evaluate $b^2 - 4ac$ to see whether this is possible.

$a = 1$, $b = -9$, and $c = 24$. So, $b^2 - 4ac = (-9)^2 - 4 \cdot 1 \cdot (24) = -15$. This is not a perfect square, so the equation does not factor over the integers.

In fact, because $b^2 - 4ac$ is negative, there are no real solutions to this equation.

Check Graph $y = x^2 - 9x + 24$. You will see that the graph does not intersect the x-axis. There are no x-intercepts.

What percent of quadratic expressions are factorable? Try the following activity.

Activity

This activity can be done with a partner if a CAS is available, or as a whole-class activity otherwise.

There are infinitely many quadratic expressions of the form $ax^2 + bx + c$, but there are only 8,000 of these in which a, b, and c are nonzero integers from –10 to 10. What percent of these are factorable? There are too many to try to factor by hand, even with a CAS. It is possible to determine this number by programming a computer to factor all of them. But it is also possible to estimate the percent by sampling.

Step 1 Set a calculator to generate random integers from –10 to 10.

Step 2 Generate three such nonzero integers. Call them a, b, and c. Record them and the expression $ax^2 + bx + c$ in a table like the one shown below.

Trial	a	b	c	$ax^2 + bx + c$	Factorable?
1	2	–3	7	$2x^2 - 3x + 7$	Prime
2	?	?	?	?	?
3	?	?	?	?	?

(continued on next page)

> **Step 3** If you have a CAS, try to factor $ax^2 + bx + c$ over the integers. If you are working by hand, calculate $b^2 - 4ac$. If the expression is factorable, record the factors. If not, record the word *Prime*.
>
> **Step 4** Repeat Steps 2 and 3 at least 20 times. What percent of your quadratic expressions are factorable?
>
> **Step 5** Combine your results with those of others in the class. What is your class's estimate of the percent of these quadratic expressions that are factorable?

Questions

COVERING THE IDEAS

In 1–5, a quadratic expression is given. Calculate $b^2 - 4ac$ to determine if the quadratic is factorable or prime over the integers. If possible, factor the expression.

1. $x^2 - 9x - 22$

2. $36 - y^2$

3. $4n^2 - 12n + 9$

4. $-3 + m^2 + 2m$

5. $7x^2 - 13x - 6$

6. Consider the equation $ax^2 + bx + c = 0$ where a, b, and c are integers. If $b^2 - 4ac$ is a perfect square, explain why x is rational.

7. Suppose a, b, and c are integers. When will the x-intercepts of $y = ax^2 + bx + c$ be rational numbers?

8. Give an example of a quadratic expression that can be factored only if noninteger coefficients are allowed.

APPLYING THE MATHEMATICS

9. The sum of the integers from 1 to n is $\frac{1}{2}n(n + 1)$. Find n if the sum of the integers from 1 to n is 499,500.

10. What in this lesson tells you that the solutions to the quadratic equation $x^2 - 3 = 0$ are irrational? (This provides a way of showing that $\sqrt{3}$ is irrational.)

11. Find a value of k such that $4x^2 + kx - 5$ is factorable over the integers.

12. a. By multiplying, verify that $(x + 5 + \sqrt{2})(x + 5 - \sqrt{2}) = x^2 + 10x + 23$.

    b. Verify that the discriminant of the expression $x^2 + 10x + 23$ is not a perfect square.

    c. Parts a and b indicate that $x^2 + 10x + 23$ is factorable, yet its discriminant is not a perfect square. Why doesn't this situation violate the Discriminant Theorem?

REVIEW

In 13 and 14, factor the polynomial completely. (Lessons 12-5, 12-4)

13. $r^2 - 5r + 4$

14. $-2x^2 + 5x + 12$

15. Consider $w^2 + 9w + c$. (Lesson 12-2)

a. Complete the square to find the value of c.

b. Express the perfect square trinomial in factored form.

16. The surface area S of a cylinder with radius r and height h is given by the formula $S = 2\pi r^2 + 2\pi rh$. (Lesson 11-4)

a. Factor the right hand side of this formula into prime factors.

b. Calculate the exact surface area of a cylinder with a diameter of 12 cm and a height of 9 cm using either the given formula or its factored form. Which form do you think is easier for this purpose?

In 17–19, rewrite the expression with no negative exponents and each variable mentioned no more than once. (Lessons 8-5, 8-4, 8-3)

17. $\dfrac{8n^{-3}m^2}{6m^{-5}}$

18. $\left(\dfrac{a^2b}{4a^5}\right)^2$

19. $\left(\dfrac{3x^4y^{-1}}{15x^3y^0}\right)^2$

EXPLORATION

20. Look back at Question 11. Find *all* integer values of k such that $4x^2 + kx - 5$ is factorable in the set of polynomials over the integers. Explain how you know that you have found all values.

21. Use a CAS to factor the general expression $ax^2 + bx + c$. (You will likely have to indicate that x is the variable.)

a. What factorization does the CAS give?

b. Explain how you know that this factorization is correct.

c. Why doesn't the existence of factors for any quadratic expression violate the Discriminant Theorem?

Lesson 12-7

Graphs of Polynomial Functions of Higher Degree

Vocabulary

cubic polynomial

▶ **BIG IDEA** The factored form of a polynomial is useful in graphing and solving equations.

Some of the ideas that you have seen in earlier lessons of this chapter extend to the graphs of polynomial functions of degrees 3 and higher. In particular, factoring a polynomial can be a powerful tool to uncover interesting features of graphs of polynomial functions.

How Are Factors and *x*-Intercepts Related?

Activity 1

In 1–6, a polynomial function is given in factored form.

a. Graph the function with a graphing calculator.

b. Identify the *x*-intercepts of the graph.

c. How are the *x*-intercepts of the graph related to the factors?

1. $f(x) = 5(x - 1)$
2. $g(x) = (x - 1)(x + 2)$
3. $h(x) = (x - 1)(x + 2)(x - 4)$
4. $k(x) = 3(x - 1)(x + 2)(x - 4)$
5. $m(x) = (x - 1)^2(x + 2)^2$
6. $q(x) = (x - 1)(x + 2)(x - 4)(2x + 15)$

7. Look back at your work. Make a conjecture about the factors of a polynomial and the *x*-intercepts of its graph. Test your conjecture with a different polynomial function than those above.

Mental Math

A baseball player has a batting average of .245. State whether his batting average goes up or down if he plays a game where he goes

a. 1 for 4.

b. 1 for 5.

c. 2 for 6.

A graph of the function P with $P(x) = x(x - 8)(x + 6)$ is shown at the right, along with a table of values. Notice how the factors and the *x*-intercepts are related.

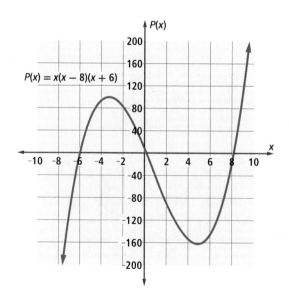

x	P(x)	x	P(x)	x	P(x)
−9	−459	−1	45	7	−13
−8	−256	0	0	8	0
−7	−105	1	−49	9	135
−6	0	2	−96	10	320
−5	65	3	−135	11	561
−4	96	4	−160	12	864
−3	99	5	−165		
−2	80	6	−144		

The graph of the function P has three x-intercepts: 0, 8, and –6. Would your conjecture from Activity 1 have predicted this result? Whether or not you predicted this, there is a simple but elegant relationship between factors and x-intercepts that holds for any polynomial function.

Factor Theorem

Let r be a real number and $P(x)$ be a polynomial in x.

1. If $x - r$ is a factor of $P(x)$, then $P(r) = 0$; that is, r is an x-intercept of the graph of P.

2. If $P(r) = 0$, then $x - r$ is a factor of $P(x)$.

The Factor Theorem is true because the x-intercepts of the graph of the function P are the values of x such that $P(x) = 0$. For the polynomial $P(x) = x(x - 8)(x + 6)$ graphed on the previous page, the equation $P(x) = 0$ means $x(x - 8)(x + 6) = 0$.

By the Zero Product Property, this is a true statement when
$x = 0$ or $x - 8 = 0$ or $x + 6 = 0$.
$$x = 8 \text{ or } \qquad x = -6$$

So, because x, $x - 8$, and $x + 6$ are factors of $P(x)$, 0, 8, and –6 are the x-intercepts of the graph of P.

GUIDED

Example 1

A polynomial function P has x-intercepts 5, 7.8, –46, and –200. What is a possible equation for the function?

Solution The polynomial must have at least four factors.

Because 5 is an x-intercept, $x - 5$ is a factor of the polynomial.

Because 7.8 is an x-intercept, ___?___ is a factor of the polynomial.

Because –46 is an x-intercept, ___?___ is a factor of the polynomial.

Because –200 is an x-intercept, ___?___ is a factor of the polynomial.

Possibly, $P(x) = (x - 5)(\underline{\ ?\ })(\underline{\ ?\ })(\underline{\ ?\ })$.

Converting from Factored Form to Standard Form

The polynomial $P(x) = x(x - 8)(x + 6)$ is the product of three factors. To convert this polynomial to standard form, multiply any two of its factors. Then multiply the product of those factors by the third factor. Because multiplication is associative, it does not make any difference which two factors you multiply first.

$$P(x) = x(x - 8)(x + 6)$$
$$= (x^2 - 8x)(x + 6)$$
$$= (x^2 - 8x) \cdot x + (x^2 - 8x) \cdot 6$$
$$= x^3 - 8x^2 + 6x^2 - 48x$$
$$= x^3 - 2x^2 - 48x$$

The standard form shows clearly that $P(x)$ is a polynomial of degree 3. It is a **cubic polynomial.** Just as a quadratic function has at most two x-intercepts, a cubic function has at most three x-intercepts.

The following example involves the function q from Activity 1. It is a polynomial function of 4th degree.

Example 2

Rewrite the polynomial $q(x) = (x - 1)(x + 2)(x - 4)(2x + 15)$ in standard form.

Solution There are four factors in the polynomial. Any two can be multiplied first. We multiply the first two and the last two.

$$q(x) = (x - 1)(x + 2)(x - 4)(2x + 15)$$
$$= (x^2 + x - 2)(2x^2 + 7x - 60)$$

Now use the Extended Distributive Property. Each term of the left factor must be multiplied by each term of the right factor. There are nine products.

$$= x^2(2x^2 + 7x - 60) + x(2x^2 + 7x - 60) - 2(2x^2 + 7x - 60)$$
$$= 2x^4 + 7x^3 - 60x^2 + 2x^3 + 7x^2 - 60x - 4x^2 - 14x + 120$$
$$= 2x^4 + 9x^3 - 57x^2 - 74x + 120$$

Check 1 In factored form it is easy to see that $q(1) = 0$. So substitute 1 for x in the standard form to see if the value of the polynomial is 0. The value is $2 + 9 - 57 - 74 + 120 = 0$. It checks.

Check 2 Use a CAS to factor the answer. See if the original factored form appears. Our CAS gives $q(x) = (x - 1)(x + 2)(x - 4)(2x + 15)$.

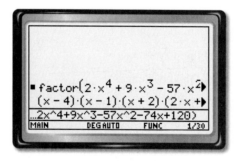

In Activity 2, you are asked to explore what happens when the same factor appears twice in a polynomial.

Activity 2

Step 1 **a.** Graph the following polynomial functions on the window
$-10 \leq x \leq 10, -500 \leq y \leq 500$. Make a sketch of each graph.

$f(x) = x(x - 3)(x + 7)$ $g(x) = x(x - 3)(x + 7)^2$

$h(x) = x(x - 3)^2(x + 7)^2$ $j(x) = x^2(x - 3)^2(x + 7)^2$

b. What are the x-intercepts of these graphs?

c. What is different about the graphs around the point $(-7, 0)$ when $(x + 7)^2$ is a factor rather than just $(x + 7)$?

Step 2 **a.** Multiply each polynomial by -1 and graph the resulting functions.

b. Describe what happens to the x-intercepts.

Step 3 Multiplying $P(x)$ by -1 means graphing $-P(x)$. The graph wiggles in the middle. But in all these functions, as you go farther to the right, the graph heads either up or down. As you go farther to the left, the graph also heads either up or down.

a. Copy and complete the table.

Polynomial	Far Right: Up or Down?	Far Left: Up or Down?	Polynomial	Far Right: Up or Down?	Far Left: Up or Down?
$f(x) = x(x - 3)(x + 7)$	?	?	$-f(x)$	?	?
$g(x) = x(x - 3)(x + 7)^2$	?	?	$-g(x)$	?	?
$h(x) = x(x - 3)^2(x + 7)^2$	?	?	$-h(x)$	?	?
$j(x) = x^2(x - 3)^2(x + 7)^2$	?	?	$-i(x)$	?	?

b. Describe the general pattern.

Step 4 **a.** Experiment to find what happens to the graph of
$P(x) = ax(x - 3)(x + 7)$ as values of a change from positive to negative.

b. Does the same situation hold for the graph of
$j(x) = ax^2(x - 3)^2(x + 7)^2$?

The Importance of Polynomial Functions

In this course, you have studied polynomial functions of degrees 1 and 2 in detail. A polynomial function of degree 1 has an equation of the form $y = mx + b$. Its graph is a line. A polynomial function of degree 2 has an equation of the form $y = ax^2 + bx + c$. Its graph is a parabola. The graphs of polynomial functions of degrees 3 and 4 have more varied shapes and graphs of higher degrees have still more varied shapes. This makes polynomial functions very useful in approximating data of many kinds and very useful in approximating other functions. Polynomials also appear as formulas in a number of situations, a few of which are mentioned in the Questions for this lesson.

Questions

COVERING THE IDEAS

In 1–4, an equation for a function is given.

    a. Identify the x-intercepts of the graph of the function.

    b. Check your answer to Part a by graphing the function. Draw a rough sketch of the graph.

    c. Write the equation in standard form.

1. $f(x) = (x + 5)(2x - 3)$ 2. $y = (x + 5.8)(2x - 3.4)$

3. $y = -3(x - 1)(2x + 1)^2$ 4. $g(x) = x(8x + 5)(10x + 2)(x - 1)$

5. Give an equation for a polynomial function whose graph intersects the x-axis at $(-9, 0)$, $(4, 0)$, and nowhere else.

6. Suppose the graph of a polynomial function has three x-intercepts: 1, –4, and 5.

    a. Give an equation in factored form for the polynomial function.

    b. Rewrite your equation from Part a in standard form.

7. a. Give an equation in factored form for a polynomial function with four x-intercepts: 2, –2, 5, and –5.

    b. Rewrite your equation from Part a in standard form.

8. Match the following equations with their possible graphs.

    a. $a(x) = (x + 2)(x - 4)^2(x - 6)$

    b. $b(x) = -1(x + 2)(x - 4)(x - 6)$

    c. $c(x) = -1(x + 2)^2(x - 4)(x - 6)$

    d. $d(x) = -(x + 2)(x - 4)^2(x - 6)$

i.
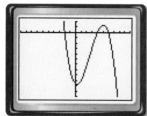

ii.
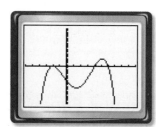

iii.
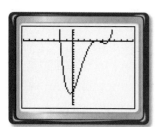

iv.
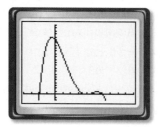

In 9–12, give a possible equation in factored form for each graph.

9.

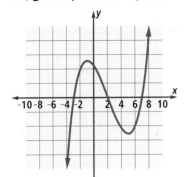

10.

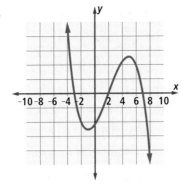

11.

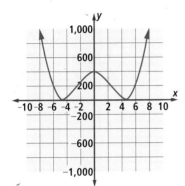

12.

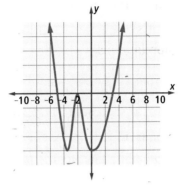

13. Let $S(n)$ = the sum of the squares of the integers from 1 to n. It is known that $S(n) = \frac{1}{6}n(n + 1)(2n + 1)$.

   a. Find $S(5)$ using the formula and verify your answer by using the definition of $S(n)$.

   b. What is the value of $S(n + 1) - S(n)$?

   c. Write the formula for $S(n)$ in standard form.

14. Explain what you know about each of the following aspects of the graph of the function $h(x) = -8(x - 11)^2(x + 5)(x + 10)^2$.

   a. x-intercepts

   b. when the graph changes direction at an x-intercept

   c. the direction of the far right side of the graph

APPLYING THE MATHEMATICS

15. a. Graph $y_1 = (x - 2)(x + 4)(x - 5)$ and $y_2 = (x - 2)^3(x + 4)(x - 5)$.

   b. Use the results of Part a to predict a characteristic of the graph of $y_3 = (x - 2)(x + 4)(x - 5)^3$.

   c. Use the results of Parts a and b to predict a characteristic of the graph of $y_4 = (x - 2)^3(x + 4)(x - 5)^3$.

   d. Generalize the results of Parts a, b, and c.

REVIEW

In 16–18, factor the polynomial. (Lessons 12-5, 11-4)

16. $9x^2y^2 - 27x^3y + 19xy$

17. $4a^2 - 16b^2$

18. $15n^2 + 1 - 8n$

In 19–22, solve by using any method. (Lessons 12-5, 12-2, 9-5)

19. $a^2 + 6a = 55$

20. $-3w^2 - 7w + 11 = 0$

21. **Multiple Choice** Which system of inequalities is graphed at the right? (Lesson 10-9)

A $\begin{cases} y \geq -2x - 8 \\ y \geq 0 \\ x \leq -9 \end{cases}$
B $\begin{cases} y \leq -2x - 8 \\ y \geq 0 \\ x \geq -9 \end{cases}$
C $\begin{cases} y \geq -2x - 8 \\ y \leq 0 \\ x \leq -9 \end{cases}$
D $\begin{cases} y \leq -2x - 8 \\ y \geq -9 \\ x \geq 0 \end{cases}$

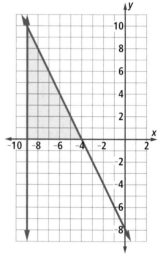

22. According to the U.S. Department of Labor, the following percentages of the adult population were employed in the particular years shown in the table at the right. Assume these trends continue. (Lesson 6-7)

a. Use linear regression to find a line that fits the pairs (year, male). Write the equation of a line of best fit.

b. Repeat Part a for the pairs (year, female). Write the equation of a line of best fit.

c. Using your equation from Part b, predict what percentage of adult women will be employed in the year 2010.

d. Using your equations from Parts a and b, predict when, if ever, the same percentage of adult men and adult women will be employed.

Year	Male	Female
1974	74.9	42.6
1979	73.8	47.5
1984	70.7	49.5
1989	72.5	54.3
1995	70.8	55.6
2001	70.9	57.0
2002	69.7	56.3

EXPLORATION

23. a. Explore the graphs of $y_1 = x^3$, $y_2 = x^4$, $y_3 = x^5$, and $y_4 = x^6$ and make a generalization about the graph of $f(x) = x^n$, when n is a positive integer.

b. If x is replaced by $x - 5$ in each of the graphs of Part a, what happens to the graphs?

c. Generalize the result in Part b.

Lesson 12-8

Factoring and Rational Expressions

Vocabulary

rational expression

lowest terms

▶ **BIG IDEA** The factored form of a polynomial is useful in writing rational expressions in lowest terms and in performing operations on rational expressions.

In Lesson 12-7, you saw how factoring can help find the solutions to polynomial equations. Factoring can also help in working with fractions that have polynomials in their numerators and denominators.

Activity

Step 1 Before reading Step 2, perform the addition of these fractions and write your answer in lowest terms. Do not use a calculator.

$$\frac{75}{100} + \frac{66}{99}$$

Step 2 Describe how you did the addition. Did you find a common denominator? If so, then you probably worked with fractions with denominator 9,900. Or, did you put each fraction in lowest terms first? Then you could do the addition with a common denominator of 12. Compare the way you added these fractions with the ways that others in your class added them.

Mental Math

Estimate to the nearest dollar the interest earned in one year in a savings account with 2.02% annual interest rate containing

a. $501.

b. $4,012.

c. $9,998.

Writing Rational Expressions in Lowest Terms

In the addition of fractions above, it is useful to write each fraction in lowest terms. As you know, this is done by dividing both the numerator and denominator of the fraction by one of their factors. Because 25 is a common factor of the numerator and denominator of the first fraction, $\frac{75}{100} = \frac{25 \cdot 3}{25 \cdot 4}$. Similarly, $\frac{66}{99} = \frac{33 \cdot 2}{33 \cdot 3} = \frac{2}{3}$.

The same idea can be used with *rational expressions*. A **rational expression** is the written quotient of two polynomials. Here are five examples of rational expressions.

$$\frac{0.7819}{x + y}$$

$$\frac{3x^3 y}{x^2 y^4}$$

$$\frac{a + \pi}{b - \pi}$$

$$\frac{4n^2 + 4n + 1}{4n^2 - 1}$$

$$\frac{6k^3 - 12k^2 + 42k - 210}{3k^3 - 6k^2 + 21k - 105}$$

A rational expression is in **lowest terms** when there is no polynomial that is a factor of its numerator and denominator. The second rational expression on the previous page is not in lowest terms because x^2y is a common factor of the numerator and denominator.

$$\frac{3x^3y}{x^2y^4} = \frac{x^2y \cdot 3x}{x^2y \cdot y^3} = \frac{3x}{y^3}$$

Technically, $\frac{3x}{y^3}$ is not exactly equivalent to $\frac{3x^3y}{x^2y^4}$ because the x in $\frac{3x}{y^3}$ can equal 0 while the x in $\frac{3x^3y}{x^2y^4}$ cannot equal 0. Often this is taken for granted, but sometimes people will write $x \neq 0$ and $y \neq 0$ because fractions do not allow 0 as the denominator.

The rational expressions $\frac{4n^2 + 4n + 1}{4n^2 - 1}$ and $\frac{6k^3 - 12k^2 + 42k - 210}{3k^3 - 6k^2 + 21k - 105}$ look more complicated than the others on page 761. But each expression can be put in lowest terms by factoring out the common factors.

GUIDED

Example 1

Write $\frac{4n^2 + 4n + 1}{4n^2 - 1}$ in lowest terms. Assume the denominator does not equal 0.

Solution

Step 1 Factor the numerator $4n^2 + 4n + 1$.

Step 2 The denominator $4n^2 - 1$ is the difference of two squares. Use this information to factor it.

Step 3 From Steps 1 and 2, fill in the blanks.
$$\frac{4n^2 + 4n + 1}{4n^2 - 1} = \frac{(\underline{\ ?\ }n + \underline{\ ?\ })(\underline{\ ?\ }n + \underline{\ ?\ })}{(\underline{\ ?\ }n + \underline{\ ?\ })(\underline{\ ?\ }n - \underline{\ ?\ })}$$

Step 4 The numerator and denominator in Step 3 have a factor in common. Divide them by that factor.
$$\frac{4n^2 + 4n + 1}{4n^2 - 1} = \frac{(\underline{\ ?\ }n + \underline{\ ?\ })}{(\underline{\ ?\ }n - \underline{\ ?\ })}$$

Because the numerator and denominator on the right have no common factor, the fraction is in lowest terms.

Check Check your answer by substituting 3 for n in the original rational expression and in the expression of Step 4.

 QY

A graphing calculator and CAS technology can be of great assistance when writing a fraction in lowest terms.

> ▶ QY
>
> Explain why
> $$\frac{6k^3 - 12k^2 + 42k - 210}{3k^3 - 6k^2 + 21k - 105}$$
> is not in lowest terms.

Example 2

Simplify the expression $\dfrac{x^3 - 2x^2 - 23x + 60}{x^3 + 8x^2 - 3x - 90}$.

Solution 1 To factor the numerator, graph $f(x) = x^3 - 2x^2 - 23x + 60$ with a graphing calculator. The graph has three x-intercepts: $-5, 3$, and 4, indicating that $(x - 4)$, $(x - 3)$, and $(x - -5)$ are factors of the numerator. To factor the denominator, graph $g(x) = x^3 + 8x^2 - 3x - 90$. This graph has x-intercepts $3, -5$, and -6, indicating that $(x - 3)$, $(x - -5)$, and $(x - -6)$ are factors of the denominator. Thus,

$$\frac{x^3 - 2x^2 - 23x + 60}{x^3 + 8x^2 - 3x - 90} = \frac{(x + 5)(x - 4)(x - 3)}{(x - 3)(x + 5)(x + 6)} = \frac{x - 4}{x + 6}.$$

$-10 \le x \le 10, -100 \le y \le 100$

Solution 2 Use a CAS. If you enter the given rational expression into a CAS, you may immediately see the expression in lowest terms.

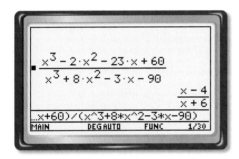

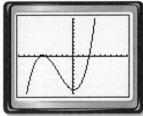

$-10 \le x \le 10, -100 \le y \le 100$

Solution 3 Use a CAS to show the steps of Solution 1. Factor the numerator and the denominator.

Thus $\dfrac{x^3 - 2x^2 - 23x + 60}{x^3 + 8x^2 - 3x - 90} = \dfrac{(x - 4)(x - 3)(x + 5)}{(x - 3)(x + 5)(x + 6)}.$

Divide numerator and denominator by the common factors.

The solution is $\dfrac{x - 4}{x + 6}$.

Caution: Notice that you *cannot* simplify $\dfrac{x - 4}{x + 6}$ by dividing by x because the x's are terms, not factors.

(continued on next page)

Check Graph $Y1 = \dfrac{x^3 - 2x^2 - 23x + 60}{x^3 + 8x^2 - 3x - 90}$ and $Y2 = \dfrac{x-4}{x+6}$ to see whether they appear to be equivalent expressions. Use the $\boxed{\text{WINDOW}}$ $-25 \le x \le 25$, $-6 \le y \le 6$.

 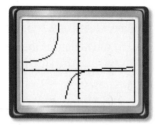

The two appear to form the same graph, so the result checks.

Adding and Subtracting Rational Expressions

To add $\dfrac{1}{9} + \dfrac{7}{15}$, you can either look for a calculator or look for a common denominator. If you do not have a calculator that does fractions, the least common denominator can be found by factoring each denominator and finding a product that will be a multiple of each denominator. Since $9 = 3 \cdot 3$ and $15 = 3 \cdot 5$, the least common denominator is $3 \cdot 3 \cdot 5$, or 45.

$$\frac{1}{9} + \frac{7}{15} = \frac{1}{3 \cdot 3} + \frac{7}{3 \cdot 5}$$

$$= \frac{1 \cdot 5}{3 \cdot 3 \cdot 5} + \frac{7 \cdot 3}{3 \cdot 5 \cdot 3}$$

$$= \frac{5}{45} + \frac{21}{45}$$

$$= \frac{26}{45}$$

You may have done most of this process in your head. We show the steps because you can add or subtract rational expressions in the same way.

GUIDED

Example 3

Write $\dfrac{a}{b} + \dfrac{c}{d}$ as a single rational expression.

Solution Since b and d have no common factors, their least common multiple is bd. This is the common denominator.

$$\frac{a}{b} + \frac{c}{d} = \frac{a \cdot ?}{b \cdot d} + \frac{? \cdot c}{b \cdot d} \qquad \text{Fraction Multiplication Property}$$

$$= \frac{?}{b \cdot d} \qquad \text{Distributive Property}$$

Check You can check by substituting numbers for a, b, c, and d. Try $a = 1$, $b = 9$, $c = 7$, and $d = 15$, since you already know the sum is $\dfrac{26}{45}$. The rest is left as a question in the Questions section.

Example 4

Write $\dfrac{6}{k+1} - \dfrac{3k+7}{k^2-1}$ as a single rational expression.

Solution 1 Use a CAS. You must be careful to include parentheses to identify numerators and denominators of the fractions. In one calculator, we entered 6/(k+1)-(3*k+7)/(k^2-1). The calculator returned the expression $\dfrac{3k-13}{(k-1)(k+1)}$.

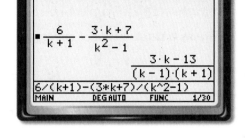

Solution 2 Work by hand. Find the least common denominator. The denominator $k+1$ is prime. The denominator k^2-1 equals $(k+1)(k-1)$. So the least common denominator is $(k+1)(k-1)$. Rewrite the first fraction with that denominator.

$$\dfrac{6}{k+1} - \dfrac{3k+7}{k^2-1} = \dfrac{6k-1}{(k+1)(k-1)} - \dfrac{3k+7}{(k+1)(k-1)}$$

Subtract the fractions as you would any fractions with the same denominator. But notice that the subtracted numerator must be treated as a quantity.

$$= \dfrac{6(k-1) - (3k+7)}{(k+1)(k-1)}$$

$$= \dfrac{6k-6-3k-7}{(k+1)(k-1)}$$

$$= \dfrac{3k-13}{(k-1)(k+1)}$$

Check You can check by substitution or by graphing. We leave these checks to you in the Questions section.

Questions

COVERING THE IDEAS

1. What is the definition of *rational expression*?

2. **Multiple Choice** Which of the following are *not* rational expressions?

   A $\dfrac{2x}{3}$ B $\dfrac{4y^0}{5y^{15}}$ C $\dfrac{z\sqrt{6}}{7}$ D $\dfrac{8\sqrt{w}}{9w}$

In 3 and 4, simplify the rational expression and indicate all restrictions on values of the variables.

3. $\dfrac{30a^4b^2c^3}{12a^4bc^5}$

4. $\dfrac{28x - 21x}{7xy}$

5. a. By factoring the numerator and denominator, write $\dfrac{2x^2 - 7x + 6}{x^2 - 4}$ in lowest terms.

   b. What values can x not have in this expression?

   c. Check your answer by letting $x = 10$.

6. **a.** Write $\dfrac{7x^2 + 161x + 910}{14x^2 + 182x + 420}$ in lowest terms.

   b. Check your answer by graphing, as was done in Example 2.

7. Complete the check of Guided Example 3.

8. Check the answer to Example 4 by graphing.

9. Check the answer to Example 4 by substitution.

In 10–13, write as a single rational expression. Check your answer.

10. $\dfrac{a}{b} - \dfrac{c}{d}$

11. $\dfrac{3}{2n} + \dfrac{3}{8n}$

12. $\dfrac{z+1}{4z-3} + \dfrac{3z}{8z^2 - 18z + 9}$

13. $\dfrac{8x^2 + 16x + 8}{5x + 5} - \dfrac{x+1}{3x^2 - 3}$

APPLYING THE MATHEMATICS

In 14 and 15, use a CAS or graphing calculator to write the expression in lowest terms.

14. $\dfrac{-3x^3 - 15x^2 - 24x - 12}{x^2 + 3x + 2}$

15. $\dfrac{x^5 - 4x^4 - 37x^3 + 124x^2 + 276x - 720}{x^5 + 20x^4 + 155x^3 + 580x^2 + 1{,}044x + 720}$

In 16 and 17, the sum F of the integers from 1 to n is given by the formula $F = \dfrac{n^2 + n}{2}$. The sum S of the squares of the integers from 1 to n is given by the formula $S = \dfrac{2n^3 + 3n^2 + n}{6}$. The sum C of the cubes of the integers from 1 to n is given by the formula $C = \dfrac{n^4 + 2n^3 + n^2}{4}$.

16. **a.** Find the values of C, F, and $\dfrac{C}{F}$ when $n = 13$.

   b. Show that $\dfrac{C}{F} = F$ for all values of n.

17. **a.** Find the values of S, F, and $\dfrac{S}{F}$ when $n = 13$.

   b. Find a rational expression for $\dfrac{S}{F}$ in lowest terms.

   c. Explain why there are values of n for which $\dfrac{S}{F}$ is not an integer.

18. Generalize the following pattern and use addition of rational expressions to show why your generalization is true.

$$\dfrac{1}{2} - \dfrac{1}{3} = \dfrac{1}{6}, \quad \dfrac{1}{3} - \dfrac{1}{4} = \dfrac{1}{12}, \quad \dfrac{1}{4} - \dfrac{1}{5} = \dfrac{1}{20}$$

REVIEW

19. If an object is thrown upward from a height of 0 meters at a speed of $v \frac{\text{meters}}{\text{second}}$, then its height after t seconds is $vt - 4.9t^2$ meters. (**Lesson 12-6**)

    a. If an object is thrown upward with speed v, how long will it take it to hit the ground?

    b. What must be true about v if the time it takes the object to hit the ground in seconds is an integer? Give an example of a v for which this happens and a v for which it does not happen.

20. Is $3x^2 - 2x + 5$ a prime polynomial? How do you know? (**Lesson 12-6**)

21. Gerardo is cutting a shape out of paper. He begins with a square piece of paper, and cuts out the upper right corner, as in the figure at the right. What is the area of the piece he cut out? (**Lesson 12-2**)

    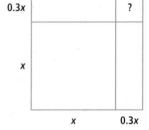

22. Nikki wants to call her friend Adelaide. She remembers that the last three digits of her number are 3, 4, and 7, but she doesn't remember the correct order. If she guesses an order at random, what is the probability that she will get the right number? (**Lesson 11-7**)

23. Marcus took a test in which there were 20 questions. In this test, every correct answer gave 6 points, and every incorrect answer subtracted 3 points from the grade. If Marcus got a 93 on the test, how many questions did he get right? (**Lesson 10-5**)

24. Is there a convex polygon with exactly 43 diagonals? Explain how you know. (**Lesson 9-7**)

EXPLORATION

25. A teacher, wanting to show students that their ideas could be used with very complicated rational expressions, used the following expression.

$$\frac{x^9 + 11x^8 - 84x^7 - 1{,}660x^6 - 4{,}874x^5 + 44{,}082x^4 + 400{,}140x^3 \; 1{,}347{,}300x^2 + 2{,}156{,}625x + 1{,}366{,}875}{x^8 - 22x^7 + 90x^6 + 882x^5 - 5{,}508x^4 - 10{,}530x^3 + 74{,}358x^2 + 39{,}366x - 295{,}245}$$

However, the teacher forgot the operation sign between x^3 and 1,347,300.

    a. If the numerator was meant to be factored, what is the operation?

    b. Use the answer to Part a to write the expression in lowest terms.

QY ANSWER

The numerator and denominator have common factors.

$$\frac{6k^3 - 12k^2 + 42k - 210}{3k^3 - 6k^2 + 21k - 105} =$$

$$\frac{6(k^3 - 2k^2 + 7k - 35)}{3(k^3 - 2k^2 + 7k - 35)} = 2$$

Factoring and Rational Expressions 767

Chapter 12 Projects

1 Combining Solutions

a. Choose an equation of the form $x^2 + bx + c = 0$ and call its two solutions: r and s. Calculate $r + s$ and $r \cdot s$. How are these related to your original equation? Do the same thing for three more equations, and write a short description of what you found.

b. Repeat Part a, but this time with equations of the form $ax^2 + bx + c = 0$.

c. The solutions to $x^3 - 6x^2 + 11x - 6 = 0$ are 1, 2, and 3. The solutions to $x^3 - 10x^2 + 24x = 0$ are 0, 4, and 6. How are these solutions related to the results you found in Part a? Can you find how the coefficient of x is related to the solutions?

d. Repeat Part c, but this time use equations of the form $ax^3 + bx^2 + cx + d = 0$.

2 Infinite Repeating Continued Fractions

Consider this sequence of complex fractions: $\dfrac{1}{5}, \dfrac{1}{5 + \frac{1}{5}}, \dfrac{1}{5 + \frac{1}{5 + \frac{1}{5}}}, \dfrac{1}{5 + \frac{1}{5 + \frac{1}{5 + \frac{1}{5}}}} \dots$

a. Calculate the values of the first five terms of this sequence.

b. As you calculate more and more terms of this sequence, the sequence approaches the value of x, where

$$x = \cfrac{1}{5 + \cfrac{1}{5 + \cfrac{1}{5 + \cfrac{1}{5 + \frac{1}{5 + \dots}}}}}$$. This x satisfies

$x = \dfrac{1}{5 + x}$. Find the value of x.

c. Complete Parts a and b, this time with a 4 replacing each 5.

3 Prime Numbers, Prime Polynomials

One of the most famous discoveries of the Greek mathematician and astronomer Eratosthenes (276 BCE–194 BCE) is an algorithm to check if a number is a prime, called the sieve of Eratosthenes.

a. Look up the sieve of Eratosthenes. Write a description of how it works. If you can, write a computer (or calculator) program that checks if an integer is a prime.

b. Do you think a similar algorithm could be invented to check if a polynomial is prime over the integers? Why, or why not?

ERATOSTHENES
En Dictylioth Lippertz

Zapf galler.

4 Public-Key Cryptography

The use of codes based on prime numbers to protect information is called *public-key cryptography*. Do research in your library or on the Internet and write an essay describing how public-key cryptography works.

5 Using Polynomials to Approximate

The graphs of polynomials of higher degree can have interesting shapes. Using a graphing calculator, to make graphs of polynomials that look like the letters of the English alphabet (both lower case and upper case).

a. For each letter you successfully create, write down the polynomial and the appropriate window.

b. Write some letters which you think cannot be drawn well this way. Why do you think this is so?

c. Which are harder to draw, lower case letters or upper case letters? Why?

6 The Bisection Method

For higher degree polynomials, there are no simple formulas that allow you to find the *x*-intercepts of the graphs. Nevertheless, in real life, it is often important to find those *x*-intercepts. One method in which approximate values can be found is called the *bisection method*.

a. Look up the bisection method in other books or on the Internet. Write a description of how it works. Include pictures to illustrate your explanation.

b. Suppose you know that there is an *x*-intercept of a graph between 0 and 1. How many times would you need to apply the bisection method to get an approximation with an accuracy of at least 0.01?

c. Use the bisection method to find the value of one of the *x*-intercepts of $y = x^5 - 2x + 5$ with an accuracy of at least 0.01.

Chapter 12 Summary and Vocabulary

○ From the **standard form of a quadratic equation,** $y = ax^2 + bx + c$, the vertex of the parabola is not visible, but if the form is converted to $y - k = a(x - h)^2$, then the vertex is (h, k). The process of converting is called **completing the square.**

○ The x-intercepts of this parabola are the solutions to the equation $ax^2 + bx + c = 0$. These can be found using the Quadratic Formula: $x = \frac{-b \pm \sqrt{b^2 - 4ac}}{2a}$. Letting

$$r_1 = \frac{-b + \sqrt{b^2 - 4ac}}{2a} \text{ and}$$

$$r_2 = \frac{-b - \sqrt{b^2 - 4ac}}{2a},$$

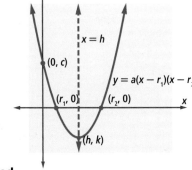

then $y = a(x - r_1)(x - r_2)$. This **factored form** is a special case of a more general theorem about polynomials: If $P(x)$ is a polynomial and $P(r) = 0$, then $x - r$ is a factor of $P(x)$.

○ Because the factored form of a polynomial enables you to see the x-intercepts, it is useful to be able to factor quadratic expressions $ax^2 + bx + c$ into two linear factors $dx + e$ and $fx + g$. In this chapter, we considered only factoring situations where $a, b, c, d, e, f,$ and g are integers. Most quadratic expressions with integer coefficients do *not* factor into linear factors with integer coefficients. The key is the value of the **discriminant $b^2 - 4ac$.** If $a, b,$ and c are real numbers and $b^2 - 4ac > 0$, then there are two real solutions to the equation $ax^2 + bx + c = 0$. If $b^2 - 4ac = 0$, then $r_1 = r_2$; there is exactly one solution to the equation, and the vertex of the parabola is on the x-axis. If $b^2 - 4ac < 0$, then there are no real solutions; the parabola does not intersect the x-axis.

○ The factoring of polynomials also helps in work with **rational expressions.** By dividing out common factors from the numerator and denominator, you can write rational expressions in **lowest terms** and can be added or subtracted.

Vocabulary

12-1
vertex form of an equation for a parabola

12-2
complete the square

12-3
factored form (of a quadratic function)

12-4
square term
linear term
constant term
prime polynomial over the integers

12-7
cubic polynomial

12-8
rational expression
lowest terms

Theorems and Properties

Parabola Vertex Theorem (p. 716)
Factor Theorem for Quadratic Functions (p. 731)

Discriminant Theorem (p.749)
Factor Theorem (p. 755)

Chapter 12 Self-Test

Take this test as you would take a test in class. You will need a calculator. Then use the Selected Answers section in the back of the book to check your work.

In 1–3, factor completely.

1. $x^2 + 3x - 40$

2. $m^2 - 17m + 72$

3. $-9h^2 + 9h - 2$

4. **Multiple Choice** Which of the following can be factored over the integers?

   A $x^2 + 22x - 9$ **B** $x^2 + 9x - 22$

   C $x^2 - 9x + 22$ **D** $x^2 - 22x + 9$

5. Determine what number must be added to $z^2 - 12z$ to complete the square.

6. Simplify the expression $\dfrac{3x^2 + 75}{2x^2 - 7x - 15}$ and indicate all restrictions on x.

7. **Multiple Choice** Which equation is graphed below?

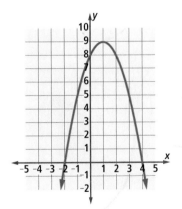

   A $y = (x + 2)(x - 4)$

   B $y = (x - 2)(x + 4)$

   C $y = (-x - 2)(x + 4)$

   D $y = -(x + 2)(x - 4)$

8. a. Give an equation in factored form for a polynomial function with 3 x-intercepts: 0, –3, and 9.

   b. Rewrite your equation from Part a in standard form.

9. A square frame is x feet on each side. The painting it holds is 1 foot shorter and 2 feet narrower than the frame. If the area of the painting is 12 square feet, what are the dimensions of the frame?

In 10 and 11, determine the vertex of the parabola with the given equation.

10. $y = x^2 - 2x - 3$

11. $y = 7 - 4x - 2x^2$

In 12 and 13, sketch the graph of the equation without a calculator.

12. $y - 4 = 2(x - 3)^2$

13. $y = (x - 5)(x + 4)$

14. Factor $3n^4 - 15n^3 + 18n^2$ completely over the integers.

15. Suppose a rectangle has an area of $486\ cm^2$, and one side is 9 cm longer than the other side. Find the dimensions of the rectangle.

16. **True or False** A quadratic expression with a positive discriminant is always factorable over the integers. Justify your answer.

17. Write a possible equation for the polynomial graphed below.

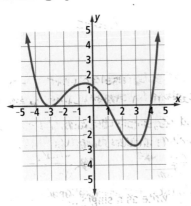

18. For the graph of the parabola, Marie wrote $y = (x + 3)(x + 1)$. Anthony wrote $y = (x + 2)^2 - 1$.

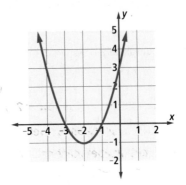

a. Are Marie and Anthony's equations equivalent? Explain.

b. What is Anthony's equation useful for finding on the graph?

Chapter 12 Chapter Review

SKILLS
PROPERTIES
USES
REPRESENTATIONS

SKILLS Procedures used to get answers

OBJECTIVE A Complete the square on a quadratic expression. (Lesson 12-2)

In 1–4, a quadratic expression is given.

a. Determine what number must be added to the expression to complete the square.

b. Complete the square.

1. $x^2 + 4x$ 　　　　2. $t^2 - 5t$

3. $z^2 + bz$ 　　　　4. $w^2 - \frac{3}{4}w$

OBJECTIVE B Factor quadratic expressions of the form $x^2 + bx + c$ and $ax^2 + bx + c$. (Lessons 12-4, 12-5)

In 5–8, factor the quadratic expression.

5. $x^2 - x - 6$ 　　　　6. $y^2 + 60y + 800$

7. $m^2 - 2m - 24$ 　　　　8. $n^2 + 4n - 12$

In 9–12, factor the trinomial.

9. $3x^2 - 2x - 8$ 　　　　10. $5x^2 + 16x + 3$

11. $6d^2 - 8d - 8$ 　　　　12. $8n^2 + 21 + 34n$

OBJECTIVE C Find the product of three or more binomials. (Lesson 12-7)

In 13–16, an equation of a function is given.

a. Identify the x-intercepts of its graph.

b. Put the equation into standard form.

13. $y = 6(x + 1)(x - 3)(2x - 11)$

14. $y = x(x - 5)(x + 2)$

15. $f(x) = (x - 4)(2x - 7)(x + 2)$

16. $g(x) = (3 - x)(4x - 1)(x + 3)(x + 1)$

OBJECTIVE D Use factoring to write rational expressions in lowest terms. (Lesson 12-8)

In 17 and 18, simplify the rational expression and indicate all restrictions on values of the variables.

17. $\dfrac{4n^2m - 8nm^2}{nm}$ 　　　　18. $\dfrac{-7rst^2q^4}{(s + 1)tq}$

In 19–21, write as a single rational expression. You may need a calculator or a CAS.

19. $\dfrac{-4n^2 + 23n - 15}{n^2 - 8n + 15}$

20. $\dfrac{3}{x + 4} - \dfrac{3x - 7}{x^2 + 3x - 4}$

21. $\dfrac{-m^3 + 5m^2 - 2m - 8}{2m^3 - 9m^2 + 3m + 14}$

PROPERTIES Principles behind the mathematics

OBJECTIVE E Determine whether a quadratic polynomial can be factored over the integers. (Lessons 12-4, 12-5, 12-6)

22. **True or False** Every quadratic polynomial whose discriminant is an integer is factorable over the integers.

23. For what values of the discriminant is a quadratic polynomial factorable?

In 24–27, determine whether the quadratic polynomial is factorable over the integers. If it is not, label it *prime*. If it is, factor the polynomial.

24. $5x^2 + 33x + 12$ 　　　　25. $15x^2 + 69x + 72$

26. $4c^2 - 14c + 8$ 　　　　27. $8x^2 + 34x + 182$

OBJECTIVE F Apply the Factor Theorem.
(Lesson 12-7)

28. $f(x) = 3x^3 - 15x^2 - 42x$.

   a. Write $f(x)$ in factored form.

   b. What does the Factor Theorem tell you about the graph of $f(x)$?

In 29 and 30, x-intercepts are given.

a. Give an equation in factored form for a polynomial function with the given x-intercepts.

b. Rewrite your equation in standard form.

29. 2 and -2 30. 0, 7, and -10

In 31 and 32, give a possible equation, in factored form, for the graph.

31.

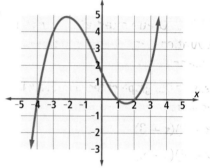

32.

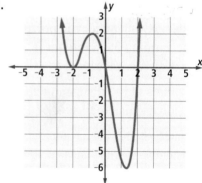

USES Applications of mathematics in real-world situations

OBJECTIVE G Solve problems involving areas and perimeters of rectangles that lead to quadratic functions or equations. (Lesson 12-1)

In 33 and 34, a rectangle is given.

a. Find its area A and perimeter P.

b. Determine the dimensions of the rectangle so that the perimeter and area are numerically equal.

33.

x

$10 - x$

34.

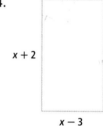

$x + 2$

$x - 3$

35. A rectangular soccer field has a perimeter of 390 yards.

   a. Write a formula for the area of the field in terms of its length x.

   b. If the width of the field must be at least 50 yards and at most 75 yards, what is the maximum area of the field?

36. A dairy cow is walking around the outside of her rectangular pasture at an average speed of 2 feet per second.

   a. If it takes the cow 20 minutes to walk around the pasture, what is the perimeter of the pasture?

   b. Write a formula for the area A of the pasture in terms of the length of one side L, and determine the dimensions of the rectangle that will maximize the cow's pasture.

37. The Irish sport of hurling can be played on a rectangular field with an area of 12,600 m². If the longer side of a hurling field is 50 m longer than the shorter side, what are the dimensions of the field?

38. The perimeter of a rectangle is 24 cm.

    a. Write a formula for the area A of the rectangle in vertex form in terms of the length x of one of its sides.

    b. What is the meaning of the vertex in this scenario?

REPRESENTATIONS Pictures, graphs, or objects that illustrate concepts

OBJECTIVE H Graph quadratic functions whose equations are given in vertex form. (Lesson 12-1)

In 39–42, sketch the graph of the equation without a calculator.

39. $y - 3 = (x - 5)^2$

40. $y - 5 = (x + 2)^2$

41. $y + 4 = 2(x + 8)^2$

42. $y + 2 = -3(x - 7)^2$

OBJECTIVE I Find the vertex of a parabola whose equation is given in standard form. (Lesson 12-2)

In 43–46, match the graph with one of the equations i. through iv. below.

i. $y = -x^2 + 6x - 14$ ii. $y = x^2 - 6x + 14$

iii. $y = -x^2 - 6x - 4$ iv. $y = x^2 + 6x + 9$

43.
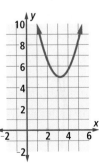

44.
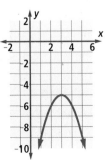

45.
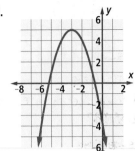

46.
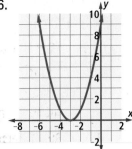

In 47–50, find the vertex of the parabola.

47. $y = 2x^2$

48. $y = x^2 + 3x - 2$

49. $y = -3x^2 + 2x - 5$

50. $y = -x^2 + 6x + 4$

OBJECTIVE J Graph quadratic functions whose equations are given in factored form. (Lesson 12-3)

In 51–54, sketch the graph of the equation without using a calculator.

51. $y = (x - 2)(x + 3)$

52. $y = (x + 4)(x - 6)$

53. $y = (2x - 1)(x + 4)$

54. $y = (3x + 7)(x + 8)$

13 Using Algebra to Prove

In previous chapters, you looked at instances and made generalizations about patterns. For example, the instances $3 \cdot 5 + 3 = 3 \cdot 6$, $7.4 \cdot 5 + 7.4 = 7.4 \cdot 6$, and $\left(-\frac{8}{99}\right) \cdot 5 + \left(-\frac{8}{99}\right) = \left(-\frac{8}{99}\right) \cdot 6$ can be described by the general pattern $n \cdot 5 + n = n \cdot 6$. In making this generalization, you have used *inductive reasoning*. **Inductive reasoning** is the process of arriving at a general conclusion (not necessarily true) from specific instances. You use inductive reasoning quite often in everyday situations. For example, if every single family house you see on a block is yellow, you may want to conclude that every house in a city is also yellow. That conclusion is wrong. There are houses in a neighborhood or city that are not yellow. But the general

pattern $n \cdot 5 + n = n \cdot 6$ does happen to be true for all real numbers. We know this because we can *prove* it mathematically.

To prove a generalization, you must use *deductive reasoning*. Deductive reasoning starts from properties that are assumed to be true. For example, we assumed the Distributive Property of Multiplication over Addition to be true: If *a, b,* and *c,* are any real numbers, then $ab + ac = a(b + c)$.

If this is true for all real numbers, then it is true when $a = n$, $b = 5$, and $c = 1$. Substituting these values for *a, b,* and *c*, $n \cdot 5 + n \cdot 1 = n(5 + 1)$.

Using another assumed property, that if *n* is any real number, then $n \cdot 1 = n$. Adding 5 and 1 then gives $n \cdot 5 + n = n \cdot 6$.

This string of justified if-then statements has *proved* that for all real numbers *n*, $n \cdot 5 + n = n \cdot 6$.

You may not have written the words *if* and *then*, but in this course you have often strung if-then statements to follow each other.

A string of justified statements that follow from each other like these is a *proof*. In this chapter, you will see many examples of proofs that use the algebra that you have studied. These proofs involve the solving of equations, divisibility properties of arithmetic, and geometric figures. They comprise one of the most important uses of algebra: showing that a statement is true when there are infinitely many cases to consider.

Lesson 13-1

If-Then Statements

Vocabulary

if-then statement

antecedent

consequent

generalization

▶ **BIG IDEA** Statements that are of the form *if . . . then* are the basis of mathematcial logic, so it is important to know how to determine if they are true or false.

If is one of the most important words in mathematics. (The words *given, when, whenever,* and *suppose* often have the same meaning.) The word *if* is often followed by the word *then*, which may or may not be written. The result is an **if-then statement.** Here are some examples.

1. If a bug is an insect, it has six legs.

2. Suppose a person likes outdoor football. Then the person will like arena football.

3. Every animal on land grows leaves.

In an if-then statement, the clause following *if* is called the **antecedent.** The clause following *then* is the **consequent.** Below we have underlined the antecedent once and the consequent twice.

If a <u>bug is an insect</u>, then <u>it has six legs</u>.
　　　 antecedent　　　　　　 consequent

Some if-then statements are *generalizations*. A **generalization** is an if-then statement in which there is a variable in the antecedent and consequent. In Statements 1–3 above, the variable is not seen but each statement can be thought of as an if-then statement with a variable.

If *B* is an insect, (then) *B* has six legs.

If *P* likes outdoor football, then *P* will like arena football.

 QY

When Is an If-Then Statement True?

An if-then statement is true if its consequent is true for *every* value in the domain of the variables in its antecedent.

Mental Math

A 28-page newspaper consists of a News section, a Classifieds section, and a Sports section. The News section is twice as long as the Sports section, and the Classifieds section is half as long as the Sports section. How long is

a. the News section?

b. the Sports section?

c. the Classifieds section?

▶ **QY**

Write Statement 3 above using a variable.

Example 1

True or False If *B* is an insect, (then) *B* has six legs.

> **Solution** The statement is true because every insect has six legs. (Having six legs is one of the defining characteristics of insects.)

An if-then statement with a variable describes a pattern. As in any pattern, a value of the variable for which both the antecedent and consequent of an if-then statement is true is an instance of the statement. A beetle is an insect and a beetle has six legs. So a beetle is an instance of Statement 1.

Beetles are the largest group in the animal kingdom, representing one-fourth of all animals.

Source: San Diego Zoo

Situations in which the antecedent is false do not affect whether an if-then statement is true. A dining room table might have six legs, but a table is not an insect. So a dining room table is not an instance of Statement 1.

A true if-then statement can be represented with a Venn diagram. The set of insects is placed inside the set of things with six legs.

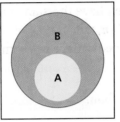

If A, then B.

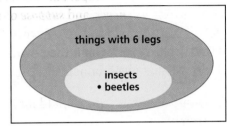

Example 2

True or False If *x* is a month of the year, then *x* has 31 days.

> **Solution** This statement is not true because there are some months that have fewer than 31 days.

If there is a value of the variable for which the antecedent of an if-then statement is true and the consequent is not true, then the if-then statement is *false*. This value is a *counterexample* to the statement. The month of November has only 30 days, so it is a counterexample to the if-then statement. One counterexample is enough to cause an if-then statement to be false.

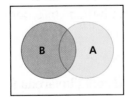

If A, then sometimes (but not always) B.

Even though there are values of the variable for which the statement of Example 2 is true, because there is a counterexample, the generalization is false.

Example 3

Draw a Venn diagram for the statement: If G is a land animal, G grows leaves.

Solution A tiger is a land animal and a tiger does not grow leaves, so the statement is false. In fact, no land animals grow leaves. So if G is a land animal, G never grows leaves. The Venn diagram has two circles that do not overlap.

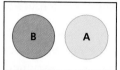

If A, then not B.

If-Then Statements in Mathematics

If-then statements occur throughout mathematics because they clarify what is given information and what are conclusions.

GUIDED

Example 4

Fill in the blanks.

If-Then Statement	True or False	Explanation
a. If $3n + 5 = 65$, then $n = 20$.	true	If $3n + 5 = 65$, then $3n = $ __?__. If $3n = $ __?__, then $n = 20$.
b. If a figure is a square, then it is a rectangle.	?	Definition of square: a square is __?__.
c. If x is a real number, then $x^2 > 0$.	?	0 is a real number and 0^2 is not greater than 0.
d. If a quadrilateral has 3 right angles, then it is a square.	false	?

Counterexamples to the two false statements in Guided Example 4 can be pictured. For Statement c, graph $y = x^2$. Notice that the graph is not always above the x-axis, so it is not the case that $x^2 > 0$ for every value of x. For Statement d, show a quadrilateral that has 3 right angles but is not a square.

This quadrilateral has 3 right angles and is not a square.

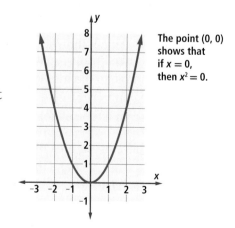

The point (0, 0) shows that if $x = 0$, then $x^2 = 0$.

Putting Statements into If-Then Form

Statements with the words "all," "every," and "no" can be rewritten in if-then form without changing their meaning.

GUIDED

Example 5

Rewrite each statement in if-then form.

Statement	If-then Form with Variables
a. Every whole number is a real number.	If x is a whole number, then ___?___.
b. All people born in the United States are U.S. citizens.	If ___?___, then P is a U.S. citizen.
c. No power of a positive number is negative.	If p is a positive number and g is any real number, then ___?___.

Questions

COVERING THE IDEAS

In 1 and 2, identify the antecedent and the consequent of the if-then statement.

1. If the sun shines this afternoon, I will be happy.

2. The world would be a better place if people did not litter.

In 3 and 4, rewrite the statement as an if-then statement with a variable in it. Underline the antecedent once and the consequent twice.

3. Every integer greater than 1 is either a prime number or a product of prime numbers.

4. When a person drives over 35 miles per hour on that street, that person is speeding.

5. Explain why this if-then statement is true.
   If $3x + 16 > 10$, then $x > -2$.

6. Explain why this if-then statement is false.
   If $3x + 16 > 10$, then $x > 0$.

In 7–9, an antecedent is given. Complete the statement with two consequents that make it true.

7. If L and W are the length and width of a rectangle, then ___?___.

8. If $x^m \cdot x^n = x^{m+n}$, then ___?___.

9. If n is divisible by 10, then ___?___.

Interstate highways nationwide usually have posted speed limits between 55 and 75 mi/h.

Source: Federal Highway Administration

In 10–13, an if-then situation is given.

a. Tell whether the statement is true or false.

b. Draw a Venn diagram picturing the situation.

10. If a figure is a rectangle, then the figure is a square.

11. If you are in the United States and in Chattanooga, then you are in Tennessee.

12. If a number is an even number, then it is a prime number.

13. If $x > 0$, then $-x > 0$.

APPLYING THE MATHEMATICS

In 14–17, a false statement is given.

a. Find a counterexample that shows it is false.

b. Find the largest domain of the variable for which the statement is true.

14. If w is a real number, then w^3 is positive.

15. If t is a real number, then t^4 is positive.

16. If r is a real number, then $2r \geq r$.

17. If x is a real number and $y = x^2 + x$, then $y \geq 0$.

In 18 and 19, draw a counterexample to the statement.

18. For all real numbers a, the graph of $y = ax^2$ is a parabola.

19. A triangle cannot have two angles each with measure over 75°.

20. Draw the following four true statements in one Venn diagram.
    a. Every rhombus is a parallelogram.
    b. Every rectangle is a parallelogram.
    c. If a figure is both a rhombus and a rectangle, then it is a square.
    d. Every square is both a rhombus and a rectangle.

In 21 and 22, rewrite the statement as an if-then statement and indicate why each statement is false.

21. All sentences have a subject, verb, and object.

22. Every president of the United States has served fewer than three terms.

REVIEW

23. **Skill Sequence** Factor each expression. (Lesson 12-4)
    a. $a^2 - 36$
    b. $n^2 - 5n - 36$
    c. $x^2 - 5xy - 36y^2$

24. **Fill in the Blank** Do this problem in your head. Because one thousand times one thousand equals one million, then $1,005 \cdot 995 = \underline{\ ?\ }$. (Lesson 11-6)

25. Tickets to a hockey game cost $22 for adults and $16 for children. The total attendance at one game was 3,150 and the total revenue from ticket sales for the game was $66,258. How many of each kind of ticket were sold for the game? (Lesson 10-5)

26. Write $2^{-3} + 4^{-3}$ as a simple fraction. (Lesson 8-4)

27. Let $g(x) = \frac{3}{4}x - 7$. (Lesson 7-6)
    a. Calculate $g(80)$.
    b. Calculate $g(-80)$.
    c. Describe the graph of g.

28. **True or False** The slope of the line through (x_1, y_1) and (x_2, y_2) is the opposite of the slope of the line through (x_2, y_2) and (x_1, y_1). (Lesson 6-6)

The Carolina Hurricanes won hockey's 2006 Stanley Cup.

EXPLORATION

29. Consider this statement: No four points in a plane can all be the same distance from each other.
    a. Write the statement in if-then form.
    b. Is the statement true or false?
    c. If "in a plane" is deleted from the statement, show that the resulting statement is false.

QY ANSWER

If A is a land animal, then A grows leaves.

Lesson 13-2

The Converse of an If-Then Statement

Vocabulary

converse

equivalent statements

if and only if

> ▶ **BIG IDEA**   The converse of the statement, "If A, then B." is the statement, "If B, then A."

You might have heard of the question, "Which came first, the chicken or the egg?" This question is difficult because: If there is a chicken, then there must have been an egg. If there is an egg, then there must have been a chicken.

These two if-then statements are *converses*. The *converse* of the statement, "If p, then q" is the statement, "If q, then p." Another way of stating this is: the **converse** of an if-then statement is found by switching the antecedent and the consequent of the statement.

STOP QY

Mental Math

Evaluate when $a = 2$ and $b = -2$.

a. $(a + b)^2$

b. $a^2 + b^2$

c. $a^2 + 2ab + b^2$

Converses of True Statements

Often the converse of a true statement is not true. Here is an example.

Statement If $x = 8$, then $x^2 = 64$. (true)

Converse If $x^2 = 64$, then $x = 8$. (False; x could also be –8.)

▶ **QY**

Give the converse of the statement: If $\sqrt{2x} = 10$, then $x = 50$.

GUIDED

Example 1

The given statement is true. Write its converse and explain why the converse is not true.

a. If a quadrilateral has 4 sides of the same length and its diagonals have the same length, then the quadrilateral is a rectangle.

b. If you live in the state of North Dakota, then you live in the United States.

Solutions

a. Converse: If a quadrilateral is ___?___, then ___?___. This statement is false because ___?___.

b. Converse: If ___?___, then ___?___ The statement is false because ___?___.

Sometimes the converse of a true statement is true. When a statement and its converse are both true, then the antecedent and consequent are **equivalent statements.** Equivalent statements can be connected by the phrase *if and only if.* Here is an example.

> **Statement** If $x = 6$, then $2^x = 64$. (true)
>
> **Converse** If $2^x = 64$, then $x = 6$. (true)

Because the statement and its converse are both true, you can write:
$x = 6$ **if and only if** $2^x = 64$.

GUIDED

Example 2

The given statement is true and so is its converse. Write the converse and then combine the statement and its converse into one if-and-only-if statement.

a. If a quadrilateral has 4 sides of the same length and its diagonals have the same length, then the quadrilateral is a square.

b. If you live in the largest country in South America, then you live in Brazil.

Solution

a. Converse: If a quadrilateral ___?___, then ___?___. You can write: A quadrilateral has 4 sides of the same length and diagonals of the same length *if and only if* ___?___.

b. Converse: If you live in Brazil, then you live in the largest country in South America. You can write: ___?___ *if and only if* ___?___.

Brazil is the fourth most populous country in the world with about 190 million people.

Source: *The World Factbook*

When you see the phrase "if and only if," then you can separate the sentence into two if-then statements.

> In Hardnox High School, a student is on the honor roll if and only if his or her grade point average is at least 3.75.

means

> In Hardnox High School, if a student's grade point average is at least 3.75, then the student is on the honor roll.

and

> If a student in Hardnox High School is on the honor roll, then his or her grade point average is at least 3.75.

Questions

COVERING THE IDEAS

1. State the converse of the statement: If there is smoke, then there is fire.

2. **Multiple Choice** If a statement is true, then its converse

    A must be true.   **B** may be true.   **C** must be false.

In 3–5, a statement is given.

    a. Is it true?

    b. State its converse.

    c. Is its converse true?

    d. If either the statement or its converse is not true, correct them so that they are both true.

3. If an integer is divisible by 3 and by 4, then it is divisible by 24.

4. If both the units and tens digits of an integer written in base 10 equal 0, then the integer is divisible by 100.

5. If $7u < 56$, then $u > 8$.

In 6–8, write the two if-then statements that are meant by the if-and-only-if statement.

6. You will receive full credit for this question if and only if you get both parts correct.

7. A quadrilateral is a rectangle if and only if it has four right angles.

8. $5x + 4y = 20$ if and only if $y = -1.25x + 5$.

In 9 and 10, rewrite the definition as an if-and-only-if statement.

9. Every linear function has an equation of the form $f(x) = ax + b$.

10. The reciprocal of a nonzero number x is the number y such that $xy = 1$.

In 11–14, are statements (1) and (2) equivalent? If not, why not?

11. (1) $x = 3$
    (2) $2x = 6$

12. (1) $y = 15$
    (2) $y^4 = 50{,}625$

13. (1) $z = 8$
    (2) $z^2 + 48 = 14z$

14. (1) $a + b = c$
    (2) $c - b = a$

APPLYING THE MATHEMATICS

In 15–18, a statement is given.

    a. Is it true?

    b. State its converse.

    c. Is its converse true?

    d. If either the statement or its converse is not true, correct them so that they are both true.

15. If $(x - 5)(2x + 3) = 45$, then $2x^2 - 7x + 30 = 90$.

16. If a polygon has 7 sides, then it is a hexagon.

17. If a parabola has an equation of the form $y = (x - 5)(x + 3)$, then its x-intercepts are -5 and 3.

18. If $3x + 4y = 6$ and $2x - 5y = 7$, then $x = 6$ and $y = -3$.

In **19–21, a statement is given.**

    a. Tell whether the statement is true.

    b. If the statement is true, give an example. If it is not true, modify it so that it is true.

19. A line is a vertical line if and only if its slope is undefined.

20. $x^a \cdot x^b = x^{a+b}$ if and only if a and b are positive integers.

21. A person can be a U.S. citizen if and only if the person was born in the United States.

A valid U.S. passport is required for U.S. citizens to enter and leave most foreign countries.

Source: U.S. Department of State

REVIEW

In **22 and 23, tell whether the given if-then statement is true or false. If it is false, provide a counterexample to the statement.** (Lessons 13-1, 9-1)

22. If a dining room table seats 8 people, then it seats 6 people.

23. If n is even, the graph of $y = ax^n$ crosses the x-axis twice.

24. **Multiple Choice** Rectangles of width x are cut off from two adjacent sides of a 12 in.-by-12 in. sheet of wrapping paper, as shown at the right. What is the area, in square inches, of the square region that remains? (Lesson 11-6)

    A $12 - x^2$ **B** $144 + x^2$

    C $144 - x^2$ **D** $144 - 24x + x^2$

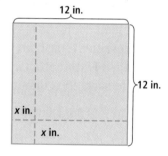

25. If 8 pencils and 5 erasers cost \$4.69 and 3 pencils and 4 erasers cost \$2.80, find the cost of 2 pencils. (Lesson 10-5)

In **26–28, simplify the expression.** (Lessons 8-6, 8-5)

26. $5(3\sqrt{x})^2$ 27. $(6 \cdot 2^{-2})^3$ 28. $\dfrac{9 \pm \sqrt{18}}{3}$

EXPLORATION

29. Write two statements from outside of mathematics that are true but whose converses are false.

QY ANSWER

If $x = 50$, then $\sqrt{2x} = 10$.

Solving Equations as Proofs

Vocabulary

justifications

proof argument

deduction

▶ **BIG IDEA**   Writing the steps in solving an equation and then checking the solutions together prove that you have found the only solutions to the equation.

An Example of a Proof Argument

Every time you solve an equation, you are proving or deducing something true. Consider solving the equation $8x + 19 = 403$. The solution is 48. You may write the steps as we show here.

Mental Math

Solve for *n*.

a. $5^n \cdot 5^4 = 5^{20}$

b. $(5^n)^4 = 5^{20}$

i. $\quad\quad\quad 8x + 19 = 403$

ii. $\quad 8x + 19 + -19 = 403 + -19$

iii. $\quad\quad\quad 8x + 0 = 384$

iv. $\quad\quad\quad\quad 8x = 384$

v. $\quad\quad \frac{1}{8} \cdot 8x = \frac{1}{8} \cdot 384$

vi. $\quad\quad\quad 1 \cdot x = 48$

vii. $\quad\quad\quad\quad x = 48$

If you include the statements that show why each step follows from the previous steps, then you have written a *proof.* These statements are called **justifications.** They indicate why you can do what you have done to solve the equation.

	Conclusion	What Was Done	Justification
i.	$8x + 19 = 403$	Given	Given
ii.	$8x + 19 - 19 = 403 + -19$	Add −19 to both sides.	Addition Property of Equality
iii.	$8x + 0 = 384$	$19 + -19 = 0$	Additive Inverse Property
iv.	$8x = 384$	$8x + 0 = 8x$	Additive Identity Property
v.	$\frac{1}{8} \cdot 8x = \frac{1}{8} \cdot 384$	Multiply both sides by $\frac{1}{8}$.	Multiplication Property of Equality
vi.	$1x = 48$	$\frac{1}{8} \cdot 8 = 1,$ $\frac{1}{8} \cdot 384 = 48$	Multiplicative Inverse Property
vii.	$x = 48$	$1 \cdot x = x$	Multiplicative Identity Property

With this argument, you have proved: *If 8x + 19 = 403, then x = 48.*
In this if-then statement, *8x + 19 = 403* is the antecedent and *x = 48*
is the consequent. A **proof argument** in mathematics is a sequence
of justified conclusions, starting with the antecedent and ending
with the consequent. The use of a proof to show that one statement
follows from another is called **deduction**.

A Justification Is Different from What Was Done

What you *do* to solve an equation is different from the justification.
What was done applies to the specific equation being solved. The
justification is the general property. In proofs, some people prefer to
see what was done. Other people prefer the justification.

GUIDED

Example 1

Prove if $-6x - 14 = 118$, then $x = -22$.

Solution

	Conclusion	What Was Done	Justification
i.	$-6x - 14 = 118$	Given	Given
ii.	$-6x - 14 + 14 = 118 + 14$	14 was added to both sides.	_____?_____
iii.	_____?_____	$-14 + 14 = 0$, $118 + 114 = 132$	Additive Inverse Property
iv.	$-6x = 132$	$-6x + 0 = -6x$	Arithmetic
v.	$-\frac{1}{6}(-6x) = -\frac{1}{6}(132)$	_____?_____	Multiplication Property of Equality
vi.	$1 \cdot x = -\frac{1}{6}(132)$	$-\frac{1}{6}(-6) = 1$	_____?_____
vii.	$x = -22$	_____?_____	_____?_____ Property

An Abbreviated Proof

Because work with additive and multiplicative inverses and identities
is so automatic, some people prefer abbreviated proofs that do not
show these steps. Here is an abbreviated proof of the statement:
If $8x + 19 = 403$, then $x = 48$.

	Conclusion	Justification
i.	$8x + 19 = 403$	Given
ii.	$8x + 19 + -19 = 403 + -19$	Addition Property of Equality
iii.	$8x = 384$	Arithmetic
iv.	$\frac{1}{8} \cdot 8x = \frac{1}{8} \cdot 384$	Multiplication Property of Equality
v.	$x = 48$	Multiplicative Inverse Property

Example 2

Prove that if $2x - 9 = 37$, then $x = 23$.

Solution Supply the justifications for the following conclusions.

	Conclusion	Justification
i.	$2x - 9 = 37$	?
ii.	$2x - 9 + 9 = 37 + 9$	?
iii.	$2x = 46$	?
iv.	$\frac{1}{2}(2x) = \frac{1}{2}(46)$	?
v.	$x = 23$	?

Justifications and Properties

In solving an equation or inequality, every justification is one of the following:

1. *Given* information (the given equation or inequality to be solved)

2. A property, of which there are three types:

   a. a *defined property,* such as the definition of slope, absolute value, or square root

   b. an *assumed property* of numbers, such as the Product of Powers Property or the Distributive Property

   c. a *previously-proved property,* such as the Means-Extremes Property or the Power of a Product Property, that were not assumed but proved using definitions or other known properties

3. *Arithmetic* (a catch-all term for all the properties you have learned that help you compute results of operations)

The Check Is a Converse

On the previous page you saw the proof of the statement: *If $8x + 19 = 403$, then $x = 48$.* When you check your work by substitution, you are proving: *If $x = 48$, then $8x + 19 = 403$.* The check is the converse of the solution. Together, the solution and the check mean $8x + 19 = 403$ *if and only if $x = 48$.*

Another way of saying this is: $8x + 19 = 403$ *exactly when $x = 48$.*

This means that 48 is a solution and no other numbers are solutions. Solving an equation means proving both a statement (to find the possible solutions) and its converse (to check that the possible solutions do work). Example 3 illustrates the importance of the check.

Example 3

Find all solutions to $\sqrt{x} = x - 6, x > 0$.

Solution

$\sqrt{x} = x - 6$	Given
$\sqrt{x} \cdot \sqrt{x} = (x - 6)(x - 6)$	Multiplication Property of Equality
$x = (x - 6)(x - 6)$	Definition of square root
$x = x^2 - 12x + 36$	Extended Distributive Property
$0 = x^2 - 13x + 36$	Addition Property of Equality
$x = \dfrac{13 \pm \sqrt{(-13)^2 - 4 \cdot 1 \cdot 36}}{2}$	Quadratic Formula
$x = \dfrac{13 \pm 5}{2}$	Simplify.
$x = 9$ or $x = 4$	Simplify.

This argument proves: If $\sqrt{x} = x - 6$, then $x = 9$ or $x = 4$. So, 9 and 4 are possible values of x. To see if they are solutions, a check is necessary.

Check When $x = 9$: Does $\sqrt{9} = 9 - 6$? Yes, $\sqrt{9} = 3$ and $9 - 6 = 3$. It checks.

When $x = 4$: Does $\sqrt{4} = 4 - 6$? No, $\sqrt{4} = 2$ and $4 - 6 = -2$. It does not check.

Consequently, $x = 9$ is the only solution to $\sqrt{x} = x - 6$. Putting it another way, $\sqrt{x} = x - 6$ if and only if $x = 9$.

In Example 3, the solution has proved: *If $\sqrt{x} = x - 6$, then $x = 9$ or $x = 4$.* The check has shown *If $x = 4$, then $\sqrt{x} \neq x - 6$ and if $x = 9$, then $\sqrt{x} = x - 6$.* So, $\sqrt{x} = x - 6$ *if and only if $x = 9$.*

Questions

COVERING THE IDEAS

1. Here is part of a proof argument. Explain what was done to get to Steps a–e and supply the missing justification.

$$40x + 12 = 3(6 + 13x)$$

a. $\qquad 40x + 12 = 18 + 39x$

b. $40x + 12 + -12 = 18 + 39x + -12$

c. $\qquad 40x + 0 = 18 + 39x + -12$

d. $\qquad 40x = 18 + 39x + -12$

e. $\qquad 40x = 6 + 39x$

f. The argument in Steps a–e proves what if-then statement?

2. Steps a–c are the conclusions in an abbreviated proof argument. Write what was done to get to each step and provide the justifications.

$$29 - 3y \le 44$$

a. $-29 + 29 - 3y \le -29 + 44$

b. $\qquad -3y \le 15$

c. $\qquad y \ge -5$

d. The argument in Steps a–c proves what if-then statement?

3. Explain the difference between inductive reasoning and deduction.

4. Give another example of inductive reasoning that is not written in this book.

5. After a month of timing her walks to school, Sula told her friend Lana, "It takes me 5 minutes less to get to school if I walk at a constant pace diagonally through the rectangular park than if I walk around two edges of its perimeter!" Lana replied, "That's a result of the Pythagorean Theorem!"

a. Who used inductive reasoning?

b. Who used deduction?

6. What five kinds of justifications are allowed in solving an equation or inequality?

7. a. Provide conclusions and justifications to prove that if $12m = 3m + 5$, then $m = \frac{5}{9}$.

b. What else do you need to do in order to prove that $12m = 3m + 5$ if and only if $m = \frac{5}{9}$.

8. Find all solutions to the equation $\sqrt{2n + 1} = n - 7$. You do not have to give justifications.

APPLYING THE MATHEMATICS

In 9–14, two consecutive steps of a proof are shown as an if-then statement. State what was done and state the justification.

9. If $d = rt$, then $r = \frac{d}{t}$.

10. If $3x + 5x = 80$, then $8x = 80$.

11. If $gn^2 + hn + k = 0$, then $n = \dfrac{-h \pm \sqrt{h^2 - 4gk}}{2g}$.

12. If $\sqrt{t} = 400$, then $t = 160{,}000$.

13. If $3x + 4y = 6$ and $3x - 4y = -18$, then $6x = -12$.

14. If $\frac{8}{3}b = 12$, then $8b = 36$.

15. Prove: If $ax + b = c$ and $a \ne 0$, then $x = \frac{c - b}{a}$. (*Hint:* Follow the steps of the solution to the first equation in the lesson.)

16. Show that if $x = \frac{c - b}{a}$, then $ax + b = c$.

17. Together, what do the statements in Questions 15 and 16 prove?

18. Use the definition of absolute value to find all values of x satisfying $|500x - 200| = 800$.

19. In Parts a and b, give abbreviated proofs.

   a. Prove: If a and k are both positive and $a(x - h)^2 = k$, then $x = h \pm \sqrt{\frac{k}{a}}$.

   b. Prove: If a and k are both positive and $x = h \pm \sqrt{\frac{k}{a}}$, then $a(x - h)^2 = k$.

   c. What has been proved in Parts a and b?

20. Prove: The slope of the line with equation $Ax + By = C$ is the reciprocal of the slope of the line with equation $Bx + Ay = D$.

REVIEW

21. Consider the following statement to be true: Every person under 8 years of age receives a reduced fare on the metro city bus. (**Lessons 13-2, 13-1**)

   a. Write this as an if-then statement.

   b. Write the converse.

   c. Is the converse true? Why or why not?

22. What value(s) can z not have in the expression $\dfrac{(2 - z)(1 + z)}{(4 + z)(3 - z)}$? (**Lessons 12-8, 5-2**)

23. a. Factor $3x^2 + 9x - 12$.

   b. Find a value for x for which $3x^2 + 9x - 12$ is a prime number. (**Lesson 12-5**)

24. a. Solve the system $\begin{cases} 2y + 3x = 7 \\ \qquad y = 6x - 1 \end{cases}$.

   b. Are the lines in Part a coincident, parallel, or intersecting? (**Lessons 10-6, 10-2**)

In 25–30, a property is stated. Describe the property using variables.

25. Product of Square Roots Property (**Lesson 8-7**)

26. Quotient of Square Roots Property (**Lesson 8-7**)

27. Power of a Power Property (**Lesson 8-2**)

28. Zero Product Property (**Lesson 2-8**)

29. Multiplication Property of −1 (**Lesson 2-4**)

30. Distributive Property of Multiplication over Subtraction (**Lesson 2-1**)

In 31 and 32, △*ACB* is similar to △*XZY*. (Lesson 5-10, Previous Course)

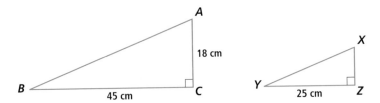

31. Find the missing lengths.

32. Fill in the Blank If $m\angle Y \approx 22°$, then $m\angle B \approx$ __?__ .

33. Two cards are drawn at random from a standard 52-card deck, without replacement. What is the probability of drawing an ace and a jack, in that order? **(Lesson 5-8)**

EXPLORATION

34. Use the Extended Distributive Property and other properties you have learned in this course to prove:
$$(a + b + c)(a + b - c)(b + c - a)(c + a - b) = 2(a^2b^2 + b^2c^2 + c^2a^2) - (a^4 + b^4 + c^4).$$

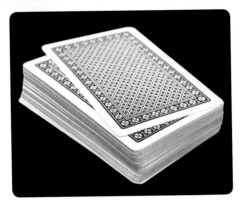

The earliest playing cards are believed to have originated in Central Asia.

Source: The International Playing-Card Society

Lesson

13-4

A History and Proof of the Quadratic Formula

> **BIG IDEA** The Quadratic Formula can be proved using the properties of numbers and operations.

The Quadratic Formula $x = \dfrac{-b \pm \sqrt{b^2 - 4ac}}{2a}$ is quite complicated. You may wonder how people used to solve quadratic equations before they had this formula, and how they discovered the Quadratic Formula in the first place. Here is some of the history.

What Problem First Led to Quadratics?

Our knowledge of ancient civilizations is based only on what survives today. The earliest known problems that led to quadratic equations are on Babylonian tablets dating from 1700 BCE. In these problems, the Babylonians were trying to find two numbers x and y that satisfy the system $\begin{cases} x + y = b \\ \quad xy = c \end{cases}$.

This suggests that some Babylonians were interested in finding the dimensions x and y of a rectangle with a given area c and a given perimeter $2b$. The historian Victor Katz suggests that maybe there were some people who believed that if you knew the area of a rectangle, then you knew its perimeter. In solving these problems, these Babylonians may have been trying to show that many rectangles with different dimensions have the same area.

Mental Math

Use the graph below to find each length.

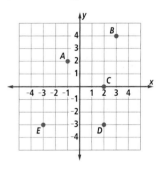

a. *ED*

b. *CD*

c. *BC*

d. *AD*

GUIDED

Example

Find the dimensions of a rectangular field whose perimeter is 300 meters and whose area is 4,400 square meters.

Solution Let L and W be the length and width of this rectangle.

Then $\begin{cases} \underline{} + \underline{} = 300 \\ \underline{} \cdot \underline{} = 4{,}400 \end{cases}$.

This system can be solved by substitution. First solve the top equation for W.

$\underline{} = 300 - \underline{}$

$W = 150 - \underline{}$

(continued on next page)

Now, substitute __?__ for W in the second equation.

$$L(\,\underline{?}\,) = 4{,}400$$

This is a quadratic equation and so it can be solved by using either the Quadratic Formula or factoring to get $L = \underline{\ ?\ }$ or $L = \underline{\ ?\ }$. Now substitute these values for L in either of the original equations to get $W = \underline{\ ?\ }$ or $W = \underline{\ ?\ }$. So, the dimensions of the field are $\underline{\ ?\ }$ m by $\underline{\ ?\ }$ m.

How the Babylonians Solved Quadratics

The Babylonians, like the Greeks who came after them, used a geometric approach to solve problems like these. Using today's algebraic language and notation, here is what they did. It is a sneaky way to solve this sort of problem. Look back at the Example.

Because $L + W = 150$, the average of L and W is 75. This means that L is as much greater than 75 as W is less than 75. So let $L = 75 + x$ and $W = 75 - x$. Substitute these values into the second equation.

$$L \cdot W = 4{,}400$$
$$(75 + x)(75 - x) = 4{,}400$$
$$5{,}625 - x^2 = 4{,}400$$
$$x^2 = 1{,}225$$

Taking the square root, $x = 35$ or $x = -35$.

If $x = 35$:
$L = 75 + x$, so $L = 75 + 35 = 110$
$W = 75 - x$, so $W = 75 - 35 = 40$

If $x = -35$:
$L = 75 + -35 = 40$
$W = 75 - -35 = 110$

Either solution tells us that the field is 40 meters by 110 meters.

 QY

Notice what the Babylonians did. They took a complicated quadratic equation and, with a clever substitution, reduced it to an equation of the form $x^2 = k$. That equation is easy to solve. Then they substituted the solution back into the original equation.

This tablet contains 14 lines of a mathematical text in cuneiform script and a geometric design.

Source: Iraq Museum

▶ **QY**

Use the Babylonian method to find two numbers whose sum is 72 and whose product is 1,007. (*Hint:* Let one of the numbers be $36 + x$, the other $36 - x$.)

The Work of Al-Khwarizmi

The work of the Babylonians was lost for many years. In 825 CE, about 2,500 years after the Babylonian tablets were created, a general method that is similar to today's Quadratic Formula was authored by the Arab mathematician Muhammad bin Musa al-Khwarizmi in a book titled *Hisab al-jabr w'al-muqabala*. Al-Khwarizmi's techniques were more general than those of the Babylonians. He gave a method to solve any equation of the form $ax^2 + bx = c$, where a, b, and c are positive numbers. His book was very influential. The word "al-jabr" in the title of his book led to our modern word "algebra." Our word "algorithm" comes from al-Khwarizmi's name.

Muhammad bin Musa al-Khwarizmi

A Proof of the Quadratic Formula

Neither the Babylonians nor al-Khwarizmi worked with an equation of the form $ax^2 + bx + c = 0$, because they considered only positive numbers, and if a, b, and c are positive, this equation has no positive solutions.

In 1545, a Renaissance scientist, Girolamo Cardano, blended al-Khwarizmi's solution with geometry to solve quadratic equations. He allowed negative solutions and even square roots of negative numbers that gave rise to complex numbers, a topic you will study in Advanced Algebra. In 1637, René Descartes published *La Géometrie* that contained the Quadratic Formula in the form we use today.

Now we prove why the formula works. Examine the argument in the following steps closely. See how each equation follows from the preceding equation. The idea is quite similar to the one used by the Babylonians, but a little more general. We work with the equation $ax^2 + bx + c = 0$ until the left side is a perfect square. Then the equation has the form $t^2 = k$, which you know how to solve for t.

Given the quadratic equation: $ax^2 + bx + c = 0$ with $a \neq 0$. We know $a \neq 0$ because otherwise the equation is not a quadratic equation.

Step 1 Multiply both sides of the equation by $\frac{1}{a}$. This makes the left term equal to $x^2 + \frac{b}{a}x + \frac{c}{a}$. The right side remains 0 because $0 \cdot \frac{1}{a} = 0$.

$$x^2 + \frac{b}{a}x + \frac{c}{a} = 0$$

Step 2 Add $-\frac{c}{a}$ to both sides in preparation for completing the square on the left side.

$$x^2 + \frac{b}{a}x = -\frac{c}{a}$$

Step 3 To complete the square add the square of half the coefficient of x to both sides. (See Lesson 12-2.)

$$x^2 + \frac{b}{a}x + \left(\frac{b}{2a}\right)^2 = -\frac{c}{a} + \left(\frac{b}{2a}\right)^2$$

Step 4 The left side is now the square of a binomial.

$$\left(x + \frac{b}{2a}\right)^2 = -\frac{c}{a} + \left(\frac{b}{2a}\right)^2$$

Step 5 Take the power of the fraction to eliminate parentheses on the right side.

$$\left(x + \frac{b}{2a}\right)^2 = -\frac{c}{a} + \frac{b^2}{4a^2}$$

Step 6 To add the fractions on the right side, find a common denominator.

$$\left(x + \frac{b}{2a}\right)^2 = -\frac{4ac}{4a^2} + \frac{b^2}{4a^2}$$

Step 7 Add the fractions.

$$\left(x + \frac{b}{2a}\right)^2 = \frac{b^2 - 4ac}{4a^2}$$

Step 8 Now the equation has the form $t^2 = k$, with $t = x + \frac{b}{2a}$ and $k = \frac{b^2 - 4ac}{4a^2}$. This is where the discriminant $b^2 - 4ac$ becomes important. If $b^2 - 4ac \geq 0$, then there are real solutions. They are found by taking the square roots of both sides.

$$x + \frac{b}{2a} = \pm\sqrt{\frac{b^2 - 4ac}{4a^2}}$$

Step 9 The square root of a quotient is the quotient of the square roots.

$$x + \frac{b}{2a} = \pm\frac{\sqrt{b^2 - 4ac}}{2a}$$

Step 10 This is beginning to look like the formula. Add $-\frac{b}{2a}$ to each side.

$$x = -\frac{b}{2a} \pm \frac{\sqrt{b^2 - 4ac}}{2a}$$

Step 11 Adding the fractions results in the Quadratic Formula.

$$x = \frac{-b \pm \sqrt{b^2 - 4ac}}{2a}$$

What if $b^2 - 4ac < 0$? Then the quadratic equation has no real number solutions. The formula still works, but you have to take square roots of negative numbers to get solutions. You will study these nonreal solutions in a later course.

Questions

COVERING THE IDEAS

1. **Multiple Choice** The earliest known problems that led to the solving of quadratic equations were studied about how many years ago?

   A 1,175   B 1,700

   C 2,500   D 3,700

2. In what civilization do quadratic equations first seem to have been considered and solved?

3. What is the significance of the work of al-Khwarizmi in the history of the Quadratic Formula?

In 4 and 5, suppose two numbers sum to 53 and have a product of 612. Show your work in finding the numbers.

4. Use the Quadratic Formula.

5. Use the Babylonian Method.

6. Suppose a rectangular room has a floor area of 54 square yards. Find two different lengths and widths that this floor might have.

In 7 and 8, suppose a rectangular room has a floor area of 144 square yards and that the perimeter of its floor is 50 yards.

7. Find its length and width by solving a quadratic equation using the Quadratic Formula or factoring.

8. Find its length and width using a more ancient method.

9. Find two numbers whose sum is 15 and whose product is 10.

10. In the proof of the Quadratic Formula, each of Steps 1–11 tells what was done but does not name the property of real numbers. For each step, name the property (or properties) from the following list.

    i. Addition Property of Equality

    ii. Multiplication Property of Equality

    iii. Distributive Property of Multiplication over Addition

    iv. Equal Fractions Property

    v. Power of a Quotient Property

    vi. Quotient of Square Roots Property

    vii. Definition of square root

APPLYING THE MATHEMATICS

11. Solve the equation $7x^2 - 6x - 1 = 0$ by following the steps in the derivation of the Quadratic Formula.

12. Explain why there are no real numbers x and y whose sum is 10 and whose product is 60.

13. In a Chinese text that is thousands of years old, the following problem is given: The height of a door is 6.8 more than its width. The distance between its corners is 10. Find the height and width of the door.

14. Here is an alternate proof of the Quadratic Formula. Tell what was done to get each step.

$$ax^2 + bx + c = 0$$

a. $$4a^2x^2 + 4abx + 4ac = 0$$
b. $4a^2x^2 + 4abx + 4ac + b^2 = b^2$
c. $$4a^2x^2 + 4abx + b^2 = b^2 - 4ac$$
d. $$(2ax + b)^2 = b^2 - 4ac$$
e. $$2ax + b = \pm\sqrt{b^2 - 4ac}$$
f. $$2ax = -b \pm \sqrt{b^2 - 4ac}$$
g. $$x = \frac{-b \pm \sqrt{b^2 - 4ac}}{2a}$$

REVIEW

15. Consider the following statement. (**Lessons 13-2, 13-1**)

    A number that is divisible by 8 is also divisible by 4.

    a. Write the statement in if-then form.

    b. Decide whether the statement you wrote in Part a is true or false. If it is false, find a counterexample.

    c. Write the converse of the statement you wrote in Part a.

    d. Decide whether the statement you wrote in Part c is true or false. If it is false, find a counterexample.

16. Solve $x^2 + 5x = 30$. (**Lesson 12-6**)

In 17–19, an open soup can has volume $V = \pi r^2 h$ and surface area $S = \pi r^2 + 2\pi rh$, where r is the radius and h is the height of the can.

17. Use common monomial factoring to rewrite the formula for S. (**Lesson 11-4**)

18. Find each of the following. (**Lesson 11-2**)

    a. the degree of V

    b. the degree of S

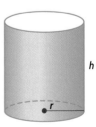

19. If the can has a diameter of 8 cm and a height of 12 cm, about how many milliliters of soup can it hold? ($1 \text{ L} = 1{,}000 \text{ cm}^3$) (Lesson 5-4)

20. Solve this system by graphing. $\begin{cases} y = |x| \\ y = \frac{1}{4}x^2 \end{cases}$ (Lessons 10-1, 4-9)

21. **Skill Sequence** Simplify each expression. (Lessons 8-7, 8-6)

   a. $\sqrt{8} + \sqrt{5}$ b. $\sqrt{8} \cdot \sqrt{5}$ c. $\dfrac{\sqrt{8} \cdot \sqrt{5}}{\sqrt{2}}$

EXPLORATION

22. In a book or on the Internet, research al-Khwarizmi and find another contribution he made to mathematics or other sciences. Write a paragraph about your findings.

QY ANSWER

19 and 53

Lesson 13-5

Proofs of Divisibility Properties

Vocabulary

closed under an operation

even integer, even number

odd integer, odd number

semiperimeter

▶ **BIG IDEA** Using algebra, you can prove that even and odd numbers have certain general properties.

In this lesson, the following statements are assumed to be true.

> The sum of two integers is an integer.
>
> The difference of two integers is an integer.
>
> The product of two integers is an integer.

The three properties above are examples of *closure properties*. A set is **closed under an operation** if the results of that operation always lies in that set. So another way of saying the above statements is:

> The set of integers is closed under addition.
>
> The set of integers is closed under subtraction.
>
> The set of integers is closed under multiplication.

But the set of integers is *not* closed under division. For example, $8 \div 3$ is not an integer. When the quotient $a \div b$ is an integer, then we say that a is divisible by b, or that a is a multiple of b.

From the closure properties and other properties of real numbers that you know, it is possible to prove criteria that describe when one number is divisible by another.

Divisibility by 2

An **even integer** (or **even number**) E is an integer that is twice another integer; that is, it is an integer that can be written as $2n$, where n is an integer. As you know, the integers are the numbers $0, 1, -1, 2, -2, 3, -3, \ldots$. So, if you multiply these numbers by 2, the results are the *even integers* $0, 2, -2, 4, -4, 6, -6, 8, -8, \ldots$.

Geometrically, a positive even number of dots can be arranged in two rows of the same length. For example, 14 dots can be split into two rows of 7.

Mental Math

A function contains
{(−16, 4.5), (−7, 4.5),
(0, 2), (1, −5), (5.5, 10)}.

a. State the domain.

b. State the range.

To tell whether a large number is even, you cannot draw a pattern of dots. You must be able to show that it is twice another integer. For example, you can show that 5,734 is an even integer because $5,734 = 2 \cdot 2,867$, and 2,867 is an integer. How did we find 2,867? We divided 5,734 by 2. The number 0 is an even integer because $0 = 2 \cdot 0$. The negative number -88 is an even integer because $-88 = 2 \cdot -44$.

Odd Integers

An integer that is not even is called *odd*. Geometrically, an odd number of dots cannot be arranged in two rows of the same length. An example of this is shown with 15 dots. Notice below that there are two rows of 7 dots plus an additional dot.

You can see that an odd integer is one more than an even integer. So we define an **odd integer** (or **odd number**) as an integer that can be written as $2n + 1$, where n is an integer. For example, $2 \cdot (-54) + 1 = -107$, so -107 is odd.

STOP QY

If two numbers m and n are positive, you know that their sum $m + n$ and their product mn are positive. But the difference $m - n$ might be positive or negative. What happens if you know whether m and n are even or odd?

By trying some numbers, fill in the following table with one of the words "odd" or "even."

> ▸ QY
>
> Let $m = 87,654$ and $n = 3,210$. Tell whether these numbers are even or odd.
>
> **a.** $m + n$
>
> **b.** $m - n$
>
> **c.** mn

Activity 1

m	n	$m + n$	$m - n$	mn
even	even	?	?	?
even	odd	?	?	?
odd	even	?	?	?
odd	odd	?	?	?

Testing pairs of numbers is not enough to show that a statement is true for *all* odd or even integers. Proofs are needed.

Example 1

Prove that the sum of two even numbers is an even number.

Solution To prove this statement, we think of it as an if-then statement: If two even numbers are added, then their sum is an even number.

Let m and n be the even numbers. Then, by the definition of even number, there are integers p and q with $m = 2p$ and $n = 2q$. So $m + n = 2p + 2q$.

By the Distributive Property of Multiplication over Addition, $m + n = 2(p + q)$.

Since the sum of two integers is an integer, $p + q$ is an integer.

So $m + n$, equal to 2 times an integer, is even.

Example 1 shows that the set of even numbers is closed under addition.

Using the idea of Example 1, you can prove that the difference of two even numbers is an even number. That is, the set of even numbers is closed under subtraction. (You are asked to write a proof of this in one of the questions at the end of the lesson.) Also, the product of two even numbers is an even number.

GUIDED

Example 2

Prove that the difference of two odd numbers is an even number.

Solution Let m and n be odd numbers. Then, by the definition of odd number, there are integers p and q with $m = 2p + 1$ and $n = 2q + 1$.

So $m - n = (\underline{\ ?\ }) - (\underline{\ ?\ }) = 2p - 2q$.

Thus $m - n = 2(\underline{\ ?\ })$.

Since the difference of integers is an integer, $\underline{\ ?\ }$ is an integer.

Consequently, $m - n$ is $\underline{\ ?\ }$ times an integer, so $m - n$ is even.

You can similarly prove that the sum of two odd numbers is an even number. The set of odd integers is *not* closed under addition or subtraction.

Example 3 deals with products.

Example 3

Prove that the product of two odd numbers is an odd number.

Solution Let m and n be odd numbers. Then, by the definition of odd number, there are integers p and q with $m = 2p + 1$ and $n = 2q + 1$.

Now multiply these numbers.

$mn = (2p + 1)(2q + 1)$
$= 4pq + 2p + 2q + 1$ Extended Distributive Property
$= 2(2pq + p + q) + 1$ Distributive Property
                         (Common monomial factoring)

Since the product of two integers is an integer, $2pq$ is an integer. Since p and q are integers, the sum $2pq + p + q$ is an integer. This means that mn is 1 more than twice an integer, so mn is odd.

Divisibility by Other Numbers

A number is *divisible by 3* if and only if it can be written as $3n$, where n is an integer. Similarly, a number is *divisible by 4* if and only if it can be written as $4n$, where n is an integer. In general, a number is divisible by m if and only if it can be written as mn, where n is an integer.

Activity 2

Step 1 Let n be an odd positive integer. Fill in the table.

n	1	3	5	7	9	11	13	15	17
n^2	?	?	?	?	?	?	?	?	?
$n^2 - 1$	?	?	?	?	?	?	?	?	?

Step 2   **a.** What is the greatest common factor of the integers in the bottom row?

        b. Is this number a factor of $n^2 - 1$ for all odd integers?

You cannot answer the last question in Activity 2 by just writing down more odd integers, squaring them, and subtracting 1. You can never show by examples that the statement is true for all odd integers. A proof is needed.

Example 4

Prove that the square of an odd integer is always 1 more than a multiple of 4.

Solution First find the square of an odd integer.

(continued on next page)

Let n be an odd integer. By definition of an odd integer, there is an integer k such that $n = 2k + 1$.

$$\text{So } n^2 = (2k + 1)^2$$
$$= (2k + 1)(2k + 1)$$
$$= 4k^2 + 4k + 1$$
$$n = 4k(k + 1) + 1$$

This shows that n^2 is 1 more than a multiple of 4.

Questions

COVERING THE IDEAS

1. State the definition of *even integer.*

2. State the definition of *odd integer.*

3. Find a counterexample to show that this statement is not always true: *If two numbers are each divisible by 2, then their sum is divisible by 4.*

In 4 and 5, use Example 1 or Guided Example 2 as a guide to write a proof.

4. Prove: The difference of two even integers is an even integer.

5. **a.** Prove: The sum of two odd integers is an even integer.
   b. Is the set of odd integers closed under addition? Why or why not?

6. Use rows of dots to explain why the statement of Question 4 is true.

7. Use rows of dots to explain why the statement of Question 5 is true.

8. Prove that the set of even numbers is closed under multiplication. (*Hint:* Use Example 3 as a guide.)

APPLYING THE MATHEMATICS

In 9 and 10, complete the fact triangle. Then state the related facts.

9.
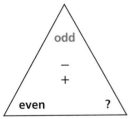

10.
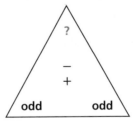

11. Prove: If a number is even, then its square is a multiple of 4.

12. Prove: If a number is divisible by 3, then its square is divisible by 9.

13. Prove: If the sum of two numbers is divisible by 35 and one of the two numbers is divisible by 70, then the other number is divisible by 35.

14. Prove or find a counterexample: If one number is divisible by 20 and a second number is divisible by 30, then their sum is divisible by 50.

15. Prove or find a counterexample: If one number is divisible by 4 and a second number is divisible by 6, then their product is divisible by 24.

REVIEW

16. Find two numbers whose sum is 562 and whose product is 74,865. (**Lesson 13-4**)

17. Find a value of b so that the quadratic expression $2x^2 - bx + 20$ is factorable over the integers. (**Lesson 12-6**)

In **18–23, solve the sentence. (Lessons 12-5, 9-5, 8-6, 4-5, 4-4, 3-4)**

18. $100x^2 + 100x - 100 = 0$

19. $x^2 - 11x + 28 = 0$

20. $\dfrac{26}{N} = \dfrac{N}{0.5}$

21. $a \cdot 11^{\frac{1}{2}} = 99^{\frac{1}{2}}$

22. $4p - 12 \le 60 - 5p$

23. $9.5 = 6x + 23.3$

24. Consider the system of equations $\begin{cases} 2x - 2y = 10 \\ -3x + 8y = -6 \end{cases}$. (**Lesson 10-8**)

    a. Write the system in matrix form.

    b. Use technology to find the inverse of the coefficient matrix.

    c. Solve the system.

25. The **semiperimeter** of a triangle is half the perimeter of the triangle. Heron's formula (also called Hero's formula) shown below can be used to calculate the area A of a triangle given the lengths of the three sides a, b, and c. (**Lesson 8-6**)

    $A = \sqrt{s(s-a)(s-b)(s-c)}$, where $s = \frac{1}{2}(a + b + c)$

    a. If the side lengths of a triangle are 15, 9, and 12 inches, calculate the semiperimeter s of the triangle.

    b. Find the area of the triangle in Part a.

Statue of Hero of Alexandria

26. If Emily reads 20 pages of a 418-page novel in 42 minutes, about how many hours will it take her to read the entire novel? (**Lesson 5-9**)

EXPLORATION

27. The numbers 1, 4, 7, 10, ..., which increase by 3, can be pictured as 3 equal rows of dots with 1 left over. These numbers are of the form $3n + 1$. The numbers 2, 5, 8, 11, ..., which increase by 3, can be pictured as 3 equal rows of dots with 2 left over. These numbers are of the form $3n + 2$.

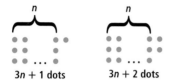

3n + 1 dots   3n + 2 dots

What happens if you add, subtract, and multiply numbers of these forms? Are the answers all of the same form? Try to prove any results you find.

28. In Activity 2, you found that, for the first 9 odd positive integers, the square of the odd number is 1 more than a multiple of 8. Prove that the result is true for all odd integers.

Lesson

13-6

From Number Puzzles to Properties of Integers

▶ **BIG IDEA**   Using algebra, you can show why divisibility tests and tricks relating to divisibility work.

In Lesson 2-3, you saw some number puzzles. In this lesson, you will see some unusual properties of divisibility that are like puzzles. Algebra shows why they work.

Activity 1

Step 1   Write down a 3-digit whole number, such as 175 or 220.

Step 2   Reverse the digits and subtract the new number from your original number.

$$\begin{array}{r} 175 \\ -\ 571 \end{array} \qquad \begin{array}{r} 220 \\ -\ 022 \end{array}$$

Step 3   Repeat Steps 1 and 2 with a few different numbers. You should find that the differences you get are always divisible by a large 2-digit number. What is that number?

Activity 2

1.   Repeat Activity 1 with a few 4-digit numbers. Does the result you got in Activity 1 work for 4-digit numbers?

2.   Does the result you got in Activity 1 work for 5-digit numbers?

Activity 3

Step 1   Write down a 3-digit whole number.

Step 2   Next to your number from Step 1 write the same 3 digits, creating a 6-digit number.

Step 3   The 6-digit number you get is always divisible by 3 different small prime numbers. What are those numbers?

Mental Math

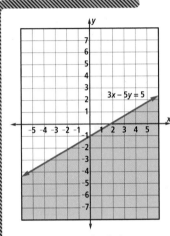

a. Describe the shaded region of the graph with an inequality.

b. Describe the unshaded region of the graph with an inequality.

Activity 4

Step 1 Write down spaces for the digits of an 8-digit number.

$$\underline{\;?\;}\;\;\underline{\;?\;}\;,\;\underline{\;?\;}\;\;\underline{\;?\;}\;\;\underline{\;?\;}\;,\;\underline{\;?\;}\;\;\underline{\;?\;}\;\;\underline{\;?\;}$$

Step 2 Choose numbers for these digits so that the sum of the 1st, 3rd, 5th, and 7th digits equals the sum of the 2nd, 4th, 6th, and 8th digits.

Step 3 Try this with a few numbers. Find a 2-digit number less than 25 that divides the 8-digit number. You may want to use the FACTOR feature of a CAS.

Activity 5

Step 1 Create a 10-digit number using each of the digits 0, 1, 2, 3, 4, 5, 6, 7, 8, and 9 once. For example, one such number is 8,627,053,914.

Step 2 Tell whether the statement is true or false.

    a. Every number created in Step 1 will be divisible by 3.

    b. Every number created in Step 1 will be divisible by 6.

    c. Every number created in Step 1 will be divisible by 9.

    d. Every number created in Step 1 will be divisible by 18.

    e. Every number created in Step 1 will be divisible by 27.

Divisibility Properties Depending on the Rightmost Digits of Numbers

You have known for a long time that in the base-10 number system the 4-digit number 5,902 is a shorthand for $5 \cdot 1{,}000 + 9 \cdot 100 + 0 \cdot 10 + 2 \cdot 1$ or, using exponents, it is a shorthand for $5 \cdot 10^3 + 9 \cdot 10^2 + 0 \cdot 10^1 + 2 \cdot 10^0$.

We say that 2 is the units digit, or the digit in the units place, 0 is the tens digit, 9 is the hundreds digit, and 5 is the thousands digit for the number 5,902. In general, if u is the units digit, t is the tens digit, h is the hundreds digit, and T is the thousands digit, then the value of the 4-digit number is

$$1{,}000T + 100h + 10t + u.$$

You can extend this idea using more variables to give the value of any integer written in base 10 in terms of its digits.

By representing the value of a number in terms of its digits, you can prove some divisibility tests that you have known for a long time. The proofs are quite similar to those used in Lesson 13-5.

Example 1

Prove that if the units digit of a number in base 10 is even, then the number is even.

Solution The proof here is for a 4-digit number N. The proof for numbers with fewer or more digits is very similar. A 4-digit number in base 10 with digits as named above has the value

$$N = 1{,}000T + 100h + 10t + u.$$

If the units digit u is even, then $u = 2k$, where k is an integer. Substituting $2k$ for u, $N = 1{,}000T + 100h + 10t + 2k.$

Notice that 2 is a common monomial factor of the polynomial on the right side. Factor out the 2.

$$N = 2(500T + 50h + 5t + k)$$

Since $500T + 50h + 5t + k$ is an integer, N is twice an integer, so it must be even.

In a similar way, you can prove divisibility tests for 4, 5, 8, and 10.

Divisibility Tests Based on the Sum of the Digits

There is a different type of divisibility test for 9: just add the digits of the number. The number is divisible by 9 if and only if the sum of its digits is divisible by 9. Proving this involves a variation of the approach taken in Example 1.

Example 2

Prove that if the sum of the digits of a 4-digit integer written in base 10 is divisible by 9, then the number is divisible by 9.

Solution Call the number N. Suppose N has digits T, h, t, and u as named above. (The same idea holds for any number of digits.)

$$N = 1{,}000T + 100h + 10t + u$$

Now separate the sum of the digits from the value of the number.

$$N = (T + h + t + u) + (999T + 99h + 9t)$$

If the sum of the digits is divisible by 9, then there is an integer k with $T + h + t + u = 9k$. Substitute $9k$ for $T + h + t + u$.

$$N = 9k + (999T + 99h + 9t)$$
$$N = 9(k + 111T + 11h + t)$$

Since $k + 111T + 11h + t$ is an integer, N is divisible by 9.

GUIDED

Example 3

Prove that if the sum of the digits of a 4-digit integer written in base 10 is divisible by 3, then the number is divisible by 3.

Solution Use Example 2 as a model for your solution.

1. Call the number N. Suppose N has digits $T, h, t,$ and u.

   $N = 1{,}000T + \underline{\ ?\ } + \underline{\ ?\ } + \underline{\ ?\ }$

2. Now separate the sum of the digits from the value of the number.

   $N = (T + h + t + u) + (\underline{\ ?\ } + \underline{\ ?\ } + \underline{\ ?\ })$

3. If the sum of the digits is divisible by 3 then there is an integer k with
   $T + h + t + u = 3k$.

4. Substitute into Step 2.

   $N = 3k + (\underline{\ ?\ } + \underline{\ ?\ } + \underline{\ ?\ })$
   $N = 3(\underline{\ \ ?\ \ })$

   Because $\underline{\ ?\ }$ is an integer, N is divisible by 3.

Reversing Digits of a Number

Consider the 3-digit number $581 = 5 \cdot 100 + 8 \cdot 10 + 1$.

Reversing the digits of this number results in the number
$185 = 1 \cdot 100 + 8 \cdot 10 + 5$.

So if a number has hundreds digit h, tens digit t, and units digit u, the number with the digits reversed has hundreds digit u, tens digit t, and units digit h. Whereas the first number has value $100h + 10t + u$, the number with its digits reversed has value $100u + 10t + h$.

Working with these numbers yields some surprising properties.

Example 4

Prove that if a 3-digit number is subtracted from the number formed by reversing its digits, then the difference is divisible by 99.

Solution Suppose the original number has the value $100h + 10t + u$.

Then the number with its digits reversed has value $100u + 10t + h$.

Subtracting the reversed number from the original yields the difference D.

$$D = 100h + 10t + u - (100u + 10t + h)$$
$$D = 100h + 10t + u - 100u - 10t - h$$
$$D = 99h - 99u$$
$$D = 99(h - u)$$

Since $h - u$ is an integer, the difference D is divisible by 99.

Questions

COVERING THE IDEAS

In 1–4, what is the value of the number?

1. The units digit of this 2-digit number is 7 and the tens digit is 5.

2. The units digit of this 2-digit number is u and the tens digit is t.

3. The thousands digit of the 4-digit number is A, the hundreds digit is B, the tens digit is C, and the units digit is D.

4. The millions digit of this 7-digit number is M, the thousands digit of this number is T, the units digit is 3, and all other digits are 0.

5. A 4-digit number has thousands digit T, hundreds digit h, tens digit t, and units digit u.
   a. What is the value of the number?
   b. What is the value of the number with its digits reversed?

6. Use Example 1 as a guide to prove: If the units digit of a 4-digit number in base 10 is 5, then the number is divisible by 5.

7. The proof in Example 2 is given for a 4-digit number. Adapt this proof for a 5-digit number, letting D be the ten-thousands digit.

8. **Fill in the Blanks** A number is divisible by 3 if and only if it can be written as __?__, where __?__ is an integer.

In 9–12, an integer is given.
   a. Tell whether the integer is divisible by 2 and state a reason why.
   b. Tell whether the integer is divisible by 5 and state a reason why.
   c. Tell whether the integer is divisible by 9 and state a reason why.

9. 259,259,259

10. 225

11. 522

12. $522 - 225$

APPLYING THE MATHEMATICS

13. **a.** Find a counterexample: If a 4-digit number is subtracted from the number formed by reversing its digits, then the difference is divisible by 99.

    b. Prove: If a 4-digit number is subtracted from the number formed by reversing its digits, then the difference is divisible by 9.

14. **a.** Give an example of this statement and then prove it: If the units digit of a 5-digit number is 5 and the tens digit is 2, then the number is divisible by 25.

    b. Is the converse of the statement in Part a true?

15. In a certain 6-digit number, the hundred-thousands and hundreds digits are equal, the ten-thousands and tens digits are equal, and the thousands and units digits are equal. Prove that this number is divisible by 13.

16. The number $46x3$, written in base 10, is divisible by 9. What is the value of x?

17. The tens digit of a 3-digit number is 4 times the hundreds digit and the number is divisible by 19. Find the number.

REVIEW

In 18 and 19, a statement is given. Prove the statement to show that it is true or provide a counterexample to show that it is false. (Lesson 13-5)

18. If a number is divisible by 5, then its square is divisible by 25.

19. If one number is divisible by 3, and a second number is divisible by 4, then the product of the two numbers is divisible by 7.

20. Give an example of an if-then statement that is false but whose converse is true. (Lessons 13-2, 13-1)

21. The triangle below has an area of 45 square inches. Find the height h of the triangle if the base is $2h + 8$ inches. (Lesson 12-4)

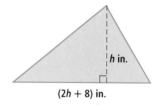

h in.

$(2h + 8)$ in.

22. A rectangular box has dimensions a, $a + 3$, and $2a + 1$.
    (**Lessons 11-5, 11-2**)

    a. Find a polynomial expression in standard form for the volume of the box.

    b. What is the degree of the polynomial in Part a?

23. Consider the quadratic equation $4m^2 - 20m + 25 = 0$. (**Lesson 9-6**)

    a. Find the value of the discriminant.

    b. Use your answer to Part a to determine the number of real solutions to the equation.

In 24–26, solve the sentence. (Lessons 8-6, 5-9, 4-5)

24. $\sqrt{m - 10} = 3$ 25. $5y - 2 > y$ 26. $\dfrac{w + 27}{9} = \dfrac{w}{3}$

27. What is the value of x in the equation $\dfrac{(h^5)^{10} \cdot h^{15}}{h^{20}} = h^x$?
    (**Lessons 8-4, 8-3, 8-2**)

EXPLORATION

28. Let h, t, and u be the hundreds, tens, and units digits of a 3-digit number in base 10.

    a. Find values of h, t, and u so that $hx^2 + tx + u$ is factorable over the integers.

    b. For your values of h, t, and u, is it true that $100h + 10t + u$ is factorable over the integers?

    c. **True or False** If h, t, and u are digits, and $hx^2 + tx + u$ is factorable over the set of polynomial with integer coefficients, then $100h + 10t + u$ is factorable over the integers.

    d. Explore this statement to decide whether it is true or false: If h, t, and u are digits, and $100h + 10t + u$ is a prime number, then $hx^2 + tx + u$ is a prime polynomial over the integers.

Lesson

13-7

Rational Numbers and Irrational Numbers

Vocabulary

irrational number

▶ **BIG IDEA**   The Distributive Property enables you to prove that repeating decimals represent rational numbers, and divisibility properties enable you to prove square roots of certain integers are irrational.

A number that can be represented by a decimal is a real number. All the real numbers are either rational or irrational. In this lesson, you will see how we know that some numbers are not rational numbers.

What Are Rational Numbers?

Recall that a *simple fraction* is a fraction with integers in its numerator and denominator. For example, $\frac{2}{3}, \frac{5,488}{212}, \frac{10}{5}, \frac{-7}{-2}$, and $\frac{-43}{1}$ are simple fractions.

Some numbers are not simple fractions, but are *equal* to simple fractions. Any mixed number equals a simple fraction. For example, $3\frac{2}{7} = \frac{23}{7}$. Also, any integer equals a simple fraction. For example, $-10 = \frac{-10}{1}$. And any finite decimal equals a simple fraction. For example, $3.078 = 3\frac{78}{1,000} = \frac{3,078}{1,000}$. All these numbers are *rational numbers*. A *rational number* is a number that can be expressed as a simple fraction.

All repeating decimals are also rational numbers. The Example below shows how to find a simple fraction that equals a given repeating decimal.

Mental Math

A school enrolled 120 freshmen, 110 sophomores, 125 juniors, and 100 seniors. What is the probability that

a. a student at the school is a sophomore?

b. a student at the school is a junior or senior?

c. a student is not a junior?

Example

Show that $18.4\overline{23}$ is a rational number.

Solution   Let $x = 18.4\overline{23}$. Multiply both sides by 10^n, where n is the number of digits in the repetend $\overline{23}$. Here there are two digits in the repetend $\overline{23}$, so we multiply by 10^2, or 100.

$$x = 18.4\overline{23}$$
$$100x = 1,842.3\overline{23}$$

Subtract the top equation from the bottom equation. The key idea here is that the result is no longer an infinite repeating decimal; in this case, after the first decimal place the repeating parts subtract to zero.

$$100x = 1{,}842.3\overline{23}$$
$$-\ x = \qquad 18.4\overline{23}$$
$$99x = 1{,}823.900$$

Divide both sides by 99.

$$x = \frac{1{,}823.9}{99} = \frac{18{,}239}{990}$$

Since $x = \dfrac{18{,}239}{990}$, x is a rational number.

STOP QY1

Rational numbers have interesting properties. They can be added, subtracted, multiplied, and divided; and they give answers that are also rational numbers.

▶ **QY1**

a. Divide 18,239 by 990 to check the result of the Example.

b. Write $4.\overline{123}$ as a simple fraction.

What Are Irrational Numbers?

The ancient Greeks seem to have been the first to discover that there are numbers that are not rational numbers. They called them *irrational*. An **irrational number** is a real number that is not a rational number. Some of the most commonly found irrational numbers in mathematics are the square roots of integers that are not perfect squares. That is, numbers like $\sqrt{2}, \sqrt{3}, \sqrt{5}, \sqrt{6}, \sqrt{7}, \sqrt{8}, \sqrt{10}$, and so on, are irrational. But notice that $\sqrt{4}$ is rational not irrational, because $\sqrt{4} = 2 = \frac{2}{1}$. All these numbers can arise from situations involving right triangles. Examine the array of right triangles shown below.

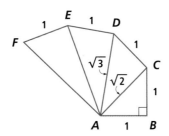

$\triangle ABC$ is a right triangle with legs of 1 and 1. Use the Pythagorean Theorem to find the side lengths AC and AD.

$$AC^2 = AB^2 + BC^2$$
$$AC^2 = 1 + 1$$
$$AC^2 = 2$$
$$AC = \sqrt{2}$$

Rational Numbers and Irrational Numbers   **817**

$\triangle ACD$ is drawn with leg $\overline{AC}$, and another leg $CD = 1$. Use the Pythagorean Theorem.

$$AD^2 = AC^2 + CD^2$$
$$AD^2 = \left(\sqrt{2}\right)^2 + 1^2$$
$$AD^2 = 2 + 1$$
$$AD^2 = 3$$
$$AD = \sqrt{3}$$

 QY2

▶ **QY2**

Find *AE* and *AF* in the figure on the previous page.

How Do We Know That Certain Numbers Are Irrational?

If you evaluate $\sqrt{2}$ on a calculator, you will see a decimal approximation. One calculator shows 1.414213562. Another shows 1.41421356237. No matter how many decimal places the calculator shows, it is not enough to show the entire decimal because the decimal for $\sqrt{2}$ is infinite and does not repeat.

Is it possible the decimal could repeat after 1,000 decimal places, or after 1 million or 1 billion decimal places? How do we know that the decimal does not repeat? The answer is that we can *prove* the decimal does not repeat, because we can prove that $\sqrt{2}$ is not a rational number. The proof uses some of the ideas of divisibility you have seen in Lessons 13-5 and 13-6. In particular, we use the fact that if a number is even, then its square is divisible by 4. The idea of the proof is to show that there is no simple fraction in lowest terms equal to $\sqrt{2}$.

Here is the proof: Suppose $\sqrt{2}$ is rational. Then there would be two whole numbers a and b with $\sqrt{2} = \frac{a}{b}$ (with the fraction in lowest terms). Then, multiply each side of this equality by itself.

$\sqrt{2} \cdot \sqrt{2} = \frac{a}{b} \cdot \frac{a}{b}$ Multiplication Property of Equality

$2 = \frac{a^2}{b^2}$ Definition of square root; Multiplication of Fractions

$2b^2 = a^2$ Multiply both sides by b^2.

So if you could find two numbers a and b with twice the square of b equal to the square of a, then $\sqrt{2}$ would be a rational number. (You can come close. 7^2 or 49 is one less than twice 5^2 or 25.)

Notice that since a^2 would be twice an integer, a^2 would be even. This means that a would be even (because the square of an odd number is odd). Because a would be even, there would be an integer m with $a = 2m$. This means that $a^2 = (2m)^2 = 4m^2$. Substitute in the bottom equation.

$$2b^2 = 4m^2 \quad \text{Substitute } 4m^2 \text{ for } a^2.$$
$$b^2 = 2m^2 \quad \text{Divide both sides by 2.}$$

Now we repeat the argument used above. Because b^2 would be twice an integer, b^2 would be even. This means that b would have to be even. And because a and b would both be even, the fraction $\frac{a}{b}$ could not be in lowest terms. This shows that what we supposed at the beginning of this proof is not true.

For this reason, it is impossible to find two whole numbers a and b with $\sqrt{2} = \frac{a}{b}$ and with the fraction in lowest terms. Since any simple fraction can be put in lowest terms, it is impossible to find any two whole numbers a and b with $\sqrt{2} = \frac{a}{b}$.

Arguments like this one can be used to prove the following theorem.

> ### Irrationality of $\sqrt{n}$ Theorem
>
> If n is an integer that is not a perfect square, then $\sqrt{n}$ is irrational.

Johann Lambert

Today, we now know that there are many irrational numbers. For example, every number that has a decimal expansion that does not end or repeat is irrational. Among the irrational numbers is the famous number π. But the argument to show that π is irrational is far more difficult than the argument used above for some square roots of integers. It requires advanced mathematics, and was first done by the German mathematician Johann Lambert in 1767, more than 2,000 years after the Greeks had first discovered that some numbers were irrational.

There is a practical reason for knowing whether a number is rational or irrational. When a number is rational, arithmetic can be done with it rather easily because it can be represented as a simple fraction. Just work as you do with fractions. But if a number is irrational, then it is generally more difficult to do arithmetic with it. Rather than use its infinite decimal, we often leave it alone and just write π or $\sqrt{3}$, for example.

Questions

COVERING THE IDEAS

In 1–3, find an example of each.

1. a simple fraction

2. a fraction that is not a simple fraction

3. a rational number

In 4–6, write the number as a simple fraction.

4. 98.6 5. $0.\overline{84}$ 6. $14.0\overline{327}$

7. **Multiple Choice** Which *cannot* stand for a rational number?

    A a terminating decimal

    B a simple fraction

    C a repeating decimal

    D an infinite nonrepeating decimal

8. Refer to the proof that $\sqrt{2}$ is irrational.

    a. If $\sqrt{2}$ were rational, what would $\sqrt{2}$ have to equal?

    b. **True or False** If the square of an integer is even, then the integer is even.

    c. **True or False** If an integer is divisible by 2, then its square is divisible by 4.

    d. In the proof, what characteristic of both a and b shows that the fraction $\frac{a}{b}$ is not in lowest terms?

In 9–11, tell whether the number is a rational or an irrational number.

9. π 10. -220 11. $\sqrt{121}$

12. Draw a segment whose length is $\sqrt{5}$ units.

13. Draw a square whose diagonal has length $\sqrt{338}$ cm.

APPLYING THE MATHEMATICS

14. Is 0 a rational number? Why or why not?

15. Is it possible for two irrational numbers to have a sum that is a rational number? Explain why or why not.

16. Using the proof in this lesson as a guide, prove that $\sqrt{3}$ is irrational.

17. **a.** Draw a segment whose length is $1 + \sqrt{3}$ units.

    b. Is $1 + \sqrt{3}$ rational or irrational?

18. If a circular table has a diameter of 4 cm, is its circumference rational or irrational?

19. A diagonal of a square has a length of 42 cm. Find the perimeter of the square. Is the perimeter rational or irrational?

20. Determine whether the solutions to the equation $x^2 - 8x - 1 = 0$ are rational or irrational.

21. Refer to the right triangle at the right.

    a. Find the exact value of a.

    b. Is a rational or irrational?

REVIEW

In 22–25, consider the spreadsheet below, which was used to compute the value of $f(x) = 3x^3 + 5x^2 - 2x$ for integer values of x from −5 to 5. (Lessons 12-7, 12-6, 11-4)

22. Complete the spreadsheet.

23. Graph the function f for $-5 \leq x \leq 5$.

24. Identify all x-intercepts.

25. Rewrite the equation in factored form.

◇	A	B
1	x	f(x)
2	-5	
3	-4	-104
4	-3	
5	-2	
6	-1	4
7	0	0
8	1	
9	2	40
10	3	120
11	4	
12	5	490

26. Solve $x^3 - 10x^2 + 16x = 0$. (Lessons 12-6, 12-5, 11-4)

27. Suppose $20x^2 + 9xy - 20y^2 = (ax + b)(cx + d)$. (Lesson 12-5)
    a. Find the value of $ad + bc$.
    b. Find b, c, and d if $a = 5$.

28. Find two numbers whose sum is 30 and whose product is 176. (Lessons 12-4, 11-6, 10-2)

29. Expand the expression $\left(\sqrt{25} - \sqrt{x^2}\right)\left(\sqrt{25} + \sqrt{x^2}\right)$.
    (Lessons 11-6, 8-6)

30. Calculate the area of the shaded region. (Lesson 11-3)

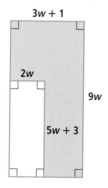

3w + 1

2w

9w

5w + 3

31. With a stopwatch and a stone, you can estimate the depth of a well. If the stone takes 2.1 seconds to reach the bottom, how deep is the well? Use Galileo's equation, $d = 16t^2$. (Lesson 9-1)

Dug wells typically used for drinking water are 10 to 30 feet deep.

Source: U.S. Environmental Protection Agency

EXPLORATION

32. Because $2 \cdot 5^2$ is one away from 7^2, 2 is close to $\frac{7^2}{5^2}$. That means that $\sqrt{2}$ is close to $\frac{7}{5}$, or 1.4. Find two other numbers c and d such that $2 \cdot c^2$ is one away from d^2. (*Hint:* There is a pair of such numbers with both of them greater than 2 less than 20.) What rational number estimate does that pair give for $\sqrt{2}$?

33. Shown here is a different way to draw a segment with length $\sqrt{n}$ from the one given in the lesson.

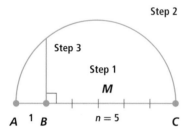

Step 1 Draw a segment $\overline{AB}$ with length 1, and then next to it, a segment BC with length n. (In the drawing here, $n = 5$.)

Step 2 Find the midpoint M of segment $\overline{AC}$. Draw the circle with center M that contains A and C. ($\overline{AC}$ will be a diameter of this circle.)

Step 3 Draw a segment perpendicular to $\overline{AC}$ from B to the circle. This segment has length $\sqrt{n}$. (In our drawing it should have length $\sqrt{5}$.)

   a. Try this algorithm to draw a segment with length $\sqrt{7}$.
   b. Measure the segment you find.
   c. How close is its length to $\sqrt{7}$?

Lesson 13-8

Proofs of the Pythagorean Theorem

▶ **BIG IDEA** There are many ways to deduce the Pythagorean Theorem using algebra.

In this book you have seen how areas of rectangles can picture various forms of the Distributive Property. The idea is to calculate the area of a figure in two different ways. Here is a picture of $(a + b)(c + d + e) = ac + ad + ae + bc + bd + be$.

Mental Math

Tell whether the three numbers can be lengths of sides in a triangle.

a. 5, 13, 5

b. 2, 14, 15

c. 1, 2, 3

	c	d	e
a	ac	ad	ae
b	bc	bd	be

You could also say that this reasoning uses area to prove that $(a + b)(c + d + e) = ac + ad + ae + bc + bd + be$.

We close this book by showing how areas of figures provide proofs of the most famous theorem in geometry, the Pythagorean Theorem. If a and b are the lengths of the legs of a right triangle, and c is the length of its hypotenuse, then $a^2 + b^2 = c^2$.

For these proofs, you need to think of a^2, b^2, and c^2 as the areas of squares whose sides are a, b, and c. This is the form in which the theorem was discovered over 2,500 years ago in many different parts of the world.

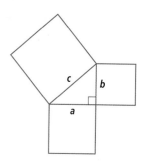

These proofs assume that you are familiar with the definitions and area formulas for some common figures. They are:

square: $A = s^2$ rectangle: $A = \ell w$

right triangle: $A = \frac{1}{2}ab$ triangle: $A = \frac{1}{2}bh$

trapezoid: $A = \frac{1}{2}h(b_1 + b_2)$

The proofs also use the properties of real numbers that you have seen in this course.

Bhaskara's Proof

Bhaskara's proof is a generalization of the idea that you saw in Lesson 8-6. Begin with right triangle DHK with side lengths a, b, and c. Make three copies of the triangle and place them so that quadrilateral $DEFG$ is a square, as shown at the right. In $\triangle DHK$, $\angle DHK$ and $\angle DKH$ are complementary. Since corresponding parts of congruent triangles are congruent, $m\angle GKJ = m\angle DHK$. So $m\angle DKH + m\angle GKJ = 90°$. Thus, $m\angle JKH = 180° - 90° = 90°$. Likewise the other three angles of $HIJK$ are right angles. So, the inside quadrilateral $HIJK$ formed by the four hypotenuses has four right angles and four sides of length c, so it is also a square.

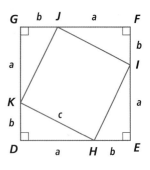

Let A be the area of quadrilateral $DEFG$. Each side of quadrilateral $DEFG$ has length $a + b$. So $A = (a + b)^2$. But the area of $DEFG$ can also be found by adding up the areas of the four right triangles $\left(4 \cdot \frac{1}{2}ab\right)$ and the square in the middle (c^2). So $A = 4 \cdot \frac{1}{2}ab + c^2$.

The two values of A must be equal.

$$(a + b)^2 = 4 \cdot \frac{1}{2}ab + c^2$$

Now use the formula for the square of a binomial on the left side and simplify the right side.

$$a^2 + 2ab + b^2 = 2ab + c^2$$

Add $-2ab$ to each side of the equation.

$$a^2 + b^2 = c^2$$

This is the Pythagorean Theorem.

President Garfield's Proof

This proof of the Pythagorean Theorem was discovered by James Garfield in 1876 while he was a member of the U.S. House of Representatives. Five years later he became the 20th President of the United States.

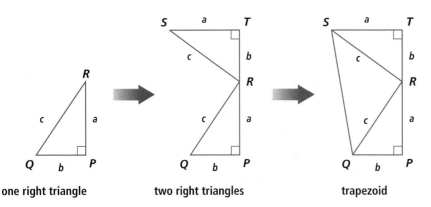

one right triangle   two right triangles   trapezoid

Major General James Garfield won the 1880 Presidential election by only 10,000 popular votes, defeating Gen. Winfield Scott Hancock.

Source: The White House

President Garfield's proof uses half the figure of the preceding proof. Begin with right triangle *PQR* as shown on the previous page. With one copy of △*PQR*, create a trapezoid *PQST* with bases *a* and *b* and height *a* + *b*. The area of any trapezoid is $\frac{1}{2}h(b_1 + b_2)$. Here the height *h* = *a* + *b*.

$$\text{Area of } PQST = \tfrac{1}{2}(a + b)(a + b)$$

But the area of *PQST* is also the sum of the areas of three right triangles: *PQR*, *RST*, and *QRS*. Look at △*QRS*. Because the sum of the measures of the angles of a triangle is 180°, m∠*QRP* + m∠*RQP* = 90°. Consequently, m∠*QRP* + m∠*SRT* = 90°. This means that ∠*QRS* is a right angle and so △*QRS* is a right triangle. Now add the areas of the three right triangles.

$$\text{Area of } PQST = \tfrac{1}{2}ab + \tfrac{1}{2}ab + \tfrac{1}{2}c^2$$

The area of the entire trapezoid must be the same regardless of how it is calculated.

$$\tfrac{1}{2}(a + b)(a + b) = \tfrac{1}{2}ab + \tfrac{1}{2}ab + \tfrac{1}{2}c^2.$$

Now multiply both sides of the equation by 2.

$$(a + b)(a + b) = ab + ab + c^2$$

Multiply the binomials on the left side and collect terms on the right side.

$$a^2 + 2ab + b^2 = 2ab + c^2$$

Subtract 2*ab* from each side of the equation and the result is the Pythagorean Theorem.

$$a^2 + b^2 = c^2$$

Other Proofs

It takes only one valid proof of a theorem to make it true. Yet in mathematics you will often see more than one proof of a statement, just as you often see more than one way to solve a problem. Alternate methods can help you to understand better how the various parts of mathematics are related. In this lesson, you have seen how areas of triangles, trapezoids, and squares are put together with binomials to prove a statement about the lengths of the three sides of any right triangle. In your next course, likely to be more concerned with geometry than this one, you will see how this theorem is related to similar triangles. Later you will learn how important this theorem is in the study of trigonometry. The algebra you have learned this year is fundamental in these and every other area of mathematics.

Questions

COVERING THE IDEAS

1. Picture the property that for all positive numbers a, b, and c,
   $a(b + c) = ab + ac$.

2. Picture the property that for all positive numbers a and b,
   $a(a + b) = a^2 + ab$.

In 3 and 4, refer to Bhaskara's proof of the Pythagorean Theorem.

3. **a.** Draw the figure of Bhaskara's proof when $a = 6$ and $b = 2$.
   b. What is the area of $DEFG$?
   c. Explain how to get the area of $HIJK$.
   d. What is the value of c?

4. $DH = a$ and $DK = b$ in the figure of Bhaskara's proof.
   a. What is the length of EF?
   b. What is the area of $EFGD$?
   c. What is the area of triangle IJF?
   d. What is the area of $HIJK$?
   e. What is the length of HK in terms of a and b?

5. **a.** Draw a trapezoid whose bases have lengths 1 in. and 2 in., and whose height is 1 in.
   b. What is the area of this trapezoid?

6. Draw a trapezoid with bases b_1 and b_2 and height h. Explain why the area of this trapezoid is $\frac{1}{2}hb_1 + \frac{1}{2}hb_2$.

7. Refer to President Garfield's proof of the Pythagorean Theorem. Let $a = 28$ and $b = 45$.
   a. Find the area of trapezoid $PQST$.
   b. Explain how to get the area of $\triangle RQS$.
   c. What is the value of c?
   d. Does the value of c agree with what you would get using the Pythagorean Theorem?

APPLYING THE MATHEMATICS

8. **a.** Find two expressions for the shaded region in the figure below.
   b. What property is illustrated by the answer to Part a?

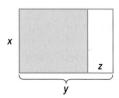

9. The square below has been split into two smaller squares and two rectangles. What property is pictured?

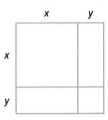

10. Quadrilateral *MNQP* at the right has perpendicular diagonals. Add the areas of the four triangles to show that the area of *MNQP* is one-half the product of the lengths of its diagonals.

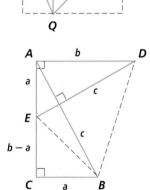

11. A proof of the Pythagorean Theorem published by W.J. Dobbs in 1916 uses the figure at the right. $\triangle ACB$ and $\triangle DAE$ are right triangles, and $AC = b$, $BC = a$, and $AB = c$. Complete each step to show the proof.

  a. What is the length of $\overline{EB}$ in terms of a and b?

  b. Find the area of $\triangle EBC$.

  c. Find the area of *AEBD,* a quadrilateral with perpendicular diagonals, using the formula from Question 10.

  d. Add the areas in Parts b and c to find an expression for the area of *ACBD.*

  e. Use the formula for the area of a trapezoid to express the area of *ACBD.*

  f. Set the formulas from Parts d and e equal to each other to show that $c^2 = a^2 + b^2$.

REVIEW

12. Prove that if the last three digits of a 4-digit number form a number divisible by 8, then the entire number is divisible by 8. (**Lesson 13-6**)

13. **Multiple Choice** Consider the following statement. If the cost of 5 pounds of ice is $2.15, then at the same rate, the cost of 32 ounces of ice is 86 cents. (**Lessons 13-2, 13-1, 5-9**)

  A The statement and its converse are both true.

  B The statement and its converse are both false.

  C The statement is true but its converse is false.

  D The statement is false but its converse is true.

14. a. Find a value of c to complete the square for $4x^2 - 12x + c$.

  b. Use your answer to Part a to solve the equation
  $4x^2 - 2x = -9 + 10x$. (**Lessons 12-3, 12-2**)

15. Leonardo and Miranda are at an amusement park and are trying to decide in which order they want to ride the 9 roller coasters in the park. **(Lesson 11-7)**

   a. How many different orders can they ride all 9 roller coasters if they ride each coaster one time?

   b. If they only have time to ride six of the roller coasters, how many ways can they do this?

16. Consider the following number puzzle. **(Lessons 8-6, 2-3)**

   Step 1 Choose any whole number.

   Step 2 Square that number.

   Step 3 Add 4 times your original number.

   Step 4 Add 4 to the result of Step 3.

   Step 5 Take the square root of the result of Step 4.

   Step 6 Subtract your original number.

   a. Follow the number puzzle with any whole number. What is your result?

   b. Let x represent the number chosen. Write a simplified expression to represent each step of the puzzle and to show why your result will always be what you found in Part a.

17. A piece of landscaping machinery is valued at $15,000. If the machinery depreciates at a constant rate of 8% per year, what will be its value in 6 years? **(Lesson 7-3)**

Out of the 710 roller coasters in North America, 628 are in the United States.

Source: Roller Coaster Database

EXPLORATION

18. A different kind of proof of the Pythagorean Theorem is called a *dissection proof.* Dissection means cutting the squares on the legs of the right triangle shown on page 823 into pieces and then rearranging these pieces together to fill up the square on the hypotenuse. Find such a proof in a book or on the Internet and explain why it works.

Chapter 13 Projects

1 Squares Surrounding Triangles

Step 1 On a piece of grid paper, draw ten squares of different sizes. (*Note:* They don't *all* have to be different from one another.) Then, carefully cut them out.

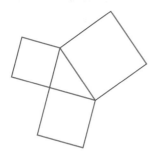

Step 2

a. Lay three of the squares on the table to form a triangle, as shown above. Refer to the longest side as *c* and the shorter sides as *a* and *b*.

b. Add the areas of the two smaller squares, and write down the sum. Is the sum $(a^2 + b^2)$ equal to the area of the largest square (c^2)? If not, is the sum greater or less?

c. Use a protractor to measure the angle across from the longest side of the triangle. Does it have the largest measure? Is it a right angle? If not, is it acute or obtuse?

Step 3 Repeat this procedure for at least ten different triangles. Record your information in a table, and look for any patterns in the data.

Step 4 Write a brief report about what you have learned about triangles, their largest angles, and the lengths of their sides.

2 Can Everything Be Proved?

At the beginning of the 20th century, a widespread belief among mathematicians was that any mathematical statement could either be proved, if it were true, or disproved, if it were false. But nobody knew for certain if this were true or not. In 1931, the mathematician Kurt Gödel settled the issue with his Incompleteness Theorems. Research to find out what Gödel discovered and how it impacted the world of mathematics.

3 Divisibility Tests

In this chapter, you saw several divisibility rules. These were just the tip of the iceberg. There are a great many known divisibility rules.

a. Find properties to check if a number is divisible by 4, by 8, by 25, and by 125. Explain how these rules work.

b. Look up a rule that can check if a number is divisible by 7, and one that can be used to check if a number is divisible by 11. Show why these methods work.

4 Conjectures

A mathematical statement may be easy to write down and understand yet still be very difficult to prove. A statement that a mathematician believes to be true but is not yet proved is called a *conjecture* or a *hypothesis*. Sometimes conjectures remain unproved for many years. One of the most famous problems in mathematics is Fermat's Last Theorem. Research to learn about Fermat and his famous theorem, and about Andrew Wiles, the man who finally proved it. Finally, find at least two conjectures in mathematics that are still unproved today.

5 If-Then Statements in Games

When solving problems in life, you use many if-then statements.

a. Start with a single Sudoku puzzle. Write the first 5 if-then statements you can use to solve it. Estimate how many if-then statements it would take for you to solve the whole puzzle.

b. In 1997, the IBM supercomputer Deep Blue won 1 out of 3 matches against world Chess champion Garry Kasparov (above at the right). Find out how many different possible chess moves Deep Blue could consider each second. Given this number, how do you think that Kasparov was able to win 2 out of the 3 matches?

6 The Euclidean Algorithm

Given two positive integers m and n, the greatest common divisor of m and n is the greatest integer that divides both of them. For example, the greatest common divisor of 8 and 12 is 4; the greatest common divisor of 12 and 15 is 3. The ancient Greek mathematicians knew an algorithm, today called the Euclidean algorithm, to find the greatest common divisor of two numbers. Look up the Euclidean algorithm and write a description of how it works.

7 Rationals vs. Irrationals

When they were first discovered, irrational numbers were an oddity. As you saw in this chapter, there are many irrational numbers. One natural question to ask is which kind of number is more common: rational or irrational? Together with a friend, prepare a debate about this question. One side should present the position that rational numbers are more common and the other side should present that irrational numbers are more common. You may use any material you can find on the subject. Be sure to include a discussion about what you mean by "more common." Present your debate before the class.

Chapter 13 Summary and Vocabulary

○ Generalizations in mathematics include **assumptions** (assumed properties), **definitions** (meanings of terms or phrases), and **theorems** (statements deduced from assumptions, definitions, or other theorems). These generalizations are often presented as **if-then statements.** For example, one assumed property of real numbers is the Distributive Property of Multiplication over Addition. It can be written in if-then form as: If a, b, and c are real numbers, then $a(b + c) = ab + ac$.

○ The **converse** of the statement, "If a, then b" is the statement, "If b, then a." The converse of a true statement is not necessarily true. When the converse is true, then the statement "a if and only if b" is true. Definitions are **if-and-only-if statements.** For example, x is an even number if and only if x can be written as $2n$, where n is an integer.

○ By putting together if-then statements of assumptions and definitions, a **mathematical proof** can be created. From the definition of even number, you can prove that if the square of an integer is even, then the integer is even. You can also prove that $\sqrt{2}$ and square roots of other nonzero integers that are not perfect squares are **irrational numbers.** Using the definition of divisibility by any number and what it means for a number to be in base 10, you can prove divisibility tests and other interesting properties of numbers.

○ Every equation or inequality that you solve showing steps and justifications can be thought of as a **proof.** Suppose you solve $8x + 50 = 2$ and obtain $x = -6$. If you can justify the steps that you used in your solution, you have proved: "If $8x + 50 = 2$, then $x = -6$." The check is the converse: "If $x = -6$, then $8x + 50 = 2$."

○ Mathematical knowledge grows by deducing statements from those that are assumed to be true or have been proved earlier to be true. Among the oldest and most important theorems in all of mathematics are the **Quadratic Formula** and the **Pythagorean Theorem.** Proofs of the Quadratic Formula use the properties that are most associated with solving equations. The proofs of the Pythagorean Theorem that we show in this chapter use area formulas for triangles, squares, and trapezoids.

Vocabulary

13-1
if-then statement
antecedent
consequent
generalization

13-2
converse
equivalent statements
if and only if

13-3
justifications
proof argument
deduction

13-5
closed under an operation
even integer, even number
odd integer, odd number
semiperimeter

13-7
irrational number

Theorems and Properties

Irrationality of $\sqrt{n}$
Theorem (p. 819)

Chapter

13 Self-Test

Take this test as you would take a test in class. You will need a calculator. Then use the Selected Answers section in the back of the book to check your work.

1. State conclusions and justifications to prove that if $8(2y - 1) = y + 37$, then $y = 3$.

2. Determine the antecedent and consequent of the statement proved in Question 1.

3. Amalia says that xy equals 0 if and only if both x and y equal 0.

   a. Write the two if-then statements that are equivalent to Amalia's if-and-only-if statement.

   b. Is Amalia correct? Explain your answer.

4. Marcus is measuring the diagonal across a piece of paper. The paper is 7 in. by 8 in.

   a. What is the exact length of a diagonal of the paper?

   b. Explain why Marcus' ruler will not give him an exact measurement of the diagonal.

5. Consider the following statement: All algebra students can solve quadratic equations.

   a. Write the statement in if-then form.

   b. Identify the antecedent and consequent for Part a.

   c. Write the converse of the statement you wrote in Part a.

   d. Decide whether the statement you wrote in Part c is true. Explain your answer.

6. Prove or find a counterexample to the statement: If the tens digit of a 4-digit number is 4 and the units digit is 8, then the number is divisible by 4.

7. What algebraic relationship is pictured by the rectangles, given that $b < a$?

8. The product of two numbers is 717, and their sum is –242. What are the numbers?

9a. Find the value of x in the diagram at the right.

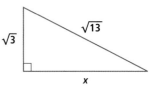

   b. Is x rational or irrational?

10. **True or False** Determine whether each of the following is true or false. Explain your answers.

   a. If a triangle is formed by cutting a square in half along one of its diagonals, then the triangle is isosceles.

   b. If a triangle is formed by cutting a square in half along one of its diagonals, then the triangle is equilateral.

11. **True or False** Determine whether the following statement is true or false and explain your answer: A person can be President of the United States if and only if he or she was born in the United States.

12. If a number is divisible by 3 and another number is divisible by 4, then their product is divisible by 12. Illustrate this statement with a picture and explain why your picture shows that the statement is true.

Chapter 13 Chapter Review

SKILLS Procedures used to get answers

OBJECTIVE A Show and justify the steps in solving an equation. (Lesson 13-3)

In 1 and 2, fill in the table for the proof.

1.

Conclusions	What Was Done	Justifications
$4x + 5 = 17$	?	?
$4x + 5 + -5 = 17 + -5$	?	?
$4x + 0 = 12$	?	?
$4x = 12$	?	?
$\frac{1}{4} \cdot 4x = 12 \cdot \frac{1}{4}$	?	?
$1 \cdot x = 3$	?	?
$x = 3$	?	?

2.

Conclusions	What Was Done	Justifications
$2n + 5 = 4n + 3$	?	?
$2n + 2 = 4n$	?	?
$2 = 2n$	?	?
$1 = n$	?	?

3. Prove: If $3t - 15 = 4t + 2$, then $t = -17$.

4. Prove: $\sqrt{16y - 16} = 2y$ if and only if $y = 2$.

OBJECTIVE B Find two numbers given their sum and product. (Lesson 13-4)

5. There are 26 students in a dancing class. If you know there are 165 possible boy-girl couples from this group, how many boys and how many girls are in the class?

In 6–9 find the two numbers that satisfy the given conditions.

6. $n + m = 10$, $nm = 24$

7. $xy = 2.3$, $x + y = 5.6$

8. $uv = 35$, $u + v = 12$

9. $p + q = -46$, $pq = 529$

10. Mrs. Violet doesn't know the dimensions of her rectangular garden, but she knows it has an area of 23.52 square meters. She also remembers that she needs 19.6 meters of fencing for her garden. Find the dimensions of Mrs. Violet's garden.

PROPERTIES The principles behind the mathematics

OBJECTIVE C Identify the antecedent and consequent of an if-then statement not necessarily given in if-then form. (Lesson 13-1)

In 11–14 identify the antecedent and the consequent.

11. If an animal has feathers then it is a bird.

12. It is spring if the trees are blooming.

13. No irrational number can be represented as the ratio of two integers.

14. James doesn't listen to music when he studies.

OBJECTIVE D Determine whether if-then and if-and-only-if statements in algebra or geometry are true or false. (Lessons 13-1, 13-2)

In 15–18, is the statement true or false?

15. A number is divisible by 3 if it is divisible by 9.

16. If $x = 7$ or $x = 3$, then $x^2 + 10x + 21 = 0$.

17. A triangle is equilateral if and only if two of its sides are equal and it has one 60° angle.

18. If only two outcomes are possible and they are equally likely, then the probability of each is 50%.

OBJECTIVE E Prove divisibility properties of integers. (Lessons 13-5, 13-6)

19. Prove that a 3-digit number abc is divisible by 7 only if the number $2a + 3b + c$ is divisible by 7.

20. Show that if n is even then n^3 is divisible by 8.

21. Show that all 6-digit integers of the form $xyzxyz$ are divisible by 13.

22. Show that if the 4-digit number $abcd$ written in base 10 is divisible by 11, then $b + d - (a + c)$ is divisible by 11.

OBJECTIVE F Apply the definitions and properties of rational and irrational numbers. (Lesson 13-7)

In 23–26, tell whether the number is rational or irrational.

23. $\sqrt{6}$ 24. $0.\overline{142857}$

25. $\sqrt{169}$ 26. $2\pi - 3$

27. Is it possible for two irrational numbers to have a product that is rational? Explain why or why not.

28. Is it possible for two rational numbers to have a product that is irrational? Explain why or why not.

USES Applications of mathematics in real-world situations

OBJECTIVE G Determine whether if-then and if-and-only-if statements in real-world contexts are true or false. (Lessons 13-1, 13-2)

In 29–32, a statement is given.
a. Is the statement true?
b. Is the converse true?
c. If either the statement or the converse is not true, change the statement so that both are true. Rewrite the new statement in if-and-only-if form.

29. A year with 366 days is a leap year.

30. If you live in France, you live within 10 kilometers of the Eiffel Tower.

31. If you are an eleventh grader, you are in high school.

32. All horses are four-legged animals.

REPRESENTATIONS Pictures, graphs, or objects that illustrate concepts

OBJECTIVE H Display or prove properties involving multiplication using areas of polygons or squares. (Lesson 13-8)

33. Picture the property that for all positive numbers a and b, $(a + b)^2 = a^2 + b^2 + 2ab$.

34. Square $ABCD$ is pictured below. Show that the area of $ABCD$ is equal to the sum of the areas of the four small triangles.

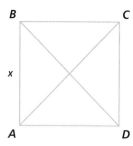

35. Draw a rectangle with dimensions a and b, and draw a diagonal from one corner to the other, making two triangles. Prove that the diagonal cuts the area of the rectangle in half.

36. Use the isosceles trapezoid below to show that $\frac{1}{2}(2b + 2x)h = xh + bh$.

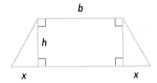

OBJECTIVE I Determine whether lengths of geometric figures are rational or irrational. (Lesson 13-7)

37. Consider the circle below. Its circumference is 32 inches.

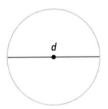

a. What is the exact radius of the circle?

b. Is this number rational or irrational?

In 38–40,

a. determine the missing length, and

b. determine whether your answer to Part a is rational or irrational.

38.

39.

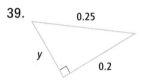

40.

41. a. Draw a segment whose length is $1 + \sqrt{8}$ centimeters.

b. Is that length rational or irrational?

Selected Answers

Chapter 7

Lesson 7-1 (pp. 398–403)

Guided Example 3: 2,000; 0.054; 18; 2000; 1.054; 18; 5154.196734; $5,154.19; $5,154.19

Questions: 1. "4 to the 10th power" or "4 to the 10th"
3. a. 343 b. 343; ⑦^③ENTER 5. $18 \cdot (-3)^4$
7. a. 100,000 people b. 250,000 people c. about 269,159 people 9. $1.02P$ 11. a. $A = P(1 + r)^t$ b. total amount including interest c. starting principal d. annual yield e. number of years 13. $2,529.55 15. a. Susana earns $20.40; Jake earns $41.60 b. No. After the first year, he has more money on which to earn interest than Susana does.
17. a. $A = 100 \cdot 1.1^t$

b.

Time since investment (in years)	Danica's account ($)
0	100.00
2	121.00
4	146.41
6	177.16
8	214.36
10	259.37
12	313.84
14	379.75
16	459.50
18	555.99
20	672.75

19. around year 15 21. a. $3W + T > 3$

b.
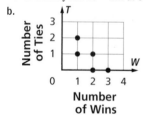
23. $\frac{5}{6}$ 25. all real numbers
27. $t = 5$

Lesson 7-2 (pp. 404–410)

1. a. $y = 11 \cdot 3^x$, where y is the population and x is the number of years after 1995. b. 99 round gobies
c. 2,673 trillion round gobies d. about 2,265 trillion round gobies 3. a. 1.045 b. $3,276.07 5. a. 1 b. 17 c. 1
7. $(-5)^0 = 1$, but $-5^0 = -1$, by the order of operations

9. a.

x	y
0	0.5
1	1
2	2
3	4
4	8

b.
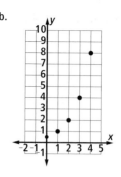

11. a. by about 3.585 million people b. about 56.190 million people 13. a. 1.04 is the growth rate; 34,277 is the 1860 population b. 1,731,158 people; 22,789 people c. about 26,956,933 people

15. a.
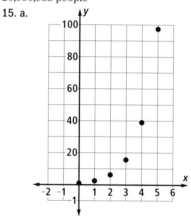

b. 1.5 c. 58.59375 d. This graph is not a line. Its rate of change increases as x increases. 17. a. $\frac{1}{31}$ b. $\frac{9}{31}$
19. 25.74

Lesson 7-3 (pp. 411–418)

Guided Example 3: a. 10; 0.97; 10; 0.97 b. 23; 23
c. 240; 240; 10; 0.97; 240

Questions: 1. 0.83 3. 1 5. a. $27,200 b. $25,600
c. $32,000 \cdot (1 - 0.01d)$ dollars 7. about 6 units;
$15 \cdot 0.97^x$ units 9. constant 11. decay
13. a. $y = 2,500 \cdot 0.98^x$ b. about 2,043 students

15. a. **Light-Panes Relation**

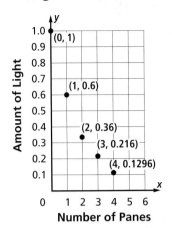

b. No, it will get infinitely close to zero.

17. a.

x	Decimals	Fractions
0	1	1
1	0.5	$\frac{1}{2}$
2	0.25	$\frac{1}{4}$
3	0.125	$\frac{1}{8}$
10	0.000976563	$\frac{1}{1,024}$
20	0.0000009536	$\frac{1}{1,048,576}$

b. no solutions

19. a.

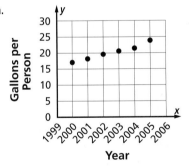

b. Answers vary. Sample answer: $y = 1.7x - 3,359.8$
c. Answers vary. Sample answer: $y = 1.7x - 3,359.8$
d. about 29.1 gal of bottled water per person

Lesson 7-4 (pp. 419–424)

Guided Example: a. $2.241 \cdot 1.218^x$ **b.** $2.241 \cdot 1.218^{24} \approx 255$; 255; 165; 165 MHz **c.** 2.241; 1.218; 44; 13,150
Questions: 1. a. 6 ft **b.** 55% **3.** 8.4 ft; about 0.83 ft **5.** about 80,817 MB **7.** c **9.** a

11. a.

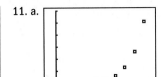

b. Let p be the number of pennies and t be the trial number. $p = 1.57 \cdot 1.49^t$ **13.** Answers vary. Sample answer: If 35% of a 14-kg block of ice melts every day, how much ice, y, remains after x weeks?

15.

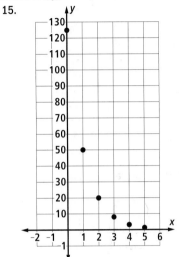

17. \$23 **19. a.** \$270 **b.** \$225 **c.** \$200

Lesson 7-5 (pp. 425–431)

Guided Example 2: all real numbers; all real numbers
Questions: 1. a. 9 **b.** 4 is the input and 16 is the output.
c. 4 is the independent variable and 16 is the dependent variable. **d.** {1, 4, 9, 16, 25} **3. a.** –1 **b.** $\frac{2}{7}$ **5.** No real number has 0 as its reciprocal because if $0 = \frac{1}{x}$, then $x = \frac{1}{0}$, which is undefined. **7. a.** {x: $-5 \le x \le 5$}
b. {y: $0 \le y \le 5$} **9.** C **11.** No; The input $x = 3$ corresponds to both outputs $y = 1$ and $y = 4$. **13. a.** false **b.** 5 **c.** the set of all real numbers **d.** {y: $y > 0$} **e.** 4

15. Answers vary. Sample answer: time is input and height is output

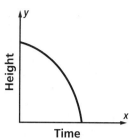

17. $\{y: 0 \leq y \leq 2\}$ **19.** domain: the set of all real numbers; range: the set of all real numbers   **21. a.** Answers vary. Sample answer: As the value of the input increases, that of the output decreases.   **b.** Khalid Khannouchi is associated with two record-setting times; that is, one input produces two outputs.   **23.** $\frac{21}{160}$ **25.** $pw \leq 1,500; p \leq \frac{1,500}{w}$

Lesson 7-6 (pp. 432–438)

Guided Example 2: 10; 121,899; 100,000 + 3,000(10); 130,000; 10; constant; 100,000

Questions: 1. f of x **3. a.** $E(25) \approx 164,061$; $L(25) = 175,000$; $C(25) = 100,000$ **b.** They are the population estimates for 25 yr from the present.   **5.** 12,800   **7. a.** $45   **b.** $135   **c.** 20   **9. a.** 506.25; It is the estimated value of the computer in four years.

b.

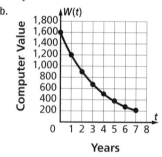

c. $t > 1.63$. This means after about 1.63 years the computer's value is less than $1,000.   **11. a.** about 325°   **b.** The temperature of the oven after it was on for 25 minutes was 325°.   **c.** $t \approx 6$ **d.** The oven reached 200° after being on for about 6 minutes.

13. No. Answers vary. Sample answer: $x = 1$ results in both $y = -2$ and $y = 0$. **15. a.** $5x - 4y = -12$ **b.** $y = \frac{5}{4}x + 3$

Lesson 7-7 (pp. 439–446)

Guided Example: Option 1: $60; $110; Option 2: $15; $22.50

Questions: 1. Answers vary. Sample answer: The rate of change varies in an exponential growth situation, but remains constant in a constant increase situation.

3.

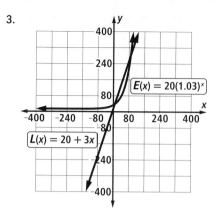

5. Answers vary. Sample answer: $E(x)$ could represent the value of a $20 investment in a bank account with an annual yield of 3% after x years. $L(x)$ could represent the amount in a bank account after x years if $20 is initially invested and $3 is added each year.   **7. a.** A2 + 13; A3 + 13   **b.** 54; 67   **c.** They will decrease to 21 and 34.   **d.** constant increase; The outputs are represented by the linear function $f(x) = 13x + 28$.   **9. a.** Next = Now + 270   **b.** Next = Now · 1.15   **c.** $L(x) = 85,000 + 270x$ **d.** $E(x) = 85,000(1.15)^x$ **e.** Answers vary. Sample answer: Yes, $L(8) = 87,160$.   **11. a.** Constant increase. Answers vary. Sample answer: Reading at 25 pages per hour is a constant rate increase.   **b.** $f(x) = 67 + 25x$ **c.** 33.32 hr
13. a   **15.** d
17. a.

	Constant	Exponential
0	2,410	2,410
1	2,270	2,270
2	2,130	2,138
3	1,990	2,014
4	1,850	1,897
5	1,710	1,787
6	1,570	1,683
7	1,430	1,585
8	1,290	1,493
9	1,150	1,406
10	1,010	1,325
11	870	1,248
12	730	1,175
13	590	1,107
14	450	1,043
15	310	982

b. 1,570, approximately 1,683; by 113   c. 170, approximately 925; by 755   **19.** true   **21.** $24x + 5y = -3$ **23.** $\frac{24}{73}$

Self-Test (pp. 450–451)

1. $\left(\frac{1}{5}\right)^2 + \left(\frac{1}{5}\right)^0 = \frac{1}{25} + 1 = \frac{26}{25}$ **2.** $8^4 d^6$ **3.** $f(1,729) = 3(1,729)^0 = 3 \cdot 1 = 3$ **4.** $g(-2) = 3(-2) - (-2)^2 = -6 - 4 = -10$ **5.** $400(1.044)^7 \approx 540.70$ **6.** Tyrone will have $400(1.044)^{10} \approx 615.26$ dollars and Oleta will have $400 + 22(10) = 620$ dollars, so Oleta will have more.
7. After 25 years, Tyrone will have $400(1.044)^{25} \approx 1,173.74$ dollars, and Oleta will have $400 + 22(25) = 950$ dollars, so Tyrone will have more money.   **8.** The value of the car is depreciating 16%, so the growth factor is $1 - 0.16 = 0.84$.
9. $m(x) = 34,975(0.84)^x$, $x \geq 0$. Because x represents years, it cannot be negative.   **10.** $m(5) = 34,975(0.84)^5 \approx$ 14,626.96 dollars   **11.** $f(1) = 5 \cdot 0.74^1 = 3.7$
12. $f(5) = 5 \cdot 0.74^5 \approx 1.11$ **13.** $f(7) = 5 \cdot 0.74^7 \approx 0.61$
14. $f(12) = |-12 - 3| = |-15| = 15$ **15.** From the graph and knowledge of the absolute value function, you can see only positive values and 0 are in the range. The range is all nonnegative numbers.   **16.** From the graph you can see the only values in the range are those greater than or equal to $f(5)$. $f(5) = |5 - 3| = 2$ so the range is all real numbers ≥ 2.

17.

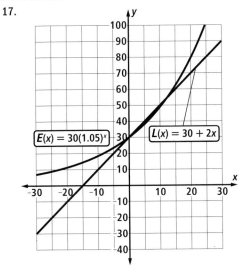

$E(x) = 30(1.05)^x$ $L(x) = 30 + 2x$

18. $L(9) = 30 + 2 \cdot 9 = 48$, $E(9) = 30(1.05)^9 \approx 46.5$; $L(9)$ is greater.   **19.** Answers vary. Sample answer: $x = 20$; $E(20) \approx 79.60$, $L(20) = 70$, $70 < 79.60$ **20.** An increase of 2.5% tells you that the growth factor is 1.025. The beginning population is 76 million, so the population p, in millions, k years after 1980, is $p(k) = 76(1.025)^k$.

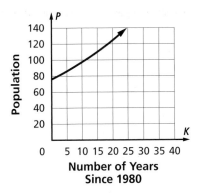

Population vs. K
Number of Years Since 1980

21. A decrease of 1% tells you that the growth factor is 0.99. The beginning circulation is 880,000, so the circulation is $c(x) = 880,000(0.99)^x$.

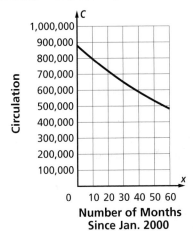

Circulation vs. x
Number of Months Since Jan. 2000

22.

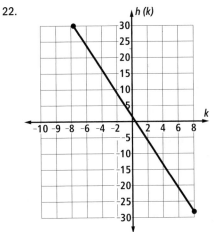

$h(k)$

23.

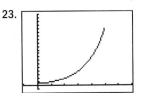

24. a. f is a linear function with negative slope, so it describes a constant decrease situation, ii. **b.** g is an exponential function with growth factor 5. Since $5 > 1$, g describes an exponential growth situation, iii. **c.** h is an exponential function with growth factor 0.4. Since $0.4 < 1$, h describes an exponential decay situation, iv. **d.** m is a linear function with positive slope, so it describes a constant increase situation, i. **25. a.** The year increases by 1, so add 1 to the value in A2. Input "$=A2 + 1$". **b.** Answers vary. Sample answer: In cell B3, input "$=1.04*B2$", and then replicate the formula from B3 to B4 through B22.

The chart below keys the **Self-Test** questions to the objectives in the **Chapter Review** on pages 452–455 or to the **Vocabulary (Voc)** on page 449. This will enable you to locate those **Chapter Review** questions that correspond to questions missed on the **Self-Test**. The lesson where the material is covered is also indicated on the chart.

Question	1	2	3	4	5	6	7	8	9	10
Objective	A	A	A	A	D	G	G	E	C	E
Lesson(s)	7-6	7-6	7-6	7-6	7-1	7-7	7-7	7-2, 7-3, 7-4	7-5, 7-6	7-2, 7-3, 7-4

Question	11	12	13	14	15	16	17	18	19	20
Objective	A	A	A	A	C	C	I	G	G	H
Lesson(s)	7-6	7-6	7-6	7-6	7-5, 7-6	7-5, 7-6	7-5, 7-6	7-7	7-7	7-2, 7-3

Question	21	22	23	24	25
Objective	H	I	H	F	B
Lesson(s)	7-2, 7-3	7-5, 7-6	7-2, 7-3	7-4	7-7

Chapter Review (pp. 452–455)

1. 4 **3.** 17 **5.** $\frac{121}{36}$ **7.** -4 **9. a.** Answers vary. Sample answer: "$= B2*1.05$" **b.** 1,050 **c.** Replicate the formula in B3 down to B12. **11. a.** x **b.** f **13. a.** $\{2, 4, 5, 10\}$ **b.** $\{200, 400, 500, 1,000\}$ **c.** $f(x) = 100x; x = 2, 4, 5, 10$
15. $918.66 **17.** (b), $1.04^8 > 1.08^4$ **19. a.** $20^5 = 3,200,000$
b. C **21.** constant increase **23.** exponential growth
25. neither **27. a.** $A(n) = 10,000,000 (1.02)^n$
b. $B(n) = 20,000,000 + 1,000,000n$ **c.** country B; $B(30) = 50,000 > A(30) = 18,113,616$ **d.** country B; $B(100) > A(100)$

29.

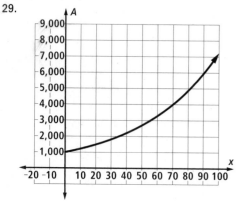

Answers vary. Sample answer: $1,000 is invested at 2% interest per year.

31.

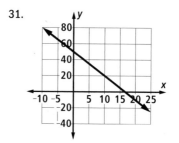

Answers vary. Sample answer: You have $50 in a bank account, and each day you take out $3.

33.

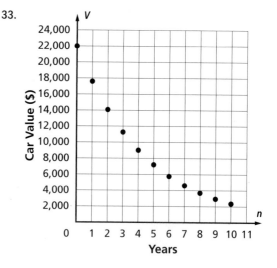

35.

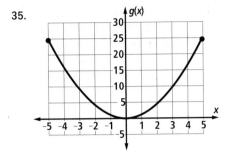

37.

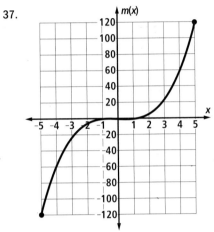

39. a. 1 b. 2 c. $\{x: 0 \le x \le 4\}$ d. $\{y: 0 \le y \le 2\}$

Chapter 8

Lesson 8-1 (pp. 458-463)

Guided Example 3: 4^{20}; 5^{10}; $(4^{20})(5^{10})$; $\frac{1}{10,737,418,240,000,000,000}$

Questions: 1. a. AA, AE, AI, AO, AU, EA, EE, EI, EO, EU, IA, IE, II, IO, IU, OA, OE, OI, OO, OU, UA, UE, UI, UO, UU **b.** 2; 5 **3.** 15,625; $1.5625 \cdot 10^4$ **5. a.** 90 **b.** To label each cell, we choose each cell among 15 columns and 6 rows, so there are $6 \cdot 15$ choices, thus 90 cells. **7. a.** 2^{10}; 1,024; $1.024 \cdot 10^3$ **b.** $\frac{1}{1,024}$ **c.** 2^Q; $\frac{1}{2^Q}$ **9. a.** $10^3 = 1,000$ **b.** $10^{-12} = 0.000000000001$ **11.** $\frac{1}{32}$ **13.** 17,069 people **15.** No, because for each value of x, there are several values of y. **17.** 108 units^2 **19.** $x = 6$ **21.** $2.8 \cdot 10^9$

Lesson 8-2 (pp. 464-468)

1. 18^9 **3.** w^7; $2^4 \cdot 2^3 = 16 \cdot 8 = 128$; $2^7 = 128$ **5.** 2^7 **7.** m^8 **9.** m^{10} **11.** $15a^6$ **13.** d^{14} **15.** a^8b^3 **17.** 65,536 sequences **19.** $x = 1$ **21. a.** $P \cdot 3^4$ **b.** 16 days **23. a.** 30 ways **b.** 6 more choices **25. a.** $y = -51.6x + 3,058$ **b.** 2,026 tickets **27.** 3.24×10^{-3}

Lesson 8-3 (pp. 469-473)

1. 2^3 **3.** 3^{m-n} **5.** 1 **7.** $6ab^5$ **9.** $4a^6$ **11.** The bases differ. **13.** 1 **15.** 2^{-3} **17.** $7 + 3m$ **19.** $4a$
21. a. about 12,410.8 barrels of oil per person per day **b.** about 158,547,936 gallons **23.** $3x^3$ **25.** $24h^7$
27. a. $\frac{1}{4^5}$ **b.** $\frac{243}{1,024}$ **29. a.** \$23.92 **b.** \$52.50

Lesson 8-4 (pp. 474-480)

Guided Example 2: a. $\left(\frac{4}{5}\right)^2$; $\frac{16}{25}$; **b.** $\left(\frac{m^2}{1}\right)^3$; $(m^2)^3$; m^6
Guided Example 4: -7; 2; -1; 2; 7; -1; $\frac{b^2}{3a^7c}$

Questions: 1. $\frac{1}{3}$; $\frac{1}{9}$; $\frac{1}{27}$; $\frac{1}{81}$; $\frac{1}{243}$ **3.** $\frac{1}{125}$ **5.** $\frac{1}{y^{24}}$ **7.** 3^{-4} **9.** 10^{-4}
11. a. $\frac{1}{w}$ **b.** $\frac{1}{wx^2}$ **c.** $\frac{y^3}{w}$ **d.** $\frac{5y^3}{wx^2}$ **13.** 1 **15.** $\frac{4a^2c^2}{b^3}$
17. The values of y seem to get extremely close to 0.
19. $x^{-2}(x^{-3} + x^4) = x^{-2}(x^{-3}) + x^{-2}(x^4) = x^{(-2+-3)} + x^{(-2+4)} = x^{-5} + x^2 = x^2 + \frac{1}{x^5}$ **21.** $m = -1$; $5^{-1} \cdot \frac{1}{25} = 5^{-1} \cdot 5^{-2} = 5^{-3}$
23. a^6; 64 **25.** $2^a b^{3a}$; 62,500 **27. a.** $m(x) = 8x + 25$
b. whole numbers less than 13 **c.** 121 and 25

Lesson 8-5 (pp. 481-487)

Guided Example 2: 3; 3; 3; 3; 3; 6; 9; 3; $-125x^6y^9z^3$
Questions: 1. a. $216x^3$ **b.** $(6 \cdot 2)^3 = 1,728$; $216(2)^3 = 1,728$
3. $-2,744x^3y^3$ **5.** $-t^{93}$ **7.** $\frac{16}{81}$ **9.** $\frac{6,859}{8y^3}$ **11.** The area is multiplied by 36. **13.** $\frac{x^5}{y}$ **15.** $144w^{10}$ **17.** 0 **19.** 225
21. $\frac{17}{3,125r^2s^2}$; $\frac{17}{7,031.25}$ **23.** $-\frac{1}{5} < p$

Lesson 8-6 (pp. 488-496)

1. a. 256 units^2 **b.** 4 units **3.** 6 **5.** 7.07 **7.** 31.623 **9.** 5
11. a. 3.31662 **b.** 11 **c.** Square of the Square Root Property **13.** 52 **15.** 1; 8; 27; 64; 125; 216; 343; 512; 729; 1,000 **17. a.** $\sqrt[3]{1,700}$ **b.** 11.935 **19.** 45 **21.** 100,995; Answers vary. Sample answer: The population 6 months from the original date **23. a.** Answers vary. Sample answer: The scarecrow's statement is an incorrect statement about isosceles triangles, while the Pythagorean Theorem is a true statement about right triangles. The statement is about the square roots of the sides, while the Pythagorean Theorem is about the squares of the lengths of the sides. **b.** No, Answers vary. Sample answer: Let an isosceles triangle with $a = 9$, $b = 9$ and $c = 4$ cm. Then $\sqrt{a} + \sqrt{b} = \sqrt{9} + \sqrt{9} = 3 + 3 = 6$; while $\sqrt{c} = \sqrt{4} = 2$, so $\sqrt{a} + \sqrt{b} \ne \sqrt{c}$. **25.** $(x^2)(y^2) = (xy)^2$ **27.** 8
29. 865,177 yr

Lesson 8-7 (pp. 497-504)

Guided Example 2: a. 7; 7; $\sqrt{98}$ **b.** 49; 49; 2; 7; $7\sqrt{2}$
Guided Example 3: 16; 4; 4 Check 6,912; 48
Questions: 1. 4 **3.** 2 **5.** $x = 18$, $y = 3$, $z = 2$ **7.** B **9.** $3\sqrt{2}$
11. $5\sqrt{2}$ **13. a.** $5m\sqrt{6n}$ **b.** $4m^2$ **15.** Quotient of Square Roots Property **17.** $3\sqrt{3}$, 5.20 **19.** $x = \sqrt{81 - y^2}$, $y = \sqrt{81 - x^2}$ **21.** Answers vary. Sample answer: Because $\sqrt{49} = 7$ **23.** $-8\sqrt{3}$ **25.** $29\sqrt{2}$ **27.** (250, 100)
29. x^5 **31.** $(6^4)^2$ **33.** Slope $= -1.5$, y-intercept $= 46$; The slope describes how many floors it descends per second, and the y-intercept is where the elevator is at 0 sec.

Lesson 8-8 (pp. 505–510)

Guided Example 2: 23; 16; 31; –11; 31; 23; –11; 16; 8; –27; 64; 729; 793; 28.160

Questions: 1. a. 2 b. 6 c. $\sqrt{40} \approx 6.325$ 3. 7 5. 22 7. $\sqrt{29} \approx 5.385$ 9. 13 11. $\sqrt{65} \approx 8.062$ 13. $\sqrt{0.0833} \approx 0.288617$ 15. $\sqrt{11.25} \approx 3.35$ miles 17. $\sqrt{b^2 + d^2}$ 19. $[(x_2 - x_1)^2 + (y_2 - y_1)^2]^{\frac{1}{2}}$ 21. 12 23. 40 25. $f(x) = \frac{8}{5}x - 10$

Lesson 8-9 (pp. 511–516)

Guided Example 4: Solution 1 –7; 35; –7; 21; –7; 14; –7; 7; 14; 7; 7; 14; 7; 14; 7; 14 Solution 2 1. $\left(9q^{-5}\right) = \left(\frac{9}{6}q^{-2}\right)^{-7}$ 2. $\left(\frac{3}{2}q^{-2}\right)^{-7}$ 3. $\left(\frac{3}{2}\right)^{-7}q^{-2 \cdot -7} = \left(\frac{2}{3}\right)^{-7} \cdot q^{14}$ Questions: 1. B 3. C 5. A special case for which the answer is false 7. true 9. no 11. yes 13. Product of Powers 15. Negative Exponent 17. $\frac{y^6}{9x^4}$ 19. 6

21. Answers vary. Sample answer: $\left(\frac{x^6}{x^3}\right)^{-2} = \frac{x^{-12}}{x^{-6}} = x^{-6} = \frac{1}{x^6}$; $\left(\frac{x^6}{x^3}\right)^{-2} = (x^3)^{-2} = x^{-6} = \frac{1}{x^6}$ 23. $2^{75}3^{50}5^{25}$ 25. 66.7 27. Yes, Answers vary. Sample answer: In an isosceles right triangle with legs of length s and a hypotenuse of length h, $h^2 = s^2 + s^2 = 2s^2$. So, $h = \sqrt{2s^2} = \sqrt{2}\sqrt{s^2} = s \cdot \sqrt{2}$. 29. $-\frac{5}{4}x + 15$

Self-Test (p. 520)

1. A, $x^{4 + 7} = x^{11}$ 2. $5^{-3} = \frac{1}{5^3} = \frac{1}{125}$ 3. $(-4)(-3) = 12$; $(-4)^{-3} = -\frac{1}{64}$; $(-3)^4 = 81.$; So, from least to greatest: $(-4)^{-3}$, $(-4)(-3)$, $(-3)^4$ 4. $\sqrt{600} = \sqrt{100 \cdot 6} = \sqrt{100} \cdot \sqrt{6} = 10\sqrt{6}$ 5. $\sqrt{25x} = \sqrt{25 \cdot x} = \sqrt{25} \cdot \sqrt{x} = 5\sqrt{x}$ 6. $2^{\frac{1}{2}} \cdot 50^{\frac{1}{2}} = (2 \cdot 50)^{\frac{1}{2}} = 100^{\frac{1}{2}} = 10$ 7. $y^4 \cdot y^2 = y^{4 + 2} = y^6$ 8. $(10m^2)^3 = 10^3(m^2)^3 = 10^3m^6 = 1,000m^6$

9. $\frac{a^{15}}{a^3} = a^{15 - 3} = a^{12}$ 10. $\left(\frac{m}{6}\right)^3 = \frac{m^3}{6^3} = \frac{m^3}{216}$ 11. $g^4 \cdot g \cdot g^0 = g^{4 + 1 + 0} = g^5$ 12. $\frac{6n^2}{4n^3 \cdot 2n} = \frac{6n^2}{8n^4} = \frac{3}{4}n^{2 - 4} = \frac{3}{4}n^{-2} = \frac{3}{4n^2}$ 13. $\frac{4w^2}{y^3}$, by the Negative Exponent Property 14. $\frac{2}{x^2} \cdot \frac{5}{x^5} = \frac{2 \cdot 5}{x^2x^5}$ Multiplication of fractions $= \frac{10}{x^{(2 + 5)}}$ Arithmetic and Product of Powers Property $= \frac{10}{x^7}$ Arithmetic 15. The prime factorization of $10(288)^2$ is $2 \cdot 5 \cdot (2^5 \cdot 3^2)^2 = 2 \cdot 5 \cdot (2^5)^2 \cdot (3^2)^2 = 2 \cdot 5 \cdot 2^{10} \cdot 3^4 = 5 \cdot 2^{11} \cdot 3^4$ 16. $\left(\frac{3}{y^2}\right)^{-3}\left(\left(\frac{3}{y^2}\right)^{-1}\right)^3 =$ $\left(\frac{y^2}{3}\right)^3 = \frac{(y^2)^3}{3^3} = \frac{y^6}{27}$ 17. 3.107 18. $1,000(1.06)^{-3} = 1,000 \cdot 0.84 \approx 840$ 19. a. Power of a Quotient Property b. Power of a Power Property c. Quotient of Powers Property d. Negative Exponent Property 20. Answers vary. Sample answer: $\frac{1}{4}$ 21. $\sqrt{(1 - 9)^2 + (-10 - 5)^2}$ $= \sqrt{289} = 17$ 22. The upper right corner of the paper has coordinates $(297, 210)$, the lower left corner has coordinates $(0, 0)$ so using the distance formula gives $\sqrt{(297 - 0)^2 + (210 - 0)^2} = \sqrt{132,309} \approx 363.7$ mm. 23. $V = s^3$, so $s = \sqrt[3]{v}$. Therefore $s = \sqrt[3]{30} \approx 3.107$ in. 24. The diagonal and two consecutive sides of the square form an isosceles triangle. The Pythagorean Theorem gives $s^2 + s^2 = 12^2$, where s is the length of a side of the square. So, $2s^2 = 144$ or $s^2 = 72$. Since the area of the square is s^2, the area is 72 m^2. 25. $26^2 \cdot 10^4 = (676) \cdot (10,000) = 6,760,000$

The chart below keys the **Self-Test** questions to the objectives in the **Chapter Review** on pages 521–523 or to the **Vocabulary (Voc)** on page 519. This will enable you to locate those **Chapter Review** questions that correspond to questions missed on the **Self-Test**. The lesson where the material is covered is also indicated on the chart.

Question	1	2	3	4	5	6	7	8	9	10
Objective	A	B	B	D	D	D	A	C	A	C
Lesson(s)	8-2, 8-3, 8-4, 8, 5	8-4, 8-5	8-4, 8-5	8-6, 8-7	8-6, 8-7	8-6, 8-7	8-2, 8-3, 8-4, 8-5	8-5, 8-9	8-2, 8-3, 8-4, 8-5	8-5, 8-9

Question	11	12	13	14	15	16	17	18	19	20
Objective	A	A	G	G	A	C	E	B	G	F
Lesson(s)	8-2, 8-3, 8-4, 8-5	8-2, 8-3, 8-4, 8-5	8-2, 8-3, 8-4, 8-5	8-2, 8-3, 8-4, 8-5	8-2, 8-3, 8-4, 8-5	8-5, 8-9	8-6	8-4, 8-5	8-2, 8-3, 8-4, 8-5	8-9

Question	21	22	23	24	25
Objective	J	U	I	I	H
Lesson(s)	8-8	8-8	8-8	8-8	8-1

Chapter Review (pp. 521–523)

1. $24m^9$ 3. $\frac{7y^4}{3x}$ 5. $\frac{1}{p^{24}}$ 7. $5a^{20} - 7a^{13}$ 9. a. approximately
$1.33x^4$ b. $\frac{4}{3}x^4$ 11. $\frac{42}{x^7y^3}$ 13. $\frac{1}{36}$ 15. $\frac{243}{32}$ 17. $129,000
19. $n = -3$ 21. a. negative b. negative 23. $3,600m^4n^6$
25. $\frac{2,187}{16,384}$ 27. $\frac{t^8}{4,096s^4}$ 29. $\frac{9z^{14}}{y^{10}}$ 31. $8\sqrt{2}$ 33. $10\sqrt{21}$
35. $\frac{2x}{y}$ 37. -2 39. 5.848 41. 0.368; $0.368^3 \approx 0.0498 \approx$
0.05 43. a. yes b. yes c. no d. It is not always true.
Part c is a counterexample. 45. Answers vary. Sample
answer: $a = 1$ 47. Power of a Quotient Property
49. Power of a Power Property or Zero Exponent
Property 51. Product of Powers Property 53. Answers
vary. Sample answer: By first applying the Negative
Exponent Property for Fractions and then the Power of a
Quotient Property, $\left(\frac{12}{13}\right)^{-4} = \left(\frac{13}{12}\right)^4 = \frac{13^4}{12^4} = \frac{28,561}{20,736}$. By applying
the Power of Quotient Property and then the Negative
Exponent Property, $\left(\frac{12}{13}\right)^{-4} = \frac{12^{-4}}{13^{-4}} = \frac{13^4}{12^4} = \frac{28,561}{20,736}$.
55. a. 243 answer sheets b. $\frac{1}{243}$ c. $\frac{32}{243}$
57. 54 different pizzas 59. $2\sqrt{2}$ units 61. x^2y^2
63. 1 m 65. a. 5 b. 3 c. $\sqrt{34}$ 67. $9\sqrt{2}$
69. $\sqrt{(a + 1)^2 + (b - 4)^2}$
71. a. yes b.

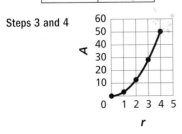

Chapter 9

Lesson 9-1 (pp. 526–531)

Guided Example 1: Step 1

A and r can only
assume positive values

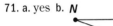

Step 2

r	A
1	3.14
2	12.57
3	28.27
4	50.27

Steps 3 and 4

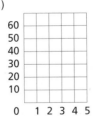

Step 5: about 2 units

Questions: 1. a.

x	$g(x) = \frac{1}{2}x^2$
-4	8
-3	4.5
-2	2
-1	0.5
0	0
1	0.5
2	2
3	4.5
4	8

b. 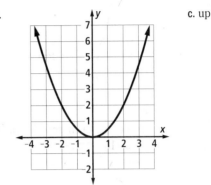 c. up

3. a. down b. maximum value c. $(0, 0)$ d. $x = 0$ 5. a. iii.
b. i. c. ii. 7. a. up b. down
9. a.

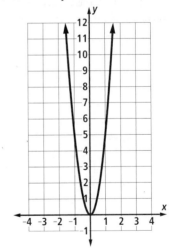

b.

x	$y = 5x^2$
-2	20
-1.5	11.25
-1	5
-0.5	1.25
0	0
0.5	1.25
1	5
1.5	11.25
2	20

c.

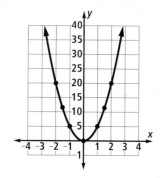

d. ≈ 1.7 and -1.7 **11. a.** $y = 0$ **b.** $x = 1$ and $x = -1$
c. $x = 2$ and $x = -2$ **13. a.** negative **b.** zero **c.** negative
d. The graph is has vertex $(0, 0)$ and opens down. **15.** 0
17. $a = -1.5$ **19. a.** $t = 5$ **b.** about 3.5 sec
21. $\sqrt{244} \approx 15.6$ in. **23.** \$2,250

Lesson 9-2 (pp. 532–536)
1. $x = \pm 5$ **3.** $x = \sqrt{40} \approx \pm 6.32$ **5.** $v = \sqrt{5} \approx \pm 2.24$
7. $a = -3$ or $a = -7$ **9. a.** about 92 ft **b.** about 2 sec
11. 5.64 units **13.** $v \pm 2.5$ **15.** about 8.50 in.
17. $m^5 n^6$ **19.** $\frac{9}{25a^2}$ **21. a.** the set of all real numbers
b. the set of nonnegative real numbers
23. a. $6x + 4y \geq 975$
b.

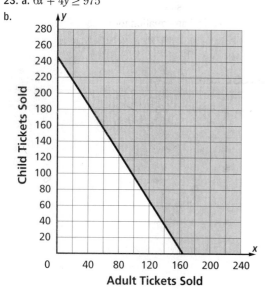

c. 121 tickets **25.** B

Lesson 9-3 (pp. 537–543)
1. the total distance traveled in the time it takes for a car to
stop **3.** 206.25 ft **5.** $a = 0.05$; $b = 1$; $c = 0$

7. a.

x	y
−3	3
−2	−2
−1	−5
0	−6
1	−5
2	−2
3	3

b.

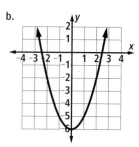

c. y-intercept: -6; x-intercepts: $\pm\sqrt{6}$; vertex: $(0, -6)$
d. $y \geq -6$
9. a.

x	y
−3	31
−2	16
−1	7
0	4
1	7
2	16
3	31

b.

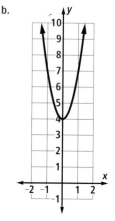

c. y-intercept: 4; x-intercepts: none; vertex: $(0, 4)$ **d.** $y \geq 4$
11. a. $(-4, 36)$ **b.** $(-2, 20)$, $(-1, 0)$, $(0, -28)$ **13.** B; Answers
vary. Sample answer: When $x = 2$, $y = 0$. Only graph B
intersects the x-axis at $x = 2$. **15.** d **17.** b
19. a. $t = \sqrt{\frac{350}{16}} \approx 4.68$ **b.** Answers vary. Sample answer: If
you drop a stone off of a 350-ft cliff, how long will it take
for the stone to hit the ground? **21. a.** 288 **b.** 352 **c.** $4\sqrt{22}$
or about 18.76

Lesson 9-4 (pp. 544–551)
Guided Example 2: a. 0; 90; 90 **b.** 90; 90; 18.37; 4.3
Guided Example 3: a. $-4.9t^2 + 22t + 2$ **b.** 1.1, 3.4; 1.1; 3.4
Questions: 1. Answers vary. Sample answer: A projectile is
an object that is dropped or launched and travels through
the air to get to a target. Cannonballs, baseballs, and tennis
balls can all be considered projectiles. **3. a.** $h = -16t^2 +$
$30t + 5$ **b.** 1 ft **c.** 19.1 ft **5. a.** 0 ft/sec; 40 ft **b.** $h =$
$-16t^2 + 40$ **c.** about 1.6 sec **7.** No; at 40 yards from the
kicker, the ball is only 8.6 ft high.
9. a.

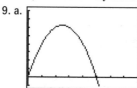

b. 31.25 m **c.** 20 m
d. between 1 and 4 sec after
launch **e.** −30 m **f.** 5 sec

11. a.

x	−3	−2	−1	0	1	2	3
y	2.25	1	0.25	0	0.25	1	2.25

b.

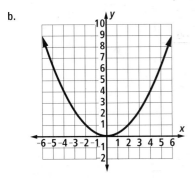

13. $A = (2, 2), B = (3, 5)$ **15.** D

Lesson 9-5 (pp. 552–557)

Guided Example 2: 4.3; –; –4.9; 10; –4.9; 214.49; 214.49; 214.49; 14.65; 14.65

Questions: 1. If $ax^2 + bx + c = 0$ and $a \neq 0$, then $x = \frac{-b \pm \sqrt{b^2 - 4ac}}{2a}$
3. 3 and –6   **5.** $t = -2$; Check: Does $(-2)^2 + 4(-2) + 4 = 0$? $4 + -8 + 4 = 0$ Yes, it checks.   **7.** $y = -4$ or $y = \frac{25}{3}$; Check: Does $3(-4)^2 = 13(-4) + 100$? $3(16) = -52 + 100$ Yes, it checks; Does $3\left(\frac{25}{3}\right)^2 = 13\left(\frac{25}{3}\right) + 100$? $3\left(\frac{625}{9}\right) = \frac{325}{3} + 100$; Yes, it checks.   **9.** $p = -5.48$ or $p = -0.85$
11. a. $x = -3$ or $x = 5$

b.

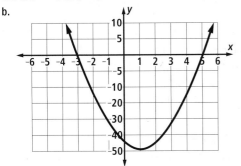

c.

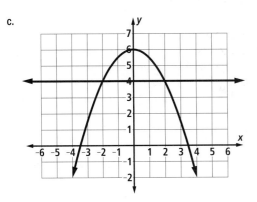

13. a. $t = 1.91$ sec and $t = 13.09$ sec   **b.** 15 sec   **15.** 2
17. 5 units   **19. a.** 2   **b.** 3   **c.** $\frac{5x - 1}{x + 1}$

Lesson 9-6 (pp. 558–564)

Guided Example 1: b. 1, 1, 1   **c.** 0, 0
Guided Example 3: 2; 16; 32; $(16)^2 - 4(2)(32)$; 256 −256; zero; 1

Questions: 1. a. $-x^2 + 2x = 0$ **b.** yes, twice   **3. a.** 0   **b.** 1   **c.** 2
5. a. 1   **b.** 0   **c.** 2   **d.** 2   **7. a.** 0   **b.** There is one real solution.
c. $n = 7$ **9. a.** 120   **b.** 2   **c.** $x = \frac{6 - \sqrt{30}}{2}$ or $x = \frac{6 + \sqrt{30}}{2}$
11. negative   **13. a.** 25   **b.** 2   **15.** 1   **17.** No; All parabolas of the form $y = ax^2 + bx + c$ contain the point $(0, c)$.
19. $x = \frac{-2\sqrt{5}}{3}$ or $x = \frac{2\sqrt{5}}{3}$ **21. a.** 48 ft   **b.** about 3.5 ft
23. down

Lesson 9-7 (pp. 565–570)

1. The cable can be placed either 87.87 ft away or 512.13 ft away from the left side of the bridge.   **3.** No, a polygon cannot have exactly 21 diagonals.   **5.** 120   **7. a.** $x + 7$ **b.** 9
9. 5.7 units   **11.** It is equal to 0.   **13.** 1   **15.** 0
17. a. $a = 36$ **b.** $b = 28$ **c.** $c = 10.25$ **19.** 26 ft
21. a. Answers vary. Sample answer:

$$m = \frac{1 + 24}{2 - 7} = -5$$
$$y - 1 = -5(x - 2)$$
$$(31) - 1 = -5((-4) - 2)$$
$$30 = 30$$

Since we can find the slope of the line between $(2, 1)$ and $(7, -24)$, we can find an equation for the line containing those two points. We then check to make sure that $(-4, 31)$ is also on the line, which it is.   **b.** $5x + y = 11$

Self-Test (pp. 574–575)

1. $x^2 = 81$; $\sqrt{x^2} = \sqrt{81}$; $x = 9, -9$
2. $n^2 - 8n - 10 = 0$

$$n = \frac{-b \pm \sqrt{b^2 - 4ac}}{2a}$$
$$n = \frac{-(-8) \pm \sqrt{(-8)^2 - 4(1)(-10)}}{2(1)}$$
$$n = \frac{8 \pm \sqrt{64 + 40}}{2}$$
$$n = \frac{8 \pm \sqrt{104}}{2}$$
$$n = \frac{8 \pm 2\sqrt{26}}{2}$$
$$n = 4 + \sqrt{26}, 4 - \sqrt{26}$$
$$n \approx 9.10, n \approx -1.10$$

3. $5y^2 - 11y - 1 = 0$

$$y = \frac{-b \pm \sqrt{b^2 - 4ac}}{2a}$$

$$y = -(-11) \pm \frac{\sqrt{(-11)^2 - 4(5)(-1)}}{2(5)}$$

$$y = \frac{11 \pm \sqrt{121 + 20}}{10}$$

$$y = \frac{11 + \sqrt{141}}{10}, \frac{11 - \sqrt{141}}{10}$$

$$y \approx 2.29, y \approx -0.09$$

4. $24 = \frac{1}{6}z^2$

$6 \cdot 24 = \frac{6 \cdot 1}{6z^2}$

$144 = z^2$

$z = 12, -12$

5. $v^2 - 16v + 64 = 0$

$(v - 8)(v - 8) = 0$

$v = 8$

6. $3p^2 - 9p + 7 = 0$ If there are any real solutions, then $b^2 - 4ac$ must be greater than or equal to 0.

$b^2 - 4ac = (-9)^2 - 4(3)(7)$

$= 81 - 84$

$= -3$ There are no real solutions. **7.** 2 because the discriminant is positive **8.** A

9. a.

x	$2x^2$
-3	18
-2	8
-1	2
0	0
1	2
2	8
3	18

b.

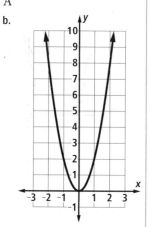

10. a.

x	$-x^2 + 4x - 3$
-3	-24
-2	-15
-1	-8
0	-3
1	0
2	1
3	0

b.

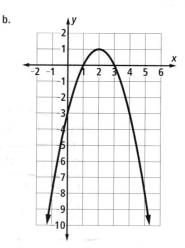

11. $h = 0.049(20)^2$; 19.6 m   **12.** $44 = 0.049v^2$;
$897.96 = v^2$; 29.97 m/sec   **13.** $h = 0.049(35)^2$; 60 m
14. $n(n + 1) = 1{,}722$; $n^2 + n = 1{,}722$; $n^2 + n - 1{,}722 = 0$;
$n = 41$ or $n = -42$; $n = -42$ or $n + 1 = -41$
15. $2x + 2(x + 6) = 24$; $4x = 12$; $x = 3$; $A = 3 \cdot 9 = 27$;
πr^2; $8.59 \approx r^2$; $2.93 \approx r$ **16.** -1.6 **17.** $-3, 1$ **18.** $x = -1$
19. $0 = -16t^2 + 40t + 50$;

$$t = \frac{-b \pm \sqrt{b^2 - 4ac}}{2a};$$

$$t = \frac{-40 \pm \sqrt{(40)^2 - 4(-16)(50)}}{2(-16)};$$

$$t = \frac{-40 \pm \sqrt{1{,}600 + 3{,}200}}{-32};$$

$$t = \frac{-40 \pm \sqrt{4{,}800}}{-32};$$

$$t = \frac{-40 \pm 40\sqrt{3}}{-32}$$

$t = -0.92$, $t = 3.42$

$t = 3.42$ sec

20. $0 = -16t^2 + 40t - 20$

$$t = \frac{-b \pm \sqrt{b^2 - 4ac}}{2a}$$

$$t = \frac{-40 \pm \sqrt{(40)^2 - 4(-16)(-20)}}{2(-16)}$$

$$t = \frac{-40 \pm \sqrt{1{,}600 - 1{,}280}}{-32}; t = \frac{-40 \pm \sqrt{320}}{-32}$$

$$t = \frac{-40 \pm 8\sqrt{5}}{-32}$$

$t = 0.69$, $t = 1.81$
21. false   **22.** $b^2 - 4ac = 1$; $(-5)^2 - 4(a)(3) = 1$
$25 - 12a = 1$
23. $b^2 - 4ac$; $12a = 24$; $a = 2$
$= (12)^2 - 4(-3)(-7)$
$= 144 - 84$
$= 60$; There are two real solutions since the discriminant has a value greater than 0.

24. $b^2 - 4ac$;
$= (-4)^2 - 4(1)(4)$
$= 16 - 16$
$= 0$; There is one real solution since the discriminant has
a value of 0.

The chart below keys the **Self-Test** questions to the objectives in the **Chapter Review** on
pages 576–579 or to the **Vocabulary (Voc)** on page 573. This will enable you to locate those
Chapter Review questions that correspond to questions missed on the **Self-Test.** The lesson
where the material is covered is also indicated on the chart.

Question	1	2	3	4	5	6	7	8	9	10
Objective	A	B	B	A	B	B	C	G	G	H
Lesson(s)	9-2	9-5, 9-6	9-5, 9-6	9-2	9-5, 9-6	9-5, 9-6	9-6	9-1	9-1	9-3

Question	11	12	13	14	15	16	17	18	19	20
Objective	F	F	F	F	E	H	H	H	D	D
Lesson(s)	9-7	9-7	9-7	9-7	9-2, 9-7	9-3	9-3	9-3	9-2, 9-4	9-2, 9-4

Question	21	22	23	24
Objective	C	C	C	C
Lesson(s)	9-6	9-6	9-6	9-6

Chapter Review (pp. 576-579)

1. $x = 13, x = -13$ **3.** $k = \pm\sqrt{85}$ **5.** $m = 3, m = -9$
7. $v = 4.75, v = 3.25$ **9.** $m = -3, m = -4$ **11.** $y = -0.46$,
$y = 6.46$ **13.** $p = -5$ **15.** $n = -2, n = 0.2$ **17.** $b = -7.9$,
$b = 2.5$ **19.** $x = \frac{-b \pm \sqrt{b^2 - 4ac}}{2a}$ **21.** 48   **23.** $b = 4$ or $b = -4$
25. 0   **27.** 0   **29. a.** 3,600 ft **b.** about 19 sec
31. a. 15.1 m **b.** about 1.0 sec and 3.1 sec **c.** 4.1 sec
33. a. $A = 60x - x^2$ **b.** $x = 30$
35. about 98°C   **37. a.** Yes, the company's profits will
exceed $100 million. **b.** 4.8 yr after 2005, or in late 2009
39. a.

x	$\frac{3}{5}x^2$
-2	2.4
-1	0.6
0	0
1	0.6
2	2.4

b.

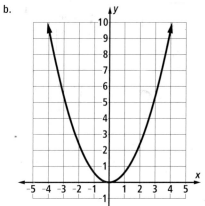

41. B   **43. a.** 5
b. $x = 8$
c. $A = (6, 1)$,
$B = (7, 4)$
45. true
47. (24, –50)

49. a.

x	$-x^2 - 4x + 3$
-5	-2
-4	3
-3	6
-2	7
-1	6
0	3
1	-2

b.

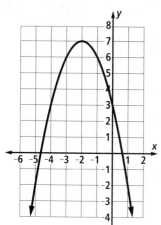

c. maximum

50. A

Chapter 10

Lesson 10-1 (pp. 582–588)

Guided Example 3: 1. zero **2.** –1 **3.** parallel **4.** no

Questions: 1. true **3. a.** $-8 = 4(-2)$ and $2(8) + 3(-2) = 16 + -6 = 10$ **b.** Answers vary. Sample answer: $x = 8$ and $y = -2$; $(x, y) = (8, -2)$

5. a. $\begin{cases} 3x - y = 3 \\ y = -2x + 7 \end{cases}$ **b.** $(2, 3)$ **c.** $3(2) - 3 = 3$ and $2(2) + 3 = 7$

7. a. $(6, 6)$

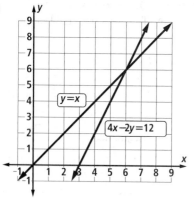

b. $6 = 6$; $24 - 12 = 12$ **9. a.** $\begin{cases} y = 3,800 + 4.25x \\ y = 12.5x \end{cases}$

b. Answers vary. Sample answer: $x$min $= 400$, Xmax $= 800$; Ymin $= 3,800$, Ymax $= 8,000$ **c.** about $(461, 5,758)$ **d.** yes

11. $(5, 15)$

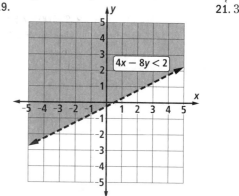

13. a. Answers vary. Sample answer: men: $y = -0.1235x + 522.17$; women: $y = -0.311x + 680.23$ Yes; both times will be equal in 2074. In 2076, the women's time will pass the men's time.

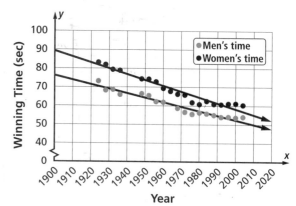

15. a. $-\frac{3}{5}$ **b.** -1 **c.** $-\frac{1}{2}$, 3 **d.** $-1.137, 2.637$ **17.** $625x^{28}y^{36}$

19.   **21.** 3 days

$4x - 8y < 2$

Lesson 10-2 (pp. 589–593)

Guided Example 3: $4t$; $10 + 3t$; $4t$; 10; $3t$; 10

Questions: 1. a. $(3, 5)$ **b.** $3(3) - 4 = 5$; $5(3) - 10 = 5$

3. a. $(-18, 8)$ **b.** $-\frac{1}{9}(-18) + 6 = 8$; $\frac{5}{3}(-18) + 38 = 8$

5. a. $(-144.6, -22.2)$ **b.** $8(-22.2) + 33 = -144.6$; $3(-22.2) - 78 = -144.6$ **7.** $d = 15 + 3t$, $d = 4t$; The solution is $(15, 60)$, so Bart's sister will win.

9. a. $\begin{cases} d = 60t \\ d = 65\left(t - \frac{1}{10}\right) \end{cases}$ **b.** $(1.3, 78)$; after 1.3 hours

c. 78 miles **11. a.** about 8.42 yr before 2000 (1991)

b. about 4,189,474 people **13.** $2\frac{1}{2}$ hr **15. a.** $(1, 4)$ and $(-8, 85)$ **b.** $2(1^2) + 5(1) - 3 = 4$ and $1^2 - 2(1) + 5 = 4$; $2(-8)^2 + 5(-8) - 3 = 85$ and $(-8)^2 - 2(-8) + 5 = 85$

17. $(-18, 8)$

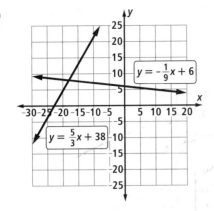

$y = -\frac{1}{9}x + 6$

$y = \frac{5}{3}x + 38$

b.

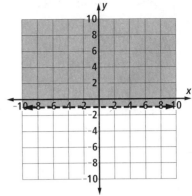

19. a. $y^2 - 5y + 1$ **b.** $y = -0.076$ and $y = 13.076$
21. $18x + 25y$ dollars

Lesson 10-3 (pp. 594-600)

Guided Example 3: $100 - x$; $100 - x$; $100 - x$; 3,000; 30x;
   $-10x$
1. 1,190 adults, 2,380 children **3.** $56.00 by the
drama, $224 by the service club **5. a.** $n = 16, w = -2$
b. $16 + 5(-2) = 6$ and $-8(-2) = 16$ **7. a.** $x = 6, y = 5$
b. $6 - 1 = 5$ and $4(6) - 5 = 19$ **9. a.** $(-4, 12)$
b.

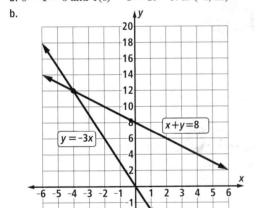

$y = -3x$

$x + y = 8$

11. $(40, -50)$ **13.** $T = \$870,000, L = \$750,000$

15. a. $\begin{cases} m = v + 40 \\ m + v = 1{,}230 \end{cases}$ **b.** $m = 635, v = 595$

17. no solution **19.** $x = -2$
21. a.

Lesson 10-4 (pp. 601–607)

Guided Example 3: $3N + 2M = 488$; $-3N - 2M = -488$;
$4M = 76$; 19; 150; 19; $150; $19
Questions: **1. a.** when the coefficients of the same
variable are opposites **b.** to eliminate one variable from a
system **3. a.** $x = \frac{-35}{4}, y = \frac{45}{4}$ **b.** $3\left(-\frac{35}{4}\right) + 9\left(\frac{45}{4}\right) = 75$;
$-3\left(-\frac{35}{4}\right) - \frac{45}{4} = 15$ **5.** 1,634 and 142 **7.** when one of the
coefficients for a variable in one equation is the same as
the variable's coefficient in another equation
9. $(x, y) = (6, 15)$ **11.** $3(150) + 6(19) = 564$,
$3(150) + 2(19) = 488$ **13.** $(x, y) = \left(12, -\frac{5}{3}\right)$ **15. a.** Yes; by
the Generalized Addition Property of Equality **b.** Answers
vary. Sample answer: Yes; because $\frac{3}{5} = 60\%$, they are
simply different ways of writing the same value.
17. $(x, y) = (0.9, -1.2)$ **19. a.** $x = -7, x = 4$ **b.** $-7, 4$
21. a. $\left\{x : x \geq \frac{9}{2}\right\}$ **b.** All nonnegative numbers **23.** $-\frac{b}{a}$
25. $x = 212$

Lesson 10-5 (pp. 608-615)

1. a. Answers vary. Sample answer: second; $-3, d$
b. $(x, d) = (69, -112)$ **3. a.** Answers vary. Sample answer:
The first equation can be multiplied by 2 and the second
equation can be multiplied by -7. **b.** The first equation
can be multiplied by 5 and the second equation can be
multiplied by 3. **c.** $(r, s) = (3, 4)$ **5. a.** 31 musicians and
26 flag bearers **b.** No, it is not possible. **7.** $(x, y) = \left(-\frac{5}{4}, \frac{10}{3}\right)$
9. $(x, y) = \left(-\frac{13}{5}, -\frac{3}{5}\right)$ **11.** $(x, y) = (-5.\overline{1}, -8.47\overline{2})$ **13.** 5 ER,
30 MC **15. a.** 11 cows, 16 chickens **b.** Answers vary.
Sample answer: By assuming there will be 14 chickens
and 13 cows, a person would count 80 legs. For every cow
replaced by a chicken, we lose 2 legs. Therefore, someone
could conclude that there were 16 chickens and 11 cows.
17. $(x, y) = (12, 4)$ **19. a.** 15 weeks **b.** $1,050 **21.** $-\frac{1}{4}$
23. a. true **b.** true **c.** true

Lesson 10-6 (pp. 616-621)

Guided Example 2: 1. $36x - 30y = 6$ 2. $-36x + 30y = -6$
3. $0 = 0$

Questions: 1. They are equal.

3. a.

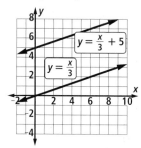

b.

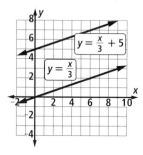

c. $y = \frac{1}{3}x$ 5. Answers vary. Sample answer:

$\begin{cases} y = 2x + 3 \\ 2y = 4x + 6 \end{cases}$ 7. a. coincident

b.

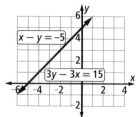

9. a. none b. Answers vary. Sample answer: The system
$\begin{cases} x + y = -2 \\ \frac{x+y}{2} = 1 \end{cases}$ has no solution.   11. coincident lines
13. two intersecting lines   15. Yes, she got her
15% discount.   17. a. $t + u = 16, t + 3u = 28$
b. $t = 10, u = 6$ c. $6 + 10 = 16, 10 + 18 = 28$ 19. a. $2d^4$
b. $\sqrt{2^8 + 3(2)^8} = 32 = 2(2)^4$ 21. a. $x = -6$ b. $y = 18$

Lesson 10-7 (pp. 622-628)

1. a. 2×3 b. a, b, c c. f 3. a. $\begin{bmatrix} 5 & -2 \\ 3 & 4 \end{bmatrix}$ b. $\begin{bmatrix} -4 \\ 34 \end{bmatrix}$

5. -4 7. $\begin{bmatrix} 18.5 & -32 \\ -20 & 44 \end{bmatrix}$ 9. Answers vary.

Sample answer: $\begin{bmatrix} 2 & -1 \\ 1 & 2 \end{bmatrix} \cdot \begin{bmatrix} 3 & -1 \\ -3 & 2 \end{bmatrix} = \begin{bmatrix} 9 & -4 \\ -3 & 3 \end{bmatrix}$,

$\begin{bmatrix} 3 & -1 \\ -3 & 2 \end{bmatrix} \cdot \begin{bmatrix} 2 & -1 \\ 1 & 2 \end{bmatrix} = \begin{bmatrix} 5 & -5 \\ -4 & 7 \end{bmatrix}$ 11. -10 13. Answers

vary. Sample answer: $M = \begin{bmatrix} 1 & 1 \\ 1 & 1 \end{bmatrix}, N = \begin{bmatrix} 2 & 1 \\ 1 & 2 \end{bmatrix}$,

$P = \begin{bmatrix} 0 & -1 \\ 3 & 1 \end{bmatrix}$ a. $MN = \begin{bmatrix} 3 & 3 \\ 3 & 3 \end{bmatrix}$ b. $MN(P) = \begin{bmatrix} 9 & 0 \\ 9 & 0 \end{bmatrix}$

c. $NP = \begin{bmatrix} 3 & -1 \\ 6 & 1 \end{bmatrix}$ d. $M(NP) = \begin{bmatrix} 9 & 0 \\ 9 & 0 \end{bmatrix}$

e. It might be associative.   15. two intersecting lines, by
comparing the slopes and y-intercepts   17. $(2.5, 0)$
19. a. $(0.5, 3), (5, 3), (5, -6)$ b. $4.5, 9$, and approximately
10.06 c. 20.25 units^2 21. approximately 27.9%

Lesson 10-8 (pp. 629-634)

1. $(7, -3)$ 3. $\begin{bmatrix} 1 & 0 \\ 0 & 1 \end{bmatrix} \begin{bmatrix} x \\ y \end{bmatrix} = \begin{bmatrix} 7 \\ -3 \end{bmatrix}$

5. $\begin{bmatrix} 1 & -2 \\ 5 & 4 \end{bmatrix} \cdot \begin{bmatrix} \frac{2}{7} & \frac{1}{7} \\ -\frac{5}{14} & \frac{1}{14} \end{bmatrix} = \begin{bmatrix} \frac{2}{7} & \frac{1}{7} \\ -\frac{5}{14} & \frac{1}{14} \end{bmatrix} \cdot \begin{bmatrix} 1 & -2 \\ 5 & 4 \end{bmatrix} = \begin{bmatrix} 1 & 0 \\ 0 & 1 \end{bmatrix}$

7. a. $\begin{bmatrix} 3 & 5 \\ 2 & 3 \end{bmatrix} \begin{bmatrix} x \\ y \end{bmatrix} = \begin{bmatrix} 27 \\ 17 \end{bmatrix}$ b. $\begin{bmatrix} -3 & 5 \\ 2 & -3 \end{bmatrix}$

c. $(x, y) = (4, 3)$ 9. a. $\begin{bmatrix} 2 & -6 \\ 7.5 & -15 \end{bmatrix} \begin{bmatrix} m \\ t \end{bmatrix} = \begin{bmatrix} -6 \\ -37.5 \end{bmatrix}$

b. $\begin{bmatrix} -1 & 0.4 \\ -0.5 & 0.13 \end{bmatrix}$ c. $(m, t) = (-9, -2)$ 11. a. $\begin{bmatrix} 0.992 & -.413 \\ -1.281 & 0.950 \end{bmatrix}$

$\begin{bmatrix} -5.5 \\ -1.1 \end{bmatrix}$ b. $(x, y) = (-5, 6)$ c. $2.3(-5) + 6 = -5.5; 3.1(-5) +$

$2.4(6) = -1.1$ 13. a. III; $\begin{bmatrix} 4 & -5 \\ 12 & -15 \end{bmatrix}$ b. Answers vary.

Sample answer: Error: Singular matrix.   15. $\begin{bmatrix} -20 & 17 \\ -8 & -4 \end{bmatrix}$

17. $a = 8$ 19. intersecting at only one point
21. a. $x = 12, x = -12$ b. $x = 10, x = -10$ c. $x = 5, x = -5$
d. $x = -5.5$ 23. $\$2,154.76$

Lesson 10-9 (pp. 635-639)

Guided Example 3: 1. parallel

2.

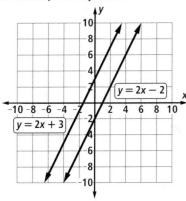

3. below; above. No, because the half-planes can intersect even if the lines do not.

4.

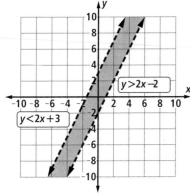

Questions: 1. IV **3. a.** It is the intersection of the half-planes below or on the line $y = 4x + 1$ and above $y = 2x + 1$. **b.** half-plane **c.** Because $\leq$ means less than or equal to, not just less than **d.** No, it is not because it is on the boundary line $y = 2x + 1$.

5.

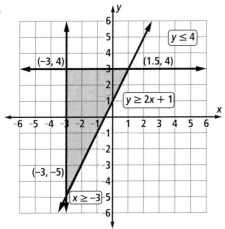

7. Yes it is possible. If there are no solutions satisfying both conditions, then the solution is Ø.

9. $\begin{cases} y \leq 0 \\ 3x + 7y < 10 \end{cases}$ **11. a.** $\begin{cases} 10L + 8P \leq 60 \\ P \geq 0 \\ L \geq 0 \end{cases}$

b.

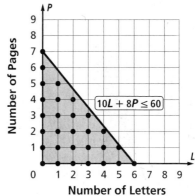

13. a.

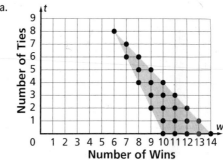

b. 25 **15. a.** $\begin{bmatrix} 6 & 4 \\ -2 & -3 \end{bmatrix} \cdot \begin{bmatrix} x \\ y \end{bmatrix} = \begin{bmatrix} 14 \\ -18 \end{bmatrix}$

b. $\begin{bmatrix} \frac{3}{10} & \frac{2}{5} \\ -\frac{1}{5} & -\frac{3}{5} \end{bmatrix}$ **c.** $(-3, 8)$ **17.** $(6.5, -10.25)$ **19. a.** -10 ft

b. The rocket has already landed.

Lesson 10-10 (pp. 640-644)

Guided Example 1: 7; 12; –2, 7; 3, 12

Questions: 1. (–3, –1) 3. (0, 0) 5. (4, 61), (–3, –2)

7.

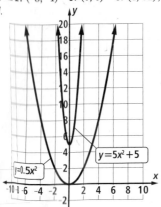

no solution

9. (3, 0)

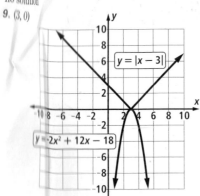

11. $\begin{cases} y = x^2 + 6x + 11 \\ y = -x^2 + 6x - 9 \end{cases}$; multiply the second equation

by –1: $\begin{cases} y = x^2 + 6x + 11 \\ -y = x^2 - 6x + 9 \end{cases}$; then add: $0 = 2x^2 + 20$.

So, $2x^2 = -20$, $x^2 = -10$ which there is no solution.

13. a. The system must have exactly one solution.
b. 0.41 sec c. about 2.76 ft d. Answers vary. Sample answer: No, the graph represents the height with respect to time; if the graph were of height with respect to distance traveled, then the graph would be of the ball's flight. 15. $n = 5$ 17. $45,604

Self-Test (pp. 648-649)

1. $(x, y) = (-18, -25)$; $x - 7 = 1.5x + 2 - 0.5x = 9$; $x = -18$; $y = -25$ 2. $(d, f) = (6, 3)$; $4f = 12$; $f = 3$; $d = 6$

3. $(g, h) = \left(\frac{-6}{13}, \frac{10}{13}\right)$; $\begin{cases} 7h + 3g = 4 \\ 6h - 3g = 6 \end{cases}$ $13h = 10$; $h = \frac{10}{13}$; $g = -\frac{6}{13}$

4. (15, 7)

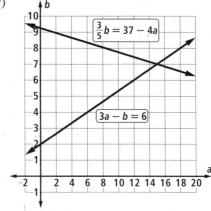

5. (1, –1) and (2, 5). Answers vary. Sample answer: $6x - 7 = x^2 + 3x - 5$, $x^2 - 3x + 2 = 0$, $x = 1$ or $x = 2$. When $x = 1$, $y = -1$. When $x = 2$, $y = 5$. 6. This is a linear system of 2 lines with different slopes. Thus there is one solution.

7. $\begin{bmatrix} 2 \cdot 3 + 7 \cdot 4 \\ 1 \cdot 3 + 0 \cdot 4 \end{bmatrix} = \begin{bmatrix} 34 \\ 3 \end{bmatrix}$

8. $\begin{bmatrix} 3 \cdot 2 + 5 \cdot 1 & 3 \cdot 8 + 5 \cdot 7 \\ 4 \cdot 2 + 6 \cdot 1 & 4 \cdot 8 + 6 \cdot 7 \end{bmatrix} = \begin{bmatrix} 11 & 59 \\ 14 & 74 \end{bmatrix}$

9. $\begin{bmatrix} 3 & 5 \\ 1 & -1 \end{bmatrix} \begin{bmatrix} p \\ q \end{bmatrix} = \begin{bmatrix} 5 \\ 7 \end{bmatrix}$

$\begin{bmatrix} \frac{1}{8} & \frac{5}{8} \\ \frac{1}{8} & -\frac{3}{8} \end{bmatrix} \begin{bmatrix} 3 & 5 \\ 1 & -1 \end{bmatrix} \begin{bmatrix} p \\ q \end{bmatrix} = \begin{bmatrix} \frac{1}{8} & \frac{5}{8} \\ \frac{1}{8} & -\frac{3}{8} \end{bmatrix} \begin{bmatrix} 5 \\ 7 \end{bmatrix}$

$\begin{bmatrix} p \\ q \end{bmatrix} = \begin{bmatrix} 5 \\ -2 \end{bmatrix}$

10. $\begin{cases} 3d + 6t = 6,795 \\ 4d + 4t = 4,860 \end{cases}$, $\begin{cases} -6d - 12t = -13,590 \\ 12d - 12t = 14,580 \end{cases}$, $6d = 990$, $d = 165$, $t = 1,050$; DVD players cost $165 each; high-definition televisions cost $1,050 each. 11. Answers vary. Sample answer: $m = n = 5$, $c = d = 4$ 12. All points with integer coordinates in the shaded region below.

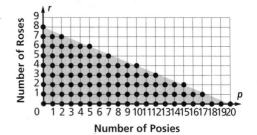

13. $(0.4, 6.2)$

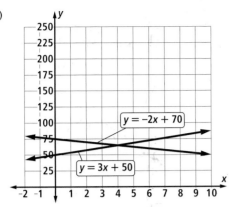

14. $\begin{cases} 2j + 2w = 1{,}000 \\ 2.5j - 2.5w = 1{,}000 \end{cases} \begin{cases} 2j + 2w = 1{,}000 \\ 2.5j - 2.5w = 1{,}000 \end{cases}$,
$j = 500 - w$, $2.5(500 - w) - 2.5w = 1{,}000$, $1{,}250 - 2.5w - 2.5w = 1{,}000$, $5w = 250$, $w = 50$, $j = 450$ airplane's speed: 450 mph; speed of jet stream: 50 mph

15. a.

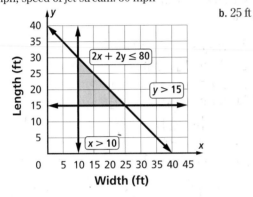

b. 25 ft

16.

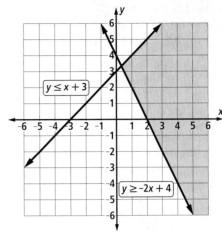

17. $\begin{cases} q + d = 15 \\ 0.25q + 0.10d = 2.40 \end{cases}$;
$q = 15 - d$, $0.25(15 - d) + 0.10d = 2.40$, $3.75 - 0.25d + 0.10d = 2.40$, $-0.15d = -1.35$, $d = 9$, $q = 6$; 9 dimes and 6 quarters

18. $\begin{cases} y < 7 \\ y \geq 2x - 7 \\ y \geq -\frac{3}{4}x + 4 \end{cases}$

The chart below keys the **Self-Test** questions to the objectives in the **Chapter Review** on pages 650–653 or to the **Vocabulary (Voc)** on page 647. This will enable you to locate those **Chapter Review** questions that correspond to questions missed on the **Self-Test**. The lesson where the material is covered is also indicated on the chart.

Question	1	2	3	4	5	6	7	8	9	10
Objective(s)	A	B	B	I	E	F	C	C	D	G
Lesson(s)	10-2, 10-3	10-4, 10-5	10-4, 10-5	10-1, 10-6, 10-10	10-10	10-6	10-7	10-7	10-8	10-2, 10-3, 10-4, 10-5, 10-6

Question	11	12	13	14	15	16	17	18
Objective(s)	F	J	I	H	J	J	G	K
Lesson(s)	10-6	10-9	10-1, 10-6, 10-10	10-9	10-9	10-9	10-2, 10-3, 10-4, 10-5, 10-6	10-9

Chapter Review (pp. 650–653)

1. $m = 2$, $n = 2$ **3.** $(-0.2, 4.6)$ **5.** $(a, b) = \left(-\frac{1}{3}, -\frac{13}{9}\right)$

7. $(f, g) = \left(\frac{102}{7}, -\frac{19}{7}\right)$ **9.** $(v, w) = \left(-\frac{29}{27}, \frac{44}{27}\right)$ **11.** $\begin{bmatrix} -2 \\ 41 \end{bmatrix}$

13. $\begin{bmatrix} 26 & -2 \\ 19 & -13 \end{bmatrix}$ **15. a.** $\begin{bmatrix} 3 & 2 \\ 5 & 7 \end{bmatrix} \begin{bmatrix} x \\ y \end{bmatrix} = \begin{bmatrix} 7 \\ 9 \end{bmatrix}$

b. $\begin{bmatrix} \frac{7}{11} & -\frac{2}{11} \\ -\frac{5}{11} & \frac{3}{11} \end{bmatrix}$ c. $\begin{bmatrix} x \\ y \end{bmatrix} = \begin{bmatrix} \frac{31}{11} \\ -\frac{8}{11} \end{bmatrix}$ 17. a. $\begin{bmatrix} 5 & -7 \\ 4 & -8 \end{bmatrix} \begin{bmatrix} p \\ q \end{bmatrix} = \begin{bmatrix} 20 \\ 14 \end{bmatrix}$

b. $\begin{bmatrix} \frac{2}{3} & -\frac{7}{12} \\ \frac{1}{3} & -\frac{5}{12} \end{bmatrix}$ c. $\begin{bmatrix} p \\ q \end{bmatrix} = \begin{bmatrix} \frac{31}{6} \\ \frac{5}{6} \end{bmatrix}$ 19. $(-1, -2)$, $(1, -2)$

21. 0 solutions 23. 1 solution 25. When $a \neq b$, since equating y and subtracting mx from both sides yields $a = b$. 27. slope 29. Austin: 280 mi, Antonio: 70 mi
31. after the fourth year 33. $\frac{8}{3}$ pints of the 15% solution and $\frac{16}{3}$ pints of the 30% solution

35.

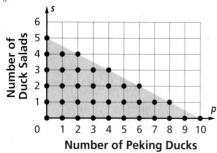

37. a.

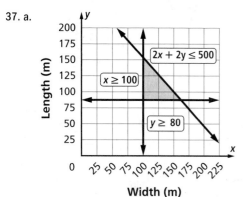

b. 650 ft c. 670 ft 39. $(5, -4.5)$ 41. infinitely many solutions 43. $(-4.2, -2.8)$, $(2.7, 7.6)$

45.

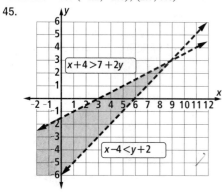

47.

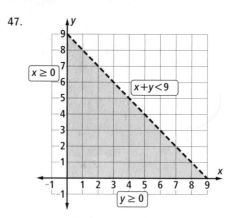

49.

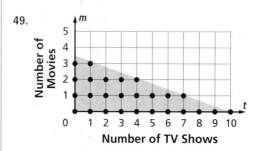

51. $\begin{cases} y \leq 0 \\ y \geq -5 \\ y \leq -2x + 7 \\ y \geq -2x - 5 \end{cases}$

Chapter 11

Lesson 11-1 (pp. 656–662)
Guided Example 2: $100; 100; 3; $120; $120x^2$; $140; $140x^1$ $160
Questions: 1. a. $4,071 b. $125.90 3. a. $75x^3 + 85x^2 + 95x + 105$ b. $225x^3 + 255x^2 + 285x + 315$ 5. Kelsey is correct. 7. $84,267 = 8 \cdot 10^4 + 4 \cdot 10^3 + 2 \cdot 10^2 + 6 \cdot 10^1 + 7 \cdot 10^0$
9. $515 11. a. $200x^2 + 300x + 250$ b. $200x^3 + 300x^2 + 250x + 300$ c. $200x^4 + 300x^3 + 250x^2$ $300x$ d. $200x^5 + 300x^4 + 250x^3 + 300x^2$ 13. D 15. $54n^2 + 65n - 21$
17. $6x^3 + 2x^2 - 2x + 2$ 19. $x = \frac{2}{9}$ 21. $7y^2 + 4y - 22$
23. $0.56 25. a. $h = \frac{1}{2}$ b. h can be any real number but $\frac{1}{2}$.
27. a. cross-fertilized: skewed left; self-fertilized: symmetric b. Cross-fertilize the plants because the mean is greater than that of self-fertilized plants.

Lesson 11-2 (pp. 663–668)
Guided Example: 1. $22w + 8$ 2. 2 3. $x^3 - x^2 - 12$; 3
4. $2x - 2$; 1 Questions: 1. $3x^2 + 4$ is a sum of monomials, while $\frac{3}{x^2} + 4$ includes a quotient of monomials.
3. a. a monomial b. 11. 5. a. a monomial b. 2 7. xyz is not a trinomial, it is a monomial because there is only one term. 9. $-3x^5 + 8x^2 - 4x + 12$ 11. $3x^2 + 2x + 5$

13. never; Polynomials with the same degree are like terms; to find their sum you add the coefficients. Thus, the degrees of the sum may be less than or equal to, but will never be greater than the degree of either addend.
15. a. $-140x^2$ b. 2   17. a. $2xy$ b. 2   19. a. 3 b. 3 c. 3
d. 3   21. 1   23. 2 25. a. Answers vary. Sample answer: x^{70} b. Answers vary. Sample answer: $x^{35}y^{35}$
27. a. Answers vary. Sample answer: $x^5 + x + 1, x^5 + x + 6$
b. Answers vary. Sample answer: $x^5 + 6x + 8, -x^5 + 4x + 2$
29. a. $1,000x^{18}$ b. $2,406.61   31. 2 m   33. $n^2 + 52n$

Lesson 11-3 (pp. 669-674)

1. $55x^2$ 3. a. $3h^2 + 15h$
b.

h	1	1	1	1	1
h	h^2	h	h	h	h	h
h	h^2	h	h	h	h	h
h	h^2	h	h	h	h	h

5. a. $4x^2 + 2x$ b. $2x(2x + 1)$
c. $4x^2 + 2x = 2x(2x + 1)$
7. $ab - ac + ad$
9. $-25x^3 - 5x^2 + 31x$
11. $-2ab^2 + a^2b - 5ab$

13. a. $(2 + h)C + (2 + h)B + (2 + h)E$ b. $h(C + B + E) + 2(C + B + E)$ c. $(2 + h)(C + B + E)$ 15. $4x^2$
17. $2m^4 + 2m^3 + 6m^2$ 19. $4xy$ 21. $20n^2 + 9n - 10$
23. a. not a polynomial b. The term $2a^{-2}$ is not a monomial and polynomials are all monomials or sums of monomials.   25. Answers vary. Sample answer: $x^4 + x + 1$
27. $c > \frac{4}{3}$ 29. $\frac{10}{9m}$ 31. $y = \frac{1}{2}(x - 1)$

Lesson 11-4 (pp. 675-679)

Guided Example 3: 4; a; $4a$; $5a^2b$; 2; $-3a^4b^2$; $5a^2b$; 2; $3a^4b^2$
Questions: 1. 1, 3, 11, 33, $x, x^2, x^3, x^4, 3x, 3x^2, 3x^3, 3x^4$, $11x, 11x^2, 11x^3, 11x^4, 33x, 33x^2, 33x^3, 33x^4$ 3. a^2b
5. a. The greatest common factor of $15c^2 + 5c$ is $5c$. So $15c^2 + 5c = 5c(3c + 1)$.
b.

	c	c	c	1
c	c^2	c^2	c^2	c
c	c^2	c^2	c^2	c
c	c^2	c^2	c^2	c
c	c^2	c^2	c^2	c
c	c^2	c^2	c^2	c

7. The factor of both x^2 and xy is x and thus, it is factorable.   9. $6n^4 + 5n^2$
11. $33(a - b + ab)$
13. $4v^9(3 + 4v)$ 15. $7rh$

17. a. 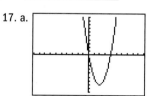 b.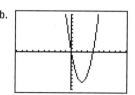

c. The two graphs are the same because $2x(x - 4)$ is a factored form of $2x^2 - 8x$, so the two equations describe the same graph.   19. $2\pi r(r + h)$

21. $-50n^{98} - 40n^{78} + 30n^{58}$ for $n \neq 0$
23. $2k^3 - kn + 4n^2$ 25. B   27. 121

Lesson 11-5 (pp. 680–684)

Guided Example 1: $5x$; (-3); $5x$; (-3); $5x$; (-3); $5x^3$; $(-3x^2)$; $(-20x^2)$; $12x$; $40x$; (-24); $5x^3$; $-23x^2$; $52x$; -24
Questions: 1. a. $(y + 12) \cdot (y^2 + 5y + 7)$ b. $y^3 + 17y^2 + 67y + 84$ 3. a. $12x^2 - 22x - 20$ b. $(2(10) - 5) \cdot (6(10) + 4) = 960$; $12(10)^2 - 22(10) - 20 = 960$
c.

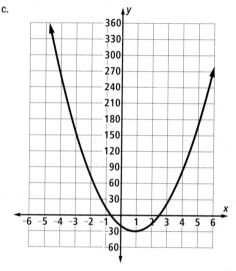

5. $2n^3 + 5n^2 + 2n - 1$ 7. $4x^4 + 16$ 9. $5c^2 + 28d^2 - 39cd + c - 7d$ 11. a. $12x^2 + 26x + 10$ b. $12x^2 - 26x + 10$
c. The expansion of $(a - b)(c - d)$ is the same as the expansion of $(a + b)(c + d)$, except the second term has the opposite sign.   13. $\frac{1}{25}x^2 - 1.08x + 7.29$ 15. $n = 5$ or $n = -\frac{31}{2}$ 17. $-5x^2 - 8$ 19. a. $\frac{33}{16}$ b. 6 c. 69

Lesson 11-6 (pp. 685-690)

Guided Example 2: Solution 1: $2 \cdot 7c \cdot 5$; 5^2; 49; 70; 25
Solution 2: $7c$; 5; $7c$; $7c$; 5; 5; 49; 70; 25
Solution 3:

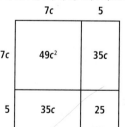

$49c^2 + 70c + 25$
Check: 26; 676; 49; 70; 25; 49; 70; 25; 676

Questions: 1. $g^2 + 2gh + h^2$ 3. $g^2 - h^2$ 5. Answers vary. Sample answer: $x^2 + 2x + 1$

7. a.

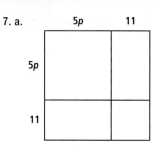

b. $(5p + 11)^2$ **c.** $25p^2 + 110p + 121$ **9.** $x^2 - 10x + 25$ **11.** $n^4 - 16$ **13.** $81 - 36x + 4x^2$ **15.** $9x^2 - y^2z^2$ **17. a.** 900; Answers vary. Sample answer: $30^2 = (3 \cdot 10)^2 = 3^2 \cdot 10^2 = 900$ **b.** 899; Answers vary. Sample answer: $29 \cdot 31 = (30 - 1)(30 + 1) = 30^2 - 1^2 = 899$ **c.** 896; Answers vary. Sample answer: $28 \cdot 32 = (30 - 2)(30 + 2) = 30^2 - 2^2 = 896$ **d.** 891; Answers vary. Sample answer: $27 \cdot 33 = (30 - 3)(30 + 3) = 30^2 - 3^2 = 891$ **19.** 40,401; Answers vary. Sample answer: $201^2 = (200 + 1)(200 + 1) = 200^2 + 2 \cdot 200 \cdot 1 + 1^2 = 40,401$ **21.** perfect square trinomial **23.** perfect square trinomial **25.** difference of squares **27.** Answers vary. Sample answer: because the largest area, when the perimeters are equal, always comes out of a square. **29.** $18x^2 + 2y^2$ **31. a.** $2,000 **b.** $800 **c.** Answers vary. Sample answer: $x = 1.03$; $10,453.31 **33.** Answers vary. Sample answer: the volume of a cube with side e **35.** Answers vary. Sample answer: the area of the region between a circle with radius s that is inside a circle with radius r

Lesson 11-7 (pp. 691-696)

Guided Example 2: without; 11; 10; 9; 11; 10; 9; 990
Questions: 1. a. Answers vary. Sample answer: ABCD, ABCE **b.** 360 permutations **3.** $n(n - 1)$ **5. a.** Answers vary. Sample answer: VWXYZ, ZYXWV **b.** 120 permutations **7.** $n!$ **9.** 56 **11.** $\frac{1}{272}$ **13.** Yes, $n! = n \cdot (n - 1)!$, for $n \geq 1$ **15. a.** 24 **b.** 3157; 3159; 3175; 3179; 3195; 3197; 3517; 3519; 3571; 3579; 3591; 3597; 3715; 3719; 3751; 3759; 3791; 3795; 3915; 3917; 3951; 3957; 3971; 3975 **17.** ABCD, ABDC, ACBD, ACDB, ADBC, ADCB **19.** The smaller circle has $8\pi(r - 2)$ square units less area. **21.** $6x^4 + 2x + 4, x \neq 0$ **23.** Answers vary. Sample answer: $-3x^3 + 4x^2 + 7$

Lesson 11-8 (pp. 697-702)

1. how different a set of actually observed scores is from a set of expected scores **3.** for expected frequencies less than 5 **5. a.** 23.7 **b.** Yes, the chi-square value of 23.7 for 7 events occurs with probability less than 0.001. **7.** The spinner seems to be fair. **9.** The chi-square value of 44.9 for 4 events occurs with probability less than 0.001, so there is evidence for the view that more tornadoes occur at certain times of the year (spring) than at others. **11. a.** 120 **b.** 720 **13. a.** $4x^2 + 4xy + y^2$ **b.** $4x^2 - 4xy + y^2$ **c.** $4x^2 - y^2$ **15.** $9k^4 - 36k^3m + 54k^2m^2 - 36m^3k + 9m^4$ **17. a.** 3.6 cm/day **b.** 25.2 cm/wk

Self-Test (pp. 706-707)

1. $3x(10 - 4x + x^3) = 30x - 12x^2 + 3x^4 = 3x^4 - 12x^2 + 30x$ **2.** $(2b - 5)^2 = (2b - 5)(2b - 5) = (2b)^2 - 2(2b)(5) + 5^2 = 4b^2 - 20b + 25$ **3.** $(8z + 3)(8z - 3) = (8z)^2 - 3^2 = 64z^2 - 9$ **4.** $6a(2a^2 + 9a - 1) = 12a^3 + 54a^2 - 6a$ **5.** $(5a^2 - a)(5a^2 - a) = (5a^2)^2 - 2(5a^2)(a) + a^2 = 25a^4 - 10a^3 + a^2$ **6.** $(2 - 6c)(4 + 3c) = 2(4 + 3c) - 6c(4 + 3c) = 8 + 6c - 24c - 18c^2 = -18c^2 - 18c + 8$ **7.** 3 **8.** In standard form the polynomial is $19x^3 - 9x^2 + 2x - 5$ and has four terms, so it is not a monomial, binomial, nor a trinomial. **9.** $6x^2y^2(2x - 4y + 5y^2)$ **10.** $(20n^2 - 8n - 12) + (16n^3 - 7n^2 + 5) = 16n^3 + (20n^2 - 7n^2) - 8n + (5 - 12) = 16n^3 + 13n^2 - 8n^2 - 7$ **11.** $9p^4 + p^2 - 5 - p(3p^3 + p - 2) = 9p^4 + p^2 - 5 - 3p^4 - p^2 + 2p = 6p^4 + 2p - 5$ **12.** False; the expression has three terms so it is a trinomial, but the highest power of a variable term is 2 so it has degree 2. **13.** $\frac{28w^3 - 18w}{2w} = \frac{28w^3}{2w} - \frac{18w}{2w} = 14w^2 - 9$ **14.** area of rectangle: $(2n + 2)(2n - 2)$; area of triangle: $\frac{1}{2}(n + 3)(n - 1)$; area of shaded region $= 4n^2 - 4 - \frac{1}{2}n^2 - n + \frac{3}{2} = \frac{7}{2}n^2 - n - \frac{5}{2}$ **15.** 840; There are 7 swimmers to choose from to swim first, then 6 left to choose the second swimmer, 5 left to choose the third swimmer, and 4 swimmers left to pick the final racer. Thus, there are $7 \cdot 6 \cdot 5 \cdot 4 = 840$ possible orders. **16.** 13,800; There are 25 students who could get 1st place, then 24 remaining who could get 2nd place, and 23 remaining to get 3rd place. $25 \cdot 24 \cdot 23 = 13,800$ different permutations. **17.** For each year that she has had a certain amount of money she receives interest on that amount at the rate of x, thus M dollars received n years ago will be worth Mx^n dollars. So on her 21st birthday she will have $200x^5 + 150x^4 + 300x^3 + 300x^2$ dollars. **18.** $200(1.03)^5 + 150(1.03)^4 + 300(1.03)^3 + 300(1.03)^2 = 1,046.77$; she would have $1,046.77 on her 21st birthday. **19. a.** $9x^2 + 18x$ **b.** $3x(3x + 6)$ **c.** No, 3 can be factored out of the parentheses and it can be factored completely to get $9x(x + 2)$.

20.

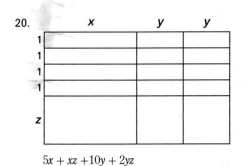

$$5x + xz + 10y + 2yz$$

21. The probability of the chi-square value of 11.03 for 6 events is between 0.10 and 0.05, so the results aren't very far from a random distribution; the die is probably not weighted.   **22.** $x^2 + 8x + 16$; See students' work.

The chart below keys the **Self-Test** questions to the objectives in the **Chapter Review** on pages 708–711 or to the **Vocabulary (Voc)** on page 705. This will enable you to locate those **Chapter Review** questions that correspond to questions missed on the **Self-Test**. The lesson where the material is covered is also indicated on the chart.

Question	1	2	3	4	5	6	7	8	9	10
Objective	B	D	B	B	D	B	E	E	C	A
Lesson(s)	11-3, 11-5, 11-6	11-6	11-3, 11-5, 11-6	11-3, 11-5, 11-6	11-6	11-3, 11-5, 11-6	11-2	11-2	11-4	11-1, 11-2

Question	11	12	13	14	15	16	17	18	19	20
Objective	A, B	E	C	I	G	G	F	F	C, I	I
Lesson(s)	11-1, 11-2, 11-3	11-2	11-4	11-3, 11-5, 11-6	11-7	11-7	11-1	11-1	11-3, 11-4, 11-5	11-3, 11-5, 11-6

Question	21	22
Objective	H	I
Lesson(s)	11-8	11-3, 11-5, 11-6

Chapter Review (pp. 708–711)

1. $4k^3 - 17k$ **3.** $5.4s^4 + 3.7x^3 + 9.8s^2 - 5.2s - 4$ **5.** -21
7. $9p^4 + 9p^3 - 54p^2 + 45p$ **9.** $\frac{1}{7}q^{11} - 2q^{10} + 16q^9 - \frac{5}{7}q^8$
11. $b^2 - 9$ **13.** $-72w^2 + 2$ **15.** $n^3 - 9n^2 + 26n - 24$
17. $\frac{51}{2}x^2 - \frac{11}{2}x - 1$ **19.** $uv(u - v)$ **21.** $15a^3b^2(3a^6b^3 + 4a^3b^2 - a^2b + 28)$ **23.** $p^2 + 12p + 36$ **25.** $2{,}025z^2 - 990z + 121$ **27.** B   **29.** Answers vary. Sample answer: $xy^3z + 3y + 9$ **31.** b and c   **33.** c   **35. a.** $1{,}200x^3 + 700x^2 + 500x$ **b.** \$373.05   **37.** 2,520 different ways
39. 10,000 different ways   **41.** 4,536 different ways
43. 504 different ways **45. a.** The company expected 36 pieces of mail each day Tuesday through Friday and 109 pieces on Monday. **b.** 5.523 **c.** There is no evidence for the belief that there was too much mail coming on Monday. The probability of a chi-square value of 5.523 for 5 events is greater than 0.1, so it is likely the deviation from the expected amount of mail was due to random chance.
47. a. $ab + 2a + 6b + 12$ **b.** $(a + 6)(b + 2)$ **c.** Yes, the answers are equal.   **49. a.** $3x(2x + 1)$ **b.** $6x^2 + 3x$

51.

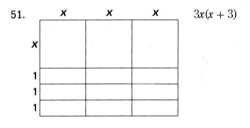

$3x(x + 3)$

Chapter 12

Lesson 12-1 (pp. 714–722)

Guided Example 4: a. $24 - 2L$; $12 - L$; $12 - L$; $(12 - L)$
c. 9 units; $3 \cdot 9$; 27 units^2; 2 units; $10 \cdot 2$; 20 units^2; 36 units^2; 6 units; 6 units
Questions: 1. a. $(-8, -16)$ **b.** $x = -8$ **3.** because $(x - 5)^2$ is never negative, $-4(x - 5)^2$ is never positive, and the greatest nonpositive number is 0, and so the greatest value of $-4(x - 5)^2 + 7$ is 7.   **5. a.** $(15, 21)$ **b.** $x = 15$ **c.** up
7. a. $(-6, -0.5)$ **b.** $x = -6$ **c.** down   **9.** All 3 graphs have $(4, -8)$ as their vertex, c opens up wider than a, and a opens up wider than b.   **11.** $y - 9 = -(x + 12)^2$

13. $y + 6 = -0.5x^2$ **15.** Answers may vary. Sample:
$y + 18 = -(x - 5)^2$ and $y + 18 = -2(x - 5)^2$ **17.** (23, 5)
19. Answers may vary. Sample:

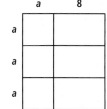

21. $m = \pm\sqrt{3}$ or $m = \pm2\sqrt{3}$ **23.** 5:20 P.M.   **25. a.** $x = 0$
b. $x < 0$

Lesson 12-2 (pp. 723–728)

1. $x^2 + 14x + 49$ **3.** $100; x + 10$ **5. a.** 1 **b.** $x + 1$
7. a. 12.25 **b.** $r - 3.5$ **9. a.** $\frac{1}{4}b^2$ **b.** $w - \frac{1}{2}b$
11. a. $y + 1.25 = (x - 1.5)^2$ **b.** -1.25 **13. a.** (1, 22)
b. maximum   **15.** No, because the minimum value of y is
0.75 since the vertex is (0.5, 0.75).   **17.** $x = \sqrt{137} - 12$ or
$x = -\sqrt{137} - 12$ **19.** The data do support the hypothesis.
The chi-square statistic yielded a value of approximately 4.
For $n = 3$, this occurs with a probability greater than 0.10.
So there is no reason to question the expected values of
the hypothesis.   **21.** 7.5   **23.** $120.83

Lesson 12-3 (pp. 729–735)

1. 8; –4   **3.** $x = 32$ or $x = -89.326$ **5.** $p = 0$ or $p = -19$
7. a. –15 and –7 **b.** (–11, –16)
c.

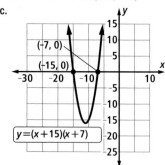

d.

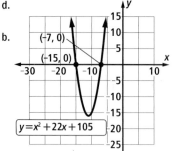

$y = x^2 + 22x + 105$
9. a. 0 and $-\frac{11}{4}$
$\left(-\frac{11}{8}, \frac{121}{16}\right)$

c.

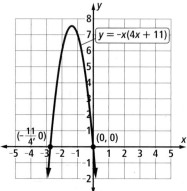
$y = -x(4x + 11)$

d.

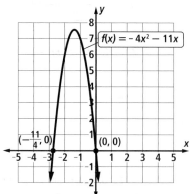
$f(x) = -4x^2 - 11x$

11. a. $x = -6.5$ **b.** Answers may vary. Sample: $y = 3(x + 11) \cdot$
$(x + 2), y = (x + 11)(x + 2), y = 50(x + 11) \cdot (x + 2)$
13. a. –5 b. $y = 2(x - 1)(x + 5); y + 18 = 2(x + 2)^2;$
$y = 2x^2 + 8x - 10$ **15. a.** $y - 5 = -(x - 5)^2$ **b.** (5, 5)

c.

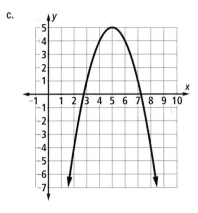

b.

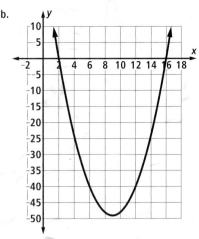

17. $25n^2 - 64$ 19. a. $(2, -4)$ b. $(a, 0)$ c. (r, s)

Lesson 12-4 (pp. 736-741)

Guided Example 2:

Product is −30	Sum of Factors
−1, 30	20
−2, 15	13
−3, 10	7
−5, 6	1
−6, 5	−1
−10, 3	−7
−15, 2	−13
−30; 1	−29

−6; 5; 6; 5 **Check 1:** 6; 5; 5; 6 **Check 2:** 6; 5
Guided Example 4: 1. −24; 5   **2.** 1   **3.** $m + 8$; $m - 3$
Check: $x + 8$; $x - 3$

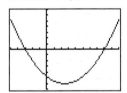

Questions: 1. a. factors: 1, 24; 2, 12; 3, 8; 4, 6; sums: 25, 14,
11, 10 **b.** $(x + 4)(x + 6)$ **c.** $(x + 4)(x + 6) = x^2 + 6x + 4x +$
$24 = x^2 + 10x + 24$ **3.** Simona's factorization is correct.
The b term in Sandra's factorization is $6 - 8 = -2$, not 2 as
desired. The c term in Steve's factorization is $(-6)(-8) = 48$,
not −48 as desired.   **5.** $(q + 1)(q + 19)$ **7.** $(v - 1)(v - 101)$
9. $(m - 2)(m + 19)$ **11.** a. $(x - 3)(x - 5)$ b. 3, 5
13. a. $y = (x - 2)(x - 16)$

15. $-(x - 8)(x - 5)$ **17.** $n = 10$ or $n = -12$. Check:
If $n = 10$, $(n - 10)(\frac{1}{2}n + 6) = 0 \cdot 11 = 0$. If $n = -12$,
$(n - 10)(\frac{1}{2}n + 6) = -22 \cdot 0 = 0$.   **19.** 20.25
21. $25a^2 - 9$ **23.** $9z^2 + 10$, $z \neq 0$ **25.** $4(7b^4 + 2b^2 + 10)$
27. slope $= \frac{1}{4}$, y-intercept $= 0$

Lesson 12-5 (pp. 742-747)

Guided Example 3: 15; 15; 1; −7; 1; 7; −1; $15y^2 + 32y - 7$;
$15y^2 - 32y - 7$; $15y^2 + 16y - 7$; $15y^2 - 16y - 7$; 1; 15;
$15y^2 + 104y - 7$; 1; 15; $15y^2 - 104y - 7$; 1; 15; $15y^2 - 8y - 7$;
1; 15; $15y^2 + 8y - 7$; $(3y + 1)(5y - 7)$
Guided Example 4: $3y + 1$; $5y - 7$; $3y + 1$; $5y - 7$; $-\frac{1}{3}$; $\frac{7}{5}$
Questions: 1. a. $8x^2 + 22x + 15$ b. $8x^2 + 26x + 15$
c. $8x^2 + 34x + 15$ d. $8x^2 + 62x + 15$ e. All of these would
be found in the process of trying to factor the trinomial.
3. a. $2(x^2 + 7x + 1)$ b. $5(n^2 + 7n - 10)$ **5.** $-(x - 3)(3x - 2)$
7. prime   **9.** $(x - 1)(17x - 19)$ **11.** $x = -\frac{3}{4}$ or $x = \frac{1}{5}$
13. $\left(\frac{3}{8}, -\frac{1}{8}\right)$ **15.** a. $n = -2$ or $n = \frac{1}{3}$ b. The solution works.
17. $p^2(5p + 3)^2$ **19.** a. $(x^4 - 4)(x^4 + 4)$ b. $(x^2 - 2)(x^2 + 2)$
$(x^4 + 4)$ **21.** $4 - \sqrt{13}, 4 + \sqrt{13}$ **23.** A

Lesson 12-6 (pp. 748-753)

Guided Example 2: 1. $2x^2 + 5x - 10$ **2.** 2; 5; −10   **3.** 105
4. no   **5.** The expression is not factorable with integer
coefficients.
Questions: 1. 169; factorable, $(x - 11)(x + 2)$ **3.** 0;
factorable; $(2n - 3)(2n - 3)$ **5.** 337; prime

7. The x-intercepts will be rational numbers when the expression is factorable. This occurs when $b^2 - 4ac$ is a perfect square. **9.** $n = 999$ **11.** Answers vary. Sample answer: $k = 8$ **13.** $(r - 4)(r - 1)$ **15. a.** $c = 20.25$ **b.** $(w + 4.5)(w + 4.5)$ **17.** $\frac{4m^7}{3n^3}$ **19.** $\frac{x^2}{25y^2}$

Lesson 12-7 (pp. 754–760)

Guided Example 1: $(x - 7.8); (x + 46); (x + 200); x - 7.8;$ $x + 46; x + 200$

Questions: 1. a. –5; 1.5

b.

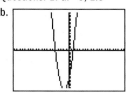

c. $f(x) = 2x^2 + 7x - 15$ **3. a.** 1; –0.5

b.

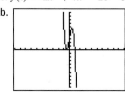

c. $y = -12x^3 + 9x + 3$ **5.** Answers vary. Sample answer: $y = (x + 9)(x - 4)$ **7. a.** Answers vary. Sample answer: $y = (x - 2)(x + 2) \cdot (x - 5)(x + 5)$ **b.** $y = x^4 - 29x^2 + 100$ **9.** Answers vary. Sample answer: $y = (x + 3)(x - 2)(x - 7)$ **11.** Answers vary. Sample answer: $y = (x + 5)^2(x - 4)^2$ **13. a.** 55; $1 + 4 + 9 + 16 + 25 = 55$ **b.** $(n + 1)^2$ **c.** $S(n) = \frac{1}{3}n^3 + \frac{1}{2}n^2 + \frac{1}{6}n$

15. a.

b. Answers vary. Sample answer: The graph crosses the x-axis at the x-intercept 5. **c.** Answers vary. Sample answer: The graph crosses the x-axis at the x-intercept 5. **d.** Answers vary. Sample answer: If a polynomial in factored form has a term of the form $(x - a)^3$, then the graph will cross the x-axis at $(a, 0)$. **17.** $4(a + 2b)(a - 2b)$ **19.** $a = -11$ or $a = 5$ **21.** B

Lesson 12-8 (pp. 761–767)

Guided Example 1: 1. $(2n + 1)^2$ **2.** $(2n + 1)(2n - 1)$ **3.** 2; 1; 2; 1; 2; 1; 2; 1 **4.** 2; 1; 2; 1

Guided Example 3: $d; b; ad + bc$

Questions: 1. A rational expression is the written quotient of two polynomials. **3.** $\frac{5b}{2c^2}, a \neq 0, b \neq 0, c \neq 0$ **5. a.** $\frac{2x - 3}{x + 2}$ **b.** 2 and –2 **c.** $\frac{2(10) - 3}{(10) + 2} = \frac{17}{12} = \frac{2(10)^2 - 7(10) + 6}{(10)^2 - 4}$ **7.** $\frac{1 \cdot 15 + 9 \cdot 7}{9 \cdot 15} = \frac{78}{135} = \frac{26}{45}$ **9.** Answers vary. Sample answer:

Let $k = 2$; then $\frac{6}{2 + 1} - \frac{3(2) + 7}{4 - 1} = -\frac{7}{3} = \frac{3(2) - 13}{(2 - 1)(2 + 1)}$ **11.** $\frac{15}{8n}$; let $n = 1$, $\frac{3}{2} + \frac{3}{8} = \frac{12}{8} + \frac{3}{8} = \frac{15}{8}$. **13.** $\frac{24x^2 - 29}{15(x - 1)}$; $x = 0$, then we have $\frac{8}{5} - \frac{1}{-3} = \frac{29}{15} = \frac{-29}{-15}$. **15.** $\frac{(x - 6)(x - 4)(x - 2)}{(x + 2)(x + 4)(x + 6)}$ **17. a.** $S = 819$, $F = 91, \frac{S}{F} = 9$ **b.** $\frac{S}{F} = \frac{2n + 1}{3}$ **c.** $\frac{S}{F}$ will only be an integer if $2n + 1$ is a multiple of 3. However, we know for some n, such as $n = 2$, $2n + 1$ will not be a multiple of 3 so $\frac{S}{F}$ is not an integer for that n. **19. a.** $t = \frac{v}{4.9}$ **b.** v is a multiple of 4.9. Answers vary. Sample answer: t is an integer if $v = 4.9$ m/sec and t is not an integer if $v = 10$ m/sec. **21.** $0.09x^2$ **23.** 17 questions right

Self-Test (pp. 771–772)

1. The product is –40, so possible factors include 10 and –4, –10 and 4, 8 and –5, and because $8 + -5 = 3$, the two factors are 8 and –5. Thus, $(x + 8)(x - 5)$ **2.** The product is 72, and the sum is negative. Therefore, possible factors include –18 and –4, –24 and –3, and –8 and –9, and since $-8 + -9 = -17$, the two factors are –8 and –9. Thus, $(m - 8)(m - 9)$ **3.** $a = -9$, so possible factors are 3 and –3, 9 and –1, or –9 and 1. $c = -2$, so the factors are either 2 and –1 or –2 and 1. Because $dg + ef = 9, d = -3, e = 2, f = 3$, and $g = -1$ as this is the only combination that works. Thus, $(-3h + 2)(3h - 1)$ **4.** B **5.** To complete the square, we add $\left(\frac{1}{2}b\right)^2$, so because $(-6)^2 = 36$, add 36.

6. $\frac{3x^2 - 75}{2x^2 - 7x - 15} = \frac{3(x^2 - 25)}{(2x + 3)(x - 5)} = \frac{3(x + 5)(x - 5)}{(2x + 3)(x - 5)} = \frac{3(x + 5)}{2x + 3}$, $x \neq 5; x \neq -\frac{3}{2}$ **7.** D **8. a.** By the Factor Theorem, the polynomial must have the factors $(x - 0) = x, (x + 3)$, and $(x - 9)$. One such polynomial is $y = x(x + 3)(x - 9)$. **b.** $y = x^3 - 6x^2 - 27x$ **9.** Let x be the length of a side of the frame. Since the area of the painting is 12 square feet, we can write $(x - 1)(x - 2) = 12$. We then put the equation in standard form, so $x^2 - 3x + 2 = 12$, which gives $x^2 - 3x - 10 = 0$. This factors as $(x - 5)(x + 2)$, so we have $(x - 5)(x + 2) = 0$. We cannot have a frame that has length –2, so the frame must have side length 5 feet. **10.** To put the equation in $y - k = a(x - h)^2$ form, we must complete the square. Thus, since $\left(\frac{1}{2}b\right)^2 = 1$, we must add 4 to both sides to get $y + 4 = x^2 - 2x + 1$. This then factors as $y + 4 = (x - 1)^2$, so the vertex is at $(1, -4)$. **11.** To put the equation in $y - k = a(x - h)^2$ form, we must complete the square. First, we move the 7 to the other side and factor a –2 out of the right hand side, which gives $y - 7 = -2(x^2 + 2x)$. Thus, because $\left(\frac{1}{2}b\right)^2 = 1$, we must add 1 into the $(x^2 + 2x)$ quantity. This gives $y - 9 = -2(x^2 + 2x + 1)$, which factors as $y - 9 = -2(x + 1)^2$.

Thus, the vertex is at (–1, 9).   **12.** By the equation, the vertex is at (3, 4) and *a* is positive, so the graph opens up.

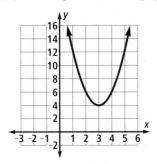

13. By the equation, the zeros of the function are at $x = 5$ and $x = -4$. Also, the axis of symmetry is $x = 0.5$, so the vertex is at (0.5, –20.25).

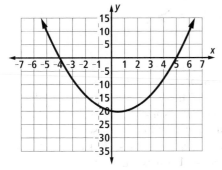

14. First, factor out $3n^2$ to get $3n^2(n^2 - 5n + 6)$. Now deal with what is in the parentheses. Because $c = 6$, possible factors include 3 and 2, –3 and –2, 6 and 1, and –6 and –1. Because $-3 + -2 = -5$, we have $3n^2(n - 3)(n - 2)$.
15. Let x be the length of the shorter side. Then $x(x + 9) = 486$, which gives $x^2 + 9x = 486$. Solving this equation gives x to be –27 or 18, but because length is positive, $x = 18$, so the dimensions are 18 cm by 27 cm.   **16.** False. A quadratic expression is only factorable over the integers when the discriminant is a perfect square, and not all positive numbers are perfect squares.   **17.** Answers vary. Sample answer: $y = 0.04(x + 3)^2(x - 1)(x - 4)$
18. a. Yes, they are equivalent because expanding each equation gives $x^2 + 4x + 3$. **b.** the vertex of the parabola

The chart below keys the **Self-Test** questions to the objectives in the **Chapter Review** on pages 773–775 or to the **Vocabulary (Voc)** on page 770. This will enable you to locate those **Chapter Review** questions that correspond to questions missed on the **Self-Test.** The lesson where the material is covered is also indicated on the chart.

Question	1	2	3	4	5	6	7	8	9	10
Objective	B	B	B	E	A	D	J	F	G	I
Lesson(s)	12-4, 12-5	12-4, 12-5	12-4, 12-5	12-4, 12-5, 12-6	12-2	12-8	12-3	12-7	12-1	12-2

Question	11	12	13	14	15	16	17	18
Objective	I	H	J	C	G	E	F	H
Lesson(s)	12-2	12-1	12-3	12-7	12-1	12-4, 12-5, 12-6	12-7	12-1

Chapter Review (pp. 773–775)

1. a. 4 **b.** $(x + 2)^2 - 4$ **3. a.** $\left(\frac{1}{2}b\right)^2$ **b.** $\left(\frac{z+1}{2}b\right)^2 - \left(\frac{1}{2}b\right)^2$
5. $(x - 3)(x + 2)$ **7.** $(m - 6)(m + 4)$ **9.** $(3x + 4)(x - 2)$
11. $2(3d + 2)(d - 2)$ **13. a.** $x = 3, x = -1, x = \frac{11}{2}$
b. $y = 12x^3 - 90x^2 + 96x + 198$ **15. a.** $x = 4, x = \frac{7}{2}, x = -2$
b. $f(x) = 2x^3 - 11x^2 - 2x + 56$ **17.** $4(n - 2m); n \neq 0,$
$m \neq 0$ **19.** $\frac{3 - 4n}{n - 3}$ **21.** $\frac{-(m - 4)}{(2m - 7)}$ **23.** perfect squares
25. $3(x + 3)(5x + 8)$ **27.** $2(4x^2 + 17x + 91)$
29. a. Answers vary. Sample answer: $f(x) = (x - 2)(x + 2)$
b. $f(x) = (x - 2)(x + 2) = x^2 - 4$ **31.** Answers vary.
Sample answer: $y = 4(x + 4)(x - 1)(x - 2)$
33. a. $A = 10x - x^2; P = 20$ **b.** $5 - \sqrt{5}$ units by $5 + \sqrt{5}$
units **35. a.** $A = x(195 - x)$ **b.** 9,000 yd^2
37. 90 m by 140 m

39.

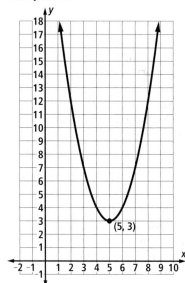

41.

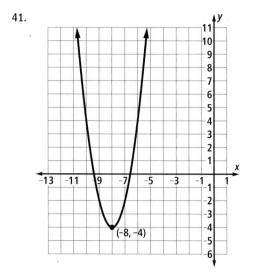

43. ii **45.** iii **47.** $(0, 0)$ **49.** $\left(\frac{1}{3}, -\frac{14}{3}\right)$

51.

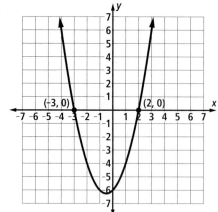

53.

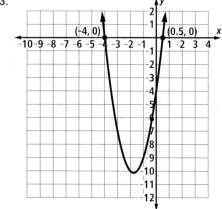

Chapter 13

Lesson 13-1 (pp. 778–783)

Guided Example 4: a. 60; 60 **b.** true, a rectangle **c.** false
d. A rectangle has 3 right angles, but it does not have to
be a square.
Guided Example 5: a. x is a real number **b.** P is a person
born in the United States **c.** p^g is not negative.
Questions: 1. the sun shines this afternoon; I will be
happy **3.** If x is an integer greater than 1, then x is a prime
number or the product of prime numbers. **5.** Solving the
inequality for x gives $x > -2$, so if the original inequality
is true, then $x > -2$ must also be true. **7.** Answers vary.
Sample answer: LW is the area of the rectangle; $2L + 2W$
is the perimeter of the rectangle. **9.** Answers vary.
Sample answer: n is a multiple of 10; n is an integer.

11. a. false **b.**

13. a. false **b.**

15. a.
Answers
vary. Sample
answer: Let
$t = 0$. Then

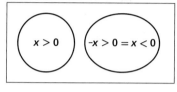

$t^4 = 0$, and 0 is not positive.
b. Answers vary. Sample answer: t can be any real
number except 0. **17. a.** Answers vary. Sample answer:
Let $x = -\frac{1}{2}$. Then $x^2 + x = \left(-\frac{1}{2}\right)^2 + \left(-\frac{1}{2}\right) = \frac{1}{4} - \frac{1}{2} = -\frac{1}{4}$, so
$y < 0$. **b.** $x \geq 0$ or $x \leq -1$
19. Answers vary. Sample answer:

$m\angle CAB = 90.00°$
$m\angle ABC = 12.59°$
$m\angle BCA = 77.41°$

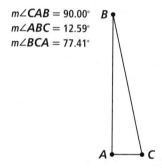

21. If something is a sentence, then it has a subject, verb,
and object; Answers vary. Sample answer: The sentence
"He went." has no object. **23. a.** $(a - 6)(a + 6)$
b. $(n - 9)(n + 4)$ **c.** $(x - 9y)(x + 4y)$ **25.** 2,643 adult
tickets and 507 child tickets **27. a.** 53 **b.** –67 **c.** Answers
vary. Sample answer: The graph is the line with slope $\frac{3}{4}$,
y-intercept –7.

Lesson 13-2 (pp. 784–787)
Guided Example 1: a. a rectangle; it has 4 sides of the same
length and its diagonals have the same length; a rectangle
can have different width and length. **b.** you live in the
United States; you live in the state of North Dakota; you
could live in any of the other 49 states **Guided Example 2:**
a. is a square; it has 4 sides of the same length and its
diagonals have the same length; it is a square. **b.** You live
in Brazil; you live in the largest country in South America
Questions: 1. If there is fire, then there is smoke. **3. a.** no
b. If an integer is divisible by 24, then it is divisible by

3 and 4. **c.** yes **d.** Answers vary. Sample answer: If an
integer is divisible by 3 and 4, then it is divisible by 12.
If an integer is divisible by 24, then it is divisible by 3
and 8. **5. a.** no **b.** If $u > 8$, then $7u < 56$. **c.** no **d.** If
$7u > 56$, then $u > 8$; If $u > 8$, then $7u > 56$. **7.** If a
quadrilateral has four right angles, then it is a rectangle;
If a quadrilateral is a rectangle, then it has four right
angles. **9.** A function is a linear function if and only if it
has an equation of the form $f(x) = ax + b$. **11.** yes
13. No, the statement "If $z^2 + 48 = 14z$, then $z = 8$" is
not true, because $z^2 + 48 = 14z$ is also true for $z = 6$.
15. a. yes **b.** If $2x^2 - 7x + 30 = 90$, then $(x - 5)(2x + 3)$
$= 45$. **c.** yes **d.** n/a **17. a.** no **b.** If the x-intercepts of a
parabola are –5 and 3, then it has an equation of the form
$y = (x - 5)(x + 3)$. **c.** no **d.** If a parabola has an equation
of the form $y = a(x - 5)(x + 3)$, then its x-intercepts are 5
and –3; If the x-intercepts of a parabola are –5 and 3, then
it has an equation of the form $y = a(x + 5)(x - 3)$.
19. a. true **b.** Answers vary. Sample answer: $x = 10$.
21. a. false **b.** A person can be a U.S. citizen if and only if
the person was born in the United States or the person was
naturalized. **23.** False; the graph of $y = ax^2$ crosses the
x-axis only once at $(0, 0)$ for all $a \neq 0$. **25.** $0.56 **27.** $\frac{27}{8}$

Lesson 13-3 (pp. 788–794)
Guided Example 1: 1. ii. Addition Property of Equality;
iii. $-6x = 118 + 14$; v. both sides multiplied by $-\frac{1}{6}$;
vi. Multiplicative Inverse Property; vi. $-\frac{1}{6}(132) = -22$;
Identity **Guided Example 2:** i. Given; ii. Addition Property
of Equality; iii. Additive Inverse Property and arithmetic;
iv. Multiplication Property of Equality; v. Multiplicative
Inverse Property and arithmetic
Questions: 1. a. $3(6) = 18$, $3(13x) = 39x$; Distributive
Property **b.** Add –12 to both sides; Addition Property of
Equality **c.** $12 + -12 = 0$; Additive Inverse Property
d. $40x + 0 = 40x$; Additive Identity Property
e. $18 + -12 = 6$; arithmetic **f.** If $40x + 12 = 3(6 + 13x)$,
then $40x = 6 + 39x$. **3.** Inductive reasoning is used to
make a general conclusion out of a specific instances,
while deduction is used to prove a specific instance of a
general case, using known facts. **5. a.** Sula **b.** Lana
7. a. (i.) $12m + -3m = 3m + -3m + 5$; Addition Property
of Equality (ii.) $9m = 0 + 5$; Additive Inverse Property
and arithmetic (iii.) $m = \frac{5}{9}$; Additive Identity Property and
Multiplication Property of Equality **b.** Show that if
$m = \frac{5}{9}$, then $12m = 3m + 5$. **9.** Multiply both sides by $\frac{1}{t}$
(Multiplication Property of Equality), and $t \cdot \frac{1}{t} = 1$ by the
Multiplicative Inverse Property. **11.** Because the
equation is quadratic, the Quadratic Formula can be
applied to solve for n. **13.** $3x - 4y = -18$ can be added to
$3x + 4y = 6$ to get $6x = -12$; Addition Property of Equality
15. (i.) $ax + b = c$ Given (ii.) $ax + b - b = c - b$ Addition

Property of Equality (iii.) $ax + 0 = c - b$ Additive Inverse Property (iv.) $ax = c - b$ Additive Identity Property (v.) $\frac{1}{a} \cdot ax = \frac{1}{a} \cdot (c - b)$ Multiplication Property of Equality (vi.) $x = \frac{(c - b)}{a}$ Multiplicative Inverse Property, Multiplicative Identity Property   **17.** $x = \frac{c - b}{a}$ if and only if $ax + b = c$ and $a \neq 0$.   **19. a.** (i.) $a(x - h)^2 = k$ Given (ii.) $\frac{1}{a} \cdot a(x - h)^2 = \frac{1}{a} \cdot k$ Multiplication Property of Equality (iii.) $\sqrt{(x - h)^2} = \sqrt{\frac{k}{a}}$ Definition of square root (iv.) $x - h = \pm\sqrt{\frac{k}{a}}$ Definition of square root (v.) $x - h + h = \pm\sqrt{\frac{k}{a}} + h$ Addition Property of Equality (vi.) $x = h \pm\sqrt{\frac{k}{a}}$ Additive Inverse Property **b.** (i.) $x = h \pm\sqrt{\frac{k}{a}}$ Given (ii.) $x - h = \pm\sqrt{\frac{k}{a}} + h - h$ Addition Property of Equality (iii.) $x - h = \pm\sqrt{\frac{k}{a}}$ Additive Inverse Property (iv.) $(x - h)^2 = \left(\sqrt{\frac{k}{a}}\right)^2$ Multiplication Property of Equality (v.) $(x - h)^2 = \frac{k}{a}$ Definition of square root (vi.) $a \cdot (x - h)^2 = \frac{k}{a} \cdot a$ Multiplication Property of Equality (vii.) $a(x - h)^2 = k$ Multiplicative Inverse and Identity Properties **c.** $a(x - h)^2 = k$ if and only if a and k are both positive and $x = h \pm\sqrt{\frac{k}{a}}$.   **21. a.** If you are under 8 years of age, then you receive a reduced fare on the metro city bus. **b.** If you receive a reduced fare on the metro city bus, then you are under 8 years of age. **c.** No. Answers vary. Sample answer: Other groups of people might receive a reduced fare as well.   **23. a.** $3(x - 1)(x + 4)$ **b.** Answers vary. Sample answer: $-\frac{3}{2} + \sqrt{\frac{119}{12}}$ **25.** $\sqrt{ab} = (\sqrt{a})(\sqrt{b})$ **27.** $(a^x)^y = a^{xy}$ **29.** $-1 \cdot a = -a$ **31.** $AB = 9\sqrt{29}$ cm $\approx$ 48.47 cm, $XZ = 10$ cm, $XY = 5\sqrt{29}$ cm ≈ 26.93 cm   **33.** $\frac{4}{663} \approx 0.006033$

Lesson 13-4 (pp. 795–801)

Guided Example: $2L$; $2W$; L; W; $2W$; $2L$; L; $150 - L$; $150 - L$; 40; 110; 110; 40; 40; 110

1. D   **3.** Al-Khwarizmi created a general method similar to today's Quadratic Formula.   **5.** $x + y = 53$ so their average is 26.5. Let $M = 26.5 + x$ and $N = 26.5 - x$. $MN = 612$, so $(26.5 + x)(26.5 - x) = 612$; $702.25 - x = 612$; $x^2 = 90.25$, $x = 9.5$ or $x = -9.5$. If $x = 9.5$, $M = 26.5 + 9.5 = 36$, $N = 26.5 - 9.5 = 17$. If $x = -9.5$, $M = 26.5 - 9.5 = 17$, $N = 26.5 + 9.5 = 36$. The two numbers are 17 and 36.   **7.** $L = 25 - W$; $W(25 - W) = 144$, $25W - W^2 = 144$, $W^2 - 25W + 144 = 0$; $(W - 16)(W - 9) = 0$; 16 yards by 9 yards   **9.** $\frac{15 + \sqrt{185}}{2}$ and $\frac{15 - \sqrt{185}}{2}$ **11.** $x = -\frac{1}{7}$ or $x = 1$ **13.** The door is 9.6 units high and 2.8 units wide.   **15. a.** If a number is divisible by 8, then it is also divisible by 4. **b.** true **c.** If a number is divisible by 4, then it is also divisible by 8. **d.** false; Answers vary. Sample answer: 12 is divisible by 4, but not by 8.   **17.** $s = \pi r(r + 2h)$ **19.** about 603mL   **21. a.** $2\sqrt{2} + \sqrt{5}$ **b.** $2\sqrt{10}$ **c.** $2\sqrt{5}$

Lesson 13-5 (pp. 802–808)

Guided Example 2:  $2p + 1$; $2q + 1$; $p - q$; $p - q$; 2

Questions: 1. an integer that can be written as $2n$, where n is an integer   **3.** Answers vary. Sample answer: 6 and 4 are both divisible by 2, but 10 is not divisible by 4.   **5. a.** Answers vary. Sample answer: Let p and q be odd integers such that $p = 2m + 1$ and $q = 2n + 1$, where m and n are integers. Then $p + q = 2m + 1 + 2n + 1 = 2m + 2n + 2 = 2(m + n + 1)$. Since m, n, and 1 are integers, $m + n + 1$ is an integer. Thus $p + q$ is an even integer. **b.** No. Answers vary. Sample answer: From Part a, the sum of the two odd integers is an even integer, not an odd one.

7.

9. even + odd = odd; odd + even = odd; odd − even = odd; odd − odd = even

11. Answers vary. Sample answer: Let m be an even number. Then there is an integer p such that $m = 2p$, so $m^2 = (2p)^2$. Thus $m^2 = 4p^2$, and since p is an integer, p^2 is an integer. Thus m^2 is a multiple of 4.   **13.** Answers vary. Sample answer: Let m and n be numbers such that $m + n = 35a$ and $n = 70b$, where a and b are integers. Then $m + n = m + 70b = 35a$, so $m = 35a - 70b$, and by the Distributive Property, $m = 35(a - 2b)$. Because a and $2b$ are integers, their difference is an integer, so m is divisible by 35.   **15.** Answers vary. Sample answer: Let m and n be numbers such that $m = 4p$ and $n = 6q$, where p and q are integers. Then $mn = (4p)(6q) = 24pq$ by the Commutative and Associative Properties of Multiplication. Because p and q are integers, pq is an integer.   **17.** Answers vary. Sample answer: $b = 13$ **19.** $x = 7$, $x = 4$ **21.** $a = 3$ **23.** $x = -2.3$ **25. a.** 18 units **b.** 54 units^2

Lesson 13-6 (pp. 809–815)

Guided Example 3: 1. $100h$; $10t$; u **2.** $999T + 99h + 9t$ **4.** $999T$; $99h$; $9t$; $k + 333T + 33h + 3t$; $k + 333T + 33h + 3t$

Questions: 1. 57 **3.** $1{,}000A + 100B + 10C + D$ **5. a.** $1{,}000T + 100h + 10t + u$ **b.** $1{,}000u + 100t + 10h + T$ **7.** A five digit number in base 10 can be written as $N = 10{,}000D + 1{,}000T + 100h + 10t + u$, where D, T, h, t, u are all digits. Separate the sum of the digits from the value of the number. $N = (D + T + h + t + u) + (9,999D + 999T + 99h + 9t)$. The sum of the digits is divisible by 9, so there is an integer k with $D + T + h + t + u = 9k$. Substituting, $N = 9k + (9999D + 999T + 99h + 9t) = 9(k + 1,111D + 111T + 11h + t)$. Since $k + 1,111D + 111T + 11h + t$ is an integer, N is divisible by 9. **9. a.** No, the units digit is odd. **b.** No, the units digit is neither 5 nor 0. **c.** No, the digits do not sum to a number divisible by 9. **11. a.** Yes, the units digit is even. **b.** No, the units digit is neither 5 nor 0. **c.** Yes, the digits sum to 9. **13. a.** Answers vary. Sample answer: $2,346 - 6,432 = -4,086$, which, when divided by 99 gives about -41.28, which is not an integer. **b.** A four digit number in base 10 can be written as $N = 1,000T + 100h + 10t + u$, where T, h, t, u are all digits. Moreover, the number with reversed digits is $1,000u + 100t + 10h + T$. The difference between these two numbers is $1,000T + 100h + 10t + u - (1,000u + 100t + 10h + T) = 999T + 90h - 90t - 999u = 9(111T + 10h - 10t - 111u)$. Since $111T + 10h - 10t - 111u$ is an integer we know that this difference is divisible by 9. **15.** A six digit number in base 10 can be written as $N = 100,000H + 10,000D + 1,000T + 100h + 10t + u$, where H, D, T, h, t, u are all digits. Our given conditions mean $H = h$, $D = t$ and $T = u$, and so our number can be rewritten as $100,000h + 10,000t + 1,000u + 100h + 10t + u = 100,100h + 10,010t + 1,001u$. We can factor 13 from this expression to get $N = 13(7,700h + 770t + 77u)$, and since $7,700h + 770t + 77u$ is an integer, N is 13 times an integer, and thus divisible by 13. **17.** 285 **19.** Answers vary. Sample answer: As a counterexample, consider 6 and 8, where $6 \cdot 8 = 48$ which is not divisible by 7. **21.** $h = 5$ **23. a.** 0 **b.** 1 **25.** $y > 0.5$ **27.** $x = 45$

Lesson 13-7 (pp. 816–822)

1. Answers vary. Sample answer: $\frac{1}{3}$ **3.** Answers vary. Sample answer: 2 **5.** $\frac{28}{33}$ **7.** D **9.** irrational **11.** rational

13.

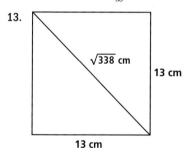

15. Yes, Answers vary. Sample answer: $\sqrt{2} + (-\sqrt{2}) = 0$, and both of them are irrational, while 0 is rational.

17. a.

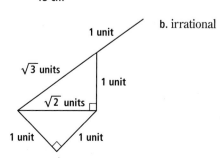

b. irrational

19. $84\sqrt{2}$ cm; irrational **21. a.** $a = \sqrt{1,606}$ **b.** irrational

23.

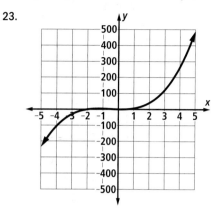

25. $f(x) = x(x + 2)(3x - 1)$ **27. a.** $9y$ **b.** $b = -4y$, $c = 4$, $d = 5y$ **29.** $25 - x^2$ **31.** 70.56 ft

Lesson 13-8 (pp. 823–828)

1. Answers vary. Sample answer:

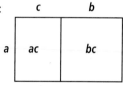

3. a.

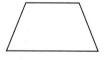

b. 64 units² **c.** Answers vary. Sample answer: Subtract four times the area of a triangle with base 6 and height 2 from the total area of 64. **d.** $2\sqrt{10}$

5. a. Answers vary. Sample answer: **b.** 1.5 in.² **7. a.** 2,664.5 units² **b.** Subtract twice the area of a rectangle with base a and height b from the total area, i.e., the trapezoid with bases a and b and height $a + b$. **c.** 53 **d.** yes **9.** The Extended Distributive Property **11. a.** $\sqrt{2a^2 + b^2 - 2ab}$ **b.** $\frac{1}{2}(ab - a^2)$ **c.** $\frac{1}{2}c^2$ **d.** $\frac{1}{2}(ab - a^2 + c^2)$ **e.** $\frac{1}{2}(ba + b^2)$ **f.** $\frac{1}{2}(ab - a^2 + c^2) = \frac{1}{2}(ba + b^2)$; $ab - a^2 + c^2 = ba + b^2$; $c^2 = a^2 + b^2$ **13.** A **15 a.** 362,880 orders **b.** 60,480 ways **17.** about \$9,095.32

Self-Test (p. 832)

1.

Conclusions	Justifications
$8(2y - 1) = y + 37$	Given
$16y - 8 = y + 37$	Distributive Property
$16y - 8 - y = y + 37 - y$	Addition Property of Equality
$15y - 8 = 0 + 37$	Arithmetic, Additive Inverse Property
$15y - 8 = 37$	Additive Identity Property
$15y - 8 + 8 = 37 + 8$	Addition Property of Equality
$15y + 0 = 45$	Arithmetic, Additive Inverse Property
$15y = 45$	Additive Identity Property
$\frac{1}{15} \cdot 15y = \frac{1}{15} \cdot 45$	Multiplication Property of Equality
$1y = 3$	Arithmetic, Multiplicative Inverse Property
$y = 3$	Multiplicative Identity Property

2. The antecedent is $8(2y - 1) = y + 37$ and the consequent is $y = 3$. **3. a.** If $xy = 0$, then both x and y equal 0; If both x and $y = 0$, then $xy = 0$. **b.** No, Amalia is not correct. Answers vary. Sample answer: The statement "If $xy = 0$, then both x and y equal 0" is not true because, for example, when $x = 1$ and $y = 0$, $xy = 0$ but x does not equal 0. **4. a.** $\sqrt{7^2 + 8^2} = \sqrt{49 + 64} = \sqrt{113}$ in. **b.** $\sqrt{113}$ is an irrational number, so its decimal is infinite and does not repeat. Marcus's ruler is not accurate for the smallest length that it measures. **5. a.** If a student is taking algebra, then the student can solve quadratic equations.

b. The antecedent is a student is taking algebra, the consequent is the student can solve quadratic equations. **c.** If a student can solve quadratic equations, then the student is taking algebra. **d.** The statement is not true. For example, a student who knows how to solve quadratic equations could be a student in geometry. **6.** True. Answers vary. Sample answer: If the tens digit of a four-digit number is 4 and the units digit is 8, then the number can be written as $1{,}000n + 48$, where n is a whole number. Then $1{,}000n + 48 = 4(250n + 12)$, and because $250n$ and 12 are integers, $250n + 12$ is an integer, so 4 divides $100n + 48$. **7.** The rectangles picture the equation $(a - b)(a + b) = (a - b)a + (a - b)b = a^2 - b^2$. **8.** $ab = 717$ and $a + b = -242$. Then $a = -242 - b$, so substitution gives $(-242 - b)b = 717$, so $b^2 + 242b + 717 = 0$. This is a quadratic equation, so solving for b gives $b = -239$ or $b = -3$. Thus, the numbers are -239 and -3. **9. a.** $x^2 + (\sqrt{3})^2 = (\sqrt{13})^2$, so $x^2 + 3 = 13$. $x^2 = 10$ so $x = \sqrt{10}$ **b.** x is irrational **10. a.** True. Because the sides of a square are all equal, two of the sides of the triangle will have equal length, so the triangle will be isosceles. **b.** False. If the length of one side of the square is a, then the length of the diagonal will be $a\sqrt{2}$, so the lengths of the sides are not all equal. **11.** False. Any person born in the United States cannot necessarily become president, since the person also needs to be at least 35 years old and have lived in the United States for at least 14 years.

12. • • •　Answers may vary. Sample: If a number is
• • •　divisible by 3 and 4, then it can be
• • •　represented as such and broken up into
• • •　rectangles of 12 dots each. Thus, it is divisible by 12.

The chart below keys the **Self-Test** questions to the objectives in the **Chapter Review** on pages 833–835 or to the **Vocabulary (Voc)** on page 831. This will enable you to locate those **Chapter Review** questions that correspond to questions missed on the **Self-Test**. The lesson where the material is covered is also indicated on the chart.

Question	1	2	3	4	5	6	7	8	9	10
Objective	B	B	B	E	A	E	H	B	A	D
Lesson(s)	13-3	13-1	13-1, 13-2	13-4	13-1, 13-2	13-5, 13-6	13-8	13-4	13-3	13-1, 13-2
Question	11	12	13	14						
Objective	G	E	F	I						
Lesson(s)	13-1, 13-2	13-5, 13-6	13-7	13-7						

Chapter Review (pp. 833–835)

1.

	Conclusions	What Was Done	Justifications
i.	$4x + 5 = 17$		Given
ii.	$4x + 5 + -5 =$ $17 + -5$	-5 added to both sides.	Addition Property of Equality
iii.	$4x + 0 = 12$	$5 + -5 = 0;$ $17 + -5 = 12$	Additive Inverse Property; Arithmetic
iv.	$4x = 12$	$4x + 0 = 4x$	Additive Identity Property
v.	$\frac{1}{4} \cdot 4x = 12 \cdot \frac{1}{4}$	Both sides were multiplied by $\frac{1}{4}$.	Multiplication Property of Equality
vi.	$1 \cdot x = 3$	$\frac{1}{4} \cdot 4 = 1;$ $12 \cdot \frac{1}{4} = 3$	Multiplicative Identity Property; Arithmetic
vii.	$x = 3$	$1 \cdot x = x$	Multiplicative Identity Property

3.

	Conclusions	What Was Done	Justifications
i.	$3t - 15 = 4t + 2$	Given	Given
ii.	$3t - 17 = 4t$	-2 added to both sides.	Addition Property of Equality
iii.	$-17 = t$	$-3t$ added to both sides.	Addition Property of Equality

5. 15 boys, 11 girls or 11 boys, 15 girls **7.** $\frac{5.6 + \sqrt{22.16}}{2}$, $\frac{5.6 - \sqrt{22.16}}{2}$ **9.** –23 and –23 **11.** antecedent: an animal has feathers: consequent: it is a bird **13.** antecedent a number is irrational; consequent: it cannot be represented as the ratio of two integers **15.** true **17.** true
19. Suppose that $2a + 3b + c$ is not divisible by 7. Then $2a + 3b + c + (14)(7a) + 7b$ is not divisible by 7. Hence, $100a + 10b + c$ is also not divisible by 7. So the three-digit number abc is not divisible by 7. **21.** Consider a six-digit integer of the form $xyzxyz$. This is equal to $100{,}000x + 10{,}000y + 1{,}000z + 100x + 10y + z$. And equivalently, this is $(7{,}692)(13x) + 4x + (769)(13y) + 3y + (76)(13z) + 12z + (7)(13x) + 9x + 10y + z$. Combining and factoring, we obtain $xyzxyz = (13)(7{,}700x + 770y + 77z)$. So all six-digit integers of the form $xyzxyz$ are divisible by 13.

23. irrational **25.** rational **27.** Yes, for example $\sqrt{2} \cdot \sqrt{2} = 2$. **29. a.** yes **b.** yes **c.** n/a **31. a.** yes **b.** no **c.** You are in high school if and only if you are in grades 9–12. **33.**

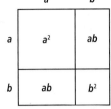

35. The area of each triangle is $\frac{1}{2}ab$. Because the area of the entire rectangle is ab, and $\frac{1}{2}ab + \frac{1}{2}ab = ab$, each of the triangles must occupy exactly half the area of the rectangle. So the diagonal cuts the area of the rectangle in half. **37. a.** $\frac{16}{\pi}$ in. **b.** irrational **39. a.** 0.15 **b.** rational **b.** irrational
41 a.

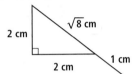

Glossary

A

absolute value (A) The distance a number x is from 0 written $|x|$. (B) $|x| = x$ if $x \geq c$; $|x| = -x$ if $x < c$. (**43**)

addition method for solving a system Given two equations in a system, applying the Addition Property if $a = b$ and $c = d$, then $a + c = b + d$, to obtain another equation that is satisfied by the solution to the system. (**602**)

Addition Property of Equality For all real numbers a, b, and c, if $a = b$, then $a + c = b + c$. (**106**)

Addition Property of Inequality For all real numbers a, b, and c, if $a < b$, then $a + c < b + c$. (**162**)

Additive Identity Property For any real number a, $a + 0 = 0 + a = a$. (**108**)

Additive Inverse Property For any real number a, $a + -a = -a + a = 0$. (**109**)

additive inverses Two numbers whose sum is zero; also called opposites. (**85**)

Algebraic Definition of Division For all real numbers a and b with $b \neq 0$, $a \div b = \frac{a}{b} = a \cdot \frac{1}{b}$. (**7**)

Algebraic Definition of Subtraction For all real numbers a and b, $a - b = a + -b$. (**7**)

algebraic expression An expression that includes one or more variables. (**6**)

algebraic fraction A fraction with a variable in the numerator, in the denominator, or in both. (**252**)

annual yield The percent of interest that money on deposit earns per year. (**398**)

antecedent The clause following *if* in an if-then statement. (**778**)

Arrangements Theorem If there are n ways to select each object in a sequence of length L, then n^L different sequences are possible. (**459**)

Associative Property of Addition For any real numbers a, b, and c, $(a + b) + c = a + (b + c)$. (**10**)

Associative Property of Multiplication For any real numbers a, b, and c, $(ab)c = a(bc)$. (**9**)

axis of symmetry Given a figure, a line over which the reflection image of the figure is the figure itself. (**526**)

B

base The number x in the power x^n. (**398**)

binomial A polynomial that has two terms. (**663**)

boundary line A line that separates two sets, e.g., solutions from nonsolutions in the graph of a linear inequality. (**381**)

boundary A point or number that separates solutions from nonsolutions on a number line. (**155**)

C

capture-recapture method The use of proportions to estimate the total number of objects in a set (e.g., the number of deer in a forest or the number of fish in a pond). (**303**)

Celsius scale The temperature scale of the metric system, developed by Anders Celsius, in which the freezing point of water is $0°$ and the boiling point of water is $100°$; also known as the *centigrade scale*. (**221**)

centigrade scale See *Celsius scale*. (**221**)

chi-square statistic A member calculated from data to determine whether the difference in two frequency distributions is greater than that expected by chance. (**698**)

circular permutation An ordering of objects around a circle. (**695**)

clearing fractions Multiplying each side of an equation or inequality by a constant to get an equivalent equation without fractions as coefficients. (**170**)

closed under an operation A set is closed under an operation if the result of the operation always lies within the particular set. (**802**)

coefficient A number that is a factor in a term containing a variable. (**73**)

coefficient matrix In the matrix equation $\begin{bmatrix} a & b \\ c & d \end{bmatrix} \cdot \begin{bmatrix} x \\ y \end{bmatrix} = \begin{bmatrix} e \\ f \end{bmatrix}$, the coefficient matrix is $\begin{bmatrix} a & b \\ c & d \end{bmatrix}$. (**622**)

coincident Two or more lines or other sets of points that are identical. (**618**)

collinear points Points that all lie on the same line. (**130**)

Commutative Property of Addition For all real numbers a and b, $a + b = b + a$. (**16**)

Commutative Property of Multiplication For all real numbers a and b, $ab = ba$. (**16**)

complementary events Two events that have no elements in common, but together they contain all the possible outcomes. (**283**)

complete factorization The representation of a polynomial as a product of prime polynomials. (**676**)

completing the square Converting a quadratic equation in standard form to one in vertex form. (**724**)

complex fraction A fraction that has a fraction in the numerator or a fraction in the denominator, or both. (**259**)

compound interest The money a bank pays on the principal and earned interest in an account. (**399, 400**)

compound sentence A single sentence consisting of two or more sentences linked by the words *and* or *or*. (**227**)

conditional probability The probability that an event will occur given that another event has occurred. (**283**)

consequent The clause following *then* in an if-then statement. (**778**)

constant-decrease situation A quantity that decreases at a constant amount in a period of time. (**130**)

constant-increase situation A quantity that increases at a constant amount in a period of time. (**130**)

constant matrix In the matrix equation $\begin{bmatrix} a & b \\ c & d \end{bmatrix} \cdot \begin{bmatrix} x \\ y \end{bmatrix}$ $= \begin{bmatrix} e \\ f \end{bmatrix}$, the constant matrix is $\begin{bmatrix} e \\ f \end{bmatrix}$. (**622**)

constant term A term in a polynomial without a variable. (**736**)

converse An if-then statement in which the antecedent and the consequent of the statement have been switched. (**784**)

conversion rate A rate determined from an equality between two quantities with different units. (**269**)

coordinates The numbers x and y that locate a point (x, y) in the coordinate plane. (**27**)

counterexample An instance for which a general statement is not true. (**23**)

cube The third power of a number x, or x^3. (**493**)

Cube of the Cube Root Property For any nonnegative number x, $\sqrt[3]{x} \cdot \sqrt[3]{x} \cdot \sqrt[3]{x} = \sqrt[3]{x^3} = x$. (**493**)

cube root If $V = s^3$, then s is a cube root of V. (**493**)

cubic polynomial A polynomial of degree 3. (**756**)

D

deduction Using a proof to show that one if-then statement follows from another. (**789**)

define a variable The process of describing the quantity a variable represents. (**14**)

degree of a monomial The sum of the exponents of the variables in the monomial. (**664**)

degree of a polynomial The highest degree of any of the monomial terms of a polynomial. (**664**)

dependent variable A variable (y) whose value is determined by the value of at least one other variable in a given function. (**426**)

deviation (A) The difference between a member of a data set and the mean of that data set. (**42**) (B) The difference between an expected number and an actual observed number. (**697**)

difference of squares An expression of the form $x^2 - y^2$. For all real numbers x and y, $x^2 - y^2 = (x + y)(x - y)$. (**687–688**)

dimensions (of a matrix) The number of rows and columns in a matrix. (**622**)

direct variation A number y varies directly with a number x if y is a constant multiple of x. (**353**)

discount The amount by which the original price of an item is lowered. (**184**)

discount rate The ratio of the discount to the original price. (**275**)

discriminant The value of $b^2 - 4ac$ in the quadratic equation $ax^2 + bx + c = 0$. (**561**)

Discriminant Property Suppose $ax^2 + bx + c$ and a, b, and c are real numbers with $a \neq 0$. Let $D = b^2 - 4ac$. Then when $D > 0$, the equation has two real solutions. When $D = 0$, the equation has exactly one real solution. When $D < 0$, the equation has no real solutions. (**561**)

Discriminant Theorem When a, b, and c are integers, with $a \neq 0$, either all three of the following conditions are true or none are true. **1.** $b^2 - 4ac$ is a perfect square. **2.** $ax^2 + bx + c$ is factorable over the set of polynomials with integer coefficients. **3.** The solutions to $ax^2 + bx + c = 0$ are rational numbers. **(749)**

Distance between Two Points in a Coordinate Plane The distance AB between the points $A = (x_1, y_1)$ and $B = (x_2, y_2)$ in a coordinate plane is $AB = \sqrt{(x_2 - x_1)^2 + (y_2 - y_1)^2}$. **(507)**

Distributive Property of Multiplication over Addition For all real numbers a, b, and c, $c(a + b) = ca + cb$. **(66)**

Distributive Property of Multiplication over Subtraction For all real numbers a, b, and c, $c(a - b) = ca - cb$. **(67)**

Dividing Fractions Property For all real numbers a, b, c, and d, with $b \neq 0$, $c \neq 0$, and $d \neq 0$, $\frac{a}{b} \div \frac{c}{d} = \frac{a}{b} \cdot \frac{d}{c}$. **(258)**

Division Property of Equality For all real numbers a, b, and all real nonzero numbers c, if $a = b$, then $\frac{a}{c} = \frac{b}{c}$. **(113)**

domain of a function The set of possible values of the first (independent) variable. **(426)**

domain of a variable All the values that may be meaningfully substituted for a variable. **(28)**

double inequality An inequality of the form $a < x < b$. (The $<$ may be replaced with $>$, $\leq$, or $\geq$.) **(156, 227)**

E

elements (of a matrix) The objects in a rectangular array. **(622)**

empty set A set that has no elements in it, written as { } or ∅. **(584)**

endpoints (A) The points A and B in the segment $\overline{AB}$. (B) The coordinates of those points on a number line. **(156)**

Equal Fractions Property For all real numbers a, b, and k, if $b \neq 0$ and $k \neq 0$, then $\frac{a}{b} = \frac{ak}{bk}$. **(253)**

equivalent equations Equations with exactly the same solutions. **(139)**

equivalent expressions Expressions that have the same value for *every* number that can be substituted for the variable(s). **(22)**

equivalent formulas Two or more formulas in which every set of values that satisfies one of the formulas also satisfies the others. **(222)**

equivalent statements When an if-then statement and its converse are both true, then the antecedent and consequent are equivalent. **(784)**

equivalent systems Systems with exactly the same solutions. **(608)**

evaluating an expression The process of finding the numerical value of an expression. **(6)**

even integer (even number) An integer that can be written as $2n$, where n is an integer. **(802)**

event A set of possible outcomes. **(280)**

expected number The mean frequency of a given event that is predicted by a probability. **(697)**

exponent The number n in the power x^n. **(398)**

exponential decay A situation in which $y = bg^x$ and $0 < g < 1$. **(411)**

exponential growth A situation in which $y = bg^x$ and $g > 1$. **(404)**

exponential growth equation If the amount at the beginning of the growth period is b, the growth factor is g, and y is the amount after x time periods, then $y = b \cdot g^x$. **(405)**

exponential regression A method to determine an equation of the form $y = b \cdot g^x$ for modeling a set of ordered pairs. **(419)**

Extended Distributive Property To multiply two sums, multiply each term in the first sum by each term in the second sum, and then add the products. **(680)**

extremes The numbers a and d in the proportion $\frac{a}{b} = \frac{c}{d}$. **(301)**

F

factors (A) A number or expression that is multiplied. (B) If $ab = c$, then a and b are factors of c. **(15)**

factored form of a quadratic function A quadratic function $y = ax^2 + bx + c$ is in factored form when it is written as $y = a(x - r_1)(x - r_2)$. **(730)**

factoring The process of expressing a given number or expression as a product. **(75, 675)**

factorization The result of factoring a number or polynomial. **(676)**

Factor Theorem Let r be a real number and $P(x)$ be a polynomial in x. If $x - r$ is a factor of $P(x)$, then $P(r) = 0$; that is, r is an x-intercept of the graph of P. If $P(r) = 0$, then $x - r$ is a factor of $P(x)$. **(755)**

Factor Theorem for Quadratic Functions The x-intercepts of the graph of $y = a(x - r_1)(x - r_2)$ are r_1 and r_2. **(731)**

fact triangle A triangle in which any pair of numbers in the triangle can be added, subtracted, multiplied, or divided to produce the third number. **(105, 112)**

Fahrenheit scale A temperature scale, developed by Gabriel Fahrenheit, in which the freezing point of water is 32° and the boiling point of water is 212°. **(221)**

fair A situation in which each outcome has the same probability; also called *unbiased*. **(281)**

Fundamental Property of Similar Figures If two polygons are similar, then the ratios of corresponding lengths are equal. **(309)**

function A set of ordered pairs in which each first coordinate corresponds to *exactly one* second coordinate. **(426)**

function notation Notation to indicate a function, such as $f(x)$, and read "f of x." **(435)**

f(x) notation Notation indicating the value of a function f at x. When a function f contains the ordered pair (x, y), then y is the value of the function at x, and we may write $y = f(x)$. **(435)**

G

general formula for the height of a projectile over time Let h be the height (in feet) of a projectile launched from Earth's surface with an initial upward velocity v feet per second and an initial height of s feet. Then, after t seconds, $h = -16t^2 + vt + s$. **(546)**

generalization An if-then statement in which there is a variable in the antecedent and in the consequent. **(778)**

Generalized Addition Property of Equality For all numbers or expressions a, b, c, and d: If $a = b$ and $c = d$, then $a + c = b + d$. **(601)**

general linear equation An equation of the form $ax + b = cx + d$, where $a \neq 0$. **(202)**

greatest common factor (GCF) For two or more integers, the greatest integer that is a common factor. For two or more monomials, the GCF is the product of the greatest common factor of the coefficients and the greatest common factor of the variables. **(675)**

growth factor In exponential growth or decay, the positive number which is repeatedly multiplied by the original amount. **(404)**

growth model for powering If a quantity is multiplied by a positive number g (the growth factor) in each of x time periods, then, after the x periods, the quantity will be multiplied by g^x. **(405)**

H

half-life The time it takes for one half the amount of an element to decay. **(414)**

half-plane In a plane, the region on either side of a line. **(381)**

horizontal line A line with the equation $y = k$, where k is a real number. **(189)**

I

if and only if A phrase used to connect equivalent if-then statements. **(785)**

if-then statement A statement that contains an antecedent and a consequent. **(778)**

independent variable A variable whose value does not rely on the values of other variables. **(426)**

inductive reasoning The process of arriving at a general conclusion (not necessarily true) from specific instances. **(776)**

inequality A mathematical sentence with one of the verbs < (is less than), > (is greater than), ≤ (is less than or equal to), ≥ (is greater than or equal to), or ≠ (is not equal to). **(155)**

initial height The starting height of a projectile. **(545)**

initial upward velocity The velocity of a projectile when it is first launched, assuming no gravity effects. **(545)**

input A number substituted for the independent variable in a function. **(221, 426)**

instance A special case of a general pattern. **(13)**

interest The amount that a bank or other financial institution pays on money in an account, based on a percentage of the principal. **(398)**

intersection of sets The set of elements in both set A and set B and written as $A \cap B$. **(227)**

interval The set of numbers between two numbers a and b, possibly containing a or b. **(156)**

inverse (of a matrix) For a matrix A, the matrix B such that AB and BA are the identity matrix. (**629**)

Irrationality of $\sqrt{n}$ Theorem If n is an integer that is not a perfect square, then $\sqrt{n}$ is irrational. (**819**)

irrational number A real number that is not a rational number. For example, the square roots of integers that are not perfect squares are irrational. (**817**)

J

justification A statement explaining why each step in a proof follows from preceding statements. (**787**)

L

least squares line The line whose squares of deviations from data set points are least. Also called the *line of best fit*. (**370**)

like terms Two or more terms in which the variables and corresponding exponents are the same. (**72**)

linear combination An expression of the form $Ax + By$, where A and B are fixed numbers. (**375**)

linear inequalities Inequalities of the form $Ax + By < C$ or $Ax + By \leq C$, where A, B, and C are constants. (> and $\geq$ can be substituted for < and $\leq$.) (**383**)

linear polynomial A polynomial of degree one. (**664**)

linear regression The fitting of a straight line through a given set of points according to specific criteria, such as least squares. (**369**)

linear term A term containing one variable with a power equal to 1. (**736**)

line of best fit A line whose equation is determined by the method of least squares and represents a linear relationship between data values. (**369**)

lowest terms (A) A fraction whose numerator and denominator have no common factors other than 1. (**761**) (B) A rational expression with no polynomial being a factor of both its numerator and denominator. (**762**)

M

markup A percent by which the original price of an item is raised. (**184**)

matrix (matrices) A rectangular array, such as $\begin{bmatrix} 3 & -4 \\ 15 & 0 \end{bmatrix}$. (**622**)

matrix form A way of expressing a system of equations using matrices. The matrix form for $\begin{cases} ax + by = e \\ cx + dy = f \end{cases}$ is $\begin{bmatrix} a & b \\ c & d \end{bmatrix} \cdot \begin{bmatrix} x \\ y \end{bmatrix} = \begin{bmatrix} e \\ f \end{bmatrix}$. The coefficient matrix is $\begin{bmatrix} a & b \\ c & d \end{bmatrix}$, the variable matrix is $\begin{bmatrix} x \\ y \end{bmatrix}$, and the constant matrix is $\begin{bmatrix} e \\ f \end{bmatrix}$. (**623**)

mean absolute deviation (m.a.d.) The average difference between individual measurements and the mean. (**48**)

means The numbers b and c in the proportion $\frac{a}{b} = \frac{c}{d}$. (**301**)

Means-Extremes Property For all real numbers a, b, c, and d (with $b \neq 0$ and $d \neq 0$), if $\frac{a}{b} = \frac{c}{d}$, then $ad = bc$. (**302**)

monomial A polynomial with 1 term. (**663**)

Multiplication Counting Principle If one choice can be made in m ways and a second choice can be made in n ways, then there are mn ways of making the first choice followed by the second choice. (**459**)

multiplication method for solving a system Given two equations in a system, applying the Multiplication Property of Equality to obtain another equation that is satisfied by the solution to the system. (**609**)

Multiplication Property of Zero For any real number a, $a \cdot 0 = 0 \cdot a = 0$. (**115**)

Multiplication Property of -1 For any real number a, $a \cdot -1 = -1 \cdot a = -a$. (**86**)

Multiplication Property of Equality For all real numbers a, b, and c, if $a = b$, then $ca = cb$. (**113**)

Multiplication Property of Inequality If $x < y$ and a is positive, then $ax < ay$. If $x < y$ and a is negative, then $ax > ay$. (**157**)

Multiplicative Identity Property of 1 For any real number a, $a \cdot 1 = 1 \cdot a = a$. (**116**)

Multiplicative Inverse Property For any real number a, where $a \neq 0$, $a \cdot \frac{1}{a} = \frac{1}{a} \cdot a = 1$. (**116**)

Multiplying Fractions Property For all real numbers a, b, c, and d, with $b \neq 0$ and $d \neq 0$, $\frac{a}{b} \cdot \frac{c}{d} = \frac{ac}{bd}$. (**252**)

N

n factorial ($n!$) The product of the integers from 1 to n. **(693)**

Negative Exponent Property For any nonzero b and all n, $b^{-n} = \frac{1}{b^n}$, the reciprocal of b^n. **(474)**

Negative Exponent Property for Fractions For any nonzero x and y and all n, $\left(\frac{x}{y}\right)^{-n} = \left(\frac{y}{x}\right)^n$. **(475)**

nonlinear system A system of equations or inequalities in which at least one of the equations or inequalities is nonlinear. **(640)**

nth power The number x^n is the nth power of x. **(398)**

null set See *empty set*. **(584)**

O

oblique A line that is neither horizontal nor vertical. **(377)**

odd integer (odd number) An integer that can be written as $2n + 1$, where n is an integer. **(803)**

odds of an event The ratio of the probability that an event will not occur to the probability that an event will occur. **(284)**

Opposite of a Difference Property For all real numbers a and b, $-(a - b) = -a + b$. **(87)**

Opposite of a Sum Property For all real numbers a and b, $-(a + b) = -a + -b = -a - b$. **(86)**

Opposite of Opposites Property For any real number a, $-(-a) = a$. **(85)**

opposites Two numbers that add to zero; also called additive inverses. **(85)**

order of operations The correct order of evaluating numerical expressions: perform operations within parentheses or other grouping symbols. Then evaluate powers from left to right. Next multiply or divide from left to right. Then add or subtract from left to right. **(6)**

origin The point $(0, 0)$ on a coordinate graph. **(44)**

outcomes A result of an experiment. **(280)**

output A number that is returned by a function after it is evaluated. **(221, 426)**

P

parabola The curve that is the graph of an equation of the form $y = ax^2 + bx + c$, where $a \neq 0$. **(526)**

Parabola Vertex Theorem The graph of all ordered pairs (x, y) satisfying the equation $y - k = a(x - h)^2$ is a parabola with vertex (h, k). **(716)**

pattern A general idea for which there are many instances. **(13)**

P(E) The probability of event E or "P of E." **(280)**

percent (%) A number times $\frac{1}{100}$ or "per 100." **(182)**

percentile The pth percentile of a data set is the smallest data value that is greater than or equal to p percent of the data values. **(292)**

perfect square trinomial A trinomial that is the square of a binomial. $a^2 + 2ab + b^2 = (a + b)^2$ and $a^2 - 2ab + b^2 = (a - b)^2$. **(687)**

period of a pendulum The time it takes a pendulum to complete one swing back and forth. On Earth, the formula $p = 2\pi\sqrt{\frac{L}{32}}$ gives the time p in seconds for one period in terms of the length L (in feet) of the pendulum. **(501)**

permutation An ordered arrangement of letters, names, or objects. **(691)**

± notation (A) $\pm x$ means (x or $-x$). (B) $a \pm b$ means $(a + b$ or $a - b)$. **(553)**

point-slope form An equation of a line in the form $y - k = m(x - h)$, where m is the slope and (h, k) is a point on the line. **(357)**

polynomial An expression that is either a monomial or a sum of monomials. **(663)**

polynomial in x A sum of multiples of powers of x. **(657)**

population The set of individuals or objects to be studied. **(302)**

power An expression written in the form x^n. **(398)**

Power of a Power Property For all m and n, and all nonzero b, $(b^m)^n = b^{mn}$. **(466)**

Power of a Product Property For all nonzero a and b, and for all n, $(ab)^n = a^n b^n$. **(481)**

Power of a Quotient Property For all nonzero a and b, and for all n, $\left(\frac{a}{b}\right)^n = \frac{a^n}{b^n}$. **(482)**

prime polynomial A polynomial that cannot be factored into polynomials of lower degree. **(676)**

polynomial over the integers A polynomial with integer coefficients. (738)

principal Money deposited in an account. (398)

probability of an event A number from 0 to 1 that measures the likelihood that an event will occur. (280)

probability distribution The set of ordered pairs of outcomes and their probabilities. (281)

Probability Formula for Geometric Regions Suppose points are selected at random in a region and some of that region's points represent an event E of interest. The probability $P(E)$ of the event is given by $\frac{\text{measurement of region in event}}{\text{measure of entire region}}$. (296)

Product of Powers Property For all m and n, and all nonzero b, $b^m \cdot b^n = b^{m+n}$. (465)

Product of Square Roots Property For all nonnegative real numbers a and b, $\sqrt{a} \cdot \sqrt{b} = \sqrt{ab}$. (498)

proof argument A sequence of justified conclusions, starting with the antecedent and ending with the consequent. (789)

proportion A statement that two fractions are equal. (301)

Pythagorean Theorem In any right triangle with legs of lengths a and b and hypotenuse of length c, $a^2 + b^2 = c^2$. (492)

Q

quadratic equation An equation that can be written in the form $ax^2 + bx + c = 0$ with $a \neq 0$. (552)

Quadratic Formula If $ax^2 + bx + c = 0$ and $a \neq 0$, then $x = \frac{-b \pm \sqrt{b^2 - 4ac}}{2a}$. (553)

quadratic polynomial A polynomial of degree 2. (664)

Quotient of Powers Property For all m and n, and all nonzero b, $\frac{b^m}{b^n} = b^{m-n}$. (469)

Quotient of Square Roots Property For all positive real numbers a and c, $\frac{\sqrt{c}}{\sqrt{a}} = \sqrt{\frac{c}{a}}$. (499)

R

radical sign (A) $(\sqrt{\ })$ The symbol for square root. (489) (B) $(\sqrt[3]{\ })$ The symbol for cube root. (493)

radicand The quantity under the radical sign. (499)

randomly (chosen) Every member of a population has an equal chance of being chosen. (302)

range (A) The difference between the maximum value M and minimum value m of a data set. (48) (B) The set of possible values of the second (dependent) variable. (426)

rate The quotient of two quantities with different units. (263)

rate of change The difference of values of a quantity divided by the amount of time between the values. The rate of change between points (x_1, y_1) and (x_2, y_2) is $\frac{y_2 - y_1}{x_2 - x_1}$. (328)

rate unit The unit of a rate. (328)

ratio A quotient of two quantities with the same units. (274, 275)

rational expression A quotient of two polynomials. (761)

rational number A number that can be expressed as a simple fraction. (816)

ratio of similitude The ratio of the lengths of corresponding sides of two similar figures. (309)

reciprocal rates Two rates in which the quantities are compared in both orders. (264)

reflection-symmetric The property held by a figure that coincides with its image under a reflection over a line. (526)

Related Facts Property of Addition and Subtraction For all real numbers a, b, and c, if $a + b = c$, then $b + a = c$, $c - b = a$, and $c - a = b$. (106–107)

Related Facts Property of Multiplication and Division For all nonzero real numbers a, b, and c, if $ab = c$, then $ba = c$, $\frac{c}{b} = a$, and $\frac{c}{a} = b$. (113–114)

relation Any set of ordered pairs. (428)

relative frequency The ratio of the number of times an event occurs to the total number of possible occurrences. (280, 289)

Repeated Multiplication Property of Powers When n is a positive integer, $x^n = x \cdot x \cdot \ldots \cdot x$ for n factors. (398)

S

sample A subset taken from a set of people or things. (302)

scatterplot A two-dimensional coordinate graph of individual points. (27)

scientific notation A number represented as $x \cdot 10^n$, where n is an integer and $1 \le x < 10$. (460)

semiperimeter Half the perimeter of a figure. (807)

sequence A collection of numbers or objects in a specific order. (20)

simple fraction A fraction with integers in its numerator and denominator. (816)

skewed left A distribution in which the lower half of the values extends much farther to the left than the upper half, leaving a tail on the left. (51)

skewed right A distribution in which the upper half of the values extends much farther to the right than the lower half, leaving a tail on the right. (51)

slope The rate of change between points on a line. The slope of the line through (x_1, y_1) and (x_2, y_2) is $\frac{y_2 - y_1}{x_2 - x_1}$. (334)

slope-intercept form An equation of a line in the form $y = mx + b$, where m is the slope and b is the y-intercept. (350)

Slopes and Parallel Lines Property If two lines have the same slope, then they are parallel. (616)

solution to an equation Any value of a variable that makes an equation true. (135)

solution to a system In a system of equations with two variables, the solution is all ordered pairs (x, y) that satisfy all equations in the system. (582)

square The second power of a number x, or x^2. (488)

Square of the Square Root Property For any nonnegative number x, $\sqrt{x} \cdot \sqrt{x} = \sqrt{x^2} = x$. (490)

square root If $A = s^2$, then s is a square root of A. (489)

square term The terms containing a variable with a power equal to 2. (736)

squaring function A function defined by $y = x^2$. (426)

standard form of an equation of a line An equation in the form $Ax + By = C$, where A, B, and C are constants. (375)

standard form for a polynomial A polynomial written with the terms in descending order of the exponents of its terms. (658)

standard form of a quadratic equation An equation of the form $ax^2 + bx + c = 0$, where $a \ne 0$. (555)

standard window The common view on a graphing calculator. (34)

Subtraction Property of Equality For all real numbers a, b, and c, if $a = b$, then $a - c = b - c$. (106)

symmetric distribution Data that are centered around one point and in which the values on the left and right sides are roughly mirror images. (51)

system A set of equations or inequalities separated by the word *and* that together describe a single situation. (582)

T

tax rate The ratio of the tax to the amount being taxed. (275)

term A number, variable, or product of numbers and variables. (15, 20, 663)

Transitive Property of Equality For any real numbers a, b, and c, if $a = b$ and $b = c$, then $a = c$. (10)

trinomial A polynomial that has three terms. (663)

trivial factors In every expression, the factors 1 and the expression itself. (675)

2 × 2 identity matrix The matrix $\begin{bmatrix} 1 & 0 \\ 0 & 1 \end{bmatrix}$. (626)

U

unbiased A situation in which each outcome has the same probability; also called *fair*. (281)

uniform distribution A distribution that has roughly the same quantity for all events. (51)

union of sets The set of elements in either set A or set B (or in both) and written as $A \cup B$. (228)

Unique Factorization Theorem for Polynomials Every polynomial can be represented as a product of prime polynomials in exactly one way, disregarding order and integer multiples. (677)

V

value of a function The output of a function obtained for a given first variable. (426)

variable A letter or other symbol that can be replaced by any number (or other object) from a set. **(6)**

variable matrix In the matrix equation $\begin{bmatrix} a & b \\ c & d \end{bmatrix} \cdot \begin{bmatrix} x \\ y \end{bmatrix} = \begin{bmatrix} e \\ f \end{bmatrix}$, the variable matrix is $\begin{bmatrix} x \\ y \end{bmatrix}$. **(622)**

vertex The point of intersection of a parabola with its axis of symmetry. **(526)**

vertex form of an equation for a parabola An equation of the form $y - k = a(x - h)^2$, where (h, k) is the vertex. **(716)**

vertical line A line with the equation $x = h$, where h is a real number. **(189)**

W

window The part of a coordinate grid that is visible on a graphing calculator. **(33)**

X

x-intercept The x-coordinate of a point where a graph intersects the x-axis. **(357)**

Xmax The greatest x-value (right edge) displayed on the window screen of a graphing calculator. **(34)**

Xmin The least x-value (left edge) displayed on the window screen of a graphing calculator. **(34)**

Xscl The x-scale of a graphing calculator. **(34)**

Y

y-intercept The y-coordinate of a point where a graph intersects the y-axis. **(350)**

Ymax The greatest y-value (top edge) displayed on the window screen of a graphing calculator. **(34)**

Ymin The least y-value (bottom edge) displayed on the window screen of a graphing calculator. **(34)**

Yscl The y-scale of a graphing calculator. **(34)**

Z

Zero Exponent Propery If x is any nonzero real number, then $x^0 = 1$. **(405)**

Zero Product Property For any real numbers a and b, if $ab = 0$, then either $a = 0$, $b = 0$, or both a and b equal 0. **(115)**

Index

Photo Credits

Volume 2 Chapters 7–13

Cover: ©Scott McDermott/Corbis, cover **front, back**. ©AFP/Getty Images. p. **830** *right*; ©age fotostock/SuperStock, p. **v** *right*; ©Mike Agliolo/Photo Researchers, Inc., p. **420**; ©Altrendo Images/Getty Images, pp. **viii** *left*, **424-425**; ©AP/ Wide World Photos, pp. **403, 549, 554, 558, 582, 621, 643, 694, 727, 783**; ©BananaStock/Jupiterimages, p. **586**; ©BananaStock/PunchStock, p. **480**; ©Jean Louis Batt/Taxi/Getty Images, p. **472**; ©Charles Bowman/Robert Harding, p. **785**; ©Tom Brakefield/Getty Images, p. **444**; ©Jiri Castka/Shutterstock, p. **404**; ©Creatas/PunchStock, p. **543**; ©Alfredo Dagli Orti/Corbis, p. **517**; ©Gianni Dagli Orti/Corbis, p. **627** *bottom*; ©Phil Degginger/Alamy, p. **572**; ©Phil Degginger/Stone/Getty Images, p. **408**; ©Digital Vision Ltd., p. **722**; ©Digital Vision/Getty Images, p. **442**; ©Digital Vision/PunchStock, p. **661**; ©Digital Vision/SuperStock, p. **692**; ©Hadi Djunaedi/iStockphoto, p. **504**; ©Dynamic Graphics Group/IT Stock Free/Alamy, p. **646**; ©Wayne Eardley/Masterfile, p. **424**; ©Sean Ellis/Stone/Getty Images, p. **695**; ©Enigma/Alamy, pp. **vii** *left*, **396-397**; ©Don Farrall/Photodisc/Getty Images, p. **v**, *left*; ©Arlene Jean Gee/Shutterstock, p. **741**; ©Getty Images/Steve Allen, p. **599**; ©Getty Images/SW Productions, p. **409**; ©Philip Gould/Corbis, p. **417**; ©The Granger Collection, N.Y., p. **824**; ©Tomasz Gulla/Shutterstock, p. **658**; ©Tom Hahn/iStockphoto, p. **496**; ©Toru Hanai/Reuters/Corbis, p. **505**; ©Gavin Hellier/Robert Harding World Imagery, Getty Images, p. **vi**, *left*; ©Hemera Technologies/Jupiterimages, p. **638**; ©Walter Hodges/Brand X Pictures/Jupiterimages, p. **590**; ©Jenny Horne/Shutterstock, p. **769**; ©Image Ideas, Inc./Indexstock, p. **627** *hammer, right*; ©INTERFOTO Pressebildagentur/Alamy, p. **819**; ©Iraq Museum, Baghdad/Bridgeman Art Library, p. **796**; ©Pekka Jaakkola/ Shutterstock, p. **794**; ©Jupiterimages Corporation, p. **531**; ©Robb Kendrick/Aurora/Getty Images, p. **588**; ©Nick Koudis/ Getty Images, p. **447**; ©Art Kowalsky/Alamy, pp. **x** *left*, **776-777**; ©Matthias Kulka/Corbis, p. **830** *left*; ©Lana Langlois/ Shutterstock, p. **592**; ©Eric Lessing/Art Resource, NY, pp. **ix** *right*, **712-713**; ©Library of Congress, Prints and Photographs Division [LC-USZ62-117122], p. **700**; ©Jim Linna/Photodisc/Getty Images, p. **779**; ©Jim Lopes/Shutterstock, p. **604**; ©Dennis MacDonald/PhotoEdit, pp. **446, 564**; ©Will & Deni McIntyre/Corbis, p. **583**; ©Ian Mckinnell/Getty Images, p. **iv** *right*; ©mdd/Shutterstock, pp. **ix** *left*, **654-655**; ©Simon Marcus/Corbis, p. **571** *bottom*; ©Jeffrey Markowitz/Corbis Sygma, p. **463**; ©Lori Martin/Shutterstock, p. **518**; ©Doug Menuez/Getty Images, p. **585**; ©Tan Wei Ming/Shutterstock, p. **620**; ©Marvin Nauman/FEMA News Photo, p. **569**; Courtesy NBA Photos, p. **606** *top, bottom*; ©Michael Newman/PhotoEdit, pp. **458, 460, 614**; ©Greg Nicholas/iStockphoto, p. **412**; ©Oleg Nikishin/Getty Images Sport/Getty Images, p. **611**; ©Phillip Novess/ Shutterstock, p. **633**; ©Shawn Pecor/Shutterstock, p. **550**; ©Photodisc/PunchStock, p. **468**; ©PhotoSpin, Inc., p. **428**; ©Frederic Pitchal/Corbis Sygma, p. **510**; ©Plush Studios/Bill Reitzel/Blend Images/Getty Images, p. **594**; ©Siede Preis/ Getty Images, p. **627** *wrench, right*; ©Adam Pretty/Reportage/Getty Images, pp. **viii** *right*, **580-581**; ©Purestock/SuperStock, p. **828**; ©Ken Reid/Taxi/Getty Images, p. **487**; ©Elena Rooraid/PhotoEdit, p. **436**; ©Deborah Roundtree/The Image Bank/ Getty Images, pp. **vii** *right*, **456-457**; ©Royalty-Free/Corbis, pp. **470, 536, 660**; ©Rubberball/Getty Images, p. **551**; ©Len Rubenstein/Index Stock Imagery, Inc., p. **462**; ©Carol Schultz/Painet, p. **537**; ©SGC/Shutterstock, p. **571** *top*; ©C. Sherburne/ PhotoLink/Getty Images, p. **787**; ©Dwight Smith/Shutterstock, p. **602**; ©Johnathan Smith/Cordaiy Photo Library/Corbis, p. **807**; ©Joseph Sohm/VisionsofAmerica.com/Photodisc/Getty Images, p. **vi**, *right*; ©Space Frontiers/Taxi/Getty Images, p. **704**; ©SSPL/The Image Works, p. **645**; ©Doug Steley/Alamy, p. **702**; ©Stockbyte/PunchStock Images, p. **781**; ©Stockdisc/ PunchStock, p. **501**; ©Rudy Sulgan/Corbis, p. **565**; ©SW Productions/Getty Images, p. **821**; ©ThinkStock LLC/Index Stock Imagery, Inc., p. **516**; ©Trip/Alamy, p. **797**; ©US Navy via CNP/CNP/Corbis, p. **448**; ©Visual Arts Library (London)/Alamy, p. **768**; ©Drazen Vukelic/Shutterstock, p. **430**; ©Stuart Westmorland/Corbis, p. **407**; ©Ross Woodhall/Taxi/Getty Images, p. **iv**, *left*; ©Yellow Dog Productions/The Image Bank/Getty Images, p. **598**; ©Kenneth C. Zirkel/iStockphoto, p. **400**;

Illustrations: Ron Carboni

Acknowledgements: It is impossible for UCSMP to thank all the people who have helped create and test these books. We wish particularly to thank Carol Siegel, who coordinated the use of the test materials in the schools; Kathleen Anderson, Aisha Bradshaw, Paul Campbell, Jena Dropela, Meri Fohran, Lisa Hodges, Rachel Huddleston, Evan Jenkins, Nurit Kirshenbaum, Lindsay Knight, Nathaniel Loman, Matthew McCrea, Jadele McPherson, Erin Moore, Dylan Murphy, Gretchen Neidhardt, Jennifer Perton, Daniel Rosenthal, Luke I. Sandberg, Sean Schulte, Andrew L. Shu, Emily Small, John Stevenson, James Thatcher, Alex Tomasik, Erica Traut, Alex Yablon, and Melissa Yeung.

We wish to acknowledge the generous support of the Amoco Foundation and the Carnegie Corporation of New York in helping to make it possible for the first edition of these materials to be developed, tested, and distributed, and the additional support of the Amoco Foundation for the second edition.

We wish to acknowledge the contribution of the text *Algebra Through Applications with Probability and Statistics*, by Zalman Usiskin (NCTM, 1979), developed with funds from the National Science Foundation, to some of the conceptualizations and problems used in this book.

Symbols

$>$	is greater than
$<$	is less than
$\geq$	is greater than or equal to
$\leq$	is less than or equal to
$=$	is equal to
$\neq$	is not equal to
$\approx$	is approximately equal to
$\pm$	plus or minus
$+$	plus sign
$-$	minus sign
$\times, \cdot, *$	multiplication signs
$\div, /$	division signs
$\%$	percent
π	pi
$|n|$	absolute value of n
$\sqrt{}$	radical sign
$\sqrt[3]{}$	cube root
A'	image of point A
$(\ )$	parentheses
$[\ ]$	brackets
$\{\ \}$	braces
$\ldots$	continuing pattern

$0.\overline{a}$	repetend bar
$\{\ \}, \varnothing$	empty or null set
$:$ or $|$	such that
$P(E)$	probability of an event E
$\cap$	intersection of sets
$\cup$	union of sets
$\overleftrightarrow{AB}$	line through A and B
$\overrightarrow{AB}$	ray with endpoint at A and containing B
$\overline{AB}$	segment with endpoints A and B
AB	length of segment from A to B; distance between A and B
$\angle ABC$	angle ABC
$m\angle ABC$	measure of angle ABC
$\triangle ABC$	triangle with vertices A, B, C
$\llcorner$	right angle symbol
n°	n degrees
(x, y)	ordered pair
$\dfrac{a}{b}$	a divided by b
$a^b, a{\wedge}b$	a to the bth power
b_1	subscript variable ("b sub 1")
$f(x)$	function notation "f of x"
$-x$	opposite of x
$n!$	n factorial
Q_1, Q_2, Q_3	first, second, and third quartiles
μ	mean